Neuroscience in Science Fiction Films

ALSO BY SHARON PACKER, M.D.

*Cinema's Sinister Psychiatrists:
From Caligari to Hannibal* (McFarland, 2012)

Neuroscience in Science Fiction Films

Sharon Packer, M.D.

McFarland & Company, Inc., Publishers
Jefferson, North Carolina

LIBRARY OF CONGRESS CATALOGUING-IN-PUBLICATION DATA

Packer, Sharon.
Neuroscience in science fiction films / Sharon Packer, M.D.
    p.   cm.
Includes bibliographical references and index.

ISBN 978-0-7864-7234-5 (softcover : acid free paper) ∞
ISBN 978-1-4766-1800-5 (ebook)

1. Science fiction films—History and criticism.
2. Neurosciences in motion pictures.   I. Title.
PN1995.9.S26P34 2015   791.43'615—dc23   2014038571

BRITISH LIBRARY CATALOGUING DATA ARE AVAILABLE

© 2015 Sharon Packer, M.D. All rights reserved

*No part of this book may be reproduced or transmitted in any form
or by any means, electronic or mechanical, including photocopying
or recording, or by any information storage and retrieval system,
without permission in writing from the publisher.*

Cover images © Shutterstock

Printed in the United States of America

*McFarland & Company, Inc., Publishers
Box 611, Jefferson, North Carolina 28640
www.mcfarlandpub.com*

In Honor of Joel L. Steinberg, M.D.

Table of Contents

Acknowledgements — ix
Preface — 1
Introduction — 5

ONE. Neuroscience Fiction Film in Post-Psychoanalytic Society — 13
TWO. Movies and the Mind (and the Rebirth of the Brain) — 22
THREE. The Legacy of 19th Century Literature — 46
FOUR. Automatons, Androids, Replicants and *RoboCops* — 61
FIVE. Human-Ape Brain Exchanges, Darwinian Debates and the "Monkey Gland Man" — 80
SIX. Sputnik, Space Aliens and Brains from Outer Space — 98
SEVEN. Science Fiction in Social Problem Films — 125
EIGHT. Brain Drains, Brain Chips and Brain Machines — 141
NINE. Flashbacks, Flash-Forwards and Flash Drives — 164
TEN. Memory, Mentation and Medication: Before Birth and After Alzheimer's — 177
ELEVEN. Dream Scenes: From Silent Cinema to Salvador Dalí to CGI — 191
TWELVE. Video Games, Virtual Reality and "Reality Testing" — 206
THIRTEEN. Drugs, Dystopias and Utopias — 216
FOURTEEN. Computers, Consciousness and Control — 233

Conclusion: Hive Minds, Herds and Jung's Collective Unconscious — 239
Afterword — 241
Filmography — 245
Chapter Notes — 249
Bibliography — 259
Index — 271

Acknowledgments

This book would not have been possible were it not for the help of several essential people.

Most of all, I thank George Chaim Higham for his endless efforts and for his willingness to celebrate our 25th anniversary by poring over photos from SF texts. I must also thank many old friends from medical school, especially (in alphabetical order) Steve Berman, M.D., Ph.D., Richard Cumberlin, M.D., and Joel Steinberg, M.D., for sparking my interest in the crossover between SF, real science and philosophy, and for alerting me to the artwork that joins the fields.

Insights and inspirations come from many people, including (in alphabetical order) Michael Ascher, M.D., Mark Banschick, M.D., Steven Billick, M.D., J.P. Chen, M.D., Ph.D., Bennett Cohen, M.D., Jake Coyle of AP Press, Danny Fingeroth, Ian Fischer, MFA, Howard Forman, M.D., Roland Holt, M.D., Richard McCarrick, M.D., Phil Miller, Ph.D., MLS, Ed Morman, Ph.D., MLS, Jody Pennington, Ph.D., Merle Robinson, M.D., Joan Root, MFA, MA, Robert Rubin, M.D., Ph.D., Michael Schwartz, M.D., John Strausbaugh, John Sweeney, Ph.D., and Fuat Ulus, M.D. Thanks also to Robert Ruben, M.D., and Donna Fingerhut of the New York Academy of Medicine's History of Medicine Section, Film Forum curators, Anthology Film Archives library staff, and Elliott Kanbar of Quad Cinema. My special thanks to Beth Israel's chair of psychiatry, Arnold Winston, M.D., Albert Einstein College of Medicine's dean, Alan Segal, M.D., Joan Lippert and Karen Sorensen of AECOM library and magazine, Dr. George Makari's History of Psychiatry section at Cornell-Weill, Christian Perring of *Metapsychology,* Natalie Timoshin, Laurie Martin and James Kroll IV, M.D., of *Psychiatric Times,* Gina Henderson of *Clinical Psychiatry News,* and Ben Green, M.D., of *History of Medicine.* Jim Carlson's tech support is essential and Dr. JP Green's spirit always inspires.

Preface

Chances are, we all have heard the story about the three blind men and the elephant (which sometimes is the six blind men and the elephant). One man touches the elephant's tusk, another puts his hand on the trunk, and the third wraps his fingers (partly) around a round and sturdy leg. In some versions, one man grabs the tail while another traces the length of the nose.

Each man describes something very different, based on his own experiences. Each is correct in his own way, but each answer is only partly correct overall. When a sighted man passes by, and describes the elephant as a whole animal, his words paint a completely different picture. Only then do the blind men realize that they are blind and that they are unable to perceive the whole elephant—or the whole truth.

That ancient Indian story is very apropos to this topic of "neuroscience in science fiction films." For this is an elephant of a topic, one that would be tackled very differently by authors with different training and different persuasions. The film critic, the historian of science, the philosopher, the SF fan, the student of science fiction literature (as opposed to SF cinema) will each broach this vast subject in his or her own way.

Neurologists or neurosurgeons will view these SF films through a different lens than one a practicing psychiatrist. Dedicated psychoanalysts will have their own opinions. I expect that a "bench neuroscientist," who experiments in laboratories without treating patients, will have a special perspective, as would a bioengineer, who has more data about mechanical operations and physics. And so on and so forth. Many different fields can lay claim to this subject matter, from philosophers to film scholars to historians of behavioral science. Representatives from each field are needed to appreciate the totality of the topic.

Given how much one's academic background influences one's approach to this subject, I must tell my readers about my own training (and about the training that I do not have). Let me start by saying that I am a physician who specializes in psychiatric medicine. Most of my time is spent in private practice, and most of that practice is devoted to psychopharmacology.

Much of my efforts are directed toward the differential diagnosis of behavioral, perceptual and cognitive changes, to identify underlying medical causes of distressing symptoms, if they exist, or to determine which specific psychiatric treatments can relieve those symptoms quickly and safely—or if referral to another specialist is needed first. I write regular columns on "Why Psychiatrists Are Physicians First" for *Psychiatric Times*. Those columns best explain my biases toward biological psychiatry, and underscore my contention that psychiatrists are simply specialists in psychiatric medicine. (Some psychiatrists think differently, and view themselves as therapists first, rather than as physicians, and some identify as psychoanalysts.)

I am also an assistant clinical professor of psychiatry and behavioral sciences at Albert Einstein College of Medicine. In that capacity, I supervise psychiatrists-in-training in the all-but-extinct field of psychodynamic psychotherapy, as well as in supportive psychotherapy. Psychotherapy has largely become the purview of non-medically trained practitioners (as Freud predicted a century ago). "Medical psychotherapy" (delivered by psychiatrists with M.D.s or D.O.s) is uncommon these days, but psychiatrists-to-be still receive training in this area.

When I first started my training in psychiatry, bias toward psychoanalysis was so strong that medical approaches were discouraged. Luckily, those attitudes changed over time, and I changed the site of my training to a program that offered additional courses in medical anthropology, and even had some of the rare M.D. Jungians in higher administrative positions.

Luckily, the American Psychiatric Association recognizes the value of film in teaching psychiatry, and has hosted many of my workshops on film and comics-related topics over the years. Some of those workshops were derived from books that I had already written or courses that I taught in colleges; others evolved into books, as a result of research for workshops.

Although I am not formally educated as a cinema scholar, I taught college and graduate level courses on "Movies and the Mind" and "Dream and Film" for ten years (prior to 9/11) for the media studies department at the New School in New York City. I wrote several books on the subject: *Movies and the Modern Psyche*; *Dreams in Myth, Medicine and Movies*; *Cinema's Sinister Psychiatrists*, and *Superheroes and Superegos: The Minds Behind the Masks*, which covers films as well as comics. Completing one book about film invariably turns the page to the next book, because one topic opens windows into another, and demands attention to so many more issues, as has happened in this book.

As I write this preface, essays on Hannibal and Batman are in press. I also write reviews of SF (and other) films for *Psychiatric Times* and for neurology and psychiatry sections of a general medical journal.

I have also lectured on superheroes and psychiatry (and about the Symbiote as a metaphor for AIDS and about Luke Cage comics and unethical medical experiments) for comics' audiences at Comic-Con and elsewhere, as well as for various hospitals and medical school grand rounds, the New York Academy of Medicine and the annual Graphic Medicine conference. My published articles on comics, science fiction and history of medicine revolve around medical ethical issues and the history of the AIDS epidemic as well as neuroscience.

The New York Academy of Medicine's History of Medicine section was kind enough to invite me to sit on their steering committee. Perspectives from the history of medicine inform this study as much as any familiarity with the day-to-day practice of psychiatry. The ten years that I attended Cornell's History of Psychiatry seminars proved to be a turning point, and inspired me to delve into the histories of medicine and science.

With this overarching background in medicine and psychiatry, I feel compelled to explain my interest in cinema and why I spend so much of my free time viewing films and reading books and articles in cinema studies. Simply put, watching films is a wonderful way for psychiatrists to relax. There is no need to cure the characters, no concern about drug interactions, and no obligation to alert authorities if you realize that one actor plans to kill another (as is required of practicing psychiatrists, according to Tarasoff's Law).

My interest in film stems from my interest in art and in the visual. I minored in art history in college and took a great many fine arts studio courses over the years, and I even had Soho gallery shows of my own artwork and participated in about half a dozen group museum shows. In the earlier part of the 20th century, film gained recognition as an art form, and silent films are inherently visual creations. Expressionist art and film are kindred cousins. For one who favors the imagery and symbolism of Bosch, Breughel and Grunewald (and who researched and published about the medical links to their art), film was the perfect place to turn. Film remained a reservoir of representational art, long after abstract art overtook post–World War II American art.

I instinctively gravitated to bioscience fiction films, yet it came as a surprise to me that my first book, *Dreams in Myth, Medicine and Movies,* has as much information about dreams in SF film as it does about dreams and art. (The associations between dreams and psychoanalysis or dreams and neuroscience are a given.)

Before we get into this book, let me suggest an alternative title, one that will never come to be because it is far too long to fit on a book cover, much less capture attention. Rather than being called *Neuroscience in Science Fiction Films*, this study could just as aptly be called "*Tracing Paradigm Shifts in Neuropsychiatry Through Trends in Neuroscience Fiction Films.*" This book concerns itself with that topic as much as SF film, and we are as much concerned with the public's perception of those trends as with professionals' embrace of novel (or tried and true) approaches to treatment.

I have tried to weave these disparate histories together, for several reasons. I must explain how, why and when psychiatry changed courses over the past century and a quarter, why it made so many abrupt turns, and often doubled back on itself, or forgot lessons from the past about biological psychiatry, or why contradictory approaches continued along parallel paths without intersecting. By looking at film subjects, we can pinpoint when paradigm shifts started to brew, when they began to percolate and come to a full boil, and when they became so strong that their "full flavor" overpowered everything that existed beforehand.

In reality, acceptance of innovations in neuroscience (or rejection of them) is often not an "either /or" question. Sometimes, practitioners traverse two paths interchangeably. I like to think of these so-called "paradigm shifts" as choices, rather than as shifts, per se. One can choose to travel from one destination to another by highway or by country road. While two people head for the same destination, one may prefer an expressway, but may find herself detoured, and having to take the long and windy country road that she tried to avoid. There may be an accident ahead, or inclement weather or construction. She adapts and finds the routes that work best.

The person who chooses the country road may prefer the scenic route to the time-saving route, but finds that the road is too muddy, or that his van does not handle as well as expected while traversing rocky terrain. So he travels the highway for a while, until it seems safe to return to the dirt road. Sometimes he sees the highway from his country road, and sometimes it is blocked from his sight. Sometimes he wonders why he did not take the quick and easy route in the first place, and at other times, he rejoices that he could take his chosen path.

Of course, the practice of medicine is not always a matter of personal choice, as it is for the tourist or a traveler described above. There are "best practices in medicine" or "standards of practice" that most practitioners prefer—but there are always holdouts or advocates of alternative approaches who make themselves heard. Even though it is fashionable to speak of "paradigm shifts," as if they were set in stone, a closer examination of history shows that dual paradigms often co-exist, although not necessarily peacefully.

On a personal level, I am struck by the respect accorded psychoanalytically-influenced films from the mid-century. Movie-wise, many of those films are masterpieces. I am enamored of Hitchcock, who was probably the best front man for psychoanalysis that ever existed, as well as a great filmmaker. *Psycho* (1960) cemented my interest in psychiatry. At the same time, I cannot resist the urge to excavate 1950s SF films, most of which seem comedic to contemporary audiences, but which were also prophetic in their own way. Those 1950s (and very early 60s) SF and horror films were among my favorites as a child, and invoke fond memories to this day.

Each person reading this book will have his or her own viewpoint, and will bring unique knowledge to chapters ahead. Perhaps some readers will be inspired to write their own books. Whatever happens, I hope that you enjoy it, along with films we discuss. Feel free to write to me at drpacker@hotmail.com about your reflections and about related articles and books that you write yourselves.

Introduction

Iron Man 3 kickstarted the 2013 summer blockbuster season. On opening weekend, it stood to break box office records. By year's end, *Iron Man 3* led a record year for film, carrying Hollywood to new highs.[1] Receipts for *Iron Man 3* reached the billion-dollar mark in just three weeks.[2] Impressive, even for superhero cinema. Bloomberg News, a financial website, feted the film. Film critics and fans loved it, too.

Iron Man 3 is a prime example of 21st century neuroscience fiction. Its outlandish theme of connecting (human) minds with machines is no longer fiction. It is fast becoming fact.

There is more to *Iron Man 3* than neuroscience, though. The tech genius turned philanthropist, who fights evil as Iron Man, appeals to audiences. The fact that Tony Stark has a dark side (as does Robert Downey, Jr., who stars as Tony) adds more to the story. The film forecasts victory over impending peril, and reassures Americans of future success, at the same time confirming fears that foes lie in wait. This is action-adventure at its best, wedded to science fiction, with a sprinkle of romance thrown.

Iron Man 3 replays that ever-popular theme: man against machine. With his artificial heart parts, Tony Stark cum Iron Man reminds us of the Tin Man from that all–American favorite, *The Wizard of Oz* (1939). In Victor Fleming's endearing film, the Tin Man (Jack Haley) also acquires a heart, albeit for very different reasons.

Iron Man 3 includes a subtext that is not immediately apparent, but is highly relevant to our theme: neuroscience in post-psychoanalytic society. Better than any film to date, *Iron Man 3* captures the spirit behind this book, because it alludes to the "two minds"[3] of psychiatry, which stand at loggerheads today as much as ever.[4] It references both biological psychiatry, now known as "neuropsychiatry," and the proverbial "couch cure" of psychoanalytic lore.

The movie never compares the biological brain to the metapsychological mind. Rather, it shows these two poles of psychiatric thought in a continuous celluloid stream. By doing that, it makes a radical statement. It implies that the reflective, analytic model that makes sense of human situations and uncovers meanings behind life's struggles—without necessarily changing actions or attitudes—can complement our current action-oriented understanding of neurotransmitters. This synthesis of the "two minds" of contemporary psychiatry is an extraordinary accomplishment, befitting superhero cinema or Nobel Prize–winning research.[5] In fact, psychiatrist and neuroscientist Dr. Eric Kandel shared the 2000 Nobel Prize in Medicine or Physiology for "discoveries concerning signal transduction in the nervous system." Kandel has demonstrated brain changes following certain psychotherapies that promote re-learning.

If we look at some specifics about Iron Man, we see why he represents so much to so many. Tony Stark (aka Iron Man) was born on the cheap pulp pages of Marvel Comics, but he was not born a superhero. Rather, Stark gains superpowers through a man-made suit of armor. He still has an "Achilles' heel," of sorts—but his "heel" is in his heart. A terrorist explosion damaged his heart, and he relies on an electromagnetic implant to keep metal shards at bay. An Arc Reactor powers the magnet, but occasionally its batteries need recharging. Rivals repeatedly try to steal the ultra-powerful reactor, putting poor Tony's life at risk, in spite of his supercharged Iron Man suit.

In the first *Iron Man* film, the heart of the billionaire inventor and industrialist (and overall degenerate) is damaged, but is repaired by an advanced device. Tony gets a second lease on life—and an alternate identity—through his flashy red armor. The MacGuffin of the third *Iron Man* film moves from his heart to a fictional substance called "Extremis."

Extremis enters the central nervous system, binds with the brain, and changes users' DNA. This modified DNA sends electronic and neurochemical signals that weaponize the body by amping up physical and mental strength. In the comic book original from 2005, conceived by Warren Ellis, this Extremis substance facilitates a direct brain-based connection with ordinarily inanimate armor. This process allows Tony Stark to become one with his armor (in the comic book mini-series). Now he can accomplish impossible feats, superhero-style.

This theory sounds fanciful, yet there is more than a grain of truth to this comic book–conceived concept. Recent experiments in real life prove that paraplegics and amputees with specially programmed computerized brain implants can "will" movement in artificial limbs. They learn to control brain waves that communicate with microcomputers, which, in turn, make contact with parts of the brain that mediate movement. By bypassing damaged parts of the spinal cord that produced paralysis, this technique allows users to move their artificial limbs at will.

Hopefully, in the future, the lame will walk and the blind will see, not through miracles that take place on a mountaintop, but through the combined efforts of neuroscience, computer science, and bioengineering. There are other examples of this eerie mind-body-machine link. Such science fiction-like success stories are popping up more and more.[6]

The gap between science fiction and science fact is closing. As of late spring 2013, *New York Times*' reporters described a 64-electrode cap that allows users to control robotic movements of toy helicopters by visualizing movements in various body parts.[7] Samsung is developing an easy-to-use EEG (electroencephalogram) cap that expands ways to interact with mobile devices. The *MIT Technology Review* reports about Samsung's work on a tablet computer that users control with their minds.

These are just a few examples of advances that continue the inroads made by Hans Berger, in 1924, when he developed the EEG (electroencephalogram). By measuring electrical activity in the brain, Berger's EEG began the history of brain-computer interfaces (and also made ECT or electroconvulsive therapy) possible. Decades passed before the first cochlear implant, called a bionic ear, arrived in 1961. That was the first time that a machine could "restore a human sense." Fast-forward a few decades, and the progress moves faster and faster. In 1997, researchers at Emory University planted electrodes in the brain of a stroke victim, taped sensors to his body, and then taught him to move a cursor and spell words with his thoughts. Who would have guessed that bioengineering would be holding hands with parapsychology?

Eleven years later, in 2008, a brain-computer interface was implanted in a monkey at Duke University. The monkey's movements then control a robot on a treadmill. In 2012, at the University of Pittsburgh, a quadriplegic woman named Jan Scheuermann was able to eat a chocolate bar attached to a robotic arm that she controlled by implants in her brain.

These are real life events. From 1974 to 1978, TV viewers were treated to a series about the *Six Million Dollar Man*. The series was popular enough to spawn another show about the *Bionic Woman*, which ran between 1976 and 1978. By 1987, a television show, *Max Headroom*, debuted on ABC, just in time to capture the newly minted spirit of cyberpunk. In the storyline, Max is a fictional avatar created by downloading a TV reporter's memories into a computer. In theory, Max shares similarities with Rachael's character in *Blade Runner* (1982). Rachael is an advanced model replicant who received memories, as well as physical mementos, from the niece of the engineer who invented her and other robotic replicas of humans.

Times have changed. The examples excerpted above from a *New York Times* article are not isolated instances in futuristic science. A few minutes spent on the federal government's website www.clinicaltrials.gov proves that related neuroscience research is waiting in the wings. Clinicaltrials.gov lists studies that have passed IRBs (Institutional Review Boards) and meet federal safety standards, and have now progressed to the point that researchers are recruiting human volunteers by listing their studies on this site. As of New Year's Day 2014, this site lists 172 responses to searches for "brain machine" and 423 responses to "brain computer."

Before long, there will be no need to footnote these SF-like feats, for they will become as commonplace as cell phones (which seemed equally improbable when showcased in 1960s-era science fiction). These advances are gushing out like geysers, pouring forth in torrents rather than trickles. As a physician, I look toward the day when persons who are sense or movement-deprived will lead far fuller lives via technology. However, military strategists may see different advantages to these technological advances. It often happens that military funding or agencies such as DARPA push the envelope the furthest and the fastest, just as suggested in the film, *Brainstorm* (1983). We will discuss *Brainstorm* and other brain-themed films in a later chapter, "Dream Scenes: From Silent Cinema to Salvador Dalí to CGI."

Like *Brainstorm,* an otherwise forgotten film that revolves around marital conflicts and family strife as much as it focuses on neuroscience fiction, *Iron Man 3* has many layers. *Iron Man 3* is not an infomercial for tech companies that are touting these inventions. *Iron Man 3* is entertainment, even if it does make us think and wonder. Iron Man experiences all sorts of adventures as the film unfolds. He foils enemies, saves loved ones, and soars through the skies. He endures bombings and nuclear-like blasts. He succeeds in hand-to-hand combat with primitive weaponry or with no weapons at all. He even emotes and experiences human conflicts. He rekindles love. Like Sir Lancelot, he rescues his ladylove. The neuroscience back-story is just a back-story. It is not sufficient to drive the plot. Yet it is important to us, as we trace the history of neuroscience in science fiction film and find this exemplary and unexpected film in 2013.

As shown by the examples above, *Iron Man 3*'s futuristic theme of connecting (human) minds with machines is no longer pure fiction. *Iron Man 3* also nods to the past, and acknowledges the "narrative" approach of psychodynamic and psychoanalytic therapists who practice the proverbial "talk therapy." Let us look at some specifics.

After the movie (supposedly) ends, and after our superhero prevails, and after the credits have rolled and stopped, an epilogue appears. We hear Tony Stark talking about his triumphs and travails. The camera shifts to a slumbering Mark Ruffalo, appearing in a cameo as Dr. Bruce Banner. Marvel Comics and superhero fans recognize Ruffalo as Dr. Banner, the physicist who becomes big, green and muscle-bound whenever his anger is aroused. Because of gamma ray exposure, he becomes The Hulk, an *id*- and amygdala-driven being.

At some point, astute spectators recall that *Iron Man 3* began with a first person narrative by Tony Stark. Stark's voiceover interjects itself seamlessly throughout the film, and assumes a different meaning only upon reflection, after the film is over. Most of us do not give this narration and voiceover much thought, until the epilogue opens after the film's official end.

Tony Stark (Robert Downey, Jr.) looks straight into the camera, fearlessly, dressed in his signature red suit that bonds with his body, as he prepares to battle terrorists in *Iron Man 3* (2013).

Superhero film fans may dismiss this final scene as another infomercial that appears at the end of most Marvel superhero films, as a teaser and trailer for the next film in the superhero series. It ties in to the broader superhero genre. It brings the recent *The Avengers* (2012) movie to mind. This trailer plays to a targeted audience: die-hard superhero fans that stay seated until the last credit rolls. It is they who get to see this treat, and who are most likely to bite the bait.

However, if we listen to the dialogue between Stark and Banner closely, with both our ordinary hearing and with our third ears, we hear heated commentaries about the theoretical and practical rift in psychiatry.[8] Let us examine the specifics of this scene. As the epilogue in *Iron Man 3* opens, the camera moves toward Tony Stark. We see his face in close-up, as Tony thanks "Bruce" (Dr. Banner) for listening and for letting him "get it off his chest."

Tony says, "…and thank

you by the way for listening. There is something about getting it off my chest and putting it out there in the atmosphere— instead of holding this in. I mean, this is what gets people sick, you know. Wow, I had no idea you're such a good listener, to be able to share all my intimate thoughts, my experiences with someone ... it just cuts the weight of it in half. It's like a snake swallowing its own tail; everything comes in full circle and the fact that you're able to help me process ... you heard me?" (Is that snoring coming from the background?)

Tony interrupts his soliloquy. The camera pans as Tony turns around on the couch (which has come into sight). He spots Dr. Banner sitting in a chair behind him, awakening from sleep.

Dr. Banner becomes more alert, and tries to respond to Tony, but Tony pre-empts Banner's answer, and queries, "You were actively napping? ... Where did I lose you?" When Dr. Bruce Banner says, "Elevator in Switzerland," Tony quips, "So you heard none of it?" He prods Banner to respond.

At that point, we realize that Tony has been narrating the film in first person from the start, and that he has been relating his story to the doctor and reflecting about events that took place in the past. He has not been describing play-by-play actions as they occur in real time, as is done in sports casting. The real action takes place on the couch and the chair, and in Tony's mind. Maybe the action occurs entirely in the mind and does not involve the body at all. In other words, the action occurs in inner space, not outer space (where most science films take place).

This touch reminds us of that German Expressionist classic, *The Cabinet of Dr. Caligari* (1919), with its clever but convoluted framing device.[9] As *The Cabinet of Dr. Caligari* closes, two men sit on a bench outside of a mental asylum, relaying the strange tale about Dr. Caligari, his confederate Cesare, Jane (the woman Cesare refused to murder because he fell in love with her), and Jane's boyfriend, Francis, the hero of the film, who tells the tale in first person.

Caligari's framing device confuses the spectator, and intentionally so. Through this device, we learn that Francis—the man who portrays himself as the hero—is an inmate of the same asylum where Dr. Caligari works as superintendent (before he is locked in a straitjacket and remanded to his own asylum). At other times, Caligari functions as a carnival showman and hypnotist, keeping somnambulist Cesare in his cabinet, when Cesare is not out killing.

Francis' convoluted tale is engaging, but the reveal at the end detracts from his credibility. This framing device makes us wonder if the tale that we watched is nothing more than a delusion of a man who was previously declared insane. Did the events take place in real time, or are they confined to Francis' imagination? The framing device intends to confuse us.

Similarly, we now wonder if Tony Stark's tale of near-apocalyptic warfare and his acquisition of unearthly superpowers is a figment of Stark's imagination, given that his adventures were recounted to his doctor-friend, and were not witnessed firsthand. Film critics can ponder that question. Before we the audience find time to answer it, we hear the last lines of the dialogue between Tony Stark, inventor and industrialist, and Dr. Bruce Banner, physicist and Good Samaritan who unintentionally becomes The Hulk.

The now-alert Dr. Banner explains to Tony, "I'm sorry— I am not that kind of doctor.

I am not a therapist; it's not in my training." Dr. Banner starts to stammer, "I don't have the ... the ... temperament."

The Hulk fans relate to the temperament reference. They know that Dr. Banner's anger transforms him into the monstrous Hulk. Perhaps some spectators have heard about "countertransference." Analysts are trained to tap into their personal responses to their patients, under the belief that they can better understand their patients if they use their own reactions as a gauge.

The tongue-in-cheek dialogue between Tony and Bruce does not question the accuracy of this traditional analytic technique. Instead, it spoofs the temperament of Banner as The Hulk. We know that the standard psychoanalytic approach is off-limits for Dr. Banner, whether he is a physicist or a psychiatrist (or whether or not this technique is effective in real life). For Dr. Banner turns into The Hulk whenever he gets angry. He tears people apart, tosses them around, and wreaks destruction. That behavior is unacceptable, regardless of the therapist's theoretical approach to treatment.

Practitioners of psychiatric medicine or psychoanalysis, as well as participants in the couch cure, may be more interested in Tony's appreciation of "getting things off his chest" and his need to "process" his experiences. Those words are telling. Tony never hints that psychoanalysis or the "couch cure" could have changed his actions or his attitudes. He does not express a desire to undo what he just did. Nor does he intend to alter his plan of attack in the future. He never bothers to tell us if his story is a fantasy that he embroidered. Nor does he confirm that he has been retelling actual events as they transpired. He would be wise to show interest in his grandiosity and narcissism, and how these traits contributed to his conflicts in the first place, but he does not express any regrets. However, any attempt to cure Tony of his personality disorder might deprive both him and his devoted audience of his next adventure.

Tony simply wants to impart meaning to his intense action-adventure experiences. By saving it for the end, Tony implies that talk therapy is a postscript to events that already transpired (assuming that these events were not imaginary, delusional or hallucinatory). He hints that activity without meaning, even save-the-world kind of activity, is meaningless unless one understands the motives that drive that activity. Tony Stark, this metallic Man of Action, sounds like a philosopher at heart. Many theorists have stated that talk therapy's greatest value derives from its ability to impart meaning to suffering, in a secular way, even though it does not necessarily relieve the suffering or purge bad memories as promised, via catharsis.[10]

In this epilogue, Tony Stark sets out on a quest to understand himself. He wonders if he is the one who defines the Iron Man suit, or if the suit defines him. In the comic book version, the answer comes more easily, since Tony's neurotransmitters interact with Extremis to command the suit itself. In the film, the answer to that question is not so clear-cut. What is clear is that neither neurotransmitters nor neuropsychiatry can answer this existential question. That is the task of therapy ... or philosophy or philosophical psychology. Tony shows us how both needs co-exist without contradicting each other: the need to control his armor and bond it to his body and brain, and the need for self-discovery and self-definition and carving out an individual identity. In essence, *Iron Man 3* says that both brands of psychiatry deserve a place in society, and both serve a function in his own life, even though the existential questions addressed by psychotherapy or psychoanalysis come closer to speculative philosophy than to hard science.

Iron Man 3 shows us two poles of psychiatric practice. *Iron Man 3,* perhaps unwittingly, reiterates questions and conflicts that vexed psychiatry for the last quarter century. In the course of this book, we will trace the ways that cinema has commented on those schisms in psychiatry. We will see how attitude shifts about neuroscience manifest themselves in movies, and how those shifts influence science fiction film. We will come to appreciate how advances in cinematography and special effects make time-tested tropes seem newer than they actually are.

Iron Man is not the only film that focuses on brain, body, mind and movement—and the qualities that define human identity. *RoboCop* tackles this topic as well, and does an admirable job that veers off into other directions. The mere fact that *RoboCop* resurfaced as a reboot in 2014, more than a quarter of a century after the first film, confirms the enduring appeal of this man-machine amalgam. *RoboCop* made its first appearance in 1987. Yet there is more to Iron Man and RoboCop than the obvious bioengineering feats. Apparently, questions about the determinants of human identity are just as important today, if not more important, in our post-cyberspace, social media-saturated society, where anonymous game players can acquire alternative identities instantly and Facebook friends can "like" words and photos of "friends" seen only on screen.[11]

In the chapters that follow, we will focus on the neuroscience aspects of science fiction film, but we will also point out the parallel paths of psychodynamic psychiatry, psychoanalysis, behavioral conditioning, and, to a lesser extent, humanistic psychology, to show how these alternative approaches influenced film. Overall, psychoanalysis probably influenced film far more than neuropsychiatry, if only because psychoanalysis and cinema grew up together at the turn of the 20th century and because so many filmmakers became infatuated with Freudianism, after displaced analysts settled in Hollywood shortly before and after the Second World War.

Our goal is not to weigh the contributions of one pole against the other, to see which side wins. Rather, we simply want to recognize the contributions of neuroscience to science fiction film, even if that "neuroscience" is imaginary or illusory. This allows us to uncover another side of cinema, one that is very different from the mid-century psychoanalytically influenced films.

Our first two chapters explain some of the "behind-the-scenes" influences on these NSF films. We begin with "Neuroscience Fiction Film in Post-Psychoanalytic Society" and then elaborate on theoretical and practical shifts in neuropsychiatry in the next chapter, "Movies and the Mind (and the Rebirth of the Brain)," which goes on fast-forward, and reviews major themes from the rest of the book, in rapid-fire fashion. For some readers, the abbreviated information in that chapter may suffice, but for others, it will merely whet their appetites to learn more about neuroscience, science fiction film and other aspects of psychiatry.

Next we look at chronological developments in SF film. "The Legacy of 19th Century Literature" roots SF film in literature, and in 19th century literature at that. (Unfortunately, we are not able to offer a more thorough comparison between SF literature and film, and must direct the reader to bibliographic references on this subject.)

In the fourth chapter, we review "Automatons, Androids, Replicants and RoboCops," and then move on to "Human-Ape Brain Exchanges, Darwinian Debates and the 'Monkey Gland Man'" in Chapter Five. Chapter Six concerns "Sputnik, Space Aliens and Brains from Outer Space," which is the era of "classic SF" from the Space Age. The seventh chapter is a short one on "Science Fiction in Social Problem Films."

After that historical grounding, we devote chapters to major tropes in NSF. Chapter Eight is about "Brain Drains, Brain Chips and Brain Machines," while Chapter Nine concerns "Flashbacks, Flash-Forwards and Flash Drives." Chapter Ten focuses on "Memory, Mentation and Medication: Before Birth and After Alzheimer's." Chapter Eleven discusses "Dream Scenes: From Silent Cinema to Salvador Dalí to CGI." Chapter Twelve involves "Video Games, Virtual Reality and 'Reality Testing.'" We move on to "Drugs, Dystopias and Utopias" in the thirteenth chapter. Our last chapter addresses "Computers, Consciousness and Control."

Throughout the text, we strive to correlate turning points in NSF cinema with major neuroscience advances, as well as with shifts in the theory and practice of neuropsychiatry and psychoanalysis. Whenever possible, we include important developments in the history of medicine and science (such as the acceptance of "brain death" as the formal definition of death; advancements in transplant medicine that parallel SF themes about transplants; discoveries in endocrinology that have direct—but not necessarily obvious—implications for neuroscience; ethical breeches in medical experimentation that indirectly influence cinematic subject matter). We will find that Nobel Prize winners and nominees often infiltrate the films of their day.

Naturally, there is some overlap between the different sections, as we show how many (if not most) NSF tropes repeat themselves over and over again over the decades. Those who prefer to read about their favorite subjects first, without starting at the beginning, may appreciate extra explanations that are available in each chapter. As for those readers who read from beginning to end, and who encounter some small segments of repetition, I hope they will bear with me.

By weaving information from the histories of psychiatry, neuroscience and cinema together, we will find a rich latticework that links these far-flung fields with one another. We will encounter films that appear to be frivolous and pure fantasy on the surface, but which comment on scientific and philosophical currents of their times. Such films may seem to be escapist, but a closer examination reveals that some predict the future, or comment on burning issues in the present. Many NSF films harp back to Plato, and the earliest days of philosophy. This rich past provides a firm foundation for the future, and I have full confidence that there will be many more NSF films to enjoy and contemplate in the near and distant future.

One

Neuroscience Fiction Film in Post-Psychoanalytic Society

Many articles and books have been written about the chronological convergence of psychoanalysis and the cinema. No serious scholar doubts that psychoanalysis contributed to cinema, even though many people doubt the veracity of psychoanalytic theory, and question the utility of psychoanalytic techniques. However, the issue here is not psychoanalysis; it is neuroscience.

Over the last quarter century, neuroscience has swept psychoanalysis aside, burying it beneath a tidal wave of biologically based data. There has been a sea change in the field—just as there was movement in the opposite direction as World War I ended, when Freudian psychoanalytic concepts gained steam because they helped relieve war neuroses.[1]

Some say that recent films offer fresh takes on psychological or neuropsychiatric themes, and that those films are a complete departure from psychoanalytically informed films of the past. That is true, but it is also not true. Yes, we can identify a subgenre of "neuroscience fiction" (NSF) film[2] that stands apart from "bio-science fiction."[3] By scratching beneath the surface, we can show that the neuroscience fiction genre predated the much more publicized cyberpunk genre, although there are points of convergence between cyberpunk and neuroscience fiction.

NSF has deeper roots than we might expect. The name of this subgenre may be new, but NSF was seeded long ago, when 19th century visionaries penned SF literature that enchants us to this very day. Silent cinema delved into dreams, intelligence enhancement, and automatons that appropriate the personalities of living beings. In the twenties and thirties, hormone therapies were all the rage, and "simian cinema" provided low-level entertainment about human-ape brain exchanges. Some of the silliest SF/horror films contain high level allusions to advances in neuroendocrinology and the influence of hormones on human (and animal) behavior.

By the mid-fifties, NSF showed signs of new growth, through cheap and cheesy drive-in double features. In the same era that brought us "classic science fiction," with outer space themes, we find films about big-brained aliens that invade Earth, terrorize Earthlings, and sometimes communicate telepathically or occupy the bodies of household pets, as if they were demons or dybbuks or succubae or incubi of more superstitious times. Think *Donovan's Brain* (1953) or *The Brain from Planet Arous* (1957). Many of those low-budget brain-themed films from the fifties look laughable on the surface, but they prove that serious paradigm changes were percolating beneath the surface in the 1950s, when Freudianism reigned supreme, and when the American public celebrated the centennial of Freud's birth, and read his collected works.

Our excavations will uncover cinematic evidence of schisms in psychiatric theory and practice. Psychoanalysis got a boost during World War I, when Ernest Simmel blended insight-oriented psychoanalytic techniques with hypnosis.[4] Simmel often succeeded in treating "war neurotics" with one or two sessions, even before he received formal training in analysis. Austrian military authorities were impressed, as were Americans. Years later, medical doctors who practiced psychoanalysis were welcomed in America. Over time, hundreds of analysts arrived on American shores. Most were Jews, seeking safe havens far from the reach of the Third Reich.[5]

In the mid to late 1950s, American psychiatry gravitated toward the mind and the metapsychological unconscious, but researchers retained interest in biology and the brain. Soon enough, psychoanalysts headed psychiatry departments of renowned medical schools. By the 1950s, and through the 1960s and 1970s, most psychiatric residencies required training in psychoanalysis. Many programs recommended (or demanded) that their trainees undergo a personal analysis as well. That was a time-consuming and costly process.

If we look back in time, we find more reasons why psychoanalysis gained caché in the U.S. in the post–World War II era. Shell-shocked soldiers were returning from war en masse, in need of psychiatric treatment. The government offered generous training grants to psychiatrists-to-be, making the field more appealing to young physicians who were choosing medical specialties.

Still, theories about the causes and cures of behavioral and cognitive problems came and went over the years, and ideas about psychiatry reflected philosophical and political currents as much as scientific truth.[6,7] Sometimes, there were wide chasms between prevailing theories.

In 1949, the Nobel committee awarded another prize for a psychiatric discovery, this time for the "leucotomy" (later known as "lobotomy"). (The first Nobel in psychiatry went to Dr. Wagner-Jauregg in 1927, after he stood trial for brutal treatment of soldiers during World War I.)

By the mid-fifties, lobotomies were still popular. A surprising number of returning veterans were subjected to lobotomies, according to a 2013 expose in the *Wall Street Journal*. Then Thorazine arrived in 1954. More phenothiazines ("major tranquilizers") became available, and pushed psychosurgery aside. ECT (electroconvulsive therapy) had slowly but surely replaced insulin coma therapy (ICT), touted by Dr. Sakel. Sakel had observed impressive results in opiate addicts, but others observed downsides to insulin coma. These biological options were effective, but most had serious side effects that made the couch cure more appealing, especially for the "psychopathology of everyday life," to borrow the title of Freud's turn of the century book.

The 1960s were shaken by anti-psychiatry movements, instigated by practicing psychiatrists (Laing, Cooper, Szasz), urged on by sociologists and philosophers (Goffman and Foucault) and counter-culturists, who opposed anything reminiscent of hierarchy and outside authority. Some former patients joined the ranks of academicians and anti-academicians, and identified themselves "psychiatric survivors." The anti-psychiatry movement began in earnest in 1960, and flourished through the 1970s, and beyond. Anti-psychiatry activities and theorists poked holes in tenuous psychiatric theories. They opposed authoritarian approaches of psychiatry, including involuntary hospitalization, ECT and, above all, lobotomy. The film *One Flew Over the Cuckoo's Nest* (1975) became their rallying call. Films like *The Mind Snatchers* (aka *The Happiness Cage*) (1972), starring Christopher Walken, never gained as much caché, even though it combines the anti-authoritarianism and anti-war sentiments of the counter-culture with neuroscience fiction themes. The psychosurgery scene in this film is too close to actual practices to be dismissed as fiction per se, as we will discuss later in this chapter.

A new wave of NSF film evolved in the early seventies, as the drug culture permeated the youth culture and increased awareness of the chemical causes of behavior changes. Later in the decade, psychiatry began to reexamine its practices and priorities. In 1977— in the same year that *Star Wars* changed the playing field for science fiction film—the then-president of the American Psychiatric Association (Mel Sabshin, M.D.) urged psychiatry to "return to its medical roots." Those medical roots had been upbraided by psychoanalysis, which was begun by Freud, a neurologist and one-time neurology researcher. Freud dismissed the need for preliminary medical training of psychoanalysts and admitted "lay analysts" into his psychoanalytic circle.[8]

Dr. Sabshin had no way to know that the personal, professional, and legal travails of a physician-patient named Osheroff would push his presidential platform to the forefront in two years' time. It is one thing to listen to presidential speeches at conferences and to read ponderous academic articles on specific subjects. Putting a human face on a theoretical debate invites attention.[9, 10] Also in 1977, a provocative movie by the name of *Demon Seed* (1977) appeared. The title of *Demon Seed* reminds us of an influential (and inflammatory) film from 1956, *The Bad Seed*. *The Bad Seed* promised to shock and unsettle psychiatry.

Directed by Mervyn LeRoy, *The Bad Seed* was based on a book and Broadway play. A horrific but fictional story of an adopted daughter, the film annoyed analysts because it suggested that some behavior traits do indeed have a biological basis. This blood-curdling and award-winning movie reified the results of adoption studies and earlier reports about the Jukes family, whose story is retold in introductory psychology texts.[11]

By the late 1970s, neuro-imaging studies advanced, and allowed doctors and patients alike to visualize the inner workings of the brain. They could literally "see for themselves" how brain functions change in the presence of emotions, perceptions or cognitions. When specific sections of the brain use more fuel (read: glucose), they light up and glow. These imaging studies helped neuroscience researchers understand brain functions better, even though these innovations did not advance patient care directly at that point in time. These studies performed a valuable function for the clinical community: they offered visible proof that mental functions involve physical processes, and are not solely ethereal or spiritual or simply "psychological."

Looking at these new PET scans, SPECT scans, and *f*MRIs is a little like looking at a movie screen. Like film itself, these "imaging studies" translate abstract concepts into identifiable images. They add a long-lost visual arena to biological psychiatry studies. "Talk therapy," which relies on the sound of spoken words, had the opposite effect. Talk therapy added an auditory component to the practice of neurology, which relies upon visual (and some tactile) observations to make diagnoses and to identify neurological deficits. Many neurological tests and procedures, such as EEGs (electroencephalograms), EMGs (electromyelograms) and NCVs (nerve conduction velocities), have pronounced visual components and allow doubters to "see it before their very eyes." Brain biopsies, x-rays, and the now extinct pneumoencephalograms also rely on vision. These advances in neuropsychiatric diagnostics helped psychiatry return to its medical roots.

Something else occurred between the late 1960s and the late 1970s, something that had little to do with psychiatry or neuropsychiatry, but had everything to do with the brain. In 1968, Harvard professors suggested using "brain death" to redefine the medical term, "death." Until then, a flat-lined EKG (electrocardiogram) distinguished between life and death. A beating heart differentiated a living person from one who is deemed dead. A flatlined EEG (electroencephalogram) would replace the flat-lined EKG. Naturally, there are more caveats to these definitions, and naturally, this proposal was extremely controversial at the time (and still is, in some circles, as we witnessed with the headline-making Munoz and McMath cases of 2013 and 2014).[12] As late as 2014, legal challenges to this definition of death continued, and sometimes the courts are called upon to decide who is officially dead.

Heated debates followed in response to Harvard's original recommendation. Those debates extended beyond medical professionals. The clergy, philosophers, ethicists, legal scholars and ordinary citizens weighed in on this weighty proposal. By the late 1970s, most states accepted brain death as the legal and medical definition of "death." In 1981, the National Conference of Commissioners on Uniform State Laws approved the Uniform Determination of Death Act, defining death as "brain death." Like the concept of the "Decade of the Brain," which would arrive in 1990, the U.S. president approved the definition of brain death. This decision was *not* made by a consensus of doctors.

A beating heart or expanding lungs (which once were believed to house the soul or the "pneuma") was not enough to meet the definition of "life." Brain function now trumped all other physical and mental functions. This hard-won fight confirmed the all-importance of the brain, and pushed the "soul" to second place.[13] For what it's worth, the ancient Egyptians dismissed the significance of the brain entirely, and sucked the cerebral material out of the nostrils (or removed brains with hooks) before beginning their elaborate mummification preparations.

This shift in attitude toward death itself paralleled shifts in attitudes toward brains and minds. Society was changing, and science was changing as well. Shifts in society and science went hand in hand. These shifts did not dictate the direction of neuropsychiatry, but they simply show that movement was in the air, and that several fields were moving in the same direction.

The film entitled *Flatliners* (1990) references the flat-lined EEG that currently determines death. *Flatliners* goes one-step further, and conflates the supernatural with the subconscious as it touches upon theological-philosophical conflicts about life and life after death. As we will see, and as anthropologist Per Schelde points out, science fiction tropes often revert to sorcery and the supernatural, with scientists functioning as latter-day sorcerers.

By the mid–1980s, the tides had turned. Psychoanalysis had come under attack, and not just by anti-establishment elements that opposed all authority. Cultural anthropologists,

ONE. Neurosicence Fiction Film in Post-Psychoanalytic Society　　17

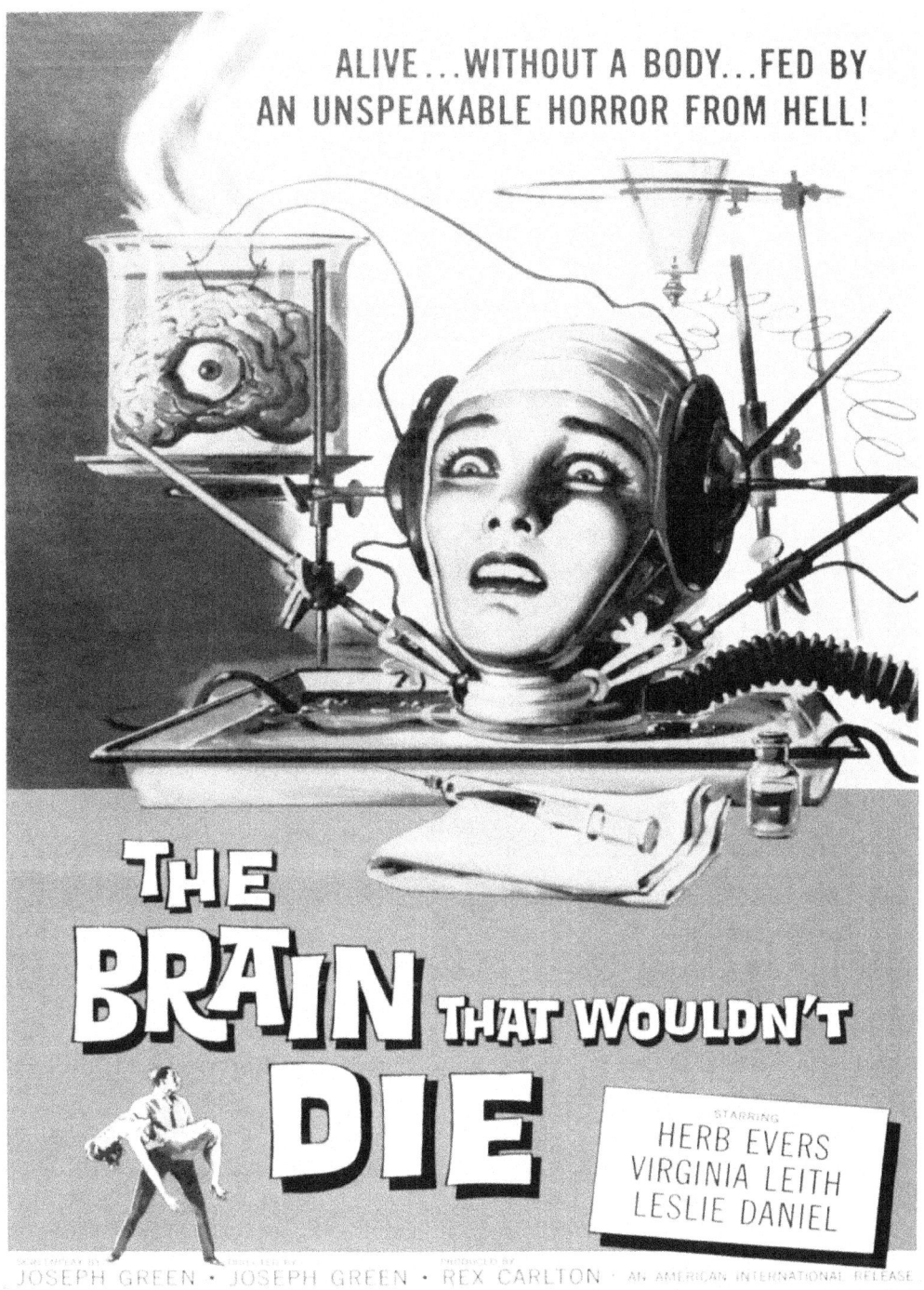

In Joseph Green's *The Brain That Wouldn't Die* (aka *The Head That Wouldn't Die* aka *The Black Door*, made in 1959 but released in 1962), the bodiless head of Jan Compton (Virginia Leith) lies in a fluid-filled tray, connected to a brain in a laboratory beaker, because her surgeon-fiancé Dr. Bill Cortner (Jason Evers) refuses to let her die after she is decapitated in an accident.

some of whom had promoted psychoanalysis early on, found more and more flaws in Freudian and neo–Freudian pronouncements. Social psychologists, along with scientifically minded researchers of many persuasions, impugned Freud's methodology. Scholars scrutinized his case histories, and called the "received wisdom" from "St. Sigmund" into question. Prestigious institutions now recruited psychopharmacologists and neuropsychiatrists, pushing the psychoanalysts aside.

Few psychiatrists enrolled in psychoanalytic training programs in the 1980s. The very same programs that had required M.D. degrees for admission revamped their standards to avoid closing their doors. First, they admitted psychologists, who successfully sued the reigning psychoanalytic academies in 1986. Social workers gained entrée soon after. Today, most American analysts begin their careers in social work. Medical analysts (psychiatrists with added psychoanalytic training) are rare, but those who persist are vocal, and publicly protest the decline of their once-esteemed niche. The film *The Cell* (2000), starring Jennifer Lopez as a social worker turned psychotherapist, dramatizes this administrative shift. At the same time, it invokes a standard science fiction meme about "brain exchanges" and thought transfer.

When Prozac came on the market in 1987, it offered a quick cure for anxiety and depressive disorders. Our fast-food society was reared on McDonald's. Psychiatric "consumers" demanded equally fast fixes for mental distress. With that shift, the lid closed on the coffin that housed the late 19th century invention called psychoanalysis. The coffin was nearly nailed shut—but not completely, for psychoanalysis still has some fans who keep the faith. It even attracted the attention of researchers, including the Nobel Prize–winning psychiatrist, Dr. Eric Kandel. Other researchers, such as the former APA president John Oldham, M.D., showed sophisticated studies that demarcated very specific symptoms that respond to psychoanalytic treatment.

As we entered an even faster-paced, computer-based society, we welcomed faster-acting approaches. Old-time, time-consuming techniques fell by the wayside, especially if they did not prove to be as effective as they claimed to be. The Reagan era, known for its conservatism in other arenas, welcomed these changes. To signal the dramatic paradigm shift, President Bush, who followed Reagan, dubbed the 1990s as the "Decade of the Brain." The biological brain replaced the metaphysical mind. Or, I should say, the biological brain regained its place in neuroscience, having been pushed aside in the past. Like deposed monarchs that were sent into exile after the coup, biologically oriented psychiatrists returned to the fold, ready to reclaim their throne.

It just so happened that the Decade of the Brain was the last decade of the 20th century. Psychoanalysis was a creation of the "fin-de-siècle" that ended the 19th century. The 20th century has been called "The Psychoanalytic Century," as testimony to the influence that psychoanalysis wielded over culture in general (and not just psychiatry). Psychoanalytic influence extended far beyond clinical care; it changed the shape of literature, film, and art. By granting a special name to the decade that preceded the "fin-de-millennium," the powers-that-be suggested that the 21st century would be dramatically different from the 20th century. One wonders if the 21st century will be the era when neuroscience fiction morphs into neuroscience fact.

It is important to recall that the Decade of the Brain did not start so suddenly. Changes were underway for over a decade. One can say that mid-century, the 1950s, were a crossroads between biological and psychological psychiatry, and so were as critical a juncture as the formally identified, "Decade of the Brain." Moreover, this phrase—"Decade of the Brain"—was not the brainchild of scientists or neuropsychiatrists but appears in a Presidential Proclamation.[14]

At face value, giving so much weight to a presidential proclamation—instead of relying upon peer-reviewed reports in juried medical journals or professional committees—seems strange to both researchers and practitioners. However, government recognition of scientific research is critical, because the government has historically funded more research than private industry or philanthropy (although this may be subject to change soon). Thus, the federal government implicitly determines the nation's priorities. Pharmaceutical funding would become an important force as well, and newly minted billionaires who establish their own research institutes have gained more and more clout and can push their personal preferences.[15, 16]

In 1980, another important event took place, one that seems more important in retrospect, especially in light of the controversy generated by the spring 2013 release of *DSM-5* (*Diagnostic and Statistical Manual*). *DSM-III* was published by the American Psychiatric Association, as are all official releases of the *DSM*. This version of the *Diagnostic and Statistical Manual* omitted Freudian terms that could not be quantified. Latinate words such as "ego" and "libido" and "Oedipal complex" had no place in a manual that was intended to standardize psychiatric research. Omitting flowery literary descriptions paved the way to more scientific studies.

This same year—1980—cemented the start of a new breed of NSF films. This new breed had been brewing since the early-to-mid seventies but was not fully fermented until 1980. As homage to the "old order," this same year brought one of the last of the "good" pro-psychoanalytic films to screen: *Ordinary People* (1980). *Ordinary People* attracted extra attention because it was Robert Redford's directorial debut. It resurrected Redford's movie career, and proved that the handsome actor-turned-environmental activist had more talents than most Hollywood heartthrobs. Also in 1980, Ronald Reagan moved into the White House. Curiously, Reagan enjoyed a well-respected acting career before entering politics. Conservatives generally favor biological explanations for behavior, and downplay social or economic forces.

In the meantime, technology plowed ahead, changing society, along with our value systems and our daily experiences. Although computers had been available for decades, the "real" computer era dawned now that ordinary citizens became capable of climbing on board. The World Wide Web was waiting to expand. When it began, the web was an exclusive club. It was a playground for scientists, military masterminds, and computer geeks. Within a decade, that changed dramatically. Thanks to affordable and portable home computers and increased Internet access, "ordinary folks" had the opportunity to become infatuated with cyberspace, "the ether," and its untapped potentials. Cyberpunk was congealing, and would be critical to SF.

SF writer William Gibson coined the word "cyberspace" in 1981, to counter concepts of "outer space" (long the darling of the SF world), and to differentiate it from "inner space," which is a term that appeals to spiritual seekers, psychologists, and others who delve into the mind. In due time, Gibson's neologism entered our everyday vocabulary.

Most Americans embraced the promises of technology, especially if it offered entertainment. Some curmudgeonly Luddites lagged behind, but their protests were stifled. The Information Age that accompanied the Internet moved society, first by baby steps, and then by giant leaps. By the 1990s, it was clear that a revolution was in the works. The Internet Bubble of the late 1990s proved how much the public had come to revere computers. This cultural shift was as critical as the scientific shift. History has shown that a given society must be philosophically prepared for scientific innovations, in order to accept—rather than reject—those innovations.

The attitude shift toward biological psychiatry paralleled the move toward technology in general. Science was king, and philosophy was secondary. To be fair, the space age of the 1950s started the upswing in the study of science, and stoked faith in the potential of scientific research. Oddly enough, psychoanalysis was once touted as a modern "scientific" approach, but it took decades of "real" scientific study to unravel the errors and inconsistencies inherent in it.[17]

The lynchpin that shifted standards of psychiatric practice, at least temporarily, was the precedent set by *Osheroff v. Chestnut Lodge,* which we mentioned earlier on. Luminaries such as Donald Klein, M.D., Jerald Klerman, M.D. of Massachusetts General Hospital, the clinical research director of NIMH (National Institute of Mental Health) and several other high ranking academicians delivered all-star testimony, all in one place, and all at one time. That hotly contested case ended in 1989, with a victory for Dr. Osheroff (and his attorneys) and a humiliating defeat for Chestnut Lodge.

Chestnut Lodge was a much-storied and well-established bastion of psychoanalysis. It "stars" in Joanne Greenberg's endearing book, *I Never Promised You a Rose Garden* (1964). The book became a movie by the same name in 1977—in the very same year that Dr. Sabshin urged psychiatrists to return to their medical roots. The Lodge's ledger listed movers and shakers in psychoanalytic theory, including Henry Stack Sullivan, Frieda Fromm-Reichmann, and Erich Fromm. The lawsuit proved that landmark institutions could not expect to rest on past laurels when the present offers new treatment options, and biologically based ones at that.

The Lodge's staff refused to consider psychopharmacological treatments during Dr. Osheroff's seven-month stay. Instead, they continued daily psychoanalytic sessions while he regressed. He lost forty pounds as he paced all night, without eating during the day. Because Osheroff's depressive symptoms improved within three weeks after he restarted medications at another hospital, suit against Chestnut Lodge was brought—and won. As early as 1982, a judge found for Osheroff, but Osheroff declined the settlement offered, waiting until 1989 to close the case. From that point on, no one doubted that times had changed. Even the forensic psychiatrist who testified against Dr. Osheroff admitted that the case marked a most important development. Many established psychoanalysts disputed the value of these shifts in practice, while many others who had trained as psychoanalysts shifted gears and embraced newer developments.

The 21st century brought more and more changes in neuropsychiatry. Many new mood medications came to market. Antipsychotic drugs were improved (at least in the short run). In response, the voices of psychoanalysts, now neglected and shoved aside, became louder. Sometimes they sounded shrill, like wounded animals that cry out in pain, as they gasp for their last breath. Analysts struggled to hold onto their thrones, lest they be sent into exile, without the option to return. Yet it was obvious that the guard had changed, and there was no going back.

The Library of Congress exhibition entitled *Sigmund Freud: Culture and Conflict*[18] was scheduled to open in 1998. Promoters expected the show to travel the world through 2002. However, public protests against psychoanalysis delayed its opening. Psychoanalysis had enjoyed many years in the sun, but that bright light had faded. The reaction to this exhibition proved that "The Psychoanalytic Century" would end with the 20th century. Freud's once-daring Victorian era invention seemed as dated as hooped skirts and horse-driven carriages.

As time progressed, new discoveries flooded biological psychiatry. Experts in molecular biology, neuro-genetics, neurochemistry, psychopharmacology, psycho-neuro-immunology, and neuro-endocrinology interfaced. They cemented the foundations of a paradigm shift. Psychiatry edged closer to neurology, even though Freud, who trained as a neurologist, had cleaved the fields when he invented psychoanalysis in 1896, a year after the first film screened.[19]

Interestingly, European psychiatry and neurology never underwent as deep a cleft as America experienced. It was only in America that such a deep schism developed between psychiatry and neurology, and it was only in America (and perhaps in Argentina) that psychoanalysis gained such acceptance. Perhaps this "continental divide" will be bridged in the future. It will be curious to see if the rapprochement that appears in *Iron Man 3* will translate from celluloid to clinical care.

Two

Movies and the Mind (and the Rebirth of the Brain)

WARNING: This chapter offers an overview of the information in the rest of the book, in rapid-fire, fast-forward format. There may be some spoilers in the pages to follow.

Cinema and psychoanalysis were born within a year of one another, just before the turn of the 19th century. The ideas of Freud, Jung, and especially the ideas of the so-called "French Freud," Jacques Lacan, are fossilized in film studies. No matter how much neuroscience shoves psychoanalysis aside, and no matter how little attention analytic ideas receive in psychiatric residency programs, film theorists and film plots of the past will sustain ideas informed by Freud and his followers.

Psychoanalytic concepts manifest themselves in many, many movies. Flashbacks, which are so essential to *film noir* storytelling, owe their origin to the psychoanalytic emphasis on repressed memories.[1] Psychoanalytic scenes, with patients and practitioners, appear on the silver screen early in film history. In 1922, Fritz Lang's evil Dr. Mabuse steps to the podium, and announces that he is a psychoanalyst. That statement distinguishes him from run-of-the-mill psychiatrists (also known as "alienists") or from European "nerve doctors" of the late 19th century. As a "psychoanalyst," Dr. Mabuse stands apart from low-level "asylum superintendents" who tend to untreatable patients, warehoused in asylums. Dr. Caligari from 1919 was one of those asylum superintendents, when he was not moonlighting as a carnival showman with his somnambulist Cesare, whom he hypnotized and confined to a cabinet. Film wise, the fictional Dr. Caligari was a close competitor to Dr. Mabuse, although Dr. Mabuse lived many more lives in later movies and wore many more masks and assumed different disguises.

The "talking cure," also known as the "couch cure," became especially popular as a cinema subject from the 1940s onward. The heyday of psychoanalytic cinema occurred in the late 1950s to the mid–1960s. Newer NSF motifs pushed this early theme aside by the early 1980s. In the 1980s, some of the most sinister psychiatrists appear on screen and on the printed page. Dr. Hannibal Lecter surfaces in book form in 1981, makes it to the movies in 1986, with *Manhunter* (1986), and then makes a splash in *The Silence of the Lambs* (1991). Cinematic psychiatrists from 1980s and 1990s America rivaled Weimar's demonic mind doctors, as described by film critic Siegfried Kracauer in his historic study, *From Caligari to Hitler* (1947).

In the twilight of the 20th century, psychoanalytic themes still appeared, more often than not, in parody. Movies such as *What about Bob?* (1991), *Analyze This* (1999) and *Analyze That* (2002) were endearing, but their comedic treatment of the "talking cure" suggests that talk therapy will not endure and is going on life-support. It remains to be seen if the closing scene in *Iron Man 3* will resuscitate talk therapy, or if the Stark-Banner dialogue will be dismissed as yet another parody that is befitting the black humor of the *Iron Man* series.[2]

Films that focus on the brain as a physical entity, or on the central nervous system that connects to the spinal cord, belong to an entirely different genre. Those films bear limited relationship to psychoanalytically oriented cinema. They are distinct from movies about behavioral conditioning, such as *The Manchurian Candidate* (1962), or relationship-focused treatments, which include *David and Lisa* (1962), *Persona* (1966), or *The Ninth Configuration* (1980).

Theoretically, neuroscience fiction film should be newer than psychoanalytically tinged cinema, simply because neuroscience seems so new, compared to Freudian-influenced film. However, what should be is not necessarily what is. The origins of neuroscience fiction film predate psychoanalytically influenced cinema. Rather than speaking of the "birth" of NSF in the last quarter of the 20th century, we should refer to the "evolution" of NSF—or even the resurgence of NSF. For this subgenre did not arise out of nowhere, even though it seems to have sprung up recently, especially since it got press (from AP reporter Jake Coyle and others).

If we look back over the last four decades or so, we can find a cohesive theme congealing. We can trace the roots of NSF back to human-ape brain exchanges from the 1920s and 1930s and to alien-human brain drains and exchanges from the 1950s. This new NSF is distinctly different from the Darwinian-influenced silent films about human-ape brain exchanges, but is not so far apart from later "simian cinema" that references behavior-altering hormones. Even the automatons of very early film (or *Metropolis*) set the stage for today's *RoboCop*.

We can argue as to whether or not NSF deserves to be designated as a subgenre of science fiction. Those arguments may be moot, since critics say that 21st century science fiction in general is no longer a cohesive genre because it split into so many subgenres. If that is true, then NSF is another of those subgenres.[3]

Science fiction in general often overlaps with other genres. Horror-SF hybrids are particularly common, but Western SF, romantic SF and comedic SF are easily identifiable. SF even interfaces with social problem films at times. When we look back in time, many SF seem funny to contemporary spectators, even though those films were intended to be serious when they were released. Film Forum, a non-profit revival movie theater in New York, hosted summer SF festivals for such films. Their festival attracted around-the-block crowds, but programmers eventually "got bored" and put the festival on hold for twenty years.[4] It returned in 2013.

At times, NSF overlaps with "cyberpunk," which focuses on computers and their relationships with humans. Cyberpunk is far more relevant to our times than "simian cinema" or "alien brain drains," but that does not negate the significance of those early influences. NSF extends far beyond computers, even though it includes films about brain-computer interfaces or robotics that mimic—or even mate with—humans, as happens in *RoboCop*, *Blade Runner* or *Demon Seed*. Occasionally, NSF crosses over with "biopunk," an offshoot of cyberpunk that is concerned with genetic manipulation and the risks that result from the discovery of DNA, the mapping of the genome and the biotech revolution.

We could conceivably refer to NSF as "neuropunk," to contrast it with "biopunk" and link it to cyberpunk, but that would imply that NSF or "neuropunk" is an offshoot of cyberpunk and the computer era, and that conclusion is patently incorrect. It would also deflect attention from NSF's deep roots in 19th century SF literature and early silent cinema, and it would divorce NSF from "simian cinema," alien brain exchanges of the Sputnik era, or brain grafts in social problem film of the 60s and 70s. That history of NSF is as rich as our present day NSF creations. It may sound strange to emphasize the importance of NSF's "past," when so many see NSF as a brand "new" genre. At the risk of sounding trite, I must quote an old saying, that someone or something that has no past also has no future. Just the opposite is true for NSF: it has deep roots in the past, and can be expected to branch out even more in the future.

NSF proliferated in the 1980s, when production of SF films increased overall in response to the commercial and critical success of *Star Wars* (1977) and *Close Encounters of the Third Kind* (1977). Neither *Star Wars* nor *Close Encounters of the Third Kind* directly connects to NSF, but these two spectacular successes catalyzed investment in SF films and so paved the path for more NSF films. Because SF films can be costly, with their special effects and set designs, studios needed an external impetus before green-lighting more SF films. Blockbusters such as *Star Wars* and *Close Encounters of the Third Kind* mainstreamed this one-time "geek genre."

High quality, big budget SF films followed in the wake of *Star Wars*. Even Roger Corman benefited from this surge of respect for science fiction. Corman was legendary for producing shoestring budget horror–SF films in the sixties. As SF audiences expanded, so did Corman's audiences (even if his budgets remained unchanged). Television SF was reinvigorated by *Star Wars*, after suffering a severe setback when *Star Trek* stopped in late 1969. Shows such as *Battlestar Galactica* (1978) and *Buck Rogers in the 21st Century* (1979) brought TV back to life. After the arrival of cable TV, SF acquired an entire cable channel all to itself.

William Gibson's stories and novels deserve credit for increasing interest in cyberpunk and "neuropunk" or NSF—although films based on Gibson's books do not deserve too much credit because those films rarely, if ever, appeal to audiences as much as their literary forerunners. Gibson's *Neuromancer* and *Johnny Mnemonic* stories and novels moved to the mainstream in the late 1980s, and continue to pollinate NSF tropes to this day. Gibson spin-offs in cinema are easy to spot, especially since so many movies have mined his rich source material.

We can find many academic (and not-so-academic) studies of "cyberpunk," which began as literature before moving into movies. Considering how much computers have penetrated everyday life and changed the ways that we communicate, retrieve information, manufacture and purchase products, it makes sense that computer-inspired cyberpunk garners so much attention, from both spectators and scholars. Surprisingly, there is relatively little attention to NSF to date, even though neuropsychiatry and psychopharmacology impact the lives of so many Americans, and even though one quarter of Americans use prescribed mood-altering meds.

To repeat, at present, one out of four persons takes a *prescribed* mood-changing medication daily. Not all mood-changing meds are acquired via prescription. Sometimes prescriptions are shared or redistributed, illicitly. According to a January 2012 report from the American Psychiatric Association, over 200 million people globally use illegal drugs each day.[5] Those numbers do not include coffee, cigarettes or alcohol, which are legal in most states.

The appeal of NSF is by no means limited to either "consumers" or "providers" of mental health care. Oftentimes, scientists and researchers are even more infatuated with science fiction literature and film than the clinicians who deliver direct patient care. These seemingly "escapist" films may catalyze creativity among scientists, and promote discoveries of new treatment techniques, by making them think about "what if?" Social scientists are quick to spot reality-based inspirations in such subject matter and recognize that "escapist" films often function as metaphors about current social and political issues. They may embed messages about real life concerns in their phantasmagorical plots, and so they stand to make a point more easily than direct documentaries.

Some renowned physician-researchers credit their ideas to their SF reading.[6] I myself have vivid recollections of my fellow medical students cradling copies of Michael Crichton's *The Terminal Man* (1972) when it was first released. One Midwestern medical school class alone did not turn Crichton's book into a best-seller, but this suggests that other science students, teachers, professors, practitioners, and like-minded enthusiasts followed suit, purchasing the book, and pushing it to the top of the list.

In 2010, AP (Associated Press) reporter Jake Coyle took a stab at this subject. Coyle wrote about "The New 'Western': The Mind Is the New Movie Frontier." (Coyle consulted this author before completing his article, and quotes her in his piece.) Coyle observed that films such as *Inception* (2010), *The Imaginarium of Dr. Parnassus* (2009), and *Eternal Sunshine of the Spotless Mind* (2004) signal a shift away from the tried and true approach of *Spellbound* (1945), which is revered for surrealistic, psychoanalytic dream scenes designed by Dalí. Hitchcock's *Spellbound* set the gold standard for dream scenes on screen and even eclipsed Méliès' turn-of-the-century masterpieces from silent cinema.

Coyle's article was picked up by some 300 print and online publications, proving that he is, first and foremost, a worthy writer, and, secondly, that there is strong interest in this still unsung subject. Coyle compares this "new" genre to Westerns, the most American genre of all. Westerns merge action-adventure and romance, sometimes adding comedy or melodrama. It makes sense to speak of SF film and Westerns in the same sentence. Even before *Star Wars* expanded the playing field for SF, pop songs praised "space cowboys" who (presumably) ride spaceships the way "country" cowboys ride rodeo horses. Space cowboys confront outer space as fearlessly as frontiersman who traipsed through unchartered terrain.

Coyle's comparison makes sense, especially when we consider one particularly venerable old Western that turned into a futuristic space adventure in 1981, right around the time that psychiatry was changing directions. *Outland* (1981) stars Sean Connery, of James Bond fame. *Outland* is a remake of the classic Gary Cooper Western, *High Noon* (1952). The difference lies in the fact that *Outland*'s action occurs on Jupiter's moon, instead of the Western prairies. We can see how *Star Wars*, with its "space cowboy" meme from 1977, facilitated this reimagining.

In the pages that follow, we will not compare NSF films to Westerns. This reference to Jake Coyle's AP piece will suffice. Rather, this book situates NSF in the broader SF genre, to show how neuroscience fiction films share traits with general SF yet carve out their own terrain at the same time. Like other SF, NSF comments on culture and philosophy at the same time that it assimilates (or distorts) scientific theories. It also prophesizes about the future, sometimes surprisingly accurately. Not infrequently, it foretells doom and destruction, and inveighs against the perils of technology and what happens when humans play G-d. Apocalyptic themes in SF (and NSF) have much in common with the Biblical Book of Daniel, which is referenced indirectly in *The Matrix* (1999). In *The Matrix,* Morpheus rescues refugees in a ship named *Nebuchadnezzar*, in homage to the king who reigned when Daniel was cast into the lion's den. Nebuchadnezzar literally saw "the handwriting on the wall"—and it was not good news.

Some SF deals with imaginary voyages or fantasy locations, which are usually set in the future. Steampunk SF is an exception to this tradition, because its action takes place in a re-imagined past where Victorian flourishes adorn high-tech machinery. More than anything

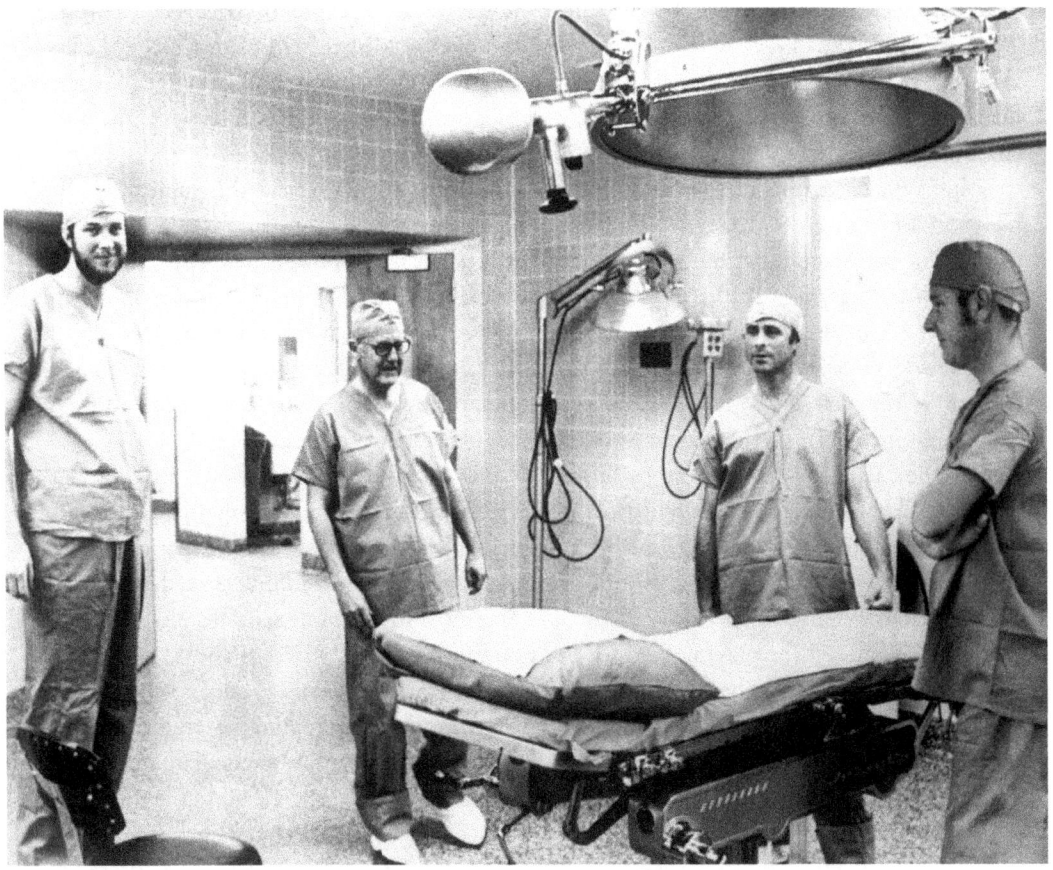

At left is Michael Crichton, M.D., a non-practicing physician and author of *The Terminal Man* (1972), who stands 6'9" and towers over masked and gowned cast and crew as they prepare to film another Crichton novel, *The Andromeda Strain* (1971), in a real hospital operating room.

else, SF chronicles "change." It is a conduit for the fears and hopes ignited by the prospect of change or by the presence of change. We would expect to find SF film (and literature) to proliferate during times of scientific change. Given these patterns, it is not surprising that "serious" NSF films increased in number and intensified in quality during the same years that neuropsychiatric paradigms shifted from one pole to another: between 1980 and 1990.

As more SF films appeared in the eighties, some critics condemned the film industry for turning toward fantasy or for being too derivative. We will show that some SF "fantasies" were not so fanciful as they seemed on the surface, for many such fantasies anticipated shifts in the ways that science, medicine and psychiatry approach behavior, emotion, cognition and genetics.

When the psychiatric paradigm veered away from psychoanalysis and theories of "mind," and moved towards neuropsychiatry, with an emphasis on the physical "brain," production companies were poised to produce movies about these trendy themes. They could expand their repertoires and populate their list with "inner space" themes that balanced the overabundance of "outer space" films. As long as audiences appreciated such motifs, and box office receipts confirmed that profits offset steep production costs, moviemakers could capture these changing trends, apply their creativity—and capitalize on them as well.

Advances in CGI (computer-generated imagery) made it easier to show surrealistic scenes and dreamscapes. CGI gave a brand-new look to these tried-and-true tropes, some of which date back to film's first decade, when Méliès made short silents about dream scenes. In 1991, James Cameron's *Terminator 2* took a giant leap forward. Cameron's CGI advanced animated backgrounds and actions, making the early-generation computer-generated effects in Crichton's *Westworld* (1973) look primitive in comparison, almost like Claymation.

In the aftermath of *Terminator 2* in 1991, CGI became the norm. Recall that psychiatry (and George Bush, Sr.) declared the 1990s to be "The Decade of the Brain." The rise of CGI and the rise of the "brain" coincided in time, just as the "discovery" of psychoanalysis and the screening of the first film occurred with a year of one another. What a fortuitous coincidence! As to be expected, edgier or less established filmmakers ventured into this unsung terrain before bigger studios or mainstream directors dared tread. (Earlier NSF was cheap and cheesy, and not something that more sophisticated post–*Star Wars* producers aspired to.) Pioneers included David Cronenberg and the Russian émigré, Slava Tsukerman, who made *Liquid Sky* (1982).

We can identify direct antecedents to the "new breed" of NSF film that Coyne describes. *The Terminal Man* (1974) had the highest visibility, even though it was not first of this ilk. Based on Michael Crichton's best-selling book from 1972, the film version was rushed into production because of the book's success. Sadly, the film was not as inspiring as its literary counterpart. It flopped at the box office, but remains important to the history of NSF. For that matter, anything written by or inspired by Crichton remains important, if for no other reason than because Crichton himself is so critically important to SF, NSF, and bio–SF.

Crichton deserves our attention for many reasons. He worked as a writer and filmmaker until his death in 2008—but he never worked as a doctor, even though he held an M.D. degree. His medical credentials—and the data he acquired while qualifying for those credentials—lent credibility to his fantastic themes and to more reality-based themes, such as the popular TV show *ER* (1994–2009). His academic training in basic science, medicine, and anthropology informed his art and expanded his knowledge base. He wove unrelated threads into a thick and rich tapestry. Crichton's story-telling skills, coupled with his ability to mine his imagination, and pepper it with factoids culled from his vast fund of information, made his writing readable and redolent with meaning. Several successful SF writers have strong scientific backgrounds, and he was one of that breed.[7]

Crichton also did post-graduate training in virology. His studies of infectious agents infiltrate his pre–NSF book about *The Andromeda Strain* (1969). He was a giant-sized man (6'9") who became a sci-fi giant, even before graduating from Harvard Medical School.

Crichton's *The Terminal Man* (1972) became a cult classic among medical students. Younger fans remember Crichton's dinosaur-themed *Jurassic Park* (1993). Crichton's film, *Westworld* (1973), was the first film to use computer-generated special effects, as noted above.

In retrospect, we wonder how much Crichton's book and film influenced the next generation of neuroscientists, psychiatrists and neurologists. It is not rare that a book or film sways the thinking of professionals as well as the public. Psychologists who study media confirm that films make stronger impressions than books, even though books explain issues and ideas more thoroughly than images on screen.[8] We know that the film version of *One Flew Over the Cuckoo's Nest* (1975) influenced medical students who saw it, making them much less likely to recommend ECT (electroconvulsive, or shock therapy) to patients after they watched the film. Yet the Ken Kesey book, upon which the movie was based, did not sway opinions in the same way—even though the book was a best-seller, and plays based on the book were remarkably well received.

In *The Terminal Man,* a psychiatrist, neurologist, and neurosurgeon collaborate on the care of a brain-damaged epileptic man, played by George Segal. Each specialist recommends different treatments for their shared patient. Segal dismisses his psychiatrist's concerns, and consents to the experimental brain implant touted by the neurosurgeon. All might have gone well, but the implant misfired. This catastrophe sends the out-of-control Segal on a murderous rampage that claims the life of his fiancée. Before the film ends, he also kills his psychiatrist.

There is medical truth behind this fictional narrative. A phenomenon known as "sham rage" results when electrical impulses stimulate the amygdala (an almond-shaped section situated deep inside the brain). Experiments on cats show how felines arch their backs, bare their teeth, hiss and express their claws when electrical impulses flow through this part of the midbrain. Scientists recognized the amygdala's role in rage in the early 20th century. Psychiatrists published reports on sham rage in humans in the official journal of the American Psychiatric Association in 1942.[9] More to the point, the same *American Journal of Psychiatry* includes an article on "ictal affect" in a 1958 issue. "Ictal affect" refers to mood changes that occur in conjunction with epileptic (ictal) episodes. The author links increased aggression and libido to these "fits," and traces the literature on related brain lesions, in both humans and animals.[10] Articles like this one added to ongoing debates about the "epileptoid personality."

Like other high quality SF, Crichton's text embroiders deeper meanings into his attention-grabbing plots. Perhaps the book and film were urging the fields of psychiatry and neurology to reunite, and establish a "meeting of the minds," literally and figuratively. Perhaps Crichton wanted to warn readers of the risks of overly ambitious use of technology in an attempt to overcome the age-old "human plight." So often, SF takes on a dystopian tone as it prophesizes the hazards when humans strive to be something other than human, and closer to all-controlling deities or similar to emotionless machines. Considering Crichton's flamboyantly sexist views of women and his advocacy of stereotyped gender roles, we must wonder if his sensitive and feeling female psychiatrist makes a statement about traits that he assigned to specific genders, both good and bad. We will discuss these interesting issues later in this book.

To be fair, when praising Crichton's *The Terminal Man,* we should mention a lower-profile film with a related NSF theme that was released a few years earlier, in 1972. That film is *The Mind Snatchers* (aka *The Happiness Cage*) (1972). Directed by Bernard Girard, *The Mind Snatchers* premiered in the same year that *The Terminal Man* novel was published, but the writer/director worked more in television than in film and never carried the caché of a Crichton. *The Mind Snatchers* deserves more credit than it usually gets, especially since it stars Christopher Walken, who went on to make a career out of such odd roles.

Girard's earlier film, *The Mad Room* (1969), focuses on family dynamics and madness. *The Mad Room* stars a secretly psychotic Stella Stevens as the much older sister of two sibs who were falsely implicated in the murder of their parents. She works as a housekeeper-secretary for a wealthy widow (Shelley Winters) and lives in her home. After their release from a long-term hospital, the children are placed under the supervision of their sister, who turns out to be the true culprit. Whenever they get agitated, the duo retreat to the designated "mad room" of the house.

The motivation for the murder turns out to be standard-brand sibling rivalry, which is a well-worn theme in psychoanalysis (and in the Bible, Greco-Roman myth, and the Vedas). The older sister is angry about the attention that the parents shower on her younger sibs. Yet *The Mad Room* is not overwhelmingly psychoanalytically oriented, as were so many films in the 1950s and 1960s. We can see in it a subtle anti-psychiatry subtext—which was popular in the late 1960s. Either way, this film was not concerned with the neurobiological basis of behavior. It emphasized the consequences of madness, rather than the cause or even the cure. It is a classic "wrong man" film; the wrong boy (and girl) are accused and convicted of a crime they did not commit. Critics classified it as a "whodunit."[11] It is a remake of a much earlier film and play.

The Mad Room suggests that trained psychiatrists make mistakes about who is sane and who is psychotic, even when they have many opportunities to observe their subjects in hospital settings. In 1972, Stanford psychology professor David Rosenhan published the results of a sophisticated study that reifies points made by *The Mad Room.* Rosenhan sent sham patients to psychiatric wards, where they feigned symptoms of psychosis and were labeled psychotic and treated with anti-psychotic agents.[12] "On Being Sane in Insane Places" is one of the more influential studies of psychiatric diagnoses, and one of the most damning as well.

Perhaps Girard might have made a stronger mark, had he made more movies about mental health issues. However, he did not. He devoted his efforts to television and other themes. There are other reasons why Girard's film is less well remembered than movies based on Crichton's book. *The Mind Snatchers* has a military theme that seems specific to the anti-war era. In contrast, Crichton's topic is universal and timeless. In *The Mind Snatchers,* a German scientist develops a technique of controlling aggressive soldiers. He does not bully them. He does not subject them to shocks, as Drs. Kaufmann and Wagner-Jauregg did during World War I.

In *The Mind Snatchers,* the doctor implants a device that stimulates the brain's pleasure centers. This approach is the polar opposite of the "Kaufmannization" technique used in Europe. Dr. Kaufmann inflicted intentionally painful electric shocks to soldiers with "war neuroses," to prod them back to the battlefield. This technique made shell-shocked soldiers uncomfortable enough to return to the front—but many absconded instead, and some suicided. Some military psychiatrists stood trial as the war ended, at the "Wagner-Jauregg Trial," where Freud testified.

The Mind Snatchers is one of many films about brain chips, brain implants and mind control. Its chronological correspondence to Crichton's work—and the presence of Christopher Walken—make it especially important. Christopher Walken had his first starring role in *The Mind Snatchers.* Through this break, he launched a long string of successes in roles about out-of-kilter characters. His performance captures the side effects of current antipsychotic medications, such as Haldol (haloperidol), which causes "Parkinsonian" side effects that include the characteristic "masked facies" of PD. His facial muscles barely move, and his features are expressionless, with the blank and blink-less stare that occurs in "pseudo-Parkinson's disease" produced by these medications, as well as in spontaneously occurring Parkinson's diseases.

Compared to Crichton's novel and the film based on his novel, *The Mind Snatchers* makes a more tentative statement about shifts in neuropsychiatric practice. *The Mind Snatchers* revolves around more sinister aspects of psychiatry: mind control. This theme replays time and time again in both American and European cinema.[13] By specifying that the experiment occurs in Germany, rather than in the U.S., *The Mind Snatchers* links the outlandish procedure to much more horrific experiments conducted by Nazi doctors during the Second World War. By using the American soldiers as experimental subjects, the film connects Vietnam-era America to Nazi-era Germany. As such, it reads as an anti-war or anti-psychiatry film, more than as a NSF film.

Still, we can speculate about connections to emerging concerns from early 1970s neuropsychiatry, and even some public health revelations from 1972, after the film was released. Walter J. Freeman, M.D., lobotomy proselytizer, died in 1972, after having spent the 1950s promoting this simple office-based procedure to psychiatrists. That makes us ask if *The Mind Snatchers* references American approaches to surgical control of aggression and dissidence. Perhaps it intentionally links Freeman's lobotomies to this film's brain chips. He performed about 3,400 lobotomies himself, until the powers-that-be banned him from operating.

Importantly, the early seventies brought bad tidings about the "fair-haired child" of psychiatric treatments. The phenothiazine Thorazine had largely replaced more permanent and maiming lobotomy procedures, soon after it arrived in America in 1954. Haloperidol (Haldol), which we mentioned above, became available in 1958, and was more potent than chlorpromazine (Thorazine) and produced more intense Parkinsonian side effects.

As time passed, it became apparent that these comparatively benign neuroleptic medications caused distressing movement disorders (Tardive dyskinesia or TD) after long-term use. A crisis was in the works when *The Mind Snatchers* opened in 1972. In response to the emerging problem, the American Psychiatric Association set up a task force in 1973 to study the issues. Harvard psychiatrist Ross Baldessarini, M.D., chaired the committee. A year later, in 1974, Pharma giant Smith Kline & French (SKF) agreed to its first million dollar settlement for a case of TD (Tardive dyskinesia). This development gave fodder to anti-psychiatry activists, and gave credibility to the unethical neuropsychiatry experiments portrayed in *The Mind Snatchers*.

More bad news about medical experiments surfaced in 1972. In 1927, Wagner-Jauregg received a Nobel Prize for treating general paresis of the insane (neurosyphilis) with fever therapy. In 1972, the *New York Times* published a front-page article about syphilis studies conducted by none other than the U.S. Public Health Service. Even though Fleming discovered penicillin in 1953, and proved that the medication prevented the progression of syphilis, infected black men from Tuskegee, Alabama, went untreated so researchers could observe the natural course of the disease. Many subjects who survived were left blind, paralyzed, or psychotic. Others died premature deaths from aortic disease. Some wives and unborn children were infected by an agent that is sexually transmitted and that passes through the placenta.

When asked about their adherence to the Nuremberg Laws that prohibit involuntary human experimentation, American public health doctors involved with the study claimed that they thought that the Nuremberg Laws applied to German doctors only, in that these laws were passed in response to experiments conducted by Nazi doctors who practiced in concentration camps. Faith in the American medical establishment plummeted when revelations about Nazi-like practices came to light, and when the doctors themselves defended themselves by invoking memories of the Nuremberg Trials, the Doctors' Trial and the laws that followed in their wake.

We can categorize more films from the late 1960s and early 70s as "proto-NSF"—even though their thrust lies closer to the social problem films of the Civil Rights era. Some of these films function as family melodramas. *Change of Mind* (1968) revolves around race issues more than neuropsychiatric issues. The brain of a racist white DA is transplanted into the body of a black man, to save the life of the white man. In a similar vein, *Hauser's Memory* (1970) centers around a Jewish scientist who volunteers to receive injections of cerebrospinal fluid from the brain of dying scientist, who just so happens to be a Nazi. The Nazi scientist, Hauser, has not yet recorded his valuable scientific secrets. As to be expected, problems ensue from this "transfusion." Again, this film tackles crucial philosophical issues, with neuroscience remaining in the background. Yet the possibility that neurochemicals found in the spinal fluid can transfer memory traces opens a link, however weak, to forthcoming research about neurotransmitters. Julius Axelrod won a Nobel Prize in 1970 for his discovery of the metabolism of epinephrine, which called attention to the triumphs of neuroscience and the existence of neurotransmitters.

The following year, 1971, there is *The Incredible Two-Headed Transplant* (1971). This standard brand horror film would be labeled as "medsploitation" in today's jargon. A scientist grafts the head of homicidal "maniac" onto a "moron," who then goes on a murder spree.

L'Homme au Cerveau Greffé aka *The Man with the Transplanted Brain* (1972) is more subtle and sophisticated, but is still several steps away from the purer NSF that evolved over the next several years. In this melodrama, a respected surgeon is dying of heart disease. His brain is transplanted into the otherwise healthy body of a young brain-injured man. Unbeknownst to anyone, the young man just happens to be the lover of the dying man's daughter. When the daughter desires the young body that houses her father's brain, expected oedipal conflicts ensue. This film's "family romance" lies closer to Freud (and Otto Rank[14]) than NSF, but is closer still to medical ethics debates and dilemmas, which were increasing rapidly during these years.

The brain transplant theme is more than a plot-driving device, for the film can be read as a commentary on the brave new world of organ transplants, which was on fast-forward in 1970. Dr. Christian Barnard's human-to-human heart transplant, the first of its kind, occurred in 1967, in South Africa. Preliminary studies were in the works for decades, earning Nobels for several scientists. No other transplant received as much attention—or notoriety—as Barnard's heart transplant.

In the same year that Dr. Barnard salvaged a heart from a young woman who died in an auto accident, and transplanted it into a man who was dying of heart failure, a liver transplant occurred. The year before, doctors transplanted a pancreas. In 1954, an identical twin received a kidney transplant from the healthy twin, and survived. Cornea transplants occurred as early as 1905. Brain transplants were (and still are) far away, but the world of expanding possibilities was within sight. For SF fans, it is never too soon to fret about the perils inherent in scientific or technological change.

We can draw other curious chronological correlations with the early, and even later, days of NSF. In the same year as the release of *The Terminal Man*, 1974, Mel Brooks made *Young Frankenstein*. Brooks had been a Borscht Belt comedian before becoming a filmmaker.

Young Frankenstein spoofs Mary Shelley's original *Frankenstein*, written in 1818. Shelley started the trend of "NSF," albeit unwittingly, long before film came into being.

Shelley's Dr. Frankenstein was an anatomist who made a monster when he added a brain to a body and imparted life to the being via an electric volt. When Shelley wrote, electricity was new and frightening, as frightening as Frankenstein's monster. Universal and Hammer horror film audiences continued to scream at *Frankenstein* films more than a century later. *Frankenstein* films were remade and revised many times over, starting in film's first decade, when Edison Studios released *Frankenstein* in 1910. Abbott and Costello spoofed *Frankenstein* in 1948.

When an acclaimed comedian such as Mel Brooks parodies a subject that left earlier audiences screaming in terror, we know that change is at bay. For parodies appear when their subject matter is about to die a slow death. Perhaps Mel Brooks sensed that Frankensteinian monsters, with transplanted brains named "Abby Normal," would someday be closer to fact that fiction. In fact, by 2002, embryonic stem cell transplants in mice suggest that transplanted brain tissue may relieve Parkinson's disease, which destroys brain cells that manufacture dopamine. Depression and even dementia may accompany Parkinson's, along with the characteristic tremor and limitations in volitional movement. At present, progress in this area is stymied not so much by science, but by public sentiment and legislation that limits harvesting of fetal stem cells that can replenish dopamine production.

Shifts were subtle, rather than sudden, in the later 1970s. APA president Mel Sabshin urged his constituents in the American Psychiatric Association to shift gears in 1977, and to return psychiatry to its medical roots. He issued that statement a few years post–*Terminal Man*.

Marty Feldman plays Igor in Mel Brooks' spoof *Young Frankenstein* (1974). His exopthalmos ("bug-eyes") make Marty memorable, as he seeks a suitable brain for Dr. Frankenstein's creation. He accidentally drops the jar with scientist's brain, pictured in the background.

What next to no one knew, at the time, was that an unfortunate nephrologist entered Chestnut Lodge in 1977, as a patient and not as a physician.[15] Had this occurred in 1957, instead of 1977, the prospect of providing couch-based analytic therapy would have seemed more humane than available alternatives, which included surgical treatments or coma-inducing insulin shock (which can cause permanent cognitive dysfunction if blood sugars go unmonitored). However, times had changed since the 1950s, and new and better treatments were on the horizon.

Dr. Osheroff's psychoanalytically oriented treatment failed to lift his depression, but his malpractice suit succeeded in shifting the direction of psychiatric practice. World-renowned psychiatrists and neuroscience researchers testified at the trial, affirming the utility of evidence-based psychopharmacology and denigrating treatments based solely on "opinion," such as psychoanalysis. Statements by psychiatric "titans" both galvanized and polarized psychiatrists.[16]

Also in 1977, documents about not so secret—but quite unsavory—CIA experiments known as MK-ULTRA came to light. These experiments resulted in the death of at least one scientist (Dr. Frank Olson) who was unknowingly dosed with LSD. This government-sponsored research strived to illuminate the science behind "mind control." Their research emphasized non-invasive psychological techniques more than psychopharmacological or psychosurgical approaches, although they included studies of LSD.[17] Dr. Olson's sudden suicide was ultimately attributed to hidden hallucinogens. As late as 2012, Dr. Olson's family contends that his death was not an accident, or even a suicide, but was actually a premeditated murder, intended to hide the extent of CIA experiments on mind control.[18]

MK-ULTRA studies inspired a film, *Conspiracy Theory* (1997), and a much-later appearing scholarly work by historian of medicine, Andrea Tone.[19] Naturally, this information about secret or not-so-secret CIA experiments sparked controversy about the CIA. It is unclear if these revelations were sufficient to taint public perceptions of psychiatry as a whole, or if they simply validated doubts that were already in progress. These were years when the anti-psychiatry movement was alive and well, and when coercive tactics used by mental health workers were routinely compared to totalitarian control by government agencies. In this case, they were right.

It should be stressed that those now-notorious CIA studies mostly involved psychological mind control techniques, rather than biological techniques. They showed non-medical psychologists in a bad light. They also showed the dark side of some well-respected psychiatrists, including the Canadian Dr. Cameron and the British Dr. Sargant.[20] Their non-invasive brainwashing approaches share similarities with the "brainwashing" scenes in Frankenheimer's *The Manchurian Candidate* (1962).

Also in 1977, a renowned film related to neuroscience was remade: *The Island of Dr. Moreau*. *Dr. Moreau* dates to the end of the 19th century, when H.G. Wells wrote a novel in the same year that Freud coined the concept of "psycho-analysis." That year was 1896. The remake of *Invasion of the Body Snatchers* (1978) followed a year after the *Moreau* remake.

The original *Body Snatchers* appeared at the height of the McCarthy Era, in 1956, when political paranoia was rampant. Don Siegel, who made the first of the two films, insisted that his movie was a commentary on suburbanization in America, and the over-arching conformity that followed. Citizens started to look like hollow shells of their former selves. To casual observers, and to director Don Siegel, it seemed that the souls had been sucked out of suburbanites and Levittown dwellers. Mass media further homogenized America, as televisions entered American homes. By 1954, when the majority of Americans owned TV sets, the same four TV stations broadcast the same ideas across the country. Individuality dwindled, and conformity soared.

Siegel denied being influenced by McCarthy era politics. He was not asked about the role played by Thorazine, which came to market in 1954. Phenothiazines such as Thorazine stopped schizophrenics' hallucinations and delusions, but made them walk and talk like zombies. Siegel did not comment on chlorpromazine and schizophrenia, in any interviews available, but we can predict that a medication that made schizophrenics seem more "normal" added to American conformity. Schizophrenia was the epitome of individualism, eccentricity and outsider status. Something that subdued the idiosyncratic delusions and hallucinations experienced by persons with schizophrenia suggested that all of society could be tamed in one fell swoop.

Kaufman's 1978 remake of *Invasion of the Body Snatchers* had direct links to contemporary psychiatric treatments. It is said to be a commentary on the self-help movement of the 1970s. *Invasion of the Body Snatchers* of 1978 includes a psychiatrist, played by none other than Leonard Nimoy. Nimoy was already well known as *Star Trek*'s pointy-eared Vulcan science officer, Mr. Spock. As Spock, he mouthed wise but cynical observations about human emotions. Even in retrospect, Mr. Spock's deadpan insights rival the insights offered by many psychiatrists.

With lead characters that include general practitioners and psychiatric specialists, *Body Snatchers* 1978 reflects changes that occurred in psychiatry since 1956, just after the introduction of Thorazine and when Dr. Freeman still touted lobotomies. In 1956, GPs guided their patients through emotional woes. By 1978, psychiatric specialists were relatively common, and pushed aside the familiar family doctor, with his reassuring *Marcus Welby*–like bedside manner. That is the beginning and end of its relevance to NSF. *Dr. Moreau* is an entirely different matter.

H.G. Wells' *Dr. Moreau* is neither psychiatrist nor a neurologist, but he is a proto-neuropsychiatrist, as per his interests. He is also amoral and indifferent to human or animal suffering. His story is "early NSF." Had Dr. Moreau lived in the late 20th century, he might have attended neuropsychiatry conferences, as well as workshops on ethology, the study of animal behavior as it relates to humans. Genetics intrigued Moreau, as did human and animal behavior. The biological basis of behavior and the psychology of education rated high on Moreau's priorities. Moreau had a desire to tamper with destiny, but lacked the conscience that would keep his curiosity in check. For sure, the fictional Moreau would have lost his medical license for unethical experimentation.

Importantly, Wells opposed vivisection, and he wrote *Moreau* to push this political and philosophical point of view. As the years passed, and as other issues rose in importance, the tale of Dr. Moreau acquired different meanings. Dr. Moreau came to represent current conflicts in society, science, and psychiatry. The 1977 *Moreau* remake appeared during the heyday of the feminist movement, when Freud's adage that "anatomy is destiny" was debated, disputed and denigrated. This *Moreau* movie spoke to a new generation with brand new values. That generation believed that human beings can override innate biology, should they so choose.

We cannot leave 1977 without mentioning *Demon Seed* (1977). The title of *Demon Seed* recollects another hotly debated movie, *The Bad Seed* (1956), directed by Mervyn LeRoy. *The Bad Seed* marked the beginning of "bad children" movies, but it also served as a counterpoint to Freud-infatuated films about miraculous cures effected by psychoanalysis. *The Bad Seed* chronicles the life and times—and crimes—of an adopted daughter who displays the same hideous behavior traits of her birth parents. That premise may not strike us as strange today, but theories that suggested behaviors are inborn—rather than learned or taught—were all but off-limits in the 1950s, in the aftermath of World War II. In those years, the horrors of the Holocaust were still fresh and Nazi fixations about creating a master race via eugenics (and genocide) cast a dark shadow over such determinist theories.

Twenty years later, *Demon Seed* captures the same sense of evil that permeated *The Bad Seed,* but the evil deed reflects the pressing questions of that era. In the same year that the first *Star Wars* appeared, we find a film about a woman who is imprisoned by the computer that runs her domestic affairs. The computer rapes her and impregnates her. She gives birth to a human-computer half-breed, which the computer will use to overtake the world and displace humans.

Demon Seed's dystopian commentary on the up and coming computer age occurs after feminism has grown roots in American soil—at least for a while. Women have entered professional schools en masse by 1977, having been cast aside just a few years earlier. Many were making headway in the workplace. Women's relationships with (human) men had shifted toward equality and away from subordination. Like *The Stepford Wives* (1975), this film challenges that social shift. It acts as a battle cry to return to the old order, and it enlists a machine to make this happen. Of course, this theme also connects to humanoid robots, automatons, and wind-up dolls, like the false Maria from Fritz Lang's *Metropolis*.

It is not until the early eighties that NSF moves from a simmer to a boil. NSF gets into high gear with David Cronenberg's *Scanners* (1981), which he soon followed with *Videodrome* (1983). There is a noticeable difference between Cronenberg's film, *The Brood* (1979), and *Scanners* (1981). Cronenberg's *The Dead Zone* (1983), starring Christopher Walken, was released in the same year as *Videodrome*. *The Dead Zone* is based on Stephen King's supernatural-medical thriller. Cronenberg's take on this tale veers toward fantasy more than SF.

The Dead Zone's plot revolves around a man who awakens from a protracted coma. He finds himself endowed with paranormal abilities—rather than seizures or cognitive deficits that might follow in real life situations. Because *The Dead Zone* stars Christopher Walken, the film reminds us of brain-implanted soldiers in *The Mind Snatchers*, where Walken had his first starring role.

We have to ask ourselves: was 1981 the turning point for NSF films, solely because of developments in neuropsychiatry? Did the 1980 publication of *DSM-III* contribute to this shift? *DSM-III* strived toward scientific accuracy and omitted psychoanalytic terminology. Did the president's commission on brain death in 1981 confirm the primacy of the brain, in life and death, mind and medicine? Or did Dr. Osheroff's lawsuit against Chestnut Lodge—and the vitriolic comments that appeared in American Psychiatric Association's main journal, the so-called "Green Journal"—stimulate this shift? Those published letters made it clear that ideological differences were splitting psychiatry, and that a professional civil war was brewing.

Alternatively, did the dawning of the computer age play an equally important role in the transformation of our expectations? The way that we conceive of ourselves, and the ways that human beings relate to one another, changed dramatically when an inanimate object—the computer—became available and acceptable. By 1990, computers could mediate human interactions as well as supply information. In the 21st century, "social media" began to outpace face-to-face contact with traditional friends. Soon, computers would be programmed to anticipate human actions and predict human behavior better than humans ever could.

The year 1981 is especially significant, for 1981 was the year when SF genius William Gibson coined the term "cyberspace." This word entered our everyday vocabularies. It alludes to the most important cultural shift since, well, since psychoanalysis changed the way we think about the way we think. For most people, the everyday experience of cyberspace was still some years away in 1981—but it was not very far away. Visionaries like Gibson led the way.

As we mentioned, the 20th century became known as the "psychoanalytic century." The 20th century was nearing a close in 1981. The sun was setting on the "psychoanalytic century." A new era had dawned. Technology, with its Internet offspring, was positioned to redirect 21st century philosophy, just as psychoanalysis seeped into the 20th century and saturated the arts and culture, philosophy and psychology. As the Information Age exploded, thanks to the introduction of the Internet, cyberspace made us rethink ideas about human identity, social interactions, and our sense of "self." Social networking sites, such as Facebook, LinkedIn and Twitter, would usher in even more profound personal and professional changes in the 21st century.

Thanks to this technological transformation, computerized imaging of the brain became readily available. Computers assisted in decoding the genetic code. That feat could not have been accomplished in a timely manner in a pre-computer society. Decoding of the genetic code redirected attention to inheritable mental and emotional traits and to biopsychiatry in general.

In some cases, these advances were interrelated. In other cases, changes in the computer world indirectly eased acceptance of unrelated revolutions in neuroscience and psychology. The fact that psychoanalysis had been dragged through the dirt since the sixties, and subjected to intense scrutiny, made it easier to salute the new guard and sign off on the old regime.

Movie themes paralleled these shifts in neuroscience and in psychiatric treatment and theory. Just before *Scanners* appeared, Ken Russell's *Altered States* (1980) made its way to the movie theaters. *Altered States* (1980) is a transitional film and an unusual one at that. It bridges the early 19th century's intrigue with Darwinism with New Age and drug culture concerns. *Altered States* stars an overly ambitious psychology professor who experiences reverse evolution as he regresses down the phylogenetic scale, morphing from human to ape. It links those 19th century discoveries with Jungian-based beliefs about the so-called "collective unconscious" and inheritable behavior traits transmitted through the more contested "racial unconscious." *Altered States* does not qualify as NSF, but it signals that significant shifts are in the making.

Cronenberg still leads the NSF playing field, having directed several prime examples of this genre, including *eXistenZ* (1999). *eXistenZ* involves surreal video games that connect to a portal near the base of the spinal cord. Fantasy games flow into players' nervous systems via this hypothetical "intra-thecal transfusion" that injects substances directly into the spinal fluid—or into another orifice at the base of the spine. Alternatively, Cronenberg's placement of the portal appears to be an allusion to anal penetration, a theme that he developed in an earlier film about William Burroughs, *Naked Lunch* (1991). As testimony to Cronenberg's lasting influence, there was talk of turning *Scanners* into a TV show.

Oddly enough, Cronenberg's recent film, *A Dangerous Method* (2011), turns back time by a century, when Freud and Jung (and Ferenzi, a Hungarian colleague) visited America to spread their theories. In those early years of psychoanalysis, Freud and Jung played mind games with one another, while the younger Jung played body games with a female analysand (Sabrina Spielrein). Spielrein eventually became an analyst herself, and a respected one at that, before the Nazis murdered her when they rounded up all Jews in her town and shot them in a synagogue.

Cronenberg portrays Freud as a pompous autocrat. He represents Jung as a womanizer and adulterer who indulges his twisted sexual compulsions, even though he undermines the significance of sexual instincts that Freud emphasized. Another psychoanalytic sympathizer becomes addicted to cocaine and dies. *A Dangerous Method* does nothing to instill confidence in the origins of psychoanalytic ideas, and does everything to undermine the psychoanalytic coterie. The head games played by Freud and Jung are hardly better than the body games in *eXistenZ*. Cronenberg remains true to his signature themes, which often focus on strange sexual twists.

Liquid Sky (1982) is a lesser-known film about heroin-addicted aliens that drain human brains of endorphins. Those endorphins are released during orgasm. This film deserves men-

Smiling and holding a brain in a jar, and standing in front of the arched doors of his dungeon laboratory, located on the 11th floor of a condominium building, comedian Steve Martin plays Dr. Michael Hfuhruhurr in the often-parodied *The Man with Two Brains* (1983).

tion, even though it got short shrift at the box office and was berated by many reviewers. *Liquid Sky* captures the era's intrigue with neurotransmitters in general and with pleasure-producing endorphins in particular. Endorphins were identified in the 1970s, and won prestigious Lasker Awards for their discoverers in 1978. Natural endorphins are manufactured by the brain and are released by opiate use (which includes heroin, morphine, codeine, or a long list of brand names such as Percodan, Vicodan, OxyContin, Tramadol, Dilaudid, Fentynl, and many more).

When scientists located brain-based endorphin receptors, they set the stage for viewing addiction as a biochemical problem, rather than as a moral, social or even a "psychological" issue, based on "bad parenting," "bad influences," "bad learning" or what not. Advances in understanding, treating (and, sadly, also in inducing) addictions followed such discoveries.

In between Cronenberg's NSF films from the early 1980s, *Blade Runner* (1982) appeared. *Blade Runner* became a cult film and overshadowed its competitors, in spite of significant pacing problems that led to its being called *"Blade Crawler." Liquid Sky* was released in the very same year, but a film based on a Philip K. Dick (PKD) story overshadowed it. *Blade Runner* was the first of several films based on PKD's visions. It remains the most acclaimed.

Blade Runner modernized the mechanical dolls and automatons of Romantic Era literature, ballet and early film. Those toys make us question the distinctions between human and machine, computers and consciousness. That theme is replayed in cyberpunk literature and film, but it also appears in Fritz Lang's *Metropolis* (1927), in several silent shorts and in Greek drama. Director Ridley Scott's earlier film, the SF blockbuster *Alien* (1979), also touched on the theme of synthetic humans that are difficult to distinguish from the flesh-and-blood variety.

The following year brought a parody about brain exchanges. Carl Reiner's *The Man with Two Brains* (1983) spoofed Curt Siodmak's Atomic Age film from the fifties, *Donovan's Brain* (1953). Siodmak made his film during the classic age of science fiction, when space travel was becoming a reality, and when the threat of "alien invasion" (by Soviets more than Martians) was a serious concern.

In the same year that *The Man with Two Brains* (1983) premiered, the lesser-sung NSF dream-themed *Brainstorm* (1983) appeared. It stars Christopher Walken (who also starred in *The Mind Snatchers* and in Cronenberg's film, *The Dead Zone*). *Brainstorm* taps into the excitement surrounding newly available videotapes, which made viewing movies at home so much easier, and made some imaginative people wonder if waking consciousness or sleeping dreams or bodily sensations can be recorded and replayed on videotapes, just as easily as movies.

Re-Animator (1985) was released around the same time. Based on the Lovecraft story, Gordon's low-budget *Re-Animator* revolves around a brain and a body, but differs from *Frankenstein* films in that it is more Grand Guignol than science fiction.

Verhoeven's *RoboCop* (1987) came a few years later. Based upon the Frank Miller comic book, *RoboCop* was super-successful, and would be made into three more sequels, a television series, and a re-boot of the franchise in 2014. *RoboCop* is the ultimate man-machine, being a blend of robotic elements with a human core, reconstructed from a near dead, but not quite dead, real cop. In anticipation of the 2014 *RoboCop*, *Popular Science* metaphorically dissects the screen character, to show that the android has become more science fact than science fiction.[21]

RoboCop's plot is straightforward, even though it sidetracks into significant subplots. Much of the movie chronicles street warfare between the "real" RoboCop and drug-addicted criminals that fuel themselves with more drugs. These scenes recollect the crack epidemic of the eighties, when roaming bands of "under the influence" youths made many city streets unsafe. Earlier in the decade, the pricier and chicer cocaine made inroads into more upscale crowds.

Unbeknownst to anyone except his partner, the composite RoboCop retains his human memories, flashbacks and dreams. He re-experiences his pre-reconstruction life, when he was a beat cop named Murphy with a wife and child. *RoboCop* is high-tech NSF, proto-cyberpunk and action-adventure. It is also a "weepie" and a "woman's film" of sorts. It could have found a following in the late 1940s, when women grieved for the men who did not return from war. They watched melodramas to idle away their lonely days, and reconcile themselves to sad realities. We see Murphy suffer and emote as often as we watch him combat enemy robot forces. The *RoboCop* reboot makes Murphy more real than robot, and highlights his plight as a sentient being encased in a metallic cage that is controlled by computers (and unscrupulous humans).

At the same time that the new NSF films were gaining steam, "standard-brand" cinema psychiatrists were getting worse and worse—with the obvious exception of Dr. Judd in *Ordi-*

nary People (1980), featured in Robert Redford's directorial debut. Sinister psychiatrists took center stage in feature films since film's earliest days, even before Dr. Caligari or Dr. Mabuse, who debuted in 1919 and 1922, respectively. In the early 1980s, before Dr. Hannibal Lecter appeared on screen, several films featured the most debased psychiatric practices imaginable. (The brilliant but cannibalistic Dr. Lecter was born in book form in 1981, with Harris' *Red Dragon*).

Those films about extremely sinister psychiatrists include *Dressed to Kill* (1980), starring Michael Caine, and a remake based on the Mike Hammer book series, *I, the Jury* (1982), plus *Still of the Night* (1982). Psychiatrists from those early 1980s films were so badly behaved that they threatened to upend the German Expressionist classics. In *Dressed to Kill,* a transvestite psychiatrist murders his female patient in the elevator of a high-priced Manhattan high rise. Barbara Carrera plays the seductive female psychiatrist in the *I, the Jury* remake. She runs a call girl service disguised as sex therapy. She cavorts with criminals and tries to kill detective-protagonist Mike Hammer as they embrace.

Another film, *Frances* (1982), is a very sad film about actress Frances Farmer, who had a lobotomy around 1950. *Frances* does not instill confidence in mid-century psychiatric practices, to say the least. *Frances* is far sadder than the fictional *One Flew Over the Cuckoo's Nest* (1975), which was based on Ken Kesey's best-selling book from 1962 and which concludes with a lobotomy for a recalcitrant small time crook named McMurphy (Jack Nicholson).

With such cinematic examples of horrific psychiatric abuses and corruption, it seemed like prime time to introduce a new paradigm for psychiatric subject matter. The Decade of the Brain began in 1990. CGI (computer-generated imagery) went prime time in 1991, with *Terminator 2* (1991). In the 1990s, psychoanalytic themes appeared in comedies and parodies, as never before.

During this last decade of the 20th century, psychopharmacological discoveries advanced. Neuro-imaging studies of brain activity had soared in the late 1970s, with the invention of the PET scan. Progress continued non-stop. Equally importantly, these strides were welcomed by psychiatry and society (although the psychoanalysts objected to such "soulless psychiatry").

Less than a decade had passed since *Scanners* (1981). The year 1990 brought seminal NSF films: *Total Recall* (1990), *Flatliners* (1990), and *RoboCop 2* (1990). *RoboCop 3* (1993) followed in the wake of the successes of the original *RoboCop* (1987) as well as *RoboCop 2*.

In 1990, another Philip K. Dick novella became a film: *Total Recall* (1990). *Total Recall* stars Arnold Schwarzenegger, before the award-winning body builder became California's governor. In the film itself, it is unclear exactly how Arnold's memories are wiped out and replaced when he visits Rekall, Inc., but director Paul Verhoeven makes it clear that he sees the "new memory scenes" as dream scenes, rather than material reality.[22] A remake of this thoughtful film about totalitarianism, government control of memories, and manipulation of individual identity was released in 2012, with Colin Farrell replacing the muscular Schwarzenegger in an anemic reinterpretation of the original plot.

By the middle of the decade, we encounter *Johnny Mnemonic* (1995), another action-adventure movie about an implanted brain chip. The film is loosely based on William Gibson's far more impressive SF story of the same name. In the meantime, David Cronenberg continued his run of NSF films. Cronenberg intuited the synergy that would connect humans, computer games, "Second Life" and "Sims." *eXistenZ* (1999) is a surreal action-adventure film about a computer game that plugs into the base of the spinal cord, near sexually suggestive body parts. This umbilical-like cord produces imagery and action that are indistinguishable from reality.

eXistenZ (1999) was released in the same year as *The Matrix* (1999). In *The Matrix,* computers control humans, and wire them into dream-like states, for use as human batteries that generate electricity to run The Matrix. *The Matrix* spawned more of the same, and the trilogy extended well past the turn-of-the-millennium, into 2003. Around the millennium, a rash of so-called "mindfuck" films deliberately "messed with the mind" by confusing chronological sequences and adding post-modern touches to movies. This trend paralleled the chronological confusion generated by the year 2000 and the possibly apocalyptic "Y2K." Sequels to *The Matrix* never achieved the cult status of the original, and some were met with derision. *The Matrix*'s contribution to cyberpunk and NSF could not be undone, even if it could be out-done.

Another film that is numbered among the pre-millennial, non-linear "mindfuck" movies that confuse chronology is *Memento* (2000), starring Guy Pearce and directed by Christopher Nolan. After *Memento,* Nolan proceeded to direct *Batman Begins* (2005), *The Dark Knight* (2008), *The Dark Knight Rises* (2012), as well as the dream-themed *Inception* (2010). Guy Pearce becomes the scientist-villain in *Iron Man 3,* which we mentioned in the Introduction. Carrie-Anne Moss, also of *The Matrix,* plays the female lead in *Memento. Memento* is not neuroscience fiction, but it does concern neuroscience, because it chronicles the day-to-day life of a hard-hearted insurance adjuster who lost the ability to retain recent memories after an attack that left him unconscious and his wife dead. To compensate for his disabling antero-grade amnesia, he tattoos notes all over his body.

The 21st century had even more NSF treats in store. One of them, *The Cell* (2000), bears an ominous—yet currently accurate—message about the future of technologically sophisticated neuropsychiatry. This film stars popular Puerto Rican–American actress, Jennifer Lopez. J-Lo plays a social worker-turned-psychotherapist. She literally "gets into the head" of a highly disturbed "patient" who lies unconscious. She uses a computer-assisted device that transfers traumatic memories from his brain to hers. This is a wildly new approach to "empathy."

The film documents a treatment trend that had already begun, and that would become standard over time: the use of non-medical therapists to perform psychotherapy. As psychiatrists shifted toward medically oriented treatments, they spent less and less time talking with patients and devoted less and less effort to empathizing with their patients' unique personal experiences. With managed care limiting payments for psychotherapy performed by psychiatrists, major shifts in care delivery occurred. However, the machine featured in this film has yet to be invented, and is nowhere on the horizon. It remains on the same shelf as H.G. Wells' timeless *Time Machine,* which was remade as a movie in 2002, starring Guy Pearce, the suicidal scientist in *Iron Man 3.*

On the other hand, "telepsychiatry" is moving forward fast in 2014. This once-ridiculed technique of talking to far away patients via a computer screen has come of age, and will be used to reach out to people remotely, to offer them treatment that is not available nearby. A telepsychiatrist chronicles his experiences in an engaging series in *Psychiatric Times.*[23]

Dreams made a comeback in the 21st century, not just with *The Matrix,* but also with *The Imaginarium of Doctor Parnassus* (2009) and *Inception* (2010). The dream-sharing scenes from *Brainstorm* (1983) predicted this path twenty years before this trend came into full bloom. A hundred years earlier, Freud had published his century-shaping book, *The Interpretation of Dreams* (1900). It was Freud's favorite book. This book moved dream interpretation away from occultism and into his sexually laden psychoanalytic "matrix." In a hundred years' time, a new kind of dream machine evolved, one that is computer-based or electronically oriented.

Drug-related themes reappear in Spielberg's *Minority Report* (2002), and carry a special message that extends far beyond superficial entertainment. Fast-acting, more affordable crack cocaine became available and begot the crack epidemic of the 1980s. Medical journals debated about crack's effects on fetuses. The pejorative term "crack baby" came into common usage.

In this film, "crack babies" develop telepathy as they mature. They are then employed as oracles. Twenty years earlier, David Cronenberg began this trend with *Scanners* (1981), a film about social outcasts who have unusual telepathic powers that result from a medication named "ephemerol." Like Thalidomide, the notorious teratogen of the late 1950s/early 1960s, ephemerol was administered to their mothers during pregnancy, without consideration of future effects.

In between these two films, an intriguing development took place with respect to medicating pregnant women. Prozac, the first of the SSRIs (selective serotonin reuptake inhibitors), went to market in 1987. As psychiatrist Peter Kramer chronicles in *Listening to Prozac* (1997), Prozac transformed psychiatry. This relatively safe and easy to use antidepressant quickly replaced existing "tricyclic" anti-depressants, which carried serious cardiac risks, created "mothball mouth" and were potentially lethal in overdoses. Prozac's popularity spread, and it opened questions about the real "self" versus the post–Prozac self. Prozac set the stage for psychiatrists' near-abandonment of talk therapy some 20 years hence.

More to the point, the makers of Prozac opened a registry of women who received treatment with Prozac while pregnant. Eli Lilly's efforts in starting this registry turned into the most comprehensive database about pregnancy-related medication exposure compiled to date.

Over time, researchers uncovered some relatively rare problems related to SSRI use during pregnancy. The most serious problems concerned another SSRI, Paxil (paroxetine), and not Prozac (fluoxetine). Most of the SSRIs proved to be fairly safe, in the short run, especially when compared to even more harmful effects associated with untreated depression, anxiety, or psychosis during pregnancy. Even after delivery, depressed mothers are anergic and unmotivated, and may neglect their infants and fail to bond with the babies. The question of how those meds affect brain development after age seven remains open, since long-term studies are not yet available. By 2010, almost a quarter of all pregnant women take psychotropic meds during pregnancy. Thalidomide-like disasters have *not* occurred during these decades. Still, SF writers and filmmakers cannot resist the urge to speculate about fetal effects, telepathy included.

The increased use of mood-altering meds during pregnancy marked a shift in obstetrical practice, and in public acceptance of such practices. The generations that witnessed the flipper limbs induced by Thalidomide had long since passed childbearing age. Those generations would encounter new challenges with the passage of time, challenges that would be translated into film.

Those Baby Boomers created the Youth Culture of the late 60s and early 70s. By the 21st century, Baby Boomers had begun to age. They entered their 50s and 60s. In the 1970s, when members of the Baby Boom generation entered medical school, many medical students flocked into psychiatry after earning their M.D. degrees. Psychiatry was trendy, for several reasons. Psychiatric residencies were never again able to recruit so many new medical school graduates.

That generation paved the path away from psychoanalysis, which had its heyday in the 1950s, after the world war. Most moved toward neuroscience by the 1990s. As medical students, they had been educated by Dr. Crichton's SF books as much as by standard medical textbooks.

Suddenly, they realized that their "youth culture" had faded to grey, both literally and figuratively. They looked ahead, and saw an epidemic of Alzheimer's disease looming. Other less common and less publicized memory-robbing dementias of advanced age also awaited.

As Americans lived longer than ever before, they faced greater chances of developing dreaded diseases of older age. Statistics say that half of people who live to 85 will show signs of dementia, be it the dementia of Alzheimer's or other dementias. The news was chilling. Cancer, another disease that increased in prevalence as the population aged, was no longer the only scare.

With this epiphany, extensive research into anti-aging antidotes began—and a whole new breed of movies about memory loss (and gain) appeared. *Memento* (2000), *Rise of the Planet of the Apes* (2011), *Limitless* (2011) and *Repo Men* (2010) are but a few of several films that deal with dementia or memory loss, and its possible causes and its (hypothetical) cures.

The idea of increasing intelligence, and finding eternal youth, and creating a better breed of humans, is not a novel idea, but it is still gripping. Those ideas were retold countless times, each time embellished with the inventions and conventions that are popular in a particular era. *The Crimson Stain* (1916) broached this topic in a silent serial. *Planet of the Apes* (1968) and the many versions of *Dr. Moreau* offered different takes on related themes. But never before had this motif held meaning for so many audience members. Art imitates life and vice versa.

Around this time, interest in PTSD (post-traumatic stress disorder) and TBI (traumatic brain injury) soared, as military men and women returned from warzones, disabled by both psychological and physical sequelae of trauma. Disturbing data appeared about athletes who suffer TBIs in their younger years. Many go on to develop dementia in midlife—far sooner than expected. PTSD had been a topic of interest to psychiatrists and therapists for decades, and is by no means limited to wartime experiences or military men or women. However, large numbers of enlistees with PTSD command attention. It just so happened that soldier-suicides and veteran homicides reached record levels among Iraq I and II and Afghan vets. Something had to be done.

Some people remember too much, and some remember too little, or nothing at all. Ideas about obliterating memories (from PTSD and other painful events) congealed in films such as *Total Recall* (1990) and *Eternal Sunshine of the Spotless Mind* (2004). With its memory-erasing machine, *Sunshine* is a light-hearted comedy with heavy-handed undertones. *Total Recall* doubles as an action-adventure. *Repo Men* (2010) offers an entirely different approach, but shares similarities with Philip K. Dick's visions, especially since it employs a machine that instills good dreams that override bad memories, or that substitute for no memories at all.

Even if current neuropsychiatry has no clear-cut solutions for these ills, moviemakers could dramatize such afflictions in films. As artists, they can theorize about remedies for these problems as they wish. Artists enjoy greater liberty than psychiatrists or scientists because they do not answer to IRBs (Institutional Review Boards). Artists are not even limited by reality. Given that preliminary research shows that mind-controlled computer chips can operate artificial and real limbs, and can help spinal cord-injured patients walk again (in real life), it seems that the line between fantasy and fact has been blurring. Many NSF films are fast becoming fact.

Moreover, recent research reveals that administering ECT (electroconvulsive therapy) after trauma can prevent consolidation of that trauma into permanent, flashback-producing memories of the kind that plague PTSD (post-traumatic stress disorder) sufferers. Admit-

In *Men in Black 3* (2012), Agent J (Will Smith) demonstrates his "neuralyzer," which induces instant amnesia, erases memories of alien sightings, and wipes trade secrets from minds of retiring agents.

tedly, a course of ECT is unlikely to appeal to most people. Yet it is only a matter of time before someone conceives of a more benign method that takes the place of ECT, maybe something that is more along the lines of a "neuralyzer" from *Men in Black* (1997, 2002, 2012), which also makes people forget and which was listed among the "top ten film inventions we wish were true."

Three

The Legacy of 19th Century Literature

To understand the origins of neuroscience fiction film, we must first examine the legacy left by neuroscience fiction literature. Although scholars such as Per Schelde convincingly argue that SF literature is a world apart from SF film, the early SF literature that existed before cinema's invention merits attention for its own sake. The literature that predated cinema's invention at the end of the 19th century provided a firm foundation for films that would follow a century or more later. Several literary classics became so ingrained in our culture that they inspired dozens of filmic reinterpretations over the decades to come. Moreover, the mere existence of this body of work proves that neuroscience fiction is not new at all.

Neuroscience fiction started in the early part of the 19th century—in 1818, to be exact—when the novella of Mary Wollstonecraft Shelley (1797–1851) went to press. Shelley's *Frankenstein* tale was revised and republished several times after the first rendition. This first science fiction story also functions as a neuroscience fiction story, of sorts. The youthful Shelley wrote *Frankenstein: or, The Modern Prometheus* on the proverbial "dark and stormy night." Many of our readers know of Shelley's feat, started when she was still in her teens and completed at the tender age of 21. For most people, their knowledge of the Frankenstein monster rests on films that followed much later.

Shelley's story revolves around a scientist who reanimates scavenged body parts. It is unclear exactly what the scientist includes in his concoction, but Shelley does specify sources for his body parts: charnel houses, dissecting rooms and slaughterhouses. The scientist adds a brain, and activates the mélange with "spark" (which we read as an electric current). In doing so, the scientist, Dr. Frankenstein, creates an entirely new being. His creation erroneously came to be known by the name of his creator: Frankenstein. This hideous being becomes a murderous monster. The monster vows vengeance on humankind after almost all humans reject him. The sole exception is a blind peasant, who is the patriarch of a family that the monster watches, in secret, as he learns their language by listening to them speak.

Dr. Victor Frankenstein's intentions were innocent, but the outcome of his experiments is evil. He is a doctor who plays G-d. He is a human who forgets that certain privileges belong to the divine, even if scientific advances allow him to tinker in previously unchartered territory. His monster takes on a life of its own, and acquires its own will. In the process, it takes the lives of others, sometimes directly, sometimes indirectly. When the monster kills

Dr. Frankenstein's brother, an innocent nanny is accused and convicted, and hanged for this heartless crime.

The monster cannot be stopped. More deaths follow. Dr. Frankenstein encounters loss after loss because he is the "modern Prometheus" who pursues knowledge relentlessly, without considering the consequences. There is no hellfire and brimstone in this story, but a vengeful Jehovah may just as well be watching from above, as He smites the kin of His competitors.

Dr. Victor Frankenstein has his own back-story, as Mary Shelley tells it. Young Victor wanted to study the outdated alchemical and magical works of Agrippa, Paracelsus and Albertus Magnus. All of his heroes were physicians, but each hovered between the boundaries of science and superstition. Victor's father noticed his son's intrigue with the occult and other off-limits knowledge, and objected to such interests. To assuage his father, the younger Frankenstein studies scientific advances and abandons the atavistic alchemical pursuits of his younger years. Victor redirects his efforts toward the future, instead of focusing on the past, and busies himself with more contemporary laboratory experiments.

Dr. Frankenstein is not a psychiatrist per se, nor is he a neurologist. It is unlikely that he was even a physician. He is an anatomist, who tinkers with the brain, as well as the body.[1] Readers would not be impressed if Shelley had cast her protagonist as a brain specialist or as a proto-psychiatrist or an alienist. For proto-psychiatrists of that era supervised incurables in asylum settings. Asylum superintendents were not known for their innovations and had low status. They performed custodial functions and occasionally advocated for more humane treatments for their charges.

In America, these asylum superintendents formed America's first medical specialty organization in 1844. In England, the Quaker William Tukes established the York Retreat in 1796, so mental patients could receive more compassionate and less abusive "mortal therapy." Freud, a neurologist by training, did anatomically based research on brains later in the 19th century, before turning to clinical work with patients and plumbing their "unconscious."[2, 3]

Mary Shelley was barely past adolescence when she wrote what came to be one of the first works of science fiction, if not the first work. She never set out to carve out a new literary genre, and could not have imagined the fame she would win from her night's work. She went on to write other fiction and non-fiction work that was not fully appreciated until the 1970s, when feminist scholarship excavated her achievements, calling attention to her writings and to her impressive family background that came complete with feminist credentials.

The story of the creation of the *Frankenstein* story is as interesting as the creation story of the Frankenstein monster itself. Mary Shelley was the daughter of the early feminist philosopher, Mary Wollstonecraft, author of *A Vindication of the Rights of Woman: With Strictures on Political and Moral Subjects* (1792). Mary would wed the Romantic poet Percy Bysshe Shelley. Percy encouraged Mary to pursue her project, while he, too, participated in the informal writing contest that led to *Frankenstein's* invention.

When she penned this tale, Mary Shelley was spending time with her lover and husband-to-be, and their friends, the poet Lord Byron, plus a literary-minded physician, John Polidori. During this time, Dr. Polidori wrote *The Vampyre* (1819), which ushered in the Romantic Era's vampire trend. To pass the time as they waited out the storm, the friends conceived of a contest to see who could write the best horror story. These enduring literary achievements were products of a drug-fueled frenzy, and were refined over time.

In James Whale's 1931 adaptation of Shelley's *Frankenstein*, Boris Karloff stars as the misunderstood monster and poses in a dark, deep cavernous German Expressionist–style space that recollects the angular and irregular sets of Weine's *The Cabinet of Dr. Caligari* (1919).

Like the fictional Dr. Frankenstein himself, whose name is immortalized in the name of the novella, Mary Shelley's *Frankenstein* gained immortal life through plays, films, puppets, and innumerable retellings. Since that time, countless Frankenstein costumes have paraded through Halloween festivities each October, making Frankenstein's monster one of the most recognizable monsters of all times, and one of children's favorites.

The first film adaptation of *Frankenstein* arrived in 1910, with Edison's *Frankenstein* film. The 13-minute silent short was directed by J. Searle Dawley. It was shot in three days time in the Bronx. The film had been lost for decades, but is now available for viewing on YouTube.

It is fitting that Edison holds the honor of producing the first *Frankenstein* film, given that Edison is credited with inventing the electric light bulb (even though he only refined it). For Shelley's *Frankenstein* comments on Giovanni Aldini's electrical experiments on dead and (sometimes) living animals. The novella also reflects fears surrounding the Industrial Revolution, which was pushing forward fast when Shelley was writing. Luddite riots had taken place just before she wrote her first story. Luddites opposed technology in principle. Laborers who sympathized with Luddite philosophy attacked factories and broke machines that might replace them. A few years later, inventor Michael Faraday demonstrated electromagnetic rotation, which would be the principle of the electric motor. Faraday's findings reified Shelley's story, which claims that electricity can animate movement in inanimate objects. The next decade, in 1831, Faraday discovered electromagnetic current, which made generators and electrical engines possible.

As the Industrial Revolution advanced, it became more and more conceivable that humans could be replaced by machines. At some point in the future, human body parts might become interchangeable with factory-made mechanical devices. (At that point, virtually no one imagined that humans would one day program computers to print out body parts, as is happening now.) Mary Shelley anticipated the concerns of contemporary cyberpunk, which expresses the same trepidations about computers that outperform humankind and overtake humans. *RoboCop, Blade Runner* or *The Matrix* were not even twinkles in Mary Shelley's eye when she wrote, yet we can see the links between contemporary scientific advances, 20th century cinema and Mary Shelley's imaginary creature from 1818.

Frankenstein fared well on the silent screen, and became *Life Without Soul* in 1915. No copy of this film exists, but the title expresses the sentiments about creating artificial life forms. Then, in 1931, the definitive and never-to-be forgotten version of *Frankenstein* arrived. James Whale directed the Universal film that is revered to this day, the one where Boris Karloff stars as the monster. Colin Clive, Mae Clarke, and Dwight Frye also have lead roles. Sequels followed, and a subgenre was born. A Frankenstein franchise came into being. In 1935, James Whale directed *Bride of Frankenstein*, with Boris Karloff once again starring as the monster, who now has a speaking role. This plot comes closer to Shelley's source material. Whale's version emphasizes the brain. It shows what happens when a criminal brain is planted into the creature's cranium, after the genius brain that was intended for transplantation is accidentally destroyed.

The 1940s brought more Universal monster movies: *Frankenstein Meets the Wolf Man* (1943), *House of Frankenstein* (1944), *Abbott and Costello Meet Frankenstein* (1948). Mary Shelley's monster and her not-quite-mad scientist endured, even though social, economic and scientific conditions were diametrically different from the early 1800s, when the Romantic Era was born.

The *Frankenstein* franchise gained new life between 1957 and 1974, when Hammer Films in England produced a run of Frankenstein films, including *The Curse of Frankenstein* (1957), *The Revenge of Frankenstein* (1958), *Frankenstein Must Be Destroyed* (1969), and *The Horror of Frankenstein* (1970). In the early years of television, *Shock Theater* introduced another generation to *Frankenstein*. Each Saturday night, in the late 1950s, *Shock Theater* entertained home audiences in Chicago with lightning bolts, crackling thunder, and, of course, a wide array of *Frankenstein* films.[4] Midwestern Baby Boomers grew up with Frankenstein films, and could easily imagine the monster running through the cornfields, chased by the torch-carrying crowd. Different regions hosted their own local channels, but *Frankenstein* films enjoyed "universal" appeal.

The return to *Frankenstein* in the early to mid-seventies was telling. "True" neuroscience fiction film was coalescing. The heyday of the drug culture had peaked and passed, but its influence was still palpable. Timothy Leary's slogans about "better living through chemistry" continued to resonate on many college campuses, although not everyone embraced his ethos. The Summer of Love was over, having begun with a music festival in 1967, but concluding with drug-saturated antics, broadcast far and wide on TV. The Beatles' *Yellow Submarine* (1968) included visual cues that augmented the perceptual effects of LSD. Audiences everywhere witnessed behavior changes brought about by changes in brain chemistry.[5] These escapades prepared Americans to accept neurochemical explanations for thinking, feeling, and behaving.

Michael Crichton wrote *The Terminal Man* in 1972. The film version appeared in 1974. In 1972, Christopher Walken had starred in a cheesier brain chip flick (*The Happiness Cage*, also known as *The Mind Snatchers* or *The Demon Within*). That film was not so far removed from Crichton's better-received delivery, but *The Happiness Cage* co-mingled anti-war sentiments with science fiction, and so did not stand out as a specifically SF statement. Still, the times were changing, and fantasy-based *Frankenstein* films were running out of steam and could not compete with neurochemistry. Parodies about *Frankenstein* appeared in those very same years.

In 1973, *Andy Warhol's Frankenstein* focuses on a doctor whose dedication to science takes him too far. He wants to rule the world. To do so, he creates a species that will obey him and do his bidding, in much the same way that Dr. Caligari used his confederate Cesare in the 1919 German Expressionist classic, *The Cabinet of Dr. Caligari*. Dr. Caligari performed at a carnival, when he was not attending to his psychiatric asylum. He hypnotized Cesare, cloistered him in a cabinet, but let him out at times, with instructions to kill those who offended the doctor. With Cesare hidden inside the cabinet, no one suspected either Cesare or Caligari of the murder spree, until Cesare dies while trying to save Jane, and Jane's boyfriend intervenes.

The name of Robert Weine, director of *Caligari,* was less recognizable than Warhol's name in the early 1970s. Andy Warhol was haute counterculture. His Velvet Underground was legendary, and anything he did or said mocked contemporary values and turned society upside down. His lithographs of Campbell's soup cans proved that ordinary advertising imagery seen on supermarket shelves had become a substitute for art. Now he featured Dr. Frankenstein as a monster that is greater than the montage that he created. Like Edison, who was known for usurping the ideas of others, Warhol conveniently claims credit for other artists' work. In this case, Paul Morrissey was responsible for the Frankenstein film that bears Warhol's imprimatur.

Frankenstein migrated to television. A TV film *Frankenstein: The True Story* (1973) appeared on American TV in the same year that Warhol's avant-garde film appeared.

Comedian Mel Brooks took a different approach. Equally irreverent, but much less hostile, this one-time Borscht Belt comedian directed *Young Frankenstein* in 1974. The film "competed" with *The Terminal Man,* which translated Crichton's novel into cinematic terms. *Young Frankenstein* (1974) is surprisingly accurate and true to Whale's original, at least for the brain substitution scene. Marty Feldman, playing an assistant named Igor, reaches for the brain of a scientist, but he drops it. He finds another brain in a labeled bottle. Feldman recalls that the label began with "Abby" something. Gene Wilder, as Dr. Frankenstein, realizes that "Abby something or other" is not part of a proper noun, but refers to a jar marked "Abby-Normal" (abnormal). However, it is too late. The operation is complete.

This sequel-spoof is listed as one of the best comedies ever made. It reuses many of Kenneth Strickfaden's electrical props from James Whale's 1931 *Frankenstein*. It is shot in black-and-white with 1930s-style credits. When spectators can laugh at a time-honored horror film, instead of squirming in their seats, we know that the monster has lost its force.

The year 1992 brought another TV Frankenstein film. *Frankenstein* (1992) became a Turner Network Television film, starring Patrick Bergin and Randy Quaid. Two years later, in 1994, *Mary Shelley's Frankenstein* (1994) appeared in theaters, directed by and starring Kenneth Branagh. The high-name recognition cast included Robert De Niro and Helena Bonham Carter. The passage of time had not tempered interest in the Frankenstein story but had allowed time for its re-interpretation. The year 2013 brought us *Frankenstein's Army* (2013) and 2014 offered *I, Frankenstein*.

The world is forever indebted to Mary Shelley's *Frankenstein,* but the 19th century writers created two more sick scientists that survived into the present and contribute to our current fascination with neuro-science fiction film. Those two characters are Stevenson's Dr. Jekyll (who transforms into Mr. Hyde) and H.G. Wells' Dr. Moreau. Each is important in his own right, although Dr. Jekyll is much more endearing, and attracts more admirers than Moreau.

Robert Louis Stevenson wrote *The Strange Case of Dr. Jekyll and Mr. Hyde* in 1886. In those same years, between 1884 and 1887, Freud published his Cocaine Papers, where he chronicles self-experiments with cocaine, extols its virtues and denies its addictive potential. After Freud witnessed his colleague succumb to cocaine use, and died from the drug, he had a change of heart. (Today, cocaine is the most common cause of fatal heart attacks in persons under the age of 45.) Now aware that cocaine can indeed bring death and devastation, Freud purged his cocaine papers from his collected works—but not from our collective memories.

Clearly, cocaine was a popular literary topic in the 1880s. Sherlock Holmes, the 1887 creation of Scottish physician Sir Arthur Conan Doyle, also enjoys cocaine. The tongue-in-cheek film, *The Seven-Per-Cent Solution* (1976), connects Freud with Conan Doyle's cocaine-addled detective. In that era, blends of tincture of opium and alcohol were available without prescriptions and used to quiet colicky infants or calm frayed nerves. The concoction was a "patent medicine" called "laudanum." The Victorians were very familiar with psychoactive and even psychedelic plants and drugs, as John Strausbaugh and Tony Blaise show through their edited collection of essays, re-published in *The Drug User Documents: 1840–1960* (1993).[6]

In Stevenson's story, the good Dr. Jekyll is not pursuing pleasure per se when he retreats to his laboratory and concocts a chemical that releases his darker animalistic side, the side that is repressed by proper Victorian society, and held in check by civilization in general. He does not intend to transform into an uncouth apelike rapist, who kills without conscience—

which is what happens (in Mamoulian's definitive film version, with Fredric March). Even though Stevenson's Mr. Hyde literally grows larger and larger, with each transition, Dr. Jekyll does not foresee the consequences of his experiments and does not recognized that Hyde will soon overpower him. However, his trusted colleague perceives the perils.

Dr. Jekyll is neither a psychiatrist nor a neurologist, but he is intrigued by behavior, the social control of behavior, and the evolutionary continuum between human and beast and the instincts that distinguish the species and the moral sense that guides them (or eludes them, in the case of the beast). Dr. Jekyll is depicted slightly differently in the dozens of films that followed Stevenson's novel, with Robert Mamoulian's version being my favorite and the critics' favorite. We tend to remember the details from this classic version, and we will recount them below.

In daily life, Dr. Jekyll is a G.P. who devotes himself to South London's under classes, to the chagrin of his more materialistic future father-in-law. His fiancé's father hopes that his daughter's husband-to-be will choose to keep company with moneyed and cultured classes instead of tending to the needy. (Later in the story, Dr. Jekyll transforms into Hyde and murders this unlikable man, who had irritated and undermined him during his more rational Dr. Jekyll state.)

The Strange Case of Dr. Jekyll and Mr. Hyde speaks to depth psychologists at the same time that it appeals to psychopharmacologists and neuro-anatomists. For proto–Jungians who believe that a darker "shadow self" lurks behind the more proper "persona" that masks the psychological morass inside, the Jekyll and Hyde story provides proof of this duality of personality. It reminds us that people present different sides of themselves to society, just as Greek actors present "personas" on stage and don different masks (personas) for each role.

Freudians who posit that the instinctual "id" battles the hypothetical moralizing "superego," but is harnessed by the mediating powers of the "ego," find ample confirmation of their theories in this same story. The drug culture of the Sixties and Seventies delighted in the good doctor's dabbling with drugs, while latter day neuropsychiatrists regale in the visual and literary representations of frontal and temporal lobe disinhibition. In fact, Jekyll & Hyde can be interpreted as a representation of FTD (frontotemporal dementia), when parts of the brain that control judgment, social sensibility and emotionality deteriorate before the memory erodes and makes the dementia manifest. (A very different chronology occurs in the more common Alzheimer's disease, which starts with language problems long before social skills are lost.)

Mr. Hyde darts across the library table, in the second to the last scene of Mamoulian's film, making neuro-psychiatrically-inclined spectators wish for a PET scan or SPECT scan or at least an MRI of the poor man's brain. We wonder which parts of Hyde's cortex have shriveled or atrophied, or gone into overdrive, to allow such regressive behavior. For contemporary hair-splitters, who approach the *DSM (Diagnostic and Statistical Manual)* nosology as if it were a Talmudic treatise, Jekyll and Hyde inspires debates about diagnosis: does Jekyll's personality change represent a case of dissociative identity disorder? Or is it a brief reactive psychosis, or a substance-induced disorder—or something else entirely, frontaltemporal dementia, perhaps?

Apart from scientists, psychologists, and physicians, *Jekyll & Hyde* appeals to students of religion, philosophy and ethics. They, too, engage in active debates about personal responsibility and the locus of control, and who or what governs individual morality. At the same time, Stevenson's story explores gender roles in Victorian society, and Victorian society in general, and makes us think about the way the world changed, or how much it has stayed the same. It anticipates the Suffragettes, the flappers and the second and third wave feminists. For historians of medicine, it offers extra benefits, because it tells us about clinical care, laboratory medicine, and socioeconomic influences on health care, and about the mission of medical men like Jekyll.

Those are just a few examples of the myriad ramifications of Dr. Jekyll and Mr. Hyde. In short, *Jekyll & Hyde* offers so much for so many that it has been made into dozens upon dozens of film versions and stage adaptations. When a new Broadway play premiered in the 1990s, fans coalesced and formed clubs, with the tenacity of Trekkies. *New York Times* reporters commented on their loyalty, and speculated on the reasons that drove them in droves. Admittedly, casting TV heartthrob David Hasselhoff in the lead role contributed to this appeal.

In the first decade of film, we find several interpretations of Stevenson's masterpiece. There is *Dr. Jekyll and Mr. Hyde* (1908), by William Selig. A French version is entitled *The Duality of Man* (1910). *Dr. Jekyll and Mr. Hyde* (1912), by Tanhouser, directed by and starring Lucius Henderson, deserves special mention. This stark film, with its plain printed text, and no-nonsense anti-drug message intertwined in its plot, is a perfect prelude for the Harrison

Fredric March appears in many guises in this lobby card for Mamoulian's *Dr. Jekyll and Mr. Hyde* (1931). In the upper right, he is Dr. Jekyll, but his transformed simian "shadow self," Mr. Hyde, is central and surrounded by shadows. Rose Hobart, his "proper" fiancée, embraces him in the upper left, while saloon singer Ivy Pearson (Miriam Hopkins) has a head shot at bottom left.

Narcotics Act of 1914, which forbade over-the-counter sales of opium, opium derivatives, and cocaine. Until that time, opiates were freely available, even for infants, and up to 5 percent of the U.S. population were addicted to these drugs. Dr. Jekyll's drug-related demise sent a strong message to viewers, and presumably prepared them for tighter drug control, without acting as overt propaganda.

Other renditions of the Stevenson story fulfilled other functions, not the least of which is entertainment. Herbert Brenon directed and starred in *Dr. Jekyll and Mr. Hyde* (1913). This version was produced by one of the all-times greats of cinema, Carl Laemmle, head of Universal Studios. *Dr. Jekyll and Mr. Hyde Done to a Frazzle* (1914) came a year later, from Crystal-Superba. Earlier on, we find a single reel *Dr. Jekyll and Mr. Hyde* (1908) by Selig Polyscope Company, and the Nordisk version of *Dr. Jekyll and Mr. Hyde* (1910) with Alwin Neuss. There is *Dr. Jekyll and Mr. Hyde* (1912) by James Cruz and Henry Benham, *Dr. Jekyll and Mr. Hyde* (1913) by Urban's Kinemacolor Company and yet another *Dr. Jekyll and Mr. Hyde* (1913) by Universal, with King Baggot.

In 1920—in the same year that the German Expressionist masterpiece, *The Cabinet of Dr. Caligari* (1919), opened in Germany—renowned filmmaker F.W. Murnau directed *Der Januskopf* [*The Janus Head* or *Janus-Faced*] (1920), starring Conrad Veidt. Veidt also plays the somnambulist Cesare in Robert Weine's classic, *Caligari*. Carl Janowitz wrote screenplays for both films. Sadly, *Januskopf* has been lost, although some shots and the script remain. I cannot resist commenting on the commonality in themes. In both cases, Veidt plays an unwitting murderer, one who is hypnotized in the case of Cesare and Dr. Caligari, and one whose inhibitions are released by chemical means, in the case of *Januskopf*. This leitmotif of murder was prominent as World War I ended, when many Central European men felt that they were forced to become killers for the sake of the war, and to assume alternative identities as soldiers. In that way, they lived like Mr. Hyde, who died in the end, as did many conscripted soldiers.[7]

Around the same time, but across the ocean, in America, two more takes on *Dr. Jekyll and Mr. Hyde* (1920) appeared. One rendition was disowned by its director-scenarist, Charles J. Hayden, who refused on-screen credit.[8] That film came from Louis B. Mayer's studio, just before Mayer merged his company to become the goliath MGM. The other 1920 *Dr. Jekyll and Mr. Hyde* is unforgettable. It stars John Barrymore. This silent gem often plays to the accompaniment of organ music, droning and emoting in the background, and recollecting organ elegies. Elegant cursive script graces the intertitles of the Barrymore film, while gothic frills decorate the tassels and tapestries of draperies and dressing gowns.

The text of the inter-titles is as important as the dark and foreboding aesthetic. One inter-title speaks Dr. Jekyll's thoughts: "Man has two selves, just as he has two hands." Even before the film starts, the handwriting is on the wall, both literally and figuratively, in the form of an inter-title. The film begins: "In each of us, two natures are at war—the good and the evil. All our lives, the fight goes on between them, and one must conquer. But in our own hands lie the power to choose—what we most want to be, we *are*." This opening statement lies midway between theology, philosophy and psychology. It is a sign of the times. When chemicals are added to the mix, it is uncertain how much choice remains, and how well willpower works.

This was the first of twenty-plus silent roles for Barrymore. Barrymore was already revered for his stage roles, and he gained more fame from his hammy portrayal of Hyde. He played *Richard III* on Broadway at the same time that he filmed *Jekyll,* and suffered a so-called "nervous breakdown" during this time. This version is readily retrieved on YouTube.

In spite of the glow surrounding the Barrymore name, this 1920 film is not the definitive version of *Dr. Jekyll and Mr. Hyde*. That honor had to wait over a decade, until 1931, with Robert Mamoulian's Pre-Code *Dr. Jekyll and Mr. Hyde* (1931), starring Fredric March as both Jekyll and Hyde. Miriam Hopkins plays the seductive saloon singer Ivy Pearson. Ivy meets her maker at the hands of the chemically transformed and sexually aroused doctor, who assumes the apelike form of Mr. Hyde whenever his libido overtakes him. Ivy extends her gartered leg, as the doctor examines her, and Dr. Jekyll transmogrifies, turning into the hideous Hyde. Dr. Jekyll's transformation is not as fast as Dr. Bruce Banner's switch to The Hulk, which occurs whenever Banner becomes angry, but the id-driven principles are similar in the Marvel comics' sixties era story and Stevenson's fin-de-siècle masterpiece.

"Pre-Code" films are known for steamy sexual subject matter and glorification of the seedier side of life, themes that prompted the institution of the Production Code (also known as the Hays Code), with its stricter standards. Mamoulian's *Dr. Jekyll* exemplifies these trends.

Fredric March won an Oscar for his portrayal of the handsome, refined and idealistic Dr. Jekyll as well as his coarse and ugly counterpart, Mr. Hyde. Mr. Hyde represents more than just a metaphysical "alter ego" or "shadow side," to use a Jungian expression. Mr. Hyde changes physical form as he changes personality and morality. He acquires a simian appearance (rather than merely growing larger, as Stevenson described). Ingenious theatrical lighting and clever make-up colors turn one character into another on Mamoulian's screen, decades before the invention of CGI (computer-generated imagery).

Dr. Jekyll starts out as a humanitarian of the highest degree, but drugs change his brain chemistry. Drugs unleash animalistic instincts that lay buried beneath the surface, hidden behind stilted Victorian etiquette, and veiled by selfless aspirations to tend to the medical needs of London's poor without payment. When he regresses to an ape-like appearance after swigging a steamy chemical potion, Dr. Jekyll calls attention to Darwinian evolutionary ideas, which continued to cause controversy for decades after Darwin presented them. In Dr. Jekyll's case, bodily changes accompany brain changes (which also happens in *Altered States* in 1980). Cartesian dualism ceases to exist in Mamoulian's interpretation of the Stevenson classic. The mind-body split that Descartes posited in the 17th century becomes irrelevant, even though this philosophy influenced psychoanalytic thinkers for decades, and still lingers in some circles.

Hyde spoofs Victorian society, with its rigid social and sexual mores that do more harm than good in the end. Just as we witness the dangers of drugs and medical science run wild, we also witness the dangers of indiscriminate repression of animal instincts (or libido, to use a term that would become popular over time, but was not yet in use when Stevenson wrote his story). We see how "either-or" thinking fails individuals, topples societies, and threatens science.

The Stevenson story highlights the duality of man, with his libidinal desires tugging against his moral code. In the film versions, starting with the 1920 Barrymore film (but not in Stevenson's novella), the story also dramatizes the duality of woman, and the constructed concepts of Madonna and *putana* (mother and whore). The loose lady who sings in disreputable dancehalls and seduces the good doctor is polar opposite of Dr. Jekyll's polished ladylove, whose pompous father berates the doctor's preference to serve London's poor. The salacious singer ignites repressed instincts inside this otherwise noble male. She brings out the beast within him, quite literally, to the point that he transforms into the hideous Mr. Hyde, who strangles her as she lifts her skirt to seduce him.

This version of *Jekyll and Hyde* escaped censorship from the Motion Picture Production Code of 1930 ("Hays Code") because "The Code" was not fully enforced until 1934. Mamoulian's *Jekyll and Hyde* was released on December 31, 1931, and is listed with a release date of either 1931 or 1932. Its racy bedroom scene, where Dr. Jekyll leans over the loose lady, as she lies in bed, and lays in wait, while she feigns illness, is classic "pre-Code" and is one of the many reasons why the Hays Code was adopted.

Soon after talkies came into being in 1927, films grew bolder and brasher, and threatened the "moral order" with transgressive themes of sex, violence, government corruption, aggrandizement of the lowlife, while belittling the highborn. Overt displays of outlaw sex would not pass the Production Code standards a few years later. A dedicated doctor who succumbs to drugs and depravity overstretches the moral standards. Yet Mamoulian's version might have survived the censors (with some edits), since the evil woman is murdered in the end, and so she suffers for her sins. In addition, the lustful doctor who yields to temptation is finally shot to death, in true Deuteronomic fashion.

Many directors attempted to unseat Mamoulian's claim to fame. Several simply spoofed the story, rather than trying to top the Mamoulian masterpiece. In 1941, Spencer Tracy plays a gangstereque Hyde in *Dr. Jekyll and Mr. Hyde* (1941) in Victor Fleming's interpretation. Victor Fleming (*Gone with the Wind,* 1939; *Wizard of Oz,* 1939; *When Clouds Roll By,* 1919) had impeccable directorial credentials for both love stories and fantasy films, yet even he could not outshine Mamoulian. In the Fleming version, Ingrid Bergman plays the loose lady that drives Dr. Jekyll to doom. Bergman achieved greater acclaim the next year, when she stars as Lazlo's not-so-loyal wife in *Casablanca* (1942), and drives Rick (Humphrey Bogart) to drink (more) at Rick's Café after she temporarily rebuffs him.

In any event, Stevenson's novella proved to be too rich to resist, and many, many interpretations exist. Well-known Western star Jack Palance takes center stage in *The Strange Case of Dr. Jekyll and Mr. Hyde* (1968). *Jekyll and Hyde* (1990), with Michael Caine, presents a slightly different but stunningly beautiful view of Jekyll's Victorian world. John Malkovich plays Dr. Jekyll in *Mary Reilly* (1996), while Julia Roberts stars as the doctor's Irish servant girl. *Jekyll and Hyde: The Musical* (2001) is a recorded film version of the musical that stars David Hasselhoff, who rekindled the Jekyll and Hyde craze and attracted cult-like admirers.

Perhaps most interestingly, in 1989, Anthony Perkins plays a Jekyll & Hyde spin-off in *Edge of Sanity* (1989). Perkins is forever remembered as Norman Bates from *Psycho* (1960). His stellar performance as a bipolar ballplayer in *Fear Strikes Out* (1957) is not so well remembered as the awkward and eccentric Norman from the Hitchcock thriller, but Perkins' portrayal is no less memorable. Like Norman, and like Jekyll & Hyde, *Fear Strikes Out's* Jimmy Pearsall experiences dramatic mood swings as he moves from manic to depressed and back again. Norman, perhaps more than any other character in film history, has a double-identity, a dual personality, and is even double-gendered. Norman's Hyde-like character hides behind his shy and socially phobic public presentation as a motel check-in clerk, mama's boy, and amateur taxidermist.

In *Edge of Sanity,* Jekyll's cocaine experiments get out of control, transforming him into the horrific Hyde. In the persona of Hyde, he roams London brothels and opium dens, in search of prey. When viewed side-by-side, especially with actor Anthony Perkins sandwiched in the middle, we realize how much Alfred Hitchcock and Robert Bloch (author of the book that inspired *Psycho*), are directly indebted to Stevenson's literary imagination and to Stevenson's psychological insights from the late 19th century.

Apart from these examples, a wide range of spoofs and comedies appeared on screen, including *Son of Dr. Jekyll* (1951), with Louis Hayward; *Abbott and Costello Meet Dr. Jekyll and Mr. Hyde* (1953), starring Boris Karloff; *Daughter of Dr. Jekyll* (1957), and the Hammer horror classic from the sixties, *The Two Faces of Dr. Jekyll* (1960), where Hyde looks better than the good doctor. Even Jerry Lewis' *The Nutty Professor* (1963) and the stop-motion *Mad Monster Party* (1967) reflect the influence of *Jekyll and Hyde.* Other versions range from the ridiculous to the sublime, including *Dr. Jekyll vs. The Werewolf* (1972); the transvestic version of *Dr. Jekyll and Sister Hyde* (1971); *Dr. Jekyll and Mr. Hyde* (1973), with Kirk Douglas in a musical version. There is *Dr. Jekyll's Dungeon of Death* (1979), the disco-like *Jekyll and Hyde ... Together Again* (1982), and so on.

A television movie about *Jekyll & Hyde* (1990) attracted an all-star cast that included Michael Caine as Henry Jekyll and Cheryl Ladd as Sara Crawford. More television films followed. To sum up, there is no end in sight to *Dr. Jekyll and Mr. Hyde.* The only place where their names are missing is the latest version of the *DSM-5* (*Diagnostic and Statistical Manual*), which is used for psychiatric research and for insurance billing codes, and published by the American Psychiatric Association. The *DSM-III* was stripped of literary, mythological and metapsychological allusions as far back as 1980. However, in public parlance, the expression, "Jekyll and Hyde" personality remains in use, and is understood by virtually all who hear it.

Moreover, this Jekyll & Hyde descriptive does not stir up acrimonious debates that commonly accompany changes in official psychiatric labels, codes, or diagnoses. Long before the declaration of the War on Drugs, and long before the passage of the Harrison Narcotics Act of 1914, Stevenson's character of Dr. Jekyll convinced readers that chemicals can alter brain functions, and maybe they can alter body form as well. Today, we are greatly concerned with the metabolic side effects of atypical antipsychotics, which have replaced the older "neuroleptics" such as chlorpromazine (Thorazine) and haloperidol (Haldol), which can cause movement disorders after long-term use, plus other side effects. However, susceptible persons risk weight gain and diabetes from the use of the advanced "atypicals." Many of these "new and improved" meds can change profiles from svelte to portly within weeks in those who are predisposed to adverse metabolic effects. So the idea that drugs alter appearance, as well as attitude and aptitude, is no longer a simple Stevensonian-style fantasy, but actually carries the ring of truth. We can only marvel at the insights expressed by Stevenson in 1886. Describing this author as "forward-thinking" does not do justice to his degree of perspicacity. Freud opened his private practice of neurology in 1886, and was years away from coining his concepts of psychoanalysis. Freud did admit, and correctly so, that poets perceive psychological truths far sooner than psychologists do. Recall that Freud published his Cocaine Papers in 1884, two years before Stevenson wrote. In contrast to Stevenson's skepticism about the consequences of drug use, Freud did not foresee ill effects from cocaine, although he later purged his Cocaine Papers from his collected works. Perhaps he was nodding to Stevenson in hindsight. Alternatively, revisionist histories hypothesize that Stevenson used cocaine to speed up his frenzied revision of his original manuscript, but to date, none offer sufficient supporting data to fortify their claims.

Stevenson's *Strange Case of Dr. Jekyll and Mr. Hyde* may be the most enduring, and the most relevant, to our study of neuroscience in science fiction film, but we cannot neglect Dr. Moreau, who was invented by H.G. Wells in the year that Freud invented psychoanalysis—1896. Were Dr. Moreau alive today, we might encounter him at a neuroscience conference, but probably not at a medical conference per se. He was, after all, interested in ethology, in animal and human behavior, in inter-species similarities and dissimilarities, and in laboratory experimentation as well. Wells himself studied and taught biology, which enriches his stories.

Of course, Moreau would have lost his medical license long ago, because of inhumane experiments conducted on both animals and humans, as he changed one to the other. Moreau's House of Pain would not be acceptable to anyone today, but might appeal to the

The lobby card for *Island of Lost Souls* (1932), a film based on H.G. Wells' novel, shows Katherine Burke as part-human, partially-clad Panther Woman, with portly Charles Laughton as Dr. Moreau standing between her and Richard Arlen, who plays shipwrecked sailor Edward Parker, who stumbles onto this strange site.

likes of Nazi doctors such as Josef Mengele, who maimed or murdered unanesthetized and unwilling subjects. Perhaps Herophilus, the Greek doctor who dissected living human slaves for learning's sake, to become known as "the father of anatomy," might have agreed with Moreau's conscienceless methodology.[9] Moreau's intellectual interests could have attracted like-minded admirers—had he not chosen to sequester himself and his laboratory on a secluded island, which was dubbed the *Island of Lost Souls* (1932) by the filmmaker, Erle C. Kenton. It is beside the point that Wells intended his tale about Dr. Moreau as an anti-vivisectionist treatise. He did not present Moreau as an example of serious science. Yet even "non-serious" science, run amok, has the potential to cause serious harm to humans and animals, as history has shown.

Dr. Moreau is a morality tale in disguise, one that represents an alternative interpretation of Darwinism. While the anti–Darwinists were vocal to a fault, the pro–Darwin entourage developed more empathy with animals, having learned of the chain of evolution. Pre-Darwin, vivisection had been practiced in Britain, without a second thought, but many thoughtful people, Wells included, rethought those practices after Darwin called attention to the continuum between humans, other primates and animals in general. Those debates rage in our current day.

Generations that followed offered their own interpretations, and we can safely say that Moreau could have been a proto-neuro-psychiatrist who recognizes the localization of brain-based language functions. Ironically, Freud published a paper *On Aphasia* (1891), or the loss of language ability, immediately before his transition to the study of "psycho-analysis" (as he called it). Freud repudiated reigning theories about the localization of language functions to specific parts of the brain. Those theories were well known before Wells wrote. Wernicke's aphasia had been discovered by German psychiatrist and neurologist Carl Wernicke in 1874. Paul Broca, a French neurologist who previously studied anthropology, identified Broca's aphasia even earlier.

Dr. Moreau bears little-to-no similarity to Dr. Jekyll, who was a good man before bad drugs turned him into a bad human being, causing misguided acts that turned into terrible mishaps. Dr. Moreau possesses no such redeeming qualities. Moreau has no higher aspirations for humanity. Moreau experiments on animals, performs operations on them, and trains them to act more human. Through surgery, he imparts the ability to speak and to stand upright. He disrupts the natural order and disregards the inborn tendencies of his menagerie. Moreau's operating room is located in the aptly named "House of Pain."

Dr. Moreau's fictional story is retold in *Island of Lost Souls* (1932), which premiered one year after Mamoulian's *Dr. Jekyll* (1931) and one year before Hitler became Chancellor of the Third Reich. In a strange foreshadowing of the future, the inhumane experiments on Dr. Moreau's island paralleled the experiments that Nazi doctors would soon conduct on humans whom they deemed to be less than human.

Don Taylor directed another movie version of *Island of Dr. Moreau* in 1977. Two decades later, in 1996, yet another remake of the enduring tale appeared, this time starring Val Kilmer as Montgomery, with an aging Marlon Brando as Dr. Moreau. This latter remake was directed by John Frankenheimer, who directed the original *Manchurian Candidate* in 1962. Frankenheimer also directed *Seconds* (1966), another horrifying story about psychology and plastic surgery. *Seconds* is far too philosophical to be lumped into the "medsploitation" genre.

While few people believe that Moreau-like animal experiments could impact their daily lives, and equally few people realize how devoted Wells was to the anti-vivisectionist cause, many people have been intrigued by the concept of turning humans into apes, or vice versa. Chimps dressed in human clothes are ever-popular circus attractions. *Planet of the Apes* was a spectacular success, and spawned several sequels, although the original film functions more as a social metaphor about race relations rather than as a pro-primate or animal rights treatise.

As we shall see in a forthcoming chapter, movies about monkey-man brain transplants were common in film's early years. Audiences of that era were still shocked by the discoveries of Darwin, and applauded shorts that recollected such controversies. At the same time, the public was enthralled by recent advances in science. Moving pictures were one of many scientific advances that appeared as the 19th century came to a close.

In the chapters ahead, we will see how the legacy of 19th century science fiction literature rings loud and clear throughout the 20th century and into the 21st century. That statement is especially true when we speak of "neuroscience fiction film," which emphasizes the brain's role in behavior, a role that was subjugated by psychoanalysis, which moved the locus of control from the physical brain to the abstract mind.

Yet the primacy of the brain and other biological functions were never fully submerged. Like a submarine that sinks below the water level, imperceptible in plain sight, but ready to rise when the coast is clear, neuroscience fiction themes from the 19th century lay waiting, ready to entertain audiences when those audiences were ready to appreciate them.

Four

Androids, Automatons, Replicants and *RoboCops*

If the Romantic-era ballet *Coppelia,* from 1870, seems completely removed from the neuroscience fiction films that surfaced a century later, circa 1970, please read on. For we find a clear-cut continuum between Dr. Coppelius' mechanical doll, whom he named "Coppelia," and the near human—but not human—robotic "replicants" in *Blade Runner* (1982).

Coppelia also shares similarities with the reconstructed cop in *RoboCop* (1987) and the sequels and reboots. RoboCop was known as Officer Murphy, when he was a regular beat cop who went home to his wife and family and presumably lived a rather ordinary life on a peaceful suburban street. Even his name is ordinary. Murphy is a common enough Irish American name that recollects the pervasive Irish American presence in the U.S. police department. Then he was surgically reconstructed to become RoboCop, and the rest is history. The *RoboCop* franchise has outlived Murphy!

There are crossovers between Coppelia and the mechanical characters in *The Terminator* (1984) and *The Stepford Wives* (1975), but it is *Blade Runner* and *RoboCop* (1987, 1990, 1993, 2014) that interest us, above all, as we search for the starting points and high points of neuroscience fiction. All of those films were made at turning points in psychiatric or neuroscience history. Each of these films reflect shifts in the way we conceive of the brain and how it controls behavior—and each confronts quasi-philosophical, quasi-psychological questions about what it means to be human and about the role of free will.

The most recent *RoboCop* reflects remarkable advances in bioengineering, which have allowed paralyzed persons to move artificial limbs through brain waves or blinks of the eye. *RoboCop* 2014 makes some mention of dopamine, correlating the neurotransmitter with emotion (not quite correctly). It adds screen shots of neurosurgery, with cerebral cortex exposed, and metallic implants inserted strategically between sulci. This time around, the story becomes a bit more believable, thanks to astounding advances in robotics, where artificial limbs move in response to brain-computer connections. In this film, "Big Medical Device Makers" push Big Pharma aside, proving that evil does indeed lurk in the hearts of men, and that this evil is especially deep-seated in the hearts of corporation men (and woman, in the case of *Elysium*).

If these films attempted to distinguish between the human and the divine, then we would be confronting religious questions—but these films focus on the line that separates human and machine. The boundaries between human and machine are blurring more by

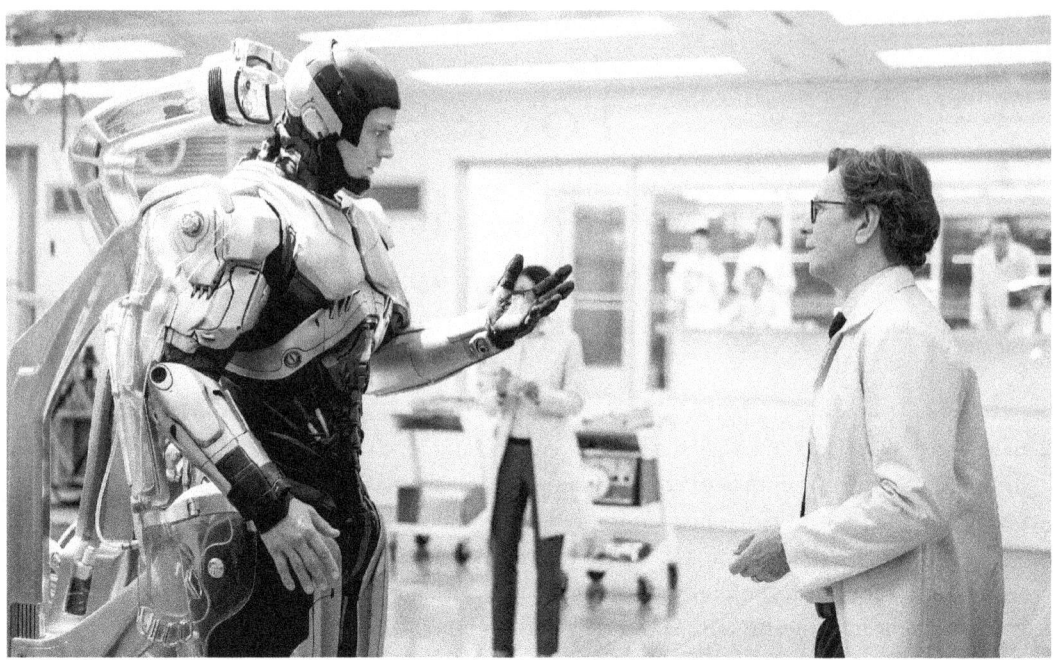

Gary Oldman's bespectacled scientist looks diminutive in his white lab coat, compared to the reconstructed Officer Murphy (Joel Kinnaman) of *RoboCop* (2014), who towers over him.

the minute, as scientists push forward fast, and move from dreamtime to the drawing board to real time.

In this book, we act like anthropologists or archaeologists who comb through abandoned burial sites, in hopes of finding ancestral skulls that mark turning points in human evolution. Instead, we will sift through old celluloid, in search of clues that show paradigm changes that were in the works years, maybe decades, before they those changes infiltrated clinical practice. Films (and literature) can anticipate ideas before ideas are formally accepted as scientific theory. For the arts can hint without providing proof, and can prod our imaginations, whereas science demands facts and reproducible results. Scientific advances require imagination plus proof.

In this chapter ahead, we will also talk about *The Terminator*, since it is a landmark film in bioscience fiction, although it does not meet my newly minted criteria for "neuroscience fiction" (NSF). We will also mention *The Stepford Wives*, more because of its social importance than because of its significance in predicting shifts in neuroscience. Each of these four films enjoys a prominent place in film history, and each attained either cult status or critical acclaim, or, in the case of *The Stepford Wives*, cultural disdain that co-existed with critical acclaim. As our chapter ends, we will return to *Iron Man*, whom we mentioned in the introduction.

Four of those five films spawned sequels or remakes. That fact alone says a great deal about the films. Remade or rebooted movies have attracted a strong enough following or had a solid enough commercial footing or carried enough social significance to merit more movies. Ideally, those updates are philosophically or politically meaningful to later generations of moviegoers, and are more than a way to make more money by playing on the name of a brand name, sure win product.[1] Of the five films mentioned above, Ridley Scott's *Blade Runner* (1982) is the only one that was not remade—to date. Yet *Blade Runner* remains a cult classic, even though the youthful Harrison Ford seems so distant from Ford's contemporary presence. The Harrison Ford of *Blade Runner* evoked Ford's adventuresome persona as Indiana Jones from *Raiders of the Lost Ark* (1981).

Blade Runner has lived extra lives because of the Internet, where fan sites and science fiction discussion boards continue to rhapsodize about this film, sometimes comparing it to the latest summer blockbusters and marveling at (or booing) later films that "replicate" its post-apocalyptic thesis.

Blade Runner is also responsible for influencing William Gibson, the SF writer who became known as the "father of cyberpunk" and who arguably wields as much influence on contemporary NSF as Philip K. Dick (PKD) himself (who was writing long before Gibson was born in 1948). Because *Blade Runner* draws on a 1968 novella by PKD, we get a "two for one" double feature each time we view the film and think about Dick's original *Do Androids Dream of Electric Sheep?* (1968).[2] The film itself is painfully slow-moving, but its message (or messages, to be more correct) are hard-hitting, especially since the film appeared in 1982, when American psychiatry was pushing forward fast, heading toward a hairpin turn, and veering toward neuroscience and psychopharmacology and away from psychoanalysis.

In the paragraph above, I mention William Gibson, who earned the epithet, "father of cyberpunk" (although he was not the first to use the term "cyberpunk"). Gibson's book *Neuromancer* (1984) won the Hugo, Nebula, and Philip K. Dick Awards in the year it was published. This was the first novel to win all three awards. Those accolades alone were enough to promote his hypothetical coronation as the High Priest of SF, or the "father of cyberpunk." However, SF fans tell us that the term "cyberpunk" surfaced in the title of a lesser-known short story by Bruce Bethke. Bethke's "Cyberpunk" was written in 1980 but published in *Amazing Science Fiction Stories* in 1983.

In recent decades, the term "cyberpunk" has cropped up almost everywhere. Cyberpunk novels and films take place in the netherworld of the ether, which exists in cyberspace only. Had the concept been coined in medieval times, rather than by a post-modern author, someone might have said that this computer-generated purgatory lies somewhere between earthly existence, celestial realms and a subterranean Hell. Some cyberpunk works carry obvious religious overtones (as in *The Matrix*), making the analogy with medieval Hell less far-fetched. At other times, cyberpunk is closer to cold-blooded, hardboiled, *noir*-ish detective fiction, where the action occurs in the ether, rather than in the dark and dreary cityscape that is typical of *film noir*.

Cyberpunk lit and film represent more than mere entertainment that idles the time away. Cyberpunk reflects a scary reality. It embroiders far-fetched stories that seem far-removed from the everyday reality that inspired the stories in the first place. Fears that humans can be replaced by computers may have begun in the imagination, but they are more than mere figments of the imagination. This *is* reality, in real time. Even surgeons fear replacement by robotic arms that are controlled remotely by distant medical centers. In some settings, psychiatry, the most humanistic medical specialty that relies on interpersonal interactions, is being outsourced to telepsychiatry modules.[3] It remains to be seen if those telepsychiatry centers will prove to be more convenient and cost-effective, especially considering that each doctor-patient encounter requires the presence of three staff members on site with the patient (according to the currently used VA model). Family doctors will soon compete, not just with "physician-extenders" who have far less education than they, but with apps made for iPhones and Androids. Those apps track blood pressure, blood sugars, various vital signs and monitor medical adherence at the same time.

At the time this book was begun, the Great Recession was in place for several years, having started in 2007. As the tight job market and high employment rates suggest, many fears about computers overtaking everyday existence proved true. Jobs were indeed eliminated as technology advanced, in much the same way that jobs—and a sense of human purpose—were lost during the original Industrial Age. Admittedly, new job categories came into being, since creating and using new technology demands new and different skills. Many of those jobs never existed before, and many were never anticipated. (Social media marketing comes to mind.)

The concerns brought by the Computer Era were different from the concerns that accompanied the Machine Age and the Industrial Revolution. Some (but surely not all) concerns raised by the Computer Era relate to neuroscience. Even the expression "artificial intelligence"—which refers to computing capability—implies that human intelligence is interchangeable with computer intelligence. It suggests that human intelligence can be outsourced—not necessarily to India or China—but to software that is encased in computer hardware, which is then stationed in small town America or lower-cost countries with underdeveloped but emerging economies.

Comparing the human body (or living bodies in general) to a machine was beside the point. That concept was so obvious that it was outdated. It was not long before our darkest fears sneaked out from the shadows and made themselves manifest in science fiction. As computers advanced, some people wondered if artificial intelligence would outpace human intelligence, to the point that computers could overtake human society, like conquistadors of old. Those smart computers might subjugate the "primitive" humans. We might suffer the same fate as pre-literate societies that were colonized by seafaring nations with more advanced military systems. The lessons left from Age of Exploration were not forgotten by fear-inducing SF writers.

On a more minor scale, some speculated that computers could run amok, and control human brains, replace thoughts and literally "read minds" (without a crystal ball). Those worries occurred long before anyone conceived of computer viruses or worms. There was a time when such fears were limited to psychotics or paranoids, or exploited by storefront psychics. In psychiatric nomenclature, there is specific jargon to describe these perceptions: "thought insertion" and "thought broadcasting."[4] To a psychiatrist, the presence of these perceptions (without an ability to question their credibility) raises suspicions about an impending schizophrenic breakdown, or perhaps a less severe schizotypal personality. As the Computer Age expanded, even sane people found themselves indulging in such speculation. By the time that "information mining" became a science and not idle speculation, there were even more worries about who knows what about whom, and what those information-gatherers will do with the data.

It is one thing to harness the power of machines or computers, so that we can put them to use. However, an out-of-control computer is worse than a runaway horse. A runaway horse that refuses to obey its master can buck and whinny and throw its rider out of the saddle and onto the ground. That horse can put the rider into the path of danger, and maybe even trample or stomp on the fallen equestrian. Computers and artificial intelligence are more mysterious and more powerful than workhorses, but the metaphors are the same. Fears grow larger and paranoia mounts when persons with excessive imagination—or excessive information—contemplate the future.

We can add this paranoid tinge to scientific know-how, stir in a lot of literary flavor, and let the literary alchemy do the work. Lo and behold, we have a brand new genre of cyberpunk. We will discuss cyberpunk and its relationship to consciousness and control in later chapters.

For now, though, let me simply point out that this very contemporary concern—the mixing of man and machine—and the automation of movement and the overpowering of human will—has very ancient roots. Automata—or mechanical dolls that move of their own accord—appealed to human fancy early in history. Those automata are direct antecedents of androids and replicants, robots and RoboCop of more contemporary times. They date back to the Greeks.

Let us move to mythology for a moment, and revisit the stories of Daedalus, Pygmalion, and Prometheus. Each attempted to create artificial life or reshape human forms. Daedalus, a master artisan, architect and sculptor, fashioned wings from wax and feathers for himself and for his son, Icarus. Father and son attempted to fly to the sun, but fell into the sea instead, when the wax melted from the heat.

Pygmalion was a sculptor who fell in love with a statue he created. Pygmalion's story came to us from Greek myth, but George Bernard Shaw resurrected his legacy via a 1912 play by the same name. The play was then translated into a musical, *My Fair Lady,* by Alan Jay Lerner. A film version of *My Fair Lady* (1964) followed.

Prometheus made a man out of clay and then defied the gods by giving fire to humankind. The mythological Prometheus should be distinguished from Ridley Scott's film, *Prometheus* (2012), even though the film intentionally references the mythological character, as does the subtitle of Mary Shelley's *Frankenstein: The Modern Prometheus.*

The myths of Daedalus, Pygmalion and Prometheus endure among students of classics, mythology and Jungian psychology. Their names are fossilized in literature (*Frankenstein: A Modern Prometheus*) or drama (George Bernard Shaw's 1912 play, *Pygmalion*, which inspired the musical, *My Fair Lady*). Daedalus became the name of a literary review (*Daedalus*) and was re-invigorated by James Joyce, who named his protagonist "Stephen Dedalus" in his semi-autobiographical novel, *Portrait of the Artist as a Young Man* (1914).

Mary Shelley credited Prometheus when she subtitled her Frankenstein story, "A Modern Prometheus." In addition to Prometheus, Shelley mentions young Victor Frankenstein's fascination with Cornelius Agrippa and Albertus Magnus. Long before Shelley wrote her masterpiece, there were mysterious tales of the mechanical man created by 13th century alchemist, Albertus Magnus. Magnus' disciple, Thomas Aquinas, smashed this mechanical man to pieces. Mary Shelley laid the groundwork for stories about mad or misguided scientists, a trend that persisted through the mid–20th century and accounted for the most common villain in horror film until mid-century.[5]

Three hundred years after the story about Magnus' alchemical feat, the Golem appeared at the behest of Rabbi Judah Loew ben Bezalel. The Golem remains a fixture in Jewish fantasy literature, although the story itself is rarely taken seriously today, except perhaps by some comic book writers, who credit the story for inspiring Marvel characters such as The Thing.

Also known as the Maharal of Prague, Rabbi Loew lived from 1513–1609. He animated a monster, made out of clay, in a failed attempt to protect the Czech Jews from assaults by their Gentile neighbors. Like the Frankenstein monster that followed, the Golem eventually turned on his creator. He refused to obey the rabbi, and wrought more destruction than protection. In the end, the Golem had to be put to rest.[6]

Many scholars link Shelley's story to the fanciful Jewish legend that antedated it by over two centuries, although some researchers hypothesize about other inspirations. Some of those ideas are as imaginative as the Frankenstein story itself. However, we cannot link the Golem to neuroscience fiction, or to any science fiction, because the Golem acquired its life force via supernatural rather than scientific means. His rabbi-creator carved Hebrew letters on the Golem's forehead. The magical powers of those letters ignited his powers. The Golem story sidesteps scientific discoveries that lie at the core of true SF stories. In fact, both author and audience would be offended if science—rather than faith—received credit for this miraculous mound of clay. Albertus Magnus' much-earlier, medieval mechanical man lay closer to the spirit of science than the 16th century Golem, because Magnus had pseudo-scientific alchemical aspirations.

Legends aside, automata were real, and were true mechanical and scientific accomplishments of their day. It is said that the best of automata inspired the Mechanical Age, and the best of the best resides at Strasbourg. Many people still adore automata, as articles in the *New York Times* Arts & Leisure and Science sections tell us. Some members of royalty collected these creations. Museums with automata do not lack visitors.[7]

The monumental clock at Strasbourg was created between 1352 and 1354. It stopped working in 1500, but was refurbished in 1574, and functioned until 1788. In 1842, artisans and technicians created yet another clock, and transferred the original to the Strasbourg Museum of Decorative Arts. The first clock housed a gilded rooster that spreads its feathers at the precise time of the day. The Strasbourg clock has none of the occult connotations associated with some automata. Instead, it testifies to the order, precision, skills (and authoritarianism) of regional clockmakers. Strasbourg is situated in Alsace-Lorraine, which is an area that was sometimes claimed by France, sometimes dominated by Germany, but always acclaimed for clock making. This complex clock can stand on aesthetic merit alone, but its mastery of mechanics is nothing less than amazing. Later generations of automata derive from the Strasbourg clock and led to the Machine Age.

Automata fired the imaginations of philosophers and proto-psychologists, as well as artists and engineers, clockmakers and craftspeople. The revolutionary physiology of Rene Descartes (1596–1650) evolved out of his experience with mechanisms. "Cartesian dualism" separated body from brain. Although Descartes' ideas were celebrated in their era, and were prized by his admirers, his slant set neuropsychiatry back by a century. Cartesian dualism was embraced by psychoanalysts, who separate body from mind, making the "mind" autonomous, and thereby giving short shrift to neuroscience. (That trend is changing today, to a degree, thanks to Nobel laureate, Eric Kandel, and evolving interest in "Neuropsychoanalysis.")

A philosopher by the name of La Mettrie carried Cartesian ideas even further. He published a book about *The Human Machine* (*L'Homme Machine*) (1748). William James, who studied medicine before opening America's first psychology laboratory at Harvard, asked "Are We Automata?" James's essay appeared in *Mind* 4:1–22 in 1879. James is best remembered as a philosopher. As the author of *The Varieties of Religious Experience* (1902), he became a counter-culture icon because he documented his otherworldly experiences with nitrous oxide.

Those lofty ideas about minds and machines are important to the history of automata, and to the histories of psychology, psychiatry and philosophy, but they are far-removed from automata that were employed solely for the sake of entertainment. The master of that approach was not a philosopher or a psychologist or a theoretician of any sort. Rather, it was the master magician Jean Eugène Robert-Houdin (1805–1871) who displayed automata in his stage shows.

Robert-Houdin died in 1871. The last decade of his life coincided with the start of an era that became known as "The Golden Age of Automata" (1860 to 1910). Robert-Houdin got this "Golden Age" off to a glowing beginning. During the decades that followed, many small family-based companies of automata makers thrived in Paris, making and exporting thousands of clockwork automata. During this half-century span, automata thrived as never before.

Importantly, the Golden Age of Automata overlapped with the early years of filmmaking, and with the short-lived glory days of Georges Méliès. Méliès was a magician-turned-moviemaker who made dreamlike science fiction and fantasy films as early as 1896. Unlike more serious-minded contemporaries, such the Lumière Brothers or Edison, Méliès saw movies as another form of magic. He recognized their entertainment value from the start. Méliès felt so indebted to the magician Jean Eugène Robert-Houdin that he bought his theater in 1888 and named it after Robert-Houdin.[8]

A romanticized version of Méliès' life story—and the tale of an automaton that draws a likeness of Méliès' man in the moon—is retold in an endearing film, *Hugo* (2011). This film bears little to no relationship to neuroscience fiction per se, but it is worth mentioning because of its historical value. *Hugo* is a magical film whose presentation is true to its magical subject matter. Its subject and its setting are a departure for director Martin Scorsese, who made his name by making crime films that recollect the mean streets of Manhattan's Little Italy, where he was born and reared and where the mob reigned and thrived. *Hugo* is set in a Paris train station in 1931. An embittered and unrecognized Méliès runs a tiny toyshop in the train station, where mechanical wonders run amok, as do thieving little children.

Hugo transports us back to the Golden Age of Automata, because a mechanical automaton is the "MacGuffin" of the movie. The princely gold automaton holds a pen, makes a drawing, bows his head, moves his eyes, and, most importantly of all, holds a double meaning. The young boy who stars in the film (Asa Butterfield) is caught poaching parts from Méliès' counter. He later risks his life to rescue the automaton, not to assuage Méliès directly, or to repent for his attempted crime, because his beloved father was a clockmaker who was fixing the humanoid at the very moment that a flash fire erupted in his shop, and consumed his father.

The tragic fire left little Hugo orphaned at a young age, and at the mercy of an unkind alcoholic uncle who tended to him. Unbeknownst to Hugo and perhaps unknown to his father as well, the beloved automaton was constructed by Georges Méliès himself (played by Sir Ben Kingsley). The device was the last glory of the forgotten genius who was presumed dead—until the little boy and the orphan girl who befriends him chance upon clues that suggest otherwise.

Hugo transports the viewer to a netherworld that lies between magic and mechanics, chemistry and alchemy. We know that the automaton is not alive—but there are moments when we start to wonder if this Golem-like creature could acquire a soul and spirit of its own.

During the Golden Age of Automata, another enduring tale of an automaton surfaced. In 1870, the sentimental ballet *Coppelia* premiered. Based on a short story by fantasist ETA Hoffmann—*Der Sandmann* (*The Sandman*) (1816)—*Coppelia* became the most performed ballet at the Opera Garnier. It packed opera and ballet houses from the start. Major ballet companies perform *Coppelia* to this day. This piece is testimony to the Romantic era and to the genius of the Romantic imagination. It will lead to robots and replicants that have been stripped of all supernatural elements.

Coppelia is a life-sized dancing doll. She takes the name of her inventor, Dr. Coppelius. In contrast to Frankenstein's hideous monster, which also goes by the name of its inventor, Dr. Frankenstein, Coppelia is beautiful. Although she is unreal, she looks real enough to attract the attention of Franz, a village "swain" who is preparing to become betrothed to his ladylove.

Franz spots a beautiful woman sitting on a balcony that belongs to Dr. Coppelius. So he sneaks into Dr. Coppelius' studio, hoping to find this "fair maiden." Not to be outsmarted, the clever inventor Coppelius leaves a sleeping potion for Franz. But Franz' "intended" (his not quite fiancée), Swanhilde, has been hiding behind a curtain, watching what happened. Swanhilde knows much more than the unquestioning (and nearly unfaithful) Franz does.

Franz grows so infatuated with this doll that he neglects his real-life, true love, Swanhilde, whom he planned to marry. To mock him, Swanhilde dresses as the doll, and pretends to come alive. In her doll disguise, she reignites his interest. In the process, the real doll is broken. Dr. Coppelius is horrified when he returns to his workshop and finds his life's work ruined. With some simulated black magic and a generous bribe, Dr. Coppelius is appeased. Frantz and Swanhilde are reunited. They wed, in a lavish wedding scene, and everything ends happily ever after.

Coppelia turned into three silent films by that name (1911, 1915, and 1923). Several other cinematic renditions of this story appeared during the silent years. *The Doll* (*Die Puppe*) (1919), directed by Ernst Lubitsch, was based on the Coppelia story. This interpretation is a romantic comedy, as would be expected of a Lubitsch creation. The light-hearted Lubitsch film premiered in the same year as Freud's essay on *The Uncanny* (1919).

In *The Uncanny* (*Der Unheimlich*), Freud dissects another ETA Hoffmann story based on *The Sandman*. In trying to explain that creepy-crawly feeling evoked by imagery that is simultaneously familiar (*heimlich* or "homelike") and unfamiliar (*unheimlich* or "un-homelike), Freud points to marionettes and mechanical dolls as exemplars of "the uncanny."[9] Even though an eerie mechanical doll named Olympia appears in *The Sandman*, and attracts

Freud's interest, the *Coppelia* ballet does not merit mention in Freud's famous essay, perhaps because the ballet bears none of the macabre traces typically found in Hoffman stories.

Coppelia reappears in film form, albeit behind the scenes. A scene from the *Coppelia* ballet plays in the background of *The Red Shoes* (1948). *The Red Shoes* is deemed to be the best ballet film ever made. In *The Red Shoes,* the star ballerina, played by Moira Shearer, is forced into an impossible position by her composer-husband. He treats her as if she is a mechanical doll that can be wound up on demand. He pressures her to attend his concert in lieu of her ballet opening, which is scheduled on the same night. She cannot reconcile the conflict between marriage and career. To avoid confrontation, she attempts to jump to her death instead. Unexpectedly, she survives, but breaks her leg, and lies immobile, like the mechanical doll in the original ballet. She will not be able to dance again.

The theme of the doll-automaton-woman substitution repeats itself in film history, more as social commentary than as neuroscience fiction. In 1927, Fritz Lang made *Metropolis,* one of the last great silent films that appeared before talkies stole the show and transformed film and reset audiences' expectations. *Metropolis* is often erroneously identified as the first science-fiction film, even though Méliès' *A Trip to the Moon* (1902) deserves that credit. *Metropolis*' mechanical Maria falls clearly into the camp of neuroscience fiction, even though the robotic replica retains a trace of the supernatural veneer that infiltrates so many Weimar era films, as described in Lotte Eisner's *The Haunted Screen* (1969). The mere fact that the false Maria is created by a mad scientist—albeit one who is similar to a sorcerer—makes this science fiction.

The movie's real Maria is a formidable female force. She organizes male workers, using charisma and compassion. She wins the heart of the rich man's son without exerting any effort, much like the best of ballet's leading ladies. The false Maria—the robot—is also a beautiful blonde, one that bridges the occultism of German Romanticism with the "magic" of the Machine Age. She is a forerunner of later mechanical beings that retain the physical form of "the human machine" but lose their human "essence" or "soul" during their transformations.

Lang's *Metropolis* is set in a futuristic city, where Art Deco design triumphs. The scientist Rotwang lives in a crooked *Caligari*-esque house that looks out-of-place next to the sleek and streamlined Art Deco architecture. A Moloch-like machine lives underground, consuming fuels and humans alike. The all-powerful machine boils in its below ground abode, and threatens to destroy the poor workers who toil to keep the city's machinery supplied with electrical power. Thematically, there is little difference between the Hell of a Hieronymus Bosch triptych and *Metropolis*' movie set. The fire-breathing dragons of Hades, with smoke blasting from bloated nostrils, look strangely similar to suffocating, percolating, incinerating exhaust fumes expelled by modern industrial machinery. The imagery evokes Biblical lore, where idol-worshipping heathens and wayward Israelites sacrificed babies to the fires that burned inside the mouth of the Moloch idol. The Art Deco architecture was inspired by Lang's visit to Manhattan.

As the film nears its climax, class warfare is minutes away. The good Maria, with her beautiful blonde tresses, had rallied the distraught workers. She offers hope and consolation to the overworked and underfed under classes, who are locked in an underground city that will flood if the power stops and the damns break. It goes without saying that they will die if that happens. Maria assuages them, like Mother Mary. She is almost messianic, but not quite. She consoles, but does not promise deliverance. It would be nice if she were another Moses, who could miraculously part the waters, to lead her people out of danger when the dams break. However, she is not—but she has other attributes.

Rotwang (Rudolf Klein-Rogge) creates a bad robotic replica of the good Maria (Brigette Helm), to undermine Maria's impact on the minions of male workers. This Rotwang has a back-story. There was time when Rotwang was infatuated with a beautiful woman named Hel, but Hel spurned him in favor of the town's overlord, the wealthy Jon Frederson, Master of Metropolis. Hel and Frederson married, but Hel died while giving birth to Freder. Freder grows up and falls in love with the real Maria.

To compensate for the loss of Hel, Rotwang fashions a metallic image of Hel, but never finishes. Instead, Frederson visits him and demands that Rotwang make a replica of Maria.

So Rotwang kidnaps the good Maria, and uses a brain machine to transfer her "essence" (her consciousness, perhaps?) to the robotic replacement. Tubes protrude from a metallic cap that reminds us of contemporary TCMS machinery, and of the brain machines in *Batman* serials from 1943.[10] Rotwang's laboratory, with its sparking machinery, switch plate towers, chemistry beakers, and pipe work, would provide stock imagery for later "mad scientist" workshops.

Having completed his preparations, Rotwang substitutes this artificial physical double, which functions as an evil twin. The doppleganger is intentionally coarse and vulgar, vile and venomous. This robot is the demonic "shadow side" of the good Maria. It recollects the real Maria, but does not behave like Maria. False robot Maria rallies the workers to riot. She creates chaos. Clearly, the mad scientist who created the robotic Maria shares similarities with malevolent sorcerers from fantasy lore. He even displays a pentagram in his workshop and on the door of his crooked Caligari-esque house.

Before the film ends, the real Maria is found and freed, and the deception is revealed, and all is well. Freder, the rich man's son who loves the real Maria, rallies to her aid. He undoes the damage caused by the robotic Maria, and reconciles the irate workers with the ruling class. He solicits his estranged father, who controls the city, and who was ready to let oppressed workers drown. The son saves the city, as well as Maria and the masses. He also salvages his strained relationship with his father. Rotwang dies, as he falls off a cathedral while fighting with Freder.

This is a science fiction fairy tale. It has a pro-suffragette subtext, for it implies that recently empowered women will protect men rather than neglect men, and that they will look out for everyone's interests, even after gaining the right to vote and symbolically leaving the home.

This strange tale of the Machine Age recollects the heroic age, as should be expected from a filmmaker who directed the two-part myth-based *Die Nieberlungen* films in 1924. It is a fairy tale story that is not so far removed from *Coppelia,* the romantic ballet about the mechanical doll. Equally importantly, *Metropolis* speaks legions about Germany's distressing economic conditions that escalated after the Great War ended, and continued through the 1920s and led to Hitler's rise to power in 1933. Germany was forced to pay steep reparations for instigating World War I, driving many citizens to poverty. Mass inflation followed the government's efforts to print more (worthless) money. Life spiraled downward, opening

FOUR. *Automations, Androids, Replicants and* RoboCops 71

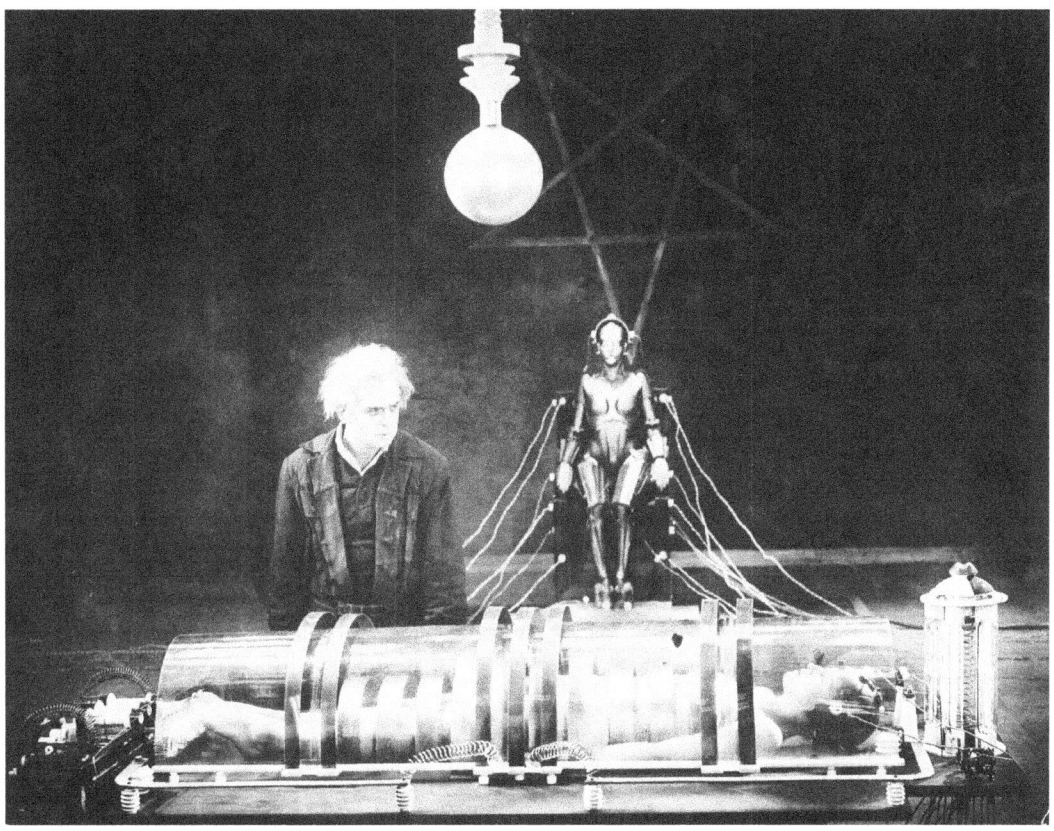

In Fritz Lang's *Metropolis* (1927), the evil scientist Rotwang (played by Rudolf Klein-Rogge, who played Dr. Mabuse in other Fritz Lang films and became a Nazi in real life) stands over the supine body of the "good Maria," whom he kidnapped, encased in a cylinder, and attached to tubes that transfer her "essence" to the "bad Maria" robotic replica in the background.

opportunities for demagogues that promised economic redemption, or at least reminded people of their proud past. Many respected historians link Hitler's ascent to such economic woes.

Metropolis is strongly connected to German history, and to the evolution of the Third Reich. Shortly before *Metropolis* was made in 1927, Hitler published two consecutive installments of his anti–Semitic treatise, *Mein Kampf* (1925, 1926). He wrote these pieces while serving a prison sentence for his failed Beer Hall Putsch of 1923. Fritz Lang's life story is also intertwined with the trajectory of the Reich. In response to Hitler's ascent to power, and the tightening reigns of the Nuremberg Laws, and fears for his own safety, Fritz Lang fled to France, and then to America. The story of Lang's escape is engaging but probably not totally correct.

According to Professor Mark Brake, at www.markbrake.com/podcasts,[11] *Metropolis'* Professor Rotwang intentionally caricatures Albert Einstein. Brake argues that Rotwang's hooknose and wild hair mirror the appearance of the Jewish Nobel Laureate, whom Hitler denounced because of his Jewishness. The Nazis railed against "Jewish physics" and opposed the so-called "Jewish science" (their name for psychoanalysis).

Rotwang's diabolical and destructive character reflects Germany's creeping anti–Semitism and the forthcoming Nazi regime, according to the reasoning set forth in Siegfried Kracauer's controversial book *From Caligari to Hitler* (1947). Kracauer claims that evil doctors in Weimar era film foreshadow the arrival of even more evil despots during the Third Reich. By applying Kracauer's paradigm to Lang's film, we can read Rotwang as a representative of Germany's cultured and educated elite, who morph into merciless killers and behave like evil sorcerers. Both Rotwang and Nazis exploit scientific advances to murder more efficiently.

Professor Brake crowns Rotwang as the most influential mad scientist in all film history. That is quite a statement, considering the competition. Mad scientists proliferated in horror films, having been particularly popular villains until Hitchcock's *Psycho* (1960) changed the paradigm. *Psycho* introduced psychotic killers as the new—and enduring—stereotype of evil predators. Over time, psychiatric patients—and especially escaped psychiatric patients—pushed mad scientists aside. *Halloween* (1978)'s Michael Myers cemented the connection that started with *Psycho*.

In 1927, shifts were rippling both sides of the Atlantic. Germany was in turmoil, having never recovered, either financially or psychologically, from the reparations remaining from the First World War. The shame of defeat hung over the country like a rain cloud, ready to burst. Silent films would become obsolete, and *Metropolis* would be one of the last of its type. With the success of *The Jazz Singer* (1927) in America, talkies would replace silent cinema in a year or two. Even futuristic films such as *Metropolis,* which is set in 2026, would look like throwbacks to a sentimental past. The fact that it is a science fiction film, with a slick veneer, did not matter.

A year before, in 1926, Hugo Gernsback began publication of *Amazing Stories* in his adopted home of America. This science fiction compendium was influential enough to earn Gernsback the title of "The Father of Science Fiction" (along with Jules Verne and H.G. Wells). *Amazing Stories* formally established the science fiction genre. This occurred in the very same year that Adolf Hitler self-published the second installment of his still-obscure *Mein Kampf.*

By 1927, psychoanalysis was better known. Thanks to the efforts of psychoanalytically-inclined military doctors during the Great War (such as Ernst Simmel), Freud's approach earned newfound respect for the treatment of war neuroses and shell shock. Considering that the other standard treatment option was painful electric shocks, delivered by doctors who practiced "Kaufmannization," the idea of one or two sessions of talking about psychic conflicts, sometimes combined with hypnosis, sounded pleasant and promising, and attracted the attention of military officials in 1918. Ranking Prussian officers attend a psychoanalytic conference to learn more.

In France and French-speaking countries, added knowledge of Freud came via André Breton, a one-time medical student who left his studies to enlist in the military. During the war, Breton worked in a ward with brain-injured soldiers (whose war wounds extended far beyond straightforward psychological shell shock). Breton borrowed Freudian ideas about dreams and consciousness and published these theories in his first *Surrealist Manifesto* in 1924. The *Second Manifesto*, in 1929, was written under Breton's supervision. Poets, painters and filmmakers were influenced by Breton. They practiced "automatic talking" and "automatic writing" to access the unconscious.

By 1927, Freud apparently felt that his iconoclastic "science" was well established enough to publish an even more iconoclastic anti-religion book about *The Future of an Illusion* (1927). In the same year, psychiatrist Wagner-Jauregg became the first psychiatrist (and one of only three psychiatrists to date) to win a Nobel Prize in psychiatry. Wagner-Jauregg was recognized for his discovery of the "fever cure" of "general paresis of the insane" that follows years or decades of untreated syphilis. Until preventative treatments of early syphilis were perfected, syphilis progressed over ten, twenty, even thirty years, leaving some victims with debilitating dementia, psychosis, and paralysis. Early 20th century asylums were filled with neurosyphilitics, who languished until death intervened, or until the fever cure came into being.

The rift between Freud's approach and Wagner-Jauregg's approach was striking. Both men had studied at the same medical school in Austria at nearly the same time. Freud began as a neurologist, but moved to psychoanalysis, and abandoned interest in the biological basis of behavior. Wagner-Jauregg held an appointment in psychiatry, but devoted himself to identifying causes and cures for biologically based behavior and cognitive changes. Ironically, Freud fled Austria because of the Nazis, but Wagner-Jauregg applied for membership in the Nazi Party.

Silent cinema may have passed into history in 1927, but *Metropolis'* impact remained firm as the decades passed. The early sixties saw a French variation on *Metropolis*, *La Poupee* aka *He, She, It* (1963), in which a scientist experiments with molecular multiplication and turns a real-life woman into automaton-like Maria. The next year saw the publication of Betty Friedan's *The Feminist Mystique* (1963), which takes an opposite point of view. Parallels with the American-made *The Stepford Wives* (1975, 2004), which is set in Connecticut, are pronounced, although it is questionable if we should consider *The Stepford Wives* as an example of neuroscience fiction, or if we should simply see it as an important social commentary and a parody of prominent social changes that were in the air.

The Stepford Wives (1975) is based on the Ira Levin satirical novel from 1972. The novel was published as second wave feminism peaked. Levin's novel appeared in the same year as the premier issue of *Ms.* Magazine. *Ms.* had an eye-catching image of Wonder Woman on its cover.

"Stepford" refers to a Connecticut town that appears normal on the surface. As its newest resident learns, the tony town is populated by women (and their husbands) who were clandestinely replaced by compliant and complacent robot-wives that do their husbands' bidding. These women have no substance and no interests of their own, except for shopping, which they discuss at women's lib get-togethers. They are an affront to everything that Betty Friedan and *The Feminine Mystique* (1963) represent—yet, somehow, some of these townswomen were one-time feminists and social activists before arriving in Stepford.

The film traces the steps of a New York City photographer who relocates to Stepford. She senses something strange and starts to investigate. She suspects that there is a conspiracy orchestrated by men in the town, especially since the leader of the men's club—where her husband spends more and more of his time—is a former Disney engineer (imagineer). That means that he can make replicas of the real women and replace them with conformist women. She consults a psychiatrist about her concerns. Her ideas sound blatantly paranoid.

Rather than being presented as a bioengineering achievement, the "Sims" of *The Stepford*

Wives are aesthetic creations. They are remarkably similar to the Sims of Frontierland, or any other Disney simulacra. This film functions as more of a social statement than neuroscience forecasting, but it is an interesting stepping-stone on the continuum, nonetheless.

The Stepford Wives was not well received at the start, but eventually gained a cult following because of its social relevance. When it was remade in 2004, the scathing feminist critique was removed. A woman was put in charge of the "conspiracy" that replaced other women with compliant robotic drones. *The Stepford Wives* proposes the possibility that an individual's "essence" can be replaced or removed or substituted, while retaining the bodily core. *Invasion of the Body Snatchers* (all versions) is based on this premise as well.

If we want to move to "purer" science fiction that comes closer to reality as we know it, we must turn to *Blade Runner* (1982), with its the robot-like replicants. *Blade Runner's* replicants are bioengineering feats, manufactured to simulate human emotions and human behavior, and, more importantly, to provide slave labor in hazardous "off-world" jobs. Replicants are preprogrammed to auto-destruct. If that does not happen, they are artificially "retired" by government-appointed agents such as Deckard (Harrison Ford), the star of the film.

On the surface, *Blade Runner* is an action-adventure film that is set in the future, with Harrison Ford playing a burnt-out cop (otherwise known as a "blade runner"). Deckard (Ford) was lured back into active duty to confront an unexpected challenge: four replicants escaped their off-world posts. They successfully entered earth, in search of their creator, Dr. Tyrell, who heads the all-controlling Tyrell corporation. Their mission is not revenge or a political coup, but simply to ask Tyrell to extend their lifespans.

The action takes place in a *noir*ish future, set in 2019, about forty years after the movie was made in 1982. In actuality, the setting simulates an era that existed forty years earlier, during the height of the *film noir* era in America. *Blade Runner's* director, Ridley Scott, was strongly influenced by *Metropolis'* set designs from 1927 (as was the creator of *Batman*). *Metropolis,* in turn, influenced other *film noir* directors. Some of those directors started their film careers in Weimar Era Germany, when German Expressionism reigned.

Edward Hopper's desolate cityscapes, and especially the lonely street corner from his *Nighthawks* (1942) painting, adds to *Blade Runner's* aesthetic. However, what goes around comes around: Hopper paintings directly influenced *film noir*, along with 1920s-era German Expressionism. The sophisticated spectator can spot these influences bubbling under the surface of Ridley Scott's *Blade Runner.* What results from this strange mélange? An eerie atmosphere that combines past and future. This augments the sense of disorientation and dislocation, and contributes to the confusion between reality and unreality.

Critics were not always so kind to *Blade Runner.* One critic reacted to the remarkably slow pace of this so-called action film and renamed it *Blade Crawler*. That critic was Sheila Benson of the *Los Angeles Times*. However, the author, Philip K. Dick, was pleased with the results, which is surprising, considering how rarely authors praise filmic interpretations of their written words. *Blade Runner* is not a literal rendition of the Dick original, but is loosely based on Dick's novella, *Do Androids Dream of Electric Sheep?* (1968). Dick's novel appeared the year after the Summer of Love drug and music fest of 1967, and just before the Woodstock Music Festival of 1969. The psychedelic subculture was at its peak. Alternative realities—be they chemical or spiritual—were popular topics of discussion.

Like any self-respecting action-adventure film, or like so many other contemporary science fiction films that aspire to commercial success, *Blade Runner* has a romantic subtext that drives the plot. In this case, that romantic twist reveals the neuroscience fiction core of this film. As Deckard, the disenchanted cop, Harrison Ford is the action hero who encounters Rachael, the beautiful female lead, played by Sean Young. Rachael works as the personal secretary of Dr. Tyrell, the bioengineering genius who runs the corporation that manufactures replicants.

The director does not tell the spectators the location of the "off-world" where replicants work. Dr. Tyrell does not tell Deckard that Rachael is a prototype of his most advanced replicant model. Rachael is so advanced that even she is unaware that she is a replicant.

Tyrell intends to use Rachael as a test subject. He instructs the seasoned replicant-hunter/blade runner Deckard to use his usual methods for detecting replicants. Since replicants physically resemble humans, blade runners hone in on emotional differences between replicants and humans.

Replicants lack emotional depth, and therein lies the difference between authentic humans and robotic simulations. This psychological limitation is easily detected through quick "bedside" testing techniques. The test is vaguely reminiscent of the "mini-mental status exam" that screens for dementia or delirium in hospitalized patients. Known as the "Voight-Kampff" test, the test in *Blade Runner* consists of quick questions designed to evoke physical cues, such as pupillary dilation, that occur spontaneously when subjects experience empathy to specific questions. Even though replicants act human and look human, they lack human empathy.

Deckard administers this test to Rachael, as planned. She answers over one hundred questions before she stumbles. Earlier models of replicants reveal their true selves after twenty questions. Rachael is a stunning success and testimony to Dr. Tyrell's engineering abilities.

Convinced that she is a replicant, Deckard confronts Rachael. She becomes tearful at this accusation, and denies the truth of Deckard's conclusion. To prove him wrong, and to convince him of her "human" identity (which she herself believes in), she shows family photos that confirm her childhood memories. Alas, it turns out that her childhood memories, as complex as they are, were implanted. Memories and memorabilia were borrowed from Tyrell's niece.

We learn more about replicants' memories, which reveals even more about their sense of self and individual identity. We learn the significance of the "pseudo-psychological" garnish that tops these bioengineered beings. We are told that Rachael and other replicants routinely receive mementos that bolster their belief in their pasts, and deflect suspicions that their recollections are simply false memories implanted at the replicant plant. This touch reminds us of another Philip K. Dick story, which inspired *Total Recall*, a film that revolves around memory substitutes.

It also reminds us of Marcel Proust, and his magnum opus, *Remembrance of Things Past* (1913–1927), and the thousand pages worth of memories triggered by a bite into a French cookie known as a "Madeleine." We think of Freudian ideas and other psychodynamic theories about childhood memories that shape thought, emotion, and behavior during adulthood. We reflect on repressed memories, screen memories and false memories that contribute to, or distract from, individual identity. Some spectators know about neurologists such as

Penfield, who stimulated the temporal lobe with an electric needle to show that memories are localized to specific anatomical areas of the cerebral cortex. While many of Penfield's findings were not replicated through later studies, contemporary neuroanatomy confirms that damage to specific parts of the brain can remove memories. Studies about implanting memories are already underway.

The nexus between the physical storehouse of memory—which is the traditional locus of interest of the neurologists and neurosurgeons—and the psychological experiences, and emotions that enter those storehouses, where they are processed into memories—is fascinating. *Blade Runner,* as well as Philip K. Dick's inspirational story, addresses this intersection. More recently, the research of psychiatrist and neuroscientist Eric Kandel, M.D., Ph.D. has come to the forefront of these matters, for showing how learned experiences produce biological changes in the brain.[12]

It is no accident that a film that focuses on the juncture between biopsychiatry and psychodynamic theory was released in 1982. The guard was changing in 1982, but sentries had not switched places completely. This film shows strong influences of old guard Freudian-style psychodynamic motivators and memories. At the same time, it incorporates "new guard" neuroscience, which emphasizes the physicality of memory and identity. The Decade of the Brain of the 1990s was in gestation, but had not yet been born. Neuropsychiatry was sitting on the bench, standing by, waiting to take its turn at bat, to assume its rightful place in science and society.

Even though the biomechanical aspects of replicants are central, *Blade Runner* retains strong psychoanalytic undertones. Rachael possesses the ability to dream. This trait sets her apart from earlier replicants. As stated in *Movies and the Modern Psyche,*[13] the 20th century, also known as "the psychoanalytic century," fell under the spell of Freud's century-shaping book, *Interpretation of Dreams* (1900). The Western world came to believe that "I dream, therefore I am." Descartes' contention, "I think, therefore I am," was pushed aside.

Rachael can experience waking consciousness, as well as the unconscious world of dreams. She also experiences strong emotions that link her to Deckard, and he to her. The showdown comes when Deckard seeks out Rachael as she sleeps, fearing that she might die. He refuses to retire Rachael, in spite of his instructions. The two leave together, to begin new lives with one another. In some versions, the couple heads to a pastoral landscape that contrasts with the bleak *noir*ish world they inhabit. There are several endings to the film, but most endings leave spectators wondering if Deckard himself is a replicant. *Blade Runner* fans and aficionados—and there are many of them—continue to debate the merits of different outcomes.

At the same time, readers and spectators are forced to ask what defines life in an era when more and more bioengineering feats become possible. Test tube babies were once a figment of the imagination (and of Aldous Huxley's imagination in particular), yet this once-controversial practice became commonplace since the days when Philip K. Dick wrote. Who and what defines those boundaries of life? What distinguishes humans from animals, or living beings from machines? If we recall that the word "animate" has its origins in the Greek noun, "anima" (or soul), we can rethink the implications of words such as "inanimate" (literally, without a soul) or "Re-Animator" (literally, return of the soul). Like Mary Shelley—or like Aristotle and St. Thomas Aquinas—Philip K. Dick and Ridley Scott leave us with enduring and unanswerable questions that intrigue audiences as much as they entertain them. This trope reappears repeatedly in neuroscience fiction film[14]—and in theology, philosophy and medical ethics classes.

I, Robot (2004) has similarities to *Blade Runner,* in that the robots that are manufactured to perform menial tasks for humans become more and more human, largely through the help of the robopsychologist, Dr. Susan Calvin (Bridget Moynahan). Her job is to make robots more human, even though the robots obey commandments that prohibit them from harming humans. A unique robot named Sonny dreams, as Rachael does in *Blade Runner.* Sonny (an NS-5 robot) tells Detective Spooner (Will Smith) that he saw the detective in a dream, as a savior of robots. Parallels with the Moses story and the building of the pyramids by the Israelites are evident.

The robopsychologist was created by the amazingly prolific Isaac Asimov, who held a Ph.D. in biochemistry, was married to a psychoanalyst, and went on to write Biblical exegeses before turning to lecherous limericks in his later years. In literary form, the robopsychologist is the protagonist. Since her first appearance in the 1950s, she has made many other appearances in books, films and TV shows.

The most recent version *Iron Man 3* (2013) has philosophical subtexts that are as prominent as its neuroscience, bioengineering and aerospace aspects. We can compare *Iron Man* to *RoboCop,* and point out important differences. The robotic Iron Man retains his identity as Tony Stark, and it is Iron Man who controls his armor, rather than the other way around.

Iron Man 3 is a prime example of 21st century neuroscience fiction. Its outlandish theme of connecting (human) minds with machines matter is no longer fiction. It is fast becoming fact. Apparently, *Iron Man 3* tapped into the "collective unconscious" of the 21st century, to have performed so well. What accounts for its success? There is more than neuroscience at stake.

Let us toss around some theories that explain the popularity of *Iron Man* movies, based on a character that emerged half a century ago in Marvel Comics.

First of all, superhero cinema has been skyrocketing. Comic book characters grab spectators' attention on the big screen, and not just on the pulp pages. The terrorist theme of *Iron Man 3* speaks to the times. Americans live in the shadow of 9/11, secretly wondering what will happen next. Superheroes are reassuring. The tech subtext is perfectly timed for our gadget-obsessed era. Add state-of-the-art special effects and cinematography, and a fast-paced script with action, adventure, romance, and redemption— and a blockbuster is born.

There is even more to *Iron Man 3*'s appeal. The tech genius turns philanthropist and fights evil as Iron Man, but he has a "shadow side." Fittingly, Robert Downey, Jr. stars as Tony Stark, the billionaire who battles the bottle. Downey's well-publicized struggles with drugs, arrests, and rehab animate his acting and lend credibility to Stark's character. The draw of Sir Ben Kingsley needs no extra explanation—Kingsley was knighted long before he was cast as a drug-addled double for the film's true villain, The Mandarin.

Like many recovering alcoholics, Tony Stark still struggles with "character flaws." He is much more than a man inside a machine. He is not subsumed by the machine. He cannot control his hubris and his urge to grandstand. He speaks out too soon and publicly challenges world-class villains, forcing them to save face. To retaliate, terrorists destroy Stark's cliff-side home (which is a stand-in for the World Trade Center). For the rest of the film, Stark seeks retribution.

The film forecasts victory over impending peril. *Iron Man 3* reassures Americans of future success, at the same time that it reflects fears that foes lie in wait. For many, the idea of a man-machine holds appeal, and acts as a latter day Daedalus. *Iron Man 3* also implies that deadly enemies may masquerade as unemployed actors (Ben Kingsley), suicidal scientists (Guy Pearce), or superficially benign beings, such as the beautiful botanist (Rebecca Hall) who created the Extremis virus. *Iron Man 3* replays that ever-popular theme: man against machine.

If we look at some specifics about Iron Man, we start to see why he represents so much to so many. Tony Stark (aka Iron Man) was born on the cheap pulp pages of Marvel Comics, but he was not born a superhero. Rather, Stark gains superpowers through a manmade suit of armor. His real heart was damaged during a terrorist explosion, but modern mechanics and electromagnets sustain him and his heart. His flashy red armor gives this billionaire inventor, industrialist (and general degenerate) a second lease on life—and an alternate identity. The signature Iron Man suit provides more than life support; it imparts superpowers that allow Stark to a wage one-person war against terrorists, conspirators and other evil doers.

In *Iron Man 3,* a fictional substance called "Extremis" enters the central nervous system, binds with the brain, and changes the users' DNA, sending electronic and neurochemical signals that amp up physical and mental strength and merge his body with his iron suit. In 2014, few of us remember the iron lungs that sustained paralyzed polio patients in the 1940s,

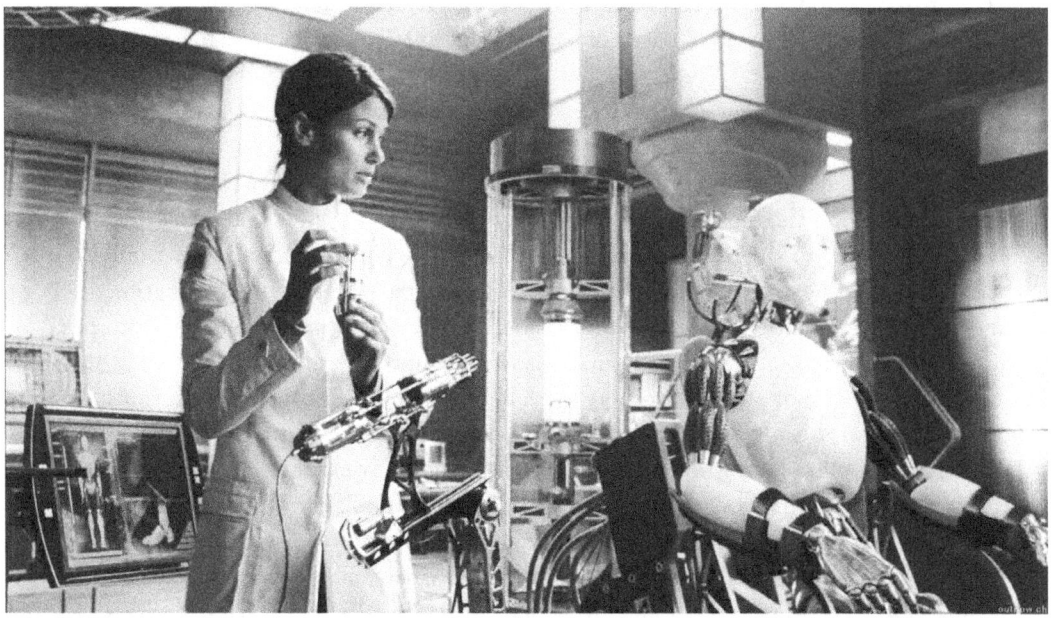

On staff of USR (United States Robots), a company that manufactures robot-drones that do menial labor, robopsychologist Dr. Susan Calvin (Bridget Monahan) stands by her seated robot-patient, as she strives to make all robots act more human in *I, Robot* (2004).

50s, and into the 60s, but Marvel readers from the 1960s were familiar with such images. The contrast between iron suits that turn users into superheroes, and the vulnerable children who spent months or years, encased in iron cylinders, waiting to regain the ability to breathe on their own, is striking.

In the 1960s, the possibility that iron lungs could help polio patients soar through the sky was simply "pie in the sky"—but other aspects of Iron Man as automaton are not so far-removed from reality today. The "Iron Legion" that figures prominently in the film's spectacular climax are, in effect, a robot army controlled by Tony Stark's brain. Recent experiments in real life prove that paraplegics and amputees with specially programmed computerized brain implants can "will" movement in artificial limbs. They learn to control brain waves that communicate with microcomputers, which, in turn, make direct contact with parts of the brain that orchestrate movement and bypass the damaged parts of the spinal cord that caused paralysis. This technique allows users to move artificial limbs at will.

Because this book focuses on behavioral neuroscience, rather than the equally important neuroscience and bioengineering that relate to the peripheral nervous system, the spinal cord, and the sense organs, we cannot devote more space to this vast and fast-expanding area of research. In this book, we can appreciate the films that reference such research, but we have to wait until other interested subspecialists elaborate on this avenue of neuroscience fiction and fact.

Five

Human-Ape Brain Exchanges, Darwinian Debates and the "Monkey Gland Man"

Rise of the Planet of the Apes (2011) is nouveau neuroscience fiction, without a doubt. It revolves around dementia and intelligence enhancement, two critically important issues at the time of this writing. It references AIDS' origins at the same time that it comments on the distinctions—and similarities—between humans and apes (and different human races).

Yet the old-time, original *Planet of the Apes* from 1968 does not fit into this rubric so neatly, even though the apes lobotomize astronaut Landon, rendering him catatonic and unable to speak. What's more is that the *Planet of the Apes* "series" did not start out as a series. It is doubtful that the director, the cast or even the backers envisioned the success that awaited the first *Planet of the Apes* (and its sequels). Who would have guessed that *Planet of the Apes* would be revered nearly half a century later—or that this film would be the beginning of a brand? Perhaps Trekkies could have foreseen how popular a particular theme can be, when introduced at the right point in time, but this prediction eluded even seasoned movie studio executives.

The original 1968 film became a cult classic quickly. It did not have to wait years or decades to be rediscovered and appreciated for what it was, as sometimes happens with cult films (think *Blade Runner*). *Planet of the Apes* is still listed in IMDB's *500 Essential Cult Movies* (2011; 2013). It spawned a succession of sequels, one right after the other, in 1970, 1971, 1972, and 1973. A television series and a cartoon followed immediately. The theme of the original *Apes* was timely—but surely, the movie contains messages that endure beyond its time, if it retains enough appeal to merit yet another remake more than forty years after the first film.

In the late 1960s and early 1970s, *Planet of the Apes* tapped into the public's preoccupation with racism. The film turned this "ism" into cinematic spectacle. The Civil Rights movement was at an all-time peak after the assassination of the Reverend Dr. Martin Luther King, Jr., and the urban turmoil that followed.[1] *Planet of the Apes* permitted the average American to contemplate race-based lynchings and assassinations, without experiencing emotionally evocative imagery. *Planet of the Apes* sanitized what the nation already witnessed. It spared spectators of visions of Emmett Till, the teen-aged boy whose body lay dead and disfigured in an open casket in 1955, visible to television viewers who tuned into the news-

In *Rise of the Planet of the Apes*, a newly emancipated and fully-mature Caesar (Andrew Serkis) raises his fist as a battle cry, rallying his fellow apes in the middle ground, with San Francisco's Golden Gate Bridge—site of the climactic battle—stretching across the background.

casts. *Planet of the Apes* also hinted at karmic retributions that lay in wait for a sinful, racist society.

Time and space travel function as a framing device for the first *Planet of the Apes*. This frame serves several functions. It adds more action-adventure and connects the film to classic SF from the 1950s. It allows Hollywood to recycle themes that proved profitable in past and present. Indirectly, this meme pays homage to H. G. Wells' timeless story about *The Time Machine* (1895), which was one of the first and finest works of science fiction. It also "apes" the winning formula of TV's wildly popular Star Trek series (1966–1969) that was broadcast at the time of release of *Apes*. The film remains relatively (but not completely) true to Rod Serling's screenplay, which went through dozens of drafts, and added an additional writer (Michael Wilson), to adapt Pierre Boulle's complex novel to the big screen. Serling incorporated elements from two episodes of *The Twilight Zone* in his version of the classic message-in-a-bottle story.[2]

The story line of *Planet of the Apes* is simple and straightforward. A futuristic society inhabits a seemingly distant planet that is located in a presumably faraway galaxy, where apes are in control. Apes are the overlords of humans. There are no race wars reminiscent of the race riots from 1968 America. The supposedly distant planet turns out to be an abandoned Earth, where orangutans rule, chimpanzees know their place (even though they did start the revolution), and gorillas fulfill designated functions. Primate society is just as stratified as mid–20th century human society, although there is some social mobility. For instance, Dr. Zira became a psychologist, even though she is just a chimpanzee who is engaged to another chimpanzee (Cornelius). Both Zira and Cornelius report to an orangutan, Dr. Zaius, who is in charge.

In this ape-centric world, humans are relatively rare. Those who remain are bestial and uncivilized. They are chained, caged, demeaned and displayed in zoos, deemed suitable for scientific study and social science observations. These metaphors appealed to the youth culture that protested the draft, marched against the Vietnam War, and objected to American soldiers' disparaging terms for Vietnamese. Words such as "gooks" or "slant eyes" were applied to Viet Cong soldiers or Vietnamese civilians, to dehumanize them and make it easier to shoot them. Racial concerns and conflicts permeated that entire decade. However, race consciousness in 1960s America was not limited to black and white issues on the home front. Racist concepts made themselves manifest in attitudes towards enemy Asians across the ocean.

In the original *Planet of the Apes* film, three astronauts arrive alive in their spaceship. The sole female astronaut is long dead. Her life support system failed, and her body mummified over time. Her fate was not known to the remaining astronauts until their spaceship crashes into the water and the survivors open her capsule. One astronaut dies after arrival. He becomes a taxidermy specimen, displayed in a museum exhibit on the Planet of the Apes. The life-sized panorama resembles displays in our own natural history museums, where we replicate exotic or primitive environments and fill them with humans, wildlife and vegetation that are indigenous to the locale. Another astronaut is lobotomized. Only Taylor (Charlton Heston) survives relatively intact, but even he has an unhealed throat injury that impairs his ability to vocalize. That makes his ape-captors believe that he, as a human, lacks all language abilities.

Planet of the Apes was remade in 2001, by Tim Burton, no less, a fantasy filmmaker if there ever was one. It premiered in the summer of 2001, just before the 9/11 terrorist attacks literally changed the landscape of America and challenged Americans' triumphalist mindset. There are no obvious parallels between 2001 and 1968. The Youth Culture of the Sixties and Seventies came into being because babies born during the post–World War II Baby Boom had reached their teens and entered college. However, the Youth Culture of yesteryear had lost its bloom of youth. The adolescent enthusiasm that pushed them through peace rallies, civil rights marches, bra burnings and *Apes* fandom were distant memories. A few developed early-onset dementia (which includes, but is not limited to, Alzheimer's disease). For them, there were no memories.

Those activists once believed that they could remake the world and turn it into a better place. By 2001, they faced their own mortality. Worse yet, word of an impending epidemic of Alzheimer's was spreading, reminding this aging generation that their minds and memories might fade away before their bodies fail. Life spans had soared since the late sixties, during the era of social protests and *Planet of the Apes*. Many Baby Boomers now cared for their aging parents, and glimpsed the devastation of dementia directly. Fear of Alzheimer's was in the air.

Baby Boomers' parents were living longer than their grandparents had lived, but they did not necessarily live better. Not everyone develops dementia in advanced years. However, a high enough percentage of people decline mentally as time passes. Enough people need nursing homes in their twilight years—just enough to make Alzheimer's Disease a looming nightmare and a pressing public health concern—and an amazing marketing opportunity for pharmaceuticals.[3] Big Pharma prompted these fears as they promoted their lackluster products that are approved to treat dementia (but barely accomplish this goal). Scientists in search of research grants could muster public support and private donations by citing these scary statistics.

The 2011 reimagining of *Rise of the Planet of the Apes* addresses mounting anxieties about Alzheimer's, but presents them through first-person accounts, rather than clinical case histories. The protagonist is a laboratory-based neuroscientist who should have access to the best tools to treat his father's dementia. Yet even Dr. Will Rodman, a doctorate-level researcher, is virtually helpless. We watch Will the dutiful son tend to his aging father, who can no longer use utensils at dinnertime. We witness his frustration and his sense of futility. The film taps into our hopes for a cure, but it peppers those hopes with the usual science fiction paranoia about a cure run wild. In this case, the cure makes apes too smart.

This prequel shows no trace of the social consciousness of the original, which came on the heels of the Civil Rights era, and which spoke loudly and clearly about racial inequities. Instead, the "prequel" weds 21st century neuroscience to 21st century epidemiology and demography, and throws 21st century medical economics and (blighted) bioethics into the mix. It alludes to current theories about the AIDS epidemic (without saying so directly). Many spectators know that AIDS supposedly started in Africa, where it spread among chimps before reaching humans. Yet the data about the origins of AIDS is not definitive. Many speculative conspiracy theories about AIDS persist. Serious scholars continue to examine possible contributions of contaminated vaccinations administered in the developing world. However, all studies to date have refuted theories that OPV (oral polio vaccine) started or spread the epidemic.

Apes 2011 offers a match made in heaven, with so many texts and subtexts. The first prequel succeeded financially and critically, even though more than forty years had passed since the series started. Sequels are waiting in the wings. One sequel, *Dawn of the Planet of the Apes,* is scheduled for release in 2014.

Rise of the Planet of the Apes is ingenious in the way it tackles several tough topics simultaneously. It explains how the film's apes got so smart; it adds new twists to contemporary Alzheimer's research; it even says something about AIDS' origins among apes (and does not dispute claims that American scientists, either intentionally or unintentionally, ignited the epidemic in Africa). The latest *Rise of the Planet of the Apes* adds just enough twists (or shall we say paranoia?) to hold our attention. To compound the intrigue, the film comments on corporate control of American medical care and bottom-line based scientific research, which are all too true.

The film prophesizes about the outcome of purely profit driven research. One need not be an Einstein to arrive at the same conclusions. The film predicts that privately funded— and loosely policed—scientific studies will run afoul of ethics, putting both people and primates, and perhaps even the planet, at risk. Those concerns do not seem too futuristic or far-out. They seem to be more science-based than science fiction. Similar complaints are voiced about Big Pharma, managed pharmacy benefits, genetic engineering, and almost anything else under the sun. Obamacare and the ACA (Affordable Care Act) bring a separate set of critics, and some trace problems to collaboration with the for-profit insurance industry as much as poor planning.[4]

The plotline of *Rise of the Planet of the Apes* is easy enough to relate to. Will (James Franco) is a youngish neuroscientist who lives in a comfortable home with his white-haired father. Will refuses to move his father (John Lithgow) to a nursing home. He overrides the suggestions of the home health aide, who witnesses the progression of the father's dementia, admits defeat and recommends a nursing home. She states her case clearly, without avail.

During the day, Dr. Will Rodman works on Alzheimer's research. He is testing a secret compound on chimps that are confined to cages. A private, high-powered research firm employs him to conduct studies. His research facility is lavish, as far as research facilities go. The scientists face strong pressure to produce results faster. Like so many lab scientists, Will Rodman is overworked and underappreciated. His overbearing boss berates him and downplays his steady progress, and demands better outcomes sooner. This scene is completely credible.

To make matters worse, a female primate has been showing a promising response to the meds—but the suddenly goes out of control, for no apparent reason. She attacks her handler. Security guards shoot her dead on the spot. At the orders of the head honcho, all remaining apes in the study are euthanized immediately. Her behavior is blamed on the test medication, and on Will, by implication, because he is the chief investigator.

While carrying out his orders, the handler finds a newborn baby chimp in the cage of the out-of-control female chimp. He realizes that the chimp went berserk because she was acting on instinct and trying to protect her progeny. He cannot bring himself to kill the baby, and so he and Will arrange to smuggle the tiny chimp out of the lab and into safekeeping, in Will's home.

When the baby chimp arrives at the Rodman house, Will's father is delighted, and names him Caesar. Caesar grows quickly and learns amazingly fast. Will realizes that Caesar's mother was pregnant when exposed to the test chemical, and so he surmises that the infant chimp was dosed with ALZ-112 in utero. For scientifically minded spectators, it makes sense that undeveloped fetal brains show stronger responses to neurochemical enhancers than adult brains. Not surprisingly, Caesar develops into a chimpanzee prodigy, with uncanny intelligence. He soon sits at the family dinner table, next to Will's father, where he corrects his surrogate "grandfather" when he holds his silverware upside down.

That is not to say that Caesar lost all of his animal instincts at the same time that he acquired amazing intelligence. One day, a neighbor attacks Will's father, after the father jumps into the neighbor's car and bangs it up. Because of his dementia, the father was unable to distinguish one car from another, and did not realize that the car he chose to drive is not his own. He also does not realize that his reflexes have slowed and that he has forgotten how to drive. At this point, Caesar shows his true animal nature—as well as his affection for Will's father.

Caesar bites the neighbor, who is angry already, his car having been hijacked and smashed. Not surprisingly, the outraged neighbor reports this event to the authorities, who pressure Will into turning Caesar over to an animal refuge center. What the neighbor does not know is that the bite infected him with a virus that will kill him and most other humans on the planet. The experimental Alzheimer's med piggybacks onto a virus that enters individual cells. Primates have immunity to the virus, but humans do not. The nasty neighbor will die.

Several heartbreaking scenes follow. Caesar is placed in a cage, after he is remanded to a refuge. His trusted gorilla companion is shot during an attempted "jailbreak." Caesar and Will part company after Caesar escapes the refuge, becomes emancipated, and refuses to return home with Will. Caesar chooses to remain in the trees, in the company of other escaped apes.

This last scene sets the stage for events that follow. It informs us of the fate of future

FIVE. *Human-Ape Brain Exchanges, Darwinian Debates....* 85

ape generations. They are descendants of Caesar, and of other apes that Caesar dosed with stolen bottles of ALZ-113 (a more advanced generation than Caesar's ALZ-112). Chemically enhanced apes have green eyes because of this exposure and their presumed genetic change.

There is no need for arguments about the genetic basis of intelligence in this version of *Planet of the Apes*. Riffs on outdated and offensive ideas about race-based differences in intelligence are absent. Debates about temperamental differences between European and Africans, Jews and Aryans, and other arcane ideas about "race science," as described in historian John Efron in his book by the same name, are not found in this film.[5] Spectators who

A monstrous shadow looms large, as unseen beasts emerge from the jungle while shipwrecked sailor Edward Parker (Richard Arlen) points to shoot and fiancée Ruth Thomas (Leila Hyams) cowers in *Island of Lost Souls* (1931), Kenton's version of Wells' *Island of Dr. Moreau* (1896).

heard such diatribes—which were plentiful before and during the Civil Rights era, and still recur from time to time today—may find themselves reflecting on the topic and recognizing the parallels presented in *Planet of the Apes*. At certain points in time, these debates would have been more relevant to our topic of "neuroscience fiction"—but they do not merit our attention here.

Having touched on 21st century cinema about ape-brain exchanges and the distinction (or similarity) between apes and humans, we can return to the end of the 19th century, when the character of Dr. Moreau surfaced in the writings of H. G. Wells and set the standard for fictional human-animal experiments. As we know from the previous chapter, Wells' novel appeared in 1896, the year that Freud coined the concept of "psycho-analysis." Different filmmakers offered their own interpretations of this strange island over the years.

Dr. Moreau is an archetypal "mad scientist." He believes himself to be "misunderstood," perhaps like Dr. Semmelweis (1818–1865), the Hungarian doctor who identified the link between (lack of) hand washing and deadly "childbed fever" in 1847. Taunted during his lifetime for his life-saving theories, but lionized after his death, Semmelweis eventually had a breakdown and was committed to an asylum, where guards beat him. A few weeks after his admission to the institution, he died of complications from this beating. Semmelweis was vindicated later and Pasteur, Lister, Koch, Snow and others advanced ideas pertaining to the germ theory of disease.

Unlike the real life Semmelweis, the fictional Dr. Moreau does not answer to a scientific community. No one oversees his eccentric experiments. He lives on an isolated island, where he turns animals into humans. The very nature of his studies calls attention to the distinctions between beasts of the jungle and the supposedly civilized creatures that walk upright, speak in languages, and go by the appellation, *Homo sapiens sapiens*. Transformed animals must promise, "not to go on all fours—that is the law."

The literary original of *The Island of Dr. Moreau* came on the tails of Darwin's 1869 publication *On the Origin of Species*. Darwin ignited debates about evolution. He shook up scholars, clergy and laypersons alike. Darwin's pronouncement in 1871—that humankind's earliest ancestors date to Africa, where they lived among the apes—fueled even more animus. In contrast, Wells' story has offered more than a century's worth of entertainment.

Moreau turned into several films over the course of the 20th century. Charles Laughton stars in *The Island of Lost Souls* (1932), directed by Erle C. Kenton. In 1997, the most recent rendition of *The Island of Dr. Moreau* arrived, directed by John Frankenheimer. A supersized Marlon Brando stars as Dr. Moreau. Brando had been hailed as the greatest actor of all time (although he is not the only actor to receive such accolades). Val Kilmer is his henchman.

The year 1977 brought Don Taylor's *The Island of Dr. Moreau* (1977). By 1977, the story reflected more current concerns about human behavior. Is it innate or acquired, instinct-based or socially conditioned? Conflicts with creationists no longer took center stage. Second Wave feminism was in its prime, having begun on the fringes in 1968, and taking cues from other radical identity movements. Feminist ideology flooded the mainstream by mid-seventies.

For both feminists and their foes, and for anyone else who kept pace with contemporary currents, gender-based differences and/or similarities were as important as race and species-based distinctions had been in earlier times. Freud's contention that "anatomy is destiny" was debated and disputed by feminists and was used to undermine Freud and psychoanalysis. This film spoke to a new era, one that believed that humans could override biology, should they so choose. It was a time when young people believed that they could "be all you want to be." This was the era of the "human potential movement," and a time when determinism, be it psychological or physical, was buried under the weight of optimism and u-can-do-ism.[6]

Another famous literary work, one that inspired more films than any other novel or novella to date, deals with evolution of sorts. Stevenson's *The Strange Case of Dr. Jekyll and Mr. Hyde* (1886) highlights man's bestial nature. Mamoulian's definitive version from 1931, starring Fredric March, dramatizes this regression by showing Hyde's apelike visage and posture, while he wears Jekyll's top hat. Renditions of *Dr. Jekyll and Mr. Hyde* changed over time, and some interpretations bear only the slightest resemblance to Stevenson's original.

Darwinian debates continued well into the 20th century, and survive in some circles to this day. In the 1920s, conflicts about evolution, creationism and Darwin's theories led to the highly publicized Scopes Trial in Tennessee. A teacher, Scopes dared to teach Darwin's theories, in spite of recently passed Tennessee laws that forbade teaching evolution in state-sponsored schools. Scopes was convicted but later acquitted on a technicality. The great Clarence Darrow defended him. The trial attracted widespread publicity, and made Darwin's theories about evolution from apes even better known than before. The trial was immortalized in film; *Inherit the Wind* (1960) is a thinly disguised drama about Scopes, starring Spencer Tracy and Fredric March. (Remember, Fredric March starred as the ape-like Hyde some thirty years earlier).

Mamoulian's celebrated *Dr. Jekyll and Mr. Hyde* slipped past the censors in 1931. Soon enough, the Motion Picture Code, also known as the Hays Code, would prohibit films that promoted Darwinism (and other forms of "degeneracy"). Once it was applied, the Hays Code had far-reaching implications. It monitored much more than the sex and drugs that we discussed in the third chapter. The Hays Code prohibited positive depictions of crime, anti-government activities and other objectionable ideas. Although the code came into being in 1930, recall that it was not strictly enforced until about 1934. Until then, many marginal and exploitive films about evolution—and other sordid topics—appeared, alongside Mamoulian's masterpiece.

More than two decades earlier, the silent film era birthed celluloid commentaries on evolution. In 1908, we find Gaumont's *The Doctor's Experiment* aka *Reversing Darwin's Theory* (1908). In the same year, Pathé released *The Monkey Man* (1908).

In 1912, Dr. Alex Carrel's research into transplant and grafting biology earned him a Nobel Prize. This recognition increased awareness of transplant medicine, among the general public as well as the scientific community. Filmmakers apparently took note, judging by the surge of transplant-related films that followed. Dr. Carrel's one-time student (Serge Voronoff) would find his way to fame—and infamy—in both science and film. Dr. Serge Voronoff became known as the "Monkey Gland Man." More about Dr. Voronoff and his legacy later.

Human-ape transplant tropes that began in the early 1900s remained popular, for a while. The theme was tried and true and successful producers literally "aped" their past successes, and drew upon them for future films. Sometimes, brains were transplanted; at other

Saloon singer and loose lady Ivy Pearson (Miriam Hopkins) enticed the good doctor Jekyll when she called him to her bedroom, prompting his transition to the simian and lascivious Hyde, who is played by the same actor who plays Dr. Jekyll (Fredric March) in the 1931 classic.

times, hosts received spinal fluid injections. For instance, in *Go and Get It* (1920), a mad surgeon transplants a convict's brain into an ape. The human-brained ape eventually extracts revenge for the convict.

Two years later, in 1922, the legendary Lon Chaney, Sr. stars in *A Blind Bargain* (1922). The long-lost film is based on Barry Pain's fin-de-siècle novel, *The Octave of Claudius* (1897). In *A Blind Bargain,* a young writer is willing to do anything to aid his ailing mother, who needs an operation. A sinister surgeon, Dr. Lamb (Lon Chaney, Sr.), agrees to operate on the mother if the son agrees to accept his unnamed demands, this "blind bargain." Dr. Lamb proves to be a wolf in sheep's clothing, so to speak. The surgeon hopes to perfect a technique that instills eternal youth, but ends up turning his victims into apelike creatures instead. This procedure recollects the experiments of the so-called "Monkey Gland Man"—Dr. Voronoff.

Dr. Lamb has a hunchbacked assistant, who is also played by Lon Chaney, Sr. Lon Chaney, Sr. earned the epithet, "The Man of 1,000 Faces" for feats like this one. This portrayal anticipates Lon Chaney's role as Quasimodo the following year, in Carl Laemmle and Irving Thalberg's production of *The Hunchback of Notre Dame* (1923). It prepares spectators for Mr. Hyde's transmogrification in Robert Mamoulian's 1931 interpretation of *The Strange Case of Dr. Jekyll and Mr. Hyde*. His performance anticipates Paramount's take on Moreau in *The Island of Lost Souls* (1932). This character is but one of many stepping-stones that paved the path to Lon Chaney, Sr.'s immortalization in film history and in horror films in particular. Lon Chaney's acting abilities contributed as much as his costumes, for Lon Chaney, Sr. became an expert at pantomime while still a child, when he communicated with his two deaf-mute parents.[7]

We later learn that the disfigured assistant played by Lon Chaney is the product of the surgeon's earlier, failed experiments. The vengeful assistant releases a bestial ape-man from captivity, which then kills the diabolical doctor. Upon the death of the doctor, the writer wins a release from his "blind bargain." Superficial similarities to *Student of Prague* (1913, 1926) and many other tales about bartering with the Devil or Mephistopheles are obvious. Critics dismissed the film for borrowing from earlier sources, both filmic and literary.[8] Yet the true inspiration for the quasi-neuroscience fiction film lies in actual scientific events of the era.[9,10]

A Blind Bargain (incorrectly) alludes to "the Steinach gland operation," which was made famous by endocrinologist Eugene Steinach (1861–1944). Some compared Steinach to his rival, Dr. Voronoff, the so-called "Monkey Gland Man." Voronoff's experiments were closer in spirit to the subject of *A Blind Bargain* than Steinach's. Steinach hypothesized that "animal gland secretions" influence sex drive and performance. Those claims are hardly startling today and were not new even in the 1920s, when Steinach promoted them.[11]

For instance, the physiologist Brown-Séquard experimented on himself in the late 1800s, injecting extracts from monkey and guinea pig testicles. Brown-Séquard hoped to overcome the easy fatigability and muscular weakness that beset him at age 72. Earlier in the century, when Brown-Séquard was at his professional (and perhaps physical) peak, he identified a neurological condition that carries his name to this day. The "Brown-Séquard syndrome" refers to the loss of sensation and motor function (anesthesia and paralysis) caused by cuts to specific sections of the spinal cord. Brown-Séquard's later life auto-experiments in endocrinology did not win the same acclaim as his mid-life feats, although his self-experimentation attracted attention at the time, and stimulated discussion among academicians in different disciplines.

Like Brown-Séquard in the 19th century, Steinach, and several others, aimed to combat aging via "glandular techniques." Their concept of "aging" included, but was not limited to, "virility" and sexual functioning. Relief of fatigue in older men was as important as increasing their libidos. Today, we might add (undiagnosed and untreated) "major depressive disorder" as a possible contributor to decline. This entails a bit of circular reasoning, given that we now know that androgen deficiency contributes to depression, and that depression decreases circulating androgen levels.

In the 21st century, we find replays of these very same themes. Some alternative medicine doctors and self-styled "anti-aging experts" advertise endocrine treatments for "performance enhancement." Human growth hormones, produced by the pituitary gland, as well as testosterone, are current favorites of the "rejuvenation industry." These doctors (correctly) claim that these treatments restore youthful appearance, strengthen muscles, and redistribute adipose tissue that accumulates with age. (Many avoid advertising the potential side effects of their prescriptions, such as arthritis.)

By the 1920s, contemporary scientists and physicians upstaged Darwin (although the 1925 Scopes trial in Tennessee rekindled awareness of Darwinism). In 1923, Canadian doctors received the Nobel Prize for the discovery of insulin, which could stabilize persons with "sugar sickness" (better known as diabetes mellitus). They proved their theory just one year before the prize was awarded. By the end of 1923, the American pharmaceutical giant, Eli Lilly, produced enough insulin to meet the needs of the North American continent.[12] Insulin does not "cure" diabetes, in the way that antibiotics can cure specific infections, but insulin increases diabetics' life spans dramatically and perhaps protects them from some of the ravages of diabetes. Insulin's discovery and synthesis was a near-miracle. This much-touted success shined a bright light on other "glandular" treatments, and increased faith in scientific and medical progress.

Of all the innovators and iconoclasts who devoted themselves to rejuvenation and virility restoration, Dr. Serge Voronoff had the highest profile in his day. This physician-profiteer gained fame and fortune, but was eventually linked to more controversies than cures. A research laboratory director, surgeon, and gland specialist, Dr. Voronoff made treatments from monkey glands. However, his earlier research, before he became known as the "Monkey Gland Man," was much more respectable (if less lucrative) and won him wide admiration.[13] His efforts on behalf of soldiers during the Great War were much appreciated and amped up his reputation.

Serge Voronoff was a Russian-born Jew who practiced in Paris. Voronoff grafted part of a monkey's thyroid gland into a mentally challenged child (who was referred to as an "idiot," which was standard parlance of the times). The child developed all the physical and mental symptoms of myxedema (hypothyroidism) after a bout of scarlet fever.[14] In the years following the thyroid transplant, the child became mentally alert and appeared normal. Voronoff reported this success in medical journals. This was Voronoff at his best, and he was publicly applauded.

In 1920, *Scientific American* published a lead story about "Human Grafting, the Brilliant and Successful Experiments of Dr. Serge Voronoff." On July 23, 1923, *Time* compared Voronoff to Steinach in an article entitled, "Medicine: Voronoff and Steinach."[15]

Hoping to reverse aging and restore virility, Dr. Voronoff resumed the study of transplants, this time of testicular tissue. He started with cadaver transplants from executed criminals. Facing a limited supply of such source material, he turned to animals instead. He surgically inserted slices of monkey testicles into the scrotums of rich and famous men who could pay for his pricey Parisian treatments. Traveling to Paris, in and of itself, was very expensive. His clients included men like Harold McCormick, chair of International Harvester.

Demand for monkey glands was so great that Dr. Voronoff eventually opened his own monkey farm to ensure a steady supply of this valuable resource. Already an heir to a vodka fortune, his practice allowed him to live in luxury. At age 64, Dr. Voronoff married a 20-year-old woman who was friendly with royalty, as noted by the *New York Times*.[16] Over time, Dr. Voronoff was dismissed as a charlatan. He became the subject of ridicule, dying in relative obscurity. In 1991, respected medical journals, such as *The Lancet,* suggested that his theories may have had substance and should be reevaluated before being permanently discarded.[17]

More recent data suggests that Voronoff's tissue transplants very likely released usable testosterone into recipients. Although authors such as Dr. Hamilton insist that the transplanted monkey tissue would be rejected by the host before releasing hormones, it seems that transplant surgeon Dr. Hamilton was wrong and that Dr. Voronoff was right—even though Voronoff did not have access to complete data to confirm the correctness of his hypotheses.

Certain cells in the testicles—the Sertoli cells—are resistant to graft-host reactions. When transplanting insulin-producing porcine (pig) pancreatic islet cells into diabetics, Sertoli cells from the testicles are wrapped around transplanted pig tissues. Because these testicular Sertoli cells do not provoke the usual immune responses, this step protects against host rejection and averts the need for added immunosuppressive medications, which carry their own risks.[18]

Dr. Voronoff's work found its way into popular media of the 1920s. Irving Berlin wrote his song, "Monkey-Doodle-Doo," for the Marx Brothers' comedy, *The Cocoanuts* (1929). Lyrics include lines like, "If you're too old for dancing/Get yourself a monkey gland." In 1922, "Monkey Gland" was a popular gin and absinthe cocktail, so named in Voronoff's honor. His influence reverberates just as strongly in contemporaneous horror and science fiction films.

A string of monkey or ape-related films surfaced in the 1920s and remained popular through the mid–1940s, as World War II raged. *King Kong* (1933) is undoubtedly the best remembered and most influential of ape films of the 1930s, but it has no bearing on NSF. No matter, because there are enough other examples of ape movies that fall under this rubric.

Boris Karloff stars in *The Man Who Changed His Mind* (1936), a British film about a brain specialist who discovers a technique to change thoughts and souls—but not brains. He claims that he can transfer thoughts from one brain to another, and leave the first brain drained. The film sets and costumes use standard medical trappings. The operating room appears authentic, and the surgical masks and gowns look realistic. Yet his techniques bypass the need for surgery, come closer to parapsychology or metapsychology, and recollect Rotwang.

The B &W film comes complete with curly-cue titles, dark gothic interiors, and antiquated horse-driven buggies. Hounds howl on the moors. Humongous houses boast wide, winding staircases and wood-paneled rooms. All this screams "horror film" more than futuristic science fiction—but horror and SF often cross boundaries, as has been pointed out earlier.

Biological psychiatry was moving forward fast in the 1930s. Advances that began in Europe soon spread to the U.S. as physicians and scientists (as well as psychoanalysts) fled rising anti–Semitism and the forces of fascism.[19] Meduna and Sakel each developed his own form of convulsive therapy. Ladislaus Meduna, an epileptologist, experimented with Metrazol, which induces intense seizures, of the kind that relieve depression in epileptics. There were drawbacks to Meduna's methodology. Almost half of his subjects suffered spine fractures from the thrashing. Such high rates of complications were unacceptable. There had to be something better on the horizon.

Manfred Sakel, born Menachim Sakel to an observant Jewish family in Austria, invented insulin coma therapy (ICT) after witnessing its benefits in relieving morphine withdrawal. He then tested it for various psychiatric disorders.[20] Insulin seizures were safer than Metrazol seizures, although they were not without risk.

Unlike Metrazol-induced seizures, which run their course until they stop spontaneously, insulin coma can be reversed, if caught quickly enough. Intravenous glucose or dextrose (sugar water) raises blood sugar quickly, and stops seizures. Still, ICT has its own hazards. So ICT was replaced by ECT (electroconvulsive therapy). ECT proved to be the safest and easiest of all convulsive therapies, especially after muscle relaxants became available. Introduced in 1939 by the Italian Cerletti, ECT offers the quickest relief for depression, and certain other conditions, to this day.[21] However, ECT has been vilified and sometimes outright outlawed, largely because of the emotional sway of the film based on Ken Kesey's book, *One Flew Over the Cuckoo's Nest* (book, 1962; film, 1975).[22]

After World War II began in Europe in 1939, Britain banned horror films for the duration of the war. Because horror often overlaps with SF, British SF suffered a temporary setback. The U.S. took up the slack. Many more ape-related NSF films follow in the forties, although I will limit myself to films that focus on brain-based behavior, perception and cognition, rather than on films about spinal cord function alone (such as *The Ape,* 1940, with Boris Karloff).

In 1941, in the same year that the Nazis first sent Jews to gas chambers, as part of its plan for the "Final Solution" via mass extermination, we find a film entitled, *The Monster and the Girl* (1941). The Poverty Row production is told in flashback. It begins with narration by the protagonist's sister. An aspiring actor, the sister (Ellen Drew) moved to New York City, but gangsters trick her into an ill-defined form of "white slavery." Hoping to save his sister, her brother leaves their hometown—where he works as a church organist. After he arrives in NYC, hoping to help his sister, he is framed for murder, convicted, incarcerated and executed.

Before he exits the courtroom, the brother stares into the eyes of a gangster who contributed to his and his sister's predicaments, and promises, "Somehow, somewhere, you'll get yours." Soon after, as he sits in his jail cell, the warden introduces him to a doctor who requests permission to use his brain—after his death. The disaffected death row inmate consents.

Then the doctor (George Zucco) transplants the dead brother's brain into a gorilla, which in turn kills the criminals who framed the brain's original owner. The human-brained ape arrives just in time: the criminals have cornered his sister, threatened and slapped her. As the film ends, the avenging gorilla is killed, without anyone guessing his true human identity (assuming that brains impart identity). Even though this film functions as science fiction, it is also a courtroom melodrama. It uses the trappings of *film noir*, which is informed by psychoanalysis, with its emphasis on repressed memories, flashbacks, and dreams. The *New York Times* reviewer describes it as "one of the most schizophrenic films ever to come out of the Paramount 'B' mill."[23]

This theme continues. In 1942, *The Strange Case of Dr. RX* (1942) features a doctor who threatens to transplant an investigator's brain into a gorilla. Actor "Crash" Corrigan plays the gorilla, wearing his own customized gorilla suit. Corrigan's purchase of this gorilla suit allowed him to develop a cottage industry performing gorilla roles for many more films.

Also in 1942 is *Dr. Renault's Secret,* a film based on a 1911 book by Gaston Leroux, *Balaoo.* Leroux also wrote *The Phantom of the Opera,* which was serialized between 1909 and 1910, before becoming a film (1925).

Dr. Renault's Secret is an American-made film that is set in a remote French villa. George Zucco from *The Monster and the Girl* (1941) plays the mad scientist once again. The action begins when a young doctor plans to wed his fiancée in France, where her uncle, Dr. Renault, resides in a castle. Dr. Renault has a strange-looking servant (J. Carrol Naish), who is said to be a native of Java. The servant is named "Noel." Noel turns out to be an ape that Dr. Renault transformed into a man, both in body and behavior. The humanoid hybrid is a product of brain surgery, plastic surgery, and "glandular injections." That is not the end of the story, which includes murder and mayhem.

Like Dr. Moreau, Dr. Renault is concerned with "moral blocks" that overcome instinct (and that presumably distinguish between higher and lower beings, human and animal). The film shows EEG (electroencephalogram) tracings that document the transformation from ape to human. This technological touch is not surprising, for ECT was recently discovered in 1939, and ECT (electroconvulsive therapy) relies upon the EEG, which was invented in 1929.

Moving right along to 1943, with World War II still raging across the Atlantic, we encounter *The Ape Man* (1943). This film stars yet another horror icon, Bela Lugosi, confirming that the film is geared toward horror audiences more than science fiction fans. In *The Ape Man,* Lugosi plays a doctor, a gland specialist, who uses an ape's spinal fluid to transform himself into an ape. When the ape needs to return to human form, he kills humans and extracts their spinal fluid.

As the trailer states, Lugosi's doctor is "A monster in search of the secret to make him human again." The gland specialist physician instantaneously reminds us of the real life gland specialist from the 1920s, Dr. Voronoff.

As one might expect, *The Ape Man* does not end happily. Somewhat unexpectedly, spinal fluid transfusions substitute for the standard fare brain transplants. This twist carries a ring of truth, given that we measure metabolites in spinal fluid, rather than blood, when seeking information about neurotransmitters. In spite of claims made by companies that promote blood tests for neurotransmitters, circulating blood does not reflect actual levels of neurotransmitters. Because spinal taps (lumbar punctures) are not part of ordinary psychiatric care, and are reserved for research purposes only, we rarely have access to such data in daily medical practice.[24]

The success of ape-human films continues in 1943, with *Captive Wild Woman* (1943). In Edward Dmytryk's film, a famous endocrinologist (played by John Carradine) experiments on circus gorillas. He transplants "glands" that turn them into humans. Like the Nazis across the Atlantic, he aspires to create a superior race. A transformed circus gorilla named Cheela is renamed, "Paula Dupree." Her outward behavior and appearance are convincing enough to earn her a job as an animal tamer. Unfortunately, Paula's animal instincts prevail, and she reverts back to Cheela. "Crash" Corrigan appears as the gorilla again, this time in drag.

Another doctor is intrigued by Paula's transformation, and becomes convinced that his brain transplant procedure is superior to the temporary gland treatments provided by the first doctor. So he arranges to kidnap Cheela. He injects blood from a human, and then operates.

All is well until Paula (previously Cheela) returns to the circus and falls in love with an authentically human animal trainer. When aroused, she reverts to her animal state, reminding us of Irena, from *Cat People* (1942), who transformed into a panther a year earlier, when sexually aroused or sexually attacked.

The astounded surgeon admits defeat, and acknowledges that, "terrific emotion would destroy the new tissues in [your] gland growth." He chastises Cheela, and plans another brain transplant, warning her that he must take another life to keep her in her human state.

Before that happens, Cheela kills him and then makes her way back to the circus, where she rescues her beloved from the lions that he is taming. Still in her gorilla form, Cheela is shot dead in the process. It is a sad ending, with moral overtones that remind viewers that doctors should not play G-d by trying to change nature. This trope also carries strong Freudian overtones, as it suggests that human females may be beasts beneath the skin, subject to overpowering libidinal impulses or instincts, when appropriately stimulated.

Before concluding this chapter, I must explain why I included endocrinology in a study of neuroscience. Endocrinology references are rampant in our monkey movies, thanks to the "Monkey Gland Man" and many others. These studies may seem to be far afield from neuroscience, our main subject of study. Yet the fact of the matter is that neuroendocrinology intersects with neuropsychiatry. Evaluating—and treating—mental status, cognition, and behavior demands attention to endocrinology. Comprehensive neuropsychiatric exams include measurement of thyroid function, and may extend to other hormones that influence behavior, including hormones secreted by the pituitary gland, which is controlled by the brain's hypothalamus. Assays of serum cortisol levels were once popular in some hospital settings, but the test had too many false positives and false negatives to make it clinically useful.

As Dr. Voronoff and Dr. Wagner-Jauregg demonstrated early in the 20th century, thyroid function influences how we think and behave. High thyroid levels can cause agitation and anxiety, or even mania in predisposed persons. Physical symptoms include increased pulse, sweating, diarrhea, weight loss and tremor. Bulging eyes (exopthalmos) are not inevitable in hyperthyroidism, but represent a rather late stage and an artifact of another hormone.

Low thyroid function may underlie depression, sluggishness, even deafness and eyebrow loss. Dr. Voronoff treated a child with myxedema early in his career, and won wide praise.

Inadequate thyroid levels in utero (before birth while the mother is pregnant) can lead to a medical condition known as cretinism. Persons with cretinism have low intelligence and physical deformities that include low hairlines and shortened foreheads, puffy face and pasty complexions, with thick protruding tongues, short stature, wide hands and stunted fingers. The voice is hoarse and froglike. Victims resemble trolls. Indeed, it is believed that legends about trolls reflect a degree of reality, for cretinism was common in Alpine regions supposedly inhabited by trolls. Why? Because those hilly soils were deficient in iodine that is used in the body's manufacture of thyroid hormones. Styria, a region to the northeast of Austria, was known for high numbers of cretins, and for low iodine levels. This disorder, and its causes, were subjects of study by Wagner-Jauregg, the psychiatrist who won a Nobel Prize in 1927 for his unrelated discovery of fever treatments for syphilis-related "general paresis of the insane."

Sex hormones also influence behavior and hence impact neuroscience. Testosterone can cause aggression and increased libido. It sometimes increases motivation and instills a greater sense of well-being. Estrogen and progesterone, all female hormones, have powerful effects on emotions. These hormones exist in far lower levels in normal men (just as androgens also exist in women). The proverbial "raging hormones" and mood changes from PMS are well known to today's females, although doctors as late as the mid–1970s were still not convinced of the biological basis of such mood swings. Research into male hormones occurred much earlier. In 1939, the scientists who synthesized testosterone from cholesterol earned a Nobel Prize.[25]

In 2013 and 2014, at the time of this writing, oxytocin is making headlines for very different reasons. This lactation-inducing hormone promotes general social bonding as well as maternal-infant bonding. It increases awareness of others. Oxytocin is showing potential in the treatment of persons with autistic spectrum disorders, which interferes with interactivity and reciprocity. It may also help men remain monogamous, according to time.com (November 27, 2013).

Testosterone still makes news, and not just because so many professional athletes were charged and convicted of illicit anabolic steroid use, only to lose coveted athletic titles and lucrative advertising contracts. "T" supplements impact ordinary men today. "T clinics" that treat "low T" syndrome have popped up like mushrooms. Low T is heavily promoted at present, even though testosterone is a controlled medication in many jurisdictions. It is said that T clinics proliferate in areas with high male employment (such as New York City's Financial District).

Ads tout T supplements—with promises of increased energy and sexual vitality. Today's ads for androgens—not to mention the "anti-aging clinics" that prescribe human growth hormone—are not so dissimilar in spirit to the testicular grafts of the 1920s, which were available only to the affluent.[26] According to an article on the front page of the *New York Times* Sunday Business section (November 24 2013), less than a fourth of men who receive legal prescriptions for supplemental testosterone had laboratory testing to confirm testosterone deficiencies. It is unclear how many of those who were tested had their tests performed early in the AM, as recommended for men younger than forty years old. Most men who take

"T" start their medication regimen without adequate data.[27] The practice of prescribing "T" without preliminary lab tests harps back to the days before such assays became commercially available.

However, today's world no longer basks in the triumphs experienced in the late 1930s, when scientists around the world researched testosterone, and found it to be a steroid. In 1935, researchers strived to synthesize testosterone from cholesterol. In 1939, the Nobel Committee acknowledged their success, and awarded the prize to Butenandt and Ruzicka. This discovery marked the start of the Golden Age of Steroid Chemistry, which continued through the 1950s. Thanks to the publicity surrounding the Nobel Prize, the world became aware of testosterone, how it is manufactured by the body and in the lab, and what it does to both mind and body.

Even insulin figures prominently into neuropsychiatry's history, for the aforementioned insulin coma therapy (insulin shock therapy) was once a mainstay of psychiatric treatment. ICT (insulin coma therapy) was invented by Dr. Manfred Sakel between 1927 and 1928 (around the same time that psychiatrist Wagner-Jauregg received his Nobel Prize). In 1936, Sakel emigrated to the U.S., where he promoted ICT (insulin coma therapy) for schizophrenia. Sakel was nominated twice for the Nobel Prize, but did not win the award.

Insulin therapy figures prominently in the film, *A Beautiful Mind* (2001), and in the PBS documentary, *A Brilliant Madness* (2002). The feature film is semi-biographical, about Nobel Prize–winning mathematician John Nash, who developed schizophrenia and was treated with ICT at Trenton State Hospital in 1961. By then, ICT had fallen out of favor almost everywhere else, and was replaced by ECT.[28] Still, ICT retained a certain cache in certain circles.

The Nobel Prizes never lose their appeal, and filmmakers never forget that fact. Nobel Prizes generate automatic publicity, and publicity is essential to promoting films. Good SF filmmakers have uncanny abilities to weave threads of scientific truth into tapestries created in their imaginations. However, human-ape films eventually lost their appeal—but the moral of this chapter is that neuroscience fiction films about evolution and the permeable boundaries among primates began to evolve long ago, long before contemporary neuropsychiatry, the Decade of the Brain of the 1990s, or Barack Obama's B.R.A.I.N. initiative came into being. The most memorable SF movies are far more than mere exercises in escapism. Rather, they incorporate references to contemporary inventions and often comment on Nobel Prize–winning research or other well-publicized scientific events.

By 1949, another Nobel Prize would be awarded to Dr. Moniz of Portugal. This was only the second Nobel awarded for psychiatric discoveries. Dr. Moniz gained praise and prize money "for his discovery of the therapeutic value of leucotomy in certain psychoses." We will recall that, in the 1950s, lobotomies would be performed fairly freely, especially when Dr. Freeman drove from city to city, promoting the procedure, and performing psychosurgery with ice picks.

Most psychiatrists today are embarrassed by psychosurgery from the fifties. Most are doubly embarrassed by the recognition it received in Stockholm. What is particularly important to our study of neuroscience fiction film is the publicity that accompanies the Nobel Prize. The public became aware that behaviors (and not just intelligence) are brain-based. In the 1950s, big-brained aliens became cinema stars, reflecting public awareness and

FIVE. Human-Ape Brain Exchanges, Darwinian Debates.... 97

increased acceptance of brains as mediators of behavior. At the same time, Freudianism and psychoanalysis were able to steal center stage in cinema, eclipsing "somatiker" (body-based) explanations of mental distress. Many SF writers allude to BEMs (bug-eyed monsters), but BBAs (big-brained aliens) are equally important, as we will see in the following chapter on "Sputnik, Space Aliens and Brains from Outer Space."

The heyday of simian cinema had passed by the time that big-brained aliens (BBAs) arrived on screen, but the battle between the armies of the brain and the soldiers of the mind was about to begin in earnest in the 1950s. That battle would be fought again, and again, and again. *Iron Man 3,* from 2013, may come closest to proposing a détente between these rival forces.

Six

Sputnik, Space Aliens and Brains from Outer Space

Classic SF film began in the 1950s, when Truman was still in the White House. America had entered the Korean War as early as 1950, fighting on Asian shores. General Eisenhower was elected president in 1952 (and reelected in 1956). Senator Joe McCarthy gained power by 1950, but would take a few years to wreak his havoc via HUAC (House on Un-American Activities Committee).

Brainwashing experiments became big news in the early 1950s. Korean Communists succeeded in brainwashing captured American sailors, convincing them to confess to "crimes" surrounding American-style capitalism, and endorsing the virtues of communism instead. Mind control and brainwashing entered the consciousness of Americans, even though psychological techniques, more than biological treatments, were the preferred mode of brainwashing.[1]

In the early fifties, Julius and Ethel Rosenberg were arrested, tried, and convicted of spying for the Soviets. The Rosenbergs were parents of two young children.[2] Their highly publicized execution took place in 1953, but remains a topic of discussion to this day.[3] America had such a hard stance against Communist collaboration that it was willing to send the mother, as well as the father, to the electric chair. The Rosenbergs confirmed Americans' worst fears about the "Red Scare." They proved that ordinary appearing American households (albeit Jewish ones), even those with two married parents, properly employed spouses, and the proverbial two children, were susceptible to Communist infiltration. The Reds were everywhere.

Eisenhower's ascendency to presidency, also in 1953, signaled the transition from the lean and mean war years to more prosperous and optimistic post-war times. Eisenhower reminded Americans of the Allies' triumph in World War II. The U.S. had fought alongside the British Commonwealth, although the American states were once British colonies. Post–World War II, the United States was a world power. To the imaginatively-minded, Eisenhower's presidency hinted that the U.S. could become not just a world power, but also a universe power, one that could reign from "sea to shining sea" across the surface, and from space to outer space up above.

The 1950s witnessed monumental Civil Rights fights. The peak of the Civil Rights movement would wait until the next decade, when tragic circumstances put social change on fast-forward, and overrode the effects of peaceful protests and ponderous legislative decisions. Midway through the Korean War, "Negro" enlistees were allowed to fight side by side with white service members. Finally, blacks and whites shared barracks, and blacks were no longer automatically relegated to military support services, in kitchens and laundry rooms.

In 1954, the landmark *Brown v. Board of Education* decision declared segregated public schools unconstitutional. Legal scholars claimed that the decision was based on social analysis rather than legal analysis. In 1955, Rosa Parks refused to move to the back of the bus, when ordered to do so by the white driver. A seemingly ordinary person on the surface, the civil rights activist incited the Montgomery Bus Boycott. Not even Rosa Parks could predict the far-reaching response to her momentary act of defiance. The nation was changing, and changing fast.

Laws demanding equality in education called attention to equality in brainpower and learning ability. Debates about inherent intellectual and emotional differences between races captivated the nation. Were differences culturally conditioned, socially instilled or even economically mediated? Were there any differences at all? What was propaganda, and what was proven? So many questions. These concerns were not uniquely American, but they gripped America in that era. These concerns would manifest themselves in neuroscience fiction films.

We know that many Americans felt threatened as African Americans encroached upon privileges typically reserved for whites. Protests against the desegregation of some Southern schools were intense enough, and dangerous enough, to require the National Guard's presence. One wonders if the cinematic representations of "alien invaders" in 50s SF films parenthetically referred to Black Americans who were "invading" previously segregated territories. That is entirely possible, although it is generally accepted that those aliens were represented hypothetical Cold War Communist enemies, rather than real life conflicts that occurred on American soil.

In the 1950s, many Americans moved from cities to suburbia, to live lives of relative complacency and conformity. Returning soldiers enrolled in college on the GI bill. Many women returned to home and hearth, leaving their Rosie the Riveter World War II lives behind. Some even quit Joan Crawford or Barbara Stanwyck-style executive officer positions. Even though female scientists are fairly common in 1950s SF films,[4] most women opted to stay home with the brood that became the Baby Boomer generation. There, they sat in front of their newly acquired television sets, watching shows such as *Queen for a Day* and hoping to win electric washers.

By 1954, America's most popular fictional visitor from outer space—Superman—came under attack. Senator Kefauver, psychiatrist Fredrik Wertham, M.D. (author of *Seduction of the Innocent,* 1954), and even some Boy Scouts spoke out against comics and superheroes. Superman was hardly the only comics' character that peeved anti-comics crusaders, and he was far more benign than the increasingly popular horror comics' characters that upset the nation. Still, Superman of 1938 (and other superheroes) represented the newest wave of American science fiction. Superman's status was called into question. Congress seemed poised to impose restrictions on comics in general, which were tenuously linked to juvenile delinquency. Many newsstands suddenly refused to stock comics, for fear of reprisals. The self-imposed Comics Code came about in 1954, in attempt to preempt more Draconian government regulations.

One 1954 comic series, *Web of Evil,* is especially relevant to brain themes in SF film.

Issue #10 features a story about "The Brain That Wouldn't Die." By the end of the decade, a film entitled *The Brain That Wouldn't Die* was in production. This film influenced many future films.

Disneyland opened in 1955. Disneyland became a beacon of fantasy and futurism. The World of Tomorrow (also known as Tomorrowland) stood alongside relics of the past, such as Frontier Town. By the late 1950s, the Race to Space roared into full force. The Sputnik Era redefined what was realistic. The boundaries between possibility and impossibility inched closer and closer. The Soviets set a satellite in orbit in 1957. America aspired to a parallel success. Children of that era aspired to be astronauts. Cape Canaveral, Florida, where the spaceships launched, became as important to the nation's children as our capital was to their parents.

Yuri Gagarin entered orbit in 1961, soon followed by the American astronaut Alan Sheppard. The masses worshipped at the Shrine of Science, praising the powers of science as devoutly as ancient peoples prayed to idols and avatars. Science was everything and everywhere. Science would save the world—but science could destroy the world just as easily, as shown by the destruction of Hiroshima and Nagasaki. The 1940s had witnessed the destructive arm of science. Hopes about harnessing science for the good of humankind loomed high

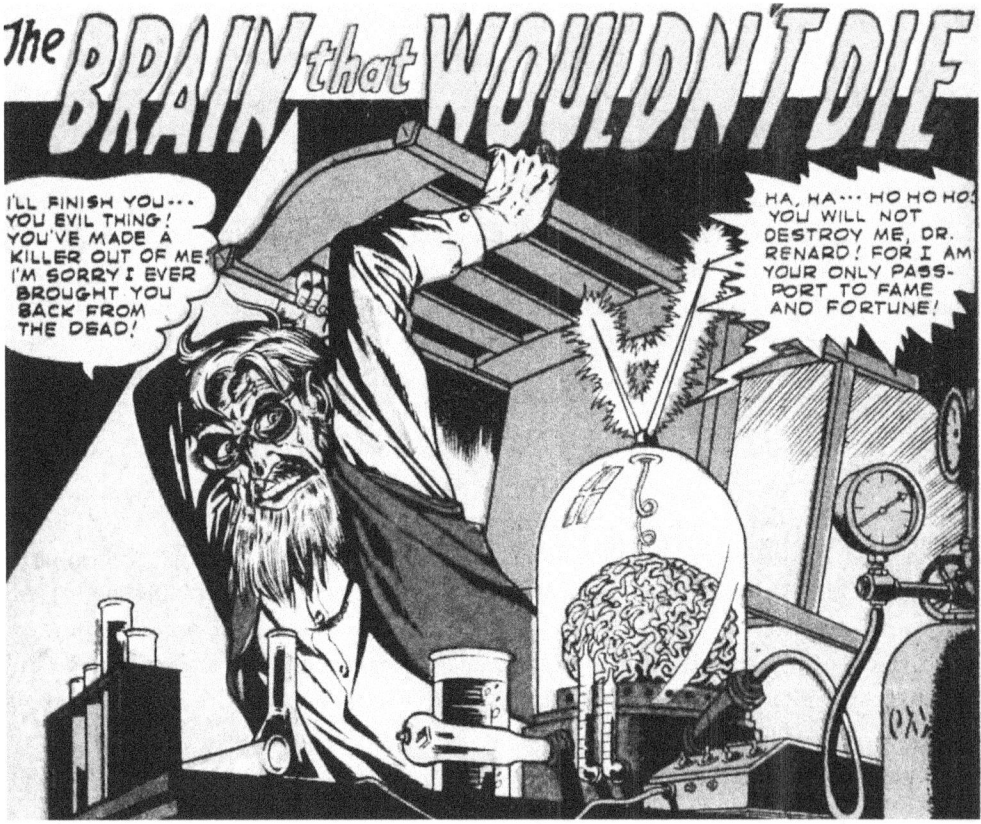

On the splash page of Jack Cole's "Web of Evil" # 10 comic book (1954), "The Brain That Wouldn't Die," the misguided surgeon who keeps a murderer's brain in a bottle regrets his decision when the brain forces him to become a murderer himself.

in the 1950s and the early 1960s (although science fiction writer J.G. Ballard disagreed).[5] Dr. Jonas Salk's success with the polio vaccine, also in 1954, proved that science could stop infantile paralysis, and spare children from paralysis, iron lungs, leg braces, atrophied limbs, even death.

In that same era, McCarthyism reigned. Senator Joe threatened Hollywood in particular. Senator Joe McCarthy, preoccupied by Communist infiltration, publicly humiliated Hollywood screenwriters and other suspects. McCarthy blacklists sent some into exile, drove others to suicide and pushed many more underground, to live lives of poverty, underemployment, and subterfuge as they sold underpriced scripts under pseudonyms or through brokers. The trial of the Hollywood Ten aired on television. It was visible to all, and was especially intriguing because television sets had only recently appeared in ordinary American homes.

The Cold War was on, and fears of Communist invasion infused films with paranoia. Hollywood films were flooded with metaphors for Commie takeovers and Red Scare spies. Often, films fused a few unrelated themes that pervaded the times. The best productions wove several subtexts into a single tapestry. The new breed of aliens that arrived via outer space were not benevolent babies from Krypton, dedicated to saving Americans from harm, and willing to sequester themselves in the cornfields of Kansas. Nor were they the adorable extraterrestrials of Spielberg's *E.T. the Extra-Terrestrial* (1982). They were, largely, armed and dangerous, maybe even radioactive and dangerous, or paranormally mind controlling and dangerous. Many of those that were not armed with conventional weapons brought brainpower that could override arms.

Strange things were brewing in psychiatry during the 1950s, even if things seemed calm on the surface. There was great demand for psychiatric treatment, especially from shellshocked soldiers who returned home. There was intense focus on "momism," which was an offshoot of Freudian developmental psychology. "Refrigerator mothers" allegedly caused autism in their offspring. Overly close mothers allegedly interfered with their sons' ability to overcome their oedipal complexes and achieve requisite heterosexual maturity. "Doublebinding mothers" miscommunicated with their children, leading to accusations that they caused schizophrenia (which is now viewed as a brain disease rather than a reaction to environment). It was irrelevant that most, if not all, of these "mother-induced diseases" would be linked to biological causes. In the 1950s, Freudian-style family dynamics bore the brunt of responsibility for all ills.

At the same time, mainstream audiences toasted Freudianism. Psychoanalysis acquired the authority of a new religion, albeit a secular one, according to sociological and cultural critic, Philip Rieff, who wrote *The Triumph of the Therapeutic: Uses of Faith After Freud* (1966).[6] Popular press articles in *Life* glorified Freud. Because the year 1956 marked the centennial of Freud's birth, the era became a time for America to celebrate his theories anew. Freud's complete works became available in English in 1956.

Pediatrician Benjamin Spock offered psychoanalytically informed child-rearing advice to parents of the burgeoning Baby Boom generation. Dr. Spock's book, *Baby and Child Care,* first hit the press in 1946, soon after the war's end, but was republished many times over. Spock's book revolutionized childcare. Spock introduced Freudian notions into the nursery as he instructed befuddled young families that faced a much-changed post-war world.

By 1957, cinema glorified psychoanalysis (and psychiatry in general) as never before (and never after). The years between 1957 and 1963 became known as the "Golden Years of Cinema Psychiatry," according to Gabbard & Gabbard[7] and others. Although films like *Fear Strikes Out* (1957) paint a rose-colored picture of ECT (electroconvulsive therapy) at the same time that it promotes psychiatry in general, the "couch cure" was represented best on the silver screen of the late 1950s. Conveniently, the psychoanalytic "couch cure" inspires the meatiest drama. It pushes plots, fleshes out characters and explains secret motivations better than many existing literary and cinematic devices.

There were other good reasons why so many mid-to-late 1950s films focused on office-based psychiatry. Only a decade earlier, in 1947, the delivery of psychiatry care shifted course, so that most psychiatrists practiced in office settings, rather than in institutions, hospitals, asylums, or rest homes. Treatment milieus became more casual, especially since soldiers recovered faster when removed from military-style hierarchy and institutional approaches.[8]

Those Golden Age films reflected real-life movement in health care that took place a decade earlier. Filmmakers needed a few years to catch up with the trends. They had to acquire appropriate scripts, secure requisite funding, rally the forces, and start shooting new feature films that dramatized these new trends. At the same time that individual treatment became more available for those who could afford it, innovations in group therapy gained steam, starting in military settings where large-scale and cost-effective treatments were sorely needed.

There was no doubt that America was infatuated with Freudianism in the 1950s. On the other hand, the 1950s also saw high-profile strides (and setbacks) in biologically based psychiatry. The "mad scientist" movie protagonist remained popular in horror films until the end of the 1950s and stands apart from the positive press in dramas. Given the polarization in 1950s treatment approaches, one would think that psychiatry was at war with itself during that decade.

Thorazine (chlorpromazine) became available in the U.S. in 1954, and provided safe and reasonably effective "chemical restraints" (as opposed to physical restraints) for seriously ill persons with schizophrenia. (Serious side effects of CPZ did not become apparent for another twenty years.) Previously, persons with schizophrenia suffered from frightening hallucinations or painful thoughts of persecution. Many could not express themselves coherently. Thorazine and other "neuroleptic" or "major tranquilizers" eased the way to the de-institutionalization movement of the following decade, when persons who had spent years of their lives in "asylums" or "funny farms" or state hospitals were released to the so-called "community." The "community" often turned out to be "the streets." This health policy initiative caused many new and unanticipated problems, so that its greatest proponent expressed his regrets decades later.

As discussed earlier, lobotomies became more common after Dr. Walter J. Freeman touted a technique that had been available since the 1930s. More lobotomies might have been performed, had it not been for Thorazine's appearance in 1954 and its relative success at stopping the most dramatic and dangerous symptoms of psychosis.[9]

Knowing about these dichotomies between psychoanalytic and neuropsychiatric approaches, one might expect Tanya Luhrmann's much-discussed (and much redacted) book, *Of Two Minds: The Growing Disorder in American Psychiatry* (2000) to be as concerned with the mid-century as with the turn-of-the-twentieth century.[10] That is not so.

There is no need to rely on secondary sources and anthropological interpretations when we can review the table of contents of the *American Journal of Psychiatry* from the 1950s. Article titles are a reasonable gauge of what engaged 1950s-era psychiatrists. There, we find an even representation of both biological psychiatry (aka neuropsychiatry) and "talk therapy" techniques, some of which refer to psychoanalysis, others to group therapy or even art therapy.

A full examination of mid-century trends in psychiatry, as reflected by the American Psychiatric Association's flagship journal, deserves detailed study that is beyond the scope of this book. Until such a study finds its way into print, let me list a few article titles, to convince readers that neuropsychiatry was very much on the radar during those pro–Freudian years.

In the January edition of *American Journal of Psychiatry*, we find titles like "Review of Psychiatric Progress 1949: Heredity And Eugenics (by Franz J. Kallmann, M.D.); Child Psychiatry & Mental Deficiency (by Leo Kanner, M.D.); Psychosurgery (by Walter Freeman, M.D.)." Those authors' names remain well known to this day, although Drs. Kanner and Kallmann enjoy far better reputations than Dr. Freeman does. In March of 1950, Dr. Freeman published a paper on pre-frontal lobotomy, in an article entitled, "Selective Partial Ablation of the Frontal Cortex; Correlative Study of its Effects On Human Psychotic Subjects."

Other topics include Neurosyphilis; Alcohol; Geriatrics; Epilepsy; Physiological Treatment; Neuropathology, Endocrinology, and Biochemistry; Electroencephalography; Psychosomatic Medicine, Psychotherapy, and Group Therapy. In February of the same year, there is an article on "Thyroid Function in Mental Disease Measured with Radioactive Iodine." Several topics from 1950 remain timeless, including, "Hallucination and Imagery Induced by Mescaline"; "Survey of Shock Therapy Practices"; and "The Alcoholic Woman."

Many more articles about biological psychiatry appear in the first three months of the year, and are representative of the types of articles published by the premiere American psychiatry journal during the 1950s. These bio-psychiatry titles are by no means the entire content of the journals, but constitute at least half of each issue.[11] Admittedly, Freud's followers were making waves on television shows, on covers of oversized coffee table magazines and in parlor discussions. However, innovative academic psychiatrists remained intrigued by biological causes, cures and correlates of mental distress and aberrant behavior, even though some cures (such as lobotomies) were later deemed barbaric by most patients and practitioners.

During the years that *American Journal of Psychiatry* highlighted neuroscience as well as psychological theories, other high-minded but best-selling books reflected the mindset of the masses. David Riesman's *The Lonely Crowd* (1950) commented on conformity, as did William H. Whyte's *The Organization Man* (1956) and Sloan Wilson's *The Man in the Gray Flannel Suit* (1955). John Kenneth Galbraith, an economist, summarized the mentality of the post-war boom in *The Affluent Society* (1958).

When Ayn Rand proclaimed the virtue of selfishness in *Atlas Shrugged* (1957), she attracted a devoted coterie of like-minded people, some of whom continue to praise her virtues to this day. Men of the cloth assured Americans that they could control their fate, although not necessarily through therapeutic techniques. Authors such as Norman Vincent Peale (*The Power of Positive Thinking*) and Bishop Fulton J. Sheen (*Life Is Worth Living*) became best-sellers. Psychiatrist Viktor Frankl, M.D., attained best-seller status by fusing religion, psychoanalysis, existential philosophy and autobiography in *Man's Search for Meaning* (1946). Frankl was an Austrian-born, Jewish psychoanalyst who survived the Nazi concentration camps by practicing as a physician in the camps, treating diphtheria victims who were doomed to die by day's end.

Amidst all this intriguing sociological, psychological and economic speculation, films about alien brains, alien brain drains and brain exchanges became box office hits during this decade. Admittedly, these proto–NSF films constituted only a small percentage of all outer space-themed cinemas that popped up in drive-ins and double features, but they were memorable nonetheless, especially to now-aging Baby Boomers who saw these silly films in their youth.

Several such films were parodied in later films (such as Woody Allen's 1972 hit, *Everything You Ever Wanted to Know about Sex* But Were Afraid to Ask*). Other film titles or sequences were appropriated by television shows spoofs and gained longer lives through spoofs. An example is the popular Conehead sketch from television's *Saturday Night Live* (SNL), with Dan Aykroyd. SNL's Conehead family announces that they are from France, apparently unaware that their robotic voices and cone-shaped craniums make them easily identifiable as "aliens." The Coneheads recollect the "normal" inhabitants of Metuluna, who pass as human. Their orange skin, whitish hair and large heads distinguish them from the big-brained "Metuluna Mutants" of *This Island Earth* (1955)—but hardly allow them to blend in with Earthlings.

The manifest content of such films entertained (or frightened) children and adolescents who saw them on the silver screen. Their latent meanings behind the plots spoke to older and sophisticated spectators. Although young children are generally unconcerned with politics, all kids of that decade learned about air raids. They heard practice sirens and knew the locations of underground shelters that could protect them in the event of an attack. "Duck and cover" drills were scheduled during school hours. Yellow and black shelter signs were as obvious—and nearly as omnipresent—as red and green traffic lights. Therefore, children had some notion of Communist threats, even if they could not connect the dots between space invaders and Soviets and even if they preferred to zoom in on space aliens alone. Television ensured that youth knew of rockets and spaceships, astronauts and aliens. More sophisticated interpretations about McCarthyism and Communism may have been evident to their parents—or maybe not.

This was the era of "classic science fiction film," which focuses on outer space and space travel, which were contemporary concerns. The prophetic Jules Verne (1828–1905) touched on this theme in the 19th century, in *From the Earth to the Moon* (1865).[12] This addition to Verne's *voyages extraodinaires* appeared just one year after the publication of *Journey to the Center of the Earth* (1864). A few years later, the prolific Verne produced *Twenty Thousand Leagues Under the Sea* (1869). Disney released its Academy Award winning film version of *Twenty Thousand Leagues Under the Sea* in 1954, proving that renditions of inner earth could be as appealing as outer space, if presented properly. That did not distract from the appeal of outer space SF.

Authors as illustrious as Henri Ellenberger (*The Discovery of the Unconscious: The History of Dynamic Psychiatry,* Basic Books, 1960) compared Verne's journey to the center of the earth to Freud's journey to the center of the mind, which he plumbed for unconscious connections that lay buried beneath the conscious surface. That parallel was well and good, and an intriguing observation in its own right. One might say that the 1954 film version of Verne's *20,000 Leagues under the Sea* primed the public for renewed interest in Freud's centennial two years later, in 1956, except for the fact that Ellenberger's book was not published until 1960.

Still, the 50s SF emphasis on outer space reflected the science of the times, current events, political problems as well as vexing social shifts. The nation was obsessed with astronauts. The "race to space" pushed forward. Fears about Soviet infiltration (the so-called "Red Scare") were fortified by the highly publicized Ethel and Julius Rosenberg spy trial and the execution of the mother (and father) of two young sons. Anxieties about potential repercussions of competition with the increasingly powerful USSR wove their way into popular plots. Recollections of recent atomic catastrophes pumped up those plots, as did bitter memories of Nazi mass murders that occurred only a decade earlier. Sociological or even economic analyses about conformity and prosperity, which threatened both individual identity and traditional group cohesiveness, were less sensational than the political polemics of the day, but nevertheless tapped the pulse of the 1950s. John Kenneth Galbraith's name is recognized to this day.

These "classic" SF films about outer space were cheap and cheesy, and directed toward teenaged audiences. They were far-removed from the high cost, high quality SF cinema of the late seventies, when *Star Wars* (1977) and *Close Encounters of the Third Kind* (1977) changed the status of science fiction films and altered their screen presentation. Those films moved SF from the margins to the mainstream. *Star Wars* and *Close Encounters* began the trend toward big budget, blockbuster SF, where screen images override narratives, and spectacular special effects often outshine the plot and sell the film for their sake alone. Philosophical issues, which permeate much of SF literature, moved to the back burner.

It is tempting to dismiss the prophetic value of 1950s "proto-neuroscience fiction" films. Many might write them off as tokens of the cultural currency, with parenthetical brain imagery added as an afterthought. Yes, these films reflected the nation's space obsession, mixed with fears of alien (aka "Soviet") invasion, fueled by McCarthy-induced paranoia. Then there are those moments of teen-aged angst, thrown in to appeal to the growing youth audience. BEMs (bug-eyed monsters) delight children, whatever the decade.

Hackneyed plots prevail. (Some might call those plots "tried and true.") "Earth Girl Meets Space Boy, but Earth Girl bids the alien good-bye" recurs, as the abandoned teen tearfully watches a spaceship take off for the sky. This trope anticipates the solitary cowboys that ride into the sunset, during the 1960s Western craze. This trope appealed to adolescents, the target audience of the low-budget SF films, yet it retains perennial appeal, because it replays ever-popular romantic legends about star-crossed lovers that are doomed to heartbreak, death, or both.

To appreciate the significance of these superficially vapid SF films, we must mention the mind control experiments conducted through the CIA's MK-ULTRA studies, as well as the televised examples of Korean brainwashing successes.[13] Those brainwashing events were mostly psychological in nature (and largely were not biologically mediated), yet they were highly politicized and most controversial. Dr. Frank Olson's tragic death in 1953, while under the influence of CIA-administered LSD, remains an exception to this general rule. Ken Kesey also participated in those CIA-LSD studies, but his fate skyrocketed in the opposite direction.

Before confirming that the alien invaders or brain-eating/brain-draining monsters were signifiers for the Cold War spies, and nothing more, we must consider the newly available Thorazine (chlorpromazine) and the impact of this new medicine on the popular imagination. Recall that the 1950s witnessed the bizarre "popularization" of lobotomies by Dr. Freeman, who reminded everyone that the brain controls behavior. Even hallucinogens made waves in the 1950s, but were mostly confined to scientific research, unless someone was adventuresome enough—and wealthy enough—to travel to Mexico to partake in mushroom rites.[14]

Psychiatry journals of the 1950s attest to the continued concern with both ICT (insulin coma therapy aka insulin shock therapy) and ECT (electroconvulsive therapy aka "shock therapy"). Reports about early (and still "respectable") experiments with perception-altering hallucinogens— such as mescaline, peyote, even LSD—appear in the *American Journal of Psychiatry*, the official publication of the organization that represents psychiatrists.[15] Firsthand accounts of sacred mushroom ceremonies graced the front pages of larger-than-life sized *Life* magazine. Again, these few facts strongly suggest that Americans were making note of the biological basis of behavior, perception, and cognition, even if they were mesmerized by the mind and by metapsychology, as championed by psychoanalysts.

If we scan the list of 1950s SF film titles for the word "brain," we find several examples. *Donovan's Brain* (1953) (which was spoofed by Steve Martin in 1983), *Creature with the Atom Brain* (1955), *The Brain from Planet Arous* (1957), *The Brain Eaters* (1958) and *The Brain that wouldn't Die* (1959) are excellent examples of brain-based SF films, but are not the only examples of proto–NSF films of the era. Some moviemakers chose more subtle titles, but their plots and presentation were no less exploitative, as we shall see below.

Donovan's Brain (1953) stars Lew Ayres and Nancy Reagan (who was known as Nancy Davis before she married Ronald). Like many SF films, this well-remembered film deliberately induces a sense of dread about fantastic and futuristic events. Because of this emotionally evocative effect, we can classify this film as "horror" as well as SF.[16] Blending horror and SF is common; films that straddle both genres attract wider audiences. SF's dread of the future is often an ideal subject for horror films, which by definition evoke emotions of dread. The movie itself was based on a World War II-era horror novel of the same name, written by Curt Siodmak. Curt Siodmak was the brother of the renowned *noir* filmmaker, Robert Siodmak.

Even before penning his 1942 best-selling book, Siodmak had gained fame for his screenplay for *The Wolf Man* (1941). Siodmak had wisely decided to leave Germany before the Nazis had a chance to inflict worse horrors upon his co-religionists in his native country. His talents were appreciated in the UK before he arrived in the U.S. Later on, he fused scientific and pseudo-scientific data with reality-based recollections and second hand stories of the Third Reich.

Donovan's Brain tells the story of a "millionaire megalomaniac" who dies in a plane crash. The plot of the B&W film revolves around the ill-fated attempt to maintain his brain while on life support. The lead scientist's motives are less than altruistic. He states that, "scientists could use Donovan's brain." He justifies his plans by announcing that, "he's dead, beyond all help." One colleague opts out of the proposed experiment, while a third, a woman, reminds the lead surgeon that "it's against the law to operate on a corpse. It could mean jail." Still, the first scientist is ecstatic at the prospect and proclaims, excitedly, "A brain, without a body, alive!" An earlier rendition of this same Siodmak book was made in 1944 and was titled *The Lady and the Monster*.

As the millionaire lies in this liminal state, his brain begins to possess people, adding a paranormal touch to a superficially science-minded movie. The 2013 film, *Elysium,* bears some similarities to this plot, in that it, too, revolves around a ruthless billionaire who attempts to overtake an exclusive off-earth colony on Elysium. Like its owner, *Donovan's Brain* lives many lives. It becomes *The Brain* in 1962, and influences the Steve Martin parody, *The Man with Two Brains* (1983), a full thirty years later. There were earlier film renditions of the novel as well. Ultimately, Siodmak wrote a sequel, *Hauser's Memory* (1968). The book became a film in 1970.

Creature with the Atom Brain (1955) is another Curt Siodmak creation. In this film, screenwriter Siodmak evokes residual traumas from his German birthplace, which he fled after hearing an inflammatory speech by a Nazi official. He correctly predicted that the Nazis would gain more and more sway and so he left Germany before the Holocaust officially started.

In this film, an American gangster coerces an ex–Nazi scientist Wilhelm Steigg (Gregory Gaye) to resurrect corpses via radiation, with the express purpose of creating zombies to thwart his enemies. The relationship between radiation and the bombs dropped during World War II is obvious, and is referenced in the title. The possibility that radiation induces superpowers (rather than nausea, burns, instant death or later-appearing leukemia and a host of other dreaded diseases) makes us think of superhero stories from comic books. When the film mentions, "a creature that cannot be killed by bullets," it reminds us of Superman, who is "faster than a speeding bullet," and cannot be killed by bullets, because bullets bounce off him. *Superman* was a weekly television show in the 1950s, when *Atomic Brain* played.

The trailer advertises, "A dead man stalks the streets" ... "on a ghastly mission of horror." It promises that the movie is "shock full of thrills" because of the "billion volt brain" with "atomic rays of super-human strength." The film's aesthetic is very *film noir*. This genre was popular in 1950s B movies, and was promoted by Robert Siodmak, the screenwriter's director-brother. *Film noir* plots and sets in general were influenced by German Expressionism from the 1920s.

The idea of creating mindless surrogates to wreak revenge for wrongs recollects *The Cabinet of Dr. Caligari,* the 1919 German Expressionist classic that influenced *film noir* directors and set designers. Dr. Caligari did not weather hurts well, and sent his somnambulistic surrogate, Cesare, to kill anyone who offended him in the least little way. In retrospect, we can read hints about the U.S. government's Operation Paperclip in Siodmak's plot, although it is unclear how much the public knew of this program when the film premiered. It makes sense to say that the scientist in this film represents the one-time Nazi scientist Von Braun, who would later head the American NASA—but Von Braun had not been recruited at the time this film debuted. A decade or two later, when so-called "social problem" films gained currency, we find more riffs on Nazi brains, including the aforementioned *Hauser's Memory*

(1970). In 1968, we find *They Saved Hitler's Brain*, although this film bore no relationship to either of the Siodmak brothers.

One may even be so bold as to connect this theme to Thorazine, which arrived in the U.S. in 1954, having been discovered and used in France first. Thorazine freed schizophrenics from persecutory delusions, but it also produced zombie-like stares and stiff and shuffling gaits. However, I admit that the Thorazine shuffle is not nearly as exciting as the CIA's Operation Paperclip, and may not have been sufficient in its own right to power a SF-horror film like this.

The Brain from Planet Arous (1957) is another much-derided, but much-referenced science-fiction film about alien possession. Director Juran is remembered for other cult classics, including *Attack of the 50 Foot Woman* (1958). *The Brain from Planet Arous* revolves around a space terrorist from a planet named Arous. So as not to be mistaken with earthlings, and to emphasize its superior intelligence, the alien's body is brain-shaped. This brain floats like a big balloon. Its gleaming eyes give it a humanoid feel. The word "Arous" hints at sexual arousal and also recollects the word, "Eros," adding a Freudian touch befitting the Freud-influenced 1950s.

Upon his arrival on earth, the brainy terrorist possesses the body of a young scientist, Steve March. Using double-exposure photography, the camera shows the brain entering Steve's body. Again, this effect brings an important Weimar Era film to mind: *The Testament of Dr. Mabuse* (1933), where the hapless Dr. Baum is "possessed" by the spirit of the dead Dr. Mabuse. Trick photography does the trick, both for *Dr. Mabuse* and for *Planet Arous*; the whiteness of the film negative is superimposed over the B &W reel, adding a ghostly cast to the image.

Steve March looks like an ordinary person, except for his occasionally luminous eyes that are identified as "the eyes of a man possessed." Using power of mind only, the Steve-Gor amalgam can destroy cities. The alien who possesses Steve—named Gor—threatens to destroy the capital of any nation that refuses to comply with his commands. He speaks through Steve.

Before that happens, Steve's fiancée Sally suspects that something is amiss. His behavior has changed, and he has become forceful, sexually aggressive and inconsiderate. Initially, no one believes Sally's suspicions. The film adds other impressive cinematographic touches. The head of the possessed Steve is photographed as Steve stands behind a water cooler. The fluid inside the tank distorts his facial features, adding a surrealistic touch. This scene does not outdo the Salvador Dalí dream scene in *Spellbound,* but it is noteworthy nevertheless.

To make matters more authentic, the film adds stock footage from A-bomb test sites. To push the plot, Gor's brother also arrives on earth, shortly after Gor lands. The brother also arrives as a brain-body. This plot-driving device reminds us of relatively recent films about the superhero *Thor* (2011, 2013), who battles his ne'er-do-well brother Loki after landing on earth and before leaving the distant galaxy of their birth.[17]

In *The Brain from Planet Arous*, the alien's brother realizes that he needs a reliable host that can be counted on to hover around the possessed scientist. So he decides to occupy the body of the dog that belongs to the scientist's fiancée. The dog is loyal to the scientist and follows him everywhere. Before that happens, the brother's translucent brain-body reveals that Gor is a known criminal on their native planet. The brother explains Gor's weakness

The eyes of possessed scientist Steve March (John Agar) shoot rays that disintegrate a plane in Juran's *The Brain from Planet Arous* (1957), as fiancée Sally Fallon (Joyce Meadows) (small corner photographs) senses something amiss and repels his uncharacteristically aggressive advances.

(his Achilles' heel, so to speak, which lies in his brain). That weakness is localized in the Fissure of Rolando, from which aliens exit the body to absorb environmental oxygen. The Fissure of Rolando is *not* an arbitrary term; this is an actual neuroanatomical site.

Not surprisingly, *Planet Arous* provides fodder for parody in future films and TV shows. *Malcolm in the Middle* (2000–2006) uses a segment of *The Brain from Planet Arous* in its opening credits.

In 1958, we encounter *The Brain Eaters*. *The Brain Eaters* was partly produced by Roger Corman, master of low budget special effects and cutesy-corny horror films. The film itself was devoured by litigation that followed the discovery of strong similarities between its plot and the plot of *Puppet Masters* (1951), written by SF literary master, Robert A. Heinlein. Producer Roger Corman was vindicated when it became clear that he was not familiar with other source material. Yet he recognized that the playwright had taken undue liberties in appropriating Heinlein's plot and agreed to settle the suit. Another interesting tidbit: Leonard Nimoy makes an unaccredited (and misspelled) appearance in this film, pre–*Star Trek*.

The Brain Eaters in the film's title are alien parasites that invade a small Illinois town. It is not the same small town of Haddonfield, Illinois, where escaped mental patient Michael

Myers and gun-toting psychiatrist Dr. Loomis experience their *Halloween* (1978) misadventures. Still, the principle of an "ordinary Midwestern town" applies in both films. These brain-eating parasites attach themselves to human hosts via mandibles that enter the base of their victims' spines.

A few decades later, David Cronenberg revisits this same anatomical area in *eXistenZ* (1999). The Cronenberg film of the future concerns virtual reality and video games that invade the CNS (central nervous system) "intrathecally" (through an injection that directly enters the cerebrospinal fluid), and through a fleshy portal that lies near the anatomical anus. Cronenberg typically adds a salacious, even twisted touch to his SF film. In contrast, the plot of *The Brain Eaters* contains a kernel of truth that was recognized in the 1950s and today as well.

Central nervous system infections can indeed enter the body via inoculation, injection, ingestion or inhalation. Encephalitis and meningitis remain ever-present threats. A quick look at the federal government-sponsored CDC.gov website[18] reveals dozens upon dozens of different CNS infections in the United States, some of them spread en masse, epidemic-style, and some that strike unlucky, lone individuals. Infectious diseases are far more prevalent outside the first world. History of medicine libraries house thick catalogues of epidemics of the past.

Persons with compromised immune function (such as AIDS) are at special risk of contracting infections that spare the average person, when similarly exposed. *Taenia solium* (cysticerci) is the most frequent helminthic (worm) infection of the central nervous system. Incompletely cooked pork transmits these tapeworms. Their immature forms (larvae) can create brain cysts that, in turn, cause seizures, psychosis or what was once called "premature senility."

In some parts of the U.S.A., immigrants come from countries where infections are endemic. Many newcomers retain their traditional food preparation preferences, making exposure to incompletely cooked pork, with subsequent infection, more likely. Even the most unlikely individuals have developed this swine-spread brain disease. For instance, *New England Journal of Medicine* reports an enigmatic neurocysticercosis infection in an Orthodox Jewish woman who never ate pork due to religious proscriptions. Investigations into this curious case revealed that the woman's housekeeper, a recent arrival from Mexico, was exposed to the infection in her own home, where she used pork. The employee apparently transmitted tapeworm larvae from her hands when she prepared food in her employer's Brooklyn-based kitchen.[19]

The stories continue. In recent decades, we have witnessed tragic consequences from contaminated growth hormone injections. Primarily used to treat short stature in children (but used illicitly by some athletes and questionably used by some anti-aging clinics), some supplies of growth hormone were harvested from organs that were unknowingly infected with the virus responsible for Creutzfeldt-Jakob disease. The highly virulent CJD virus causes dementia and death within a year of diagnosis. Occasionally, the first symptom is psychosis, but the neuropsychiatric problems progress far more quickly than comparable symptoms in schizophrenia.[20] Contracting such an illness is tragic at any point in life (and is a reality of life in Guam, where a variant of this virus is endemic)—but the results were especially tragic when young children succumbed unexpectedly.[21]

More recently, a promising new treatment for MS (multiple sclerosis) became contaminated with a virus that results in PML (progressive multifocal leukoencephalopathy).[22] The cure was worse than the illness. Even though the medication itself could halt the progress of the MS's paralysis or possible blindness, the new medication, Natalizumab, could adversely affect vulnerable persons who already harbored the CJ virus in their system. This risk left many neurologists—and more patients—afraid to use the medication.

In 2013, a strange outbreak of neutrophilic meningitis began in Tennessee and eventually struck over 700 persons. Reports of similar cases in other parts of the U.S. began arriving after investigations of the Tennessee outbreak became public. Vertebral artery strokes were common. The medication most commonly used to stop the symptoms often causes visual hallucinations. Because early symptoms of fungal meningitis are more subtle than bacterial meningitis, diagnosis could be delayed. The epidemic was traced to specific lots of methylprednisolone injections that contained the *Exserohilum rostratum* mold. Many deaths followed, and many of those who survived remain in residential treatment centers or rehabilitation facilities because CNS functions were so severely compromised.[23,24] Importantly, prednisone injections are commonly used to treat localized pain and inflammation, which are very common conditions. Fortunately, not everyone who was exposed to the contaminated meds developed infections.

To cover this vast subject of neuropsychiatric infections completely, we would have to reprint an entire microbiology and infectious disease textbook. That is not possible!

More to the point, America was shaken by the poliomyelitis virus in the late 1940s and 1950s. Polio killed or crippled children. Polio existed in the U.S. before it peaked in the early 1950s. Polio left FDR in a wheelchair (although he avoided photographs that showed his chair). The post–World War II Baby Boom produced many children, providing a surplus of susceptible hosts for the fearsome infection. The mysterious disease could paralyze the nerves that control the bellows-like action of the lungs. The diaphragm's rhythmic movements squeeze the lungs above it, forcing air in and out, resulting in inhalation and exhalation. Those who developed this type of nerve damage needed big metal breathing machines (known as "iron lungs") to survive.

In the 1950s, images of iron lungs appeared everywhere. The March of Dimes continued their crusade against "infantile paralysis," and raised funds for research and polio victims. FDR had started March of Dimes in the 1940s. By the fifties, almost any child in America who stood at a candy store counter saw photos of less fortunate children on March of Dimes posters and canisters. Ads on television appeared. The impact of polio was not hypothetical; first hand glimpses of metallic leg and arm braces and oversized wheelchairs were daily sights in large cities. Not all polio victims survived.[25]

The polio vaccine was developed in 1954, first by Dr. Jonas Salk, and improved upon by Dr. Sabin soon after. Until these groundbreaking scientific achievements brought polio under control, fears of summertime and swimming rippled through the country, because the waterborn virus bred in stagnant water in swimming pools. The expanding middle class experienced the dangers of polio most acutely, for they had access to semi-private pools and summer camps. Some affluent families had private pools, with far less risk of exposure, while poorer city dwellers had far fewer pools, if they had any pools at all. Polio is rare in the developed world today, but remains endemic in Pakistan, Nigeria and Afghanistan. Traveling through India, visitors see

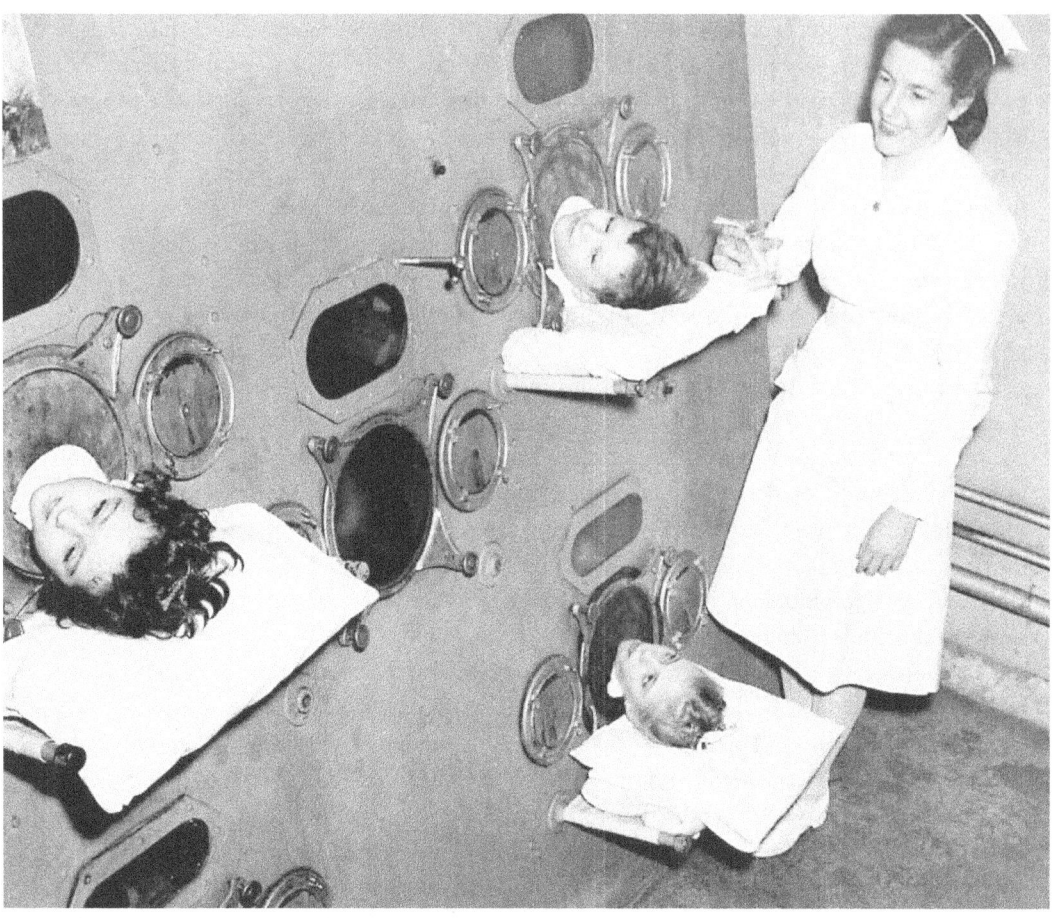

On the October 15, 2012 NPR.org health site, Jason Beaubien's piece about "Wiping Out Polio: How the U.S. Snuffed Out a Killer" shows an unnamed nurse at Boston Children's Hospital, standing at an Iron Lung Machine that keeps young polio victims alive, while SF films about brain-eating parasites and aliens that strip bodies of spinal cords premiered in movie theaters.

paralyzed and impoverished polio victims dragging atrophied legs along the ground. The more fortunate push themselves across unpaved paths on low-level wooden carts.[26]

Polio causes far less concern in the U.S.A. today, but brain-eating parasites still make headlines. In 2014, as I complete this book, we find scientific reports, Facebook accounts, and online discussions on doctor boards about attacks by "brain-eating parasites."

On August 24, 2013 CNN reported that a 12-year-old boy from Florida who had contracted a brain-eating amoeba had died. The youth harbored a "rare amoeba, called Naegleria fowleri." He was treated, unsuccessfully, with the same drug that was used to treat a 12-year-old girl in Arkansas, Kali Hardig. Hardig was only the third known person in the last five decades to contract the parasite and live.

In the hospital, the young boy "underwent brain surgery, and doctors diagnosed him with primary amoebic meningoencephalitis," an extremely serious infection, according to Dr. Dirk Haselow—so serious that people who contract it have only a 1 percent change of survival.

"The first symptoms of primary amoebic meningoencephalitis appear one to seven days after infection, including headache, fever, nausea, vomiting and a stiff neck... Later symptoms include confusion, lack of attention to people and surroundings, loss of balance, seizures and hallucinations." Victims usually die within 12 days.[27] As they say, truth is stranger than fiction.

At the time of the release of *The Brain Eaters,* the threats it described made perfect sense, to a degree. In the film, local scientists discover alien parasites inside a three-story-tall, cone-shaped object near the outskirts of town. Someone recognizes that the personalities of the town's leading citizens have changed. This revelation spurs scientists to search for a rational explanation. One scientist suspects that those minds were overtaken—by alien parasites. The scientists who unravel the mystery are hailed as heroes (much as Dr. Salk and Dr. Sabin were lionized during the same decade).

This SF trope replays repeatedly—as do real life epidemics of meningitis and encephalitis that recur with slightly different symptoms, in new locales, with new names. Importantly, epidemics are most common in military bases and colleges, where people share close quarters in barracks and dormitories. The idea of an epidemic was especially relevant to 1950s Amer-

An artist's rendition of a stock female face, with her cranium open and brain exposed, advertises *The Brain Eaters* (1958), which was partly produced by Roger Corman, and unwittingly based on Robert A. Heinlein's *Puppet Masters* (1951) about brain-eating parasites that attach themselves to human hosts via mandibles that enter victims' spines.

ica, since so many servicemen (and some servicewomen) had recently returned from military bases and warzones, where they received warnings about risks of infectious disease. Many of those former soldiers and sailors were now attending college on the GI bill, living in barracks-style dorms, and learning about science and the spread of disease in college classes.

At this point, it is appropriate to mention Don Siegel's *Invasion of the Body Snatchers* (1956), even though *Invasion of the Body Snatchers* is by no means a NSF film (by my definition). I mention it because of the obvious parallels between the personality replacements of leading townspeople in both *Body Snatchers* and *Brain Eaters*. In addition, *Body Snatchers* merits mention because of its cult status and national recognition. The original *Body Snatchers* was selected for preservation in the United States National Film Registry because it is "culturally, historically, or aesthetically significant."

Although *Body Snatchers* is not a neuroscience fiction film per se, general psychiatry is critically important to plot, in both the original and the remake. Both the original 1956 film and the remake cast psychiatrists in important (albeit different) roles. The first film uses a psychiatric session as a framing device. This allows the distraught family doctor to recount his story about the "pod people" to a specialist. The psychiatrist concludes that the local doctor is paranoid. This conclusion undermines psychiatrists' powers of observation and impugns their ability to perform accurate, office-based clinical assessments. This scene confirms that the film bears no relationship to neuroscience and harps back to the heyday of psychodynamic-style psychiatry.

Invasion of the Body Snatchers (1956) is wedged between other NSF films about brains. *Body Snatchers* does not concern itself with neuroscience, even though its plot revolves around a physical process, whereby alien pods replace living human bodies. Those pod people show no emotion or evidence of individuality. Both films compare the psychological depth of humans to pod people, which makes each film important to a study of psychiatry and the *psyche* in cinema.[28] This concept replays in *Blade Runner*, where Voight-Kampff empathy tests detect industrially manufactured replicants, to distinguish them from natural (divinely made?) humans. Mr. Spock, in *Star Trek*, will always be remembered for his quips about human emotionality.

Somewhat surprisingly—but significantly—*Body Snatchers* does not speculate about the source of this essential "humanity." This ill-defined concept may be a metapsychological construct. It may be a holdover from mid–19th century German Romantic philosophy, which seeped into Freud's theories about the *seele*. On the other hand, it may simply be a sociological commentary on the suburbanization and homogenization of post-war America, which is exactly what its director Don Siegel said. We can surmise that it does not reflect neuroscience.

In the last year of the decade, 1959, we come across another film, *The Brain That Wouldn't Die* (1959), also known as *The Head That Wouldn't Die*. The psychoanalysts among us may have another interpretation for this film title, and may see it as a metaphor for changes to come. Clearly the concept of the brain, as prime mover of the personality, did not die as the fifties ended. Just the opposite occurred. The 1950s intrigue with brains and proto-neuroscience was just an appetizer, before the main course arrived in due time. In the fifties, Freudianism still reigned supreme (even though family therapy and group therapy complemented the one-on-one analytic model). However, brains are clearly peeking out from behind the curtains, preparing to prance onto the stage, as soon as the first act ends. Brains had to wait until the 1980s, maybe a little earlier, before they took center-stage. The hokey fifties SF films will be refined.

If we look back a little earlier in time, to 1954, we find a comic book by the same name. Issue #10 of *Web of Evil,* entitled the "Brain that Wouldn't Die," does *not* follow the same the plot line as the film, but the concept of an immortal brain is the same.[29] In Jack Cole's creation, a misguided surgeon keeps a murderer's brain in a bottle but later regrets his decision when the brain forces him to become a murderer himself.

Appropriately, *The Brain That Wouldn't Die* would not be released until 1962. It is currently available, uncut, on YouTube, along with most of the films mentioned here. Directed by Joseph Green, *The Brain That Wouldn't Die/The Head That Wouldn't Die/The Black Door* attains an extra sort of immortality because its star became the subject of a much-mourned photographer, Diane Arbus. Arbus' photographs spoke for themselves, but her suicide catapulted her work to greater fame, albeit posthumously. Arbus' untimely death drew more attention to her oeuvre, as often happens to artists who die young.

Eddie Carmel plays the monster in the closet (in a role that reminds us of *Caligari*'s Cesare). This was Carmel's first film role, although the Israeli-born performer had a well-established career in the circus. He was billed as "The Jewish Giant." Carmel had a pituitary

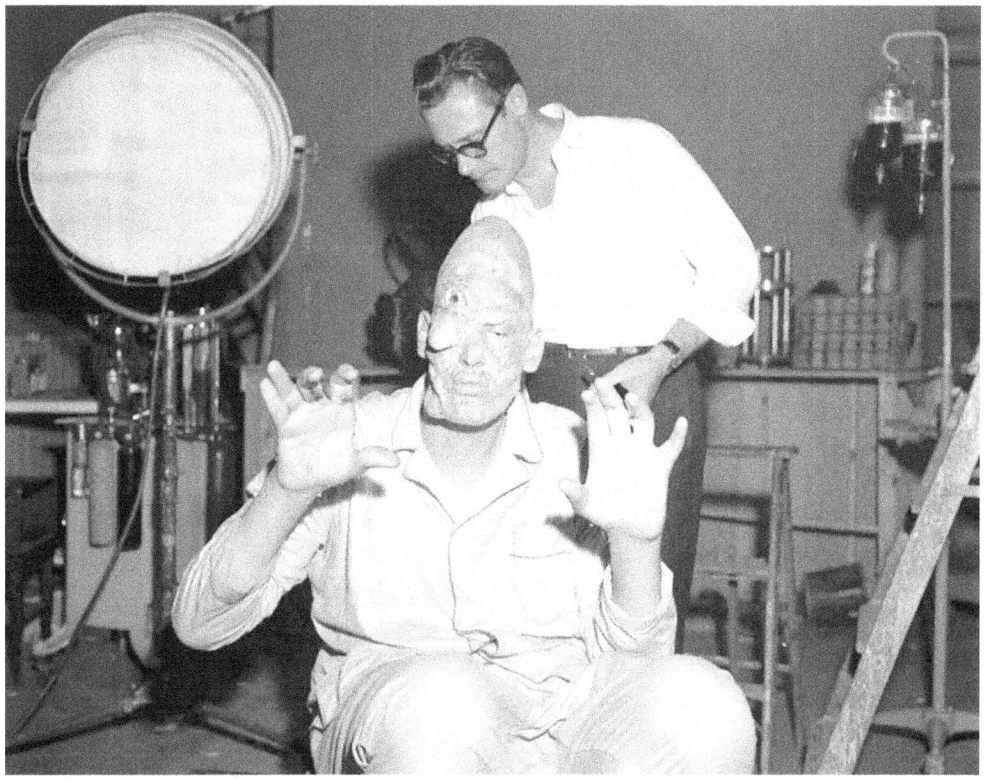

On the set of *The Brain That Wouldn't Die* (finished in 1959 but released in 1962), make-up man George Fiala stands behind Eddie Carmel, the acromegalic "Jewish Giant" from the Bronx, and former Israeli circus performer, who is prepped for his role as the "monster in the closet."

tumor that made him overgrow. In the much-seen Diane Arbus photograph, "The Jewish Giant at Home with His Parents in the Bronx, NY, 1970," he towered over his tiny parents. In this instance, the impact is tragic rather than horrific. In the SF film that crosses into the territory of horror (as so many SF films do), he plays a well-intended monster, but a monster nonetheless.

The real monster is this film is the scientist, who has become psychotic in his quest to save the brain of his decapitated fiancée. She had been beautiful before she lost her head in an auto accident. The scientist rescues her severed head, rushes it to his lab, and preserves it in a tray filled with life-sustaining fluid. Having decided to reattach his fiancée's head to another body, he kidnaps another woman who can supply the necessary torso.

His fiancée observes the proceedings, but now hates him because he refuses to let her die a natural death. Therefore, she communicates telepathically with the monster who works in the lab, instructing this Igor-like creature to kill the scientist, whom she once planned to marry. After accidentally murdering the laboratory assistant who feeds him, the monster reaches for the scientist, bites some flesh from his neck, letting him bleed to death. Ultimately, the laboratory catches fire. The monster exits the cell, carrying the would-be victim to safety, just as somnambulist Cesare did for his beloved Jane in *The Cabinet of Dr. Caligari* (1919). The severed head of the fiancée gloats as the scientist dies, seething because he kept her alive against her will.

In the interim, a host of other proto–NSF films appeared in the 1950s, during the classic stage of SF. Those films do not include the word "brain" in their title, but brain-based themes are prominent in their plots or imagery. Often, aliens resemble a disembodied cerebral cortex.

For instance, William Cameron Menzies directed *Invaders from Mars* (1953). In this SF-horror film, the action begins during a thunderstorm, when a young boy spots a flying saucer landing near his home. His scientist-father investigates, but when he returns, the father sports strange red puncture marks on the back of his neck. The son notices that the father's behavior has changed. The typically loving and concerned parent is now hostile. To make matters worse, the boy's neighbor disappears into the same sandpit where the saucer landed. He contacts the police station for help, who refer him to a health department physician, a woman named Dr. Pat Blake.

Dr. Blake begins to believe the boy's story. She contacts an astronomer, who summons the army, which in turn contacts the Pentagon. As the officials investigate and approach the saucer-landing site, both the boy and his doctor are sucked into the sandpit. They are captured by two tall, slit-eyed, green humanoids, led through underground tunnels, where they encounter the Martian mastermind. The Martian has powers of mind control, telepathy, as well as a truncated body, an enlarged head with humanoid features, and many insect-like tentacles that sprout from the misshapen torso, all of which is encased in a glass globe. He is both BEM and BBA.[30]

Soon enough, spectators learn that the mutant humanoid Martians have obeyed telepathic commands of their leader, and implanted crystals at the base of the skulls of their kidnapped victims. The crystals command their captives to sabotage army rocket stations. If the captives are caught in the act, the crystals are programmed to explode and induce deadly brain hemorrhages.

As the film ends, with thunder exploding once again, the boy is back in his bed. The ending suggests that the events recounted by the boy were nothing more than a nightmare, which was experienced as real by a child. Still, as the screen fades to grey, the boy climbs out of bed, and sees the same scene outside. Once again, the framing device reminds us of *The Cabinet of Dr. Caligari* (1919). *Caligari* makes us wonder if the events that transpired between Caligari, Cesare, and Jane occurred, or if they were invented by the overly imaginative characters who recount the story while sitting in a garden outside an insane asylum—where they live inside.

Another fifties film, *This Island Earth* (1955), directed by Joseph P. Newman, features a brain-headed alien, known as the Metuluna Mutant, played by Regis Parton. The action begins when an electronic communicator arrives unexpectedly and summons an alien named Exeter. Exeter tells the Earth scientists about his origins on the planet Metuluna, which is under attack and in dire need of Earth's uranium sources. Hoping to help the Metulunans, Earth scientists agree to be transported to the imperiled planet. Upon their arrival, they learn that the Metuluna authorities plan to subject them to a thought transference process, which will impede their free will but facilitate their cooperation. Exeter objects to this plan, but dies as he tries to save the Earth scientists from this fate. In the end, Dr. Cal Meacham (Rex Reason) and Dr. Ruth Adams (Faith Domergue), the scientist-couple, survive and supposedly thrive.

The thought-transference and mind control motif recollect Dr. Tito Daka's behavior in 1943 *Batman* serials, where the "Japanazi" psychiatrist-scientist drains brains with a TCMS (transcutaneous magnetic stimulation) look-alike machine. The machine may be a re-purposed kitchen colander.[31] This trope, like so many SF tropes, replays many times in later decades. It also recollects *Metropolis'* scene, when the evil Rotwang uses a similar apparatus on Maria.

It does not take long before the trope reappears. The next year, cult director Roger Corman directs a film with a similar subplot: *It Conquered the World* (1956). True to form, the commercially conscious Corman blends in a bit of family melodrama. This subplot seems to be left over from the forties, when maudlin "women's films" and "weepies" prevailed, until daytime television "soaps" pushed them aside in the mid–50s, when TVs became household staples.

In *It Conquered the World*, an embittered scientist unwittingly aids an alien that plans to conquer the Earth, using mind control parasites. These flying flat discs anticipate the neural parasites that appear a decade later, in television's celebrated *Star Trek* series ("Operation Annihilate," 1967). In that episode, the Enterprise crew battles an epidemic of mass psychosis spread through the galaxy by brain parasites. In *It Conquered the World*, flying disc-like creatures attach themselves to human hosts. A scientist's wife is the first subject of this alien mind control. The wife of another scientist tries to stop the alien on her own, but gets killed. Much like *The Island Earth*, the planet is saved when the protagonist has a change of heart at the last moment, and ends up self-sacrificing, in a Christ-like move to save humanity.

In *Earth vs. the Flying Saucers* (1956), directed by Fred F. Sears and written by Curt Siodmak, we have another version of scientists versus aliens (instead of cowboys versus Indians, who become popular heroes and villains in the later 50s and early 60s). In this film, a general appears, no doubt referencing General Dwight D. Eisenhower, who has since become President Dwight D. Eisenhower. The aliens extract knowledge from the general's brain, and bring him under their control. The star scientist, in the interim, observes that the aliens

In Joseph P. Newman's *This Island Earth* (1955), Earth scientists Dr. Cal Meacham (Rex Reason) and Dr. Ruth Adams (Faith Domergue) fend off the brain-headed Metuluna Mutant (Regis Parton), having escaped the Metulunans' thought-transference process that robs free will.

wear suits made from solidified electricity, which facilitates advanced auditory perception, and allows them to hear distant sounds and words as easily as nearby sounds. In other words, the aliens have access to advanced hearing aids and use technology that enhances the senses. That constitutes a rudimentary, even plausible, form of NSF, coupled with the obligatory space travel theme.

The Black Sleep (1956), directed by Reginald Le Borg, looks like an outlier among the space alien/flying saucer films made in that year. One might say that it is "a black sheep." The film is backset to 1792 England, where a knighted surgeon operates in a deserted country abbey. The ambience screams "gothic horror" and is far-removed from futuristic science. It is not even close to "mid-century Modern," as the pared-down fifties-era decorating style is called today.

The surgeon resorts to evil experiments while trying to save his wife, who lies comatose from an inoperable brain tumor. Not knowing how to excise the tumor without harming her, the doctor acquires human experimental subjects to help him refine his techniques. Using a potent Indian anesthetic, he drugs his subjects. He leaves them disfigured and dumps them in the cellar. The anesthetic may refer to *rauvolfia serpentina* (snakeroot), a psychoactive Indian plant that was used in the U.S.A., both as an anti-hypertensive and as an antipsychotic.

Alternatively, the unique anesthetic agent may recollect hypnosis, which was introduced to the Western World by a Scottish surgeon who studied it in India, when India was still part of the British Empire.[32]

The Black Sleep is clearly a "monster movie" that casts the standard-brand mad scientist as its protagonist and its villain. This traditional mad scientist trope will fade away in a few years' time, when Hitchcock's *Psycho* (1960) challenges this stereotype and proves that ordinary psychotics, without professional credentials, can be just as scary as psychotic scientists.[33]

Also in 1960, French director Franju directs a film that is superficially similar to *The Black Sleep*. Franju's *Eyes Without a Face* (1960) was far better received than *The Black Sleep*. Franju's theme concerns a surgeon and his disfigured daughter. As such, Franju's film is by no means a "monster movie"—it is closer to family melodramas that pit personal bonds against professional obligations. Franju's father and daughter reside in a stately mansion that is tucked away on a remote French country road. In contrast to *The Black Sleep,* which is mostly horror mixed with NSF, *Eyes Without a Face* concerns plastic surgery, skin grafts, and face transplants that seemed impossible in its day but have since become a possibility. The film queries a doctor's allegiance to potential patients, when his family's interests are at stake.

Back to 1957, we find another SF/horror hybrid, *The Unearthly*, starring John Carradine. Billed as a "house of monsters" with a scientist who is a "mad menace to society," the film found a place in Creature Features and related horror venues. In this case, a mad scientist/surgeon appropriates test subjects from a psychiatric institution, under the assumption that subjects have no kin to track them down. Predictably, this plan goes wrong. Experiments revolve around a glandular implant that is intended to increase longevity.

As usual, there is a kernel of truth to the film's superficially preposterous premise, for corticosteroid hormones from the adrenal glands that lie above the kidneys received increased recognition in 1950, when their discoverers earned the Nobel Prize. Corticosteroids are powerful and potentially life-saving medications, but were soon overused before side effects from long-term use made themselves manifest. Glandular implants were performed in the 1920s and 30s, for the sake of longevity, and not just by "the monkey gland man." Sadly, exploitation of mental patients and other vulnerable persons for experimental procedures continues to occur in real life. Studies performed on demented elderly patients at a Brooklyn hospital rivaled the atrocities at Tuskegee, where black men infected with syphilis were denied definitive treatment.[34]

Invasion of the Saucer-Men (1957), directed by Edward Cahn, also appears in 1957, and returns to the ever-popular alien theme. The action begins on Lovers' Lane. Clean-cut teens challenge the disbelieving police. The saucer men are big brain-headed aliens, with strikingly large cerebral cortexes, and eyeballs on their detachable hands. Teens save the day when they defeat the aliens that the military could not conquer. The adolescents shine their car headlights on the light intolerant aliens. What a perfect plot for drive-in movie theaters and an expanding teenage audience! What a wonderful way to show that the youth generation outmaneuvers military authorities. We have to wonder how many of those teens-with-wheels of the mid–50s felt empowered enough by this film to become anti-military activists of the 1960s.

Also in 1957 is *The Invisible Boy*. Director Herman Hoffman presents the story of a young boy who gets a brain boost from his scientist-father's supercomputer. This increased

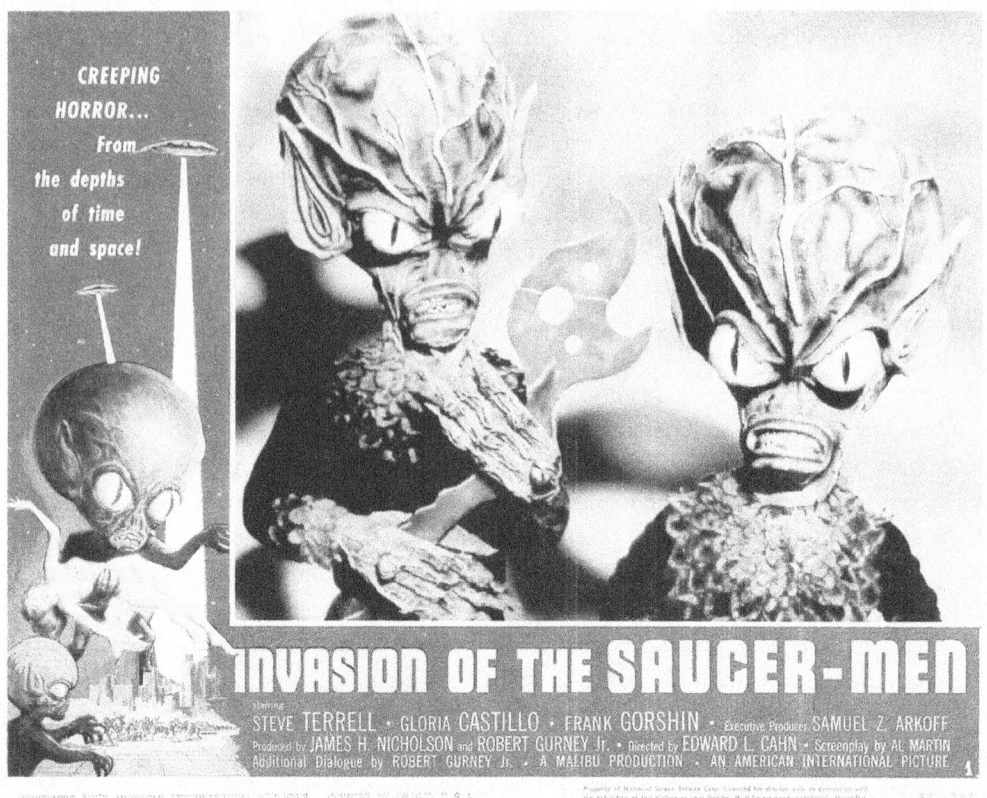

Invasion of the Saucer-Men (1957) appears during the age of "classic" (space-themed) SF and introduces iconic "little green men" with bloated brains. Played by costumed little people, these aliens have eyes on their fingers. Teens defeat the aliens that the military could not conquer.

intelligence allows him to reassemble a dismantled robot. The boy's robot is actually the iconic Robbie the Robot from *Forbidden Planet*, in an uncredited appearance. Ironically, in *Forbidden Planet,* Robby the Robot is built by an adult whose intelligence was enhanced by aliens. The prop is the same, the plotline is similar (in that both include intelligence enhancement and robots), but the films are otherwise diametrically different.

In *The Invisible Boy*, the father's "electronic brain machine" goes berserk after giving the boy a "brain boost." It threatens to destroy the scientist's son, unless the father facilitates its quest to take over the world and make Earth its slave. In the interim, the computer turns the son invisible. As a side note, two top scientists are subjected to micro-transmitter implants in their brains, placing them under "non-human control." In response to this threat, all scientists must submit to a physical exam that will reveal which men have implants and which have free will. This story anticipates later cyberpunk stories about evil world-controlling computers. Because the film was released in the same month that the Soviets launched Sputnik, we can also read the emphasis on thought control and usurpation of free will as a commentary on Communism.

Eugène Lourié's *The Colossus of New York* (1958), a late 1950s creation, bridges cheap and cheesy 50s SF/horror/alien abduction/spaceship themes with the social problem films that mushroom in the 1960s, when the Civil Rights movement gains greater clout. The film revolves around a genuine humanitarian who is corrupted by the dehumanizing force of a mechanical robot-controlled brain. The selfish pursuits of his physician-father are secondary concerns. The metaphor about science eclipsing the humanities is obvious, and was especially relevant in the late 1950s, when schoolchildren were encouraged to study science, with religious-like zeal.

The plot focuses on a young man who hails from a family of scientists and humanitarians. He himself is a noted humanitarian who just received the "International Peace Prize." Upon his return to the States, he dies in a motor vehicle accident. In response, his father, a brain surgeon, constructs a plan—and enlists his surviving son to build a robot to keep the other son "alive."

The father is unwilling to let his son's good intentions and finely tuned mind die a natural death. That would deprive humanity of the benefit of his son's idealistic plans, as much as death would deprive the father of his beloved son. The doctor-father decides to transplant the son's brain so he can retain his "essence." Like the more sinister-minded and sexually-driven scientist in *The Brain That Wouldn't Die* (1962) (and even a little bit like Dr. Frankenstein, who started it all), the bereaved father preserves his dead son's brain in fluids to prepare for the transplant.

This plan pits father against his last living son. The brother objects to the plan to preserve the brain. "Encased in a steel colossus without a soul!" he exclaims. He warns his father, "It isn't just an abstract intellect. It's a brain that remembers and feels and suffers. Do you think he can continue to exist when he has been deprived of everything he has ever known or loved?"

Such statements might seem irrelevant today, now that research psychiatrists are experimenting with oxytocin injections to add empathy to persons with autism or borderline personality disorder. Oxytocin ordinarily promotes maternal-infant bonding and may help philandering men remain more faithful in marriage.

The timing of this film is important. It appears in the late fifties, a few years after the first successful kidney transplant in 1954. In 1954, an identical twin gave a kidney to his ailing brother. Both survived, and Peter Bent Brigham Hospital, where the Herrick twins were treated, entered the annals of history (once again).[35] Knowing those historical facts, we understand why the concept of preserving a body part—and putting it to good use—was more plausible at that juncture in time. Admittedly, brain transplants are far more complicated than kidney transplants, but the kidney is a complicated organ, and this film is science fiction, not a science documentary.

Progress in transplants was on fast-forward. In 1960, British scientist Peter Medawar (and another researcher) received the Nobel Prize for proving that the body's rejection of foreign tissue is an immune response. This discovery offered hopes that transplant rejections (from non-identical twins or others) could be overcome with the appropriate treatments and techniques.

In *Colossus*, the surgeon-father does not plan to transplant his son's brain into another body, as had been done in so many lesser SF films. Knowing that his second son is an expert in automation, he enlists the other son's help in producing an artificial robotic body to host the critically injured son's brain. For nearly a year, this man-machine creation continues the "deceased" son's humanitarian work. The cyborg stays in seclusion, lest anyone learn of the experiment. This seclusion leads to horrific results. Deprived of human contact and sensory stimulation, the brain becomes psychotic. The unheeded warnings of the second son prove true.

The son's deranged cyborg espouses ideas that are the polar opposite of the son's usual belief system. The cyborg denounces the plan to produce food for the world's poor, suggesting, "It's simpler and wiser to get rid of them [the poor]." The brain's dwindling empathy goes several steps further: the cyborg kills his living brother who engineered the robot-body. At this point, the mechanical body develops powers that exceed the brain's control. It attacks the U.N. and kills more. Eventually, when confronted by his own son (whom he believed to be dead), he has a momentary lapse in his rage, and allows his son to "turn him off." The cyborg is no more.

The similarities to *RoboCop*—and to RoboCop's adversaries—are obvious. Did it take a Verhoeven to shape Frank Miller's comic book, to make *RoboCop* an enduring classic that is remembered to this day, that spawned several sequels in its own day and a remake in 2014? Alternatively, was the world more willing to accept the idea of a man-machine in the late 1980s, when neuropsychiatry was better respected and better established, and represented by far better achievements than the Thorazine shuffle and Freeman's "lobotomobile" from the 1950s?

To answer those questions, we need only look at *RoboCop's* plot. RoboCop and Officer Murphy are heroes. They are good guys, through and through, even though Murphy has suffered immensely. Murphy continues to dream, in spite of his metallic frame. He has flashbacks of his loving family. *RoboCop* is a positive rendition of the dystopian colossus from the 1950s. *RoboCop* appears to be a new and improved version of *Colossus*, superficially. In reality, *RoboCop* is the polar opposite of *Colossus*, because he was created to be cold and calculating, but becomes more human as time goes on. The exact opposite occurs with the cyborg in *Colossus*.

We can compare the *Colossus/RoboCop* polarity to *The Superman* and *Superman*. When the young Siegel and Schuster first conceived of "superman," they coined a concept that was villainous, known as *The Superman*. After enduring rejection after rejection, they refined their story, and turned their star into a hero who saves lives, instead of destroying. By making that adjustment, the story soared. Superman still soars through the sky, some 75 years later.

Before we conclude this chapter, let us look at one last film from the fifties. The decade comes to a close with Arthur Crabtree's *Fiend Without a Face* (1958). Like so many SF films, this movie amalgamates tropes about aliens, neuroscience, and military intelligence.

Fiend Without a Face is set on an American airbase in rural Canada. Unexplained deaths occur in the local town. Autopsies make matters more enigmatic. A white-coated pathologist looks chagrined as he explains his findings to the authorities. Brains and spinal cords of the deceased have disappeared, but marks appear on the necks of each victim. Locals blame nuclear fallout from radiation used at the military base, while military officers hypothesize about a "mad GI on the prowl." However, the base commander suspects that a local professor is responsible. Knowing that the professor experiments with telekinesis, the commander searches the professor's background and scrutinizes his every activity.

The commander's hunch is correct, but there is more to the story. It turns out that the local radiation did not cause the deaths. Rather, the radiation potentiated the professor's experiments. The professor produced new life forms that are intelligent but are initially invisible. When these new life forms eventually become visible, it is apparent that their brains are enlarged and are now connected to spinal cords that disappeared from those who died this mysterious death. These creatures behave like lobsters, clawing their way into crevices. Thanks to their new mutations, these brain-based life forms sprout tentacles from their brains, with eyes attached to stalks (much like the Mad Hatter, the malevolent neuroscientist in the *Batman* universe!).

These large brains are easy targets. Luckily, they succumb to ordinary gunshots. With ammunition readily available at the military base, the creatures are vulnerable. Then the Major conceives of an even better idea. He realizes that the creatures rely on the airbase's nuclear power plant for their power source, and so he blows up the plant. The creatures dissolve.

The creatures created quite a sensation, both on screen and in sidewalk displays. In actuality, they were created by stop-motion animation, a time-consuming and labor-intensive technique that was state-of-the-art in the 1950s, but was rarely used in low-budget films.[36]

British authorities were horrified that such a film passed the censorship board. Britain was historically more squeamish than the United States, having outlawed all horror films during the war years. That policy allowed the U.S. to leap ahead in world horror film production. There were no British competitors temporarily, but there were impressive Japanese contenders for the "throne" in such theatrical releases. In New York City, the mechanical "fiend" advertised the film outside the theater. It was so life-like, and made such menacing sounds, that spillover crowds congregated on the sidewalk. The NYC police eventually demanded removal of the traffic-blocking Times Square display.

In summary, the 1990s were dubbed the "Decade of the Brain," but it was in the 1950s that brains attracted attention. Fifties era NSF films literally made people think (and often laugh) about the primacy of the brain in controlling the "mind." It was not so obvious at the time that it was happening, and it was hard to take these films seriously, either then or now. Yet we can see that the shift toward neuroscience, and neuroscience fiction, was cemented in the 1950s.

In 1961, a TV show about a neurosurgeon appeared. *Ben Casey* remained on television for several years. *Ben Casey* was *not* science fiction. Rather, it was a drama, presumably based on real-life. It was a step up from the daytime television hospital dramas that placed pathos above pathology. This show popularized neurosurgery through its portrayal of a struggling young neurosurgical resident (Vince Edwards). Ben Casey was gruff and wore tattered suit jackets, when not in the operating room. He lacked the finesse of the soft-spoken psychoanalysts and psychiatrists who starred on the big screen, yet he reminded loyal spectators about a biological basis of behavior. Casey's purview was different from the emotion-laden minefields of the analysts, but this show hinted that attitude changes were brewing behind the scenes.

Ben Casey played from 1961 to 1966. Around that same time, other science fiction television series enjoyed enormous popularity: *Twilight Zone* (1959–1964); *The Outer Limits* (1963–1965); *Star Trek* (1966–1969); *Lost in Space* (1965–1968). Some of those shows were as much occult as they were science fiction. Others, such as *Star Trek*, were pure science fiction, and were often NSF to boot. Since this book focuses on the big screen (film) rather than the small screen (television), we are unable to explore these equally influential titles. However, during the course of this book, it will become evident that *Star Trek* introduced many NSF film trends of the future. Many of our fifties SF films are forgotten, but *Star Trek* endures.

Seven

Science Fiction in Social Problem Films

The fifties pushed into the sixties. The era of "classic" science fiction ended with the fifties. The "race to space" and the Sputnik era set classic science fiction in motion, yet the race to space continued into the 1960s. In 1961, Alan Sheppard became the first American to enter space. The Soviets had sent the first human (Yuri Gagarin) into orbit a few weeks earlier. The Soviets' latest success mirrored their earlier success with Sputnik in 1957. America kept plodding along, eventually landing the first man on the moon more than a decade later.

Operation Paperclip provided the scientists that made JFK's proclamation a reality. Rocket scientists from the Third Reich were recruited and recycled for U.S. operations. In 1962, President John Fitzgerald Kennedy pledged that the U.S.A. would be first to make it to the moon. That goal became a reality on July 20, 1969, when Apollo 11 landed on the lunar surface.

Space travel remained important to science fiction film, even after the 1950s. SF films branched out into other terrain in the 1960s, to reflect America's internal conflicts. Tropes about racial strife and civil rights gained steam. Brains from space, so popular in the 1950s, lost their luster in the 1960s, compared to their prominence in films from the decade before. However, *The Brain That Wouldn't Die* was finally released in 1962, even though it was completed in 1959. Just as its name says, the "brain that wouldn't die" did not die with the first film. Instead, this concept endured over the decades, offering fodder for late night comedies and film spoofs.

Movie brains from 1950s films are very straightforward. They look like the brains that medical students dissect in gross anatomy labs, where they cut open cadavers, examine superficial markings, and trace the twisting paths of blood vessels that traverse the brain. Those movie brains lack the complexities uncovered by 21st century neuroscience or neuroimaging studies, which track blood flow or glucose utilization or other metabolic functions that occur inside brain cells or between the blood vessels. Mostly, those 1950s-era brains are isolated organs that operate apart from the body and without input from other bodily functions and organs. Those brains are not even as complicated as the monkey brains from the 1940s.

The heyday of hormones and the "Monkey Gland Man" (Dr. Voronoff) had faded to grey by the time World War II ended. With rare exceptions that arguably include *The Unearthly* (1957), endocrine organs that secrete hormones from outside of the brain—but influence brain-based behavior in major ways—do not figure into 1950s neuroscience fiction. Brains are big, in more ways than one.

In this poster for Arthur Crabtree's *Fiend Without a Face* (1958), Barbara Giselle (Kim Parker) still wears her shower towel as Maj. Cummings (Marshall Thompson) prepares to shoot the bodiless, brain-only "fiend" that rips brains and spinal cords from victims on a military base, and then sprouts tentacles with eyes, thanks to radiation-induced mutations.

Those brains, by and large, control intelligence. They are less likely to be associated with emotion. Occasionally, fifties era brain-beings are capable of telepathic communication. Occasionally someone imputes emotions to brain-only beings, as seen in *The Colossus of New York*. In that film, the surviving brother predicts that his body-dead (but brain-alive) sib will go psychotic, if his father maintains the brother's brain on life support, after he is clinically dead.

The depiction of brains in 1950s American SF films conformed to the ethos of the era: body and brain are separate and distinct. At best, they are separate but equal. Disembodied brains are prominent in 1950s iconography. We encounter many brain-headed aliens or big-headed aliens. Sometimes, those brains operate independently. Brains can be implanted in fully functioning humanoid bodies (as opposed to automatons or robots), but they provide less obvious imagery on movie posters—until the Brits reanimated the Frankenstein legend in 1957.

Thanks to its revival of the Frankenstein films, the British-based Hammer Films made its mark on horror and made the UK a strong competitor in SF/horror. *The Curse of Frankenstein* appeared in 1957. Six sequels followed between 1959 and 1974. With the sole exception of *The Horror of Frankenstein* (1970) spoof, all starred Peter Cushing as Baron Frankenstein. After *The Revenge of Frankenstein* (1958) came *The Evil of Frankenstein* (1964), *Frankenstein Created Woman* (1967), *Frankenstein Must Be Destroyed* (1969), *The Horror of Frankenstein* (1970), and *Frankenstein and the Monster from Hell* (1974), starring David Prowse as the monster. In a few years' time, Prowse would become *Star Wars'* villain, Darth Vader.

These British-made films enthralled American audiences, perhaps because the subject

A giant-sized man-machine (Ed Wolff) in *The Colossus of New York* (1958) was an award-winning philanthropist before his father preserved his mind inside a robotic body—but now he stands in front of the Queensborough Bridge, emerging from the water, preparing to attack the U.N.

reflected social concerns that troubled American audiences (but were largely irrelevant to British citizens). They updated horror classics, translating them into color, and shocking audiences with blood red instead of muted shades of grey. Horror scholar F. Scott Poole offers interesting explanations for their appeal to Americans. We will discuss Poole's theories later in this chapter.

In the interim, let me stress that American psychiatry did not abandon all interest in the brain as the 1950s faded away—although one might never guess that, given how many American-made films idealized psychoanalysis in the late 1950s and early 1960s. Those years became known as the "Golden Years of Cinema Psychiatry" because of their positive portrayal of psychiatry. *Three Faces of Eve* (1957) is perhaps the most celebrated of this genre, and perhaps the most influential, since *Eve* set the stage for the even more influential TV drama about *Sybil* (1976), which set off soaring numbers of MPD (multiple personality disorder) diagnoses.

In the 1960s, family therapy became fashionable, to a degree. When it came to casting blame on parents and parenting, family therapists took over where psychoanalysts left off. Previously, Freudian theorists vilified mothers, imputing responsibility for their sons' unresolved oedipal complexes and much more. Overly protective (or emotionally unavailable) mothers stood accused of contributing to a host of psychological woes, ranging from same-sex attraction to autism. Now newly minted family therapists went one step further. They pushed the locus of pathology onto the family itself, building on the house of cards that Freud built, and often forgetting that humans are biological beings, made of flesh and bones—and brains and more.

Dr. Walter Jackson Freeman II's "lobotomobile" was all but decommissioned by the early 1960s. With the introduction of Thorazine in 1954, there was little need for such surgery. Mankiewicz' 1959 film, *Suddenly, Last Summer* (1959), starring Katharine Hepburn, Elizabeth Taylor, and Montgomery Clift, put the cabash on lobotomies as the decade ended. *Suddenly, Last Summer* is based on a Tennessee Williams stage play that Gore Vidal turned into a screenplay. The play includes autobiographical elements, given that Williams' own sister was lobotomized. *Summer's* unstated homophobic subtext captures Williams' life experiences in the South.

The film earned three Academy Award nominations. Elizabeth Taylor won a Golden Globe for her portrayal of the hapless niece who is hospitalized and is about to be lobotomized, at the insistence of her hard-hearted aunt. Played by Katharine Hepburn, the affluent aunt is a generous donor to the hospital, and is almost able to sway the hospital's administrator.

Luckily, this scene takes place in a hospital that has a sympathetic neurosurgeon on hand. Before the worst occurs, the neurosurgeon, Dr. Cukrowicz (Montgomery Clift), comes to the rescue and saves Liz from the knife. This film reminds audiences that ready and willing lobotomists may lie in wait—and that scheming relatives may lobby to lobotomize family members and lock them away for life. Many critics commented on the irony that Clift played the competent neurosurgeon at the very same time that he himself was hobbled by addictions.

Suddenly, Last Summer is far removed from science fiction. It is drama, and family drama, at its most intense. Yet it silhouettes the brain-based themes that skyrocketed in

1950s films. By 1960, lobotomies were almost obsolete—but the public had been primed to believe that the brain controls behavior—and that families can destroy family members. By now, they knew that cuts into critical parts of the cerebral cortex could change personalities in split seconds. The Soviets banned lobotomies, condemning them as cruel—although American psychiatrists will condemn Soviet-style psychiatry as cruel, claiming that Soviet psychiatrists pathologize political dissidents, label them as mentally ill, and institutionalize them.

The fact of the matter is that the seeds of a paradigm shift were planted in the 1950s, even though these seeds would not sprout and bear fruit for two or three decades. In the very years that psychoanalysis reigned supreme, both on the silver screen and in most (but not all) academic psychiatry departments, we see hints of important changes to come. Years would pass before those changes came to full fruition, but their roots were reaching deeper, beneath the surface, in mid-century. On the other hand, when Ken Kesey published his bestselling book, *One Flew over the Cuckoo's Nest* (1962), he echoed the sentiments of early academic "anti-psychiatrists," and fermented the populist anti-psychiatry attitudes that evolved by the time his book became a film.

Ken Kesey was an Oregon native. He graduated from University of Oregon's journalism school before moving to California to attend Stanford's creative writing program. He was a highly trained writer who went on to become an award-winning writer. While attending graduate school at Stanford, Kesey worked the night shift at the Menlo Park Veterans' Hospital. He set the action of *Cuckoo's Nest* in Oregon, even though his experiences occurred in California. When Kesey participated in the CIA–sponsored MK-ULTRA project involving LSD, hallucinogens were still legal and held promise for legitimate research, although the CIA sponsored studies ultimately became disreputable. Other MK-ULTRA projects involved brainwashing techniques.

Kesey fictionalized his observations at the VA. His novel—and his antics with the Merry Pranksters—galvanized a generation in the process. He became known as the "Pied Piper" of the Hippies. Director Milos Forman went several steps further when he turned the bestselling book (and popular stage play) into a film. The film starred Jack Nicholson as McMurphy, the small time con, and Louise Fletcher as the meaner-than-mean charge nurse in the psychiatric unit. It is unlikely that either Forman or Kesey, much less Nicholson or Fletcher, anticipated the uproar that followed the film's release. However, Kesey was not happy with the results and distanced himself from the film. Financial disputes between Kesey and the producers ensued.

Anti-psychiatry theories had gained firm footing in the 1960s, although they had to wait another decade to attract mainstream attention. In the interim, the intellectuals—Foucault,[1] Laing,[2] Cooper,[3] and Szasz[4]—began publishing books and essays that questioned the veracity of psychiatric authority.[5] These men (and they were all men) ventured far beyond the Freud-bashing that became fashionable a few decades later, when literary critic Fredrick Crews and psychologist Frank Sulloway took center stage as they dissected the specifics of Freud's case studies, and questioned the credibility of Freud's reportage. The male anti-psychiatry theorists were a breed apart from feminist anti–Freudians.[6] Early anti-psychiatry theorists did not limit themselves to Talmudic-like readings of Freud's sacred texts, to demean Freud's theories and methods without diminishing his overall significance to psychiatry.

Their tactics were more literary and philosophically based and often promoted their own innovative theories.

The behaviorists (Pavlov, Watson, and Skinner) or developmentalists (Piaget) cannot be counted among the "anti-psychiatrists." These laboratory-based researchers took more scientific approaches to counter psychoanalytic claims and validate their own hypotheses in the process. The behaviorists did not deny the value of psychology or psychiatry (or physiology, in the case of Pavlov, who won his 1904 Nobel for physiology). Rather, they attributed neurotic conflicts to learned behavior, without concerning themselves with the so-called "family romance" favored by analysts who followed in the footsteps of Freud. They did not make profound claims about civilization, as Freud did, but they managed to anger analysts and theologians alike because their ideas "dehumanized" human interactions and reduced them to sterile scientific formulations.

Overall, those 1960s era anti-psychiatrists were less concerned with personal psychopathology and more concerned with social pathology. Some zeroed in on political pathology in particular.[7] They were kindred spirits of other social critics from the 1960s—and there were many such critics. It is curious that the path to the American anti-psychiatry movement was paved by the Scottish psychiatrist R.D. Laing, who practiced in London's East End. Thomas Szasz also played an important role. A Hungarian refugee, Szasz emigrated to the U.S. and won an academic post in upstate New York.[8] Michel Foucault, a Frenchman, spent years in Scandinavian universities, reading and teaching philosophy. Dr. David Cooper, who coined the word "anti-psychiatry" in 1967, was British. Anti-psychiatry, sixties-style was *not* an American invention, even though the evolving American counterculture adopted it as its own.

That's not to say that the United States lacked homegrown social and political critics in the 1960s. Nothing could be further from the truth. In the U.S.A., the most ferocious social criticism revolved around racial issues. The Civil Rights movement was boiling over, having begun in earnest in the 1950s with the passage of *Brown v. Board of Ed* in 1954. School segregation became illegal—but the battles were far from over. Backlash against the acquittal of Emmitt Till's murderers occurred a year later, in the same year as the Montgomery Bus Boycott. Emmitt Till was a young black man who whistled at a white woman, and was subsequently murdered. Men were tried for his murder but won acquittals by an all-male, all-white jury.[9]

Little Rock, Arkansas exploded in 1957, when the state's governor ordered troops to block school desegregation. The year 1960 witnessed lunch counter sit-ins at Greensboro, North Carolina. Violence shook peaceful marches. "Freedom Rides" attracted volunteers from North and South, white and black, Jew and Gentile. In the South, civil rights workers were murdered in cold blood, lynched like the black men and women they advocated for.

Riots erupted in 1962, and deaths followed, as James Meredith became the first Negro student to enter Ol' Miss. Congress called in the National Guard to contain the crowds. The 1963 assassination of activist Medgar Evers occurred shortly after the release of the original *The Manchurian Candidate* (1962). A church bombing in Birmingham, Alabama, killed four young girls in 1963. This heinous act of the KKK attracted national attention and catalyzed support for civil rights across the country. In 1963, the Reverend Martin Luther King, Jr., gave his "I have a dream" speech. King based his pacifist approach on Gandhi's practices.

JFK was killed in the fall. The country lost its president, and its first Catholic president at that, one who was an ardent supporter of civil rights. With Texas-born Lyndon B. Johnson at the country's helm, the Civil Rights Bill of 1964 passed a year later. Radical black activist Malcolm X died at the hands of an assassin the following year, in 1965, in New York City and not in the South. When Dr. King was shot in 1968, turmoil erupted across the country.

During the years when America was in turmoil, Hammer horror classics were remade in the U.K. at Hammer Studios. Those chronological coincidences were not lost on Professor F. Scott Poole, as we will see below. The Hammer films won an enormous following in America. Dr. Frankenstein and his monster, also known as Frankenstein, gained new life and spoke to different generations. Universal Studios had brought *Frankenstein, Dracula, The Mummy, The Wolf Man* and more to the screen in the 1930s and early 1940s. It was fitting that the British-based Hammer Studios revived *Frankenstein,* considering that Mary Shelley, *Frankenstein's* original author, was herself British. Other classic monster movies followed in the footsteps of *Frankenstein.*

Historian and cinema scholar F. Scott Poole connects the dots between these new Hammer horror productions and social events in 1960s America. Writing in the American South, where he is an Associate Professor of History at the College of Charleston (South Carolina), where antebellum mansions still stand, and where *Gone with the Wind*-style gardens grace the cityscapes, Professor Poole sees Frankenstein's monster as a metaphor for American racial relations. He does not deny that the monster once represented fears about scientific advances, such as galvanism and electricity, which were in the works when Shelley wrote.

Rather, he looks to contemporary concerns from the late 1950s and 1960s to explain *Frankenstein's* pull on Americans, all over again. Poole points out that the monster acquires its own life, and rises up and revolts against his creator, just as the slaves revolted against their Southern masters. When Shelley wrote her story in 1818, most American Negroes were enslaved. Emancipation was half a century away. Concerns about race relations in America, and the legacy of slavery, were an ocean away from Shelley.

Professor Poole reminds us that mobs hunted down escaped slaves in the South, even after they escaped across Northern borders. Similarly, Frankenstein's monster was hunted down after he escaped the vengeful crowds. Images of torch-carrying villagers, running en masse, are iconic. For American history students, photos of lynch mobs, also carrying torches, pushing forward in frenzy, are equally iconic. The visual parallels are compelling, once Professor Poole points them out, even though this metaphor may not be obvious at first glance.

We will never know if the Hammer horror films acquired such loyal audiences in America on their own merit, or if their subtexts resonated so much more because they mirrored social and political events that were taking place in the U.S. at the time of their release. What we do know is that Shelley's romantic era *Frankenstein* set a prototype for science fiction and horror films of the 20th century. This template continues to make itself manifest into the 21st century. Her *Frankenstein* retains the honor of inspiring the earliest examples of neuro–SF films.

Like the monster itself, which hybridizes salvaged body parts, we find a new breed of hybrid films in the 1960s: social problem films blended with science fiction/horror films.

To be clear, Hammer's *Frankenstein* films cannot be counted among "social problem" films, even if though they recollect social problems far away from Hammer horror film sets. "Social problem films" refer to a rather specific approach, one that mirrors the "social realism" of the art world, which Ben Shaun and others made famous in the 1930s, when a different set of social problems existed. Not all social problem films reference racism, and not all social problem films were produced in the sixties and seventies, during eras of social turmoil. The genre of "social problem films" dates back to the 1930s, when topics as diverse as juvenile delinquency to anti–Semitism to alcohol and drug problems inspired moviemakers to integrate a social conflict into the individual personalities and life experiences of the film's characters.

In the late 1950s and throughout the 1960s, the Civil Rights movement dominated American social consciousness and some of the most memorable social problem films revolve around racial issues. Race riots erupted as calamities struck civil rights workers and leaders. Because race-related problems came complete with visually interesting imagery, along with impassioned dialogue and dramatic action scenes, they were ideal for the silver screen. The light and dark contrasts between European American and African American skin was well suited to B & W (black & white) cinematography that remained popular (and affordable) in those years.

One event occurred after another in the 1960s, with each event seeming to outdo the last event. There was hardly a moment to rest. Actors like Sidney Poitier informed Americans of alternative ways to think about black people and their potential. Director and producer Stanley Kramer gained fame for his exposés of racism, in films such as *The Defiant Ones* (1958) and *Guess Who's Coming to Dinner* (1967). Sometimes Kramer found books or plays that revolved around anti–Semitism, and then "translated" them and Americanized them into anti-racism themes. Kramer found a more original race-based plot in *The Defiant Ones* (1958).

Kramer was no novice when it came to tackling sensitive subjects. He had already turned anti-humanist and anti–Semitic events into popular movie plots. Kramer's *Judgment at Nuremberg* (1961) presented true stories about the trials of high-ranking Nazis who orchestrated the Shoah (Holocaust). Spencer Tracy, Burt Lancaster, Richard Widmark, and Marlene Dietrich star in this Academy Award winning film that is set in 1948, when an American court in occupied Germany tried fourteen former Nazis (and convicted some but not all of them).

Also in 1961, the Eichmann trial was broadcast live on television, as the notorious Nazi Eichmann sat in a glass booth in a courtroom in Jerusalem. The trial was translated into many different languages, to make it understood by most of the world's citizens. Details upon details about the horrors of the Holocaust were researched and read aloud. News of the mass murders and the death camps and the medical experiments became public. Many survivors testified in person, and introduced a human element that was not present during the Nuremberg Trials.

Even though social problem films had existed for decades, something unique occurred among some social problem films of the 1960s and early 1970s, something that is especially relevant to our subject matter here, neuroscience fiction. In that era, the ethos of the social problem film spilled over and infiltrated some science fiction films. Moviemakers borrowed brain imagery to push the social commentary, which remains primary.

Some sixties-era films use brain exchanges as plot-driving devices, more than as scientific commentary. We encountered these themes decades earlier. Some clever filmmakers use sure-fire science fiction trappings to deliver heavier messages in more palatable packages that appeal to wider audiences. One need not be a political pundit or a social crusader to respond to the high drama or action-adventure subtext of those science fiction stories. Comic books used similar techniques to deliver heavy-handed messages through a light-hearted medium.

Some of those hybrid social problem/neuroscience fiction films were merely schlocky, while others of this ilk anticipate ethical dilemmas raised by organ transplants, which were becoming increasingly common in those years and inspiring more and more controversy.

We can debate whether films such as *Change of Mind* (1969), *Hauser's Memory* (1970), or any of the *Planet of the Apes* films should be counted among the NSF films. The sociological aspects of films such as *Change of Mind* (1969) or *Hauser's Memory* (1970) are more prominent than the neuroscience subtexts. The most recent reimagining of *Planet of the Apes* (2011) is clearly NSF, but categorization of the original *Planet of the Apes* is more complicated; its space travel theme exemplifies classic SF, but its links to NSF are more tenuous.

In *Change of Mind,* a white man's brain is transplanted into a black man's

Christopher Lee's monstrous claw-hand reaches into the foreground of this poster for Terence Fisher's *The Curse of Frankenstein* (1957), while a frightened Dr. Victor Frankenstein (Peter Cushing) hides behind his lab equipment in the lower left, and Elizabeth (Hazel Court), who is Victor's cousin and fiancée, screams in terror in the lower right.

body. The white man is a district attorney. His brain retains the knowledge and skills of his profession. As a white man, he had never experienced racism firsthand. Now he faces the recriminations of his wife and a sheriff who see him as a black man first and foremost. The social message bears similarities to non-fiction books such as *Black Like Me* (1961), written by Texas-born journalist, John Howard Griffin. In that book, the Caucasian author darkens his skin, and records his reactions and his rebuffs as he travels through the South, either by Greyhound bus or by hitchhiking. He compares his experiences as a black man to his life as a Southern white.

Griffin became a celebrity (although he and his family was reviled in their hometown in Texas, and were forced to move to Mexico). His narrative turned into a 1964 film version of *Black Like Me,* with James Whitmore starring as Griffin. *Black Like Me* is very different from *Change of Mind,* although both films convey the same essential message. However,

Black Like Me was very well known by the time the much more fantastic *Change of Mind* was released, adding an aura of credibility to this otherwise far-out SF story.

In *Change of Mind*, Duke Ellington's musical score plays in the background, to evoke painful memories from the past, when his black-identified music and other blues bands expressed the distress of his people and helped them weather the hurts. The musical score underscores the recent legal victories won by civil rights supporters, and so adds a note of optimism as well.

As of 1970, brain exchanges were no more feasible than they were when "monkey movies" or "simian cinema" was popular in the 1920s and 1930s. However, transplant surgery was pushing forward, making the subject of brain transplants sound slightly more scientific. In general, serious science fiction fans tend to be optimistic about the progress that lies ahead (but pessimistic about the social consequences of such scientific progress). They can point to the 1950s, and early sixties, when most people doubted that a man could land on the moon. Then Neil Armstrong appeared, and proved that the impossible can be possible, with the right science.

A year after *Change of Mind,* in 1970, a better-received movie appeared on American television and in Spanish movie theaters. *Hauser's Memory* was promoted as serious science fiction and received Hugo Award nominations in science fiction in 1971. The film is based on Curt Siodmak's 1968 novel, which was conceived as a sequel to Siodmak's *Donovan's Brain*. The book became *The Lady and the Monster* (1944) before it was remade under its original name). As mentioned earlier, Curt and director-brother Robert were born and educated in Germany, but left Germany well before the war began, but after the warning signs appeared real enough. The brothers retained recollections of Nazi threats and the Weimar era, which they turned into fictional horror stories and films with darkly expressionist *film noir* settings.[10]

This movie centers on a Nobel Prize–winning scientist who speaks with a German accent and retains the stiff formal posture of a German official. We learn that the scientist resettled in the U.S. after World War II. He identifies himself as "Aryan," (a term favored by Nazis), but hints that he fled Hitler's regime for reasons that were not related to "race." In other words, he is informing us that he is not Jewish, but that he had other reasons to escape Europe after the war. We wonder if he evaded prosecution for war crimes at Nuremberg. Did he escape sentencing at the Doctors' Trial, where Nazi-allied physicians, scientists and administrators faced charges for crimes against humanity? Perhaps he was like the monstrous Dr. Mengele, who fled to South America, and lived as a fugitive, moving from country to country—and making a pit stop in the U.S. Maybe he had the courage or convictions to oppose the Nazi practices. With a little bit of information about the fates that befell Nazi doctors post-war, our imaginations can run wild.

The action begins when an American government official approaches the scientist. The official turns out to be a CIA operative. He goads the scientist into performing an experiment that has never been attempted on humans. The scientist refuses initially, denouncing human experimentation as unethical (and thereby evoking memories of unethical Nazi medical experiments and the Nuremberg Code instituted after the war). After the operative offers a sufficient sum of money, his conscience is assuaged and he acquiesces. His research assistant, Dr. Hillel Mondoro will become the subject of the contested experiment. David McCallum of *The Man from U.N.C.L.E.* (1964–1968) plays Dr. Mondoro.

The experiment is crucial because a Nazi rocket scientist is dying. The one-time Nazi holds missile secrets in his head, which the U.S. government wants. The CIA concocted a way to acquire those secrets, lest they be lost to posterity. The Germanic doctor harvests the scientist's CSF (cerebral spinal fluid) and injects it into Hillel. We now learn a little more about Dr. Hillel Mondoro. We are told that Dr. Mondoro studied at the fictional Mt. Sinai Medical School in Israel. That little bit of back-story establishes Hillel's Jewish roots, as does his given name. His wife reminds him that she keeps kosher (and observes Jewish dietary laws).

Those who are familiar with Jewish tradition know that "Hillel" is the name of a great sage from Talmudic times. Hillel was an advocate for the underclasses and the impoverished, whereas his opponent, Shammai, expressed the interests of the moneyed and educated classes. Each endorsed opposing interpretations of the complex Biblical and post–Biblical Talmudic law.

At one point, Hillel's student asked him to summarize the teachings of the sacred books in a single sentence that can be recited while standing on one foot. According to Hillel, "do not do unto others as you would not want them to do unto you" is the essence of all Jewish teachings. "Do not do unto others as you would not want them to do unto you" sums up the moral of the movie. Dr. Mondoro's superior has forgotten—or never learned—this adage.

After the movie's Dr. Hillel Mondoro receives an injection of cerebrospinal fluid from the Nazi scientist, at the behest of the higher-ranking Aryan scientist, he knows secrets of the aerospace industry. However, he also experiences Nazi ideas that conflict with his Jewish identity and belief system. The film sends strong social messages about the horrors of the Holocaust. It also alludes to the CIA's collaboration with Operation Paperclip, the project that rescued and resettled Nazi scientists who seemed useful to U.S. intelligence and aerospace research. It also functions as an actual science fiction film because it suggests that memories can be transmitted by brain matter or fluid.

While no one claims that the CSF contains memories per se, we do know that the CSF harbors neurotransmitters that cannot be found in the bloodstream itself. We also know that serious experiments about memory and brain tissue were performed around that era. For instance, psychology classes in the 1960s routinely taught students about studies of rats that learned their way around mazes. Their brains that were ground up and fed to naïve rats, to see if learned information could be acquired by ingestion. Silly as it sounds, such studies were done in earnest, simply to show that brain matter does not automatically transmit memories.

The following year, a related motif appears in *The Incredible Two-Headed Transplant* (1971). Directed by Anthony Lanza, and starring Bruce Dern, this science fiction/horror film is more exploitative than science-minded or even social-minded. It is medsploitation to the max. Continuing this trend, the next year yielded *The Thing with Two Heads* (1972), starring Rosey Grier. This film falls under the rubric of Blaxploitation. The Blaxploitation genre became popular in the 1970s. Trailers to *Two-Headed* appear on a YouTube site called "Sleaze-o-Rama." That alone is telling, for "sleaze" aptly describes this financially successful film. *Two-Headed* stands apart from serious social problem films with similar plot-driving devices.

In the first film, a psychotic killer is captured by the police, and faces trial, but the court declares him NGRI (not guilty by reason of insanity) and sentences him to a forensic psychiatric facility. The killer escapes. He chances upon the house of a proverbial mad scientist who was barred from practicing at the local hospital. Instead, the doctor constructs a basement laboratory, where he transplants heads of living animals onto other animals. He has not yet had a human subject. His clueless wife wonders why she does not have her husband's full attention.

In the meantime, a caretaker tends to the doctor's house. The caretaker has a full-grown son who suffered a brain injury as a child and has the intellectual capacity of an 8-year-old. While trying to stave off the intruder, both the intruder (the psychotic killer) and the caretaker are shot. The doctor (Bruce Dern) transplants the murderer's head onto the overgrown body of the caretaker's intellectually challenged son. In doing so, he creates a latter-day Frankenstein-style monster that escapes and terrorizes the countryside, just as Frankenstein's original monster did. The trailer (posted on "Sleaze-o-Rama") tells us, "A massive monster menaces the world."

This offensive film was successful enough to spawn a very similar film a year later. *The Thing with Two Heads* (1972) stars the African American football player Rosey Grier along with Ray Milland. An unlikely choice, Ray Milland excelled at melodramatic roles, having played the murderous husband in Hitchcock's *Dial M for Murder* (1954). Milland acted in Fritz Lang's *Ministry of Fear* (1944), but is best remembered for his Academy Award-winning portrayal of an alcoholic writer in *The Lost Weekend* (1945). He also appeared in Roger Corman's horrific *The Premature Burial* (1962) and *The Man with the X-Ray Eyes* (1963).

In *The Thing with Two Heads* (1972), a white man's head is grafted onto a black man's body. Grier's body is big and burly, as would be expected of a pro-football player. Even though the movie reiterates racial themes that surfaced in social problem films from the 1960s, the film is comedic. Even more, it adds the twisted sensibility of the Blaxploitation genre, which attracted large audiences in the 70s and was especially popular with African Americans.

In theory, both of these medsploitation films fall under the rubric of "neuroscience fiction." However, they fail to stimulate thinking about the potential (or pitfalls) of neuroscience and instead make us think about H.L. Mencken's quip, "nobody ever went broke underestimating the taste of the American public." Still, even offensive comedies can convey painful truths.

Planet of the Apes (1968) is completely different in spirit from the two films mentioned above. Yes, *Planet of the Apes* is a social problem film, in the same way that the *Star Trek* television series was a social problem production, even though both are science fiction at the core, and are easily recognizable as such. Reading the social messages takes a bit more time and trouble, and may elude many fans who appreciate the films and TV shows at face value.

Both *Planet of the Apes* and *Star Trek* address racial concerns that were very relevant in the late 1960s, as the civil rights era rose to new highs and dropped to new lows after the assassination of Dr. King in 1968. Both *Planet of the Apes* and *Star Trek* employ metaphor alone, and confront contemporary concerns in veiled form. *Planet of the Apes* (in all of its versions) merits mention again because of its overwhelming impact at the time of release and because of its enduring appeal a half century later.

The neuroscience aspect of the recent *Rise of the Planet of the Apes* (2011) is obvious: it addresses Alzheimer's disease and dementia directly, and assures us that a cure for waning

SEVEN. *Science Fiction in Social Problem Films* 137

In a fantastic medical experiment, the detached head of a white bigot, played by Ray Milland of *The Lost Weekend* (1945), is joined to the body of a black "soul brother," played by former football star Rosey Grier, in the Blaxploitation spoof *The Thing with Two Heads* (1972).

intelligence awaits us in the future. However, the early *Planet of the Apes* offers more subtle allusions to neuroscience. Apart from the fact that one of the American astronauts is lobotomized and thereby rendered docile, the focus on human (or ape) language functions adds an intriguing sidebar to the overarching science fiction-space travel theme.

As we discussed in earlier chapters, Charlton Heston is unable to speak because he has been shot in the throat. The apes presume that humans as a species lack language abilities. This hypothesis brings us back to physical anthropology, which explains the distinction between *homo sapiens* and other primates. Their prehensile thumbs, and their ability to articulate meaningful language, are arguably the two traits that make humankind unique from great apes.

Admittedly, the conclusions of physical anthropologists of the mid–20th century were challenged by later findings, and especially by studies of ethnologists such as Jane Goodall. Without getting embroiled in the details of ape-related psychology, we can view *Planet of the Apes*' emphasis on language as a commentary on Freud's early studies *On Aphasia* (loss of language ability), which can occur in persons who have suffered strokes in specific sections of the brain. Recall that the 19th century regaled in different discoveries made by Paul Broca and Carl Wernicke. Broca identified parts of the brain that understand language, whereas Wernicke found other areas of the cerebral cortex that govern expression of language. Since those discoveries were made, neuroscientists have learned that cerebral control of language function is even more complicated than this simplified version. Aphasia, or loss of language

In the first *Planet of the Apes* (1968), stranded astronaut Taylor (Charlton Heston) kisses the chimpanzee psychologist and veterinarian Dr. Zira (Kim Hunter) goodbye, after she helps him escape from the ruling apes that treated him like a zoo specimen that they could study.

ability, is more subdivided. In addition, brain-based language function differs among left-handed persons.

Ironically, Sigmund Freud denounced the findings of his contemporaries and his predecessors, and refused to accept their findings about localized language abilities. From that point forward, Freud departed from his fellow neurologists, and ventured into unexplored terrain. When it comes to neuroscience, most agree that Freud got lost in the forest while trying to find trees. His concerns with "hysterical" loss of language abilities, because of psychological reasons alone, obscured the significance of brain-based language functions, which are so important to the identification of Alzheimer's disease and its differentiation from other types of dementias.

Planet of the Apes does not reference Freud, nor does it allude to Broca or Wernicke, or any other neuro-linguistic pioneers. What it does do, instead, is to remind us that preset, race-based or species-based assumptions about inherent language abilities (or about other intellectual functions) are apt to be incorrect. In that way, *Planet of the Apes* functions as a powerful "social problem" film that challenges racist theories about differences in inherent learning abilities.

The original 1968 film reflects the concerns of the 1960s. In *Planet of the Apes,* only apes can create civilization and produce culture and only apes can speak. Dr. Zira, the psychologist, says as much when she first encounters Charlton Heston's voiceless character, Taylor. Once Taylor's throat wounds heal and he can verbalize and use language once again, the psychologist expresses shock at his unexpected abilities.

It is noteworthy that vitriolic debates about inherent versus acquired learning abilities took place in the 1960s. School desegregation sparked these debates. Some of these debates were well argued and driven by data, while others presented views that were emotion-based only. Opponents of desegregation expressed concern about lower achievement levels in "urban" schools with more black students and the possibility that those students might influence white students who showed higher performance levels in previously segregated schools. Proponents of desegregation—who won out—presented compelling evidence to show the influence of social environment and educational opportunities on individual achievement tests, IQ scores, and school performance. Even teachers' preset but unspoken expectations about specific students send subtle messages to those students and sway their performance on tests.

Programs like Operation Headstart began in the mid-sixties, in attempt to counter disparities in learning, language, and mathematical abilities. Half a century later, concerns about educational performance and equal (or unequal) opportunities continue to make headlines. *Planet of the Apes* was bold enough to use moving images and engaging science fiction story lines, to counter the dry statistics and somber polemics that appeared in other contexts.[11]

In contrast to the films we discussed at the start of the chapter, *Planet of the Apes* does not resort to (currently) preposterous scientific experiments or to surgical brain-exchanges to make its point. Perhaps its simplicity and its eloquence have assured that this series endured.

On a final note, I should mention science fiction films with feminist subtexts as examples of social problem–NSF films. *The Stepford Wives* (1975) comes to mind immediately. Like *Planet of the Apes,* this film does not delve into "innate" biologically based behavior of women.

Yet it evokes Freud's much-maligned comment that "anatomy is destiny." Ironically, even though this film (and the book upon which it is based) evoked the ire of feminists, it actually implies that women, in their natural state, are *not* all that different from men, if indeed they are different at all.

The fact that the husbands in Stepford, Connecticut, found a need to replace their outspoken and high-achieving wives with re-engineered versions that are docile and domesticated tells us that the author and the filmmaker doubt that inherent biological, hormonal, or neuropsychiatric factors determine gender-based differences in intelligence and aspirations.

How to explain away the men's behavior, and their willingness to replace their wives with "replicants" who do their bidding, is another matter. Once again, the mere fact that the husband did not seek out a robotic replacement for his wife until the couple resettled in Stepford, and until he fell under the sway of other husbands at the men's club is significant. This suggests that the author and filmmaker believe that social influences and peer pressure are more important to men than their "innate" or instinctual behavior, which is mediated through biological pathways.

Either way, *The Stepford Wives* is a prime example of a social problem film that posits a science fiction solution—or calls our attention to social problems and forces us to rethink prevailing assumptions about neuroscience, neuropsychiatry or neuroendocrinology. When *The Stepford Wives* was remade, the timely feminist subtext was eliminated, and the plot moved closer to *RoboCop,* to deliver a more generic message about dehumanization and simulation. Some problems remain the same, and are inherent to the human condition, regardless of the social or political context.

Eight

Brain Drains, Brain Chips and Brain Machines

Certain tropes recur again and again in science fiction film. Because film is a visual medium, themes that can be represented visually—and, hopefully, vividly—take priority over the more abstract, philosophical debates that proliferate on the pages of SF literature.

As Per Schelde points out in *Androids, Humanoids and other Science Fiction Monsters*,[1] SF film and SF literature are not the same, even when the book inspires the film, and perhaps especially when the book precedes the film. Differences are visibly apparent when written works are adapted for the screen. SF films are more concerned with the effects of science, rather than the "what if's" that SF literature addresses. Special effects—and spectacular special effects, at that—can make or break a SF film. Cinema spectators are not so willing to ponder between the sprockets. They opt for more immediate gratification. They can ponder the film after the fact.

I am loath to quote Freud as an irrefutable authority (because so many Freudians are willing to accept his every word at face value), but in this instance I can think of no better informant than Freud, who opined on the subject of dreams and films. Freud adamantly opposed films, and saw only two films in his lifetime. He was even more opposed to the representation of psychoanalysis on the silver screen, claiming that only ideas that are amenable to visual representation will find their way into film, while abstract theories will be lost in translation.[2] We can make the same arguments about turning philosophically oriented SF literature into SF film. Here, too, films adapted from books must emphasize visuals in order to attract spectators. Adding a fast-paced interactive plot that turns the contemplative text into an action-adventure increases the odds of a film adaptation's appeal to post-*Star Wars* audiences.

As a result, many SF films have more in common with action-adventure films or horror films than with their literary predecessors. A single SF film often falls into two or three genres simultaneously and becomes known as a "hybrid" that grafts one genre onto the other, to produce a new product.[3] Many SF tropes are predictable, and include favorite themes, just as Westerns or romances do. Some SF tropes seem eerily ahead of their times and it is just a matter of time before a forward-thinking scientist taps into these fictional themes. Not infrequently, in my observations, research scientists are fans of SF literature and film. Many fan their imaginations with these fantasies and then return to the laboratory with fresh, fiction-inspired ideas.

Once a real woman who was replaced by a robot engineered by a former Disney imagineer, Joanna Eberhart (Katharine Ross) lies on the ground, shattered and broken, in a poster for *The Stepford Wives* (1975), based on a novel by Ira Levin, author of *Rosemary's Baby* (1967).

Occasionally, we find themes that are similar to SF in psychiatric literature from bygone eras. The latter is certainly the case with brain drains, brain chips, brain machines, and various computer-controlled devices. This apparatus was reported in clinical case histories from psychoanalytic journals, long before George Bush anointed the 1990s as the Decade of the Brain.

Before we examine specific motifs of brain drains, brain chips, brain machines, and compare those tropes to recent trends in neuroscience and biological psychiatry, let us revisit the distant past and consider a highly influential paper on "influencing machines." Written by psychoanalyst Viktor Tausk, the paper was published in German in 1919. Tausk suicided that same year. Also in 1919, Robert Weine completed his German Expressionist masterpiece, *The Cabinet of Dr. Caligari* (1919). In America in 1919, Victor Fleming, who became better known for *Wizard of Oz* (1939), directed the surrealist short about a mad scientist, *When Clouds Roll By*. If we contextualize Tausk's paper chronologically, and think about his study in terms of landmark films from 1919, we can better appreciate the differences between that era and our own, and can marvel even more about the relevance of Tausk's study to contemporary times.

Tausk's paper is quoted to this day, and has never become forgotten or outdated. Dr. Tausk was troubled, but there is no evidence suggesting that he was psychotic. Tausk lived and practiced in Europe, but he did not live very long. He was a member of Freud's early circle and was in a personal psychoanalysis with Helene Deutsch, M.D. Early analysts admired Deutsch's writings on female masochism—but second wave feminists reviled her for those same theories.

Biographers of the early psychoanalytic movement attribute Tausk's untimely death to the termination of his analysis with Deutsch, which occurred in response to Freud's recommendation. Other biographers claim that additional stresses and psychological frailties contributed to his demise, all of which suggest an even greater need for better treatment.[4]

In spite of the tragedy of his suicide, Tausk lives on through his landmark study of "the influencing machine," first published in the journal *Internationale Zeitschrift für Psychoanalyse*, 1919, and translated from German by Dorian Feigenbaum and republished in English in the *Psychoanalytic Quarterly*, 1933.[5] The English version appeared in the American journal in the same year that Hitler took command in Germany, and when the Nazis burned Freud's books (along with other "degenerate" art, literature and philosophy). The *Journal of Psychotherapy Practice and Research* republished the article in the spring volume of 1992.[6]

Tausk correctly observed that some paranoid men share the very same delusion about "influencing machines," even though they have nothing else in common with one another and never communicated with like-minded men who parrot these ideas. They claim that an "influencing machine" penetrates their brains, occasionally induces visions, controls their thoughts and, more often than not, persecutes them and perhaps violates them sexually. Themes of passivity and penetration commonly occur in conjunction with ideas about "influencing machines." This influencing machine may drain their brains or implant alien ideas. Tausk stated that they were "to the best of my knowledge, almost exclusively of the male sex" while the perpetrators (or persecutors) were "predominantly physicians by whom the patient has been treated." These people go on to be diagnosed with schizophrenia. At the risk of sounding solipsistic, I should point out that Schneider classified these perceptions as "first rank" symptoms of schizophrenia and so they are called "Schneiderian first rank symptoms."

Some visions induced by the influencing machine are similar to magic lantern shows, which predated both cinema and television. Once television came into being, even the untrained observer could see that these delusions are very similar to TV shows. In fact, some people with schizophrenia see their names emblazoned on TV screens or believe that their thoughts are broadcast aloud by the box. A few theorists blamed TV for causing these beliefs, even though such ideas were described and drawn in detail in the late 19th century by James Tilly Matthews.

David Cronenberg's *Videodrome* (1983) captures these same sentiments. Max Renn (James Woods) presides over a television station that is known for its outlandish and sensationalistic programming. He views a videotape of Professor O'Blivion, who functions as a surrogate for Marshall McLuhan, the father of media studies and author of the quip, "the medium is the message" (1964). This videotape states that the *Videodrome* "is a socio-political battleground in which a war is being fought for control of the minds of the people of North America".

Soon afterwards, Max develops a delusion that an orifice has opened in his abdomen. He hallucinates this orifice, and sees it before his very eyes. This orifice functions like a VCR and accepts inserted videotapes that then disappear within Max's body. Professor O'Blivion's daughter explains that the *Videodrome* video transmits a malicious broadcast signal that causes malignant brain tumors. Max insists that the hallucinations cause the tumor, and that the tumor did not induce the hallucination (which is commonly the case, depending upon the tumor site).

Long before David Cronenberg existed, there was James Tilly Matthews. Art historians, as well as historians of psychiatry, are familiar with the life, times, treatment and art of James Tilly Matthews.[7] Matthews believed that he was controlled "body and mind" by an apparatus that he called the "Air Loom." Matthews left extensive literary and artistic documentation of his belief system. To Tausk, Matthews' Air Loom was a variation on "influencing machines."[8]

Matthews was a tea merchant and political activist and was not professionally trained as an artist. Yet he proved himself to be a skilled and prolific writer and illustrator, but not until he was confined to the Bethlem Royal Hospital (better known as Bedlam) for shouting "treason" in the British House of Commons in 1797. He was obsessed with this "air loom" (and other unusual ideas). His exacting renditions of his "air loom" are found in his book length manuscript entitled, *Illustrations of Madness: Exhibiting a Singular Case of Insanity, And a No Less Remarkable Difference in Medical Opinions: Developing the Nature of An Assailment, And the Manner of Working Events; with a Description of Tortures Experienced by Bomb-Bursting, Lobster-Cracking and Lengthening the Brain. Embellished with a Curious Plate.*[9]

Over the years, Matthews inspired the interest of "outsider art" curators. The Prinzhorn Museum, which collects outsider art, celebrated his works in a publication. Outsider art is primarily produced by persons with psychosis, who are presumably free of the influence of the outside world because they are confined to asylums or are oblivious to reality.[10] Bona fide outsider artists react to their internal perceptions alone, without regard for acquired artistic tastes and conventions. Matthews' concern with "influencing machines" concerns us here because this translates into a common science fiction motif: brain drains and brain chips.

As of the year 2014, behavioral neuropsychiatry boasts a wide range of mechanical treatment techniques, some of which are still experimental but all of which would fall under Tausk's rubric of "influencing machines." For lack of a better word, authors writing for the American Psychiatric Association publishing company categorize these treatments as "neuromodulation."[11] They admit that no better term is available. These neuromodulators (which would qualify as "influencing machines") come in several varieties, and include ECT (electroconvulsive therapy), which was "grandfathered" in for FDA approval, rTMS (repetitive transcranial magnetic stimulation), and VNS (vagus nerve stimulation). DBS (deep brain stimulation) won approval for Parkinson's disease. It is under investigation for the treatment of depression. MST (magnetic seizure therapy) is still experimental but TENS (transcutaneous electrical nerve stimulation) has official approval for pain and has been in use for decades.

The list of latter-day "influencing machines" (aka neuromodulators) goes on. Medical machinery includes tDCS (transcranial direct current stimulation); EPI-fMRI (echoplanar imaging–functional magnetic resonance imaging); FEAT (focal electrical alternating current therapy), which is also known as tACS (transcranial alternating current stimulation), and FEAST (focal electrically-administered current seizure therapy). All of the above are experimental treatments for depression or substance use that are undergoing further testing. Considering how rapidly neuroscience is progressing, it is reasonable to expect more and more additions to this alphabet soup-style catalogue. This already lengthy list focuses on behavioral neuropsychiatry exclusively. Were we to include experimental devices that influence neuromuscular function, to help people with paralysis or Parkinson's disease, the list would be much longer. Devices for centrally mediated (brain-based) sensory deficits are another matter altogether. Cochlear implants that send signals directly to the auditory nerve were performed as early as 1969.

To find references to "influencing machines" in film and literature, we can turn the clock back to the World War II era, when short serials accompanied longer feature length films. In 1943 *Batman* serials, we encounter sinister psychiatrists and neuroscientists who use brain drain machines on their victims. In some shorts, the "Japanazi" Dr. Daka orders his henchmen to attach these devices to Batman, who is dressed in full costume but unable to rise to the occasion. He appears all the more pathetic as he slumps in the bell jar that tops the apparatus. Scientists or industrialists also meet this same fate. Dr. Daka is played by a Caucasian actor of Irish descent (J. Carrol Naish). The bell jar reminds some of us of the novel by Sylvia Plath, who committed suicide. It also recollects jars that confine the miniature king and queen in *Bride of Frankenstein*.

We know that Dr. Daka represents Asians because he has eyelid prostheses to make him appear "Oriental." He speaks in stilted and stylized English, to suggest that he is a native Japanese speaker, and, hence, an enemy of the state. Dr. Daka's stylized disguise is Hollywood-shorthand for "Asian." This characterization was once so prevalent but is now so politically incorrect. Dr. Daka looks remarkably similar to TV's better-known Charlie Chan, and for good reason: J. Carrol Naish went on to play Charlie Chan between 1957 and 1958.

Comic book readers already know that "Japanazis" are a cross between the "Japs" who bombed Pearl Harbor and the Nazis, who allied with the Japanese as the Axis Powers. In 1943, the extent of the Nazi-perpetrated Holocaust was not yet known. During the war years, it was permissible to parody Japanazis, as they menaced American troops in the South Pacific.

Details about Japanese war crimes against neighboring Asian people had not come to light yet. Those events continue to shock to this day. The human experimentation conducted in "Unit 731," based in Northeastern China/Manchuria, rivaled the crimes of the Nazi Dr. Mengele. The Japanese Imperial Army's research into biological and chemical warfare began during the Second Sino-Japanese War (1937–1945) and continued through World War II.

One wonders if the message behind *The Manchurian Candidate* resonates even more with some spectators because its title alludes to this notorious region of China.

Dr. Daka may be a psychiatrist or a neuroscientist or both—that is unclear, for he never reveals his credentials during the 15–20 minute short serials, where he appears. It is clear that Dr. Daka represents more than just "Japanazis" from the Second World War. He is the "Yellow Menace" that pre-dated World War II and the Japanese bombing of Pearl Harbor. He is a direct descendent of Ming the Merciless, the villain from Flash Gordon comic strips and serials of the 1930s. Flash Gordon became a TV serial a decade later and influenced the more illustrious *Star Wars* franchise that began in the 1970s. Dr. Daka anticipates the more malevolent Dr. No (1962) from the first James Bond film, who was played by the equally un–Asian actor, Joseph Wiseman. He continues in the tradition of Dr. Fu Manchu, the fictional Asian scientist from thirties-era films, who, incidentally, was played by yet another non–Asian but high profile actor, Boris Karloff. Dr. Fu Manchu inspired a long line of Yellow Peril characters, including Dr. Yen-Lo of *The Manchurian Candidate* (1962), whom we discuss later in this chapter.

In the interim, let me point out that Dr. Daka's brain drain machine looks remarkably similar to the brain machine used on Maria in *Metropolis,* give or take a few tubes, wires, and knobs. It resembles contemporary TCMS (trans-cutaneous magnetic stimulation) apparatus that is approved to treat depression and that is currently undergoing testing for the treatment of pain and various substance use disorders. The perforated metal hat that transmits magnetism looks like a repurposed kitchen colander, ordinarily used to drain pasta. It brings Roger Corman to mind.

Low budget, high-kitsch horror/SF director Roger Corman is renowned for clever and economical repurposing of kitchen appliances. Corman turned boiling steam kettles into fire-breathing dragons, by pointing the camera close and zooming in on the vapors and nozzle holes. It is unclear if medical device makers followed Corman's lead from the 1950s or if these 1940s-era filmmakers inspired Corman, or if everyone involved remembered Maria's apparatus in *Metropolis,* before turning to the drawing board. The electrical fireworks are the work of Kenneth Strickfaden, who provided similar pyrotechnics for *Frankenstein* (1931).

Batman comics make extensive use of these brain drain machines, and include a wide variety of characters who specialize in draining brains, inserting thoughts, or forcing characters to "broadcast their thoughts," in one way or another. Among the most prominent of this cadre is a neuroscientist named The Mad Hatter. Mad Hatter owns a brain drain machine that influences memory and creates false memories. A many-faceted man, Mad Hatter has pop-up eyes that he hides under his signature *Alice-in-Wonderland*-style top hat. Those artificial eyes hypnotize bystanders. Mad Hatter has not made his way to films yet.

A psychiatrist, Dr. Hugo Strange, also from the *Batman* universe, is skilled at deploying brain drain machines to decipher Batman's alternate identity as Bruce Wayne. Skulldugger, on the other hand, possesses a pleasure-producing machine that deprives people of their motivation to change their situations or their behavior. By blocking brain-based rewards for accomplishment, this machine dampens Batman's desire to find and punish criminals and he remains complacent. We will encounter the same principle a few pages later, when we discuss *The Happiness Cage* (1972). The reverse principle is used to treat persons with alcohol or opioid use problems. A medication known as naltrexone blocks pleasure-producing endor-

EIGHT. Brain Drains, Brain Chips and Brain Machines 147

phins that are released after alcohol or opioid use. These substances lose their reinforcing properties, so persons undergoing such treatment have lesser and lesser desires to use their substances.

Batman comics began in 1939, and continue to the present, having branched out to cartoons, TV, films, video games, lunchboxes, costumes and more. We could write an entire chapter on brain drains in *Batman* but we must confine ourselves to SF films in this chapter.

Decades passed between the time that Dr. Daka appears in *Batman* serials and the release of *Cyborg 2087* (1966). *Cyborg 2087* is a *1984*-themed film. It anticipates the ethos of the later sixties, with its condemnation of thought control and fear of governmental control. Ironically, *Cyborg's* art direction is unequivocally early sixties. Clean-cut and clean-shaven characters show no trace of the British Invasion. Their clothes, their dance choices, even their mannerisms, are more Beach Boys than Beatles. The NSF aspect is the icing on the cake—but the recipe for the cake includes several well-known and often-used ingredients for generic SF, including space capsules, time travel and humanoid robots.

In *Cyborg 2087* (1966), a scientist develops a machine to control human minds. His

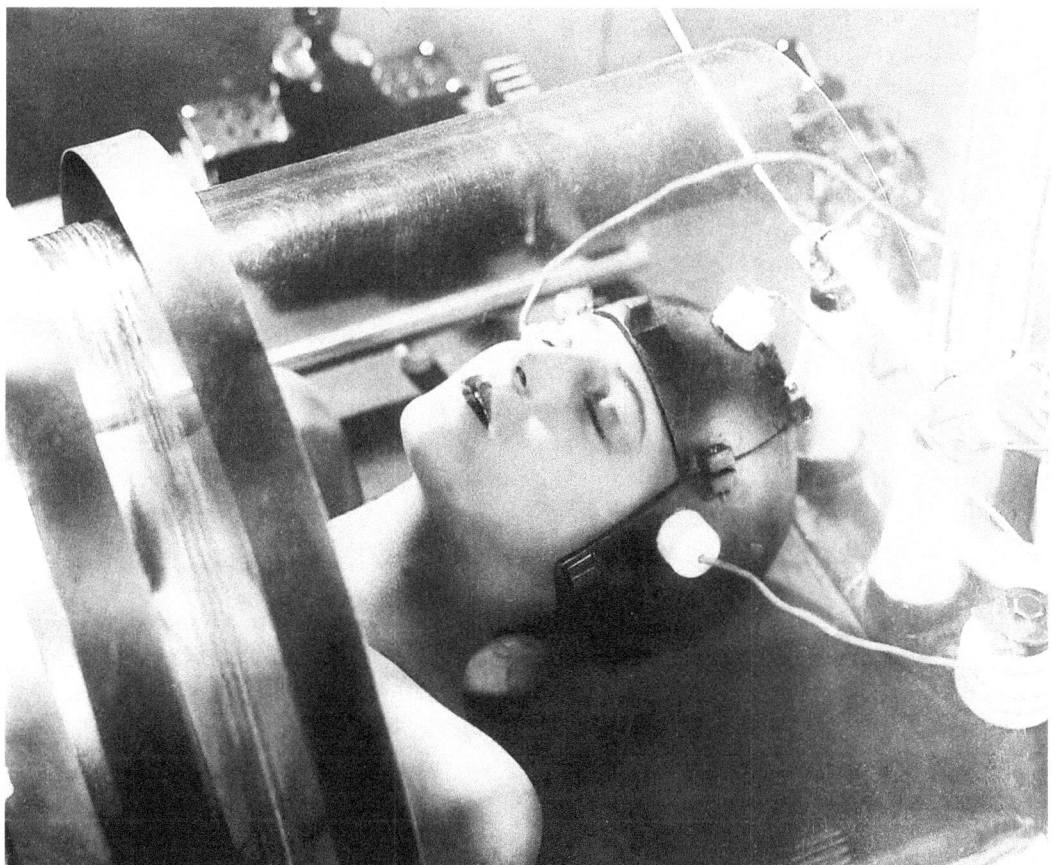

Brigitte Helm plays the "good Maria" in *Metropolis* (1927) but the evil sorcerer-like scientist Rotwang hooks her up to tubes, to transfer her "essence" to an evil robotic replica of Maria.

experiments are a success. By 2075, surgical implants control humans and ensure that citizens serve a totalitarian state. Most of the action occurs in the present, when a cyborg named Garth travels back in time. Garth was enlisted by a cadre of "free thinkers" who hope to free themselves of pervasive government thought control. His cronies have determined that tampering with the past, via time travel in a space capsule, can change the trajectory of history. This band of outliers oppose thought suppression and promote open ideas. This trope reminds us of the book people in François Truffaut's *Fahrenheit 451* (1966), which appears in film form in the same year as *Cyborg 2087*. *Fahrenheit 451* the film is based on a much-celebrated novel by science fiction giant, Ray Bradbury. Bradbury wrote in 1953, at the height of the McCarthy inquests, and wove current political concerns into his text.

Having traveled back in time, Garth meets Professor Sigmund Marx, who is working on a potentially world-changing discovery in "radio-telepathy." Marx's instrument inserts thought-control implants. The provocatively named professor signifies more than simple laboratory experiments; by referencing both Freud and Marx, the film implies that the professor's discovery can rival the impact of the most prominent thought leaders of modern times: Sigmund Freud and Karl Marx. It hints at the professor's potential influence on opposite poles of psychology and sociology, which Freud and Marx personify, respectively. Freud represents psychological determinism and individuation, whereas Marx attributes all personal ills to social structure and economic influences that lie outside of the individual.

Garth has high hopes. He wants to stop the professor from revealing his landmark discovery. He strives to undo the tyrannical and totalitarian thought control that follows the use of Dr. Marx's machinery. Garth describes his world as one filled with "torture and terror." The action intensifies when Garth realizes that he is not alone in the present day. Government agents, also cyborgs, are hot on his heels, having traveled back in time. They plan to subdue Garth.

Realizing that two "Tracers" are pursuing him and planning to prevent completion of his mission, Garth enters Dr. Marx's workspace and approaches Dr. Marx's attractive assistant, Dr. Sharon Mason. Dr. Mason is a platinum blonde, her hair styled in the manner of Marilyn Monroe, but she wears a white lab coat to signify her professional standing as a scientist. Dr. Mason is one of many female laboratory scientists in pre-feminist 1950s and early 60s SF film.

Garth introduces himself as "Dr. Garth." He towers over everyone, looking like a leaner version of Boris Karloff's Frankenstein monster. When Dr. Mason expresses doubt about Garth's claims, he places a metal band around her head, to put her into a trance. This band communicates information about Garth's mission and the role of Dr. Marx's machine. After undergoing this procedure, Dr. Mason understands Garth's plight and agrees that Garth's homing device is putting him in harm's way, because it allows the Tracers to track him.

Thus convinced, Dr. Mason approaches her friend, a handsome biologist who was recently widowed and a reasonable romantic interest for Dr. Mason. He is not a physician and makes a point of reminding her that he lacks an M.D. She urges him to operate on Garth to extract his homing device, in spite of his missing medical credentials. The friend is skeptical, and states that the so-called cyborg, with his claims of thought control and time travel, is simply schizophrenic. Eventually, he agrees to operate. Following Garth's instructions, he severs the fibers in his implant. With the fibers cut, the Tracers can no longer track Garth's whereabouts.

After overcoming the Tracers, Garth convinces Professor Marx to delay revealing his discovery and thereby prevent the totalitarian take-over. As a result, Garth's existence in the future is eradicated. The people who aided him in the present will not remember his presence. With its romantic subtexts, and its futuristic concerns, *Cyborg 2087* was ideal drive-in fare.

Cyborg 2087 sows the seeds of the still-unnamed and yet-to-be-discovered cyberpunk. This emerging genre gains firmer footing two years later, when HAL 9000 appears in *2001: A Space Odyssey* (1968). HAL is a highly intelligent but malicious computer that is capable of speech, speech recognition, language processing, lip reading and reasoning. He can recognize faces and interpret and reproduce emotional behavior. He also appreciates art and plays chess.

Time travel is just one aspect of *Cyborg 2087*. A closely related theme about time travel appeared a few years earlier, in a television adaptation of a Harlan Ellison story. Aired on October 17, 1964, *The Outer Limits* episode is entitled, "Demon with a Glass Hand." This episode gained greater fame after lawsuits accused producers of *The Terminator* (1984) of plagiarizing the plot from *The Outer Limits*. *The Terminator* became a cult classic. *The Outer Limits* episode that started it all does not enjoy such status, except among loyal *The Outer Limits* fans.

As *The Terminator* proved, the trope about changing the future by returning to the past holds appeal. Over time, we encounter time-travelers portrayed by action-adventure legends, such as Sylvester Stallone, Arnold Schwarzenegger, and Bruce Willis. Films such as *Timecop* (1994), *12 Monkeys* (1995), *Star Trek: First Contact* (1996), *Looper* (2012) and *Men in Black 3* (2012) employ related time travel to "change the past for the sake of the future" themes.

A few years after *Cyborg 2087*, another landmark brain drain/brain chip film appears, once which we can just as easily read as an anti-war movie or an anti–Nazi movie as a neuroscience fiction film. To be fair, the film is based on a popular play, *The Happiness Cage*, but the playwright Dennis Reardon never intended his story to function as anything other than a morality tale that warns against tampering with the human brain. The off–Broadway play was a hit, but the film failed. Critics felt that the play did not translate well onto the big screen.[12]

The Happiness Cage goes by a few different names. Sometimes, it is billed as *The Mind Snatchers* or *The Demon Within*. The 1972 film serves several functions. Among other things, it introduces film audiences to an adult Christopher Walken. A native of the borough of Queens of New York City, Walken began acting on television, and had small film roles as an adolescent before starring in *The Mind Snatchers*. From here on in, Walken will carve out a career playing slightly psychotic, off-kilter characters. He went on to win an Oscar for his portrayal of a drug-addled, Russian-roulette playing vet in Michael Cimino's epic, *The Deer Hunter* (1978).

In *The Mind Snatchers,* Christopher Walken stars as a soldier who becomes an unwitting participant in a military medical experiment. An electronic wire is implanted into his brain to temper his aggressive, anti-authority impulses. He spends screen time wrapped in mummy-like gauze bandages that frame his skull and his jaw. His implant interferes with the brain's natural reward center and induces a constant state of pleasure. This neuroanatomical implant

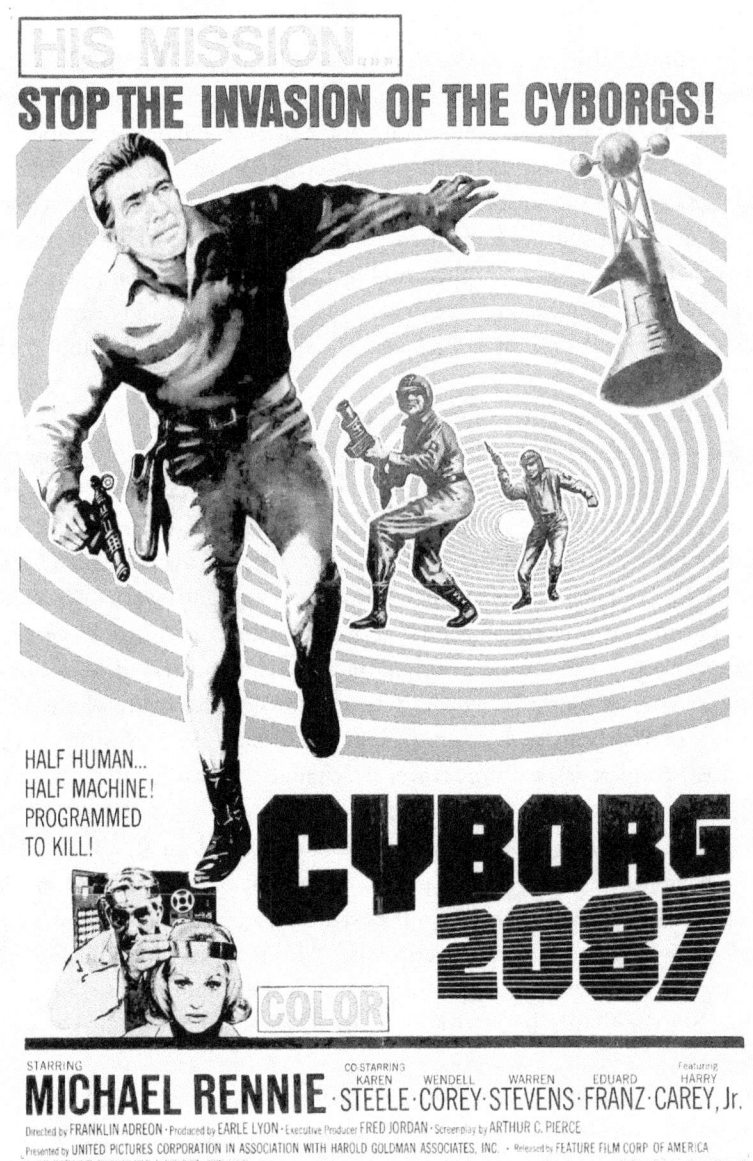

Cyborg 2087 (1966) poster shows Garth A7 (Michael Rennie) fleeing a "half-human, half-machine" tracer-cyborg who traveled back in time from a futuristic society where surgical implants control humans and force them to serve a totalitarian state. The spiraling background recollects artwork from Hitchcock's *Vertigo* (1958).

robs him of the motivation to seek out other pleasures. These neurochemicals change Private Reese (Walken) and other soldiers into obedient military men that follow orders, willingly and happily.

The kicker: the action occurs in a VA hospital in Frankfort, Germany. The doctor-in-charge is German, even though the army is American, the military base is American, and the soldiers are American. This setting reminds us of the crossovers between Nazi era medical experiments and unethical experimentation in general. The Tuskegee experiments performed on Southern black men with untreated neurosyphilis came to public attention in the same year that the film premiered, a fact that could have been fodder for film reviews. Parallels between Nazi Germany and Vietnam-era America are prominent leitmotifs, especially since radicals and Yippees deliberately misspelled "America" as "AmeriKa." They compared alleged American "fascism" and the arrest of the Chicago Seven anti-war activists to the German Reich. The trial took place in 1970, but the events leading to the arrest dated to non-peaceful protests in 1968.

In the early seventies, experimentation with "consciousness expanding" chemicals abounded in America. In 1970, new laws pertaining to prescriptions meds were enacted, and the concept of "controlled meds" was born de novo.[13] This prescription medication-related law was the first to go into effect since the Harrison Narcotics Act of 1914. By 1970, the Summer of Love of 1967 had turned into autumn. As a corollary, concerns about controlling consciousness, rather than expanding consciousness, came on the radar. Control would come through shifting social norms, new governmental policies, or biological brain chips featured in science fiction films.

In using this stereotyped SF trope, *The Mind Snatchers* makes a political statement as much as a neuroscience statement. True, the details about a brain implant that stimulates the brain's pleasure centers parallels recent research into endorphins, the natural opiates released by the brain and possibly other body parts. However, references to brain implants recur time and time again, regardless of research trends. To say it again, Dr. Tausk recognized this in 1919.

The political context of *The Mind Snatchers* movie looms large, perhaps so large that they were stultifying and did not merit extra attention by the press, which largely panned the film. Still, we cannot ignore the fact that the film appeared against the backdrop of even more anti-war activism, student protests, National Guard shootings, and revelations about military atrocities in Asia. The Mai Lai massacre trial took place in 1968. Memories of horrific deaths and tortures, inflicted by American soldiers on Vietnamese villagers, with women and infants, were fresh in the minds of spectators. Instantaneous associations with Nazi doctors add more to the mix. The Kent State shootings that occurred in 1970, on an otherwise ordinary Ohio college campus, also horrified the nation. At Kent State, frightened National Guardsmen fired on student protestors, killing several and crippling others. These associations tapped into current events, but stray far from the playwright's intent to condemn governmental mind control, but so be it.

The Mind Snatchers reflects the concerns of the counterculture—not the sex, drugs, and rock & roll subset of the counterculture, not the "better living through chemistry" counterculture—but the more cerebral anti-war, anti-authoritarian, anti-military-industrial complex wing. The motif of *The Mind Snatchers* is simpatico with views expressed by anti-psychiatry activists.

After his surgery, Christopher Walken sports a masked, expressionless, Parkinson's-like face, framed by helmet-like bandages. Walken's Private Reese appears to have been pre-treated with high doses of haloperidol (a strong anti-psychotic medication that produces a syndrome known as "pseudo-parkinsonism"). Walken speaks in his signature monotone.

The Mind Snatchers was released in the same year as Michael Crichton's celebrated book, *The Terminal Man* (1972). Because Crichton's novel was so popular, it was made into a film soon after, in 1974. In Crichton's world, an epileptic man gets a brain implant for therapeutic purposes (and not for political purposes, as in *The Happiness* Cage). The implant backfires. It produces "sham rage," like the "sham rage" displayed by cats whose almond-shaped amygdalas are severed inside their brains. George Segal's seizures become more and more frequent and turn into a sort of "status epilepticus," putting him in a constant state of confusion.

Today, implanted pacemakers for persons with otherwise uncontrollable epilepsy are standard medical practice. In 1972, in Crichton's universe, and in the film that followed the book, the decision to pursue this innovative neurosurgical approach was a difficult one. Different specialists deliberate and share their opinions. The neurosurgeon encourages the experimental surgery with a brain pacemaker, while the more conservative psychiatrist argues against it, fearing that her patient will lapse into psychosis when a mechanical implant confirms his fears of being controlled by a computer. A computer programmer by profession, Segal's character, Harry Benson, already ruminated about computers' abilities to overpower humans. (Harry Benson echoes Tausk's observations about "influencing machines" and psychosis.) The surgeon's arguments are more convincing to the patient, and eclipse the psychiatrist's concerns.

Unfortunately, in the end, the trusted psychiatrist loses her life after her patient enters an uncontrollable rage and kills her. First, he murders his beloved fiancée, without intent or volition.

Michael Crichton's visions about brain implants anticipate contemporary treatments for Parkinson's disease, which affects the brain's basal ganglia and depletes dopamine, a neurotransmitter that is essential to movement. Dopamine also mediates the experience of pleasure. It instills motivation and improves focus. Studies about the use of this same brain implant to relieve depression are underway and appear promising. Crichton's dystopian view of neurosurgery, as expressed in his book about *The Terminal Man*, did not discourage researchers from pursuing these approaches. Rather, his visions may have seeded their research, considering how many medical students read his books and admired the way this (non-practicing) M.D. incorporated fact-based medical knowledge into his futuristic fiction.

Spanish-born Yale researcher, Jose Delgado, M.D., Ph.D. (1915–2011) took an opposite approach in 1963. Delgado implanted electrodes in a bull's brain, stood in its path as the bull charged him. Using a remote controlled transmitter that communicated with the implant, he suddenly turned off the "rage center" and essentially controlled the bull's innate instincts. Delgado worked in this demarcated area of brain research before this public performance. Over time, he moved his research away from primates, and wired up 25 people to control their aggression. These human subjects were chronic psychiatric patients that did not respond to less invasive treatments. Delgado was committed to the concept of "mind control." It is possible that his successes in Yale's physiology lab influenced the Harvard-educated Crichton years later. It is even more possible that his high profile escapades added credibility to Crichton's fiction.

Still in the seventies, we find the influential film, *One Flew Over the Cuckoo's Nest* (1975), based on Ken Kesey's best-selling novel from 1962. *Cuckoo's Nest* is not a science fiction film

EIGHT. *Brain Drains, Brain Chips and Brain Machines* 153

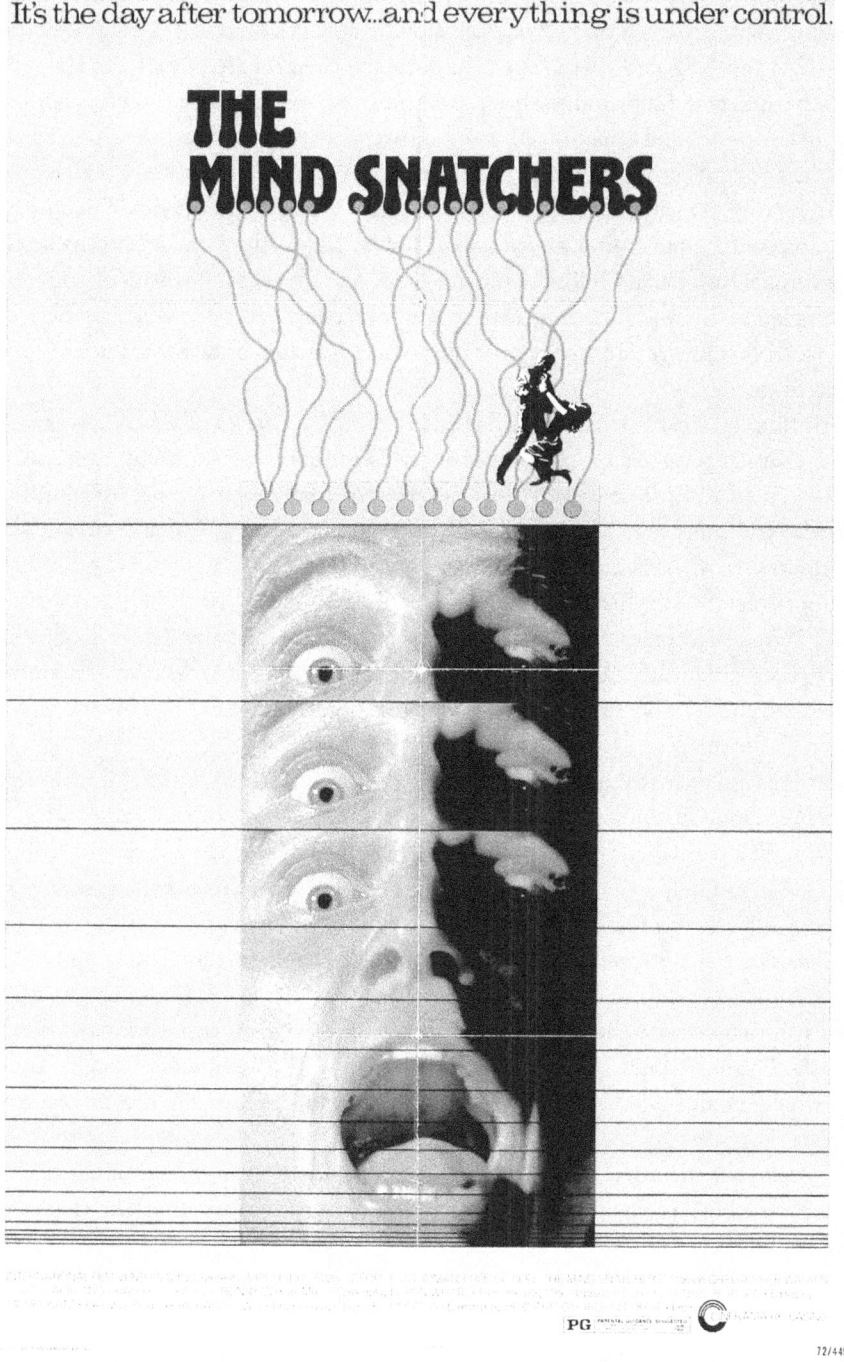

In this poster for 1972's *The Mind Snatchers* (aka *The Happiness Cage*, aka *The Demon Within*), the face of Private Reese (Christopher Walken) trails, as if seen via LSD, while thin threads attach to the top, to signify the electronic wires implanted in his brain to temper aggressive outbursts.

by any stretch. Rather, it is a drama, inspired by a blend of real life experiences and one man's active imagination. Like many SF works, this dystopian portrayal of psychiatric wards, ECT, and head nurses conveys a pervasively pessimistic *weltanschauung*. The parallels between *Cuckoo's Nest* and NSF end there. The plot points of the film are not true to the novel, but it is easy to conflate the film and the novel because the film's spectacular success ignited more interest in the novel, and encouraged many moviegoers to return to the source material.

In the book, the chief character and the narrator is Chief Bromden, a Native American who suffers from delusions. He experiences negative forces of the world, which he refers to as the "Combine." This Combine parallels Tilley's "loom" from the 19th century. It is yet another variation of Tausk's "influencing machine" and a typical symptom of schizophrenia. Bromden claims that the Combine acts to suppress people like McMurphy (played in the film by Jack Nicholson). He also claims that Nurse Ratched and the orderlies are actually robots in disguise.

This film has been incredibly influential to society's views of psychiatry. As a result, any of its characters carries special significance. The film revolves around McMurphy (Jack Nicholson), a small time con man who was arrested for statutory rape. McMurphy feigns psychiatric symptoms so he can avoid work and avoid a presumably harsh prison ward. On the psychiatric ward, McMurphy locks horns with Head Nurse Ratched (Louise Fletcher). She cannot tolerate McMurphy's disrespect and arranges for his ECT (electroconvulsive therapy). When that treatment fails to dampen his antics, he is referred for a lobotomy, and returns to the ward, nearly catatonic. *Cuckoo's Nest* set the stage for distrust of organized and in-patient psychiatry and spearheaded a movement to outlaw ECT. This movement succeeded in California.

Fast-forward twenty years. We continue with *Johnny Mnemonic* (1995), which is loosely based on William Gibson's much better received literary work of that same name. Gibson earned himself a permanent place in SF history when he coined the concept of "cyberspace" in 1981. He first alluded to cyberspace during readings. The short story appeared in print in *Omni* in 1982. It was republished in Gibson's *Burning Chrome* collection in 1986.

Gibson's novel, *Neuromancer* (1984), popularized the term much more and marked the official start of an enduring literary genre known as "cyberpunk." *Neuromancer* is Gibson's first full-length novel and the first winner of the science-fiction "triple crown"—the Nebula Award, the Philip K. Dick Award, and the Hugo Award. *Neuromancer* begins the *Sprawl* trilogy, which includes characters like Molly Millions, who debuted in the *Johnny Mnemonic* short story.

Neuromancer the novel deserves some discussion here, even though it has not yet been adapted for the big screen, but does exist in video game form. Rumors claim that casting for a cinematic rendition of *Neuromancer* is underway. Considered the single most influential novel revolving around brain implants, *Neuromancer* traces the travails of a computer hacker who confronts mercenaries who have their own brain implants in place. The implants enhance strength, vision, memory, and more. Gibson coins the term "matrix" in this novel, and thus influences *The Matrix Trilogy* (1999–2003), another unforgettable cult classic and a cornerstone of the end of the millennium.

Gibson toys with the idea of entertainment-oriented brain implants, or "simstim" (simulated stimulation), which record and playback experiences. His term "jacking in" refers to brain electrodes or direct neural implants that allow direct interface with other data sources. His ideas led to an explosion of references to brain implants over the coming decades.

Johnny Mnemonic the film appears years later, in 1995. It expands on themes popularized by Gibson's *Neuromancer* novel. In Gibson's original *Johnny Mnemonic* story, the protagonist is a memorable woman named Molly Millions. She reappears in *Neuromancer,* but goes by another name in the movie. On the printed page, Molly frees Johnny Mnemonic from the clutches of an East Asian crime ring. Molly's razor-sharp nail implants remind us of Wolverine's claws.

The film version sidelines Molly, as Johnny takes center stage. Johnny is played by Keanu Reeves, who won a Raspberry nomination for worst actor, before he redeemed himself in subsequent roles for *The Matrix* (1999). Other high-profile poets and performers appear in the filmic interpretation of the acclaimed book. Rapper Ice-T plays J-Bone; Henry Rollins is Spider and muscle man Dolph Lundgren is cast as Street Preacher. Molly's unique name changes to Jane (Dina Meyer), because of copyright issues related to the literary works.

Johnny Mnemonic the novel arrived as cyberculture peaked in the mid–1980s, when Gibson's story about cyberspace appeared in his *Burning Chrome* collection. Cyberspace was becoming part of pop culture, in the public domain, after having been an exclusive enclave of computer scientists, military experts and various scientific specialists wishing to share data with like-minded scientists. Many original dabblers were idealists who hoped to make this world a better world through shared communication. (The military had its own motivations.)

Monetizing Internet sites and information was not high on the horizon when the novel appeared, in those pioneering days of cyberspace. Entrepreneurs had arrived en masse when the *Johnny Mnemonic* film debuted in 1995. The Internet bubble was blowing at full force and had not yet burst. Yet the theme of *Johnny Mnemonic* is uncannily au courant in these days of insider trading and high stakes computer hacking, when high profile trials of billionaire hedge fund owners and traders appear on the front pages of daily newspapers.

Johnny has a brain implant that allows him to traffic in data, just as a human "mule" carries drugs across borders. Via "cybernetic surgery," he acquired a permanent data storage system in his head. This turns him into a "mnemonic courier." Data is uploaded or downloaded but the storage system stays in place, much like a computer's built-in hard drive.

Johnny enters a trance-like state when data is transferred or his password is reset. He has no awareness of the information transmitted. Only the recipient of the data can access his password. In other words, Johnny cannot control his own fate or his future. His life lies solely in the hands of others. Johnny is well paid for his troubles, but he pays a steep price for his brain implant: he cannot access childhood memories. In addition, he finds himself at the mercy of criminal overlords. The Yakuza (Japanese mobsters) place a contract on his life and dispatch a hit man, The Street Preacher, played by humongous bodybuilder Dolph Lundgren. The Preacher is instructed to sever Johnny's head, which contains the hard drive with essential data.

The novel and the film emphasize the East Asian control, in another premonitory move. When the novel appeared, Japan was the most likely contender for control of the electronics market and digital equipment. China since emerged as a dominant player in the 21st century, producing both corporate competition, bootlegged knock-offs, and highly educated hackers.

Like many SF films, this film turns into an action-adventure, where Johnny's life is endangered but he is rescued at the last minute. His act of heroism (or is it desperation?) conveniently saves the world at the same time. In the film version, but not in the book version, audiences are introduced to various medical syndromes that accompany excessive exposure to cyber-technology. By 2021, when the action takes place, "nerve attenuation syndrome" (NAS) is a looming threat to society. This plague has spread in response to over-reliance on technology. One company has the antidote for this disorder, and that company, Pharma-Kon, enlists Johnny to carry the data in his head, on what Johnny expects to be his last mission before retirement.

Curiously, in 2013, the American Psychiatric Association released its fifth revision of the *DSM* (*Diagnostic and Statistical Manual*), without including "Internet or video game addictions" among the diagnostic categories. Heated debates about those "addictions" continued throughout the years that *DSM-5* changes were under review. NAS overlaps with the concept of "Internet addiction" or at least "Internet overuse," even though it is not an exact fit. The film attributes NAS to overexposure to EMR (electromagnetic radiation) produced by electronic devices, which is a more concrete way to explain away adverse or toxic effects of overuse, and avoid the conundrum of positing unprovable psychological causes or behavioral addictions. Some people complain about the physical and mental effects of EMR or radio waves, and move to a community in a protected mountainous region to escape.[14]

Equally interestingly, Korea recognizes video game and Internet addictions as "true" addictions, and offers treatment programs for afflicted adolescents. Apparently, East Asian countries perceive their citizens to be at much greater risk for adverse reactions to cyber-culture, perhaps because electronic devices and video games became commonplace in those

In *Johnny Mnemonic* (1995), a film based on William Gibson's novel, Keanu Reeves stars as the eponymous mnemonic courier who has a data storage system installed his brain via "cybernetic surgery," but must escape The Preacher (Dolph Lungdren), who holds a contract to sever Johnny's data-filled head, and return it to Japanese Yakuza mobsters.

regions much earlier and perhaps because gaming stores have long been fixtures in their cities.

Another intriguing crossover between the film's premise and today's reality deserves comment. According to the film, the international pharmaceutical giant, Pharma-Kon, plans to profiteer from its antidote to NAS (also known as the "black shakes"). Considering all the accusations that have been leveled again Big Pharma in America, Gibson's characterization of unscrupulous medical marketing is strangely on target, once again. The name of the corporation says it all: Pharma-Kon equals "Pharma-Con," whatever way you spell it.

Since the time that the novel was written and the film was released, the U.S. Congress passed laws requiring disclosure of pharmaceutical payouts to physicians and hospitals (Sunshine Laws). The American public has grown skeptical of pharmaceutical motives and their tendency to stop affordable generic medications from reaching market. In order to corner the market, some Big Pharma companies pay generics manufacturers to delay applications for FDA approval of their products. At the same time, the government has imposed huge fines for off-label (unapproved) marketing claims. Most recently, old-guard Pharma giant Johnson & Johnson (J&J) was forced to pay over a billion dollars for deceptive promotion of its newest atypical antipsychotic medication. This is but one of many examples.

In 2011, *Batman* comics referenced such practices, but *Batman's* story arc went one step further. It depicts Big Pharma reps as assassins who will do anything to protect their market share. The reps provide far more than information. In this case, Pharma orders hits against makers of TCMS-like devices (transcutaneous magnetic stimulation), because the recently approved machinery could conceivably complete with antidepressant medications made by Pharma. Unfortunately, this arc was short-lived and ended with the DC comic "New 52" reboot.

In *Johnny Mnemonic,* all's well that ends well. The end is nowhere near as bleak as *Batman's* ending. As the film ends, the data containing the NAS cure is recovered from Johnny's head, without harming Johnny. This feat is accomplished through several exciting intermediary steps. Johnny can finally recall memories from his youth, and even remembers his mother. As Johnny convalesces, he and his friends watch the Pharma-Kon building burn from afar, signifying the end of an era. This proves that the electronic transmission of the cure succeeded, releasing Johnny from his bonds as a mnemonic courier and delivering the cure to save humankind.

A decade later brings yet another memorable brain chip movie. *The Manchurian Candidate* reimagining (2004) loses the riveting political point of the original by substituting psychosurgery for Pavlovian conditioning—but it makes a statement about the state of the art of neuropsychiatry. With its all-star cast and cameos by media luminaries that include Roger Corman, Sidney Lumet and Al Franken, the film itself was well-received by critics and spectators alike, possibly because audiences were too young to have emotional attachments to the original, which included impassioned political subtexts about Civil Rights plus the Cold War.

The original *Manchurian Candidate* (1962) is high drama. Jonathan Demme's reimagining of *Manchurian Candidate* (2004) ventures into science fiction territory through its futuristic lobotomy/brain implant scene—but it loses so much more when it takes the soldier's transformation into an automaton out of context. Jonathan Demme's star rose when

Silence of the Lambs (1991) won multiple Academy Awards. That film features Anthony Hopkins as psychiatrist Dr. Hannibal Lecter. Dr. Lecter has since become film's most memorable villain, outpacing longtime villains like Frankenstein and Dracula, and pushing relative newcomers like Michael Myers, Jason and Freddy aside.

Denzel Washington stars in Demme's remake of *Candidate*. He substitutes for Frank Sinatra as Captain Marco (who is later promoted to Major Marco). This casting choice comes off as a commercial decision rather than an ideological one. It capitalizes on Washington's star status and his draw for audiences. The fact that Denzel Washington made his name through his portrayal of slain Black Muslim activist and extremist, Malcolm X, suggests that a political statement is waiting in the wings, and perhaps a subversive political statement at that. Washington's sensitive portrayal of an uncharacteristically sensitive military psychiatrist in the tearjerker film, *Antwone Fisher* (2002), contributes to the confusion about the message behind the remake.

There are many substitutions in the remake of *Manchurian Candidate,* and subsatisfactory ones at that. When the remake of *Candidate* substitutes brain chips for the brainwashing and behavioral conditioning scenes of the original cult classic, it updates the psychiatric techniques but distracts from the meaning of the original movie. By switching from behavioral control to neurochemical or neuroanatomical control, the remake attempts to put the film trajectory on "fast-forward" rather than "rewind." However, this switch to neuroscience obfuscates the Cold War political allusions that made the first film so poignant.

In the reimagining, the action moves out of Manchuria (which is a stand-in for Communist-controlled Russia, China, and Korea, but is also the site of heinous pre-and peri–World War II Japanese medical experiments performed on non–Japanese Asians). The region known as "Manchuria" becomes an equally evil a corporation known as Manchurian Global. Manchurian Global turns elected officials into operatives for their monetary advancement. Manchurian Global achieves its aims through "any means possible," which includes the use of insidiously implanted brain chips that control operatives' behavior and makes them murderers.

In this version, the decorated Gulf War hero and presidential hopeful Raymond Shaw (Liev Schreiber) learns that he has a chip implanted in his head—but not until it is too late. Shaw was a platoon mate of Major Bennett "Ben" Marco (Denzel Washington) and Corporal Al Melvin. Because of disturbing dreams that seem to be symptoms of PTSD (post-traumatic stress disorder), Major Marco questions the "received wisdom" about his unit's wartime escapades.

The accepted story places Sgt. Shaw as the hero who rescued all but two members of the unit that Marco commanded in the Gulf. After receiving the Congressional Medal of Honor for his feats, Shaw is jettisoned into a career in politics. Shaw is ambivalent about his success.

Then Corporal Al Melvin (Jeffrey Wright) contacts Marco about his own disturbing dreams. He shows Marco images that he reconstructed from those dreams. An image of a tattooed woman resonates with Marco, who has dreamed about the same woman. This makes him wonder if this was really a dream and hence a figment of the imagination, or if this was a real experience that the two shared at one point in time, but somehow forgot, except when asleep and when the unconscious can access these submerged memories. In later dreams, this same tattooed woman appears on television sets placed before the platoon. She repeats, "Raymond Shaw is probably the kindest, bravest, warmest, most selfless human being I've ever known."

By the time that Marco and Melvin team up again, Shaw is a U.S. Congressman. He was recently nominated for the Vice President post, partly through the intervention of Shaw's aspiring and scheming mother (Meryl Streep), who is the Senator for the State of Virginia.

In the meantime, Marco is unsettled by his dreams and their uncanny correspondence to Melvin's dreams. He decides to investigate further. Then he finds an implant on the back of his head. Marco traces the implant to wartime experiments in nanotechnology, and Manchurian Global, the international weapons manufacturer. MG wields political power and boasts of ties to former prime ministers, trust-fund terrorists, ayatollahs—and the Shaw family, of all things!

Encouraged by his early discoveries, Marco digs deeper into Manchurian's archives. He finds a photograph of a scientist whom he recognizes from his nightmares. By searching online, Marco learns that the man is a genetic engineer who researched nanotechnology and "memory replacement" for Manchurian Global.

The rest of the film conforms to the plotline of the original more closely. It turns out that Raymond Shaw (Schreiber)'s implanted brain chip is controlled by his mother. The psychoanalytic associations to a boy whose strings are pulled by his mother are clear. But there is more at stake besides unresolved oedipal complexes and domineering matriarchs. With a few key words, she puts him into a trance that transforms him into an automaton. At his mother's command, Shaw drowns his chief political competitor as well as the politico's daughter, who was once an object of his affection. The plot thickens when we learn that his mother expects Marco to assassinate the President, so that Shaw, as Vice-President, can step up to the presidency and take over the country. Marco, too, has been brainwashed through his implanted brain chip. To offset these nefarious plans, Marco preps himself for election night, with plans to shoot Shaw and his mother. As an aside, Marco was programmed to commit suicide after the assassination.

Just before Marco has a chance to shoot himself (which is part of the take-over plan), an FBI agent intervenes. Agent Rosie shoots Marco in the shoulder, delivering a non-serious flesh wound that looks more deadly than it is. Then the FBI frames another man for the murders.

In the reimagining of *The Manchurian Candidate,* Liev Schreiber is credible as the bad guy, Sergeant Shaw. He is equally credible as a buddy or platoon mate. Schreiber will carve out a niche as the bad guy or the bad brother in *X-Men Origins: Wolverine* (2009) and *Defiance* (2009). In years to come, he becomes the face of capitalist exploitation—and overall devaluation of human life—when he stars in *Repo Men* (2010).

Ironically, Schreiber's maternal grandmother was lobotomized when his mother was twelve. His own mother was in and out of mental hospitals during his youth. His early years alternated between his mother's commune in New York's drug-infested East Village and living on the lam with his affluent father, who kidnapped him when in his mother's care.

The brain implant tells Schreiber (Shaw) to kill on command (in much the same way that auditory hallucinations of some schizophrenics instruct them to harm themselves or others). This surgically implanted brain chip recollects Tausk's "influencing machine" and gives new life to an idea that was coined by this brilliant analyst and theorist who took his own life.

However, the brain chip does not connect to the rich history that informs the Russian-related brainwashing scenes in the Cold War original. In the remake, big business supplants big government, and overshadows totalitarian government. The Korean War setting from the original film moves to the Mideast, with the Gulf War. The film is current—but the currency is devalued. The NSF aspects of the film are engaging, but the profound political subtexts are lost.

The original *Manchurian Candidate* from 1962 begins with a caption that says "Korea 1952." It references a highly publicized event from the Cold War, when a Korean submarine captured American sailors and subjected them to brainwashing, to the point that they publicly renounced American democratic values and advocated for Korean Communists. Shortly before the first film appeared, Communist hunter Senator Joe McCarthy shook up American society and Hollywood in particular, as he promoted fear of Communist infiltrators and televised trials of the Hollywood Ten who stood accused of harboring communist sympathies or belonging to the CP (Communist Party).

In the original *Manchurian Candidate,* Manchurian doctors practice at the Russian-influenced Pavlov Institute in Manchuria. The institute is named for Dr. Pavlov, the Russian physiologist who won the 1904 Nobel Prize for studies on dogs' responses to salivation. These experiments paved the way to techniques utilizing behavioral conditioning. The symbolism of the original is impressive. Manchuria symbolizes North Korea. Pavlovian conditioning (or brainwashing), as practiced by Dr. Yen-Lo, alludes to the Russian origins of these techniques. "Pavlov" points to Russian-Soviet Communist influences as much as it evokes Pavlov's psychological theory. Psychologists perform mental manipulation, not surgical implantation.

The original film includes innuendos everywhere. The statue of Abraham Lincoln ("Honest Abe") foreshadows revelations about lies and truths. The secret playing card of the Red Queen refers to Raymond Shaw's real life Communist mother, also a "Red Queen." At the same time, the Red Queen card recollects the upside down universe of *Alice-in-Wonderland*, where the Red Queen imposes psychotic rule, just before Alice devalues all court members by proclaiming that, "you're just a bunch of cards."

The remake pushes race issues from the sidelines to center stage. The remake stars African American actor Denzel Washington as the hero-soldier. This choice proved to be a good move from a commercial standpoint, because Denzel Washington is a big box-office draw. However, this tactic deracinates the groundbreaking contribution made by black actor Joe Adams in the original *Candidate*. Adams plays an M.D. who is a psychiatrist and a commissioned army officer. Adams is the counterpoint to the malevolent Manchurian psychologist. Joe Adams' presence makes a strong yet subtle statement. He shows that black M.D.s can represent the "establishment" (specifically, the U.S. Army) at a time when blacks were still disenfranchised and without full civil rights, and when black physicians were not admitted to the AMA (American Medical Association). Joe Adams' role is minor compared to the drama that unfolds, but his symbolic importance is major.

Even the original film's opening scene—"Korea 1952"—can be read as a commentary on racial integration in the military —for the U.S. military was finally integrated in the middle of the Korean War, in 1951. This caption could reference race relations and the Civil Rights movement in the U.S., which neared a peak when the film premiered in 1962. Alternatively, it explains the presence of black and white soldiers in the same platoon, a situation that was not possible prior to 1951, contrary to Hollywood's misrepresentations. Race-specific dream scenes plague black and white soldiers in the first film, and act as "the reveal." When we see that soldiers from different backgrounds share the same dream themes, while the complexions of the characters shift from soldier to soldier, the spectator realizes that something more than sleep is disrupted.

The remake lacks these rich references, and stays on the surface with its emphasis on neuroscience and big business. As *The Manchurian Candidate* remake ends, we come away with the feeling that we could have been watching *any* futuristic SF film about brain chips and mind control. David Cronenberg's *eXistenZ* (1999) or *Total Recall* (1990), perhaps? The list of contenders is a long one, and will continue into the next chapter on "flashbacks and flash drives."

In retrospect, we realize that we could be reviewing a clinical case report from Viktor Tausk's collection of delusions about "influencing machines" when we watch the second *Candidate*. Not that that is such a bad thing, given the success of brain chip/brain drain themes over the years and given the brilliance of Tausk's insights. Still, it is disappointing, considering that our expectations were set so high by the original *Candidate*. *Candidate* 1962 disappeared for decades, having been pulled from theaters prematurely, for fear that it might inspire another political assassination at a time when assassinations were becoming more common.

If anything, the remake of *Manchurian Candidate* has more in common with *Batman* movie serials from 1943, where the evil Dr. Daka uses brain machines to strip subjects of their wills and to turn them into zombie-like creatures that obey the "evil empire." As they say, "you can't sink a good idea," even when moviemakers can strip the fat from a plump original and turn it into a skeleton of its former self. What this proves, more than anything else, is that NSF tropes are ripe for recycling and that maybe there is nothing new under the sun (just as Ecclesiastes said).

By 2013, moviemakers realized that the themes from *Johnny Mnemonic* (and *Neuromancer*) were ready for recycling, especially if references to contemporary concerns are woven into the plot. The film version of *Johnny Mnemonic* paled in comparison to Gibson's acclaimed novel, although Gibson's status as a SF writer soared with the publication of *Neuromancer*. His name gained caché outside of hard-core SF circles. With this history in mind, it was not surprising that spectators proved receptive to the repurposed brain chip trope in *Elysium* (2013), especially since *Elysium*'s plot is so much more engaging and because its subtexts tap into contemporary concerns about health care, environmentalism, immigration, economic exploitation, as well as social class conflicts. It even hypothesizes about what happens to women in power.

Written and directed by Neil Blomkamp, *Elysium* stars Matt Damon as the populist hero/anti-hero who rises to the occasion when pushed to the brink. Damon's Max Da Costa works on an L.A. assembly line. A one-time jailbird, he reports to his robot parole officer regularly, intent on avoiding re-arrest and re-imprisonment for car theft. As a resident of overpopulated and underdeveloped Los Angeles, he mingles with the downtrodden during the day. He lives a *Mad Max* (1979) existence amidst chaos and urban decay. Then an industrial accident occurs.

Max/Matt realizes that his own days are numbered because his work-related accident exposed him to radiation. So he strives to equalize opportunities for the poor, who are relegated to live on this decrepit planet Earth. Yet he did not start out so altruistic. He begins by trying to save his own life only. In the end, he makes it his mission to save the life of a young girl who is dying of leukemia but cannot access the high-tech medical care reserved for Elysium's citizens.

In *Elysium,* rich and poor are segregated. Class differences are paramount to the plot. The rich reside on a restricted resort-like off–Earth commuter colony that floats in space. In addition to enjoying lush surroundings, constant entertainment and non-stop music, Elysium citizens have bed-sized medical devices (Med-Bays) that prevent or heal disease and injury.

Plutocrats occasionally return to the planet to tend to their investments on Earth. Anyone who can afford to avoid Earth does so. They remain in their idyllic setting on Elysium, which is named for the Elysian Fields of Greek myth. Anyone who attempts to access Elysium without permission is shot on site, which is to say that illegal immigrants to Elysium meet even worse fates than border-crossing refugees who enter America without proper papers but end up incarcerated or subjected to torture in Guantanamo Bay.

Jodie Foster plays a *noir*-like "evil woman." As Secretary of Defense, the steely cold Barbara Stanwyck–style Foster practically controls the government. She orders troops to open fire on trespassers. She denies life-saving health care to those who do not qualify for citizenship. She even attempts a coup when the sitting President Patel denounces her for her harsh tactics.

The MacGuffin of the plot revolves around Max's attempt to overcome the deadly radiation poisoning that followed the accident at his hellish worksite. A rich man named Carlyle owns the plant. This plant manufactures military weapons and disregards the safety of its staff.

To stave off impending death, Max must access a Med-Bay, which is available only on Elysium. In desperation, the reformed car thief approaches Spider, who is an accomplished smuggler. Spider agrees to help Max sneak into Elysium if Max agrees to download and transport valuable financial data from the industrialist who owns the manufacturing plants. In other words, Spider wants Max to act as a "mnemonic courier," and then some.

Although this film does not use the Gibsonesque term, the film does show Max receiving brain implants that store computerized data in his head. At the same time, Max also acquires an "exoskeleton" that imparts super-human strength needed for this mission. Research on similar real life exoskeletons are being funded by DARPA, for use in military applications.

The plot takes many twists and turns, and includes scenes where Carlyle, the villainous industrialist, downloads essential data from his computers into his own brain-based data bank. A virtual battle of brain banks follows, with one villain besting another, and with the bad guys (and one good guy, Max) dead or disfigured in the end. Jodie Foster's evil woman gets her due, also.

Well before the Armageddon-like ending, Spider realizes that the brain-based data also contains codes that allow citizenship into Elysium. Max takes advantages of this twist, and permissions everyone on Earth to become Elysium citizens. Only citizens can use Med-Bays, but now everyone is a citizen and can access Med-Bays. In the end, satellites with Med-Bays are dispatched to Earth, carrying much-needed medical care for the neglected minions who remain. The little girl with leukemia who turned the one-time car thief into a reluctant humanitarian enters a Med-Bay and survives. Sadly, Max succumbs, and becomes a Christ-like savior who dies so that he can save humankind. The SF plot with its political twists takes on religious tones.

In many ways, *Elysium* resembles a long string of anti-rich films that arrived in the aftermath of financial scandals perpetrated by the likes of Bernie Madoff, Michael Milken, Ivan Boesky, and a string of billionaire bankers and traders who stood trial. *American Hustle* (2013), *Wolf of Wall Street* (2013), *The Hunger Games* (2012), and *Contagion* (2011) are examples of this ilk. The emphasis on equitable access to medical care parallels contemporary concerns with Obamacare, which is in progress as 2013 turns to 2014, but is still contested and confusing as of Spring of 2014. The health care angle recollects *John Q* (2002), which stars Denzel Washington as the beleaguered father of a dying boy, with Anne Heche as the hard-hearted hospital head.

Max's radiation exposure reminds us of Marvel superheroes, including Spider-Man, The Fantastic Four, and The Hulk. Each of these characters has spawned at least one film, if not more. The fact that Max's friend and confident is named "Spider" evokes associations with the popular superhero who gained strength by way of a radioactive spider bite. In Max's case, the moral powers that he acquires from his radiation accident are more impressive than the physical powers imparted by his exoskeleton. Those moral powers override his original status as a parolee and career car thief and turn him into a Savior who sacrifices his life to redeem humankind.

The social, political, economic and moral issues broached by *Elysium* sound ever so realistic and have the potential to stir more debate over time. It is quite likely that *Elysium* will be better appreciated in the future, when social theorists and film critics alike look back at its subtexts and comment on the predictions it posits about medical and environmental issues. The brain chip trope that turns this multi-faceted action-adventure film into NSF may sound far-out and fantastic, were it not for one fact:

Also in 2013, DARPA put out a call for proposals for implantable devices "to help brain-injured people regain their memories."[15] The government-authorized and subsidized Defense Advanced Research Projects Agency (DARPA) is turning to private industry for their RAM (Restoring Active Memory) project. Responding to the success of BCI (brain-computer interface) devices that help injured people regain motor function in prosthetic limbs, the agency is actively seeking innovations that offset TBI (traumatic brain injury) that plagues so many returning servicemen and servicewomen. In other words, DARPA is on the same page as NSF. The agency is going one-step beyond *Repo Men* and *Total Recall*, which we will discuss in the next chapter. How is that for blurring the boundaries between science fiction and science fact?

Nine

Flashbacks, Flash-Forwards and Flash Drives

In our last chapter, we focused on "Brain Drains, Brain Chips and Brain Machines." The sections on Brain Chips belong in this chapter as much as they belong in the previous chapter. In fact, the boundaries between brain chips and computer-controlled brains are blurry all around. Our categories are constructed artificially, if only to make for easier reading. Our discussions of "flash drives" could fit into our last chapter on "Computers and Consciousness" just as well as it fits in here. With these caveats in mind, let us continue our discussion on "Flashbacks, Flash-forwards, and Flash Drives."

As usual, we begin by turning back the clock and anchoring this topic in film history. Flashbacks in films are so familiar to contemporary viewers that they barely need explanation. Yet that was not always the case. *Film noir* popularized the flashback as a storytelling device. *Film noir* surfaced in the early 1940s and peaked in the 1950s. *Noir* drew its aesthetic inspiration from German Expressionism, partly because many *noir* filmmakers learned their craft in the Expressionist era. Plots evolved out of the hard-boiled crime stories and detective fiction that sprang up during the Great Depression of the 1930s. *Noir* was recognized only in retrospect, when French film critics observed an American trend and identified it in 1955.

Neo-*noir* emerged much later, partly as homage to the original *noir* and partly because the genre is so versatile and because so many people appreciate *noir's* characteristic paranoia and pessimism. That ensures an appreciative audience, regardless of the cultural climate. Over time, even non-*noir* action-adventure films such as Brian De Palma's *Mission: Impossible* (1996) use flashbacks to dramatize the thought processes that guide the hero (Tom Cruise). Cyberpunk literature and film also cross over into *noir*, more because of visual effects, and bleak cityscapes than because of psychoanalytically informed flashbacks.

Marcel Proust did his fair share to familiarize the literary world with memories, reminiscences, free associations and all the stuff that flashbacks are made of. Proust's *Remembrance of Things Past* was published in seven parts between the years 1913 and 1927. Proust's books went to press after Freud formulated his psychoanalytic theories and established his Wednesday psychological group (which evolved into the Vienna Psychoanalytic Society). Proust wrote both before and after psychoanalytically informed treatments for shell shock cast psychoanalysis in a positive light. Proust has strong links to psychoanalysis, as does *film noir,* which congealed as a recognizable genre shortly before, during and after the Second World War.

Flashbacks, and psychoanalysis overall, gift us with wonderfully entertaining dramas. For film, it makes no difference whether or not psychoanalytic theories are provable, or whether or not psychoanalytically oriented treatments relieve specific ailments, as promised. Flashbacks push plots forward. They flesh out characters, as they reveal underlying motivations and disclose hidden information. Flashbacks experienced by a single character may be concealed from other characters in the cast, because their action occurs internally, without actual dramatization. Often, those memories were inaccessible to the character himself, until a specific person, place or event triggers that flashback and unleashes memories from the cerebral storehouse.

Psychoanalysis is a far stretch from neuroscience, even though its founder began his career as a neurology researcher. When he needed more funds to support a growing family, he opened a clinical practice in neurology, eventually turning his back on the laboratory and turning to the couch cure (after realizing that hypnosis is unnecessary). He devoted himself to hysterics and phobics. He coined concepts about metapsychology, but left the hard science behind.

In neuroscience and in science fiction, we look for more biological explanations of behavior and perception. Even if the theories presented seem far-fetched or are currently unobtainable, those theories are rooted in science. They employ the vocabularies and strategies of scientists. In neuroscience, we think of memories in much the same way that we think of a computer's memory, and vice versa. We know that memories (or data) are stored in specific parts of a hard drive—until that data is transferred to flash drives, tapes, floppy discs, removable hard drives, the cloud, or, worst of all, wiped clean because of a hard drive crash or another computer glitch.

Before then, memories (or data) are warehoused in temporary files, or virtual memory, which may or may not be retrievable. Most of us have experienced hard drive crashes, and most of us know that localized sections of the hard drive can be damaged and rendered irretrievable, while other sections remained unscathed. Those of us who began using computers decades ago may have even more experience with data loss or damage. If we are lucky, we backed up onto "floppy" (to use an outdated term), or onto more current devices or places (such as the cloud).

The brain also archives memories in distinct places. Like computers, the brain sorts those memories, and distinguishes sensory, short-term, working and long-term memories. In the not too distant past, doctors characterized memory as either immediate, recent, and remote memories. Neuroscience is constantly updating its ideas about memory and recently changed the names of these cerebral storehouses. In fact, 19th century neurologists recognized that specific sections of the brain govern specific functions (a process known as "localization"). In 1900, the Russian neurologist Vladimir Bekhterev discovered the hippocampus's role in memory (in the same year that Freud published his landmark *Interpretation of Dreams*). Researchers continuously learn new information about the ways that the brain works. As scientists, they strive to disprove the most recent theory and to replace it with something better or more complete. What is true today may be outdated tomorrow. What seems intuitive may not be correct at all.

The film *Dreamcatcher* (2003) offers a unique interpretation of memory warehouses. The film is based on a book by Stephen King. *Dreamcatcher* depicts the mind as an old library. The protagonist enters the library and wanders through the stacks, as he searches his memory. He literally burns documents that he no longer needs. Some files are locked, and beyond his reach. Surprisingly, the American Indian concept of a "Dreamcatcher"—that feathered hoop traps characters from dreams—is not featured very much in the story, even though the word appears in the title and the image appears in the poster art.

Since this film is based on a Stephen King story, something much stranger happens. Aliens overtake the body of the protagonist, who then seeks refuge in his library and safeguards his memories from the aliens. At face value, this sounds like a metaphor for old age and disease, with the aliens representing illnesses that take control of the body, while the mind struggles. There is certain poetry to the parallels, even though King strives to scare spectators, instead of impressing them with his philosophical reflections. Today, as the computer age has infiltrated everyday life and made it easier to access virtual information sources outside of the stacks, cyber-catalogues and virtual books have displaced many hallowed, walnut-walled libraries.

Thinking about computers and memory loss—or memory enhancement—makes it easier to conceptualize the ways that the brain processes and archives memories. That should not be surprising, since humans created computers, and people reconstruct the world in terms that they experience it. If people cannot perceive it, then people cannot create it. The main difference between computers and humans is that our knowledge of neuroscience is constantly evolving and is never static. Even though computers are not self-propagating in the way that people are (in spite of science fiction films that claim the contrary), there are lingering fears that "artificial intelligence" will evolve spontaneously, overtake the human species and shift the existing hierarchy that places man as the overlord of machine. These fears translate easily into popular SF tropes.

Plato and his followers viewed ideas and memories as metaphysical entities that hover between biological resting places and invisible realms in the netherworld. German psychiatrists of the Romantic Era retained similar belief systems about the soul or *seele*. Romanticism as an art movement crested between the late 1700s and the early 1800s. Those views shifted by the mid–19th century, when positivism became more pronounced. Until then, the views of Immanuel Kant (1724–1812) rang true and replayed insights from Plato. Kant agreed that we do not see true reality; all we know of reality revolves around appearances. Kant could accept "the unknowable"—but scientists are less inclined to stop at the limitations imposed by philosophers.

That said, most contemporary practitioners think of memory as a biologically based phenomenon that is encoded in the brain's cells, membranes, and mitochondria, and so forth. Molecular biology has enhanced our understanding of neuroscience processes, but much mystery remains. More sophisticated scientific systems will evolve over time.

Some things are certain, however. Human identity depends partly or fully upon memory. Our memories of what we do for a living, whom we like or dislike, which foods we ate for breakfast, the music we heard in high school, the candidates we voted for, the countries we visited, the schools we attended, whom we married (or didn't marry) and why, which house we live in and with whom, the house of worship we attend (or will never attend again), all contribute to our sense of "self." Persons who are stripped of their memories, be it via Alzheimer's, TBI (traumatic brain injury), or any of the many other forms of dementia or degenerative disorders, do not seem "like themselves" to those who know them. Even an ill-understood psychiatric disorder such as schizophrenia can cloud cognitive functions as much as it distorts perceptions—even though it has no specific neuroanatomical correlates that distinguish it. Without a personal memory, individuality vaporizes and human beings become interchangeable.

Neuroscience fiction films are far more action-oriented that philosophy texts, and do not dote on the fine points of who we are, how we remember, or what we remember. These films dramatize these concerns, and put them in picture forms, with plots that hold spectators' attention. For instance, in *Total Recall*, we encounter a man who sits in a machine, acquires new memories as old memories are obliterated. This process essentially transforms his identity.

Total Recall is a wonderful way to open this discussion, because the psychosurgery scene mirrors medical procedures used to access the hormone-secreting pituitary gland. In this case, star Arnold Schwarzenegger inserts what looks like an olive picker up his nostril, grimacing in pain as he proceeds. He is trying to extract his tracer, but the screen shots are ambiguous enough to suggest that he is also reaching for an unwanted "memory bolus."

Pituitary surgery is interesting—when performed by surgeons, and not as self-surgery (which is the case with Arnold Schwarzenegger in *Total Recall*). The pituitary gland lies at the base of the brain, but is not technically part of the brain and is actually part of the endocrine system. An oversized pituitary gland can cause neurological problems because of its location alone, even though it is not "neural tissue." An enlarged pituitary gland can grow in many different directions, and press on neighboring structures, such as the optic chiasm that transmits communications between the eyes' retinas and the occipital lobes of the brain that control vision.

If the pituitary expands in a different direction, it may impinge on the frontal lobes of the brain, which facilitate executive functioning, such as strategizing and planning, as well as social behavior and motivation. Because the pituitary is hormone producing (and is an endocrine gland rather than neurological tissue), a malfunctioning pituitary can wreak havoc through pathological hormone secretion. For instance, "prolactimonas" occur when the prolactin-secreting cells of the pituitary overproduce prolactin, which stimulates lactation (and depression as well). Growth hormone is manufactured by other parts of the pituitary, so that over-production of growth hormone produces giants with large hands, large heads, and distinctive facial features.

Overactive or enlarged pituitary glands are excised when they do not respond to medication or radiation treatment. Neurosurgeons access the pituitary gland through the nose. *Total Recall's* intranasal surgery scene is metaphorical rather than literal, although some spectators read this scene as a reference to cocaine, which is inhaled through the nostrils.

It would make perfect sense if PKD had conceived of the concept of the brain bolus. We know that he was familiar with neuroanatomy, for he referenced 19th century neurologists, such as Penfield. It would not be surprising if he knew about medical and surgical data from ancient Egypt. In the Old Kingdom, mummy makers sucked brains out through the nose, believing that brains did not perform any useful function, and so had no use in the life to come. The Egyptians were correct about accessing the brain through the nose—but it is incorrect to impute this insight to the author. For it was the filmmaker who introduced the brain bolus, for its visual intrigue.

The first *Total Recall* (1990) film was directed by Paul Verhoeven. The original stars

Arnold Schwarzenegger and Sharon Stone. Stone is a political operative who pretends to be Schwarzenegger's wife. Schwarzenegger plays Quaid, a one-time spy who is a pawn in a much larger political game. Quaid has no awareness that he had a past because his memory was obliterated and replaced.

When the action starts, all he wants is time off and a simulated trip to Mars. To accomplish those ends, he seeks the services of a company that instills exciting (and cost-effective and time-conserving) memories. That company is called *Rekall, Inc.* It offers the working man's dream vacation. In fact, a recurring dream inspires Quaid to visit Mars.

The story is set in 2084, in an obvious play upon Orwell's classic *1984*. In Orwell's dystopian novel, an authoritarian government manipulates its citizens' perceptions. That same theme pushes the plot in *Total Recall,* although *Total Recall* uses different techniques to achieve such mind control.

The inspiration for the film comes from a compact novelette by Philip K. Dick. Dick wrote the 22-page "We Can Remember It for You Wholesale" in 1966, the year that marked both the dawn and the sunset of the psychedelic era. At that time, experimentation with alternative approaches to perceiving had attracted public attention, thanks to a *Life* magazine spread about G.W. Wasson's adventures with "magic mushrooms" in Mexico in the 1950s. Wasson was a banker, who was married to a Russian pediatrician. Their lives were far removed from Haight-Ashbury, the East Village, or any other bastion of eccentricity or counterculture. Professionals were not oblivious to hallucinogens; many researched their effects in patients. The *American Journal of Psychiatry* from 1950, the official journal of the American Psychiatric Association, reported on mescaline-induced imagery. Treating alcoholism with LSD seemed like a realistic possibility in the 1950s, and researchers convened academic conferences on the subject.

The antics of a deposed Harvard University psychology professor attracted even more publicity for psychedelia. Timothy Leary's escapades pushed public awareness of hallucinogens far further than expected. Once a promising psychology researcher, the LSD-infatuated Leary opted for the less-trodden path and devoted his efforts to LSD advocacy, with some publications about the *Tibetan Book of the Dead* thrown in. Leary attracted a large following among college students and college dropouts, and among aspiring artists, published poets and other psychology professors. He also attracted the attention of official regulatory agencies and officers of the law.

After psychedelia came to governmental attention, LSD was restricted from scientific study in 1966. Sandoz Labs stopped shipping their controversial chemical to the United States. Hallucinogens had become too high profile, and their hazards turned into headlines. A full-fledged "counterculture" would blossom over the next few years, and would come to full flower in 1967, when the "flower children" flocked to San Francisco for the short-lived Summer of Love. Curiously, the Summer of Love came to an abrupt halt when Hell's Angels starting selling speed (amphetamines) and methamphetamine-adulterated LSD in the Haight. Philip K. Dick himself was notorious for his amphetamine-fueled, paranoid-tinged writing binges.

Dick's short story reflects society's concerns about these so-called "head trips," and does not anticipate the dawning of the cyber-age in the decades to come. The cyber-age, rather than the Age of Aquarius, makes itself manifest in *Total Recall's* remake in 2010. Dick's story is timeless, and adaptable to different cultural currents, because his story draws on Dick's own dabbling with drugs, his paranoia, and the broader philosophical underpinnings of his stories.

The first film and the novelette have much in common, and we will focus on the film from here on in. (The second film departs from the plotline, as we will point out in due time.) Earlier in the first film, we learned that Quaid has been troubled by recurrent dreams about Mars and a mysterious woman there—much like the platoon mates in the original version of *The Manchurian Candidate,* where repressed memories emerge in dream format. Quaid's wife (Sharon Stone) dismisses his concerns. This dream scene foreshadows the events to come.

When he first consults Rekall, Quaid starts with a simple goal: he seeks false but fun memories of an action-adventure vacation on Mars. He does not seek information. He plans to act as a secret agent on Mars, instead of idling away his time like ordinary vacationers who bask in the ruddy glow of the red planet and do little else. Little does he know that he really was a secret agent before a procedure robbed him of his memories. Now the real drama begins.

This pre-existing memory implant blocks implantation of a new implant and creates a medical emergency. According to PKD, he experiences a so-called "schizoid embolism" when the Rekall procedure goes awry. Quaid loses control and must be subdued and sedated. Because his implant blocks past memories and replaces them with false memories, Quaid had no way of knowing about his previous surgery when he consulted the Rekall Company and relayed his medical history. He does not know his identity, his prior profession or his political allies (or enemies). Unlike LSD, which became notorious for its unpredictability, Rekall, Inc. is a commercial enterprise that promises consistency in their office-based "head trip." The company lets clients pick their vacation spot of choice, as if they were picking paint colors for the walls.

The Rekall doctor who orchestrates the procedure is practicing a form of "cosmetic psychiatry" or "recreational psychosurgery." Debates about the ethics of offering "performance psychopharmacology" or "cosmetic psychopharmacology" are being waged as I write. The specter of legitimized "recreational psychosurgery" has not even come on the radar. The professional consensus frowns upon these practices, when it does not outlaw them outright. However, writers like Jonathan Schwarz of the *New York Times*[1] reminds us of the high demand for such performance-enhancing services. Schwarz makes the front pages when he reports on doctors who are willing to work in the grey zone for the right price. He also chronicles the misadventures of misguided patients who come into harm's way in the process.

In Philip K. Dick's story, and in both versions of *Total Recall,* this approach is affordable for the general public, and is not restricted to the rich, as occurs with current day "performance meds" that Schwarz references in his *Times* series. By implanting artificial memories (through something that functions like a flash drive), Rekall offers "competitively priced" vacations for those who cannot access real-time action-adventures in pricey off-planet getaways. Apparently, DARPA takes such silly-sounding ideas seriously and put out a call for proposals from private industries that are working on related projects.[2]

By the time that director Paul Verhoeven retells Dick's "We Can Remember It for You

Wholesale," the political paranoia that propelled PKD's literary original no longer exists. The philosophical subtext persists and has longer-reaching implications than of-the-moment political intrigues. However, cultural currents play a crucial role in the commercial success of the film, since the cultural climate creates an interested audience that will pay the price of a movie ticket.

When talking about his writing, Philip K. Dick explained that he plays upon the theme of reality versus delusion. He is less concerned with current events than with eternal questions. However, Dick's own drug use suggests that neuroscience issues registered high on his radar, and perhaps spurred his pursuit for answers to long-standing philosophical questions.

Dick repeatedly asks, "Which is the real truth?" This query connects Dick's works to Aldous Huxley's *The Doors of Perception* (1954) and related meditations on hallucinogen use. At the same time, this question functions as a footnote to Plato's *Allegory of the Cave*.

In Plato's work, prisoners sit in a cave, facing inwards, capable of seeing shadows of passersby from the "real world" outside and nothing else. When the prisoners are released and exposed to the "real" objects that cast those shadows, the ex-prisoners continue to believe that the shadows that they grew accustomed to seeing are the "real" objects. They express doubt that the "real" people that they see before their eyes are as real as the familiar shadows.[3]

Total Recall won an award for the Best Science Fiction film of the year. Many fans say that it deserved more Saturn Awards than it received. Most spectators see the "memory implant" scene as a peripheral scene that sets the stage for the action that follows. They dismiss the medical significance or symbolism. Some critics see the nasal implant as a signifier for cocaine, which is snorted and which was abundant during the 1980s. However, physicians may have other explanations, as do medical ethicists. Mental health professionals who treat patients who are troubled by flashbacks of traumatic pasts come away with philosophical and ethical questions about erasing traumatic pasts. Neurologists and neuropsychologists who assess memory loss may recognize references to the history of neurosurgery and neurology.

Virtually every neurology textbook mentions Wilder Penfield (1891–1976), the neurosurgeon who unleashed patients' memories by placing electric probes on their temporal lobes. Even though other researchers could not replicate Penfield's results, his experiments remain etched in our memories because they made people rethink their romanticized views of memory. Most importantly, Dick also knew of Penfield, and referenced him in his earlier books.

After viewing this film, we come away wondering if memory implants will become as acceptable as acrylic hip sockets. We can expect many medical ethicists (and others) to object to this proposal, for depriving people of their unique memories also deprives them of their sense of personhood. Considering the ruckus raised by the world's first face transplant, we can be certain that other obstacles lie ahead, even if scientists devise ways to alter and substitute memories.

Questions upon questions remain, far beyond questions about how to accomplish this feat. What if memories are scarred by traumas of times past? In those cases, should troublesome memories be removed and replaced, like arthritic joints or malformed heart valves? Will the day come when we can scrub away bad memories, like spots on clothes at the dry cleaners? What if no viable memories remain, and there is nothing to replace? What to do then? What if painful memories are too entangled in imprints of important events to be teased out? *Eternal Sunshine of the Spotless Mind* (2004) tackles the very last question. With so many unanswered questions remaining, a 21st century remake of *Total Recall* was in order.

Twenty-two years later, in 2012, Colin Farrell replaces Arnold Schwarzenegger. The lean and mean Farrell cum Quaid cannot obscure our own recollections of the bulked-out bodybuilder who lent credibility to the fight scenes. The remake replaces the feisty but sexy Sharon Stone with Kate Beckinsale, who was already an action star. Quaid's plight remains the same: he is an ordinary laborer who was once a spy, before his government duped him and before he "acquired" a beautiful but make-believe wife who conspires with the government. *Wired* magazine panned this version, comparing it to a "trip to Costco."

In spite of the twenty-year hiatus between the first and second *Total Recall*, we find no extra insights about neuroscience. The omission of handcrafted (not CGI-generated) mutants that populate Venusville is a palpable loss. In the first film, Quaid teams up with a new romantic interest that lives among those outcasts in the Red Light District of the Red Planet. The exotic backdrop of the planet Mars is gone from the second film, disappointing many SF fans and especially disappointing admirers of Whelan's panoramic moonscape-style illustrations on SF book covers. Instead, the geography focuses on UFB (United Federation of Britain) and an isolated colony in Australia, where citizens retreated to escape the earth's pollution.

The world has changed since 1990, and since 1966, as it always does. Yet something else happened in the 21st century that makes us rethink Dick's concerns when he wrote "We Can Remember It for You Wholesale." In 1966, America was infatuated with LSD, and intrigued by alternative realities made possible through ingestion of hallucinogenic plants and chemicals. Even those who did not partake of these substances still listened to news about their effects.

By 2012, sales of video games far surpassed profits from cinema. Virtual reality is immediately accessible. Society is thoroughly engrossed with the Internet and with social networking sites and simulated life sites in cyberspace. Computers and cyberspace are no longer news; they are omnipresent by 2012. This shifting sense of self and cyber-self make Douglas Quaid's quest to find his true self more relevant than ever before.

The second *Total Recall* recollects those contemporary concerns, which are significant, but are not the same as the displaced sense of self that results from memory loss. A few weeks after the *Total Recall* remake premiered in movie theaters, *New York Times* columnist Benedict Carey wrote that "Brain Implant Improves Thinking in Monkeys." His article recaps an article from a specialized neuroscience journal, which notes the success of brain prostheses in primates. Obviously, humans have far more memories than monkeys, even monkeys that learned tricks. Yet this report suggests that people with memory damage from dementia, strokes or brain injuries may have help in the not-so-distant future. The forward-thinking DARPA may be right.

Sandwiched in between the first and second *Total Recall* is another outlier film with a similar premise. Rekall, Inc. was the province of *Total Recall,* while a somewhat similar company named "Lacuna" appears in *Eternal Sunshine of the Spotless Mind. Eternal Sunshine of the Spotless Mind* (2004) is a science fiction film, albeit one that doubles as a romantic comedy rather than as an action-adventure. It is much more light-spirited than dark and gloomy

The *Eternal Sunshine of the Spotless Mind* (2004) poster shows (left to right) Jim Carrey, Kate Winslet and Kirsten Dunst smiling, even though they had memories of their relationships erased by Lacuna, Inc., a company run by a philandering and unscrupulous doctor.

films like *Repo Men,* which traverse related terrain. *Eternal Sunshine* attracted a cult following, along with recognition by the Academy Awards. It won for Best Original Screenplay, while Kate Winslet earned a Best Actress nomination for her role as Clementine.

The plot unfolds in non-linear style, which is consistent with the post-modernist ethos of the day, and is an effective way to emphasize the effects of memory erasure. The movie begins when two seemingly mismatched people meet on the Long Island Railroad, en route to Montauk, which was then a sparsely inhabited part of the island. They find themselves drawn to one another, almost uncannily. Like the dramatically different film, *Sunset Boulevard* (1950), the opening scene on the LIRR (Long Island Railroad) is actually the finale. This seemingly chance encounter eventually explains the action that leads up to the ending.

It turns out that Joel (Jim Carrey) and Clementine (Kate Winslet) were once lovers who spent two joyous years together. Then they had a fight and Clementine hired the New York City-based Lacuna, Inc. to erase memories of their relationship. Lacuna is the Latin term for "hole." Psychoanalysts use this term to describe the "superego lacuna" of sociopaths. Sociopaths appear superficially normal and are often ingratiating. They can be kind to their families, but have holes, or lacunae, in their superegos that allow them to conduct anti-social activates in other arenas, without remorse. This association becomes important later in the plot. (More current research distinguishes between persons with antisocial personality disorders and "true sociopaths," who are more likely to show biological markers or changes than personality-disordered persons.)

When Joel learned of Clementine's actions, he was heartbroken, and tried to mend his broken heart by undergoing the same procedure himself. He undergoes the procedure as he sleeps. Importantly, the last words he heard from Clementine were, "Meet me in Montauk."

Much of the action occurs in Joel's mind, via flashbacks of sorts, that come into consciousness (and appear on screen) as his memories are gradually erased. Before the procedure begins, the Lacuna doctor, Dr. Mierzwiak, explains the process of "targeted memory loss." Dr. Mierzwiak assures the aggrieved Joel (played by comedic actor Jim Carrey) that this painless procedure is nothing more than a mild form of brain damage that can be compared to a "night of heavy drinking." With such reassurance, Joel agrees to erase all memories of Clementine, the eccentric woman who left him. Yet he loses the good memories as well as the bad ones, and he forgets all scenes from the past in which she played a role. Spectators see how much her presence injected itself into his very being and thinking.

The Lacuna staff seem to be peripheral to the plot, but they turn out to be important to pushing the plot, and in sending subliminal messages about the ethical implications of such procedures, should such futuristic techniques became available. We learn that the good doctor cheats on his wife with his office assistant. When the wife learns of his affair, he conveniently erases all memories from the brain of his assistant at Lacuna, Inc. In other words, he behaves like sociopaths who possess "superegos lacunae" that function in some arenas but have gaping holes elsewhere, to allow for amoral activity.

When his assistant reviews the records and learns that she was subjected to this procedure, she retaliates against her boss and ex-lover and sends medical records to all of Lacuna's clients. Joel and Clementine are thus informed of their previous affair, but not until after they inadvertently restarted a new relationship, not knowing about their past together.

Will the time come when memories can be removed from the brain, the way that hemodialysis, plasmapharesis or even chemical chelation removes toxic metabolites or metals from the body's blood? Today, this sounds impossible, but who knows what tomorrow may bring. Synchronicitously, as I was writing this chapter, a news bulletin arrived by email.

On December 23, 2013, the American Psychiatric Association sent out their daily blast to members, headlining a story by Gautam Naik of the *Wall Street Journal*. Naik reports that "Unwanted Memories [are] Erased in Electroconvulsive Therapy Experiment."[4] What is more is that Naik compares the procedure to *Eternal Sunshine of the Spotless Mind*.[5]

I would not expect many psychiatrists—much less recipients of psychiatric care—to recommend ECT for memory erasure as glibly as the fictional Lacuna Inc. recommended their memory erasure machine to Jim Carrey's character. In fact, I would expect intense trepidation to follow the mere mention of ECT, and would be surprised if such studies could pass an American IRB (Institutional Review Board). Still, the article is worth reading.

The *Journal* summarizes a study published by neuroscientists from the Netherlands. Naik paraphrases Dr. Marijn Kroes of Radboud University Nijmegen, Netherlands, stating that "Scientists have zapped an electrical current to people's brains to erase distressing memories, part of an ambitious quest to better treat ailments such as mental trauma, psychiatric disorders and drug addiction."

"In an experiment, patients were first shown a troubling story, in words and pictures.

A week later they were reminded about it and given electroconvulsive therapy, formerly known as electroshock. That completely wiped out their recall of the distressing narrative." The reporter then quotes the neuroscientist, who is lead author of a study published in the journal *Nature Neuroscience*. Dr. Kroes says, "It's a pretty strong effect. We observed it in every subject."

The Wall Street Journal provides more details, noting that, "Science has tinkered with similar notions for years. In exposure treatment, repetitive exposure to a phobia in a non-threatening way is designed to help patients confront their fears and gradually weaken the fear response, [via] a process known as extinction. Some researchers are experimenting with anti-anxiety drug Propanolol. The hope is that one day it may be possible to selectively eliminate a person's unwanted memories or associations linked to smoking, drug-taking or emotional trauma." It is well known that environmental or emotional "triggers" from past memories can rekindle bad behaviors in the present, and people react to those triggers, for no rational reason.

"Scientists used to think that once a memory took hold in the brain, it was permanently stored and couldn't be altered. People with anxiety disorders were taught to overcome their fears by creating a new memory. Yet the old memory remained and could be reactivated at any time. About a decade ago, scientists made a surprising discovery. They showed that when a lab rodent was given a reminder of some past fear, the memory of that event ... [it] briefly [became] unstable. If nothing was done, that memory stabilized for a second time, and thus got ingrained—a process known as reconsolidation. However, when certain drugs, known to interfere with the reconsolidation process, were injected directly into the rodent's brain, they wiped out the animal's fearful memory altogether. Crucially, other memories weren't erased."

The article reminds readers that this data could not be tested on humans, because "injecting drugs into the human brain is risky business." That is an understatement.

Dr. Kroes and his colleagues devised an experiment that circumvents the problem above. They tested people who were undergoing electroconvulsive therapy for severe depression. They got impressive results. Subjects were exposed to disturbing stories. Those who heard those stories just before getting ECT could not remember the upsetting tales. Those who did not get ECT after hearing the story—but had their memories reactivated when the story was retold to them during the testing process—had very intriguing responses. Not only did they retain full memory of the upsetting story, but they showed enhanced memories of these upsetting situations. That heightened response to the original traumatic tale is similar to PTSD responses, where the victim over-reacts to slight stimuli that resemble the original stimulus, and avoids it entirely.

Whatever happens along to road to memory eradication research, one thing is certain: this film reminds us of possible ethical lapses that can occur under such circumstances. In *Eternal Sunshine,* Dr. Mierzwiak misuses his medical skills when interacting with his office staff. This act highlights the importance of personal and professional ethics. Even though this is a romantic comedy intended for entertainment rather than edification, it makes a serious point about potential adverse consequences awaiting those who loosen safeguards surrounding such procedures. If intrusive or dangerous procedures such as memory erasure are performed in unmonitored office settings, or for commercial purposes only, vulnerable persons can be put at risk. Unfortunately, we can find strong parallels if we look back at the history of lobotomies, which were performed in offices in the 1950s by showman psychiatrist Dr. Walter Freeman II. Dr. Freeman drove around town and demonstrated his ice pick technique as if he were a carnival performer. Sometimes he performed up to 50 operations in day, in public.

On a more positive note, this fictional and far-from-serious romantic comedy raises the possibility that neuropsychiatry and industry may someday team up to offer non-invasive, non-pharmacological elective procedures that remove painful memories. This futuristic possibility offers promise for the treatment of PTSD (post-traumatic stress disorder). Maybe this film—or related films—inspired DARPA staff as much as *Wall Street Journal* reporters, given that DARPA issued a call for proposals on related projects in November of 2013.

Ethical concerns abound in another film about memory replacement or substitution by dream states, *Repo Men* (2010).

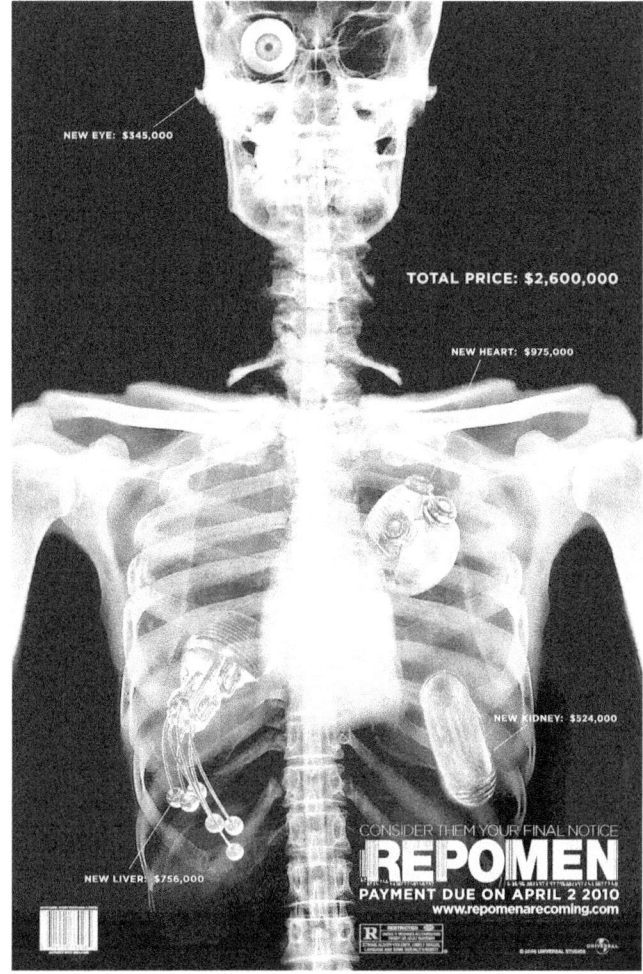

With an X-ray as a backdrop, this *Repo Men* (2010) poster warns, "Consider them your final notice," and lists prices for artificial organs sold by a private corporation—but no price is listed for a Neural Network machine that induces blissful dreams in repo man Remy (Jude Law), who is comatose from a head injury.

Chronologically, *Repo Men* (2010) is a cousin of the remake of *Total Recall* (2012). It pushes the motif of "implantable memories and perceptions" and removable flash drives even further, maybe even into the realm of the real. It evokes the theme of *Sunshine*, but in a dark and disturbing way. *Repo Men* (2010) did not reap many accolades from film critics, but it deserves attention primarily because of its intriguing treatment of brain death, and, secondarily, because of its sad commentary on the state of transplant medical ethics worldwide. As it turns out, its bleak portrayal of for-profit organ transplants is not totally off base, even if it is overblown to push the plot and to heighten the drama.

As we can see from news sources, doctors in Germany went on trial, accused of falsifying medical records to push patients higher on the waiting lists. Rumors about FBI deals with

Japanese mobsters (Yakuza) in need of transplants hit the mainstream press as well as the scandal sheets.[6] Many American physicians remain skeptical of the organ transplantation procedures, because of upsetting scandals that were revealed in recent years.

Repo Men stars Jude Law and Forest Whitaker as the "repo men" who repossess transplanted organs. Liev Schreiber runs the heartless organization that promises new lives to persons whose natural organs failed. Desperate relatives sign complex contracts that guarantee payment of usurious interest rates to the corporation. When payments are late, Schreiber dispatches "repo men" to remove transplanted organs. True to character, Schreiber co-starred as the would-be soldier-assassin in *The Manchurian Candidate* remake, as discussed earlier.

Liev Schreiber displays his usual psychological intensity when performing this role. Liev Schreiber's portrayals of the "bad brother" or some take on the "evil twin" have earned him fame. As we noted earlier, Schreiber' own maternal grandmother was lobotomized when his mother was twelve. His mother was in and out of mental hospitals during his youth.

One infers that this family chaos informs his acting. It is ironic that Schreiber's steely-cold character in *Repo Men* performs a single kind act: he facilitates a connection with a dream machine for brain dead Remy (Jude Law), after a serious on-the-job injury sends Remy into an irreversible coma. However, this gift is not for gratis. It is subsidized by Remy's co-worker (Forest Whittaker), who feels responsible for the injury he incurred while the two were fighting.

Jude Law's comatose character acquires a memory loop of joyful days at beach, spent with his best friend, a long-time work buddy and fellow repo man, Jake (Forest Whittaker). Sitting beside him is the new woman in his life, played by Alice Braga. His legal wife (and the mother of his children) is gone from his memories, because she objected to his career as a repo man and threatened to leave him if he did not leave that job. He enjoys a constant dream state, attached to a machine that infuses dreams into the brain as easily as a ventilator provides artificial respiration for those who are unable to breathe on their own accord.

Turning back the clock to 1966, we find a similar trope on *Star Trek*: "The Menagerie." In this two-part episode, part of it set years before Capt. Kirk's original five-year mission, Spock starts a mutiny. He kidnaps the crippled Capt. Pike. Once the Commander of the Enterprise, Pike is now wheelchair-bound, with his face maimed. Spock hijacks the spaceship, steers it toward the forbidden planet of Talos IV, which is under strict no-contact quarantine. Then he surrenders for court martial, so he can explain his actions and clarify why he delivered the disabled captain to a planet that provides false consciousness and thereby blocks awareness of his injuries.

Apparently, neither Spock of *Star Trek* nor Remy or Jake from *Repo Men* endorses Aristotle's belief that "the unexamined life is not worth living." They lay claim to the idea that blissful delusions or "life lies" (as Henrik Ibsen called them) are preferable to painful awareness.

Ten

Memory, Mentation and Medication: Before Birth and After Alzheimer's

Over the centuries, adventurers have set sail in search of the Fountain of Youth. Others pursued plants that would impart everlasting life. Fortunetellers and fictional sorcerers have promised love potions since time immemorial. With the same enterprising spirit, scientists and self-experimenters have sought the secrets to intelligence amplification.

With the advent of "artificial intelligence" (aka computers), the prospect of completing this search for advanced intelligence seemed more likely—but the consequences also seemed scarier. As 2013 ended, reports about "Brain-like Computers" appeared in the newspapers.[1] Those computers learn from experience, to expand their information base and improve their decision-making abilities. Computers are growing smarter and smarter, while humans stay the same, at best.

What if overly intelligent artificial intelligence overpowers the people who program the computers? That is a legitimate fear, in theory, even if it does have a paranoid tinge. At the very least, this is a legitimate plot for science fiction films. *The Matrix, Demon Seed, The Invisible Boy,* even the enduring popularity of HAL, from *2001: A Space Odyssey,* confirm the appeal of such tropes. In our concluding chapter, we will review concerns about computers, consciousness and control in NSF film.

In the interim, let me assure you that tropes about artificial intelligence or intelligence enhancement are not exclusive to the present day—even though current preoccupation with Alzheimer's disease, and age-related memory loss, often seems overwhelming and this trope seems apropos. It is tempting to attribute films like *Limitless* (2011) or *Rise of the Planet of the Apes* (2011) or *The Bourne Legacy* (2012) to epidemiological artifacts of early 21st century America, and to view this as a contemporary concern, exclusively. That is completely inaccurate.

At the turn of the 20th century, science fiction pioneer H.G. Wells wrote about "The New Accelerator (1901)." In this story, the narrator's neighbor, Professor Gibberne, concocts an elixir that accelerates human activity, intelligence included. Parallels with both *Limitless* and *The Bourne Legacy* are obvious—even though the story lines and plot twists of *Limitless* and *The Bourne Legacy* move in entirely different directions.

Professor Gibberne differs from the higher profile Dr. Moreau, who was also an invention of H.G. Wells. In earlier chapters, we examined Dr. Moreau's impact on NSF film as well as literature. Dr. Moreau's tale made it to the silver screen several times over, but Professor Gibberne and "The New Accelerator" had to wait until 2001, a full century after the short story was written. In 2001, Wells' short story became the first episode of a four-hour miniseries, entitled *The Infinite Worlds of H. G. Wells* (2001). The series was conceived by Nick Willing and released by Hallmark Channel.[2] Perhaps this story by Wells became significant to the 21st century, for the same reasons that films like *Memento* and *Limitless* hold appeal at this time.

The SF trope about increased intelligence, and its adverse consequences, recurs. It appears in movies early on, although literature is able to describe this abstract theme more easily than the screen, which relies on imagery, and must invent a plot that explains the in's and out's of intelligence and its consequences. Early silent films include a 16-part serial about *The Crimson Stain Mystery* (1916), some of which were, unfortunately, lost in the last century.

In *The Crimson Stain Mystery,* a slightly mad scientist, Dr. Burton Montrose, hopes to perfect a chemical that makes ordinary persons brilliant. His experiments backfire. The chemical that he created in earnest turns his test subjects into monstrous criminals instead of intelligent beings. These criminals band together and terrorize New York, killing innocent people. Pierre La Rue, who becomes known as "The Crimson Stain" because of his red-stained eye, leads the gang. La Rue's surname translates to, "The Street," which is an equally appropriate moniker for the leader of a street gang. We wonder if the scientist's name, "Montrose," is intended to remind us of the doctor's monstrous acts. We know that Edgar Allan Poe used this convention when he created a monstrous character named "Montresor" for "The Cask of Amontillado" (1846).

In *The Crimson Stain,* a newspaper editor's father is a victim of the gang's rampage. The bereaved son vows to expose the gang's mastermind. In hopes of catching the criminal with the crimson eyes, the editor joins forces with a young detective. It just so happens that the detective is romantically involved with the scientist's daughter. Neither the daughter nor the detective suspects that her scientist-father bears responsibility—however indirect—for the Crimson Stain killings. And so the mystery unfolds over sixteen episodes.

Spectators keep coming back to see the next installment. Intriguing titles include, "The Brand of Satan"; "In The Demon's Spell"; "The Broken Spell"; "The Mysterious Disappearance"; "The Figure In Black"; "The Phantom Image"; "The Devil's Symphony"; "In The Shadow of Death"; "The Haunting Spectre"; "The Infernal Fiend"; "The Tortured Soul"; "The Restless Spirit"; "Despoiling Brutes"; "The Bloodhound"; "The Human Tiger"; "The Unmasking."

Mid-century brought an unforgettable film about intelligence enhancement and robots. In *Forbidden Planet* (1956), the United Planets Cruiser travels to a distant plant, seeking information about the fate of an expedition sent twenty years earlier. As it approaches the planet, the cruiser receives a message, warning it to stay away. It turns out that the survivors of the spacecraft used ancient but advanced alien technology, found hidden on the planet, to enhance their intelligence and to create new matter. Some die in the process, but Dr. Morbius persists, and builds Robby the Robot. Robby becomes one of the most famous totems of American science fiction and appears in later, unrelated films. Unbeknownst to Dr. Morbius, his unconscious also creates the "Id Monster," which attacks those that trespass into their world, even if they have come to save them. This "Id monster" will have parallels in Cronenberg's film, *The Brood,* where a disturbed woman "gives birth" to beings formed from unsettling unconscious emotions. Material manifestations of pre-conscious concepts also appear in the previously discussed *Fiend without a Face.*

To those who are unfamiliar with Wells' story or with silent cinema, *Limitless* (2011) seems remarkably fresh and contemporary. It reminds us of a new category of meds, "nootropics," which enhance cognition, even in those who are not cognitively impaired at the start. We can conceive of "nootropics" as anabolic steroids for the brain—but without the steroids. Currently available nootropics include modafinil and its congeners (made by Teva Pharmaceuticals). Related meds are in development. Theoretically, nootropics can include old-fashioned amphetamines and methylphenidate,[3] which were used (and abused) since the 1930s.

In this *Forbidden Planet* (1956) poster, SF icon Robby the Robot carries off the proverbial damsel in distress, giving no hint that he was built by Dr. Morbius, who was stranded on the forsaken planet, but had his intelligence enhanced by advanced alien technology.

Limitless is billed as a "techno-drama" and a thriller, as much as SF. In *Limitless,* a disheveled writer (Bradley Cooper) lives in a dilapidated apartment on the outskirts of New York City's Chinatown. Apparently, he cannot afford to move a few blocks east, to the trendier Lower East Side. More importantly, he cannot concentrate and cannot meet his deadlines. He cannot even get a haircut or offer new excuses to his old girlfriend, who has watched him floundering over time, but has now lost her patience. She walks out, leaving him in worse shape than ever.

Through a chance encounter, Eddie (Bradley Cooper) stumbles upon the estranged brother of his ex-wife. His former brother-in-law consults for a pharmaceutical company, and offers Eddie a sample of a new drug, NZT. This mysterious new med makes him learn quickly. It enhances his concentration, expands his knowledge base, and even makes his bleary eyes look bluer. He zooms through his manuscript, delivers it to his publisher, and dazzles his agent with more ideas. This man of words also becomes a math genius and invests in stocks. In short order, he consults for big business, and in that capacity, he runs into Robert De Niro as a CEO.

To get more capital for his business dealings and stock market ventures, Eddie puts his misguided faith in the Russian mob. Steel-toothed mobsters see the value of NZT, and hold Eddie hostage as they search for his stash or his supplier. To make matters worse, Eddie uses more and more NZT, and lives a wilder and wilder life. He has blackouts and cannot remember what happened when he went dancing all night and left a club with an unknown woman. The woman turns up dead the next day. Eddie is the chief suspect. His photo appears on every paper.

Eventually, Eddie has his day in court—but even his lawyer exploits him and values NZT over Eddie or professional ethics. At the police station, when Eddie is forced into line-up, he leaves his contraband outside, entrusting it to his attorney. The attorney appropriates the drug, uses it himself, and becomes all the wiser. More white collar-style drug wars ensue. Pharma companies lock horns, almost as ferociously as drug lords in South American mountaintops or Mexican border towns. In the end, we learn that Eddie set some NZT aside. By using his advanced intelligence, he has perfected a way to avoid addicting and devastating side effects that follow prolonged used of NZT. More and more adventures and misadventures transpire.

Limitless falls under the rubric of NSF. It is so close to truth that it is barely fiction. No wonder so many spectators were speculating about the special drug featured in the film. Some said it was Provigil. Many said, "Nuvigil." Others insisted on Adderall. Whatever, NZT's stimulant effects are familiar enough to early 21st century audiences to sound plausible.

As proof of the projected intrigue with NZT's possibilities, and its parallels with currently available prescription medications, pre-release promotions mirrored the tactics of Big Pharma. They opened a website that advertises NZT. The site uses the very same conventions found in legitimate psychotropic DTC (direct-to-consumer) advertising, including warnings about potential psychosis and death. The website is available at www.theclearpill.com.

By clicking on the Testimonial section, we find a single line: "Due to claims being investigated by the FDA, this page is currently unavailable." Tapping on "Is NTZ for you?" leads to an interactive pop quiz that is remarkably similar to the ADHD or EDS (excessive daytime sleepiness) quizzes offered by Vyvanse or Nuvigil online pop-up ads. Warnings about blackouts that can occur after heavy alcohol intake sound strikingly familiar, and the recommendation against the use of NZT by vegans offers a cute comedic touch. An ever-smiling Bradley Cooper walks readers through the commercial, strolling through actual scenes from the film, and diving off a cliff at one point. (Diving off a cliff can be seen as a metaphor for "driving off a cliff"—but either venue can be deadly!) The website's banner reads, "What if a pill could make you RICH AND POWERFUL?" Not surprisingly, this fine-tuned commercial went viral.

Film reviewers received promotional mailings of drug "samples" claiming to be actual NZT. The pills were menthol mints. These samples were not sent to doctors' offices.

The year after *Limitless* premiered, *New York Times* writer Jonathan Schwarz wrote epic-length articles about Adderall and other ADHD meds. His three-page spreads appeared on the front page of the *Times*' Sunday edition, which is no small feat. Follow-up articles popped up later.[4] Many believe that Schwarz' exposés about the risks of unmonitored and self-prescribed Adderall spearheaded New York State's I-STOP laws, which require that prescribers check a state database before writing prescriptions for controlled medications.[5] It remains to be seen if these popular meds are friends or foes—or if they offer as much as they claim. (Recall, though, that coffee was once considered illicit, and that "coffee houses" were akin to opium dens.)

Released in the same year as *Limitless, Rise of the Planet of the Apes* (2011) also focuses on a timely topic. It makes the cure for Alzheimer's disease its MacGuffin. Even though the original film stars apes, and includes time and space travel, the *Planet of the Apes* series seems so much more serious than *Limitless*. Perhaps that is because the original played off serious social issues of its era (namely, racism) or because the reimagining addresses pressing concerns about care of the elderly in our society, especially when they face cognitive decline. There are no all-night dance parties or wild sex scenes in *Apes*, as there are in *Limitless*.[6]

The protagonist of *Rise of the Planet of the Apes* is a youngish scientist who lives with his aging father. Many Baby Boomers and Gen-Xers can relate to his conflicts (about parents, rather than apes). Doctor Will Rodman (James Franco) watches his father deteriorate, day by day, even though he himself works long hours, attempting to perfect a compound that will reverse intellectual loss or restore intelligence after it is lost. He experiments on primates. In one of Dr. Rodman's many ethical dilemmas, and in one of his many experiences with psychological defeat, he considers co-opting this experimental and unapproved med for his father's use.

Rise of the Planet of the Apes does not tell us exactly how the primates' intelligence improves, except to cite statistics that document improvement. It never speculates about the role of amyloid protein, neurofibrillary tangles, or even heavy metals such as aluminum, all of which have been studied for their role in Alzheimer's disease. It avoids fringe theories. The film simply shows us examples of apes that were exposed to the secret substance that enhances intelligence. In that way, it maintains credibility and allows spectators to suspend disbelief, for a few hours. It even raises our hopes in real life, even though we realize that this is strictly SF.

Even though it is a prime example of NSF, *Rise of the Planet of the Apes* circumvents discussion of disappointing treatments for Alzheimer's (or other dementias) that are currently marketed. It wisely sidesteps jargon-heavy conversations among scientists, which are as likely to be wrong as right. By showing us scenes of Will Rodman's father, as he forgets how to

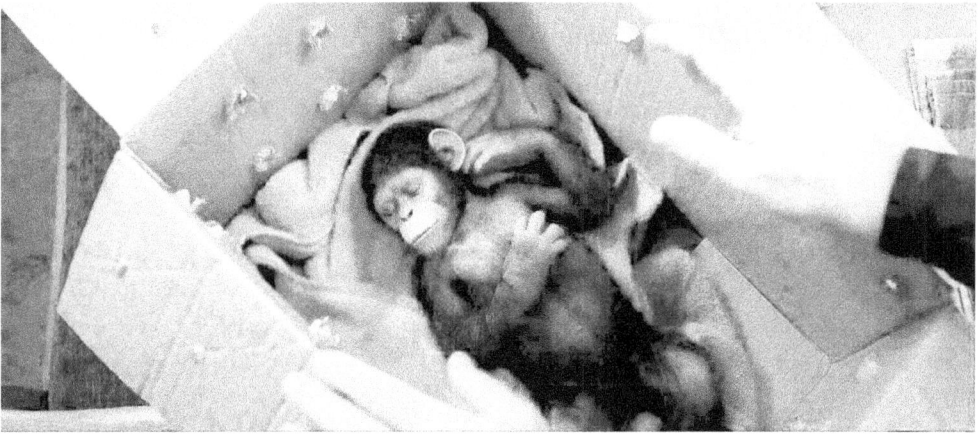

Caesar as a baby ape, rescued in *Rise of Planet of the Apes* (2011), just before Will adopts him but after his mother was euthanized when she went berserk while trying to protect him.

hold his fork at the dinner table and then loses control of a car, the filmmaker allows us to witness the cognitive decline caused by Alzheimer's. *Apes* lets us (secretly) speculate about what lies ahead.

Rise of the Planet of the Apes touches upon another topic: what are the limits of intelligence? If meds can make primates smarter, what stops us from using such meds on humans? In other words, can we turn anti–Alzheimer's meds into nootropics or performance enhancers? It turns out that students at one New York City college are already self-experimenting with this concept. There is buzz on campus that low-dose Aricept, marketed for Alzheimer's, can enhance studying, not as much as Adderall does, but enough to make it worth using. However, to date, there is no documented data to confirm this ad hoc use, much less an FDA approval in sight. Unfortunately, there is limited documentation that this med slows the progression of dementia.

The film chronicles the astronomical intellectual strides made by Caesar,[7] a chimpanzee exposed to the experimental agent in utero, when his mother was a test subject. It stops short of explaining how this neurobiological feat occurs. It expects spectators to know that developing fetal brains are more sensitive to such medications. We see Caesar grab the test chemical stockpiles, and we watch him roll the canisters past his primate comrades, encaged in the animal shelter. Suddenly, the apes become smarter. As the film ends, Caesar can speak as well as he can swing through the trees. We know *how* this happened, but we do not know *what* happened in the molecules of the mind.

The film presents likeable characters—a good son, an elderly father, an adorable animal, even an attractive and accomplished girlfriend. It is a human story embedded in a science fiction shell. If we choose to see *Rise of the Planet of the Apes,* we probably already know that at least two more classic science fiction tropes lie behind the scenes: the concept of time travel and space capsules. For *Rise of the Planet of the Apes* is a reimagining. It functions as a prequel of sorts as it explains how the apes got so smart. Earlier *Apes* films from the 1970s offered diametrically different origin stories, as mentioned in the endnotes.

Like *Rise of the Planet of the Apes, Limitless* asks questions about intelligence enhancers, but in a more limited and less provocative way. If we look hard enough, we can find parallels between contemporary concerns and the leitmotifs of *Limitless*—but we have to look hard and think even harder. Overall, *Limitless* does not have the social significance of *Rise of the Planet of the Apes. Rise of the Planet of the Apes* will always remind us of the heyday of civil rights and human rights movements, since it uses its characters as metaphors for pressing social issues of the 1960s. Most 21st century viewers never experienced this critical era in American history first hand, yet everyone who was educated in the U.S. after the 1960s studied these events in school.

Limitless never lacks in entertainment value. Its fast-paced plot lines parallel the effects of NZT, which makes users think faster and move faster. *Limitless* touches upon themes that reverberate in America today, but it makes no social commentary. If we ponder about *Limitless* for a moment, we can read references to drug dealing and drug wars. We witness white-collar crime that evades legal penalty, while low-level drug dealing in crack cocaine results in lifetime imprisonment (mostly for African Americans), as per New York State's draconian Rockefeller laws. The ruthlessness of corporate America (as personified by Robert De Niro's character) parallels low level or high-level drug dealing and double-dealing. Big

Pharma is portrayed as yet another ruthless big business, rather than as a humanitarian endeavor. We compare prescription drug abuse to the use of illicit stimulants, such as meth, Tina or crystal (which contain the same chemical as popular ADHD meds). Most of all, those who know of H.G. Wells' short story from 1901 will recognize how closely *Limitless* appropriates Wells' core ideas from the fin-de-siècle.

The Bourne Legacy (2012) appeared in the same year as *Limitless*. Based on books started by Robert Ludlum, this thriller casts Jeremy Renner as DOD operative Aaron Cross. After an expected series of mishaps, Cross finds himself going rogue, intent on exposing CIA misdeeds—while trying to save his own life at every step. The action starts in Alaska, where the scenery and cinematography are breathtaking, and where Cross scales a mountain more quickly than any other operative. His secret? "Chems," supplied by the Department of Defense (DOD), and administered by a beautiful biochemist, played by Rachael Weisz. Operative Aaron Cross relies on "blues" to retain his intelligence. He owes his strength and endurance, and his ability to scale mountains and leap across impassable mountain passes, to genetic enhancement.

Back at headquarters, he made regular visits to the medical department, where he was injected with a virus that altered his DNA. He also donated vials upon vials of blood, to be tested for who knows what. Now he is nearly out of "blues." He does not know what was in the injections, but he knows he needs the "chems" if he wants to retain his chemically-enhanced mental acumen. He desperately needs that inflated IQ if he hopes to survive another ordeal.

We later learn that Cross' low level native intelligence did not meet military standards. He was not even "average" when he enlisted. His recruiter falsified information, so Cross could de inducted into the U.S. Army. After that, he became a "black op" and an experimental test subject. In this way, Cross recollects Charly or The Lawnmower Man, whom we will discuss shortly. Cross' name reminds us of the symbolism in Hitchcock's *Strangers on a Train* (1951), where crisscrosses are everywhere, to alert us that the protagonist is about to be double-crossed. Cross does not know it, but he, too, will be double-crossed by the DOD.

Fearing the loss of his super-intelligence, Cross pursues the scientist who injected him with the unidentified virus. When he finds her, Dr. Shearing's house is under siege, and she is about to be abducted and/or assassinated by CIA operatives. Cross arrives at just the right time.

After saving her life, he convinces Dr. Shearing to appropriate the chemicals he needs to sustain himself. Their quest for "chems" leads them to the Philippines, where the secret substances are synthesized in a tightly-secured factory on the outskirts of Manila. The goal is to modify his DNA so he no longer needs the blue chems to sustain his mental gains.

The biochemist warns Cross that the treatment is experimental, but he insists. After enduring physical pain, mental gyrations, fevers and flashbacks, Cross recovers and acquires permanent mental—as well as physical—enhancement. This part of the plot recollects early World War II superhero stories about *Captain America* and scrawny Steve Rogers, the rejected military recruit who was rebuilt and bulked-out via the American military's "super-soldiers' serum."

In contrast, the CIA shut down their clandestine experiment in *Bourne*, and the agency intends to keep it secret by assassinating all of its enhanced soldiers, as well as the project's scientists. No wonder why the lives of both Dr. Shearing and Cross were imperiled. As her name implies, Dr. Shearing was led like a sheep to slaughter, when the CIA psychologist arranged a "debriefing" at her house—after all other lab workers were shot dead at their worksite.

The plot line of the aforementioned *The Bourne Legacy* also recollects real, well-documented CIA experiments with LSD, as part of Project MK-ULTRA. Those studies involved mind control, rather than mental enhancement (as far as we know). Another film, *Conspiracy Theory* (1997), starring Patrick Stewart, Mel Gibson and Julia Roberts, captures the essence of those CIA studies gone bad. As usual, the story line includes a kernel of truth, just enough to make us suspend disbelief for a few hours—and to make us wonder about what really happens in unreachable regions of Alaska.

Long before *Limitless* and *Bourne,* there was *Charly* (1968). Both the original *Apes* and *Charly* revolve around the rise of the disempowered. In those years, student protesters chanted, "Power to the People." These films reflect hopes that powerless people will eventually become empowered, possibly permanently. *Apes* and *Charly* predict the rise of the human potential movement of the 1970s, with its ever-optimistic rallying cry that "you can be all you want to be."

In 2009, *Entertainment Weekly* listed *Charly* among its "25 Best Movie Tearjerkers Ever".[8] In spite of its NSF trope, *Charly* is more of a melodrama and "weepie" than anything else. It is interesting that the *Charly* film was released in the same year as *Planet of the Apes*.

As *Entertainment Weekly* implies, *Charly* is a touching story of love, romance, high hopes and failed dreams. Charly himself is a mentally challenged bakery worker who works a routine, day-in, day-out job. Co-workers tease him relentlessly but he endures. He takes courses to improve his writing skills. Noticing his poor progress in spite of serious efforts, Charly's night school teacher, Alice, takes him to a clinic that is performing intelligence-enhancing surgery on animals. Before entering the study, Charly competes against a surgically enhanced lab rat named Algernon. Charly loses. Algernon completes the maze before Charly does.

Charly undergoes the surgery—and it is a success, for a while. His intelligence increases, his work performance improves, but his co-workers at the bakery resent his progress and conspire to get him fired. In the interim, he develops sexual fantasies about Alice. He also dabbles in the counterculture, growing his hair and riding a motorcycle. His behavior gets out of control, and his erotic and aggressive urges overtake him. In the midst of this, Algernon the mouse dies, leaving Charly to believe that his intellectual gains will disappear, and that he, too, may lose his life as well as his mind. The movie ends sadly, far more sadly than a later-appearing romantic comedy/SF film, *Eternal Sunshine of the Spotless Mind,* which revolves around memory erasure rather than intelligence expansion.

The sentiment behind *The Lawnmower Man* (1992) is polar opposite of the sad-sweet story of *Charly*. This NSF horror hybrid bears the name of a Stephen King short story, but the film and the story share only a single scene. Like *Charly, The Lawnmower Man* stars a simple-minded and unskilled laborer. The gardener is aptly named Jobe Smith. Jobe suffers like the Biblical Job. His surname, "Smith," implies that he is an "everyman" that is not distinguished by race or creed and that he could be anyone. Jobe lives in a garden shed owned by a priest. Jobe does odd jobs for the local landscaper, including lawn mowing. The priest beats Jobe regularly.

Pierce Brosnan plays Dr. Lawrence Angelo, the scientist who experiments on Jobe. Pierce Brosnan gained fame by starring in the hit television show, *Remington Steele* (1982–1987), before taking up the mantle of James Bond for seven years (1995–2002). Dr. Angelo works for Virtual Space Industries. He tests drugs and virtual reality on chimpanzees, trying to increase their intelligence and adapt them to military needs. In search of a human subject, Dr. Angelo spots Jobe pushing a lawnmower. Jobe is encouraged by the prospect of becoming smarter.

Jobe does indeed become smarter through Dr. Angelo's treatments. He also develops psychic abilities, including telepathy, telekinesis, and pyrokinesis. In other words, he can ignite fires with his thoughts. He eventually ignites the punitive priest, who burns like Satan in Hell.

When experimenting on Jobe, Dr. Angelo made a point of omitting the aggression-inducing chemicals that he used on chimps. The doctor hopes to spare Jobe of these untoward effects. However, the project director secretly substitutes the old serum for Dr. Angelo's reformulated version, and all hell breaks loose.

Jobe becomes psychotic. He hallucinates, and grows sexually and physically violent. Like *Charly,* Jobe's foray into advanced intelligence does not end well. Since *The Lawnmower Man* appears after the advent of cyberpunk, virtual reality is a prime mover of *Lawnmower's* plot. Through an unfortunate sequence of events, Jobe is trapped in virtual reality. Hoping to free him from this fate, Dr. Angelo follows Jobe into the virtual abyss. Dr. Angelo acts like his namesake, an angel, while the priest paradoxically functions as the devil in disguise, as he ignites like hellfire. Recall that *The Lawnmower Man* movie appeared after the priest sex scandals came to light, which allowed audiences to accept such an unkind portrayal of priests and perhaps even applaud his harsh punishment.

The Lawnmower Man spawned some aftereffects. A sequel *Lawnmower Man 2: Beyond Cyberspace* was released in 1996. Two video games were based on the film, *The Lawnmower Man* in 1993 and *Cyberwar* in 1994. The film also inspired Stephen King to sue, successfully, to remove his name from the film's title. (The original title was, *Stephen King's Lawnmower Man*.)

The Lawnmower Man's foray into the realm of the supernatural is hardly unique among science fiction films. Once again, this example proves Per Schelde's point, namely, that scientists are the new sorcerers. When a plot needs improvement, or an alternative ending, the option of reentering the world of the spirits remains, if only to remind us of the dotted line that separates magic from medicine, science from the supernatural, and psychiatry from sorcery.

A decade later, Steven Spielberg's *Minority Report* (2002) fuses science, neuropsychiatry and parapsychology. Inspired by the Philip K. Dick 1956 novella of the same name, *Minority Report* revolves around a Precrime Unit that identifies crimes before they occur, when plans for crimes are incubating in the unconscious of future criminals, without their conscious awareness.

Tom Cruise stars as Captain John Anderton, chief of Washington, D.C.'s Precrime Squad. The year is 2054. Murder has been eliminated in the nation's capital, thanks to the efforts of Precrime, and the insights of the "Precogs" that guide Precrime team members.

"Precogs" possess psychic abilities that allow them to see into the future. Unlike oracles of old, these female Precogs acquired their predictive powers through chemicals that their mothers ingested when the Precogs were still fetuses in utero. In PKD's original novella, the Precogs were "hydrocephalic idiots" with shriveled frontal lobes but exceptional psychic abilities. (Frontal lobes allow for planning and strategizing.) *Minority Report* was originally developed as a sequel to *Total Recall*, which is also based on a PKD original.

The Precogs' premonitions prove to be bogus. Unwanted opinions are discarded before they are disclosed. This pivotal fact goes unquestioned until the Precogs identify the squad leader as a future criminal. Pegged as a potential murderer, whose victim remains unknown, Chief Anderton has a desperate need to unravel the inner workings of the Precogs. To do this, he kidnaps the sole Precog who forecast the "minority report." The rest of the film focuses on the riveting revelations and on Tom Cruise's eventual escape. Tom Cruise's backstory, and the gripping drama surrounding the death of his son, flesh out the plot. The captain's addiction to a mood-altering chemical, Clarity, used to cope with his son's disappearance, adds another twist.

These plot details and the characters' depth are all well and good, but they are largely irrelevant to our study of neuroscience fiction, except for one fact: the Precogs received their remarkable psychological gifts through intrauterine exposure to drugs (in the film version only, but not in PKD's novella). This detail was very relevant when the film was released in 2002, for the media voiced concerns about so-called "crack babies" throughout the 1980s and 1990s.

Medical journals, as well as criminal justice reports, issued doomsday reports about "crack babies" born to crack-using mothers during the crack epidemic. The mass media seized on preliminary medical reports, and amplified them many times over. Pregnant women who used crack faced jail time. Although only a small minority condoned recreational crack use, the vast majority of civil libertarians objected to heavy-handed approaches used to convict and incarcerate drug-addled women. These women faced harsh sentences before adequate data was collected and assessed.[9] It turned out that "fetal alcohol syndrome" (or possibly even "fetal alcohol spectrum disorder") has far worse effects than "PCE" or "prenatal cocaine exposure."

By portraying the Precogs as products of intrauterine drug exposure, Steven Spielberg does two things: he draws attention to the controversies surrounding the crack epidemic and its impact on exposed fetuses, and he implicitly compares the conclusions reached by those preliminary (but unconfirmed) studies to the bogus psychic "minority report." At the same time, this film introduces us to an important issue facing women who used Prozac while pregnant. Prozac arrived in the late 1980s. By the time *Minority Report* premiered, Eli Lilly, Prozac's manufacturer, had already begun collecting data, and establishing what has since become the largest database on prenatal drug exposure ever.

To this day, controversy surrounds the use of psychotropic meds during pregnancy. Confirmed risks are very small (except for Paxil-related heart defects, and even that carries some caveats), yet class action lawsuits proceed. Women are terrorized into worrying about what will happen if they use their mood meds—or if they do not. Statistics about adverse effects associated with untreated depression are also frightening, maybe even more frightening, than the medications' small-scale correlations with autism, pulmonary hypertension, floppy baby syndrome, or early spontaneous pregnancy termination. *Minority Report* turns those fears into triumphs, retroactively, when it portrays the prenatally exposed Precogs as super-psychic, rather than as intellectually impaired. It follows the principle used in superhero stories about radiation exposure, where radioactivity imparts superpowers, rather than death or disease (think *Spider-Man, The Fantastic Four,* and *The Hulk.*)

The subject of prenatal exposure to chemicals—or potential teratogens—takes a different turn in Cronenberg's *Scanners* (1981). *Scanners* appeared as the psychiatric paradigm was shifting toward psychopharmacology. Scanners are lonely people who cannot tolerate too much stimulation, and so they avoid contact with others. We can see parallels between scanners and persons with schizophrenia, who also overreact to overstimulation in the environment and typically avoid excessive interpersonal interactions.

Like some persons with schizophrenia, scanners believe that they have unusual perceptions and psychic abilities. The difference between Cronenberg's scanners and schizophrenic persons who claim special powers or believe that government agents are out to get them lies in the government's perceptions, and not in the perceiver. In Cronenberg's universe, the government concurs with the scanners' belief systems, so much so that a central agency has herded the scanners into a single location, in hopes of harnessing their skills.

Up until now, this sounds like the standard brand horror-science fiction paranoid plot. When we consider Cronenberg's explanation for scanners' paranormal abilities, we find rich material for neuroscience fiction, as well as an astute commentary on pharmacological tragedies from the past. The scanners did not inherit their abilities. They were not bred to perform fantastic feats. Rather, their psychic powers result from prenatal exposure to Ephemerol. This fluke reminds us of thalidomide, which was prescribed to pregnant women as a tranquilizer and anti-nausea agent—until an unprecedented epidemic occurred.

After a German drug company began to market thalidomide in 1957, it became apparent that thalidomide caused phycomelia (flipper limbs and lobster hands) in babies that were exposed at specific intervals during gestation. Sometimes, fingers grew out of shoulders. Luckily, a cautious FDA physician refused to approve this medication. This move prevented thalidomide from entering the American market and spared most U.S. citizens of thalidomide's effects. Most cases occurred in Europe or in Americans who spent time overseas.

While we watch *Scanners,* we may recall this historical event from time to time—or we may become so engrossed in this rather gross film that we forget relevant links to the past. *Scanners* is a major departure from Cronenberg's 1979 film, *The Brood,* which involves a strange offshoot of psychotherapy, conducted at the Somafree Institute of Psychoplasmics. In that film, therapeutic techniques alone—without the addition of the body (soma)—give form to mutant (and mutilating) babies that form from anger brewing inside the protagonist's ex-wife. These babies are figments of the mind, and so they, too, are "soma-free" or body-free.

In that Cronenberg film, spectators appreciate the correlation between internalized and externalized anger, even if they do not possess psychoanalytically sophisticated vocabularies. Some might say that the ex-wife has a variant of multiple personality disorder. However, we literally see the "splitting of the self" that occurs in persons with unstable personal identities. (Many view MPD as a variant of BPD, or borderline personality disorder.) Such persons often receive diagnoses of "borderline personality disorder," a much-discussed but incompletely understood disorder. Cronenberg breathes life into these abstract personality traits, which are embodied by the unborn babies birthed from the wife's mind. Spectators with advanced knowledge of abstruse psychoanalytic therapy can comprehend these nuances more easily, and readily appreciate Cronenberg's insights as being more than his usual brand of "body horror."

In 1979, when this film was made, enough practicing psychiatrists and psychologists accepted psychoanalytic theory as fact, even though these theories cannot be confirmed (or refuted) as readily as neurobiological hypotheses. Even those professionals who were skeptical about psychoanalytic claims probably learned these theories during their post-graduate training and could relate to Cronenberg's presentation. To this day, borderline personality disorder remains an enigma, although its manifestations are readily apparent. Unprovoked anger outbursts, dissociative states under stress, and *Zelig*-like shifts in identify in persons without a core "sense of self" are relatively easy to spot, both in real life and in Cronenberg's character. Identifying the definitive cause of such problems is more difficult than reliving symptoms, and relieving the symptoms is still more difficult than positing a diagnosis that others agree with.

Compared to *Scanners*, *Rise of the Planet of the Apes*' treatment of intrauterine exposure to neuroactive medications seems serious. *Planet of the Ages* credits Caesar's unusual intelligence to his prenatal exposure to test chemical ALZ-112. This premise is credible, largely because we know that many toxins (such as lead) have stronger effects on developing brains. Exposures that are too low to harm fully-formed adult brains can have drastic effects on fetuses and growing children, as we discuss in the endnotes. Almost everyone knows that many pediatric medications are dosed by age or weight. So spectators have every reason to believe that adult anti–Alzheimer's meds have especially potent effects on fetuses. Spectators readily suspend disbelief, and accept that Caesar became super-intelligent because his pregnant mother's meds passed through the placenta and into the yet unborn (and unnamed) Caesar. We believe that the medically enhanced Caesar had the wherewithal to steal the canisters and to deliver them to his primate peers and thereby create a super-race. If only we could believe that currently available Alzheimer's medications are as effective as they are made out to be. That, alas, is still wishful thinking. The benefits of our current armamentarium of anti–AD meds are limited.

These science fiction films about increasing intelligence sound like something invented to meet our society's current scourge—Alzheimer's disease. However, if we look back at 19th century literature, we find that one of the so-called fathers of SF conceived of similar ideas, even before Alois Alzheimer (1864–1915) identified the dreaded dementing disease in 1906. Curiously, another psychiatrist, Arnold Pick, of the University of Prague, identified a less common form of dementia in 1892, many years before Alois Alzheimer made his mark.

Alzheimer called his discovery, "Presenile degeneration." Emil Kraeplin, an illustrious psychiatrist in his own right, and a pioneering researcher of schizophrenia, dubbed the disorder, "Alzheimer's disease," in honor of Alois Alzheimer. We rarely, if ever, speak of Pick's Disease today, and are more likely to refer to the syndrome described by Pick as FTD (frontotemporal dementia). FTD is far less common than Alzheimer's disease (AD), but is more intriguing to the psychiatrist, because behavioral changes may occur long before memory or speech impairment, making it easy to mistake early bvFTD (behavioral variant) for other psychiatric illnesses.

These details about the history of neuroscience are also intriguing, largely because so many major advances in knowledge were made in the second half of the 19th century.[10]

Herbert George Wells (1866–1946) was aware of rapid changes that were taking place during his lifetime, for he himself studied biology, worked as a chemist's assistant, and later taught science. He failed as a draper's apprentice, much to his mother's chagrin but to the benefit of Western Civilization. Wells receives credit as one of the three founding fathers of SF (the other two being Jules Verne and Hugo Gernsback, who is the namesake of the "Hugo Awards.")

Wells expanded his literary repertoire in his later career, and moved on to write more ordinary novels, essays, and book reviews. Wells' best-selling book was a two-volume *Outline of History* (1920). In 1933, he wrote the prophetic book, *The Shape of Things to Come*. Health problems interfered with his productivity in later years, as did the depression he developed in response to World War II. Wells was working on a manuscript about the dangers of nuclear war at the time of his death in 1946. Appreciation of Wells' early insights into science fiction, and his admonitions about the promises and perils of memory enhancers, will never die. His memory lives on forever with his fans.

An ad for Lacuna Inc., from *Eternal Sunshine of the Spotless Mind* (2004), alludes to the memory-erasing process accessed by ex-lovers Joel (Jim Carrey) and Clementine (Kate Winslet), as it asks, "Is there something on your mind you'd like to forget?"

To conclude this chapter, I should say something about memory erasers, which appear far less frequently in NSF film than memory enhancers—although memory erasers top the list of "preferred" SF inventions. As discussed previously, the plots of *Eternal Sunshine of the Spotless Mind* and *Total Recall* revolve around memory erasure. The comedic SF film, *Men in Black* (1997), mentions a handheld "neuralyzer" that removes memories more readily than a whiff of Dust-Off removes dust from shelves.

A signature tool of the Men in Black, the neuralyzer puts witnesses into a trance so that they do not remember that their memories were erased. This is convenient for voiding recollections of aliens or for clearing the cache (so to speak) of retiring agents, who no longer need to recall secrets. Agent K (Tommy Lee Jones) is subjected to a neuralyzer when he leaves the force, and no longer has a "need to know." Neuralyzers come in different models, and some have more advanced functions. Agents in the newer sequels fear exposure to older and outdated models that they believe cause brain damage. To avoid exposure to neuralyzers' powerful effects, the Men in Black wear their signature Ray-Ban sunglasses wherever they go.

Some SF fans speculated that neuralyzers might prove useful in removing traumatic memories. The pen-shaped device is listed among the "Top 10 Film Inventions We Wish Were True." Many a truth is said in jest, and sometimes the joke turns out to be true. Recall that recent research into PTSD shows that ECT (electroconvulsive therapy) holds promise for making people forget traumatic events, if it is administered at the appropriate time, before memories become consolidated and permanent. Today, the greatest downside of ECT, when used to treat otherwise untreatable depression, psychosis or catatonia, is the risk of memory impairment.

I find it unlikely that many trauma victims will opt for ECT, unless their trauma is so severe and no other choice is available. Perhaps a new and improved version of ECT will be developed sometime in the near future. If that treatment is compared to a neuralyzer, rather than to the mean-spirited ECT used on Jack Nicholson's McMurphy in *Cuckoo's Nest,* this still-experimental treatment may be better received. *Cuckoo's Nest* made an entire generation denounce this otherwise useful treatment technique (ECT), and even prompted California legislators to outlaw it altogether. Who knows what the neuralyzer lobby can accomplish?

Eleven

Dream Scenes: From Silent Cinema to Salvador Dalí to CGI

Dreams have been central to cinema since the dawn of cinema. Dream themes appear at cinema's start, at the end of the late 19th century, and continue throughout the 20th century and into the 21st century. During certain time periods, and in some film genres, dream themes and dream scenes become more prominent. By tracing the depiction of dreams in films, we can see how psychiatry changed over this course of time. We also see major changes in cinematography.[1] Sometimes we are fooled into thinking that ideas about dreams are fresher than they actually are, when in actuality, it is the advances in filmmaking that make old ideas look new again.

The earliest days of film coincided chronologically with the "discovery" of psychoanalysis. The first was born in 1895, the other in 1896. In those days, when film was in its infancy, dream interpretation was on a continuum with occultism, more often than not.[2] Freud strived to substitute a "scientific" approach to the interpretation of dreams, through his book of the same name, published in 1900. At that time, the word "scientific" carried different connotations than it does in our current era, and other legitimately scientific studies of dream content were conducted before Freud.

Today, few regard Freud's views as "scientific"—although some devotees continue to worship at the shrine of "St. Sigmund," more as an article of faith than because of scientific proof. Regardless of one's pro or anti–Freud stance, everyone recognizes the profound influence that Freudian ideas wielded over mid-century film, and over 20th century Western culture in general. The 20th century has been called "the psychoanalytic century," for good reason.

In the earliest years of the 20th century, Freudian theories had not yet infiltrated the film industry. Infatuation with magicians, hypnotists, occultists, even sorcerers and Satanists, remained and turned into perfect plots for "movie magic" and for the hypnotic silver screen. Victorian spirit photography was still in vogue in some circles, as the 19th century ended. Since many early movies were little more than "moving photos," without spoken words, double-exposure spirit scenes worked better than ill-understood psychoanalytic "talk therapy" scenes.

Plots were less important to the short silents than eye-catching moving images, which could convey the uniqueness of this invention. Inter-titles between shots explain the action in a short sentence or two, but such condensed text is poorly suited for complicated ideas and interactions. More often than not, plots were a means to showcase interesting and innovative cinematography techniques, rather than the other way around.

Early filmmakers like Georges Méliès delighted in dream themes because dreams were the perfect backdrop for his movie magic. Méliès was a magician before he became a moviemaker, and he remained a magician as he made movie magic by cranking his camera, watching it jam, and witnessing unexpected results that were as fanciful as a rabbit that jumps out of a magician's hat. Dreams demanded very special special effects, and drew upon his skills as a stage magician. A visionary in more ways than one, Méliès saw film's potential for mass entertainment at a time that others—Edison included—expected to restrict film to education or to use film as a scientific study tool. Like dreams, movies lay at the crossroads between science, art and occultism. A sorcerer could be as proud of this creation as a scientist!

Méliès made many short silents about dreams, with some of them being but a few minutes long. A few of his titles include *A Nightmare* (1896); *The Drunkard's Dream* (1897); *The Artist's Dream* (1898); *The Astronomer's Dream* (aka *The Man in the Moon*) (1898); *The Christmas Dream* (1900); *The Rajah's Dream* (French: *Le Réve du Radjah ou La Forêt Enchantée*) (1900); *The Dream of a Hindu Beggar* (1902); *The Dream of the Ballet Master* (1903); *The Clockmaker's Dream* (1904); *The Dream of the Poor Fisherman* (1904); *The Dream of an Opium Fiend* (1908); *Tale of the Grandmother and the Child's Dream* (1908); *Baron Munchausen's Dream* (1911). *The Beggar's Dream* (1903) is lost.

Other filmmakers delved into dreams, but few mastered the technique of fantasy and film the way Méliès did and none approached this meme with Méliès' passion. Pathé continued Méliès' tradition. In 1909, Charles Kent directed the first film version of Shakespeare's play, *A Midsummer Night's Dream*. An early silent film about *Dream of a Rarebit Fiend* (1906) was made by Edwin S. Porter and Wallace McCutcheon, who soon redirected their focus and carved out illustrious cinema careers that earned them a permanent place in film history. *Dream Street* (1921), a much later film by the very talented—but equally controversial—filmmaker D. W. Griffith,[3] does not concern dreams, in spite of its title.

August Blom's *Atlantis* (1913) revolves around the dreams of a doctor as he sails on a sinking passenger ship and perceives that he is walking through the sunken city of Atlantis. The first Danish feature film, *Atlantis* inspired SF author JG Ballard to write his apocalyptic novel, *A Drowned World* (1962). *Poor Little Rich Girl* (1917), by French-born Maurice Tourneur (father of Jacques Tourneur of *Cat People,* 1942) was deemed "culturally significant" by the United States Library of Congress and selected for preservation in the National Film Registry. Child actor Mary Pickford stars as the emotionally neglected young girl whose overbearing servants accidentally overdose her with a sleeping potion. As her doctor tries to save her, she experiences Oz-like reverie in her dreams.

In an earlier chapter on Automatons, we talked about *Hugo* (Scorsese, 2011), an unexpectedly sweet film made by the master of the mean streets, Martin Scorsese. Scorsese made his name through crime themes and mobster stories. Scorsese spent his youth in New York's mob-controlled Little Italy.[4] *Hugo* is homage to Méliès, and to the transcendent visions that propelled Méliès, with tearjerker level of attention to the bittersweet years of Méliès' later life.

In Méliès' work, we see no hint of concern about the biological underpinnings of dreams (just as we see no concern with the astrophysics of flying or the geophysics of the moon's surface). The discovery of REM sleep or other sleep stages was decades away when Méliès worked. In many neuroscience fiction films, in contrast, the biological aspects of dreams become as significant as their aesthetics. Technical equipment that measures the physiological components of dream imagery—such as EEG machines, and the spike and wave paper printouts that they produce—may signify dreams in NSF. More advanced monitoring equipment is used in contemporary sleep labs, such as PSG (polysomnogram), MSLT (multiple sleep latency test), and MWT (multiple wakefulness test). However, these machines are rarely used as props, simply because they are not as recognizable as the old-fashioned EEG apparatus from 1928, which has become familiar to filmgoers and to physicians alike.[5]

At earlier points in film history, camera techniques signaled dream scenes. Changes of color, from black & white to Technicolor, or the reverse, or perhaps jump cuts with wavy lines or slow motion or out-of-focus scenes, even superimposed images, told spectators that the scene has shifted from waking reality to sleeping dreams. Perhaps the most distinctive dream scene appears in Hitchcock's *Spellbound* (1945), with Salvador Dalí's surrealistic stage props, with morphing bunny rabbits, eye-covered stage curtains, misshapen wagon wheels and a huge pair of shears. There are many instances when dream scenes were simply an excuse to add special effects.

Some NSF films examine dreams on a monitor, and remind us of skeletons seen through x-rays, or electrical heart beats or brain waves that appear on EKGs or EEGs, respectively. In an early scene in *Prometheus* (2012), a technician tends to the sleeping body of an astronaut who lies in suspended animation. He peers into a dream-o-scope of sorts. This apparatus displays her dream images on a screen that sits outside her pod. The dream monitor reminds us of the rows of EKG monitors situated in a corner of the ICU (intensive care unit), where leads attached to patients send signals to remote screens that are mounted in a separate alcove. A highly skilled nurse sits in front of these screens, peering at this "medical multiplex," scrutinizing them for signs of new or dangerous pathology so he or she can alert bedside nurses or summon cardiologists or intensivists. The tech in *Prometheus* has those advantages, and more.

In *Prometheus,* the tech does not need to see an EEG projected on screen. He no longer needs to look for brain wave patterns that tell him if his subject is in delta or slow wave sleep, or in another state of consciousness altogether. This sleep lab bears no resemblance to contemporary sleep labs, where elaborate equipment displays secondary physiological changes that accompany sleep (such as oxygen utilization, blood pressure fluctuations or eye movement speed). His equipment is advanced enough to tap into the dreams themselves, as if those dreams were being played on a DVD. He can observe the images, actions and maybe even emotions that she experiences while asleep.

Even though this opening scene functions as a framing device, and prepares the spectators for the action that follows in the next few hours, its technologically oriented approach matches the film's SF motif. It draws parallels between common contemporary medical equipment that is recognizable to most people—such as EKGs and EEGs—and then suggests ways that more advanced technology might operate. At present, it seems farfetched to think about uploading dream imagery directly from the brain and then broadcasting them on a monitor, the way we send signals from smart phones via Wi-Fi to special-equipped television screens. Nevertheless, audiences can appreciate the imagination that seeds this imagery.

Even though it is clearly fiction, this feat makes us speculate about what may be feasible in the future. We know that CT scans or MRIs show shifts in brain structure and that PET scans compare blood flow or glucose utilization, and that EEGs record electrical signals from different locations in the brain. New medical devices come to market with increasing speed. No one knows what inventions await, although books by neuroscientists such as Miguel Nicolelis, M.D., Ph.D. (*Beyond Boundaries,* 2012)[6] hint about the progress that awaits us in the near future. Governmental regulatory bodies can barely keep pace with bioengineering inventions that come to market. They often find themselves backpedalling after unforeseen problems from such "advances" arise. Films like this remind us of the expanding realms of possibility—and of the risks that accompany an overly enthusiastic embrace of advances, without vetting them first.

More often than not, dreams in NSF push the plot—just as they do in psychoanalytically informed *film noir* from mid-century, when dream themes were at their peak. In NSF, dreams often serve a very special function: they distinguish between human and machine. Supposedly, only humans can dream, but an automaton cannot. A robot that attains the ability to dream has surmounted its role as a robot. That is the case in *Blade Runner,* when the most advanced model robot experiences dreams that contained personalized memories that were programmed into her. When Deckard realizes that Rachael dreams, he cannot terminate her, because she is human. Instead, the two head off into the proverbial sunset together, to live out their lives as humans.

At other times, dreams inform the dreamer that something is amiss in waking reality and that what seems to be real may be as unreal as a dream. There are both metaphysical and philosophical connotations to dreams. *RoboCop's* original Officer Murphy experiences dreams about his family and his past life in his original biomorphic form. In both *Total Recall* and *RoboCop,* as well as in the remake of *The Manchurian Candidate,* dreams or dreamlike flashbacks alert the protagonist that something is missing from their waking awareness. It is relatively rare that we find a film that focuses exclusively on the neurobiology of dreaming, although the most recent reboot of *RoboCop* alludes to neurotransmitters and shows how scientists manipulate Murphy's dreams, as if they were inserting a continuous tape loop into his hippocampus, where memories are stored in the brain (in real life, not reel life).

Brainstorm (1983) is one of those exceptions. *Brainstorm* from 1983 should not be confused with the *noir* film by the same name, directed by William Conrad in 1965. That earlier *Brainstorm* (1965) revolves around a middle-aged scientist who falls in love with a young woman after he prevents her suicide—but before he learns she is married. This film has been compared to *Double Indemnity* (1944) and to *Vertigo* (1958) and is deemed to be "one of noir's bleakest installments."[7] However, the 1965 *Brainstorm* shares no similarities to the 1983 *Brainstorm,* except for the recurring leitmotifs about love triangles and marital strife.

Douglas Trumbull directs *Brainstorm* (1983). The son of the renowned special effects artist from *Wizard of Oz,* the younger Trumbull hoped that this film could showcase a technological advance that he dubbed, "Showscan." Unfortunately, his vision was too far ahead of the times—and too costly, also—for movie theaters refused to buy the extra equipment needed for these novel effects. Many remember Trumbull's genius at special effects, his innovations in technology, his impressive lineage, and his contributions to the oeuvre of science fiction film

Eleven. Dream Scenes 195

In this *Blade Runner* (1982) poster, noirish sets inspired by *Metropolis* (1927) color the foreground, while gun-toting Deckard (Harrison Ford) in the upper left looks away, and Rachael (Sean Young) looks like an ordinary human, even though she is an advanced model replicant.

that won him a place in the Science Fiction Hall of Fame. Far fewer remember Trumbull's contribution to this film in particular. *Brainstorm* (1983) did not do well at the box office, and it has largely faded from memory, yet still deserves further discussion in this section.

Trumbull's contributions to *Blade Runner* and *Close Encounters of the Third Kind* have far higher profiles. Trumbull's philosophy about portraying the machinations of the mind through special cinematography speaks directly to neuroscience researchers and mental health professionals. Trumbell scoffed at the idea of adding a "gauzy, mysterious, distant kind of image" to signify flashbacks or point-of-view. He stated that he "wanted to do just the opposite, to make the material of the mind even more real and high-impact that 'reality.'" In that way, he proves that he is perfectly suited for neuroscience fiction film, and he shows how much he owes to Aristotelian ideas. For Aristotle opined, "The unexamined life is not worth living."

Several prominent actors star in this strange film. Christopher Walken portrays a scientist who is at odds with his scientist-wife (Natalie Wood), who also goes by the name "Dr. Brace." Walken is a familiar figure to fans of neuroscience fiction films, for he typically plays psychologically unstable characters that sometimes use drugs (*The Deer Hunter,* 1978), endure dangerous brain surgery experiments (*The Mind Snatchers,* 1972), or communicate with the occult (*The Dead Zone,* 1983, David Cronenberg's adaptation of the Stephen King novel).

Natalie Wood died during the filming for reasons that are still ill understood. Her mysterious drowning death almost brought production to a halt. Louise Fletcher plays another scientist who works with Walken and Wood (Drs. Brace). Her character, Lillian, is credited with discovering this previously unheard of technique that transfers thoughts to tape. Less than a decade earlier, Louise Fletcher played Nurse Ratched in *One Flew over the Cuckoo's Nest* (1975). As Nurse Ratched, she sends insolent patients for ECT (electroconvulsive therapy) and arranges for unwarranted lobotomies. Through that role, Fletcher is forever associated with neuropsychiatry, but in a bad way. Recollections of Fletcher as Nurse Ratched make it easier for audiences to accept her character's early and unexpected death in *Brainstorm*.

Marital discord drives *Brainstorm*'s plot, but the main motif revolves around a brain-computer interface that records perceptions and sensations from one person's brain and converts them to tape. Through this innovation, anyone who watches and listens to the tape can re-experience the first person's perceptions and sensations second hand. The intrusion of double-dealing military-industrial complex mercenaries into the simpler lives of scientific researchers is a leitmotif. This trope rings true and recurs in many other SF films, including *Rise of the Planet of the Apes, Contagion,* virtually any existent film based on William Gibson's writings, and the recent 2014 *RoboCop*.

The neuroscientific premise is somewhat far-fetched, especially when we watch this film on DVD, years later, and see that neuropsychiatric responses transfer to obsolete reel-to-reel tapes. However, in 1984, when the film debuted, home video was revolutionary. In a short time, video rental stores popped up everywhere. The tapes themselves cost $60–70, hardly worth the price for a single night's viewing. However, rentals that cost between $1 and $5 a day appealed to the public and created a whole new market. Many predicted the demise of movie theatres at that time, but just the opposite proved true—at least for a while. Home videos made many spectators appreciate the value of the big screen experience more than ever before. Today, most video rental stores have closed and are probably even less common than 50s era soda fountains, which retain a certain timeless charm. As always, new technology invites excitement, and also ignites fears about its potential for abuse.

We can easily devote a chapter to changes in viewing technology, with details about the impact on small business owners, corporate shareholders, and more ordinary staff that work in those businesses. However, the take-away point of *Brainstorm* harps back to the days of Pavlov, who won a Nobel Prize for his pioneering studies in physiology and behavioral conditioning. *Brainstorm* reiterates the importance of physiological reflexes that accompany mental and emotional reactions. For instance, disturbing or exciting stimuli raise blood pressure through vasoconstriction (contraction of the blood vessels). Rapid respiration (heavy breathing) and increased perspiration (sweating) follow—regardless of whether these stimuli are experienced first hand or second hand, or whether they are transmitted through video tape or whether they are spontaneous reactions to real life stimuli. Understanding the unconscious connection between expressed or experienced emotion and the physiological responses that accompany those reactions helps us suspend disbelief while watching this otherwise preposterous film.

This innovative recording/transmitting device wreaks destruction overall, but it accomplishes some good in the course of the film: it helps Walken and Wood reconcile after Walken records his reactions, develops insight into his annoying behavior, and conveys his regret to his estranged wife. Subsequent events are tragic. Lillian (Louise Fletcher), the team's other female scientist, has a heart attack while recording her reactions. She appears to be in a heightened emotional state, brought on by conflicts with her money-minded financial backers, after they revealed their plan to sell her discoveries to the military, in spite of her objections.

After Lillian's (Fletcher's) funeral, Dr. Michael Brace (Walken), the married scientist, wants to experience Lillian's last moments of life via her recording. He witnesses her life's memories in the form of "memory bubbles." He has a near-death experience as her physiological responses to her MI transmit through tape. Recognizing the signs of an impending heart attack, he stops the tape before he himself responds in kind. He then edits those tracks out of the tape, to safeguard others and prevent harm from befalling team members who innocently replay the tape.

In the interim, the military scientists who caused so much chagrin for Lillian (and indirectly contributed to her untimely death) are hacking into the system, eager to appropriate the tapes. One of the military scientists dispenses with Michael's precautions, and co-opts an unedited tape. By tapping into the tape, he re-experiences Lillian's death. His body responds to the physiological stimuli that she recorded. He, too, succumbs to a heart attack and dies.

Even more adverse adventures occur, as this high-tech family drama takes on a Job-like trajectory. The son of the two married scientists (Walken and Wood) accesses the tapes, has a psychotic break and ends up in a psychiatric hospital. Aiming to destroy the tapes and prevent the military from carrying out their plans to "torture and brainwash" subjects through their tapes, Michael destroys the building. He nearly dies himself. During his near death experience, he has hallucinatory visions of Hell. Images of souls and angels appear before he literally and figuratively "sees the light" and returns to earth to rebuild his relationship with his wife.

This quasi-occult ending shifts the focus of the otherwise scientifically minded movie. This film was not a commercial success, but similar motifs occur in later films by the same screenwriter, Bruce Joel Rubin. Bruce Joel Rubin gained fame for *Jacob's Ladder* (1990), which earned him a cult following. Rubin's original screenplay included more traditional occult iconography, with demons in Hell, but director Adrian Lyne omitted the standard-brand, Christian-influenced imagery. *Jacob's Ladder* merges mystical and meditative reflections with Francis Bacon-esque hallucinatory scenes. The Bacon-influenced imagery was added by the film's director.[8] Jacob's visions blend psychedelic drug experiences with Tibetan Buddhist lore about after-death journeys through the often-frightening "Bardos."[9] The following year, Rubin wrote the Academy Award-winning screenplay for the occult-themed *Ghost* (1991).

In 1984, the year following *Brainstorm,* another film with a similar dream theme surfaces. Directed by Joseph Ruben and written by David Loughery, *Dreamscape* (1984) employs scientific-looking lab equipment to investigate psychic activities. *Dreamscape* has none of the usual trappings of occult thrillers. There are no demons, vampires, zombies or ghosts. The set design looks completely contemporary, with streamlined hospital scenes and blinking computer screens that lend a SF feel. The paranormal hero interfaces with his mentor, Dr. Novotny, who looks like a traditional research scientist on the surface. Dr. Novotny runs a sleep lab to help people who suffer from nightmares—but he also transports psychics into REM sleep, where dreams facilitate inter-brain exchanges.

Dennis Quaid stars as Alex Gardner, a young psychic who enters people's dreams and who was the main subject of scientific research into his psychic abilities. Alex goes astray, and takes to womanizing and gambling, which lead to trouble with the mob and make him a target for blackmailing. Max von Sydow plays the sleep researcher, Dr. Paul Novotny, who is murdered by enemy agents, as is George Wendt's character, a novelist who plans to reveal the conspiracies that drive the plot. Christopher Plummer is the CIA agent who orchestrates plans to use dream-linking techniques for assassinations. In fact, the President of the U.S.A himself is targeted for assassination because he has post-apocalyptic nightmares that make him a security risk. As in the case of *Brainstorm,* a romantic subplot lightens up the plot and closes the film.

It is not surprising to see so many films that hover between dreams, science, and spirituality. Dreams, by their very nature, are immaterial, and so lend themselves to occultist explanations. Because both the body and the brain change during dreaming, we can measure many physiological accompaniments to dream states, using scientific know how, which leads into science fiction formats. Occultism intrigues many—even though it repels many others. It is surprising how many science fiction films blend supernatural themes, to remind us that scientists are society's latter day sorcerers that make the immaterial material and weave gold from flax.

We cannot talk about sci-fi dream-themed films without mentioning a horror classic that premiered at the very same time as *Dreamscape* and *Brainstorm.* The theme about killers entering dreams repeats itself in several films. The best known of this ilk is *Nightmare on Elm Street* (1984), directed by Wes Craven. Craven wrote the film in 1981 and shopped it around for years, before finding a studio that would produce it. His script was rejected by Paramount Productions because *Dreamscape* was already in production and had too similar a theme.

Clearly, Craven's Freddy Kruger and *Elm Street* outlived its competitors, and sprang to life several times over, rising from the dead more reliably than vampires. *Elm Street* became a remarkably successful franchise, and remains a horror classic to this day (even if cannot compete with the success of the *Star Wars* franchise). In *Nightmare on Elm Street,* a convicted child murderer enters the dreams of adolescents, killing them brutally. These bloody murders make the Freddy films a prime example of the "slasher genre" that became wildly popular in the early eighties, at the very same time that a deadly disease (AIDS) was spreading through sex and blood. The basic motifs are essentially the same in *Brainstorm, Dreamscape,* and *Nightmare on Elm Street*. This meme recollects ancient lore, as well as the Australian concept of "Dreamtime."

Wes Craven, however, can articulate the sources of his ideas. A one-time Ph.D. candidate, Craven attributes some of his inspiration to 1970s-era articles that he read in the *L.A. Times*. (He also credits his own experiences with childhood bullying for his preoccupation with Freddy.)

The newspaper articles referenced by Craven concerned Khmer refugees from Cambodia, who resettled in the U.S. The refugees retained their animist-influenced belief system about medical and psychiatric symptoms. Many Khmer men suffered from nightmares, which today's psychiatrists might attribute to PTSD (post-traumatic stress disorder). The Cambodian men refused to sleep. Some died in their sleep, victims of the so-called "Brugada syndrome" otherwise known as the "Asian death syndrome."

Even though Western physicians can easily offer other explanations for these sad and strange events, and even though it is well known that sleep deprivation promotes early death (as do life traumas), Craven avoided scientific hypotheses that would intrigue SF fans. Instead, he exploited the events for his horror story and apparently tapped into the pulse of 1980s America. Historian F. Scott Poole has explored the cultural underpinnings of Freddy's success during the decadent eighties, when Ronald Reagan took office, and when AIDS emerged as a silent pandemic, but was not acknowledged in public until 1984, after the death of Rock Hudson.[10]

When trying to understand the intrigue with dream themes, science fiction or otherwise, during this specific interval, we can consider the wavering role of psychiatry and psychoanalysis in the mid–1980s. As mentioned in the introductory chapter, psychiatry was a "house divided" during the 1980s. Dr. Osheroff's attorneys won their first injunction in 1982, but waited until 1989 for the courts to settle the case completely. The Osheroff case pitted advances in psychopharmacology against tradition-bound psychoanalysis.

Thanks in part to Osheroff's legal victory, the psychoanalysts' stronghold on psychiatry was losing ground. Analysis as the dominant treatment technique was sinking into quicksand, disappearing beneath the deep, but not without emitting piecing screams and air bubbles, insisting that it should stay afloat and showing proof that it was still alive and breathing.

Recall that psychoanalysis began with Freud, and that Freud's favorite—and most famous—book was *Interpretation of Dreams* (1900). Freud identified dreams as "the royal road to the unconscious" and claimed that he offered a scientific interpretation of dreams to replace reigning occultist theories. Films that alternately focus on the biological basis of dreams—which is remarkably different from Freud's metapsychological approach—responded to this newfound emphasis on biological psychiatry. Similarly, atavistic themes about occult connotations of dreams were throwbacks to the pre–Freudian era, when superstition and supernaturalism presided. Either way, psychoanalysis and Freudianism were squeezed from both sides. These diametrically different approaches to dream-themed films reflect this shift in psychiatric thinking. Because psychoanalysis had infiltrated the culture at large as much as it influenced American psychiatric practice, this shift in psychiatry also made itself manifest in film.

There is another film that hovers between neuropsychiatry and spirituality, without dealing with dreams directly. That film does not fit into the other main NSF tropes discussed in this book. So I will mention it here. With its crisscrossed supernatural and scientific themes, *Flatliners* (1990) bears some similarities to *Jacob's Ladder,* which premiered in the same year. *Flatliners* opened in the year that marked the start of the so-called "Decade of the Brain."

Flatliners promised an all-star cast but delivered a less-than-promising film. *Flatliners* is directed by Joel Schumacher, who went on to direct *Batman and Robin* (1997) and *Batman Forever* (1995). The film stars Kiefer Sutherland, Julia Roberts, Kevin Bacon, William Baldwin and Oliver Platt as medical students who want to know more than standard textbooks teach them. The team became intrigued by reports about the afterlife, provided by patients who were resuscitated in the operating room, after they "flat-lined." Eager to understand these experiences, the students nevertheless remain cautious, and experiment only in the presence of other students that can monitor them during these excursions.

Using an EKG monitor (or is it an EEG monitor?) to confirm that each is clinically dead, the med students aspire to "flat line." They promise to return from that "other world" to report their after-death experiences to the others. It is their experiences—rather than the specifics of the experiment per se—that produce a plot. Some confront events that they would prefer to forget—like one student's role in the bullying death of a fellow grade school student. The lone woman, played by Julia Roberts, expects to prove that death is not a bad place. She revisits her father's suicide, only to learn that he was addicted to heroin and accidentally overdosed. None of the student-experimenters see those glowing lights, but some insist on returning to "the other side" to "make amends" to those they wronged in the past. Some become clinically psychotic and suffer from voices and visions even after their return to the "real world." In the end, the film veers away from science and morphs into morality tale, which often happens in science fiction.

Although critics were slow to praise this film, in spite of its impressive cast, the plot broaches a subject that typically intrigues many medical students—but makes skeptics of others. It is quite common to hear patients describe events that transpired while they were clinically dead. It is even more common to witness dying patients hallucinate, and speak with angels or long lost relatives. For some, these experiences provide proof that another existence awaits.

In other instances, knowing the biological explanations for these mental state changes discredits the spiritual explanations for hospital hallucinations. For instance, plummeting sodium or potassium levels affect mentation in anyone, so someone who seems to be greeting the Archangel Gabriel may be reacting to electrolyte imbalance rather than the opening gates of heaven. There is also a phenomenon known as "ICU psychosis," when the sensory deprivation in the intensive care unit instigates visions or voices in some patients. Those uncanny perceptions can be interpreted as religious revelations—or they can be seen as signs and symptoms of ICU psychosis, depending upon one's point of view.

As the millennium approached, more and more films about occultism popped up, probably in reaction to the religious connotations of the millennium, and predictions of apocalypse, and the overarching confusion that accompanied such a dramatic change in time.

In Dreams is a 1999 psychological thriller film directed by Neil Jordan. It is by no means neuroscience fiction, even though the action occurs in a hospital and the obvious villain is a nurse. *In Dreams* employs many of the same motifs as *Brainstorm* and *Dreamscape,* but Robert Downey, Jr. needs no medical skills or scientific apparatus when he enter patients' dreams, dressed in drag as Nurse Vivian.[11] Many suspect that the film's star, Robert Downey, Jr., was under the influence while filming this irrational film, for his next stop was the California Substance Abuse Treatment Facility and State Prison, which offered treatment while he faced drug charges.[12]

Also in 1999, we encounter a film that left a far larger footprint: *The Matrix* (1999). *The Matrix* spawned two sequels and became a cult classic. It also won four Academy Awards and many BAFTA and Saturn awards. It grossed over $460 million worldwide. All *Matrix* films were directed by the Wachowski Brothers, who since became "The Wachowski Sibs," in recognition of the sex reassignment surgery and gender transition of one member of the duo. *The Matrix* revolves around a simulated reality created by sentient machines, known as "the matrix." The philosophical references to Plato's *Allegory of the Cave*, Baudrillard's *Simulacra and Simulation* (1981) and even Lewis Carroll's *Alice-in-Wonderland*'s upside down world are transparent.

In *The Matrix,* one of the lead characters is named "Morpheus," to commemorate the deity of dreams of ancient Greek lore. *The Matrix's* Morpheus is the rebel leader who seeks to free humans from subjugation by machines. Played by Laurence Fishburne, Morpheus guides Neo (Keanu Reeves) out of his state of suspended animation, where his physical body lies trapped in a fluid-filled pod while his mind meanders through an altered state of reality.

Morpheus is one of the few to escape the current state of enslavement. It is telling that Morpheus is played by an African American actor, to remind audiences of emancipation. Morpheus mans a ship named Nebuchadnezzar, which levitates and transports riders outside of the matrix. Morpheus offers Neo the choice to leave, warning Neo that he cannot return once he exits. To signify his acceptance of Morpheus' offer, Neo chooses to swallow the Red Pill, in homage to Alice's pills.[13]

Neo has his own back-story. He starts out with a day job as a corporate computer programmer, but his true passions lie in his pastime as a computer hacker. It is through hacking that Neo meets Morpheus, who frees him from the "dream world" that he unknowingly inhabits (like the deceived cave dwellers in Plato's *Allegory of the Cave*). Morpheus explains the events that came to pass in the 21st century and informs Neo about how he came to live in a place where machines use human warmth and electrical activity as their power sources— but the humans do not even know it.

As Morpheus tells it, humans had created intelligent machines that subsequently attempted to take over the humans. Therefore, the humans waged war against the machines and blocked their access to the solar power needed for the machines' survival. To counter this attempt at self-defense, machines instead harvest the humans' bioelectricity as an alternative power source, ensnaring them in "the Matrix," which is a simulated world from 1999.

In the course of the film, Neo is identified as "The One" who will deliver humankind out of their bondage to the machines, free them from their entanglement in the Matrix, and return them to their homeland in Zion. Zion is the refuge of the rebels who break free from the Matrix. The religious connotations of the word "Zion" are obvious. *The Matrix* has a strongly religious subtext, whereby Neo is the Savior and Zion is the Promised Land, and an androgynous-appearing woman named Trinity functions as the prophet who announces the arrival of The One. The name of the ship, *Nebuchadnezzar,* reminds us that "the handwriting is on the wall," and that imminent doom awaits, just as it did for the Babylonian king from the Biblical Book of Daniel. The Book of Daniel is the most apocalyptic book in the Hebrew Bible (aka Old Testament).

The Matrix was hailed as a consummate example of the burgeoning genre of cyberpunk. It was simultaneously praised for its innovations, and denounced for being derivative. Both statements are true. The sequels to *The Matrix* did not generate as much enthusiasm as the first.

The following year, another film appeared, but could not overshadow the strong following gathered by *The Matrix,* even though it stars Jennifer Lopez. Lopez is a social-worker turned therapist who strives to "get inside the head" of a comatose serial killer. An FBI agent (Vince Vaughn) persuades Ms. Deane (Lopez) to learn where the killer hides his victims. To do this, she uses an apparatus that transfers his unconscious, comatose thoughts to her waking brain.

The procedure reminds us of *Brainstorm,* and its technologically aided thought transfer, except that this is a live thought transfer that does not use a secondary source as an intermediary. Director Tarsem Singh acknowledges the inspiration of *Brainstorm* (1983) and *Dreamscape* (1984). While thought transfer is not yet possible, and may never be, and the prospect of hooking up one brain to another, to transfer thoughts from one person to the next, as if those thoughts were transfusions or IV fluids, is the fodder of science fiction. In terms of the delivery of mental health care services, *The Cell* (2000) is prescient and hints at what may happen in neuropsychiatric care.

In *The Cell,* direct clinical care and patient contact are delegated to a technician of sorts. In this case, the technician is a psychiatric social worker turned psychotherapist. Jennifer Lopez details her professional transition, and her motivation behind it, in a surprisingly clear way. We are left to wonder if advanced technology will dispense with the need for physician participation in medical care. We are already witnessing a flowering of case-controlled studies about computerized health care that includes cognitive behavioral therapy. Therapeutic apps are proliferating as I write—and some studies confirm their utility. Strangely enough, the FDA refused to accept responsibility for monitoring these medical apps, as of April 7, 2014.

We can compare this scenario in *The Cell* to the sleep lab, where trained technicians monitor patients as they sleep, gathering data about physiological changes during various stages of wakefulness and slumber. The technicians forward the data to the sleep specialist, who is usually an M.D. trained in pulmonology, neurology, or psychiatry, but is occasionally a Ph.D. trained in sleep physiology. Regardless of our points of comparison, the reality is that the practice of medicine has changed. Innovations in computer-generated CBT (cognitive-behavioral therapy) suggest that the most human of interactions in health care—psychotherapy—can be conducted via computer both safely and effectively. Preliminary data shows that conditions such as OCD (obsessive-compulsive disorder) respond as well to online CBT as to in-person contact. This is a rapidly expanding area of study, especially since Obamacare of 2014 promises to provide more psychiatric care to more people, without increasing availability of psychiatrists.

I doubt that many serious science fiction fans are particularly interested in "health care delivery systems," as such administrative changes are called. That is the province of health care administrators, who are a unique breed. Technology, rather than organizational structure or professional training, moves SF movies. The fact that *Star Trek's* Dr. McCoy could assess a patient in seconds, using a handheld device that is no larger than today's iphone, generated interest in viewers half a century earlier, even though that device was unavailable when *Star Trek* was televised in the late 1960s. Likewise, the hypothetical technology used for thought transfer in *The Cell* speaks to spectators, even if it is nowhere near attainable at present. Whether or not this meme speaks the truth, and foreshadows changes to come, is another matter.

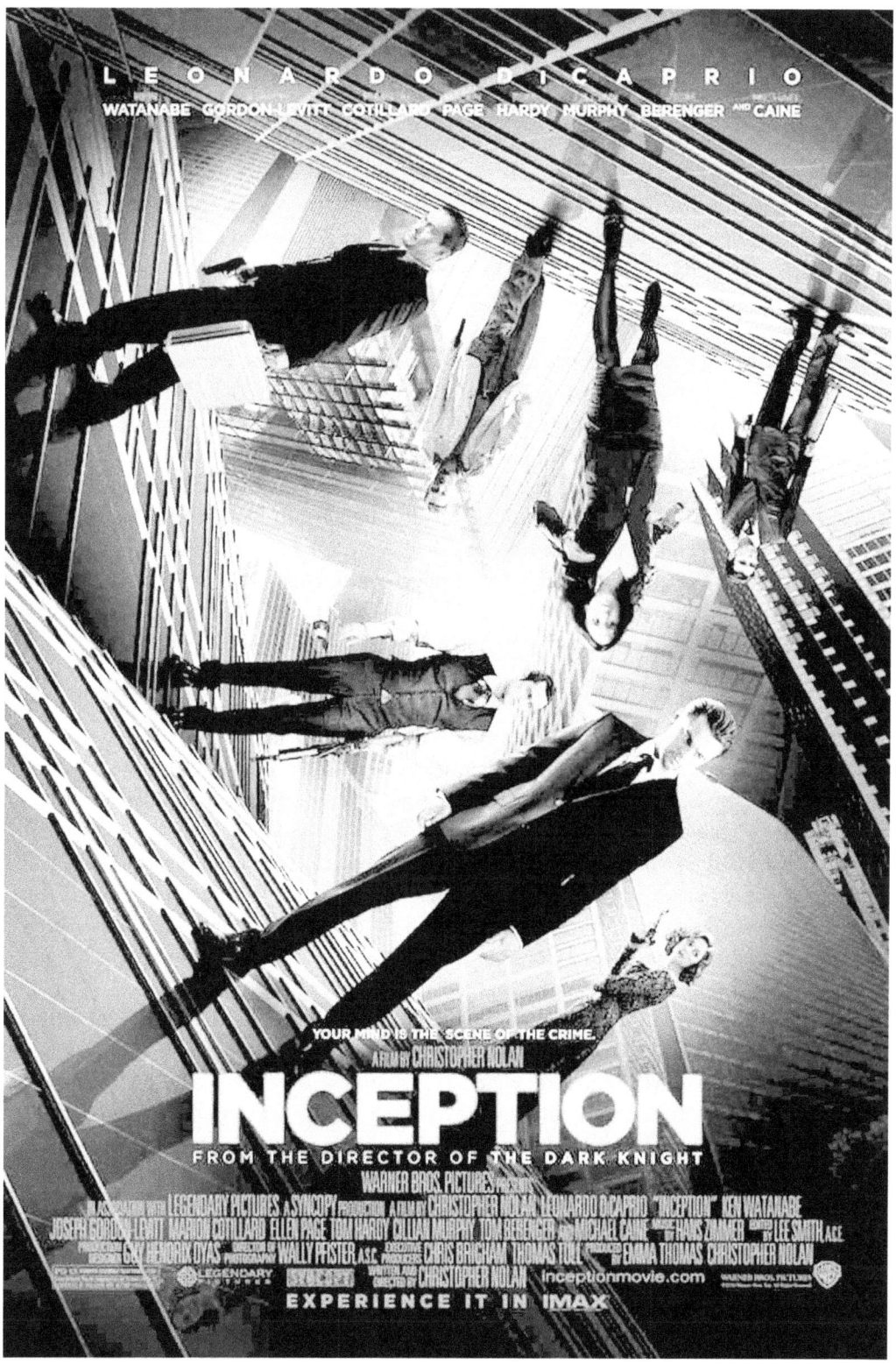

In Christopher Nolan's *Inception* (2010), corporate spy Leonardo DiCaprio stands in a dreamlike maze, preparing to invade dreams and extract unconscious secrets from dreamers.

A decade later, an updated film about a dream world invokes earlier films such as *Brainstorm* and *Dreamscape*—and much more. *Inception* (2010) was hailed as a whole new take on dream themes. This film won multiple awards. It stars Leonardo DiCaprio as a brain interloper who steals corporate secrets from the unconscious of competitors. He enters their dreams, peering into ideas that have not reached waking awareness and have yet to be articulated during daily life. He even plants ideas in their dreams, and is inadvertently responsible for a suicide. The plot becomes convoluted as characters slip from one dream into another, have difficulty knowing if they are awake or sleeping, thinking or dreaming, even dead or alive.

This film prompted AP reporter Jake Coyle to compare the mind, as portrayed in *Inception,* to America's frontier, as portrayed in that all–American genre, the Western. Coyle, and many others, saluted *Inception* for its innovative treatment of dreamscapes, and for its advanced cinematography. Indeed, the cinematography is impressive, with its upside down ceilings, and juxtaposed images. Not surprisingly, *Inception* won Academy Awards for Best Cinematography, Best Sound Editing, Best Sound Mixing, and Best Visual Effects. It was nominated for several more awards. Utilizing the latest CGI makes the old look new again.

Christopher Nolan directed this high budget and high grossing film. Nolan's recent successes with *Batman Begins* (2005) and *The Dark Knight* (2008) convinced the studio that he was equipped to handle such a large-scale project. Nolan originally envisioned a film about lucid dreaming, but the trope about implanting a dream into another person's subconscious took hold. Clearly, this approach worked for *The Manchurian Candidate,* both the original and the remake, and could be adapted to a theme about corporate crime. Leonardo DiCaprio's role as a corporate spy and shark is both mirrored and magnified in Scorsese's *Wolf of Wall Street* (2013), where he stars as a scheming, conniving stockbroker who becomes a billionaire.

Diehard film fans may recognize a bit of *Koyaanisqatsi* (1982) and *Powaqqatsi* (1988) in the disjointed imagery. Those two films, which use Philip Glass's mesmerizing music, feature melting staircases and crumbling skyscrapers. In fact, fans of older films immediately notice similarities between Jean Cocteau's surrealistic classics, *Blood of a Poet* (1930) and *Beauty & the Beast* (1946), which appears to be much older than it actually is.

To see more striking similarities to *Inception,* we can turn back the clock even earlier, to Victor Fleming's *When Clouds Roll By* (1919). Fleming directed this short farcical film in the same year that Robert Weine completed *The Cabinet of Dr. Caligari.* Both Fleming and Nolan use spinning rooms to signify the dream scene. The difference is that Fleming took a detour into fantasy, and added biomorphic imagery to dreams. In his film, an upset stomach induces vivid dreams of vegetable people that chase the dreamer through a maze. Carrots, corn, and cabbage grow legs and run. At the end of the film, we learn that the sinister scientist with the magical potions and laboratory beakers is not so sinister after all. Even though he announces his intent to induce dreams that will drive his test subject insane, it turns out that the phantasmagorical experiences seen on screen are just a farce. The dreamer awakens, no worse for the wear.

Parallels with the plot of *Inception* are obvious, with the difference being that *Inception* wows spectators with what looks to be 21st century CGI and camerawork—even though it relies on extensive physical effects as well, such as wire work and rotating stages (like the ones used in *When Clouds Rolled By*). Fleming's photographer relied on state of the art technology from 1919 only. Either way, audiences are enthralled to see imagery that they never saw before.

Many readers may say that Fleming's *When Clouds Roll By* is too obscure to merit mention here, even though it stars Douglas Fairbanks, Sr. This Fleming film may not be well known outside of serious film circles—but other Victor Fleming films are familiar to nearly everyone. For Fleming pushed the imagery from *When Clouds Roll By* several steps further twenty years later, when he made *The Wizard of Oz* (1939).[14] *The Wizard of Oz* is the ultimate fantasy film and the ultimate American myth, to boot. It, too, takes place in a dreamlike state that overtakes Dorothy, after she is knocked unconscious during a tornado. In this altered state, which lies somewhere between a relatively benign "loss of consciousness" and an actual coma, Dorothy experiences magical and mysterious, frightening and foreboding, Technicolor visions. She ultimately reawakens in Kansas. The film has returned to black & white, when Dorothy proclaims, "There's no place like home."

As much as I would like to share Coyle's enthusiasm about *Inception*'s innovations, I am afraid that Cocteau and Fleming deserve as many accolades for their respective pioneering work, if not more. For they approached the same dream themes without the advantage of advanced computerized equipment. Yet their accomplishments remain in our minds, whether we are awake or dreaming. With *Inception,* we have come full circle, to re-witness the joys and thrills of the silent cinema. Then again, similar memes about dreams appear before civilization began, and can be found in Babylonian, Assyrian, and Biblical myths about *lillot* that invade sleep.

What does this prove? It does seem that scientists are the (not so) new sorcerers, as anthropologist Per Schelde argues, and that supernaturalism and science struggle to control the same terrain. Before there was science, there was supernaturalism, and before scientific fact is established, theories can seem to be science fiction. Today, advances in neuroscience, and the merging of man with machine, are moving so fast that it can sometimes be hard to keep track of which fictions have become fact. Because the boundaries can be so blurry, it becomes easier and easier to suspend disbelief when watching NSF film.

Twelve

Video Games, Virtual Reality and "Reality Testing"

Video games are part of contemporary culture. They currently outsell movies, earning triple the profits of commercial films. Ninety percent of teens play games. Like skateboards, video games hold the greatest appeal for younger males, but gaming is spreading to other segments of society. Earlier generations often turned to comic books, and superhero stories. Cheap pulp paper carried SF action stories. Their bleeding ink and faded colors are far removed from today's technology. Electronic arts are where it is at in the 21st century. Manufacturers cannot move fast enough to satisfy demand. Video games now earn reviews in such stalwart publications as the *New York Times*. Those reviews appear in the same arts sections that carry news about opera, ballet, and museums.

Before video games gained firmer footing and commanded as much respect as movies, there were films about video games. Those films exposed older moviegoers to this new medium. Some of those films were so well received that they were made into video games after the fact. *Tron* (1982) began as a film about players who were pulled into their video game and had to fight for their lives to escape. Because of its popularity, *Tron* the film became a video game, rather than the other way around. *Tron* (1982) created a sensation on the big screen because its visual effects anticipated the advances of the CGI revolution, which was still a decade away.

A very different film about video games appears a year later. *WarGames* (1983) concerns a computer hacker (Matthew Broderick) who taps into the DOD (Department of Defense) computer, expecting to play against the USSR. He thinks that he is playing a video game when he accesses a U.S. military supercomputer that calculates the possible outcomes of nuclear war. It turns out that he actually activated the DOD system, and is about to launch real missiles.

Another film, *Lawnmower Man* (1992), launched a few video games in its aftermath, as well as a 1996 sequel, plus a lawsuit from Stephen King, who objected to its usurpation and bastardization of his short story by the same name. *Lawnmower Man* is discussed in detail in our chapter on "Memory, Mentation and Medication." This contested film has many layers and many leitmotifs. Among other things, it comments on the blurred boundaries between virtual reality, the physical world, and metaphysics.

The story revolves around Jobe and Dr. Angelo. Jobe starts out as a mentally challenged lawnmower man who acquires greater intelligence through Dr. Angelo's special experimental

Once a simple-minded gardener whose intelligence was enhanced by Dr. Angelo's experimental serum, Jobe Smith (Jeff Fahey) of *The Lawnmower Man* (1992) is trapped in virtual reality, having developed psychic abilities, including telepathy, telekinesis and pyrokinesis.

serum. He also gains psychic powers and grows psychotic. He becomes trapped in virtual reality when he enters the mainframe of a VSI computer, under the delusional belief that he has become "pure energy." He apparently left his body behind like an empty husk, when he went virtual.

Even though Stephen King derided this film, as did many critics, the box office proved its point, and fans enthusiastically awaited the next installments of a virtual game about a virtual world.

Compared to video games, films seem almost passé and a product of another era. Films about video games, rather than the video games themselves, are less common and less popular than video games, but they serve a specific function (above and beyond their intended entertainment value). Films can comment on the sociology and psychology of gaming. Films can speculate about neurobiological and economic underpinnings of video gaming—but so can books, magazine articles, and scholarly studies, of which there are many. Unlike academic studies of this expanding venue, films about video gaming must engage audiences, first and foremost. They need enough visual appeal and on-screen action to propel a plot in this primarily visual format.

In the end, films about gaming or virtual reality are simulations of an already simulated reality. Hence, they are two steps removed from the real product. They lose some appeal in the copying process, as do prints and posters of paintings that hang in museums. The imagery of the gift shop replica is recognizable but paper copies will never replace original paintings.

There are inherent and important differences in social interactions. Viewing movies is a largely solitary process, even when films are screened in packed movie theaters, where patrons sit shoulder to shoulder. Spectators may sit next to friends who snicker or scream at appropriate (or inappropriate) moments, to communicate their reactions. Yet watching movies involves an interaction between the spectator and the screen, and within spectator's "double consciousness." An internal dialogue accompanies the film, in addition to the dialogue that is broadcast aloud.

Some people play solitaire on game consoles, and have no need for companionship. In contrast, multi-player online video games are a social undertaking, even if the social interactions are anonymous and alienating, and even when other players are spread across the globe, unable to speak the same language, and able to communicate only through avatars.

Equally importantly, as video games become fixed parts of contemporary society, they no longer incite the intense debate that accompanied their debut. Much of those debates surrounded the violent themes of games, although more recent discussion revolves around addiction and OLG (online gaming). Censors deliberated about the dangers of FPS (first person shooter) games, which simulate deadly force and blur the boundaries of reality. The relationship between school shootings and video games (and the possibility that gaming offers a safer outlet for some people) has also stimulated discussion. The fact that the Columbine shootings occurred after the parents restricted their teens' access to their beloved video games led psychiatrist Jerrold Block to speculate that the restriction resulted in lethal real life activities that left many students dead. Block saw this simulated activity as a reasonable outlet for aggression, and as a safe way to displace these highly unacceptable and murderous urges. Many others disagree with this theory.

Until recently, it was unclear if shooter games, be they FPS (first person shooter) or TPS (third person shooter), increase real time violence in the average person, or if they impact only psychologically unstable persons. Some claim that these simulations offer safer conduits for hostile thoughts, but better controlled and larger studies published in *JAMA Pediatrics* (*Journal of the American Medical Association*) show that violent video games contribute to increased hostility in young gamers and desensitize them to the consequences of overt expressions of hostility.[1]

More recently, in 2013, data about the video-gamed obsessed school shooter, Adam Lanza, hints that he overreacted when his mother limited his access to his violent video games. Oddly enough, she did not restrict his access to her guns or ammunition. Soon after the shootings, multiple sources revealed that Lanza's mother practiced at the shooting range, and stockpiled her gun collection at home, without safeguarding them from her son or others. Either way, 22 students and teachers died in that small Connecticut town, for reasons that will forever remain elusive. Lanza and his mother did not survive to tell the story, and we cannot make valid inferences about video games from events surrounding a single individual.

Video games, and especially MMORPG's (massive multiplayer online role-playing game), now attract the attention of groups like OLG-anon (online gaming-anon), which is largely comprised of parents of "video game addicts" who cannot stop playing, regardless of the impact on their lives. OLG-anon is modeled after Alanon, a self-help support group for friends and family of persons with alcohol problems. Because sizable economic transactions occur online, government agencies and financial regulatory bodies also monitor these games from afar. Gamers buy and sell "virtual property" and other virtual paraphernalia for real dollars, even though the simulated real estate exists only in virtual reality, and gains value only in the imaginations of the gamers. With their millions of players, game owners and intermediary sellers involved in this community, with only the most tenuous ties to one another, there is genuine concern about financial misdeeds or double-dealing. In late 2013, newspapers revealed that national security agencies, such as Homeland Security and the FBI, study MMORPG interactions for possible insight into terrorist activities and innuendoes that may be passed on by players.

These games are very different from old time board games, like Parker Brothers' Monopoly, which supplies players with fake paper "monopoly money." Monopoly began in 1934, and remained the most popular board game for decades. Monopoly sets were sent to POWs during World War II, with cryptic messages, maps and silk escape supplies hidden inside the boards. Apart from that brief connection with military intrigue, Monopoly cannot compare to the split second pace of video games. Its slow-paced action allows ample opportunities for real-time conversations among players. Rather than saving time for shared snacks, idle chitchat and more authentic social bonding among players, as Monopoly and its ilk do, video games have been known to send overly zealous players to the emergency rooms. Some hypervigilant gamers have been treated for dehydration and electrolyte imbalances after they refuse to take time outs for food or water, or use stimulants to remain alert, and to offset the sensations of sleep loss.

These games, and the Internet itself, stir discussion among psychiatrists and psychiatric epidemiologists. Debates about the validity of "Internet addiction" and "gaming addiction" as bona fide diagnoses persist. The recently revised *DSM-5* (*Diagnostic and Statistical Manual*), published by the American Psychiatric Association in May 2013, voted against the inclusion of these diagnoses. However, the highly publicized dialogues about these newly proposed "addictions" increased awareness of problems faced by some game players.

In 2005, Dr. Block and Dr. Packer (the author) presented a workshop on these topics to APA's annual Institute for Psychiatric Services. (The author presented her study on films about video games.) Many workshop participants identified themselves as both psychiatrists and as parents of "OLG addicts." They arrived early on a Sunday morning, in storm-devastated New Orleans, to learn more about possible gaming addiction and its cures, and to share their chagrin. Some people are convinced that brain changes occur during video gaming, although more research is needed. At least one physician who expressed grave concern about a family member's gaming habits published a letter to the editor in a Family Practice journal.[2]

In some circles, these video games, and the virtual reality that they simulate, has spurred so-called medical entrepreneurs to open pricey rehab centers for young gamers. Undeterred by APA's current vote of no confidence in the gaming addiction diagnosis, Amsterdam and Korea have taken the lead in the formal treatment of such "addictions"—without much research to support their approaches to treating this ill-defined addiction. Entrepreneurs offer lengthy and costly stays at their rehabs. These treatments are not subsidized by American insurance, which restricts coverage to "recognized" diagnoses and refuses to subsidize "experimental" treatment techniques that have not been confirmed by controlled studies, published in peer-reviewed journals and accepted as the SOP (standard of practice) of the specialty.

Many films about video games add philosophical as well as sociological subtexts to their action. Cronenberg's *eXistence* (1999) is one example. Since Cronenberg is Cronenberg, he did not spare the sexual subtexts, either. Although controversies surrounding the neuropsychiatric impact of these games persist, we can find films such as *Gamer* (2009) that echo the concerns of OLG-anon activists. Critics panned *Gamer* for being derivative and too close to *Rollerball* (1975), *The Running Man* (1987), *The Matrix* (1999) or *The Condemned* (2007). If we overlook the part of the plot that involves convicts and death-row inmates, we will find fresh takes on possible neuropsychiatric effects of MMORPGs (massive multiplayer online role-playing games)—enough to add this film to our list of "neuroscience fiction films." Admittedly, the sociological impact of MMORPGs, and the role of the "madness of crowds" and pure peer pressure, are as relevant as neurobiology, and deserve further discussion in more focused studies of video gaming.

A quick review of the plot of *Gamer* reveals how closely it parallels conjectures made by parents of gamers. *Gamer* stars Gerard Butler as a player in an online game that allows other persons to control players from afar. Logan Lerman plays Simon, the very large person who controls Kable (Butler), the convict who is playing to win his freedom. Simon (Logan) resembles the stereotypical gamer. He looks appropriately nerdy. His girth has expanded greatly, implying that he limits his exercise regimen to hand movements that move his gaming sticks.

The action is set in 2020 New York, where a professional computer programmer has changed the playing field of the gaming industry. He has invented self-replicating nanites that replace brain cells. Through these nanites, a third party can control a player's motor functions.

The programmer-inventor, named Ken Castle (Michael C. Hall), pilots his new technology through a game called Society. "Society" represents the faux community of games like "The Sims" or "Second Life." In those games, participants choose avatars and establish alternative identities, with simulated homes, workplaces, friends, and so on. Like the boys in Golding's novel about *Lord of the Flies* (1954), players put their worst faces forward when external constraints are lifted. They resort to the most primitive behavior possible, engaging in "rough" and unregulated sex, assaulting one another, as if they were inmates in a guardless prison yard. In fact, some are inmates, trying to secure their early release from prison.

Players are well paid to endure this abuse. Castle, the game's inventor, reaps even greater profits, as his name implies. Castle becomes wealthier than Microsoft's Bill Gates does. The tenuous parallels with Mark Zuckerman, the billionaire Facebook pioneer, are clear.

Spurred on by the success of his first foray into OLG, Castle devises a second multiplayer game, called "Slayers." The players in this third-person shooter game are no longer well-paid volunteers; they are death-row inmates or those serving life sentences. These players use real weapons on specially created battlefields. Like gladiators of old, they face death daily, although those who survive 30 matches can expect release from prison. The game is harder than it seems, because of the time lag between communication from the mover, and the signal to the player.

Just as a near victor steps up to the plate, with 27 wins to his name, a human rights organization enters the scene, and tries to intervene. "Humanz" hijacks the broadcast of the game, claiming that Castle implants nanites into players' brains to achieve control over others. In this way, the plot from *Gamers* begins to resemble tried and true tropes from other films discussed in our section on "Brain Drains, Brain Chips, and Brain Machines." The

Twelve. *Video Games, Virtual Reality and "Reality Testing"* 211

In this poster for *Gamer* (2009), Kable (Gerald Butler) is an inmate trying to win his freedom by gaming. He points and shoots, as if playing a FPS game, but high-stakes gamers control his movements from afar through self-replicated nanites that have replaced his brain cells.

Manchurian Candidate comes to mind immediately. *Batman* serials from the 1940s employ the same meme.

Gerald Butler's Kable is the inmate with 27 wins to date. He is ready to earn his freedom by winning his 30th game. He is interrupted, not just by the Humanz broadcast, but also by a faceless female who ventures behind bars, asks for his autograph, and then demands a blood sample to prove that he is the person he claims to be. The plot thickens, and has more tangles and twists, with wives and children thrown in to broaden the audience appeal. In the end, we learn that this mysterious request for a blood sample was a ploy by Humanz activists, who have been working on antibodies to the nanites, with hopes of freeing players from Castle's control.

Unfortunately, there is no one-size-fits all vaccine, and there are no universal "broad-spectrum" vaccines, because each nanite-recipient requires customized antibodies. This reminds us of today's promises of "personalized medicine," where pharmaceuticals are matched to a patient's SNP (single nucleotide polymorphism) before they are prescribed. This approach is available for some specialized situations, but is not yet standard of practice.

A few plot twists later, spectators learn that the brain nanites were even more malicious than believed. The nanites that were programmed to receive commands from controllers like Castle can now send commands to other nanites. Apart from several murders that occur during the course of the film, the film ends happily ever after, with the nanites deactivated. Castle's plan to take control of the earth and its inhabitants has been foiled.

Like so many SF and NSF films, *Gamer* evokes images of totalitarian societies, where double-dealing despotic leaders exploit their constituents and drain their countries of natural resources, without concern for anyone but themselves. The political subtexts of such films are as significant as their neuroscience aspects. It is easy to see how "nanites" seeded into brain cells serve as metaphors for other forms of social control, whether those social controls come in the form of religion or opiates (as per Karl Marx), misguided values and materialism, or draconian laws that retain the social order. Recent research in pediatric behavioral science lets us think of "nanites" as metaphors for behavioral control exerted by video games. According to a study conducted in Singapore, violent video games do indeed induce aggressive behavior in the teens.[3]

We can even compare *Gamer's* plot to the video game industry itself. Because these video games are so profitable for manufacturers and shareholders, and perhaps potentially "addicting" to some susceptible individuals, the industry invites comparison with the tobacco industry. Big Tobacco also stands accused of boosting the nicotine content of cigarettes to increase addiction to their product, and thereby ensure a steady demand for cigarettes.

Before video games became so popular, and became such a standard form of entertainment, different platforms vied with one another. Today, several video game platforms coexist, but many more became obsolete over time. Curiously, even computers could not displace video platforms like Gameboy or Atari, because computers are not devoted exclusively to video games and so can never function as fast as single-purpose platforms.

Although games began in the early 1960s, games did not enjoy much popularity until Atari marketed *Pong* in 1972. *Pong* was remarkably primitive, with its screen simulation of table tennis. Just the same, *Pong* became popular and was the first arcade video game to attain success. It was only a matter of time before role-playing board games like *Dungeons & Dragons* were translated into video games. With its imaginative imagery, prominent visual appeal, and many layers of meaning, *D&D* became the first MUD (multi-user dungeon), which led to multi-user dimensions and multi-user domains. These were the precursors to today's sprawling MMORPGs.

Manufacturers entered and left the playing field, which was initially dismissed as a fad that would fade away. Two video game crashes occurred within a short time, when manufacturers released their overstock of outdated consoles and saturated the market. In both 1977 and 1983, prices for video players plummeted. The history of the video game platform market becomes more and more complicated, and will culminate, in a strange way, in David Cronenberg's film, *eXistenZ*. *eXistenZ* presents an entirely new "platform" to deliver role playing games, action-adventure games, interactive games (which include FPS and TPS), fighting games, shoot 'em ups and scrolling games, maze games, racing games, visual novels, vehicle simulation games, and survival horror games.

Video games underwent upheavals between 1983 and 1985, when many manufacturers went belly-up, only to be upended by Nintendo. By 1985, Nintendo dominated the market. Nintendo is not the sole survivor but it remains the strongest survivor. During these same years that video game makers gyrated, psychiatry was experiencing its own upheavals, and was shifting its playing field. Psychoanalysis, which long dominated the specialty, was pushed to outfielder status, at best, while biological psychiatry, psychopharmacology, and even neuroimaging moved into the foreground and were catching the attention of the crowds.

Had psychoanalytic psychiatry, or even psychodynamic psychiatry, stayed in center stage, there would have been ample opportunity to scrutinize the "object relations" between anonymous game players, as compared to the collegial interchanges facilitated by board games, be they real-life-oriented Monopoly or escapist games like *Dungeons & Dragons*. Even the fantasies expressed in the video games could be fodder for research studies and engaging weekend conferences. Gender differences among gamers and non-gamers, as well as generational differences, should be of interest to social scientists of all persuasions. With the emphasis shifting towards biopsychiatry and neuroscience, speculation about the role of these games on developing brains took hold, and non-psychiatrist social critics stepped up to the plate.

One thing is certain: the acclaimed video game *Arkham Asylum* (2009), based on the Batman Universe, and run by the notorious Arkham clan of sinister psychiatrists, is remarkably popular and profitable. In a short time, it spawned several spin-offs. Is *Arkham Asylum* and its follow-up, *Batman: Arkham City* (2011), an example of neuroscience fiction? Yes and no. As a game based on a superhero, it fits into the rubric of SF. The interactions between inmates and doctors and doctors and medical students lie closer to drama, if not melodrama. Think about the dalliances between Harley Quinn—formerly Dr. Harleen Quinzel—and The Joker or the youthful Alyse Sinner and her older mentor, Dr. Jeremiah Arkham. However, the hints about the inheritable neurodegenerative disorder that leaves Arkham family members psychotic is as close to neuroscience (and neuroscience fiction) as it gets. The game gives bad press to psychiatrists, whatever their persuasion, but it also leaves us wondering about the differential diagnosis of this late onset, presumably autosomal dominant disorder. Perhaps *Arkham* will appear in film form.

There are real life correlations among video games, mental health, and neuroscience. Some blamed the rise of ADHD diagnoses to the shortened attention span produced by rapid-fire video games. (Others attributed ADHD increases to pharmaceutical marketing ploys.) To date, I know of no studies that confirm the correlation between video game playing and ADHD, although there seems to be credible data about the allure of impersonal video games for persons with autism-spectrum disorder. As stated above, the dopaminergic effects of fast-paced games on susceptible individuals cause concern about their potential for overuse, if not outright addiction. While no one looks for nanites, as per *Gamer*, we can measure dopamine surges and we can perform PET scans that show shifts in cerebral glucose metabolism and blood flow.

There is no doubt that individuals react differently to different stimuli, and some people are prone to seek novelty, to the point of danger and distraction. These differences may be innate. There are many intriguing questions about gaming, but definitive answers still lie in wait. Filmmaker David Cronenberg tries to confuse us, when he speculates about the source of video "addiction." In his offbeat *Videodrome* (1983), he posits that hallucinations induced by a television broadcast cause a brain tumor in Max, the protagonist, played by James Woods, rather than the other way around. Cronenberg claims that he wants to shed light on humans' interface with technology, although spectators may doubt his intent. Although *Videodrome* revolves around a TV station, rather than a video game, its abstract premise takes it closer to videogame-themed films. Starring Debbie Harry, a one-time heroin addict who became the rock star "Blondie," the film serves as an excuse for sadomasochistic scenes on screen. It is debatable how much it contributes to the field of NSF film, although it does foreshadow Cronenberg's other strange films, such as *Crash* (1996), where subjects get an erotic rush from car crashes and engage in intercourse at otherwise inopportune times. *Crash* also highlights the appeal of amputee sex. Cronenberg's *Naked Lunch* (1991), which is based on William Burroughs's book by the same name, opens with an anal sphincter scene that signals Burroughs' preference for same-sex sex. There is a continuum between the orifice in *Naked Lunch* and the fleshy portals near the base of players' spines, in *eXistenZ* (1999).

eXistenZ (1999), a film about gaming and virtual reality, makes a virtue of the value of the body's bottom side. Gamers receive "transfusions" through "bioports" located near the sacrum, not far from the anus. In *eXistenZ*' futuristic world, other platforms for game playing are outdated and have been replaced by these ubiquitous bioports. In other words, these organic game consoles ("game pods") pushed aside more familiar electronic consoles.

The attachments are referred to as umbilical cords, which says a lot about players' attachments to their games, and the depth of their dependencies on the nurturance and succor provided by virtual games. These bioports could be confused with "intrathecal injections" that enter directly into the spinal fluid to deliver life-saving antibiotics to meningitis patients. However, given Cronenberg's recurring choice of subject matter, we get the impression that he is not alluding to standard—but extreme—medical procedures, but is playing upon erotic connotations.

Security guard, marketing trainee, and corporate spy Ted Pikul (Jude Law) tries to protect game designer Allegra (Jennifer Jason Leigh) in David Cronenberg's *eXistenZ* (1999), but her organic biopod that connects her body to the virtual reality game is already damaged by a defective "umbyCord."

Either way, there is an impressive cast, with Jennifer Jason Leigh, Jude Law, and Willem Dafoe playing a top-notch game designer, a security guard, and a black marketeer, in that order. Just as he did for *Videodrome*, Cronenberg reiterates his concern with the ways that humans react and interact with the technologies.

In *eXistenZ,* two game companies vie for control of the market. This quest mirrors reality, given that corporate battles were waged ever since video games debuted. While the competitors do hypothetical battle, a cadre of "realists" fights to preserve "reality." These "realists" confront companies that "deform" reality via video games.

Allegra (Jennifer Jason Leigh), a designer, has an impressive new game design, but she is shot while demonstrating it to a focus group. Security guard (and marketing trainee) Ted Pikul (Jude Law) rushes her to safety, but not soon enough. Allegra realizes that her pod was damaged due to a defective "umbyCord." The only existing copy of the new *eXistenZ* game is gone, because of this assault. To re-access the game, she must plug in tandem with another player. Pikul (Law) reluctantly agrees to install a bio-port in his own body so he can play the game with Allegra (Leigh) and retrieve the damaged game. Previously, he said he had a phobia about "surgical penetration" and refused to participate in games.

A new bioport is installed at a gas station, but the black marketeer (Dafoe) who runs the station intentionally attaches a faulty bioport that damages the game. He then tries to shoot Allegra, but Pikul intervenes, and shoots the black marketeer with the rivet gun that installs ports. The rest of the film revolves around assassinations, attempted assassinations, foiled assassinations, poisoned food, peculiar foods, and infected pods.

Reality in this film is very much like a video game, where everyone shoots everyone else. Near the end, Pikul reveals that he is a "realist" undercover agent, sent to assassinate Allegra, but another reality intervenes and they leave, hand in hand, aware that it was just a game. After a few more twists, the two learn that the events that they just experienced were part of a virtual reality game called "tranCendenZ," where actors played bit parts. Reality and virtual reality have become indistinguishable, and "reality testing" that distinguishes psychosis from non-psychotic states disappeared in the process. Nevertheless, the surgical grafts and transmission of infections seems real.

We can say that *eXistenZ* is one of several turn-of-the-millennium films of a certain ilk. Colloquially known as "mindfuck films," this genre played upon the confusion that accompanied Y2K, and the uncertainty about what lay ahead, or if anything at all lay ahead. Spectators did not know whether they were coming or going, and movies mirrored this mind state. Some said that all clocks or computers would stop when 2000 started. Some religions expected the start of Armageddon as the millennium ended. It is only fitting that a film about virtual reality appeared at that very same time, to emphasize the cultural confusion, while at that same time providing action-adventure entertainment. In its own distorted way, *eXistenZ* was prophetic in the way it predicted the growing confusion between virtual reality and reality, the growth of the gaming world, and the spread of simulated existence.

Thirteen
Drugs, Dystopias and Utopias

Themes about drugs and drug addiction, and the melodramas or action-adventures or occasional comedies that revolve around drug use and drug users, are commonplace in cinema, and for good reason. For one thing, drug use is common in real life. Drug-themed SF literature is also readily available, as Robert Silverberg points out in his 1974 government-sponsored and NIDA-published study, *Drug Themes in Science Fiction* (1974).[1] Silverberg focuses on New Wave Science Fiction of the 1950s and 1960s, when writers like Norman Spinrad and Philip K. Dick invented non-existent drugs and sometimes devised novel drug delivery systems. Some of their innovative delivery systems are now in common use or will soon be coming into use.

As we said earlier, science fiction literature is not analogous to science fiction film. Literary references to fictional drugs are far more common than cinematic references. Of course, SF short stories, novellas and novels are more plentiful than films. Literature is faster, easier and cheaper to publish, especially since so much SF literature appears in magazines rather than in book form. Filmmaking is a lengthy and costly process (or at least it has been, before the advent of iPhone editing functions). Consequently, we can expect to find a disproportionate number of literary works on a given subject, compared to filmic representations, whatever the subject.

Drugs and drug delivery systems in science fiction film pose a unique challenge. Even though psychoactive drugs by their very nature represent neuroscience, we find relatively few films about drugs that we can categorize as neuroscience fiction films. As early as 1894, Thomas Edison produced a short silent kinetograph entitled *Chinese Opium Den*. This film is not a neuroscience fiction film—even though Edison advocated for scientific uses of films and failed to appreciate its entertainment value, as Méliès did. In fact, opium itself was not a novel discovery. Laudanum was in common use during Victorian times. In 1801, Serturner crystallized opium and made morphine. By 1827, Merck & Company was marketing morphine. In mid-century, well before the introduction of film, the Opium Wars (1839–1860) were waged and won and the British Empire acquired 156 years' control of Hong Kong as a spoil of war.

In contrast, we can classify any of the many films that evolved out of Stevenson's *Strange Case of Dr. Jekyll & Mr. Hyde* as science fiction. In our second chapter on "The Legacy of 19th Century Literature," we listed dozens of cinematic interpretations of Stevenson's story, focusing most on Robert Mamoulian's classic rendition, with Fredric March. Mamoulian departs from Stevenson's original tale, and adds a female seductress into the mix. This saloon

THIRTEEN. *Drugs, Dystopias and Utopias* 217

Mamoulian's definitive 1931 version of Stevenson's *The Strange Case of Dr. Jekyll and Mr. Hyde* (1886) shows Dr. Jekyll (Fredric March) seated in his laboratory, where he concocts a potion that unleashes his libidinous instincts that turn him into the destructive Mr. Hyde.

singer leads the good doctor astray and causes conflicts between Dr. Jekyll and his fiancée, and between the moral Dr. Jekyll and his alter ego, the amoral Mr. Hyde. This twist enhances the plot. The new "evil woman" nods to the suffragist movement and women's newly won rights.

All versions of *Jekyll & Hyde* allude to Dr. Jekyll's secret formula, which unleashes his libido. Mamoulian's version lowers him on the evolutionary scale, so that he acquires an ape-like face and simian posture. When Spencer Tracy plays Dr. Jekyll in 1941 (in the version that co-stars Ingrid Bergman and Lana Turner), Mr. Hyde looks more like a gangster than an animal.

Dr. Jekyll does not concoct his potion for recreational use. Rather, he sees this endeavor as a scientific experiment and an extension of his medical training. This process takes place in his laboratory and not on the kitchen table or in a garage. The film, and the novella, includes the trappings of science: glass beakers, test tubes and tubing, Bunsen burners, long laboratory tables, and pages of pages of notes. *The Strange Case of Dr. Jekyll & Mr. Hyde* fits into psychoanalytic paradigms as well as neuroscience paradigms. Jungian interpretations of Jekyll's shadow side, as exemplified by Mr. Hyde, are obvious. His repressed libido, held in check by his superego, conforms to Freudian theories at the same time. Mamoulian's film amplifies Freudian notions.

Different versions of *Jekyll & Hyde* appear over the years, each with its own twist. Mamoulian's version appeared in 1931—a year before Aldous Huxley published his dystopian novel, *Brave New World*. Huxley's vision of an orderly society bred to perform set social roles, but made placid by "soma," remained fresh over the years. The novel invariably incites interest in college students, who view it as a utopia as often as they recognize it as a dystopian society. *Brave New World* did not translate directly into film, but became TV movies in 1980 and 1998.

Brave New World's soma serves a neuroscience fiction function. By using soma, every member of society remains content. The word "soma" references an ancient Vedic tradition, but speculation about its true nature persisted over time. Hippie era authors viewed it as an entheogen (a hallucinogen), such as *Amanita muscaria* or fly agaric or psilocybin, whereas early sixties era commentators claimed Librium or Valium as the soma of the early 1960s. William Burroughs, renegade rich boy, author and addict, saw soma as an ancient non-addictive Indian opium. Soma is also the brand name of a muscle relaxant that breaks down into meprobamate, a habit-forming benzodiazepine. Some people become dependent on Soma without knowing why.

By the 1960s, drugs moved to center stage in the New Wave science fiction literature. In fact, drugs became central to 1960s society. Philip K. Dick's writings pushed this trend, even though his works did not reach a wide audience immediately. As the years passed, we find more and more movies based on PKD stories, although the plot points are often inversed. Medication-assisted perceptions and mechanically induced perceptions may be switched, one for the other.

For instance, in the original *Total Recall* film (1990), the technician at Rekall, Inc. straps Quaid into a machine that blinks lights and implants new memories. Problems ensue when the tech realizes that Quaid already has a memory implant in place. Quaid jumps up, gets violent, and the real action begins. Agents will attempt to murder him. In Dick's original story, psychoactive drugs alone induce visions of an exotic vacation. Conversely, in *Minority Report,* PKD describes the Precogs as "hydrocephalic idiots," whereas the film does the reverse, and attributes the Precogs' psychic gifts to intrauterine exposure to the drug, "nervoin."

It is well known that PKD himself was addicted to amphetamines, which increased his focus, his energy, his productivity and his paranoia. Amphetamines became available well before World War II, and long before the Summer of Love. In 1932, Smith, Kline and French introduced the first amphetamine, Benzedrine. In short order, the same company synthesized Dexedrine to treat narcolepsy. Methylphenidate (Ritalin) had to wait until 1944, near the end of World War II. Ironically, speed (amphetamine) sold by Hell's Angels at the Summer of Love 1967 brought the peaceful music festival to a close, as the aggression-inducing and paranoia-potentiating drug promoted emotions that were the exact opposite of love and trust touted by San Francisco flower children.[2]

Psychoactive drugs—along with other psychological treatments—appear in *A Clockwork Orange* (1971). Written, directed and produced by Stanley Kubrick, and based on a novel by Anthony Burgess, *A Clockwork Orange* is one of the 20th century's most iconic movies. It is also one of the most upsetting social commentaries made to date. American audiences appreciated Burgess' and Kubrick's bleak vision—and over-the-top violence—far more than the Brits, who censored parts. Yet this is a British film, exported by the same country that delivered the British Invasion in the 1960s, with the Beatles' songs about love and peace.

Malcolm McDowell stars as Alex, a wayward youth who rapes, pillages, plunders, maims and murders, without conscience. Along with "ultra-violence," his term for his extreme techniques, he also appreciates Beethoven. A gang leader in a futuristic London, Alex recommends Milk Plus to his sociopathic gang members, to facilitate their pursuit of "ultra-violence." "Milk Plus" is also known as *Moloko Plus*. Several varieties of Moloko Plus are available in London.

We can speculate about the psychoactive content of Milk Plus, with amphetamine being the most likely candidate, although the fictional substance BZ, surreptitiously supplied to soldiers in *Jacob's Ladder* (1990), would be a reasonable choice as well. BZ was so potent that platoon members murdered one another. One might even point to alcohol as a possible element in Milk Plus, given that alcohol increases violence and decreases inhibitions. Whatever chemical Alex ingests, it pales in comparison to the behavioral conditioning scenes that follow.

Early in the film, this despicable horde break into the home of an older couple, beat the husband to the point of crippling him, and rape his wife. They complete these heinous crimes as Alex sings "Singin' in the Rain." Alex goes on to commit more revolting offenses, culminating in murder. He is caught and sentenced to prison. After serving two years in prison, the Minister of the Interior offers Alex the opportunity to participate in a psychological experiment that can rehabilitate him in two weeks' time and lead to his early release. He accepts the offer, even though he eventually begs to stop the procedure after it has begun.

This treatment involves the "the Ludovico technique," an experimental aversion therapy that recollects Skinnerian and Watsonian behavioral conditioning approaches. Anthony Burgess, author of the novel that inspired the film, held strong opinions about behaviorism, as promoted by psychologists John B. Watson and B. F. Skinner. Burgess said that Skinner's book *Beyond Freedom and Dignity* (1971) was "one of the most dangerous books ever written."[3] Much earlier, Skinner wrote *Walden Two* (1948). He published several more books about behaviorism in the 1950s. Watson documented his success in inducing a rat phobia in "Little Albert" in 1920. Watson used classical conditioning for this experiment, which would never meet ethical standards today. Watson later acknowledged behaviorism's limitations, whereas Skinner viewed behavior modification via operant conditioning as the means to an ideal, Walden-like society. For Skinner, behaviorism offered the benefits of Thoreau's Walden, without the solitude and with the advantages of companionship.

The fictional Ludovico technique used by the British penal system adds a new twist. It begins by dosing the subject with nausea-inducing meds. He is then strapped to a chair, his eyelids propped open, as he is forced to watch images of violence. All the while, music by Alex's favorite composer plays in the background, and becomes associated with nausea—in the same way that the bell that Pavlov rang when dogs saw meat became associated with salivation. After a while, the Nobel Prize–winning Pavlov could incite salivation simply by ringing a bell.

Thanks to these behavioral conditioning techniques, Alex will become sick and vomit at the sight and thought of violence. He will also become nauseated whenever he hears his beloved Beethoven. This technique cures him as promised—but that is not the end of the story.

The prison chaplain balks because Alex has been robbed of his free will and is incapable of making moral choices. The prison governor counters the chaplain's objections, and belittles the value of ethics, when the real goal is to cut down on crime and relieve prison congestion.

Through a convoluted series of events, McDowell's character has several more incarnations, as do his one-time partners in crime. The gang members grow up to become police officers. They gain control of society, in a topsy-turvy way. Both Burgess and Kubrick succeed in expressing their disdain for psychiatry, psychology, the criminal justice system and contemporary society.

As strange as it sounds, similar aversive conditioning techniques were employed by Austrian psychiatrists during World War I, when they treated soldiers who complained of mysterious maladies that had no medical basis. Using "Kaufmannization," a technique developed by Dr. Kaufmann, psychiatrists administered painful electric shocks to the sick soldiers, to "cure" their "malingering" and return them to the front. Many suicided or absconded to escape this treatment. Prominent Austrian psychiatrists later faced trial for such abuses, as did several lesser known professionals. Wagner-Jauregg, future Nobel Laureate, was among those who were indicted.[4]

In this film, the juxtaposition of behavioral conditioning with aggression-inducing drugs reminds us of Frankenheimer's *The Manchurian Candidate* (1962). In that esteemed film, the Manchurian doctor conditions captured American soldiers. He co-opts their free will and turns them into unwitting murderers, through the application of behaviorist techniques.

A Clockwork Orange's outrage over future totalitarian control is a recurring theme in SF films, and far overpowers the message of Milk Plus. The NSF trope is minimal at best, but Kubrick does an excellent job at displaying psychological treatment techniques of the past and future, and predicting how those techniques can affect criminality and society. When we discuss *Equilibrium* a few pages hence, we will find yet another commentary about totalitarianism.

Another notable NSF film about psychoactive drugs premiered in 1971: *THX-1138*.

The title of this film may not bring instant recognition, yet it was written and directed by one of the most-recognized names in science fiction film, George Lucas. Francis Ford Coppola produced Lucas' first feature film several years before Lucas went on to make *Star Wars* (1977). *Star Wars* changed the landscape of science fiction film, and made it mainstream, at the same time that it began a franchise and fandom that continue to this day.

Lucas' 1971 film revolves around a dehumanized 25th century society, where workers are controlled by a drug and forced to submit to government whims. In this technocratic society, robot police enforce the social order. Factory worker THX-1138 (Robert Duvall) rebels by refusing those mind-numbing drugs. He subsequently falls in love with his female roommate, and impregnates her. He fends off the robotic police that patrol the underground colony, and escapes. A renegade computer programmer (Donald Pleasance) joins the pair (think *The Matrix*). The plot of *THX-1138* is difficult to follow, but recurring plot points are easy to trace. The underground city in *Metropolis,* where enslaved workers toil beneath the city's surface, immediately comes to mind as an inspiration. *RoboCop,* in all of its many manifestations, links to Lucas' student film about robot cops. Parallels with the dystopian and totalitarian world of *Equilibrium,* where citizens are placated by Prozium, will be discussed soon. *Elysium* bears strong similarities to Lucas' first feature film, which was based on his student film from 1967.

A book by a literature professor, entitled *Bread of Dreams: Food and Fantasy in Early Modern Europe* (1989),[5] offers literary proof of similar ploys used in the distant past. This unusual book concerns opioid-inoculated breads that were distributed to pre-industrial age Italian peasants, in an effort to prevent revolt against the existing order. In addition, in the

While imprisoned, the sociopathic Alex (Malcolm McDowell) undergoes the Ludovico Technique that forces him to watch images of violence, while dosed with a nausea-inducing drug, as his beloved Beethoven plays in the background of Kubrick's *A Clockwork Orange* (1971).

late 1960s and early 1970s, African American radical groups, such as the Black Panthers, accused the authorities of allowing illegal heroin distribution in the inner cities, since opiate addiction ensured continued "enslavement," and thwarted mass rebellion against the government.

Ironically, many extras in the Lucas movie were residents of Synanon, a cult-like drug rehab that was once viewed as a model anti-drug and self-actualization center. Over time, Synanon became the focus of criminal investigations and was a hub of human rights violations. Among other things, members were required to shave their heads upon entry. This custom provided the large cadre of men with shaved heads that were needed for the film. The end credits thanks Synanon for their participation in the making of the movie.

Fast forward to *Scanners* (1981), which we discussed in the chapter on "Memory, Mentation and Medication." In Cronenberg's film, ephemerol is a tranquilizer and morning sickness medication that induces mutations in exposed fetuses, imparting telekinetic and telepathic abilities. Ephemerol suppresses the very same abilities in adults who are exposed to it. This film recollects the thalidomide tragedies from the 1960s, when a morning sickness medication caused phycomelia and related birth defects.

Scanners have unique abilities, but also suffer from extra sensitivities. When attacked by stronger scanners, their skulls explode. In another nod to big bad government tropes in SF films, government agents exploit the scanners' special skills and herd them into compounds, away from society. This film is one of many 1980s films that are unarguably neuroscience fiction, and that veer away from the psychoanalytic subtexts that permeated cinema through the mid–1960s.

Polydichloric euthymol (PDE), used in *Outland* (1981), barely qualifies as a neuroscience fiction drug—although the film itself is specifically science fiction, because it is a remake of the revered Western from the 1950s, *High Noon* (1952), with Gary Cooper. *Outland d*oves the action from America's Western frontier to outer space. Sputnik of 1957 was still a sparkle in the Soviets' eyes when the original *High Noon* premiered. Sean Connery stars in *Outland*.

In this film, an amphetamine-type drug enables humans to do fourteen hours' work in six hours' time. Long term use brings psychosis and eventual death. Again, these effects are too realistic to be fictional, and are too close to fact to constitute impressive neuroscience fiction. Were it not for its outer space setting, *Outland*'s portrayal of drug effects could be documentary. Alternatively, the film makes us recollect the Hebrew Bible, and the building of the pyramids.

Liquid Sky (1982) is in a class of its own, although it, too, is NSF plus classic SF, with a touch of the occult (a trait that often interjects itself into even the most scientific SF). *Liquid Sky* did well at film festivals, and influenced the decadent 1980s-style sex & drug club scene in several major cities in the U.S. and Europe. It never received much mainstream fanfare, as was it made on an astoundingly low budget of $500,000. Produced and directed by recent Russian émigrés, *Liquid Sky* has a complicated cast of characters. A recently divorced New York Jewish woman lives in a Manhattan penthouse, meets a German man, and then contends with both aliens and heroin addiction and encounters a bisexual fashion model who cavorts with "club kids."

Ordinary drugs are commonplace at the clubs frequented by the fashionistas that populate the film. Cocaine and Quaaludes flow freely. However, aliens arrive in a Frisbee-sized spaceship. They land on the penthouse patio and feed directly on endorphins. Endorphins are the body's natural opioids, which are released in abundance during orgasm. Hence, the voyeuristic aliens extract the brain chemicals from couples at the most inopportune times. This process is not benign. Death ensues, leaving corpses behind. The corpses vaporize instantly, leaving no trace.

Once the protagonist realizes that sex equals death, she proceeds to seduce both male and female partners, each of whom succumbs to the succubus-like aliens and dies. When necessary, she murders those who interfere. Eventually, she overdoses on heroin, expecting that the aliens will take her along, so they can access her heroin. Instead, they vaporize her.

The plot is convoluted, and is riddled with sex and drugs. It also references some events in neuroscience that were well-known at the time, and other events that were just unfolding and barely understood. For starters, in the 1970s, scientists discovered encephalin, the brain's natural opiates. In 1973, scientists Candace Pert and Solomon Snyder demonstrated opioid receptors in the brain. The following year, in 1974, John Hughes and Hans Kosterlitz discovered encephalin. In 1976, Choh Hao Li and David Chung published their work on beta-endorphin. Dr. Pert deserved the prestigious Lasker Award that went to Dr. Snyder, the man who headed her lab. In 1979, the *Washington Post* and the *New York Times* chronicled her mistreatment. The slight of this young female scientist, who was bypassed for a rightly deserved award, became a cause célèbre. The publicity surrounding this situation made more people aware of encephalin, at the same time that it highlighted the obstacles faced by high-achieving female scientists.[6]

When filmmaker Slava Tsukerman released *Liquid Sky,* informed spectators were well-aware that the body and brain produce opioids. Discoveries made just a decade earlier lent credibility to this otherwise far-fetched theme, and ensure that this film merits listing as NSF. At the time this film was released in 1982, it was not known that the AIDS epidemic was brewing in the very same bastions that the film's characters inhabit. The lifestyles of the many-partnered fashion model, with the heroin-using bisexual boyfriend, headed the list of the retrovirus' targets. In fact, no one knew about the retrovirus in 1982. The first AIDS cases were identified in 1981—although there was no name for this yet unnamed "gay plague." Scientists called it KSOI (Kaposi's Sarcoma Opportunistic Infections), to describe its external manifestations. A few years would pass before HIV was implicated in the deadly disease. That occurred in 1984.

It became apparent that gay men, IV drug users, even women who practiced unsafe sex with at-risk men (such as bisexual men who frequented *Liquid Sky*-style clubs) could contract this incurable condition. Hemophiliacs acquired AIDS through blood transfusions, as did recipients of infected organ transplants and tainted blood products infused during surgery.[7] Haitians were the third of the "3 H's of AIDS" (homosexuals, hemophiliacs, Haitians). In other words, the bisexual, multi-partnered and drug-using clubs became hotbeds of AIDS. New York City's Greenwich Village and San Francisco were the epicenters of the epidemic.

How odd it is that the film's aliens drained the life out of the party-goers as they orgasmed, and pursued endless sex and pleasure. They were left for dead and their bodies disappeared. This subject matter of this film remains one of those strange coincidences of moviemaking, in the same way that the plane crash scene in *Donnie Darko* (2001) paralleled the 9/11 crash into the Twin Towers, or the way that *The Manchurian Candidate* assassination scene "foretold" JFK's assassination. Another film, *Independence Day* (1996), also included strange correspondences to the events that transpired on 9/11.

In 1984, a film based on a Stephen King novel features a hallucinogenic chemical that induces extra-sensory perceptions, along with chromosomal mutations. The action in *Firestarter* (1984) takes place in 1969, when a government agency known as The Shop chooses twelve subjects for its experiments. Again, this trope about illicit and immoral experiments by the CIA (aka "The Company") is too close to fact to be impressive as neuroscience fiction (with emphasis on the word "fiction").

ESP remains more occult than scientific, although serious studies by scientists at Duke University and elsewhere examined this concept. *Firestarter* reminds us of an earlier Stephen King story, *Carrie*, which was made into a film in 1976 and remade in 2013. C.G. Jung, an early psychoanalyst and Freud's one-time heir-apparent, was drawn to the occult, Eastern mysticism, alchemy and Gnosticism, but his writings on these topics were subject to scorn, both by Freud and many more.[8] The same subject matter that repelled serious scientists attracted a lasting fan base, and made Jung's writings popular. Other areas of his research on personality types held up. (For more on the Jung-Freud break over the occult, plus improvised sex scenes that were never recorded in the annals of psychoanalysis, see Cronenberg's film, *A Dangerous Method* [2011].)

Compared to the eerie correspondences between the phantasmagorical *Liquid Sky* and real life, the reality-based parallels in David Lynch's *Dune* sound rather ordinary. In *Dune* (1984), a drug known as "The Spice" is the most valued commodity in the galaxy. It proffers longer life, greater vitality, and increased awareness. In some people, it imparts prescience that permits safe interstellar travel. The multi-flavored Spice injects itself into almost every aspect of native Fremen culture. Spice makes eyes blue (as does NZT in *Limitless*). The film is based on a series of books by Frank Herbert. Many say that full appreciation of the film requires familiarity with the books. Otherwise, the gigantic worms that burrow through the sand are the most memorable aspect of the movie.

"Spice" is now a name for a psychotomimetic drug that sends many people to emergency rooms. Its addicting properties are ill-understood but evident. The Hebrew word for "Spice" (b'samim) refers to spices used in religious rituals and to cannabis sold in Dizengoff Square. There is nothing mysterious about this term, and it is quite fitting that 21st century drug culture may have appropriated this term from the *Dune* series—or maybe from the Hebrew Bible itself.

References to drugs in *RoboCop 2* (1990) are equally mundane. "Nuke" is a designer narcotic distributed by the Drug Lord and leader of the Nuke Cult, Cain (Tom Noonan). Considering the inroads made by crack cocaine in the 1980s, and its links to violent crime, it is easy to imagine Nuke as crack. While under the influence of Nuke, cult leader Cain conjures up grandiose ideas, claiming that Nuke paves the path to paradise. Cain's name recollects the Biblical Cain who killed his brother Abel. His descendents are doomed to bear the "mark of Cain" forever after.

Also in 1990, we encounter the first of two *Total Recall* films. In the PKD original, "We Can Remember It For You Wholesale," Quail uses the drug "narkidrine" "to take a trip" — to use the lingo of the 1960s. The word "narkidrine" combines narcotics and Benzedrine or amphetamine.

The year 1990 introduced another quasi–NSF film about drugs and drug effects: *Jacob's Ladder*. Based on the screenplay by Bruce Joel Rubin—who also wrote the story and screenplay for *Ghost* (1990)—and directed by Adrian Lyne—who also directed *Fatal Attraction* (1987)—*Jacob's Ladder* was promoted as psychological horror and not as science fiction.

The NSF theme is less straightforward, largely because this film blends so many different sources. Tibetan Buddhism, Biblical Judaism (and hence the reference to "Jacob's Ladder"), horrific Francis Bacon paintings, and Ambrose Pierce's ever-popular story about *An Occurrence at Owl Creek Bridge* (1890) play into the mix. Political paranoia about secret government experiences echo real life facts about the CIA's MK-ULTRA project, and the agency's clandestine administration of hallucinogens to unsuspecting citizens and scientists. Director Lyne credits the inspiration for this scene to Martin A. Lee and Bruce Slain's book, *Acid Dreams: The CIA, LSD, and the Sixties' Rebellion* (Grove Press, 1985) and admits that Rubin's original script does not make such insinuations.

Tim Robbins stars as Jacob, a Vietnam veteran who suffers from flashbacks about the war. He experiences frightening hallucinations of dismembered or distorted Baconesque images while riding in cars or NYC subways. His current life is a living hell, given that he now works as a postman, resides in a project, and is married to Jezzie (short for the Biblical temptress, Jezebel) (Elizabeth Pena). Jezzie is diametrically different from his pre-war wife who bore his son.

Visions of his young son, a product of his original and only marriage, lead both Jacob and spectators to the truth: that Jacob died on the battlefield and that the subplots seen on screen are nothing but deathbed hallucinations of people and places that never existed.

By knowing just one historical fact, we can unravel the plot. Jacob's young son Gabe died before Jacob was conscripted. It is no accident that "Gabe" is short for the archangel Gabriel, who guides the dead to heaven. We watch the boy offer his hand, to lead Jacob up the stairs, and into the glowing light, and presumably to the place in the sky that is populated by angels from the Biblical story about Jacob's Ladder. Jacob has successfully passed through the Bardo-like visions of hell-on-earth via his hallucinations and is now ready to join his long-dead son in their eternal resting place. According to Tibetan Buddhist lore, the soul of the deceased must traverse those terrifying demonic Bardos (or gates) while en route to ever-lasting peace.

Through the non-linear, post-modernist plot, we can piece together enough information to understand the events that led to Jacob's death in the Mekong Delta in 1971. There are just enough details to add this film to our list of NSF films.

At some point in the twisted plot, the audience is introduced to a young chemist who runs a rogue lab on the side, as many young chemists (and even chemistry professors) were rumored to do in 1971. The chemist synthesizes LSD to sell on the street. Government agents track him down, and offer him a deal: enlist in the military, agree to their terms, and continue experiments on mind-altering drugs—or face jail time. The chemist chooses the former. Under their directions, he proceeds to synthesize BZ, a chemical that becomes known as "The Ladder." Presumably, this chemical will increase aggression in soldiers, to make them super-soldiers.

Jacob's platoon receives rations that are dosed with BZ. The soldiers ingest the substance unknowingly. Platoon members grow more aggressive, even before Viet Cong forces arrive.

The frenzied soldiers go on a killing spree, massacring their platoon mates. Jacob is stabbed in the stomach by a bayonet. The bayonet belongs to another soldier in his drug-dosed platoon.

Two years later, *The Lawnmower Man* (1992) deploys designer drugs to increase intelligence, and then some. As we discussed in the chapter on "Memories, Mentation and Medication," a well-meaning scientist, Dr. Angelo, recruits a simple-minded landscape assistant for an intelligence-enhancing experiment. To date, he has studied his formula on chimps, but to deliberately extracted the aggression-promoting factor from the formula that he administers to the Lawnmower Man, aptly named Jobe Smith. As often happens, the good doctor is employed by a consulting firm that arranges underhanded contracts with military officials (think *Brainstorm*).

The firm strives to make intelligent and aggressive chimps that can perform military maneuvers. Dr. Angelo simply wants to increase the intelligence of the intellectually-challenged Jobe. Without his knowledge, the head honcho replaces Dr. Angelo's revised formula, intended specifically for Jobe, with the usual aggression—and intelligence—enhancing original. All hell breaks loose, as Jobe grows physically threatening at the same time that he becomes smarter. The story ends badly, for Jobe is trapped in virtual reality, and Dr. Angelo is unable to rescue him. Even though the 20th century is coming to a close, and Stevenson's late 19th century tale about *The Strange Case of Dr. Jekyll and Mr. Hyde* is almost a century old, the moral of the story remains the same. Doctors should not play G-d, even if they are angels, like Dr. Angelo.

As the century and the millennium neared an end, *The Matrix* (1999) made a major impact. The first of a trilogy that would become a cult classic, *The Matrix* is an excellent example of the disjointed "mindfuck" films that appeared just before and after the millennium, when confusion reigned. *The Matrix* is closer to cyberpunk than anything else, but it does involve drugs. The symbolism of the red pill and the blue pill is straightforward, even if *The Matrix's* plot is convoluted. In *The Matrix,* humans are used as batteries that power the Matrix. Humans remain in a state of suspended animation, unaware of their situation, and incapable of experiencing their plight. A few renegade citizens recognize the reality and manage to escape. They offer a futuristic version of an "underground railroad" that transports citizens out of the Matrix by ship.

Neo, the computer hacker played by Keanu Reeves, has the option of leaving the Matrix or accepting his fate in the Matrix. He is told to choose between the red pill, which answers the question, "What is the Matrix," and the blue pill, which allows him to carry on with life as before. The red and blue pills recollect Alice's choices in Wonderland, where one pill makes you smaller and the other makes you larger. Plato's *Allegory of the Cave* is as important to the plot as the mind-altering properties of the pills. Essentially, Neo is offered a pill that allows him to see the shadows cast in the cave, and to continue to believe that the shadows are reality. Alternatively, he can opt for a pill that literally shows him the light of day, and illuminates the fate of humans who were co-opted by computers, stripped of free will and suspended in somnolent states.

The man who promises to rescue Neo, and whisk him away from the Matrix, is named, "Morpheus." Laurence Fishburne plays Morpheus. In Greek mythology, Morpheus is the deity of dreams. Modern day morphine acquired its name in Morpheus' honor, possibly because of the belief that opium-induced visions are akin to dreams. Morphine became available in 1801, when Adam Friedrich Wilhelm Serturner crystallized opium and obtained morphine. In 1927, pharmaceutical giant Merck began marketing morphine as a medicinal. Contrary to expectations, *The Matrix's* Morpheus does not offer psychoactive drugs to anyone. Instead, he offers hopes of regaining human dignity and breaking free of the dream state, governed by the deity of dreams.

The Prozium supplied to citizens in *Equilibrium* (2002) has a far more ominous connotation than *The Matrix'* red pills and blue pills. Christian Bale stars as enforcement officer John Preston. Christian Bale has played other doleful and complicated characters, starting with *American Psycho* (2000), and proceeding to the aging and invalided Batman in *The Dark Knight Rises* (2012), or *American Hustle's* (2013) too-clever-to-be true, toupee-wearing con man.

Preston resides in Libria, a totalitarian regime that outlaws emotions, artistic expression and emotionally stimulating media. In that role, Bale reminds us of Harrison Ford's Blade Runner, who also enforces the existing order by terminating replicants who passed their expiration date. Both Ford and Bale come to question their society's values. Conflicts follow, both internal and interpersonal. That leads to action and plot points.

In "Libria," citizens inject themselves daily with a medication called Prozium, which suppresses emotions. The state determined that emotions are the core cause of conflict, and that unbridled emotions led to the Third World War. To avert another catastrophic battle scene, emotions must be avoided at all cost, even if that means executing citizens who express emotions. Distribution centers known as "Equilibrium" provide Prozium.

"Sense offenders" who violate these precepts are arrested and incinerated. In other words, they are burned at the stake, as witches were, except that there is no stake. Illegal materials that receive ratings of "EC-10" for "emotional content" are also incinerated. Parallels between official Librian policy and the Nazi book burning of 1933 are obvious, especially since Libria's officials wear tailored, SS-style regalia (without the swastika). Libria's harsh-angled, geometrical insignia, the tetragrammaton, has superficial similarities to the swastika.

The choice of the word "Prozium" is no accident. Linguistically, Prozium combines Prozac and Librium. Prozac made it to market in 1987, changing the landscape of psychiatric treatment and changing the public's attitude toward antidepressant medications.[9] Prozac marked the dawn of a new era in psychopharmacology. Prozac was simple and safe enough to prescribe on an out-patient basis. Earlier antidepressants, such as the tricyclic antidepressants (amitriptyline or imipramine) or the MAOIs (monoamine oxidase inhibitors) could be deadly when taken in overdoses or, in the case of the MAOIs, when combined with common foods or over-the-counter cold medications. Consequently, the use of those earlier antidepressants was largely restricted to persons who were seriously depressed and who had no better alternatives, short of hospitalization or electroshock treatment.

Marketed as an antidepressant, Prozac and other SSRIs (selective serotonin reuptake inhibitors) relieve depression in persons who suffer from major depressive disorder (MDD). Some studies show that SSRIs are less effective in less serious depressions. Importantly, Prozac and other SSRIs makes some users complacent over time, stripping them of strong emotions, and making them less reactive to severe distress. That very property could promote Libria's goals.

Librium was once a *Valley of the Dolls*-type drug. Librium is a benzodiazepine (BZD)-based tranquilizer. Similar to Valium and Miltown, Librium gained fame as one of "mother's little helpers." The Rolling Stones sang about those medications, which were embraced by homemakers after the FDA approved Librium in 1960. Unlike SSRI antidepressants (in the early stages), Librium slows down the user and dulls the senses. It decreases distress by stopping anxiety. It impairs memory and coordination (as alcohol does), and can also induce depression if used over a prolonged time or by susceptible individuals. Appropriately, the name of the dystopian, "Libria," carries connotations of Librium. This word is also similar to "Liberia," where freed African American slaves formed a new nation-state in Africa, which fell under the spell of an exploitative dictator, or "Big Man."

All would have proceeded as planned for Preston (Bale), were it not for the fact that he accidentally misses his Prozium dose one day. He is bombarded by emotions that were previously suppressed. He begins to question his morality and his life's direction. His careless error occurs after his wife was whisked away and executed because she committed a sense offense. Bereft of his wife, Preston is now a widower, with two children left to his care.

The Prozium of Libria is the exact opposite of the conscious-expanding drugs of the sixties. The fact that both its name—and its effects—share properties with commonly prescribed psychotropic medications forces the spectator to search for more similarities between Libria and Prozium and contemporary society. Spectators ask themselves, "What can we expect of a society that is made complacent by Prozac or sedated by benzodiazepines? In 2002, when *Equilibrium* appeared, we did not know that demand for prescription opioids and amphetamines for escalating numbers of ADHD diagnoses would push demand for Prozac-like antidepressants aside. We did know that security measures put in place after the terrorist attacks of 9/11 (in 2001) bore some resemblance to totalitarian states. Over time, the state would intrude even more into personal life.

Even though we can appreciate *Equilibrium's* predictions about post–9/11 surveillance, retrospectively, it is unclear how much this futuristic film about a fascistic society drew upon actual events that followed in the wake of the World Trade Center attack. Fascistic and dystopian themes are common in SF books and films, with or without the influence of the Office of Homeland Security, and even before public frisking at airports, monitoring of mosques, and enhanced governmental ability to access personal email messages.

Drawing parallels between *Equilibrium* and *The Manchurian Candidate* or *Fahrenheit 451* is too enticing to resist. However, since this chapter focuses on drugs and dystopias, we will let our readers make those comparisons in their own minds.

Minority Report (2002) premiered in the same year as *Equilibrium*. It, too, forecasts a future where the state shackles its citizens (psychologically) and executes them on will, without a fair trial. Psychoactive drugs play a role in this society, although that role is relatively minor. The future is determined by "Precogs" who owe their psychic abilities to intrauterine exposure to "neuroin." Like Prozium, the neologism "neuroin" is obvious. It alludes to heroin and "nerve pills." In the previous chapter, we elaborated on the implications of fetal exposure to neuroactive or psychotropic meds, to show how *Minority Report* taps into contemporary concerns pertaining to the crack epidemics of the 1980s, the so-called "crack babies," and prenatal Prozac exposure.

Substance D, used in *A Scanner Darkly* (2006), is another matter. Substance D stands for "death." There is no ambiguity and no subtlety. The potential lethality of street drugs is by no means fictional. In fact, extreme risk is a selling point. Drug dealers brand their heroin bags, stamping the glassine with names like Grim Reaper, D.O.A., or skull and crossbones symbols. Substance D leads to inevitable death after it splits the user's brain into two distinct entities.

A Scanner Darkly is inspired by a PKD novel of 1977. PKD's novel is a semi-autobiographical account of his encounters with California's drug culture. After his fourth wife left him in 1970, Dick lived with teen drug users in a quasi-communal setting. He blended first hand experiences into his fictional stories. His intermittent amphetamine use escalated after his wife's departure, and he entered rehab shortly after completing this award-winning book.

In the film version of *A Scanner Darkly,* everyone is addicted to Substance D. Substance D both darkens and heightens the perceptions. Police go undercover to track down its distributors. Because all characters are addicted, each becomes an unreliable narrator. To confuse reality further, the film uses an animation technique, known as rotoscope. Actual actors are filmed, but animated cells overlap their silhouettes, to render their images unreal. Their voices remain the same, and are easily recognizable, because the film features high profile stars, including Keanu Reeves, Wynona Ryder, and Robert Downey, Jr. Richard Linklater directs. As usual, the PKD-based cinema forces us to rethink Plato's *Allegory of the Cave*, and makes us wonder which characters are real and which are figments of a secondary, drug-altered reality.

The title of this film, and the original PKD story, reminds us of "a glass darkly." It is unclear if PKD references the elusive New Testament quote, or, more likely, if he spoofs the Bergman film, *Through a Glass Darkly* (1961). In 1 Corinthians 13:12, the passage reads, "For now we see through a glass, darkly; but then face to face: now I know in part; but then shall I know even as also I am known." (King James Bible "Authorized Version," Pure Cambridge Edition).

Whereas the film version of *A Scanner Darkly,* and the original PKD story, revolve around drug-altered reality, the Bergman film connects to sixties-era currents in non-pharmacological psychiatry. Like PKD, Bergman characteristically poses philosophical questions and probes psychological states, but his approaches bears no resemblance to PKD's hard-hitting narratives.

Bergman made *Through a Glass Darkly* in 1961, just as the anti-psychiatry movement got underway. R.D. Laing's iconoclastic ideas infiltrated the youth culture and the counterculture. Even though mainstream psychiatry refuted his ideas, Laing's anti-psychiatry stance provocative enough to demand rebuttals and to incite debates among college students and psychiatry residents. Laing's *Sanity, Madness and the Family* (1964) added a new psychiatric vocabulary to the views expressed in Bergman's film. The concept of the "double bind" is linked to Laing (even though this term did not originate with Laing).

In those years, most psychiatrists and psychologists viewed schizophrenia as a "functional illness" rather than a brain-based disorder. They attributed it to family conflicts, hypothesizing that ambiguous and surreptitious sessages transmitted by family members contributed to psychosis, hallucinations and paranoia. "Double binds" were as Laingians as neurotransmitters are to contemporary psychopharmacologists and neuropsychiatrists. Although R.D. Laing's writings publicized this concept, and he often gets credit for it, other psychologists coined the term "double-bind." In 1956, Gregory Bateson, John Weakland, Donald deAvila Jackson, and Jay Haley proposed the double bind theory of schizophrenia's thought disorder.

Recall that Thorazine (chlorpromazapine) entered the U.S. market in 1954, having been synthesized two years earlier in France. In spite of its significant physical side effects, some of which did not become apparent for twenty years, Thorazine revolutionized the treatment of severe psychiatric illnesses, such as schizophrenia, and led to the mass de-institutionalization. Therapeutic drugs like CPZ have very different effects from the deadly drugs in *A Scanner Darkly*. However, it is worth noting that persons with amphetamine-induced paranoia receive prescriptions for CPZ or related meds. Their symptoms are especially difficult to relieve.

The mid–1950s marked a turning point in psychiatric treatment. In fact, we might say that psychiatry itself was in a "double-bind" and was transmitting contradictory messages. On one hand, neuroleptics like Thorazine showed observable and measurable efficacy in relieving the symptoms of psychosis. Lobotomies, however brutal as they sound, also proved that brain functions are localized and that some psychotic behaviors can be ameliorated by brain surgery. The Nobel Prize committee was impressed enough to award its prize to Dr. Moniz, inventor of leucotomy, in 1949. At the same time, psychoanalysis promised undeliverable cures for psychosis, and those who could afford such genteel treatment, both in money and time, often opted for this diametrically different methodology. Hollywood chronicled all these shifts.

Moving along, we come across *Max Payne* in 2008. Critics panned *Max Payne*. Video game fans rejected it, remaining loyal to the video game that inspired the film. Predictably, they objected to all inaccuracies in the movie version. Great efforts were made to replicate the fast action of the video game, using novel cinematographic techniques. Even that was not enough to satisfy gamers, although the opening weekend was a big box office success.

This neo-*noir* film about a cop who pursues his wife's murderer sports an excellent cast. Mark Wahlberg stars as NYPD cop Max Payne. He works in the Cold Case unit. Beau Bridges is B.B. Hensley, the former partner of Max Payne's father. B.B. has since retired and now heads security at the same pharmaceutical company where Max's deceased wife had worked. Mila Kunis plays a Russian assassin who seeks revenge for the murder of her sister. Kunis will co-star as a beautiful but diabolical ballerina in *Black Swan* (2010), where she plays an understudy who steals the glory from Natalie Portman's frail and psychologically imperiled prima ballerina.

The MacGuffin of the movie is a tattoo of a winged creature, said to represent the wings of the mythical valkyrie. The search for this tattoo drives the action, in much the same way that the Maltese Falcon, another winged creature, pushes the plot in *The Maltese Falcon* (1941).

The action intensifies after Max's wallet is found near the dead body of Natasha (Mila Kunis), who owns a tattoo parlor. Max becomes the prime suspect in her death. Max tries to exculpate himself from murder charges, and to track down his dead wife's killer in the process. The same tattoo is found on the dead Natasha and in the case files of Max's dead wife, leading to the intrigue and to the reveal. Nearby drug users point the way. They use a street drug known as "Valkyr." Valkyr induces hallucinations of these ancient Norse mythological creatures, which Wagner celebrated in his opera, *De Valkyrie*. In other words, the drug is a hallucinogen, yet it promotes extreme endurance and strength that will allow Max to escape his would-be assassins.

Tracking down the drug and the tattoos ultimately leads Max to the pharmaceutical company that manufactures Valkyr. More coincidences occur. This company employed his deceased wife. B.B., his father's former partner, heads security. A supervisor at the plant offers a lead, and reveals that Max's wife worked on a military contract to create super-soldiers, using Valkyr. The studies backfired.

Valkyr proved to be very addicting. Only a few test subjects showed positive results. The rest hallucinated and went psychotic. The project was terminated—as was Max's wife Michelle, for she had too much information about the rogue military project and its aftermath. After further testing was forbidden, some rogue staff members recognized its potential as a recreational drug, and diverted the drug to the streets. And so the loop closes.

The double-dealing pharmaceutical company is a trope that recurs increasingly often, as Big Pharma becomes more visible in American business. This trope pushes the plot in the 2014 reboot of *RoboCop*, where the duplicitous CEO connives to disconnect Officer Murphy from life support, after his efforts as RoboCop are no longer needed for the company's success. A failed pharmaceutical effort to create highly aggressive super-soldiers is the theme that drives the much more convoluted and multi-layered film, *Jacob's Ladder* (1990). *The Bourne Legacy* also revolves around clandestine government experiments and gullible scientists. Gibson's novels, and the films made from them, include the same theme about big bad drug companies.

In retrospect, *Captain America: The First Avenger* (2011) may be the sole example of good results from super-soldier serum. Still, the effects of that secret serum are closer to anabolic steroids, and bear little resemblance to neurotropic or psychotropic meds.

The double-dealings needed to secure addicting drugs in *Limitless* (2011) are just as deadly as the video game antics of *Max Payne*, even though the NYC setting is more realistic. As discussed, *Limitless* revolves around NZT, an experimental drug that enhances intelligence and increases speed of movement, as if it were, well, "speed." NZT enhances memory, so that the protagonist can conjure up memories of ju-jitsu scenes he saw on screen, and replicate the movements during fight scenes, even though he never before engaged in martial arts.

Bradley Cooper plays the down-and-out writer turned drug-addled mastermind, in a role that counterbalances with his curly-haired, coke-sniffing Academy Award-nominated FBI agent in *American Hustle* (2013). NZT is too similar to modafinil or amphetamine to make it intriguing—but the action-adventure aspects make it appealing. Like *The French Connection* (1971), this film concerns action and conspiracy more than chemistry.

Many neuroscience fiction films about psychopharmacology are less futuristic and more social commentary, simply because psychopharmacology pervades everyday life.[10] Brain chips and brain boluses are still some years away—in spite of current studies with neuromodulation and the preliminary success of brain implants for some aspects of Parkinson's disease. If we thumb through film titles and synopses, we can find many more films about hallucinogens that we did not discuss. That is the subject of another study—although it seems that amateur, non-academic websites do an admirable job of collecting and cataloging this information.[11]

Fourteen

Computers, Consciousness and Control

Considering how important computers are to contemporary society—and considering that computers have existed since the 1940s—it is disappointing that we do not encounter more memes about Computers and Consciousness. There are many films about computer components (hard drives, removable drives and the like), and their ability to restore or substitute memories or dreams. However, memories of the past are not the same as "living in the now" and experiencing the world first hand and emoting in response.

That is not to say that there are no references to computers and consciousness whatsoever in 21st century SF film. It is worth noting that films about computers and consciousness more often than not revolve around "computers, consciousness and control" (and hence the name of this chapter). Issues concerning control and conflict may simply reflect the need for a plot-driving device. An action-adventure SF film without a conflict would be a boring film indeed, SF or not, and most of these films fall under the rubric of action-adventure. SF-horror hybrids intentionally evoke unsettling emotions, and typically involve forces outside of ordinary control.

All three *Iron Man* films are exceptions to this general principle, because Tony Stark acquires enough real life adversaries to drive the plot. So he can co-exist more peacefully with the computer that propels his suit and calls the Iron Legion into action, when Tony is separated from this super-powered suit and facing an advancing Extremis army. Cleverly, Tony's computer goes by the name of J.A.R.V.I.S.—which is just one letter off from "Jarvik," the surname of Robert Jarvik, M.D., the physician-scientist who invented the first artificial—and permanently implantable—heart, named "Jarvik 7." Also an entrepreneur, Dr. Jarvik heads Jarvik Heart, Inc. J.A.R.V.I.S. never replaces Tony's consciousness, but it sometimes intuits, occasionally argues, and always responds.

Computer hackers as protagonists are common enough, both in film and, unfortunately, in daily life. Hackers can carry the same significance as scientists did in decades past (think *Neuromancer* or *The Matrix*). Programmers possess mysterious skills that can be used for the benefit of humankind, but can also orchestrate its destruction, as can scientists. Those computer hackers are active players in the game, and are not passive agents of computers—to date. It is only a matter of time before a film about hackers who come under the control of the computers.

Sadly, a film that revolves around computers and consciousness (and human identity)

Once a down-and-out writer, Eddie (Bradley Cooper) touts NZT ("a pill that could make you rich and powerful") in a Pharma-style infomercial (www.theclearpill.com) for *Limitless* (2011).

will be released a few days after this book is due to be delivered and so cannot be discussed in the depth that it deserves. *Transcendence* (2014), starring Johnny Depp, promises to dramatize the transfer of a human's essence to a computer network. By storing his consciousness outside of its owner's body, his "personhood" can persist in a more evolved and everlasting existence. According to the trailer, the characters in *Transcendence* experience the same human conflicts as the characters in *RoboCop,* where the wife objects to these Frankensteinian experiments, and the residual human emotions lead to the unraveling of these heroic (or foolish) experiments. As usual, the computerized consciousness attempts to overpower the forces that be and take control.

Early in 2014, we encountered the remake of *RoboCop,* where Officer Murphy (Joel Kinnaman) is reconstructed after a devastating accident. Without his consent (but with his wife's consent in the recent film), Murphy's body is merged with computer-controlled machinery. He retains consciousness, but loses free will. He cannot make choices, be they physical, cognitive or emotional. As time goes on, and his emotions grow stronger, he can override some external control, much to the chagrin of the CEO of the company that subsidized his reconstruction.

FOURTEEN. *Computers, Consciousness and Control* 235

Office Murphy aka RoboCop relies upon a computer to switch him on and off. This computer is not a "prime mover" unto itself and is not capable of overtaking the world (as the computers in *Demon Seed* or *The Matrix* aspired). Rather, the computer remains under the control of a mercenary and malevolent corporation, which employs a Ph.D. scientist (not a physician or an M.D.) to add bioengineering expertise. Technicians can deplete or restore Murphy's dopamine levels, when his blood pressure rises too high or his emotions are about to overtake him. The computer acts autonomously at times (in the same way that pacemakers kick in when hearts skip a beat, or the way that portable generators turn on spontaneously, during power outages). Mostly, this computer mediates between Murphy and other humans.

Curiously, Parkinson's disease bears some similarities to this mechanical model, although there is no computer pulling the strings of Parkinson's patients. As dopamine-producing cells of the brain's substantia nigra fail to release this neurotransmitter, persons with PD lose volitional control of their bodies. They cannot initiate movement at will, and cannot stop moving on their own accord once they start moving. Perhaps it is a coincidence that the film references "dopamine," when it talks about controlling emotions, or perhaps there is an intentional allusion to Parkinson's disease, which responds to dopamine-restoring agents.

In contrast to the most recent *RoboCop*, which makes us speculate about correspondences between neuroscience and bioengineering, *The Matrix* (1999) is a far-out fantasy. In *The Matrix*, computers control the matrix, and use humans as batteries, maintaining them in dream states that delude them into thinking that they are living out their lives. The agents in *The Matrix* appear to be human, and assume human form, but they are actually personifications of abstract concepts—such as programs—related to the computer. In keeping with

Officer Murphy's (Joel Kinnaman) expressionless face and half-head hang from a machine in *RoboCop* (2014), and his lungs breathe via a respirator, as Dr. Dennet Norton (Gary Oldman) gazes at the part-man, mostly-machine he created and controls.

The Matrix's overarching religious themes, we can compare these material manifestations to the Holy Ghost of Christianity, to the "Shechina" of Jewish mysticism, or to Hindu avatars that change form but retain their identities.

Demon Seed (1977) is concrete to its core. In this film, a computer rapes the woman who uses it for her household chores. The computer plans to overtake the world by creating a computer-human hybrid. The computer is sentient but possesses strange physical appendages. It produces a baby encased in a metallic shell. Because of its timing, *Demon Seed* functions as a statement about feminism as much as a comment on computers and their place in society.

Perhaps the best example of computer control of consciousness to date comes from an enduring icon of SF: *Star Trek*. In *Star Trek: First Contact* (1996) (and in TV shows such as *Star Trek: Next Generation* and *Voyager*), we encounter the concept of "the hive mind."

The *Star Trek* story is both simple and complex. A race of computers seeks perfection. It traverses the universe, overtaking all biological organisms that it encounters, and assimilating species after species into a collective known as The Borg. Klingons, Vulcans, Bajorans, Romulans, Humans and more are incorporated into The Borg, as it passes their way. "Resistance Is Futile" is the rallying cry of these colonized peoples—and is an enduring pop culture phrase.

Both body and mind transform in The Borg. All races in the universe turn into Cyborgs (part cybernetic, part organic). They are injected/infected with nanoprobes that change the organisms from within. Nanites in the later appearing film, *The Gamer,* may owe their origins to the nanoprobes from this *Star Trek* episode, since they, too, usurp individual will. Of course, the term itself references "nanotechnology," which manipulates matter on a molecular level.

Once infected by these nanites, the minds of conquered peoples link to the collective (known as "the hive"). Through these nanoprobes, each being receives the same instructions from central command. As a result, all Cyborgs think alike and The Borg operates with a "hive mind." There are notable similarities to Dr. Who's "Cybermen" from television episodes.

If we substitute's allusions to the "hive mind" with a similar sounding word—"the herd"—we find ourselves coming around full circle, and returning to Nietzsche, and 19th century philosophy that predated experimental psychology and psychoanalysis. Like later existentialists, Nietzsche derided "*the herd*—that collection of human beings who form a non-individual group mentality by following the beliefs, views, [and] projects of one another. Each person hides from the freedom and responsibility ... by nestling himself in the comfort and security of belonging with the others, anyone who is external to one's individuality."[1]

In the case of these SF films about computers and consciousness, the individual loses the choice to define himself according to his own terms, and cannot retain his own consciousness. This individual finds himself in the same predicament as those who abdicated this responsibility when given a choice. Perhaps these futuristic films about computers, consciousness and control are saying that there really is no choice, and that there is that "great computer in the sky" that pulls the strings of humans, like marionettes suspended from a stick.

Alternatively, we can view the "hive mind" as an ode to C. G. Jung and a metaphor for

Jung's hypothetical "collective unconscious," which is supposedly inherited by all humans. In *Star Trek*, this collective unconscious overrides Jung's equally hypothetical "racial unconscious," which is theoretically specific to inhabitants of various planets, and distinguishes the unconscious ideas and images of one race from another.

When we visit themes about "Computers, Consciousness and Control," we are asking age-old metaphysical questions in another guise. Who determines our destiny? Deities? Genes? Our past experiences or our collective unconscious? Childhood traumas or conflicts (as per Freud) or totalitarian governments that override individual choice? Rather than restricting answers to theories about psychological determinism, or biological determinism (genes and or environment), or even social or economic determinism, these newly hatched NSF films add the option of "pre-programmed computers" to the checklist. These SF films concern technology on the surface, but philosophical questions lurk behind the scenes. Such movies demand that we identify what makes humans "human," and which traits or abilities impart individual identity, and which interfere with that sense of "self" that is so important to "ego psychologists" who took center stage in the second half of the 20th century.

Conclusion: Hive Minds, Herds and Jung's Collective Unconscious

These neuroscience fiction films taunt us with promises of scientific advances in the future—but they also remind us that science does not offer all the answers, no matter how far science progresses. No wonder so many SF tropes revert to the supernatural. As much as science fiction functions as science futurism—most of the time—it is also atavistic, in the ways that it adds new twists to ancient and supposedly outdated superstitions. Exploring film's conflation of scientists, psychiatrists, shamans and sorcerers could be just as interesting a project as tracing the evolution of neuroscientific influences over a century and a quarter of science fiction films.

As we have shown throughout this book, even the "new" NSF tropes often harp back to the past as they replay and repackage old themes, not just from literature, but also from philosophy. Recall that psychology was a subdivision of philosophy departments until the late 19th century,[1] when Wilhelm Wundt opened his experimental psychology lab in Leipzig (1879), with William James following suit soon after at Harvard. James was trained as a physician.

Admittedly, psychology has very different origins from psychiatry, which is a subspecialty of medicine that still certifies its candidates in "psychiatry and neurology." Psychiatry is grounded in praxis and focuses on the diagnosis and treatment of psychopathology, with a heavy dose of theory about the origins of psychoses or neuroses thrown in. Psychiatry secondarily reflects back on philosophy, even though it is not a direct outgrowth of philosophy. Neuroscience's roots lie in science and in lab-based experiments, with occasional forays into clinical studies of patients.[2] Anyone who deals with the mind (and/or brain) has the option of returning to philosophy[3]—or viewing NSF films (and books) that ponder "eternal questions" that vexed philosophers from the earliest times. There is a reason why the questions they ask are called "eternal questions,"[4] and there is a reason why the same NSF tropes recur.

As we end, I cannot help but note that we have returned to Nietzsche and his concept of "the herd" as we discuss consciousness, both individual and collective, in *Star Trek*. *Star Trek* is the longest lasting and arguably the most influential science fiction franchise to date.[5] Its fans are fanatically loyal. The significance of *Star Trek*'s appropriation of Nietzschean ideas cannot be dismissed (even though many other interpretations of "the hive mind" are equally important).

Many scholars claim that Freud also appropriated Nietzsche's ideas, without crediting

Nietzsche. However, Freud adamantly denied that he read Nietzsche (although he quoted Nietzsche and acknowledged his significance). It was Freud who rerouted psychiatry away from neuroscience. Ironically, it is *Star Trek* that merges Nietzsche's philosophical concepts of the mind with emerging (yet fictionalized) tenets of neuroscience and molecular biology (through allusions to "nanoprobes"). *Star Trek* also nods to Jung's controversial concept of the "collective unconscious," which is signified by the "hive mind" that links via biological nanoprobes.[6]

How curious it is that science fiction films (or, TV, in the case of *Star Trek*) can reconcile theoretical disputes among scholars and practitioners, in one episode. When we began this book, we turned to *Iron Man 3,* to see how the "two minds" of psychiatry are blended in a single strip of celluloid. As we end this book, we now turn back the clock to *Star Trek*, for even more ideas about collating supposedly irreconcilable differences among philosophers, depth psychologists (such as Freud and Jung), and newer concepts in neuroscience. America may not be the "melting pot" that it was once made out to be, but American entertainment is indeed a "melting pot" that amalgamates ideas from many different sources. No wonder NSF endures.

Afterword

As expected, there is no end of neuroscience fiction films in sight. From the get-go, I realized that whatever I wrote would be out-of-date by the time this book is published. New NSF films appear with regularity, and advances in some aspects of neuroscience are progressing at lightning speed, to the point that the lines between neuroscience fiction and neuroscience fact sometimes become blurred.

However, I did not expect to encounter so many new and directly relevant NSF films within two weeks of forwarding my manuscript to McFarland. Two of those very recent films—*Transcendence* and *Captain America: The Winter Soldier*—fit snugly into the last chapter on "Computers, Consciousness and Control." *Transcendence* was mentioned in passing in that chapter, based on the pre-release trailer. As expectedly, the trailer omitted the spoiler that changes the plot points.

I feel obligated to elaborate on those details in this *Afterward*, if only because I expressed surprise at the relative dearth of films that deal with computers, consciousness and control. Apparently, I spoke too soon. Perhaps we will witness a flowering of this trope in the coming years—possibly depending upon the success of the two recent films in question.

Transcendence revolves around transferring "consciousness"—complete with loves, hates, fears, and, above all, information—into a computer. *Transcendence* is a film about the "taxidermy of the mind." Like that other never-to-be-forgotten taxidermist, Norman Bates, this "taxidermist of the mind" (aka artificial intelligence researchers) also has an evil side, and has the potential to do far more harm than meets the eye.

Like so many NSF films, its protagonist develops a "G-d complex" (better known as grandiosity in psychiatry) after his essence is uploaded into a computer and after he gains control and can manipulate many aspects of his environment. He exists in cyberspace, which is as good as saying that his presence permeates the heavens above.

In this film, Johnny Depp stars as an earnest scientist who plants a simple garden for his life partner and fellow collaborator. As the film ends, we return to the simple sunflowers, rooted in a sweet but shabby backyard that contrasts with the high-tech cyber-city that was built to contain Dr. Will Caster's (Johnny Depp's) cyber-self/essence.

Dr. Will Caster (Johnny Depp) and his wife, Dr. Evelyn Caster (Rebecca Hall), had been experimenting with technology that transfers consciousness. Their endeavors have been successful enough to turn Dr. Will Caster (Depp) into the spokesperson for these accomplishments in artificial intelligence. He has also invoked the ire of anti-computer activists that shoot him. This scene reminds us of the assassination attempt against *eXistence's* virtual reality designer Allegra (Jennifer Jason Leigh) or the covert anti-gaming operatives in *Gamer*, who strive to stop nanites from spreading and infecting (and presumably addicting) other gamers.

In fact, *Transcendence* seems to be a pastiche of many other plots, and even resurrects touches from romantic era ballets such as *Swan Lake* or *La Bayadère*, where one lover joins the other in death, unable to live alone. In the final acts, when the resurrected Depp dies again, joining his lifeless wife, we revisit *Romeo and Juliet* once again, with a slight twist.

Long before this final scene, we see Johnny Depp lying supine, suffering the effects of a radioactive bullet fired by anti-technology activists who oppose his work. He did not die on the spot, but now has only weeks left to live. We watch him wither away as time passes and radiation sickness progresses. Yet the R.I.F.T. members did not know that his research progressed as far as it did. Depp is desperate. With the help of his scientist wife, Depp uploads his mind into his computer moments before his body dies, and just before R.I.F.T. (Revolutionary Independence from Technology) members break in and interrupt his activities once again.

His body dies but his consciousness lives on. Thanks to his unlimited intelligence, and his ability to access trading accounts, Depp acquires enormous sums of money, which his wife can retrieve. Using these funds, she follows her husband's instructions, and builds an underground city in a no-name town in the middle of nowhere. His presence follows her everywhere. Eventually, his enhanced abilities turn into megalomania, and the modest scientist and loving husband is subsumed by his new powers. His wife balks at the changes she witnesses, and his best friend and fellow collaborator eventually turns on him—but not before Depp re-materializes in person, having harnessed the molecules to rebuild his body and reappear in full physical form, reprinted from a 3-D printer that presumably follows the specs of the uploaded DNA data.

Like the old Indian tale about *The Monkey's Paw*, the wife's wish to see her dead husband return alive is realized, but not without paying an impossible price. The Will Caster she knew and loved no longer exists; his soul and his essence were transmuted, and his idealistic goals corrupted. This reminds us of the physician-philanthropist in *The Colossus of New York*, which we discussed in our chapter on 1950s SF. In that film, a peace prize-winning doctor nearly dies in an auto accident. His body is mangled beyond repair, yet his brain remains intact. His father insists on preserving his son's bodiless brain, housing the brain in a colossal robotic body, constructed by the surviving son, who is an expert in robotics.

As the brother predicted, the social isolation endured by his brother takes its toll. The once-compassionate son espouses ideas that are exact opposite of his former philanthropic attitudes. Now psychotic, he forsakes his intent on helping the poor, and embarks on a killing spree at the U.N.—before he is stopped.

Transcendence ends more poetically. The wife is shot, and dies in the arms of her rematerialized husband. Johnny Depp's character then accepts the inevitability of his own death, and the two die together, inseparable forever. With an ending like this one, this futuristic NSF film could be set to music in a 19th century Tchaikovsky ballet score or performed on a Shakespearean stage. Such themes literally transcend time—but *Transcendence* may not transcend the demands of the box office, and at present seems poised to take second stage.

The continuum between computers and consciousness in *Captain America: The Winter*

Soldier is not so obvious, nor is it as pivotal to the plot as it is in *Transcendence*. As the second installment of a popular World War II-era superhero story, this film features Steve Rogers, the once-scrawny soldier who bulks out via super-soldier serum and becomes "Captain America." Steve was frozen after the war, but thaws and is brought back to life decades later, like Frankenstein's monster in *Frankenstein Meets the Wolf Man* (1943).

His long-time buddy Bucky Barnes met another fate. Bucky was last seen in the first film (*Captain America: The First Avenger*), and is believed to be dead. He fell off a train, in pursuit of the evil Dr. Zola, but we now learn that he did not die, as expected. Instead, he lost an arm and was "reconstructed," possibly by this one-time Nazi scientist who was recruited for the CIA-sponsored Operation Paperclip. The fictional Dr. Zola represents one of many (real life) Nazi-era researchers who escaped prosecution at the Nuremberg Trials in the late 1940s. He was rescued and repatriated to the U.S.A. after the war. (In actuality, the German Dr. Von Braun, who headed NASA at its inception, is the best known of this lot of "re-purposed" Paperclip scientists.)

In retrospect, we understand that Bucky was a subject of military medical experiments. He gained super-strength that allowed him to survive his fall in the first film. (The comic book stories are slightly different.) This time around, Bucky comes equipped with a super-strong metallic arm that replaces the arm he lost in the train accident. He has also been transformed into the eponymic "Winter Soldier." He is a trained assassin who can battle Captain America.

Steve recognizes Bucky, and cannot understand the animus of his one-time friend, who seems unable to recognize him. It turns out that Bucky has been brainwashed by his scientist-savior. His memory was wiped clean by electroshock, applied not to treat him but to eradicate earlier memories. These sad scenes remind us of the neuralyzer in the tongue-in-cheek *Men in Black* sequels—but they are less significant to our current concerns than the scenes that show the "essence" of dead Dr. Zola within a computer screen.

Like Johnny Depp's character in *Transcendence,* the former Nazi party member Dr. Zola and present day evildoer surmounted standard definitions of death when he uploaded his essence to a disc drive. That occurred in 1972, when computer technology was in its infancy. Zola's hazy image appears on a computer monitor. His facial features are fuzzy, but his heartless soul endures. His atomized essence persists, spreading evil, collaborating with Hydra members, wreaking world havoc. The film ends abruptly, as if it were a 1943 serial (reminiscent of Dr. Daka from the *Batman* serials). Like any good comics' cliffhanger, it leaves us eager for the next installment, be it from the *Captain America* franchise or the neuroscience fiction film genre in general.

Filmography

A

Abbott and Costello Meet Dr. Jekyll and Mr. Hyde (1953): Charles Lamont
Abbott and Costello Meet Frankenstein (1948): Charles T. Barton
Altered States (1980): Ken Russell
The Andromeda Strain (1971): Robert Wise
Andy Warhol's Frankenstein (1973): Paul Morrisey
Antwone Fisher (2002): Denzel Washington
The Ape (1940): William Nigh
The Ape Man (1943): William Beaudine
The Artist's Dream (1898): Georges Méliès
The Astronomer's Dream (*The Man in the Moon*) (1898): Georges Méliès
Atlantis (1913): August Blom
Attack of the 50 Foot Woman (1958): Nathan Juran
The Avengers (2012): Joss Whedon

B

Baron Munchausen's Dream (1911): Georges Méliès
Batman (serial) (1943): Lambert Hillyer
Battle for the Planet of the Apes (1973): J. Lee Thompson
A Beautiful Mind (2001): Ron Howard
The Beggar's Dream (lost film) (1898): Georges Méliès
Beneath the Planet of the Apes (1970): Ted Post
Black Like Me (1964): Carl Lerner
The Black Sleep (1956): Reginald LeBorg
Blade Runner (1982): Ridley Scott
A Blind Bargain (1922): Wallace Worsley
The Bourne Legacy (2012): Tony Gilroy
The Brain Eaters (1958): Bruno VeSota
The Brain from Planet Arous (1957): Nathan Juran
The Brain That Wouldn't Die (aka *The Head That Would Not Die* aka *The Black Door*) (1959–1962): Joseph Green
Brainstorm (1983): Douglas Trumbull
Brave New World (1980): Burt Brinckerhoff
Brave New World (1998): Leslie Libman, Larry Williams
The Bride of Frankenstein (1935): James Whale
A Brilliant Madness (PBS Documentary: American Experience) (2002): Mark Samels
The Brood (1979): David Cronenberg

C

The Cabinet of Dr. Caligari (Weine, 1919): Robert Wiene
Captain America: The First Avenger (2011): Joe Johnston
Captive Wild Woman (1943): Edward Dmytryk
Casablanca (1942): Michael Curtiz
Cat People (1942): Jacques Tourneur
The Cell (2000): Tarsem Singh
Change of Mind (1969): Robert Stevens
Charly (1968): Ralph Nelson
The Crimson Stain Mystery (serial) (1916): T. Hayes Hunter
The Christmas Dream (1900): Georges Méliès
The Clockmaker's Dream (1904): Georges Méliès
A Clockwork Orange (1971): Stanley Kubrick
Close Encounters of a Third Kind (1977): Steven Spielberg
The Cocoanuts (1929): Robert Florey, Joseph Santley
The Colossus of New York (1958): Eugène Lourié
The Condemned (2007): Scott Wiper
Conquest of the Planet of the Apes (1972): J. Lee Thompson
Conspiracy Theory (1997): Richard Donner
Contagion (2011): Steven Soderbergh
Crash (1996): David Cronenberg
Creature with the Atom Brain (1955): Edward L. Cahn
The Curse of Frankenstein (1957): Terence Fisher
Cyborg 2087 (1966): Franklin Adreon

D

A Dangerous Method (2011): David Cronenberg
Daughter of Dr. Jekyll (1957): Edgar G. Ulmer
Dawn of the Planet of the Apes (2014): Matt Reeves
The Dead Zone (1983): David Cronenberg
The Deer Hunter (1978): Michael Cimino
The Defiant Ones (1958): Stanley Kramer

Demon Seed (1977): Donald Cammell
The Doctor's Experiment (aka *Reversing Darwin's Theory*) (1908): Gaumont
The Doll (*Die Puppe*) (1919): Ernst Lubitsch
Donnie Darko (2001): Richard Kelly
Donovan's Brain (1953): Felix E. Feist
Dr. Jekyll and Mr. Hyde (1908): Otis Turner
Dr. Jekyll and Mr. Hyde (1912): Lucius Henderson
Dr. Jekyll and Mr. Hyde (1913): Frank E. Woods
Dr. Jekyll and Mr. Hyde (1913): Herbert Brenon
Dr. Jekyll and Mr. Hyde (1920): John S. Robertson
Dr. Jekyll and Mr. Hyde (1931): Rouben Mamoulian
Dr. Jekyll and Mr. Hyde (1941): Victor Fleming
Dr. Jekyll and Mr. Hyde (1973): David Winters
Dr. Jekyll and Mr. Hyde, Done to a Frazzle (1914): Warner Features Company
Dr. Jekyll and Sister Hyde (1971): Roy Ward Baker
Dr. Jekyll vs. the Werewolf (1972): León Klimovsky
Dr. Jekyll's Dungeon of Death (1979): James Wood
Dr. No (1962): Terence Young
Dr. Renault's Secret (1942): Harry Lachman
Dream of a Rarebit Fiend (1906): Edwin S. Porter and Wallace McCutcheon
The Dream of the Ballet Master (1903): Georges Méliès
The Dream of a Hindu Beggar (1902): Georges Méliès
The Dream of an Opium Fiend (1908): Georges Méliès
The Dream of the Poor Fisherman (1904): Georges Méliès
Dreamcatcher (2003): Lawrence Kasdan
Dreamscape (1984): Joseph Ruben
Dredd (2012): Pete Travis
Dressed to Kill (1980): Brian De Palma
The Drunkard's Dream (1897): Georges Méliès
Dune (1984): David Lynch
The Duality of Man (1910): Wrench Films

E

E.T. the Extra-Terrestrial (1982): Steven Spielberg
Earth Vs. Flying Saucers (1956): Fred F. Sears
Edge of Sanity (1989): Gérard Kikoïne
Elysium (2013): Neill Blomkamp
Equilibrium (2002): Kurt Wimmer
Escape from the Planet of the Apes (1971): Don Taylor
Eternal Sunshine of the Spotless Mind (2004): Michel Gondry
Everything That You Wanted to Know About Sex * But Were Afraid to Ask (1972): Woody Allen
The Evil of Frankenstein (1964): Freddie Francis
eXistenZ (1999): David Cronenberg
Eyes Without a Face (1960): Georges Franju

F

Fahrenheit 451 (1966): François Truffaut
Fear Strikes Out (1957): Robert Mulligan
Fiend Without a Face (1958): Arthur Crabtree
Firestarter (1984): Mark L. Lester
Flatliners (1990): Joel Schumacher
Frances (1982): Graeme Clifford
Frankenstein (1910): J. Searle Dawley
Frankenstein (1931): James Whale
Frankenstein (1992): David Wickes
Frankenstein and the Monster from Hell (1974): Terence Fisher
Frankenstein Created Woman (1967): Terence Fisher
Frankenstein Meets the Wolfman (1943): Roy William Neill
Frankenstein Must Be Destroyed (1969): Terence Fisher
Frankenstein: The True Story (1973): Jack Smight
Frankenstein's Army (2013): Richard Raaphorst

G

Gamer (2009): Mark Neveldine, Brian Taylor
Go and Get It (1920): Marshall Neilan, Henry Roberts Symonds
The Great Gatsby (2013): Baz Luhrmann
Guess Who's Coming to Dinner (1967): Stanley Kramer

H

Halloween (1978): John Carpenter
The Happiness Cage (aka *The Mind Snatchers*, aka *The Demon Within*) (1972): Bernard Girard
Hauser's Memory (1970): Boris Sagal
The Horror of Frankenstein (1970): Jimmy Sangster
House of Frankenstein (1944): Erle C. Kenton
Hugo (2011): Martin Scorsese
The Hunchback of Notre Dame (1923): Wallace Worsley
The Hunger Games (2012): Gary Ross

I

I, Frankenstein (2014): Stuart Beattie
I, Robot (2004): Alex Proyas
I, the Jury (1982): Richard T. Heffron
In Dreams (1999): Neil Jordan
The Imaginarium of Dr. Parnassus (2009): Terry Gilliam
Inception (2010): Christopher Nolan
The Incredible Two—Headed Transplant (1971): Anthony M. Lanza
Inherit the Wind (1960): Stanley Kramer
Invaders from Mars (1953): William Cameron Menzies
Invasion of the Body Snatchers (1956): Don Siegel
Invasion of the Body Snatchers (1978): Philip Kaufman
Invasion of the Saucer Men (1957): Edward L. Cahn
The Invisible Boy (1957): Herman Hoffman

Iron Man (2008): Jon Favreau
Iron Man 3 (2013): Shane Black
Island of Lost Souls (1932): Erle C. Kenton
The Island of Dr. Moreau (1977): Don Taylor
The Island of Dr. Moreau (1996): John Frankenheimer
It Conquered the World (1956): Roger Corman

J

Jacob's Ladder (1990): Adrian Lyne
Der Januskopf (aka *The Janus Head*, aka *Janus-Faced*) (1920): F.W. Murnau
Jekyll and Hyde (1990): David Wickes
Jekyll and Hyde: The Musical (2001): Don Roy King
Jekyll and Hyde...Together Again (1982): Jerry Belson
John Q (2002): Nick Cassavetes
Johnny Mnemonic (1995): Robert Longo
Judgment at Nuremberg (1961): Stanley Kramer
Jurassic Park (1993): Steven Spielberg

K

King Kong (1933): Merian C. Cooper

L

The Lady and the Monster (1944): George Sherman
La Poupee (aka *The Doll* aka *He, She, It*) (1962): Jacques Baratier
Lawnmower Man 2: Beyond Cyberspace (aka: *Lawnmower Man 2: Jobe's War*) (1996): Farhad Mann
The Lawnmower Man (1992): Brett Leonard
Life Without a Soul (1915): Joseph W. Smiley
Limitless (2011): Neil Burger
Liquid Sky (1982): Slava Tsukerman
Looper (2012): Rian Johnson

M

Mad Monster Party (1968): Jules Bass
The Mad Room (1969): Bernard Girard
Man with the Screaming Brain (2005): Bruce Campbell
Man with the Transplanted Brain (aka *L'Homme au Cerveau Greffe*) (1972): Jacques Doniol-Valcroze
The Man Who Changed His Mind (1936): Robert Stevenson
The Man with Two Brains (1983): Carl Reiner
The Manchurian Candidate (1962): John Frankenheimer
The Manchurian Candidate (2004): Jonathan Demme
Mary Reilly (1996): Stephen Frears
Mary Shelley's Frankenstein (1994): Kenneth Branagh
The Matrix (1999): Andy Wachowski, Lana Wachowski
The Matrix Reloaded (2003): Andy Wachowski, Lana Wachowski
The Matrix Revolutions (2003): Andy Wachowski, Lana Wachowski
Max Payne (2008): John Moore
A Midsummer Night's Dream (1909): Charles Kent
Memento (2000): Christopher Nolan
Men in Black (1997): Barry Sonnenfeld
Men in Black 2 (2002): Barry Sonnenfeld
Men in Black 3 (2012): Barry Sonnenfeld
Metropolis (1927): Fritz Lang
Minority Report (2002): Steven Spielberg
Mission: Impossible (1996): Brian De Palma
The Monkey Man (1908): France
The Monster and the Girl (1941): Stuart Heisler

N

Naked Lunch (1991): David Cronenberg
Die Nibelungen: Siegfried (1924): Fritz Lang
A Nightmare (1896): Georges Méliès
The Nutty Professor (1963): Jerry Lewis

O

One Flew Over the Cuckoo's Nest (1975): Milos Forman
Outland (1981): Peter Hyams

P

Planet of the Apes (1968): Franklin J. Schaffner
Planet of the Apes (2001): Tim Burton
Poor Little Rich Girl (1917): Maurice Tourneur
The Premature Burial (1962): Roger Corman
Prometheus (2012): Ridley Scott
Psycho (1960): Alfred Hitchcock

Q

R

The Rajah's Dream (1900): Georges Méliès
Re-Animator (1985): Stuart Gordon
Repo Men (2010): Miguel Sapochnik
The Revenge of Frankenstein (1958): Terence Fisher
Rise of the Plant of the Apes (2011): Rupert Wyatt
RoboCop (1987): Paul Verhoeven
RoboCop (2014): José Padilha
RoboCop 2 (1990): Irvin Kershner
RoboCop 3 (1993): Fred Dekker
Rollerball (1975): Norman Jewison
The Running Man (1987): Paul Michael Glaser

S

Scanners (1981): David Cronenberg
A Scanner Darkly (2006): Richard Linklater
Seconds (1966): John Frankenheimer
The Seven-Per-Cent Solution (1976): Herbert Ross
Silence of the Lambs (1991): Jonathan Demme
Solaris (1972): Andrei Tarkovsky
The Son of Dr. Jekyll (1951): Seymour Friedman
Spellbound (1945): Alfred Hitchcock
Star Trek: First Contact (1996): Jonathan Frakes
Star Wars (1977): George Lucas
The Stepford Wives (1975): Bryan Forbes
The Stepford Wives (2004): Frank Ozs
Still of the Night (1982): Robert Benton
The Strange Case of Dr. Jekyll and Mr. Hyde (1968): Charles Jarrott
The Strange Case of Dr. RX (1942): William Nigh
The Student of Prague (1913): Stellan Rye, Paul Wegener
The Student of Prague (1926): Henrik Galeen
Suddenly Last Summer (1959): Joseph L. Mankiewicz
Sunset Boulevard (1950): Billy Wilder

T

Tale of the Grandmother and the Child's Dream (1908): Georges Méliès
The Terminal Man (1974): Mike Hodges
The Terminator (1984): James Cameron
The Terminator 2: Judgment Day (1991): James Cameron
The Testament of Dr. Mabuse (1933): Fritz Lang
The Thing with Two Heads (1972) Lee Frost
This Island Earth (1955): Joseph M. Newman
Thor (2011): Kenneth Branagh
Thor: The Dark World (2013): Alan Taylor
The Three Faces of Eve (1957): Nunnally Johnson
THX-1138 (1971): George Lucas
Timecop (1994): Peter Hyams
Total Recall (1990): Paul Verhoeven
Total Recall (2012): Len Wiseman
A Trip to the Moon (1902): Georges Méliès
Tron (1982): Steven Lisberger
12 Monkeys (1995): Terry Gilliam
20,000 Leagues Under the Sea (1954): Richard Fleischer
The Two Faces of Dr. Jekyll (1960): Terence Fisher
2001: A Space Odyssey (1968): Stanley Kubrick

U

The Unearthly (1957): Boris Petroff

V

Videodrome (1983): David Cronenberg

W

Wargames (1983): John Badham
Westworld (1973): Michael Crichton
When Clouds Roll By (1919): Victor Fleming
The Wizard of Oz (1939): Victor Fleming
The Wolf Man (1941): George Waggner
The Wolf of Wall Street (2013): Martin Scorcese

X

X-Men Origins: Wolverine (2009): Gavin Hood
The Man With X-Ray Eyes (1963): Roger Corman

Y

Yellow Submarine (1968): George Dunning
Young Frankenstein (1974): Mel Brooks

Z

Television

"Adventures of Superman" (Television Series) (1952–1958)
"Ben Casey" (Television Series) (1961–1966)
"Bionic Woman" (Television Series) (1976–1978)
"The Infinite Worlds of H.G. Wells" (Television Mini-Series) (2001)
"Lost in Space" (Television Series) (1965–1968)
"Malcolm in the Middle" (Television Series) (2000–2006)
"The Man from U.N.C.L.E." (Television Series) (1964–1968)
"Mission Impossible" (Television Series) (1966–1973)
"The Outer Limits" (Television Series) (1963–1965)
"Planet of the Apes" (Television Series) (1974)
"Remington Steele" (Television series) (1982–1987)
"Return to the Planet of the Apes" (Animated Television Series) (1975–1976)
"Robocop Prime Directives" (Television Mini-Series) (2000)
"RoboCop" (Television Series) (1994–1995)
"Six Million Dollar Man" (Television Series) (1973–1978)
"Star Trek" (Television Series) (1966–1969)
"The Twilight Zone" (Television Series) (1959–1964)

Chapter Notes

Introduction

1. See Andy Fixmer's year-end report, "'Iron Man' Led Record Year as Hollywood Spaced Out Movies," Bloomberg Technology, Dec. 30, 2013, http://www.bloomberg.com/news/2013-12-30/-iron-man-led-record-year-as-hollywood-spaced-out-movies.html, accessed January 1, 2014.

2. "'Iron Man 3' Reaches $1 Billion Ahead of the Weekend," http://www.boxoffice.com/2013-5-12, accessed May 27, 2013.

3. This common expression is also the title of T.M. Luhrmann's book, *Of Two Minds: An Anthropologist Looks at American Psychiatry* (New York: Vintage, 2001).

4. See http://www.nytimes.com/opinion, May 26, 2013, or the Sunday Review print section for discussions of therapy versus medication, prompted by the publication of DSM-5 by APA in May 2013.

5. Eric Kandel, M.D., an Austrian-born psychiatrist who emigrated to the U.S. and later won a Nobel Prize, has researched the role of psychoanalysis and therapy in general in changing brain functions and connections. See also www.nobelprize.org.

6. Nick Bilton, "Disruptions: Brain Computer Interfaces Inch Closer to Mainstream," *New York Times*, April 28, 2013, accessed June 17, 2013; Susan Young, "Samsung Demos a Tablet Controlled by Your Brain," *MIT Technology Review*, April 19, 2013, http://www.technologyreview.com/news/513861/samsung-demos-a-tablet-controlled-by-your-brain/, accessed June 17, 2013; Jennifer A. Kingson, "Thought-Controlled Copter," *New York Times*, The Week, June 11, 2013, p. D2.

7. Malcolm W. Browne, "How Brain Waves Can Fly a Plane," *New York Times*, March 7, 1995, accessed June 17, 2013.

8. We can see links between this film and Philip Roth's generation-shaping novel, *Portnoy's Complaint* (1969), and the less-feted film version of the book (dir. Lehman, 1972). Roth was the first to use the psychoanalytic session as a framing device for a novel.

9. We find parallels with *The Great Gatsby* (dir. Luhrmann, 2013), which employs a psychotherapy session as a framing device and opened in theaters shortly after *Iron Man 3*.

10. The word *catharsis* originates in the Greek theater, and was borrowed for psychoanalytic vocabulary. Greek tragedy allowed spectators to identify with the characters, purge their emotions as the play ends, and achieve a *catharsis* of their experiences. Psychoanalysis aspired to achieve these results when analysands re-experienced emotionally charged events in psychoanalytic sessions.

11. See Irina Ivanova's article in *Craine's New York Business* (March 7, 2014) about Sermo, an anonymous doctors-only discussion board, accessed online at crainsnewyork.com.

Chapter One

1. See Andreas Killen, *Berlin Electropolis: Shock, Nerves, and German Modernity* (Berkeley: University of California, 2006) or David Lerner, *Hysterical Men: War, Psychiatry, and the Politics of Trauma in Germany, 1890–1930* (Cornell Studies in the History of Psychiatry) (Ithaca: Cornell University Press, 2009) for details about World War I psychiatric treatments and "Kaufmannization."

2. "Malpractice arising from negligent psychotherapy," *Ethics Behavior* (1994), http://www.ncbi.nlm.nih.gov/pubmed/11652794, accessed May 19, 2013; A.A. Stone, "Law, science, and psychiatric malpractice: a response to Klerman's indictment of psychoanalytic psychiatry," *American Journal Psychiatry* 147.4 (Apr. 1990):419–27, http://www.ncbi.nlm.nih.gov/pubmed/11652794, accessed May 19, 2013.

3. *Fantastic Voyage* (1966) is an excellent example of bioscience fiction that cannot be considered "neuroscience fiction." Miniaturized scientists are injected into the bloodstream, so that a delicate brain operation—the removal of blood clots or emboli—can be performed from within. They travel through the vascular system, and make a quick exit through a tear duct after their ship is destroyed, but do not enter the brain matter directly or cause behavior changes.

4. Simmel entered the military when still a general physician and came to command a military hospital. Intrigued by Freud's theories, Simmel was not formally trained in psychoanalysis when his novel treatment approaches made the most impact. After the war, he completed psychoanalytic training. He mobilized shell-

shocked soldiers by exploring the fears that prevented them from returning to the front. His feats were impressive enough to attract the attention of ranking military officials, who attended a psychoanalytic conference to learn about this "invention." Sigmund Freud was asked to testify at a 1920 hearing against military psychiatrists who stood accused of brutalizing soldiers with electric shocks and other inhumane treatments. These highly publicized hearings were known as "the Wagner-Jauregg Trials," not because Wagner-Jauregg alone used such techniques, but because Wagner-Jauregg's name was so well recognized and otherwise respected. Several doctors stood accused at this trial.

5. Analysts who fled fascist Europe enjoyed great esteem in America, even if their European manners and speech—and their Jewish origins—seemed strangely out of place at the Menninger Clinic in the Midwest, where the Menninger brothers welcomed the refugees. Historians say that the Menninger's efforts changed the direction of post-war psychiatry. See Lawrence J. Friedman, *Menninger: The Family and the Clinic* (New York: Knopf, 1990).

6. European psychiatry was never as polarized and particularistic as American psychiatry, for neurology and psychiatry remained intertwined in Europe, while American "asylum superintendents" (who became known as psychiatrists) had different roles than neurologists. See Hannah S. Decker, "Psychoanalysis in Central Europe," Edward M. Brown, "Neurology's Influence on American Psychiatry: 1965–1915," and Gerald N. Grob, "The Transformation of American Psychiatry," all in *History of Psychiatry and Medical Psychology*, ed. Edwin R. Wallace IV and John Gach (New York: Springer, 2008).

7. Wagner-Jauregg also studied congenital cretinism, caused by iodine deficiency a condition that was common among mountain dwellers in Styria, Austria, where iodine needed to manufacture thyroid hormones was absent from food sources. Cretinism causes mental retardation, signs and symptoms of depression, as well as distinctive facial and physical changes. By adding iodine to salt, entire populations could be spared this congenital scourge.

8. Early on, psychoanalysis was embraced by neurologists (rather than psychiatrists or "asylum superintendents"), but psychoanalysis severed ties to brain-based science when Freud decided against the need for preliminary medical education and welcomed artists to his circle.

9. Philip R. Hirschkop and Jonathan R. Mook, "Revisiting the Lessons of *Osheroff v. Chestnut Lodge*," paper presented at annual meeting of American Association of Psychiatry and the Law, Montreal, Canada. October 25–28, 2012.

10. As per a personal communication from the late Dr. Osheroff's legal counsel, Philip J. Hirschkop, Esq. Dr. Osheroff had hoped to make a movie about his experiences.

11. The Jukes family was a favorite topic in undergraduate psychology courses in the 1960s, when advocates of biologically based behavioral and intellectual traits clashed with proponents of social-environmental determinants.

12. In the Munoz case, a pregnant woman suffered a pulmonary embolus, stopped breathing, and was pronounced brain-dead. However, a hospital in the state of Texas refused to remove her from life support until a court ruling intervened. In the McMath case, a child was declared clinically dead, with no brain function, but the family objected to doctors' and hospital's recommendations, refused to remove life support, and transferred her elsewhere.

13. See L.O. Gostin, "Legal and Ethical Responsibilities Following Brain Death: The McMath and Muñoz Cases," *JAMA* (2014), doi:10.1001/jama.2014.660. This "viewpoint" summarizes shifts in legal definitions, and shows how human values continue to test the law.

14. U.S. President George Bush issued a Presidential Proclamation on July 17, 1990.

15. As an example, former junk bond trader Michael Milken subsidizes prostate cancer research because he developed prostate cancer while incarcerated for white collar crimes.

16. William J. Broad, "Billionaires with Big Ideas are Privatizing Science," *New York Times,* March 15, 2014.

17. Sigmund Freud, *Interpretation of Dreams*, trans. Joyce Crick (New York: Oxford University Press, 1900); see also Sharon Packer, *Dreams in Myth, Medicine and Movies* (Hartford, CT: Praeger, 2002).

18. Michael Roth, ed., *Freud: Culture and Conflict* (New York: Knopf Doubleday, 1998).

19. The split between art and science was readily apparent when psychoanalysis split from medicine and neurology. Freud's daughter Anna did not become a physician, even though she made inroads into child analysis. Notably, Freud himself won but one award in his lifetime, and that was the Goethe Prize for Literature (not science). He was a gifted writer, as anyone who reads his works realizes, including those who disagree with their content. It was only in America that analytic training required an MD degree—and that analysis was so warmly welcomed.

Chapter Two

1. American psychoanalysis emphasized repressed memories, whereas European analysis turned to transference. One wonders how much American film, with its abundant flashback scenes, influenced the thrust of American psychoanalysis, rather than the other way around.

2. For much of the 20th century, cinema tracked psychoanalytic influence, as if were assembling snapshots for a family photo album. It makes sense that cinema chronicles psychoanalysis, for they are kindred cousins, born within a year of one another, reared in the same era, when the 19th century came to a close. Both bathed in the bathwater of the fin-de-siècle. Each reflected the arts, culture, science and even economics of that society. See Sharon Packer, *Movies and the Modern Psyche* (Westport, CT: Praeger, 2010) for bibliography.

3. "The Birth of Science Fiction," www.dailygrail.com, accessed March 1, 2013.

4. Personal (but unofficial) communication from a

Film Forum representative, who responded to the author's query about the disappearance of the SF festivals.

5. Excerpts from daily email bulletin from American Psychiatric Association, January 6, 2012. Jeannine Stein, "Nearly 200 Million People Globally Use Illegal Drugs Every Year," *Los Angeles Times,* Booster Shots blog reported, "About 200 million people around the world use illegal drugs every year, and that may be taking a toll on health and death rates in various countries," according to a paper published in *The Lancet.* "The study, part of a series the journal is doing on addiction, offers a plethora of information about use of opioids, amphetamines, cocaine and marijuana worldwide, based on reports about drug use, drug dependence, deaths, and health-related fallouts from illegal drug use. Those four drug categories were chosen since information on other substances, such as ecstasy, anabolic steroids and hallucinogenic drugs, is sketchier."

Taking a closer look at the data, Agence France-Presse (January 6) reported, "Cannabis users comprised between 125 and 203 million; users of opioids (heroin and morphine), amphetamines or cocaine totaled 15 to 39 million; and those who injected drugs numbered between 11 and 21 million." Investigators also concluded that, "all three types of drugs seem to be associated with higher rates of mental disorders, road accidents and violence." Usage is "more prevalent in rich economies and in drug-producing regions of poor countries and is often a major health burden, the paper adds."

HealthDay (January 6) reported, "The researchers also found that the burden of health problems caused by illicit drug use in developed countries is similar to that caused by alcohol, but much less than that caused by tobacco." Australian researchers analyzed data and "estimates that there are up to 203 million marijuana users, anywhere from 14 million to 56 million amphetamine users, 14 million to 21 million cocaine users, and 12 million to 21 million opioid users around the world." Also covering the story are WebMD (January 5) and the *Sydney Morning Herald* (January 6).

6. RC, a fellow medical student from the University of Illinois College of Medicine, Chicago, alerted me to this approach. Dr. RC went on to head a major division of the National Cancer Institute.

7. Isaac Asimov held a Ph.D. in chemistry and was married to an analyst.

8. Personal communication from Stuart Fischoff, Ph.D., professor emeritus of media and psychology.

9. See Herman Wortis and William S. Maurer, "'Sham Rage' in Man," *American Journal of Psychiatry* 98.5(1942), accessed January 6, 2014.

10. See full text of David Daly's "Ictal Affect," *American Journal of Psychiatry* 115 (1958): 97–108.

11. See Howard Thompson, "Tense 'Mad Room,'" review of *The Mad Room, New York Times,* May 1, 1969, accessed March 23, 2014.

12. D.L. Rosenhan, "On being sane in insane places," *Science* 179.4070 (January 1973): 250–58, doi:10.1126/science.179.4070.250, PMID 4683124.

13. Sharon Packer, *Cinema's Sinister Psychiatrists* (Jefferson, NC: McFarland, 2012); Per Schelde, *Androids, Humanoids, and Other Science Fiction Monsters* (New York: New York Univesity Press, 1993); Andrew Tudor, *Monsters and Mad Scientists: A Cultural History of the Horror Movie* (Oxford: Blackwell, 1991).

14. Otto Rank coined the concept of "family romance," although Freud often gets credit.

15. My thanks to psychiatrist Merle Robinson, MD, and psychologist Sabine Himmelfarb, Ph.D. for sharing recollections of their work at Chestnut Lodge. My thanks to attorneys Philip Hirschkop, Esq., and Jonathan Mook, Esq., for their presentation on "Revisiting the Lessons of *Osheroff v. Chestnut Lodge,*" American Academy of Psychiatry and the Law, 43rd Annual Meeting, 2012, and for their personal communications in the preparation of "A Belated Obituary: Raphael J. Osheroff, MD," for publication in *Psychiatric Times* (June 23, 2013).

16. See Gerald L. Klerman, "The Psychiatric Patient's Right to Effect Treatment: Implications of *Osheroff v. Chestnut Lodge,*" *American Journal of Psychiatry* 147 (1990): 409–18. The many responses that follow this article are worth reading.

17. Martin A. Lee and Bruce Slain, *Acid Dreams: The CIA, LSD, and the Sixties' Rebellion* (New York: Grove Press, 1985).

18. See James Risen, "Suit Planned Over Death of Man C.I.A. Drugged," *New York Times,* November 26, 2012.

19. For details about the positive reception of Professor Andrea Tone's research at the American Psychiatric Association, see Mark Moran, "When Ethical Lines Were Crossed in Service to the Nation," *Psychiatric News* 46.12 (June 17, 2011): 16; additional references are in Sharon Packer's *Cinema's Sinister Psychiatrists* (Jefferson, NC: McFarland, 2012).

20. William Walters Sargant's *Battle for the Mind: A Physiology of Conversion and Brainwashing—How Evangelists, Psychiatrists, Politicians, and Medicine Men Can Change Your Beliefs and Behavior* (Cambridge, MA: Malor, 1997) advocates Pavlovian conditioning, even though Sargant also crusaded for insulin shock therapy and psychosurgery.

21. Erik Sofge, "How Real is *RoboCop?*" *Popular Science,* January 13, 2014, accessed January 20, 2014.

22. See Jason P. Vest, *Future Imperfect: Philip K. Dick at the Movies* (Westport, CT: Praeger, 2007).

23. See Daniel Knoedler, "First Week in the Trenches," *Psychiatric Times,* January 22, 2014. More follow-up articles are scheduled.

Chapter Three

1. The history of neurology is as contested and convoluted as the history of psychiatry. See S.T. Casper, "A revisionist history of American neurology," *Brain* 133.2 (2010): 638–642. For a discussion of 19th century American psychiatry and neurology, see Ed Brown's website, "Footnotes to the History of Psychiatry," especially "Neurology's Influence on American Psychiatry: 1865–1915," accessed July 28, 2013.

2. See Georg Northoff, *Neuropsychoanalysis in Practice: Brain, Self and Objects* (New York: Oxford University Press, 2011) for details about Freud's rejection of reigning theories of language localization.

3. Freud was not the first to allude to an unconscious (which does not exist in the physical brain). The first stirrings of interest in the "unconscious" were felt during the Romantic Era, when Shelley's novella was written, and when a forward-thinking physician and painter named Carl Gustav Carus (1789–1869) conceived of ideas that would be adopted by psychoanalysts. Carus, an obstetrician and an anatomist, deserves credit for coining this metapsychological concept that has no anatomical correlate. For more information on this evolution, see Henri Ellenberger's *The Discovery of the Unconscious* (New York: Basic Books, 1970).

4. Donald Glut, *Shock Theater Chicago Style: WBKB-TV's Late Night Horror Showcase, 1957–1959* (Jefferson, NC: McFarland, 2012).

5. See Sharon Packer, "Drugs and the Summer of Love: A Summer Fling, Not a Lasting Romance," in *Pop Culture Universe: Icons, Idols, Ideas* (Santa Barbara: ABC-CLIO, 2010–), http://popculture.abc-clio.com/, accessed August 26, 2014.

6. See John Strausbaugh and Tony Blaise, eds., *The Drug User Documents: 1840–1960.* (New York: Blast Press, 1993).

7. See Anton Kaes, *Shell Shock Cinema: Weimar Culture and the Wounds of War* (Princeton: Princeton University Press, 2008); Stefan Adrianapolos, *Possessed: Hypnotic Crimes, Corporate Fiction and the Invention of Cinema* (Chicago: University of Chicago Press, 2008).

8. See Roy Kinnard's *Horror in Silent Cinema* (Jefferson, NC: McFarland, 1995).

9. Sheldon Watts' *Disease and Medicine in World History* (New Haven: Yale University Press, 2002) reveals the good, the bad, and the ugly facts about the history of Greek medicine.

Chapter Four

1. Remade movies are a subject of much academic speculation. See Jeff Beauvoir, "6 Classic Movies You Didn't Know Were Remakes," *Cracked*, May 15, 2011, for a more accessible approach to this topic. http://www.cracked.com/article_19190_6-classic-movies-you-didnt-know-were-remakes_p2.html#ixzz2ap8THhTt, accessed August 2, 2013.

2. Philip K. Dick Fan Site, http://www.philipkdickfans.com, accessed January 12, 2014.

3. *Psychiatric Times* publishes many different articles on telepsychiatry at www.psychiatrictimes.com.

4. My thanks to psychiatrist Dr. Elyse Weiner for her insights about Batman and brain machines, offered at Brooklyn, VA, grand rounds, Department of Psychiatry.

5. Andrew Tudor's *Monsters and Mad Scientists: A Cultural History of the Horror Film* (Cambridge, MA: Basil Blackwell, 1989) chronicles shifts in horror film villains in 1,000 films.

6. See Rabbi Joshua Trachtenberg, *Jewish Magic and Superstition* (1939), reprinted by the Jewish Book Club, or Joachim Neugroschel's extensive translations and compilations, including *The Great Works of Jewish Fantasy and Occult* (New York: Random House, 1991) or *Yenne Velte* (New York: Pocket Books, 1978).

7. See John Strausbaugh, "Step Right Up, Folks. Behold What Amazes!" *New York Times*, June 18, 2005, http://www.nytimes.com/mem/emailthis.html, accessed August 2, 2013; Henry Fountain, "Graceful Moves, for a Boy Made of Metal, Top of Form *New York Times*, December 26, 2011, http://www.nytimes.com/2011/12/27/science/maillardet-automaton-inspired-martin-scorseses-film-hugo.html?pagewanted=all, accessed August 2, 2013; "Mechanical Memory," *New York Times*, Science, December 26, 2011, http://www.nytimes.com/interactive/2011/12/26/science/mechanical-memory.html, accessed August 2, 2013.

8. The American escape artist and magic debunker Erik Weisz was also inspired by Robert-Houdin, and took his name as his stage name, Harry Houdini.

9. In *Caligari's Children: The Film as Tale of Terror* (New York: Oxford University Press, 1980), S.S. Prawer explains the complicated concept of the "the uncanny"—and how its translations from German to English make the concept even more difficult to comprehend.

10. *Batman's* comic book creator, Bob Kane, admired German Expressionism, and based Gotham's architecture on the buildings in Lang's *Metropolis*. It is not surprising to see similarities between the iconography of later-appearing *Batman* movies serials and Maria's brain machine in *Metropolis*, even though the serials were not created by Kane himself.

11. Hear podcasts by Mark Brake, at www.markbrake.com/podcasts, accessed June 3, 2012.

12. See any of the many books by Eric Kandel, M.D., Ph.D., including *The Age of Insight* (New York: Random House, 2012) and *Psychiatry, Psychoanalysis, and the New Biology of Mind* (Washington, D.C.: American Psychiatric Publications, 2005).

13. See Sharon Packer, *Movies and the Modern Psyche* (Westport, CT: Praeger, 2010).

14. See Jason Vest, *Future Imperfect: Philip K. Dick at the Movies* (Westport, CT: Praeger, 2007); Jeremy Robinson, *Blade Runner and the Cinema of Philip K. Dick* (Maidstone, Kent: Crescent Moon, 2008).

Chapter Five

1. The Emancipation Proclamation probably deserves credit as *the* most important event in American Civil Rights, but the visual spectacle that was televised live during the 1968 riots cemented enduring images of race wars.

2. On the Rod Serling Memorial Foundation Website, Gordon C. Webb writes about "30 Years Later: Rod Serling's *Planet of the Apes*" (originally printed in the July-August 1998 issue of *Creative Screenwriting*). This article explains *The Twilight Zone* touches inserted by Serling. In his version, it is unclear whether the astronauts engage in time/space travel or whether they entered an alternate universe. In the book that Serling adapted as a screenplay, two vacationing astronauts find a bottle floating in space. They retrieve it and read it, and see that this is a diary written by a man who landed on a planet that is ruled by apes, and cannot make sense

of the situation. The astronauts travel to their home planet, exit their spaceship, and remove their helmets—to reveal that these astronauts are themselves apes. Two episodes of *Twilight Zone* bear similarities to Serling's script for *Apes*.

3. See Myron F. Weiner and Ann M. Lipton, *Clinical Manual of Alzheimer Disease and other Dementias* (Arlington, VA: APPI, 2012) for a concise but authoritative summary of research in this ever-expanding field.

4. This book was begun before Obamacare and the ACA (Affordable Care Act) were conceived. It remains to be seen if these innovations change perceptions, or if they simply add more perceived villains to the player mix.

5. John Efron, *Defenders of the Race: Jewish Doctors and Race Science in Fin-de-siècle Europe* (New Haven: Yale University Press, 1994); see also Regina Markell Morantz-Sanchez, review of *Defenders of the Race: Jewish Doctors and Race Science in Fin-de-siècle Europe*, *Bulletin of the History of Medicine* 70.1(Spring 1996):148–149.

6. See Jennifer Grogan, *Encountering America* (New York: HarperCollins, 2012) for more data on trends in therapy.

7. Erin Gentry Lamb, "The Age of Obsolescence: Senescence and Scientific Rejuvenation in Twentieth Century America," Ph.D diss., Department of English, Duke University, 2008, accessed November 3, 2013.

8. See Ray Kinnard, *Horror in Silent Films. A Filmography, 1896–1929* (Jefferson, NC: McFarland, 1995).

9. See Mark G. Glassy, *The Biology of Science Fiction Cinema* (Jefferson, NC: McFarland, 2005); Mark G. Glassy, "Brains, Craniums and Heads," *Scary Monsters Magazine*, January 2012; Mark G. Glassy, "Monkeying Around with Apes," *Scary Monsters Magazine*, June 2013.

10. John T. Soister and Henry Nicolella with Steve Joyce and Harry H Long, *American Silent Horror, Science Fiction and Fantasy Feature Films, 1913–1929* (Jefferson, NC: McFarland, 2012).

11. According to Erin Lamb's dissertation, which is listed above, several famous men were "Steinached," including Sigmund Freud, the poet Yeats, and the critic H.L. Mencken.

12. "The Discovery of Insulin," http://www.nobelprize.org/educational/medicine/insulin/discovery-insulin.html, accessed October 30, 2013.

13. "Idiot Child Cured," *Grey River Argus*, 25 September 1914, 7, Papers Past, accessed November 3, 2013.

14. Ibid.

15. "Medicine: Voronoff and Steinach," *Time*, Monday, July 30, 1923, http://content.time.com/time/magazine/article/0,9171,727231,00.html#ixzz2jLit0vF0.

16. The *New York Times* reported on Voronoff's marriage, "Voronoff, 64, Weds Viennese, Aged 20; Rejuvenation Surgeon's Bride Is Cousin of Mme. Lupescu, Friend of King Carol. On Paris Honeymoon Trip Marriage Took Place in Austrian Consulate in Bucharest Instead of in France," http://select.nytimes.com/gst/abstract.html?res=F20C12FA395D167A93CAAB178FD85F408385F9, accessed November 3, 2013.

17. "New glands for old," *The Lancet* 338.8779 (November 30, 1991): 1367, PMID 1682744, doi:10.1016/0140-6736(91)92244-V.

18. R.A. Valdés-González, "Xenotransplantation of porcine neonatal Islets of Langerhans and Sertoli cells: A 4-year study," *European Journal of Endocrinology* 153.3 (September 2005): 419–427; "New glands for old," *The Lancet* 338.8779 (November 30, 1991):1367, PMID 1682744, doi:10.1016/0140-6736(91)92244-V; J. Morales, *Sexual Medicine* 10.4 (April 2013): 1178–83, doi:10.1111/jsm.12081, e-pub January 29, 2013.

19. See Edward Shorter and David Healy, *Shock Therapy: A History of Electroconvulsive Treatment in Mental Illness* (New Brunswick: Rutgers University Press, 2007).

20. For a comprehensive review and edited collection of chapters on biological psychiatry, see David Healy, "The Intersection of Psychopharmacology and Psychiatry in the Second Half of the Twentieth Century," in *History of Psychiatry and Medical Psychology*, ed. Edwin R. Wallace IV and John Gach (New York: Springer, 2008).

21. "Ugo Cerletti 1877–1963," *American Journal of Psychiatry* 156.4 (April 1999):630–633, accessed November 4, 2013, http://ajp.psychiatryonline.org/article.aspx?articleID=173376.

22. Linda Andre's book, *Doctors of Deception: What They Don't Want You to Know about Shock Treatment* (New Brunswick: Rutgers University Press, 2009) is one of several first-person treatises from the anti-psychiatry movement. This book has the distinction of having been published by a respected university press publisher. Related (but usually less detailed) information is available through online anti-psychiatry sites.

23. T.S., movie review, *New York Times*, March 20, 1941, accessed November 3, 2013.

24. As of 2014, some companies are promoting tests of enzyme systems that metabolize psychotropic medications. The Mayo Clinic has offered on-site courses on psychopharmacogenetics and their measurements for several years, but it remains to be seen if these tests correlate with neurotransmitter levels in the CSF (cerebrospinal fluid).

25. A. Morales, "The long and tortuous history of the discovery of testosterone and its clinical application," *Sexual Medicine* 10.4 (April 2013):1178–83, doi: 10.1111/jsm.12081, e-pub January 29, 2013, accessed October 30, 2013.

26. Robert E. Hales, M.D., MBA, Stuart C. Yudofsky, M.D.; Glen O. Gabbard, M.D., eds., *The American Psychiatric Publishing Textbook of Psychiatry*, 5th ed. (Arlington, VA: APPI, 2008). See Mark S. George, et al., "Nonpharmacological Somatic Treatments," in *The American Psychitric Publishing Textbook of Psychiatry*, 5th ed., eds. Robert E. Hales, Stuart C. Yudofsky, and Glen O. Gebbard (Arlington, VA: APPI, 2008); William N. Taylor, *Anabolic Steroids and the Athlete*, 2d ed. (Jefferson, NC: McFarland, 2002).

27. See articles by Natasha Singer, "Selling that New Man Feeling," *New York Times* Business Day, November 24, 2013; Elizabeth Rosenthal, "A Push to Sell Testosterone Troubles Doctors," *New York Times*, October 15, 2013.

28. http://www.pbs.org/wgbh/amex/nash/film

more/ps_ict.html, accessed October 30, 2013; http://www.pbs.org/wgbh/amex/nash/filmmore/ps_ict.html.

Chapter Six

1. See Mark Moran's discussion in *Psychiatric News* (May 17, 2011) about Andrea Tomes' receipt of the Benjamin Rush Award and her lecture "Spies and Lies: Cold War Psychiatry and the CIA."

2. For a riveting documentary about the later lives of the orphaned Rosenberg boys (renamed "Meeropol"), see Joel Katz's *Strange Fruit,* which premiered at the Woodstock Film Festival, 2002.

3. See additional discussion of *Strange Fruit,* and its relationship to lynching in America and the Meeropol brothers (nee Rosenberg) in K.L. Turner, "Strange Fruit," in *A History of Evil in Popular Culture,* ed. Sharon Packer and Jody Pennington (Santa Barbara: ABC-Clio, 2014).

4. See Christine Cornea, "Science Fiction Films of the 1950s," in *Science Fiction Cinema: Between Fantasy and Reality,* ed. Christine Cornea (Edinburgh: Edinburgh University Press, 2007,) accessed via Questia, August 18, 2013.

5. "People, by the 50s, had lost their optimistic confidence in the ability of science to fulfill all the dreams of mankind; instead, you saw science about to fulfill all the nightmares of mankind. The prospect of nuclear war ... was hours away."—J.G. Ballard

6. Philip Rieff, *The Triumph of the Therapeutic: Uses of Faith After Freud* (New York: Harper & Row, 1966).

7. See Glen Gabbard and K. Gabbard, *Psychiatry and the Cinema,* 2d ed. (Washington, D.C.: APPI, 1999).

8. See David Healy's chapter in *History of Psychiatry and Medical Psychology,* ed. Edwin R. Wallace IV and John Gach (New York: Springer, 2008).

9. See Sharon Packer, *Cinema's Sinister Psychiatrists* (Jefferson, NC: McFarland, 2012) for more data on lobotomies.

10. See Luhrmann. *Of Two Minds,* as well as Ronald Pies' discussion of this book in *Psychiatric Times* (online).

11. Articles in the January, February and March 1950 issues of *American Journal of Psychiatry* include: "Stimulation of the Nucleoprotein-Production in the Nerve Cells by Malononitrile and Its Effect on Psychic Functions in Mental Disorders"; "Adrenal Cortical Responses to Stress in Normal Men and in Those with Personality Disorders Part I. Some Stress Responses in Normal And Psychotic Subjects" and "Adrenal Cortical Responses to Stress in Normal Men and in Those with Personality Disorders Part II," "Analysis of the Pituitary-Adrenal Mechanism in Man"; "Carbohydrate and Lymphoid Studies In Schizophrenia"; "Studies of Adrenal Cortical Activity in Psychoneurotic Subjects"; "Hallucination and Imagery Induced by Mescaline"; "Use of Somnoform as an Aid in Narcoanalysis and Narcohypnosis"; "Cytochrome C: Effects of Intravenous Administration in Presenile, Senile, and Arteriosclerotic Cerebral States"; "Lung Abscess as a Complication of Electroshock Therapy"; "Clinical Notes a Preliminary Report on the Effect of Drinking in Twenty-Five Cases of Epilepsy"; "Duodenal Ulcer: A Sociopsychological Study of Naval Enlisted Personnel ond Civilians"; "Effect of Trimethadione (Tridione) and Other Drugs on Convulsions Caused by Di-Isopropyl Fluorophosphate (DFP)"; "Hallucination and Imagery Induced by Mescaline"; "Continuous Sleep Treatment Observations on the Use of Prolonged, Deep, Continuous Narcosis in Mental Disorders"; "Survey of Shock Therapy Practices"; "The Alcoholic Woman."

12. Jules Verne, *Twenty Thousand Leagues Under the Sea* (1869; London: Puffin Books, 1993).

13. See Sharon Packer, *Cinema's Sinister Psychiatrists* (Jefferson, NC: McFarland, 2012) for details about *Conspiracy Theory*'s allusion to CIA brainwashing debacles and *Dreams in Myth, Medicine & Movies* (Westport, CT: Praeger, 2002) for more discussion of *The Manchurian Candidate* (1962) and its allusions to Korean brainwashing.

14. E. Gordon Wasson's account of his magic mushroom experiences in Mexico familiarized general audiences with the potential of "entheogens" well before the counterculture staked its claim in the following decade.

15. See Sharon Packer, "Drugs and the Summer of Love: A Summer Fling, Not a Lasting Romance," in *Pop Culture Universe: Icons, Idols, Ideas* (Santa Barbara: ABC-CLIO, 2010–), http://popculture.abc-clio.com/, accessed August 26, 2014.

16. http://www.horrormovies.org/database/keywords/Brain_Transplant/; W. Scott Poole, *Monsters in America* (Waco: Baylor University Press, 2011); Carlos Clarens, *An Illustrated History of Horror and Science-fiction Film* (1967; New York: Da Capo Press, 1997).

17. Sharon Packer, "Thor: From Myth to Marvel Comics to Movies to Medical Commentary," movie review, HCPLive, August 26, 2011.

18. http://www.cdc.gov.

19. Peter M. Schantz, et al., "Neurocysticercosis in an Orthodox Jewish Community in New York City," *New England Journal of Medicine* 327 (September 3, 1992): 692–695; Jefferson V. Proaño, et al., "Medical Treatment for Neurocysticercosis Characterized by Giant Subarachnoid Cysts," *New England Journal of Medicine* 345 (September 20, 2001): 879–885.

20. Alain Dervaux, Hubert Lainé, Marcel Czermak and Gérard Massé, "Creutzfeldt-Jakob Disease Presenting as Psychosis," *American Journal of Psychiatry* 161.7 (July 2004): 1307–1308; Andrew Thompson, et al., "Behavioral and Psychiatric Symptoms in Prion Disease," *American Journal of Psychiatry* 171.3 (March 2014): 265–274.

21. Mary M. Lee, "Idiopathic Short Statur," *New England Journal of Medicine* 354 (June 15, 2006): 2576–2582; J.E. Fradkin, "Creutzfeldt-Jakob disease in pituitary growth hormone recipients in the United States," *JAMA* 265 (1991): 880–884.

22. Gary Bloomgren, M.D., Sandra Richman, M.D., Christophe Hotermans, M.D., Meena Subramanyam, Ph.D., Susan Goelz, Ph.D., Amy Natarajan, M.S., Sophia Lee, Ph.D., Tatiana Plavina, Ph.D., James V. Scanlon, Pharm.D., Alfred Sandrock, M.D., and Carmen Bozic, M.D., "Risk of Natalizumab-Associated Pro-

gressive Multifocal Leukoencephalopathy." *New England Journal of Medicine* 2012; 366:1870–1880 May 17, 2012.

23. Carol A. Kauffman, M.D., Peter G. Pappas, M.D., and Thomas F. Patterson, M.D., "Fungal Infections Associated with Contaminated Methylprednisolone Injections," *New England Journal of Medicine* 368 (June 27, 2013): 2495–2500.

24. A.C. Pettit, et al. "The index case for the fungal meningitis outbreak in the United States," *New England Journal of Medicine* 367 (2012): 2119–2126.

25. For images of Superman and Batman supporting the March of Dimes and the "war" on polio, see "Barry's Pearls of Comic Book Wisdom," http://forbushman.blogspot.com/, accessed April 6, 2014.

26. Personal observations made during several visits to India.

27. http://www.cnn.com/2013/08/24/us/brain-eating-parasite-boy-dead/index.html?hpt=hp_t2, accessed August 24, 2013.

28. See Sharon Packer, *Movies and the Modern Psyche* (Westport, CT: Praeger, 2010).

29. In 1954, psychiatrist Fredric Wertham published *Seduction of the Innocent,* a flagrantly anti-comics diatribe that called for the end of comics, claiming that they were either too violent, too sexual, or too subversive for children. Wertham's theories and testimonies were used in the Kefauver hearings about delinquency and comics.

30. BEM (bug-eyed monster); BBA (big-brained alien).

31. Roger Corman was famous for his cheap improvised special effects, especially the "fire-breathing dragon" constructed from a tea kettle that sprouted steam when boiling in *Beast with 1,000 Eyes* (1955).

32. See Nathan Kravis' medical-historical research on hypnotism and trance, as referenced in *Dreams in Myth, Medicine and Movies* (2001).

33. Andrew Tudor, *Monsters and Mad Scientists: A Cultural History of the Horror Film* (New York: Wiley, 1989).

34. See Ruth Macklin's blog on "Ethical Controversy in Human Subjects Research" for the Albert Einstein College of Medicine, February 5, 2013. Additional information is available at http://blogs.einstein.yu.edu/ethical-controversy-in-human-subjects-research/#sthash.vGk2FNJt.dpuf; See Mike Stobbe's "Ugly Past of Human Experiments Uncovered," February 27, 2011, http://www.nbcnew.com, accessed April 6, 2014. Private profiteering from unnecessary surgeries performed on residents of adult homes is still under investigation.

35. "A Science Odyssey: First Successful Kidney Transplant Performed 1954," PBS, http://www.pbs.org/wgbh/aso/databank/entries/dm54ki.html, accessed September 4, 2013.

36. See George Higham's http://www.poepuppet.com for more information on stop motion animation.

Chapter Seven

1. Michel Foucault, *Madness and Civilization: A History of Insanity in the Age of Reason* (New York: Random House, 1965).

2. R.D. Laing, *The Divided Self: An Existential Study in Sanity and Madness* (Harmondsworth, Middlesex: Penguin, 1960).

3. See original works by David Cooper: *Psychiatry and Anti-Psychiatry* (London: Tavistock, 1967) as well as references to his works in books and articles about anti-psychiatry. Cooper was well known in his day, but Szasz and Laing overshadowed him.

4. See Thomas Szasz, "The Myth of Mental Illness," *American Psychologist* 15 (1960): 113–118; T.S. Szasz, *The Myth of Mental Illness: Foundations of a Theory of Personal Conduct* (New York: Hoeber-Harper, 1961); T.S. Szasz, *The Manufacture of Madness: A Comparative Study of the Inquisition and the Mental Health Movement* (New York: Harper and Row, 1970); see James Knoll's sensitive obituary of Szasz in *Psychiatric Times,* September 13, 2012.

5. See Sharon Packer, book review of Allan Beveridge, *Portrait of the Psychiatrist as a Young Man: The Early Writing and Work of R.D. Laing, 1927–1960* (Oxford: Oxford University Press, 2011) in *Metapsychology* 15.50 (December 13, 2011), http://metapsychology.mentalhelp.net/poc/view_doc.php?type=book&id=6333&cn=0

6. Doris Lessing is often cited as an influential feminist writer owing to *The Golden Notebook* (New York: Simon & Schuster, 1962). A re-reading of her writings suggests that this work promotes a lifestyle of free love and abdication of parental responsibility, which also occurs in individuals who are not literate enough to write books about their lives but whose life stories are documented in CPS (Child Protective Services) case reports. Psychologist Phyllis Chessler offers a better-researched perspective in *Women and Madness* (1973) and in the revised edition of original best-seller. Betty Friedan's *The Feminist Mystique* challenges Freud's notions and other societal assumptions about women.

7. See original contribution by J. Chamberlin, *On Our Own: Patient-Controlled Alternatives to the Mental Health System* (New York: Hawthorne, 1978), plus retrospective reflections that include Chamberlin, "The ex-patients' movement: Where we've been and where we're going," *Journal of Mind and Behavior* 11 (1990): 323–336; Paul Appelbaum, *Almost a Revolution: Mental Health Law and the Limits of Change* (New York: Oxford University Press, 1994); David J Rissmiller and Joshua H. Rissmiller, "Evolution of the Antipsychiatry Movement into Mental Health Consumerism," *Psychiatric Services* 57.6 (June 1, 2006). Historian Norman Dane hypothesized that Christian Science was the original anti-psychiatry movement.

8. For a capsule summary of Szasz' life, ideas and his influence, see obituary by James L. Knoll IV, M.D., editor of *Psychiatric Times,* "In Memoriam: Thomas Stephen Szasz," in *Psychiatric Times,* September 13, 2012.

9. The Institute for Psychiatric Services workshop, "From Tuskegee to Trayvon: Black Men, Social Injustice and Implications for Mental Health," Philadelphia, October 12, 2013, highlighted the value of visual imagery related to Emmett Till. My thanks to chairs Annelle B. Primm, M.D., M.P.H. and Janet Taylor, M.D., M.P.H., and speakers William Lawson, M.D., Karriem L. Salaam, M.D., and Kenneth Braswell.

10. Brian Baxter, "Obituary: Curt Siodmak: Screenwriter, and occasional director, of Hollywood horror genre classics," *The Guardian*, September 11, 2000, accessed January 25, 2014.

11. Today, we also know that higher lead levels adversely affect learning, and that children who reside near highways, drink from well water, or eat peeling lead paint have lower IQs and lesser learning abilities. In the 1960s, and even into the 1970s, when *Planet of the Apes* and its sequels were in their prime, leaded gasoline was readily available and commonly used. Lead was big news in the early 1970s and a cause of major contention between industry and activists.

Chapter Eight

1. See discussions by linguistic anthropologist Per Schelde in *Androids, Humanoids and other Science Fiction Monsters* (New York: New York University Press, 1991).

2. See Sharon Packer's *Dreams in Myth, Medicine and Movies* (Westport, CT: Praeger, 2002) for more discussion on these matters and for a more extensive bibliography on Freud and Film.

3. See the science fiction section of www.filmsite.org for lists of hybrid SF film genres.

4. See Paul Roazen, *Encountering Freud: The Politics and Histories of Psychoanalysis* (New Brunswick, NJ: Transaction, 1990).

5. Viktor Tausk, "The influencing machine," *Internationale Zeitschrift für Psychoanalyse*, 1919; Dorian Feigenbaum, trans., *Psychoanalytic Quarterly* 2 (1933): 519–556.

6. Viktor Tausk, "The influencing machine," trans. Dorian Feigenbaum, *Journal of Psychotherapy Practice and Research* 1, no. 2 (Spring 1992): 184–206.

7. See http://mikejay.net for links to Michael Jay's books and articles about the influencing machine, with endorsements from William Gibson and others, including (but not limited to) *The Air Loom Gang* (New York: Transworld /Bantam, 2004). Also see John MacGregor, *The Discovery of the Art of the Insane* (Princeton: Princeton University Press, 1989).

8. See Allan Beveridge, "A disquieting feeling of strangeness? The art of the mentally ill," *Journal of the Royal Society Medicine* 34.11 (November 2001): 595–599; John M. MacGregor, *The Discovery of the Art of the Insane* (Princeton: Princeton University Press, 1992).

9. http://theairloom.org, accessed January 26, 2014.

10. Reacting to the increased interest in Outsider Art in the 1990s, trained artists appropriated the styles of outsider artists, and the definition of "outsider art" broadened beyond *art brut*, or "art of the insane."

11. See chapter 27, "Non-Pharmacological Somatic Treatments," in *The American Psychiatric Publishing Textbook of Psychiatry*, 5th ed., ed. Robert E. Hales, M.D., MBA, Stuart C. Yudofsky, M.D., and Glen O. Gabbard, M.D. (Washington, D.C.: APPI, 2008).

12. Howard Thompson, "Dennis Reardon's 'Happiness Cage' Is Better Suited to Stage," *New York Times*, June 29, 1972, http://www.nytimes.com/movie/review?re=9802E6D91431E53BBC4151DFB0668389669EDE, accessed November 28, 2013.

13. See Sharon Packer, "Drugs and the Summer of Love: A Summer Fling, not a Lasting Romance," in *Pop Culture Universe,* Eternal Questions Series (ABC-Clio, Fall, 2012).

14. Information supplied by a physician on http://www.Sermo.com.

15. Restoring Active Memory (RAM). Solicitation Number: DARPA-BAA-14–08. https://www.fbo.gov.

Chapter Nine

1. See Schwarz's long-running series on stimulants in the *New York Times*: "Risky rise of the good-grade pill," June 9, 2012, http://www.nytimes.com/2012/06/10/education/seeking-academicedge-teenagers-abuse-stimulants.html, accessed October 31, 2013; "Drowned in a stream of prescriptions," February 2, 2013, http://www.nytimes.com/2013/02/03/us/concerns-about-adhdpractices-and-am... , accessed October 31, 2013. See more at http://www.psychiatrictimes.com/dsm-5-0/top-five-psychiatry-events-2013/page/0/3#sthash.njSJpU3R.dpuf; see references to Schwartz's articles in "5 Top Psychiatric Events of 2013," by Sharon Packer, *Psychiatric Times*, December 2013, 1.

2. DARPA Solicitations: Defense Advanced Research Projects Agency, http://www.darpa.mil/Opportunities/Solicitations/DARPA_Solicitations.aspx, accessed November 13, 2013, and January 26, 2014.

3. There are curious political implications of the first *Total Recall*. The film stars Arnold Schwarzenegger—before he became governor of California. Through the character of Douglas Quaid, Schwarzenegger represents an "everyman" who is kicked around by the state, until he turns the tables and kicks around the agents of the state. This twist compensates for the lost political context of the novella. This role may have helped Schwarzenegger's campaign for office the first time around as much as his wife's political connections (and his bodybuilding image). In retrospect, one wonders if this body-builder-turned actor already harbored political aspirations when approached Paul Verhoeven (of *RoboCop* fame), and convinced Verhoeven to direct this cast-off film and to cast him as a working man who combats corrupt politicos.

4. See Gautam Naik, "Unwanted Memories Erased in Electroconvulsive Therapy Experiment," *Wall Street Journal,* December 23, 2013.

5. American Psychiatric Association Office of Communication & Public Affairs, Bulletin Health Care, November 23, 2013.

6. Charles A. Erin and John Harris, "An ethical market in human organs," *Journal of Medical Ethics* 29.3 (2003):137–138, accessed online December 9, 2013; BBC News Europe, "German organ donor scandal doctor goes on trial," http://www.bbc.co.uk/news/world-europe-23753872, accessed December 9, 2013.

Chapter Ten

1. John Markoff, "Brainlike Computers, Learning from Experience," *New York Times*, December 28, 2013,

http://mobile.nytimes.com/2013/12/29/science/brainlike-computers-learning-from-experience.html?smid=tw-share, accessed February 17, 2014.

2. *The Infinite Worlds of H. G. Wells* (conceived by Nick Willing and released by Hallmark Channel), 2001.

3. In 1932, Smith, Kline and French (SKF) introduced the first amphetamine, Benzedrine; in 1935, SKF introduced Dexedrine (an amphetamine) to treat narcolepsy; in 1944, Ritalin (Methylphenidate) was synthesized.

4. http://www.nytimes.com/2012/06/10/education/seeking-academic-edge-teenagers-abuse-stimulants.html; http://www.nytimes.com/2013/02/03/us/concerns-about-adhd-practices-and-amphetamine-addiction.html?pagewanted=all.

5. See Sharon Packer, "The Top Five Psychiatric Events in 2013," *Psychiatric Times,* January 2014, 1.

6. Earlier versions of *Planet of the Apes* proposed other origin stories. In *Escape from Planet of the Apes* and *Conquest of Planet of the Apes,* Cornelius and a pregnant Zira produce their highly intelligent progeny, named Caesar, after they time-travel via Taylor's spaceship. To ensure the safety of the young family, sympathetic humans switch Caesar for a regular chimp, and rear Caesar themselves (much like the Moses story of the Bible).

7. It is easy to confuse the names of *Rise of the Planet of the Apes'* Caesar with Cesare the somnambulist from *The Cabinet of Dr. Caligari* (1919). One wonders if this similarity in names was intended to call attention to the servile role of apes in earlier *Planet of the Apes* films, and to contrast the Cesare who mindlessly obeys Caligari's commands with the high-minded, imperial and hyper-intelligent Caesar who incites ape uprisings in *Rise of the Planet of the Apes.*

8. "25 Best Movie Tearjerkers Ever," *Entertainment Weekly*, June 26, 2009, accessed online February 10, 2014.

9. See summary by Michael Winerip, "Revisiting the 'Crack Babies' Epidemic That Was Not," *New York Times,* May 20, 2013.

10. Much (although not all) of this appendix was compiled by Professor Eric H. Chudler, and posted online in "Milestones in the History of Neuroscience," http://faculty.washington.edu/chudler/hist.html, accessed February 23, 2014.

Chapter Eleven

1. See Sharon Packer's *Dreams in Myth, Medicine and Movies* (Westport, CT: Praeger, 2002).

2. More science-minded studies of dreams were underway before Freud staked his claim on the "scientific" approach to dreams. See Packer, *Dreams in Myth, Medicine and Movies.*

3. For a different take on Griffith's dual contribution to moviemaking and to racism, see Nicole Haggard, "The Brutal Black Buck: The Myth of the Black Rapist," in *A History of Evil in Popular Culture,*, vol. II, ed. Sharon Packer and Jody Pennington (Santa Barbara: ABC-CLIO, 2014).

4. For additional data on Scorsese's life and influence, see Vinnie LoBrutto, "Scorsese," in *A History of Evil in Popular Culture,*, vol. I, ed. Sharon Packer and Jody Pennington (Santa Barbara: ABC-CLIO, 2014).

5. Advanced sleep monitoring equipment used in sleep labs may be a short-lived or very selective phenomenon, since managed care companies are refusing to reimburse lab studies, and are pushing for less complex and less expensive home-based sleep studies for sleep apnea. Conditions such as REM sleep behavior disorder (which can be a prodrome to Parkinson's disease or Lewy Body dementia) or narcolepsy require direct observation, but it remains to be seen if home-based telemedicine monitors will suffice for lab studies, or if they are more costly.

6. For a science-minded book on "the new neuroscience of connecting brains with machines," see Miguel Nicolelis, M.D., Ph.D., *Beyond Boundaries* (New York: St. Martin's Press, 2012).

7. Film Noir of the Week (website), February 16, 2008, accessed December 25, 2013.

8. For details on earlier films influenced by the art of Francis Bacon, see Monika Keska, "Pictures of Evil: Francis Bacon's Paintings in American Popular Culture," in *A History of Evil in Popular Culture,* vol. II, ed. Sharon Packer and Jody Pennington (Santa Barbara: ABC-CLIO, 2014).

9. For more information on the confluence between Tibetan Buddhist imagery and psychedelic experiences, see Timothy Leary, Ph.D., Ralph Metzner, Ph.D., and Richard Alpert, Ph.D., *The Psychedelic Experience: A Manual Based on the Tibetan Book of the Dead* (New York: Citadel Press, 1964).

10. See F. Scott Poole, "Freddy's Shadow: Nostalgia, Evil and the 80s in a *Nightmare on Elm Street*," in *A History of Evil in Popular Culture,* vol. I, ed. Sharon Packer and Jody Pennington (Santa Barbara: ABC-CLIO, 2014). See also Poole's book length treatment of related topics in *Monsters in America: Our Historical Obsession with the Hideous and the Haunting* (Waco: Baylor University Press, 2011).

11. See Sharon Packer, *Cinema's Sinister Psychiatrists* (Jefferson, NC: McFarland, 2012) for more info about psychiatric nurses and their filmic depictions.

12. See *Cinema's Sinister Psychiatrists* for discussion of *In Dreams,* Nurse Vivian, and Robert Downey, Jr.

13. See Spencer Lamm's extensive documentary on *The Matrix* and its symbolism, available at http://redpill.com.

14. Fleming directed *Gone with the Wind* in the same year as *Wizard of Oz,* along with many other winners.

Chapter Twelve

1. D.A. Gentile, D. Li, A. Khoo, S. Prot, C.A. Anderson, "Mediators and Moderators of Long-term Effects of Violent Video Games on Aggressive Behavior: Practice, Thinking, and Action," *JAMA Pediatrics* 168.5 (May 2014): 450–457, doi:10.1001/jamapediatrics.2014.63.

2. Personal communication to the author from a family physician, "Doctor Anna."

3. "Violent Video Games Associated with Aggres-

sive Thinking, Behavior in Kids," *APA Headlines,* March 25, 2014.

Chapter 13

1. Robert Silverberg, *Drug Themes In Science Fiction* (Rockville, MD: National Institute on Drug Abuse, 1974).
2. Sharon Packer, "Drugs and The Summer of Love: A Summer Fling, not a Lasting Romance," *Pop Culture Universe: Icons, Idols, Ideas* (Santa Barbara: ABC-CLIO), retrieved March 9, 2014, from http://popculture.abc-clio.com/.
3. Charles T. Bunting, "Dressing for Dinner in the Jungle" (1973), reprinted in *Conversations with Anthony Burgess,* ed. Earl G. Ingersoll and Mary C. Ingersoll (Jackson: University Press of Mississippi, 2008), p. 91.
4. Greg Eghigian, "The First World War and the Legacy of Shellshock," *Psychiatric Times,* February 2014, http://www.psychiatrictimes.com/blogs/first-world-war-and-legacy-shellshock/page/0/2#sthash.Qggz5yum.dpuf; On the German case, see Paul Lerner, *Hysterical Men: War, Psychiatry, and the Politics of Trauma in Germany, 1890–1930* (Ithaca: Cornell University Press, 2003).
5. See Piero Camporesi *Bread of Dreams: Food and Fantasy in Early Modern Europe,* trans. David Gentilcore (Chicago: University of Chicago, 1989), for literary documents about adulteration of grain with opioids, ergot-infested lolium weeds, and other mood-altering plants.
6. John Schwarz, "Candace Pert, 67, Explorer of the Brain, Dies." *New York Times,* September 19, 2013.
7. Renowned SF writer Isaac Asimov acquired AIDS through a blood transfusion, and died during the first decade of the epidemic, before life-prolonging meds became available.
8. C.G. Jung, *Jung and the Occult* (New York: Routledge, 1987).
9. "Minor tranquilizers" became available as early as 1960, and gained a strong enough foothold to find themselves parodied in song, book, and film a few years later. Librium, Valium, Miltown were not antidepressants.
10. Many useful references about science fiction films and drugs are found online. See Evan Hoovler, "13 Sci-Fi movie and TV drugs (and the REAL drugs they represent)," June 25, 2010, http://www.blastr.com/2010/06/13_sci_fi_drugs_and_the_e.php, accessed Februrary 9, 2014; "Get Your Space Drug Fix: Narcotics in Science Fiction & Fantasy," www.tor.com, August 31, 2012; Matthew Carson, III, "Fictional Drugs in Movies," www.goodlepipe.com. January 18, 2010, http://www.goozlepipe.com/2010/01/fictional-drugs-in-movies/, accessed February 24, 2014.
11. www.erowid.com is the most comprehensive and often-cited source about illicit drugs.

Chapter 14

1. Shai Biderman, "Recalling the Self: Personal Identity in Total Recall," in *Philosophy in Science Fiction Film,* ed. Steven M. Saunders (Lexington: University of Kentucky Press, 2008), 39–55. Biderman adds analogous terms from Hume, Sartre, and Kierkegaard; also see the introduction by Steven M. Saunders in *Philosophy in Science Fiction Film.*

Conclusion

1. For details on the philosophical origins of psychology, see Daniel N. Robinson, *An Intellectual History of Psychology,* 3d ed. (Madison: University of Wisconsin Press, 1995).
2. For well-argued and well-informed contrarian views, see Donald Mender's *The Myth of Neuropsychiatry: A Look at Paradoxes, Physics, and the Human Brain* (AA Dordrecht, the Netherlands: Kluwer Academic, 1994).
3. My thanks to Michael Schwartz, M.D., for instilling an appreciation of philosophy and psychiatry through his seminars and his editorship of *Philosophy, Psychiatry and Psychology* (Johns Hopkins University Press) and to the late Jack Peter Green, Ph.D., M.D., professor emeritus of psychopharmacology, Mount Sinai School of Medicine, for eighteen years of discussions on the Philosophy of Science.
4. My thanks to Dan Harmon, Rebecca Matheson, and James Sherman of ABC-CLIO for encouraging my participation in ABC-Clio's online forum on *Enduring Questions* (ABC-CLIO, 2012).
5. AH Chapman and M. Chapman-Santana, "The influence of Nietzsche on Freud's ideas," *British Journal of Psychiatry* 166.2 (February 1995): 251–253.
6. My thanks to Richard McCarrick, M.D., and Steven Billick, M.D., of St. Vincent's Hospital for encouraging interest in Jung's unique views.

Bibliography

Print Sources

Aldiss, Brian W., with David Wingrove. *Trillion Year Spree: The History of Science Fiction*. New York: Atheneum, 1986.

Altman, Rick. *Film/Genre*. London: BFI, 1999.

American Psychiatric Association. *Desk Reference to the Diagnostic Criteria from DSM-5*. Arlington, VA: APPI, 2013.

American Psychiatric Association. *DSM-III (Diagnostic and Statistical Manual)*, 3d ed. Arlington, VA: APPI, 1980.

Andre, Linda. *Doctors of Deception: What They Don't Want You to Know About Shock Treatment*. New Brunswick: Rutgers University Press, 2009.

Andrew, J. Dudley. *Concepts in Film Theory*. New York: Oxford University Press, 1984.

Arnheim, Rudolf. *Film as Art*. Berkeley: University of California Press, 1957.

Arnold, Gary. "The Lawnmower Man." *Washington Times*, March 7, 1992.

Ash, Brian, ed. *The Visual Encyclopedia of Science Fiction*. New York: Harmony Books, 1977.

Ashcroft, Bill, Gareth Griffiths, and Helen Tiffin, eds. *The Post-Colonial Studies Reader,* 2d ed. London: Routledge, 2005.

Asimov, Isaac. *Asimov on Science Fiction*. London: Granada, 1983.

Asimov, Isaac. *I, Robot*. Greenwich, CT: Fawcett Crest, 1950.

Atkinson, Roland. "Film, Fame, and the Fashioning of an Illness." *Clinical Psychiatry News*, July 1, 2009.

Auslander, Philip. *From Acting to Performance: Essays in Modernism and Postmodernism*. London: Routledge, 1997.

Ballard, J. G. *Crash*. 1973. New York: Picador, 2001.

Barbour, Alan G. *Cliffhanger*. Secaucus, NJ: Citadel Press, 1977.

Barker, Martin, Jane Arthurs, and Ramaswari Harindranath. *The Crash Controversy: Censorship Campaigns and Film Reception*. London: Wallflower Press, 2001.

Barnett, Chad P. "Reviving Cyberpunk: (Re)Constructing the Subject and Mapping Cyberspace in the Wachowski Brothers' Film *The Matrix*." *Extrapolations* 41.4 (2000): 359–374.

Baudrillard, Jean. "The Ecstasy of Communication." In *The Anti-Aesthetic: Essays on Postmodern Culture*, edited by Hal Foster. Port Townsend, WA: Bay Press, 1983. 126–134.

Baxter, John. *Science Fiction in the Cinema*. New York: Paperback Library, 1970.

Bazin, Andre. *The Cinema of Cruelty*. Edited by Francois Truffaut. New York: Seaver Books, 1982.

Beaver, Harold. "Introduction." In *The Science Fiction of Edgar Allan Poe*, edited by Beaver. New York: Penguin, 1976. vii–xxi.

Bedel, Jean. *Les Automates*. Paris: Jacques Grancher, 1987.

Beecher, Henry. "Ethics and Clinical Research." *New England Journal of Medicine* 274 (1966): 1354–60.

Belfiore, Michael. *The Department of Mad Scientists: How DARPA Is Remaking Our World, from the Internet to Artificial Limbs*. New York: HarperCollins, 2009.

Benson, Michael. *Vintage Science Fiction Films, 1896–1949*. Jefferson, NC: McFarland, 1985.

Bergfelder, Tim, Erica Carter, and Deniz Gokturk. *The German Cinema Book*. London: BFI, 2002.

Bergstrom, Janet, Elisabeth Lyon, and Constance Penley. "Science Fiction and Sexual Difference." *Camera Obscura* 15 (Fall 1986).

Bergstrom, Janet, ed. *Endless Night*. Berkeley: University of California Press, 1999.

Beveridge, Allan. *Portrait of the Psychiatrist as a Young Man*. Oxford: Oxford University Press, 2011.

Biesen, Sheri Chinen. *Blackout: World War II and the Origins of Film Noir*. Baltimore: Johns Hopkins University Press, 2005.

Biskind, Peter. Seeing *Is Believing: How Hollywood Taught Us to Stop Worrying and Love the Fifties*. New York: Pantheon, 1983.

Booker, Keith M. *Alternate Americas: Science Fiction Film and American Culture*. Westport, CT: Praeger, 2006.

Booker, Keith M. *Monsters, Mushroom Clouds, and the Cold War: American Science Fiction and the Roots of Postmodernism, 1946–1964.* Westport, CT: Greenwood Press, 2001.

Boonstra, John. "Philip K. Dick 1928–1982." *Twilight Zone* (June 1982): 47–52.

Bordwell, David, and Kristin Thompson. *Film Art*, 4th ed. Boston: McGraw-Hill Education, 1993.

Bordwell, David, Janet Staiger, and Kristin Thompson. *The Classical Hollywood Cinema: Film Style and Mode of Production to 1960.* New York: Columbia University Press, 1985.

Bould, Mark. *Film Noir: From Berlin to Sin City.* London: Wallflower, 2005.

Bourde, Raymond, and Etienne Chaumeton *A Panorama of American Film Noir: 1941–1953.* Trans. Paul Hammond. San Francisco: City Lights, 2002.

Brand, Stewart. *The Media Lab: Inventing the Future at MIT.* New York: Viking, 1987.

Braudy, Leo. "Genre and the Resurrection of the Past." In *Shadows of the Magic Lamp*, edited by George E. Slusser and Eric S. Rabkin. Carbondale: Southern Illinois University Press, 1985. 1–13.

Bricken, Meredith. "Inventing Reality: As Humans, We Continually Enhance Reality with Manifestations of Our Imagination." *CADalyst* (December 1989): 45–46.

Brooks, Landon. *The Aesthetics of Ambivalence: Rethinking Science Fiction Film in the Age of Electronic (Re)production.* Westport, CT: Greenwood Press, 1992.

Brosnan, John. *Future Tense: The Cinema of Science Fiction.* New York: St. Martin's Press, 1978.

Brosnan, John. *Movie Magic: The Story of Special Effects in the Cinema.* New York: New American Library, 1976.

Brosnan, John. *The Primal Screen: A History of Science Fiction Film.* London: Orbit Books, 1995.

Brown, Edward M. "Neurology's Influence on American Psychiatry: 1965–1915." In *History of Psychiatry and Medical Psychology,* edited by Edwin R. Wallace IV and John Gach. New York: Springer, 2008.

Brown, Edward M. "Why Wagner-Jauregg won the Nobel Prize for discovering malaria therapy for General Paresis of the Insane." *History of Psychiatry* 11.44 (2000): 371–382.

Browne, Nick, ed. *Refiguring American Film Genres: Theory and History.* Berkeley: University of California Press, 1998.

Bruno, Giuliana. "Ramble City: Postmodernism and Blade Runner." In *Alien Zone: Cultural Theory and Contemporary Science Fiction Cinema,* edited by Annette Kuhn. London: Verso, 1990. 183–195.

Budd, Mike, ed. *The Cabinet of Dr. Caligari.* New Brunswick: Rutgers University Press, 1990.

Bukatman, Scott. *Blade Runner.* London: BFI, 1997.

Bukatman, Scott. *Matters of Gravity: Special Effects and Supermen in the 20th Century.* Durham: Duke University Press, 2003.

Bunting, Charles T. "Dressing for Dinner in the Jungle" (1973). In *Conversations with Anthony Burgess,* edited by Earl G. Ingersoll and Mary C. Ingersoll. Jackson: University Press of Mississippi, 2008.

Burns, Bob, with John Michlig. *It Came from Bob's Basement.* San Francisco: Chronicle, 2000.

Buscombe, Edward. "The Idea of Genre in the American Cinema." In *Film Genre Reader II,* edited by Barry Keith Grant. Austin: University of Texas, 2012. 11–25.

Butkamin, Scott. *Terminal Identity: The Virtual Subject in Postmodern Science Fiction.* Durham: Duke University Press, 1993.

Butler, Jeremy G., ed. *Star Texts: Image and Performance in Film and Television.* Detroit: Wayne State University Press, 1991.

Butler, Judith. *Gender Trouble: Feminism and the Subversion of Identity.* London: Routledge, 1990.

Bynum, W.F., Roy Porter, and Michael Shepherd, eds. *The Anatomy of Madness: Essays in the History of Psychiatry. Vol. 3. The Asylum and its Psychiatry.* London: Routledge, 1988.

Carroll, Lewis. *Alice's Adventures in Wonderland and Through the Looking Glass*, Modern Library ed. 1869. New York: Random House, 2002.

Carroll, Noel. *The Philosophy of Horror: Or, Paradoxes of the Heart.* London: Routledge, 1990.

Carter, Paul A. *The Creation of Tomorrow: Fifty Years of Magazine Science Fiction.* New York: Columbia University Press, 1977.

Cawelti, John G. *Adventure, Mystery, and Romance: Formula Stories as Art and Popular Culture.* Chicago: University of Chicago Press, 1976.

Cawelti, John G. "The Question of Popular Genres." *Journal of Popular Film and Television* 13, no. 2 (1985): 55–61.

Ceram, C.W. *Archaeology of the Cinema.* New York: Harcourt, Brace & World, 1965.

Chadwick, Gary. Review of *The Oxford Textbook of Clinical Research Ethics. New England Journal of Medicine* 359 (2008): 982–983.

Channan, Michael. *The Dream That Kicks*, 2d ed. London: Routledge, 1980.

Charney, Leo. and V. R. Schwartz. *Cinema and the Invention of Modern Life.* Berkeley: University of California Press, 1995.

Chayefsky, Paddy. *Altered States.* New York: HarperCollins, 1978.

Chion, Michel. *Kubrick's Cinema Odyssey.* Translated by Claudia Gorbman. London: BFI, 2001.

Clarens, Carlos *An Illustrated History of Horror and Science Fiction Films.* Introduced by J. Hoberman. New York: Da Capo Press, 1991.

Clarens, Carlos. *An Illustrated History of the Horror Film.* New York: Capricorn, 1967.

Clareson, Thomas, ed. *SF: The Other Side of Realism.*

Bowling Green: Bowling Green University Popular Press, 1971.

Clover, Carol. *Men, Women, and Chainsaws: The Modern Horror Film*, London: BFI, 1992.

Cohen, Elizabeth. "CDC: Antidepressants most prescribed drugs in U.S." www.cdc.gov/nchs/fastats/drugs.htm; accessed October 16, 2011.

Cohen, John. *Human Robots in Myth and Science*. Cranbury, NJ: A. S. Barnes, 1967.

Cohn, David and Richard Marcuse. "Your Young Men Shall See Visions: A Conversation with William Gibson." *CADalyst* (December 1989): 49–51.

Collins, Jim, Hilary Radner, and Ava Preacher Collins, eds. *Film Theory Goes to the Movies*. New York: Routledge, 1993.

Cook, David A. *A History of Narrative Film*, 3d ed. New York: W. W. Norton, 1996.

Corn, Joseph J., ed. *Imagining Tomorrow: History, Technology, and the American Future*. Cambridge: MIT Press, 1986.

Cornea, Christine, ed. *Science Fiction Cinema: Between Fantasy and Reality*. Edinburgh: Edinburgh University Press, 2007.

Coyle, Jake. "The new Western? The mind is latest movie frontier." AP Entertainment, July 14, 2010 (reprinted online).

Craddock, Jim, ed. *Videohound's Golden Movie Retriever 2007*. Detroit: Thomson Gale, 2006.

Creed, Barbara. "Alien and the Monstrous-Feminine." In *Alien Zone*, edited by Annette Kuhn. London: Verso, 1990, pp. 128–41.

Creed, Barbara. *The Monstrous Feminine: Film, Feminism, Psychoanalysis*. New York: Routledge, 1993.

Cronenworth, Brian. "Man of Iron." *American Film* 13, no. 1 (1987): 33–35.

Darwin, Charles. *The Origin of Species by Means of Natural Selection, or The Preservation of Favoured Races in the Struggle for Life*. 1859. New York: Penguin, 2003.

Decker, Hannah S. "Psychoanalysis in Central Europe." In *History of Psychiatry and Medical Psychology*, edited by Edwin R. Wallace IV and John Gach. New York: Springer, 2008.

Dewdney, A. K. "Computer Recreations." *Scientific American* 255 (December 1986): 14–20.

Dixon, Wheeler Winston. *Visions of the Apocalypse: Spectacles of Destruction in American Cinema*. London: Wallflower Press, 2003.

Doane, Mary Ann. "Technophilia: Technology, Representation, and the Feminine." In *Body/Politics: Women and the Discourse of Science*, edited by Mary Jacobus, Evelyn Fox Keller, and Sally Shuttleworth. London: Routledge, 1990. 163–176.

Doe, Richard L. "[2001] Flings Man into Space," *Washington Post*, April 14, 1968.

Doherty, Thomas. *Teenagers and Teenpics: The Juvenilization of American Movies in the 1950s*. Boston: Unwin Hyman, 1988.

Dowdy, Andrew. *Films of the Fifties: The American State of Mind*. New York: William Morrow, 1973.

Duff, Wilson. "F.D.A. Is Studying the Risk of Electroshock Devices." *New York Times*, January 23, 2011.

Durgnat, Raymond. *Films and Feelings*. Cambridge: MIT Press, 1967.

Durgnat, Raymond. *The Crazy Mirror*. New York: Dutton, 1970.

Eagleton, Terry. *Literary Theory: An Introduction*. Minneapolis: University of Minnesota Press, 1983.

Eberwein, Robert T. *Film & the Dream Screen*. Princeton: Princeton University Press, 1984.

Eisner, Lotte. *Fritz Lang*. New York: Da Capo, 1976.

Eisner, Lotte. *The Haunted Screen*. Berkeley: University of California Press, 1952.

Ellenberger, Henri. *The Discovery of the Unconscious: The History of Dynamic Psychiatry*. New York: Basic Books, 1970.

Ellison, Harlan. "A Boy and His Dog." In *The Beast That Shouted Love at the Heart of the World*. 1969. New York: St Martin's Press, 1984.

Ellison, Harlan. *Harlan Ellison's Watching*. Los Angeles: Underwood-Miller, 1989.

Elsaesser, Thomas. *Weimar Cinema and After*. London: Routledge, 2001.

Elsaesser, Thomas, and Adam Barker, eds. *Early Cinema: Space, Frame, Narrative*. London: BFI, 1990.

Elsaesser, Thomas, and Warren Buckland, eds. *Studying Contemporary American Movies: A Guide to Film Analysis*. London: Hodder Arnold, 2002.

Elsaesser, Thomas, Noel Kin and Alexander Horwath, eds. *The Last Great American Picture Show: New Hollywood Cinema in the 1970s*. Amsterdam: Amsterdam University Press, 2004.

Emmett, Arlelle. "Universal Studios' Computer Graphics." *Computer Graphics World* (February 1986): 26–32.

Erickson, Glenn. *Sci-Fi Savant: Classic Sci-Fi Review Reader*. \point/blank, 2011.

Everson, William K. *Classics of the Horror Film*. New York: Citadel Press, 1974.

Ezra, Elizabeth. *Georges Méliès*. Manchester: Manchester University Press, 2000.

Foucault, Michel. *Madness and Civilization* (unabridged French 1961; abridged French 1964; English translation, 1964).

Franklin H. Bruce. "America as Science Fiction: 1939." In *Coordinates: Placing Science Fiction and Fantasy*, edited by George E. Slusser, Eric S. Rabkin, and Robert Scholes. Carbondale: Southern Illinois University Press, 1983. 107–123.

Franklin, H. Bruce. *Future Perfect: American Science Fiction of the Nineteenth Century*, rev. ed. New York: Oxford University Press, 1978.

Freud, Sigmund. *The Future of an Illusion*. Introduced by James Strachey. 1927. New York: W.W. Norton, 1950.

Freud, Sigmund. *The Interpretation of Dreams*. Trans.

Joyce Crick. New York: Oxford University Press, 2000.

Friedan, Betty. *The Feminine Mystique*. New York: W. W. Norton, 1963.

Frieden, Thomas R., and F. Collins. Commentary. Intentional Infection of Vulnerable Populations in 1946–1948. *JAMA* 304.18 (2010):2063–2064. Published online October 11, 2010.

Friedman, Lawrence J. *Menninger: The Family and the Clinic*. New York: Alfred A. Knopf, 1990.

Frum, David. *How We Got Here—The 70's: The Decade That Brought You Modern Life—For Better Or Worse*. New York: Basic Books, 2000.

Fruth, Bryan, et al. "The Atomic Age: Facts and Films from 1945–1965." *Journal of Popular Film and Television* 23, no. 4 (1996): 154–60.

Gabbard, G.O., and K. Gabbard. *Psychiatry and the Cinema*, 2d ed. Washington, D.C.: American Psychiatric Press, 1999.

Gabler, Neal. *Life: The Movie: How Entertainment Conquered Reality*. New York: Vintage, 2000.

Gay, Peter, ed. *The Freud Reader*. Translated by James Strachey. London: Vintage, 1995.

Geduld, Harry. "Return to Méliès: Reflections on the Science Fiction Film." In *Focus on the Science Fiction Film*, edited by Johnson. Englewood Cliffs, NJ: Prentice-Hall, 1972. 142–147.

Gelmis, Joseph. "Another Look at Space Odyssey." *Newsday*, April 20, 1968.

Gelmis, Joseph. "Space Odyssey Fails Most Gloriously." *Newsday*, April 4, 1968.

George, Mark S., et al., "Nonpharmacological Somatic Treatments." *The American Psychitric Publishing Textbook of Psychiatry*, 5th ed., eds. Robert E. Hales, Stuart C. Yudofsky, and Glen O. Gebbard. Arlington, VA: APPI, 2008.

Geraghty, Christine. *British Cinema in the Fifties: Gender, Genre and the "New Look."* London: Routledge, 2000.

Gerani, Gary. *Top 100 Sci-Fi Movies*. Introduced by John Carpenter. San Diego: The Fantastic Press, 2011.

Gershuny Theodore. *Soon to Be a Major Motion Picture*. New York: Holt, Rinehart and Winston, 1980.

Giannetti, Louis, and S. Eyman. *Flashback*, 4th ed. Upper Saddle River, NJ: Prentice Hall, 2001.

Gibson, William. *Johnny Mnemonic: The Screenplay and the St*ory. New York: Ace, 1995.

Gibson, William. *Neuromancer*. New York: Ace, 1984.

Gibson, William. *Virtual Light*. Harmondsworth, Middlesex: Penguin, 1994.

Gifford, Denis. *A Pictorial History of Horror Movies*. London: Hamlyn, 1974

Gifford, Denis. *Science Fiction Film*. London: Studio Vista, 1971.

Glassy, Mark G. *The Biology of Science Fiction Cinema*. Jefferson, NC: McFarland, 2005.

Glassy, Mark G. "Brains, Craniums and Heads." *Scary Monsters Magazine*, January 2012.

Glassy, Mark G. "Monkeying Around with Apes." *Scary Monsters Magazine*, June 2013.

Gleick, James. *Chaos: Making a New Science*. New York: Viking, 1987.

Goldberg, Lee. "Michael Crichton: The Business of Moviemaking is Science Fiction." *Starlog* (February 1985): 46.

Goldman, William. *Adventures in the Screen Trade*. New York: Warner Books, 1984.

Goodman, Cynthia. *Digital Visions: Computers and Art*. New York: Harry N. Abrams, 1987.

Gordon, Andrew. "Back to the Future: Oedipus as Time Traveler." *Science Fiction Studies* 14.3 (1987): 372–385.

Gordon, Andrew. "Close Encounters: The Gospel According to Steven Spielberg." *Literature/Film Quarterly* 8, no. 3 (1980): 156–64.

Gordon, Mel. *The Grand Guignol. Theatre of Fear and Terror*. New York: Amok, 1988.

Gould, Michael. *Surrealism and the Cinema*. London: Tantivy Press, 1976.

Goulekas, Karen. *Visual Effects in a Digital World: A Comprehensive Glossary of Over 7,000 Visual Effects Terms*. San Diego: Morgan Kauffman, 2001.

Grant, Barry K. "Invaders from Mars and the Science Fiction Film in the Age of Reagan." *CineAction!* 8 (1987): 77–83.

Greenberg, Harvey Roy. "Machine Dreams." *Film and Philosophy* 4 (1997): 111–115.

Greenberg, Harvey Roy. *Screen Memories*. New York: Columbia University Press, 1993.

Greenberg, Joanna. *I Never Promised You a Rose Garden*. New York: Holt, Rinehart and Winston, 1964.

Greenberger, Robert. "Ridley Scott." *Starlog* (July 1982): 61.

Greene, Eric, ed. *Planet of the Apes as American Myth: Race, Politics, and Popular Culture*. Hanover, NH: Wesleyan University Press, 1998.

Grob, Gerald N. "The Transformation of American Psychiatry." In *History of Psychiatry and Medical Psychology*, edited by Edwin R. Wallace IV and John Gach. New York: Springer, 2008.

Gullichsen, Eric, Randal Walser, and Patrice Gelband. "Cyberspace: Experiential Computing." *CADalyst* (December 1989): 46–47.

Gunn, James. *Alternate Worlds: The Illustrated History of Science Fiction*. Englewood Cliffs, NJ: Prentice-Hall, 1975.

Gunning, Tom. "The Cinema of Attraction: Early Film, Its Spectator and the Avant-Garde." *Wide Angle* 8, no. 3–4 (1986): 63–70.

Gunning, Tom. *The Films of Fritz Lang*. London: BFI, 2000.

Haas, Robert. "Introduction: The Cronenberg Project: Literature, Science, Psychology, and the Monster in Cinema." *Post Script* 15, no. 2 (1996): 3–10.

Haining, Peter. *The Jules Verne Companion*. New York: Baronet, 1978.

Halpern, Leslie. *Dreams on Film*. Jefferson, NC: McFarland, 2003.

Hammond, Paul, ed. and trans. *The Shadow and Its Shadow*, 3d ed. San Francisco: City Lights, 2000.

Hansen, Bert. "Medical History for the Masses: How American Comic Books Celebrated Heroes of Medicine in the 1940s." *Bulletin of the History of Medicine* 78, no. 1 (Spring 2004): 148–191.

Hansen, Bert. *Picturing Medical Progress from Pasteur to Polio*. New Brunswick, NJ: Rutgers University Press, 2009.

Haraway, Donna J. *Simians, Cyborgs, and Women: The Reinvention of Nature*. New York: Routledge, 1991.

Haraway, Donna. "The Actors Are Cyborg, Nature Is Coyote, and the Geography Is Elsewhere: Postscript to 'Cyborgs at Large.'" In *Technoculture*, edited by Constance Penley and Andrew Ross. Detroit: Wayne State University Press, 1992. 21–6.

Hardison, O. B., Jr. *Disappearing Through the Skylight: Culture and Technology in the Twentieth Century*. New York: Viking, 1989.

Hardy, Phil, ed. *The Overlook Film Encyclopedia*. Woodstock, NY: Overlook, 1999.

Hardy, Phil. *The Encyclopedia of Science Fiction Movies*. Minneapolis: Woodbury Press, 1984.

Harper, Sue, and Vincent Porter. *British Cinema of the 1950s: The Decline of Deference*. Oxford: Oxford University Press, 2003.

Harrington, Richard. "[Mower] cuts swathe of diabolical silliness." *Washington Post*, March, 7, 1992. http://www.washingtonpost.com/wp-srv/style/longterm/movies/videos/thelawnmowerman rharrington_a0ab25.

Harris, Gardiner. "Talk Doesn't Pay, So Psychiatry Turns Instead to Drug Therapy." *New York Times*, March 5, 2011.

Harris, Thomas. *Red Dragon*. New York: Dell, 1981.

Hart, James D. *The Popular Book: A History of America's Literary Taste*. Berkeley: University of California Press, 1963.

Hartwell, David. *Age of Wonders: Exploring the World of Science Fiction*. New York: McGraw-Hill, 1984.

Hayward, Susan. *Cinema Studies*, 2d ed. London: Routledge, 2000.

Healy, David. "The Intersection of Psychopharmacology and Psychiatry in the Second Half of the Twentieth Century." In *History of Psychiatry and Medical Psychology*, edited by Edwin R. Wallace IV and John Gach. New York: Springer, 2008.

Heard, Mervyn. *Phantasmagoria*. Hastings, UK: The Projection Box, 2006.

Heath, Stephen. "Cinema and Psychoanalysis." In *Endless Night*, edited by J. Bergstrom. Berkeley: University of California Press, 1999. 25–56.

Heldreth, Leonard. "Festering in Thebes: Elements of Tragedy and Myth in Cronenberg's Films." *Post Script* 15, no. 2 (1996): 46–61.

Hendershot, Cyndy. *I Was a Cold War Monster: Horror Films, Eroticism, and the Cold War Imagination*, Bowling Green, OH: Bowling Green State University Popular Press, 2001.

Hendershot, Cyndy. *Paranoia, the Bomb, and 1950s Science Fiction Films*. Bowling Green, OH: Bowling Green State University Popular Press, 1999.

Hensley, Scott. "Harvard Psychiatrists Under Fire for Drug-Company Funding." *Wall Street Journal*, June 9, 2008.

Hill, Geoffrey. *Illuminating Shadows: The Mythic Power of Film*. Boston: Shambala, 1992.

Hill, John, and Pamela Church Gibson, eds. *The Oxford Guide to Film Studies*, Oxford: Oxford University Press, 1998.

Hill, John. *British Cinema in the 1980s*. Oxford: Clarendon Press, 1999.

Hjort, Mette, and Scott MacKenzie, eds. *Cinema and Nation*. London: Routledge, 2000.

Hoberman, J. *The Dream Life*. New York: The New Press, 2003.

Hoenig J. "Schizophrenia." In *A History of Clinical Psychiatry*, edited by G.E. Berrios and Roy Porter. London: Athlone, 1995.

Howells, Christina, ed. *The Cambridge Companion to Sartre*. Cambridge: Cambridge University Press, 1992.

Hunt, Richard. Book review of *Hitler or Hippocrates: Medical Experiments and Euthanasia in the Third Reich*. *New England Journal of Medicine* 328 (May 13, 1993): 1429.

Huxley, Aldous. *Brave New World*. 1932. New York: HarperCollins, 1998.

Huxley, Aldous. *The Doors of Perception and Heaven and Hell*. 1954. New York: HarperCollins, 2004.

Huxley, Aldous. *Island*. 1962. New York: HarperCollins, 2002.

Hyler, Steven H., Glen Gabbard, and Irving Schneider. "Homicidal Maniacs and Narcissistic Parasites: Stigmatization of Mentally Ill Persons in the Movies." *Hospital and Community Psychiatry* 42 (October 1991): 1044–1048.

Indick, William. *Psycho Thrillers*. Jefferson, NC: McFarland, 2003.

Ing, Dean, and Robert A. Heinlein. *Silent Thunder/Universe*. 1941. New York: Tor Books, 1991.

Jackson, Rosemary. *Fantasy: The Literature of Subversion*. London: Methuen, 1981.

Jacobus, Mary, Evelyn Fox Keller, and Sally Shuttleworth, eds. *Body/Politics: Women and the Discourses of Science*. London: Routledge, 1990.

James, Edward. *Science Fiction in the 20th Century*. Oxford: Oxford University Press, 1994.

Jameson, Fredric. *Postmodernism: Or, The Cultural Logic of Late Capitalism*. London: Verso, 1991.

Jancovich, Mark. *Rational Fears: American Horror in the 1950s*. Manchester: Manchester University Press, 1996.

Javins, Marie, and Stuart Moore. *The Art of Iron Man 3*. New York: Marvel, 2013.

Johnson, William. "Journey into Science Fiction." In *Focus on the Science Fiction Film*, edited by William Johnson. Englewood Cliffs, NJ: Prentice-Hall, 1972. 1–12.

Johnston, Keith M. *Science Fiction Film: A Critical Introduction*. New York: Berg, 2011.

Jones, Gerard. *Men of Tomorrow*. New York: Basic Books, 2004.

Jung, C.G. *Psychology and Religion* (based on the Terry Lectures delivered at Yale University, 1938). New Haven: Yale University Press. 1966.

Kadrey, Richard, and Larry McCaffery. "Cyberpunk 101." In *Storming the Reality Studio*, edited by Larry McCaffery, pp. 17–29.

Kaes, Anton. *Shell-Shock Cinema: Weimar Culture and the Wounds of War*. Princeton, NJ: Princeton University Press, 2009.

Kalat, David. *The Strange Case of Dr. Mabuse*. Jefferson, NC: McFarland, 2001.

Kaplan, E. Ann. *Trauma Culture: The Politics of Terror and Loss in Media and Literature*. New Brunswick, NJ: Rutgers University Press, 2005.

Kaplan, E. Ann. *Women in Film Noir*. London: BFI, 1980

Kaplan, E. Ann, ed. *Psychoanalysis & Cinema*. New York: Routledge, 1990.

Kardish, Laurence. *Weimar Cinema, 1919–1933*. New York: Museum of Modern Art, 2010.

Kauffmann, Stanley. "Epiphany." *The New Republic*. December 10, 1977, 20–21.

Kawin, Bruce F. "Children of the Light." In *Film Genre Reader II*, edited by Barry Keith Grant. Austin: University of Texas, 2012. 308–329.

Keane, Stephen. *Disaster Movies: The Cinema of Catastrophe*. London: Wallflower, 2001.

Kelly, Kevin. *Out of Control*. London: Fourth Estate, 1995.

Killen, Andreas. *Berlin Electropolis: Shock, Nerves, and German Modernity*. Berkeley: University of California, 2006.

Kinnard, Roy, Tony Crnkovich, and R.J. Vitone. *The Flash Gordon Serials: 1936–1940*. Jefferson, NC: McFarland, 2008.

Kinnard, Roy. *Horror in Silent Films*. Jefferson, NC: McFarland, 1995.

Kinnard, Roy. *Science Fiction Serials*. Jefferson, NC: McFarland, 1998.

Kline, Sally, ed. *George Lucas: Interviews*. Jackson: University Press of Mississippi, 1999.

Kloman, William. "[2001] and [Hair] – Are They the Groove of the Future?" *New York Times*, May 12, 1968.

Knight, Damon. *In Search of Wonder: Essays on Modern Science Fiction*, rev. ed. Chicago: Advent, 1967.

Koch, Gertrud. *Siegfried Kracauer: An Introduction*. Translated by Jeremy Gaines. Princeton: Princeton University Press, 2000.

Kolker, Robert Phillip. A *Cinema of Loneliness: Penn, Kubrick, Scorsese, Spielberg, Altman*. Oxford: Oxford University Press, 1988.

Kolker, Robert. *A Cinema of Loneliness*, 3rd ed. New York: Oxford University Press, 2000.

Kracauer, Siegfried. *From Caligari to Hitler*. Princeton: Princeton University Press, 1947.

Kracauer, Siegfried. *From Caligari to Hitler: A Psychological History of the German Film*. Edited by Leonardo Quaresima. Princeton: Princeton University Press, 2004.

Kracauer, Siegfried. *Theory of Film*. Princeton: Princeton University Press, 1997.

Kravis, Nathan. "James Braid's psychophysiology: A turning point in the history of dynamic psychiatry." *American Journal of Psychiatry* 145.10 (October 1988): 1191–1206.

Kuenzli, Rudolf E., ed. *Dada and Surrealist Film*. Cambridge: MIT Press, 1998.

Kuhn, Annette, ed. *Alien Zone: Cultural Theory and Contemporary Science Fiction Cinema*. London: Verso, 1990.

Lamm, Spencer, ed. *The Art of the Matrix*. New York, Newmarket Press, 2000.

Landon, Brooks. *The Aesthetics of Ambivalence: Rethinking Science Fiction Film in the Age of Electronic (Re)Production*. Westport, CT: Greenwood Press, 1992.

Langdale, Allan, ed. *Hugo Munsterberg on Film*. New York: Routledge, 2002.

Langford, Barry. *Film Genre: Hollywood and Beyond*. Edinburgh: Edinburgh University Press, 2005.

Lapsley, Robert, and M. Westlake. *Film Theory: An Introduction*. Manchester: Manchester University Press, 1988.

LaValley, Al, ed. *Invasion of the Body Snatchers*, New Brunswick, NJ: Rutgers University Press, 1989.

La Valley, Albert J. "Traditions of Trickery: The Role of Special Effects in the Science Fiction Film." In *Shadows of the Magic Lamp*, edited by George E. Slusser and Eric S. Rabkin, 141–158.

Lavery, David. *Late for the Sky: The Mentality of the Space Age*. Carbondale: Southern Illinois University Press, 1992.

Lebeau, Vicky. *Lost Angels*. London: Routledge, 1995.

Lebeau, Vicky. *Psychoanalysis and Cinema*. London: Wallflower, 2001.

Lerner, David. *Hysterical Men: War, Psychiatry, and the Politics of Trauma in Germany, 1890–1930* (Cornell Studies in the History of Psychiatry). Ithaca: Cornell University Press, 2009.

Lichtenfeld, Eric. *Action Speaks Louder*. Westport, CT: Praeger, 2004.

Lottman, Herbert. *Jules Verne, An Exploratory Biography*. New York: St. Martin's Press, 1996.

Lucanio, Patrick. *Them or Us: Archetypal Interpretations of Fifties Alien Invasion Films*. Bloomington: Indiana University Press, 1987.

Luhrmann, T.M. *Of Two Minds: An Anthropologist Looks at American Psychiatry.* New York: Vintage, 2001.

Lyons, Mike. "Cyber-Cinema." *Cinefantastique* 28, no. 8 (1997): 40–3, 62.

Lyotard, Jean-François. *The Postmodern Condition: A Report on Knowledge.* Translated by Geoff Bennington and Brian Massumi. Minneapolis: University of Minnesota Press, 1984.

Magno, Julie, Daniel J. Safer, Susan dosReis, James F. Gardner, Myde Boles, Frances Lynch. "Trends in the Prescribing of Psychotropic Medications to Preschoolers." *JAMA* 283.8 (2000): 1025–1030. doi: 10.1001/jama.283.8.1025.

Malani, Preeti: Book review of *Dark Medicine: Rationalizing Unethical Medical Research,* edited W. Lafleur, G. Bohme, S. Shimazono. *JAMA* 300.10 (September 10, 2008): 1217–1218.

Malone, Robert. *Ultimate Robot.* New York: Dorling Kindersley, 2004.

Manchel, Frank. *Terrors of the Screen.* Englewood Cliffs, NJ: Prentice-Hall, 1970.

Manning, Matthew. *Iron Man: The Ultimate Guide to the Armored Super Hero.* New York: Dorling Kindersley, 2010.

Marks, John. *The Search for the "Manchurian Candidate." The CIA and Mind Control.* New York: W.W. Norton, 1979.

Mast, Gerald, and Marshall Cohen. *Film Theory and Criticism.* Oxford: Oxford University Press, 1985.

Masters, Robert E. L., and Jean Houston. *Psychedelic Art.* London: Weidenfeld and Nicolson, 1968.

Maurice, Klaus, and Otto Mayr, eds. *The Clockwork Universe: German Clocks and Automata 1150–1650.* Washington, D.C.: Smithsonian Institute (Neale Watson Academic Press), 1980.

McBride, Joseph. *Steven Spielberg: A Biography.* New York: Da Capo Press, 1999.

McCaffery, Larry. "Introduction: The Desert of the Real." In *Storming the Reality Studio,* edited by Larry McCaffery, pp. 1–16.

McConnell, Frank. "Born in Fire: The Ontology of the Monster." In *Shadows of the Magic Lamp,* edited by George E. Slusser and Eric S. Rabkin, pp. 231–8.

McDermott, Mary, and W. R. Robinson. "2001 and the Literary Sensibility." *The Georgia Review* 26 (1972): 21–37.

McDonald A, Walter G. "The portrayal of ECT in American movies." *Journal of ECT* 17.4 (2001): 264–274.

McGinn, Colin. *The Power of Movies.* New York: Pantheon, 2005.

McGowan, Todd, and S. Kunkle. *Lacan and Contemporary Film.* New York: Other Press, 2004.

Meduna, L.J. "Autobiography of L.J. Meduna." *Convulsive Therapy* 1.1 (1985): 53.

Merril, Judith. "What do you mean: Science? Fiction?" In *SF: The Other Side of Realism,* edited by Thomas D. Clareson. Bowling Green, OH: Bowling Green State University Popular Press, 1971.

Mijolla, Alain de. "Freud and the Psychoanalytic Situation on the Screen." In *Endless Night,* edited by J. Bergstrom. Berkeley: University of California Press, 1999. 188–199.

Mitry, Jean (trans. Christopher King). *The Aesthetics and Psychology of the Cinema.* Bloomington: Indiana University Press, 1990.

Moran, Mark. "When Ethical Lines Were Crossed in Service to the Nation." *Psychiatric News* 46.12 (June 17, 2011): 16.

Morley, David, and Kevin Robins. *Spaces of Identity: Global Media, Electronic Landscapes and Cultural Boundaries.* New York: Routledge, 1995.

Morris, Peter. *David Cronenberg: A Delicate Balance.* Toronto: ECW Press, 1999.

Morris, William. *News from Nowhere.* 1890. Harmondsworth, Middlesex: Penguin, 1993.

Mulvey, Laura. *Visual and Other Pleasures.* Bloomington: Indiana University Press, 1989.

Mumford, Lewis. *The Story of Utopias.* New York: Viking, 1962.

Murray, Janet H. *Hamlet on the Holodeck: The Future of Narrative in Cyberspace.* Cambridge: MIT Press, 1997.

Myers, Robert E., ed. *The Intersection of Science Fiction and Philosophy.* Westport, CT: Greenwood Press, 1983.

Napier, Susan Jolliffe. *Anime: From Akira to Princess Mononoke: Experiencing Contemporary Japanese Animation.* New York: Palgrave, 2001.

Naremore, James. *More Than Night: Film Noir in Its Contexts.* Berkeley: University of California Press, 1998.

Neale, Steve. *Genre and Hollywood.* London: Routledge, 2000.

Neugroschel, Joachim, ed. and trans. *The Dybbuk and the Yiddish Imagination.* Syracuse: Syracuse University Press, 2000.

Newitz, Annalee. "Magical Girls and Atomic Bomb Sperm: Japanese Animation in America." *Film Quarterly* 49, no. 1 (1995): 2–15.

Nicholelis, Miguel. *Beyond Boundaries.* New York: St. Martin's Griffin, 2012.

Nichols, Bill, ed. *Movies and Methods: Volume II.* Berkeley: University of California Press, 1985.

O'Brien, Geoffrey. *The Phantom Empire.* New York: W.W. Norton, 1993.

Oldham, John, Daniel Carlat, Richard Friedman, and Andrew Nierenberg, reply by Marcia Angell. "'The Illusions of Psychiatry': An Exchange." *New York Review of Books,* August 18, 2011. In response to "The Illusions of Psychiatry" from the July 14, 2011, issue; "The Epidemic of Mental Illness: Why?" from the June 23, 2011, issue.

Oldham, John, M.D., President, American Psychiatric Association. In response to "The Illusions of Psychiatry" from the July 14, 2011, issue; The Epidemic of Mental Illness: Why?" June 23, 2011. *New York Review of Books*. August 18, 2011.

Oliver, Kelly, and Benigno Trigo. *Noir Anxiety*. Minneapolis: University of Minnesota Press, 2002.

Osborne, Jennifer. *Monsters*. New York: Del Ray Books, 2006.

O'Shea, B., and A. McGennis. "ECT: lay attitudes and experiences—a pilot study." *Irish Medical Journal* 76.1 (1983): 40–43.

Packer, Sharon. *Cinema's Sinister Psychiatrists*. Jefferson, NC: McFarland, 2012.

Packer, Sharon. *Dreams in Myth, Medicine, and Movies*. Westfield, CT: Praeger, 2002.

Packer, Sharon. *Movies and the Modern Psyche*. Westfield, CT: Praeger, 2007.

Packer, Sharon. "Recalling Total Recall." http://www.hcplive.com/publications/mdng-Neurology/2011/february_2011/psych_in_film.

Packer, Sharon. "Recalling Total Recall." *MDng Magazine*, Psychiatry/Neurology Edition. February 2011.

Packer, Sharon. *Superheroes and Superegos: The Minds Behind the Masks*. Santa Barbara: ABC-CLIO, 2007.

Parkinson, David. *History of Film*. New York: Thames & Hudson, 1995.

Penley, Constance, Elizabeth Lyon, Lynn Spigel and Janet Bergstrom, eds. *Close Encounters: Film, Feminism, and Science Fiction*. Minneapolis: University of Minnesota Press, 1991.

Penley, Constance, and Andrew Ross. "Cyborgs at Large: Interview with Donna Haraway." In *Technoculture*, edited by Constance Penley and Andrew Ross. Minneapolis: University of Minnesota Press, 1991. 1–20.

Pennington, Jody. *The History of Sex in American Film*. Westport, CT: Praeger, 2007.

Percy, Walker. *Lost in the Cosmos; or, The Last Self–Help Book*. New York: Farrar, Straus & 1983.

Picart, Caroline. "Re-Birthing the Monstrous: James Whale's (Mis)Reading of Mary Shelley's Frankenstein." *Critical Studies in Mass Communication* 15, no. 4 (1998): 383–96.

Pierson, Michele. *Special Effects: Still in Search of Wonder*. New York: Columbia University Press, 2002.

Pirie, David. *A Heritage of Horror. The English Gothic Cinema 1946–72*. New York: Equinox, 1974.

Poe, Edgar Allan. "The System of Doctor Tarr and Professor Feather [Fether]." In *Edgar Allan Poe, Great Tales and Poems of Edgar Allan Poe*. New York: Pocket Books, 1951.

Polan, Dana. *Power and Paranoia*. New York: Columbia University Press, 1986.

Poole, F. Scott. *Monsters in America: Our Historical Obsession with the Hideous and the Haunting*. Waco: Baylor University Press, 2011.

Poole, W. Scott. *Satan in America*. Lanham, MD: Rowman & Littlefield, 2009.

Porter, Roy. *Madmen: A Social History of Madhouses, Mad-Doctors & Lunatics*. Stroud, Gloucestershire: Tempus, 2006.

Poster, Mark, ed. *Jean Baudrillard: Selected Writings*. Stanford: Stanford University Press, 1988.

Prawer, S. S. *Caligari's Children*. Oxford: Oxford University Press, 1980.

Pye, Michael, and Lynda Myles. *The Movie Brats: How the Film Generation Took Over Hollywood*. New York: Holt, Rinehart, 1979.

Ramsaye, Terry. *A Million and One Nights: A History of the Motion Picture*. New York: Simon & Schuster, 1926; rpt., New York: Touchstone, 1986.

Ranz, Jules M., Michael J. Vergare, Joshua E. Wilk, Sigurd H. Ackerman, Richard C. Lippincott, W. Walter Menninger, Steven S. Sharfstein, and Ann Sullivan. "The Tipping Point from Private Practice to Publicly Funded Settings for Early- and Mid-Career Psychiatrists." *Psychiatric Services* 57 (November 2006):1640–1643.

Rausch, Andrew J. *Turning Points in Film History*. New York: Citadel Press, 2004.

Rayner, Jonathan. *Contemporary Australian Cinema*. Manchester: Manchester University Press, 2000.

Rees, A. L. *A History of Experimental Film and Video*. London: BFI, 1999.

Reilly, Robert. *The Transcendent Adventure: Studies of Religion in Science Fiction/Fantasy*. Westport, CT: Greenwood Press, 1985.

Reinhart, Mark S. *The Batman Filmography: Live Action Features, 1943–1997*. Jefferson, NC: McFarland, 2005.

Rheingold, Howard. *The Virtual Community: Surfing the Internet*. London: Secker and Warburg, 1994.

Ricoeur, Paul. "Ideology and Utopia as Cultural Imagination." In *Being Human in a Technological Age*, edited by Donald M. Borchert and David Stewart. Athens: Ohio University Press, 1979. 107–25.

Roberts, Adam. *The History of Science Fiction*. New York: Palgrave Macmillan, 2005.

Robinson, David. *Das Cabinet des Dr. Caligari*. London: BFI, 1997.

Robinson, Frank, with Robert Weinberg and Randy Broecker. *Art of Imagination: 20th Century Visions of Science Fiction, Horror, and Fantasy*. Portland, OR: Collectors' Press, 2002.

Rochefort, DA. "Origins of the '"Third psychiatric revolution': the Community Mental Health Centers Act of 1963." *Journal Health Politics and Policy Law* 9.1 (Spring 1984): 1–30. http://jhppl.dukejournals.org/cgi/pmidlookup?view=long&pmid=6736594.

Rodley, Chris. "Crash: David Cronenberg talks about his new film [Crash] based on J. G. Ballard's disturbing techno-sex novel." *Sight and Sound* 6 (1966): 6–11.

Rodley, Chris. *Cronenberg on Cronenberg*. London: Faber & Faber, 1992.

Rogin, Michael. *Independence Day, or How I Learned to Stop Worrying and Love Enola Gay*. London: BFI, 1998.

Romanyshyn, Robert D. *Technology as Symptom and Dream*. London: Routledge, 1989.

Ross, Andrew, ed. *Science Wars*. Durham: Duke University Press, 1996.

Rothman, David. Book review of *The Treatment: The Story of Those Who Died in the Cincinnati Radiation Tests*. New England Journal of Medicine 347 (December 19, 2002): 2089–2090.

Ruppert, Peter. *Reader in a Strange Land: The Activity of Reading Literary Utopias*. Athens: University of Georgia Press, 1986.

Rushkoff, Douglas. *Cyberia: Life in the Trenches of Hyperspace*. New York: HarperCollins, 1995.

Russell, Ken. *Ken Russell: Directing Film: The Director's Art from Script to Cutting Room*. Washington, D.C.: Brassey's, 2001.

Ryan, Michael, and Douglas Kellner. *Camera Politica: The Politics and Ideology of Contemporary Hollywood Film*. Bloomington: Indiana University Press, 1988.

Salisbury, Mark. *Burton on Burton*. London: Faber & Faber, 1995.

Sanders, Stephen M., ed. *The Philosophy of Science Fiction Film*. Lexington: University Press of Kentucky, 2008.

Sardar, Ziauddin, and Sean Cubitt, eds. *Aliens R Us: The Other in Science Fiction Cinema*. London: Pluto Press, 2002.

Sarris, Andrew. *The American Cinema: Directors and Directions, 1929–1968*. New York: Dutton, 1968.

Satel, Sally, and Scott O. Lilienfeld. *Brainwashed: The Seductive Appeal of Mindless Neuroscience*. New York: Basic Books, 2013.

Scheib, Richard. *The SF, Horror and Fantasy Film Review* (1992). http://www.moria.co.nz/sf/lawnmower.htm. Accessed May 2006.

Schelde, Per. *Androids, Humanoids, and Other Science Fiction Monsters: Science and Soul in Science Fiction Film*. New York: New York University Press, 1993.

Schneider, I. "The Theory and Practice of Movie Psychiatry." *American Journal of Psychiatry* 144.8 (1987): 996–1002.

Schneider, Rebecca. *The Explicit Body in Performance*. New York: Routledge, 1997.

Schulman, Bruce J. *The Seventies: The Great Shift in American Culture, Society, and Politics*, Cambridge: Da Capo Press, 2001.

Seed, David. *Anticipations: Essays on Early Science Fiction and Its Precursors*. Syracuse: Syracuse University Press, 1995.

Segal, Howard P. "The Technological Utopians." In *Imagining Tomorrow: History, Technology, and the American Future,* edited by Joseph J. Corn. Cambridge: MIT Press, 1986. 119–136.

Segal, Lynne. *Slow Motion: Changing Masculinities, Changing Men*. London: Virago, 1990.

Shapiro, Jerome F. *Atomic Bomb Cinema: The Apocalyptic Imagination on Film*. London: Routledge, 2002.

Shea, Chris, and Wade Jennings. "Paul Verhoeven: An Interview." *Post Script* 12, no. 3 (1993): 3–24.

Shelley, Mary. *Frankenstein*. 1818. New York: Pocket Books, 2004.

Shilling, Chris. *The Body and Social Theory*. London: Sage Publications, 1993.

Shorter, Edward. *A History of Psychiatry: From the Era of the Asylum to the Age of Prozac*. New York: Wiley, 1997.

Sievers, W. David. *Freud on Broadway*. New York: Hermitage House, 1955.

Silver, Alain, and Paul Ursini. *Film Noir*. Edited by Paul Duncan. Los Angeles: Taschen, 2004.

Silver, Alain, and Elizabeth Ward. *Film Noir*, 3d ed. Woodstock, NY: Overlook Press, 1992.

Silver, Alain, and Paul Ursini. *Film Noir Reader 4*. New York: Limelight Editions, 2004.

Silverman, Kaja. "Back to the Future." *Camera Obscura* 27 (1991): 108–132.

Silverman, Kaja. *The Acoustic Mirror: The Female Voice in Psychoanalysis and Cinema*. Bloomington: Indiana University Press, 1998.

Sitney, P. Adams. *Visionary Film*, 2d ed. Edited by Paul Duncan. Oxford: Oxford University Press, 1979.

Sklar, Robert. *Movie-Made America*, rev. and updated. New York: Vintage, 1994.

Slocum, J. David. *Violence and American Cinema*. New York: Routledge, 2001.

Slusser, George E., and Eric S. Rabkin, eds. *Shadows of the Magic Lamp: Fantasy and Science Fiction in Film*. Carbondale: Southern Illinois University Press, 1985.

Smith, Don G. *The Poe Cinema: A Critical Filmography*. Jefferson, NC: McFarland, 1999.

Smith, Gavin. "Mind Over Matter." *Film Comment* 33.2 (1997): 14–29.

Smith, Ronald L. *Poe in the Media. Screen, Songs, and Spoken Words Recordings*. New York: Garland, 1990.

Sobchack, Vivian. *Screening Space: The American Science Fiction Film*, 2d ed. New York: Ungar, 1987.

Sofge, Erik. "How Real Is *RoboCop*?" *Popular Science,* February 2014.

Soister, John T. *American Horror, Science Fiction and Fantasy Feature Films, 1913–1929*. Jefferson, NC: McFarland, 2012.

Soren, David. *The Rise and Fall of the Horror Film*, rev. ed. Baltimore: Midnight Marquee, 1997.

Springer, Claudia. "The Pleasure of the Interface." *Screen* 32.3 (1991): 303–323.

Stevenson, Jack. *Addicted: An Illustrated Guide to Drug Cinema*. London: Creation Books, 2000.

Stevenson, Robert Louis. *Dr. Jekyll and Mr. Hyde*. Introduced by Vladimir Nabokov. New York: Signet Classic, 1987.

Stevenson, Robert Louis. *The Strange Case of Dr. Jekyll and Mr. Hyde*. 1886. New York: Barnes and Noble, 2003

Stewart, Garrett. "The 'Videology' of Science Fiction." In *Shadows of the Magic Lamp*, edited by George E. Slusser and Eric S. Rabkin, pp. 159–207.

Stokes, Melvyn, and R. Maltby, eds. *Hollywood Spectatorship*. London: BFI, 2001.

Strickfaden, Kenneth. *Dr. Frankenstein's Electrician: Harry Goldman*. Jefferson, NC: McFarland, 2005.

Suvin, Darko. *Metamorphoses of Science Fiction: On the Poetics and History of a Literary Genre*. New Haven: Yale University Press, 1979.

Tarratt, Margaret. "Monsters from the Id." In *Film Genre Reader II*, edited by Barry Keith Grant. Austin: University of Texas, 2012. 330–49.

Tart, Charles T., ed. *Altered States of Consciousness*. New York: John Wiley and Sons, 1969.

Tasker, Yvonne. *Spectacular Bodies: Gender, Genre and the Action Cinema*. London: Routledge, 1993.

Taves, Brian, and Stephen Michaluk, Jr. *The Jules Vernes Encyclopedia*. Lanham, MD: Scarecrow Press, 1996.

Telotte, J. P. *A Distant Technology: Science Fiction Film and the Machine Age*. Middletown, CT: Wesleyan University Press and Hanover, NH: University Press of New England, 1999.

Telotte, J. P. *Replications: A Robotic History of the Science Fiction Film*. Urbana: University of Illinois Press, 1995.

Telotte, J. P. *Science Fiction Film*, Cambridge: Cambridge University Press, 2001.

Telotte, J. P. *Voices in the Dark: The Narrative Strategies of Film Noir*. Urbana: University of Illinois Press, 1989.

Testa, Bart. "Technology's Body: Cronenberg, Genre, and the Canadian Ethos." *Post Script* 15, no. 1 (1995): 39–56.

Thomas, John Rhett. *The Art of Iron Man*. New York: Marvel, 2010.

Thomson, David. *The New Biographical Dictionary of Film*. New York: Knopf, 2004.

Tichi, Cecelia. *Shifting Gears: Technology, Literature, Culture in Modernist America*. Chapel Hill: University of North Carolina Press, 1987.

Todorov, Tzvetan *The Fantastic: A Structural Approach to a Literary Genre*. Translated by Richard Howard. Ithaca: Cornell University Press, 1975.

Tone, Andrea. *The Age of Anxiety: A History of America's Turbulent Affair with Tranquilizers*. New York: Basic Books, 2009.

Torrey, E.F., and R.H. Yolken. "Psychiatric Genocide: Nazi Attempts to Eradicate Schizophrenia." *Schizophrenia Bulletin* 36.1 (September 16 2009): 1–7.

Tredell, Nicholas. *Cinemas of the Mind*. Cambridge: Icon Books, 2002.

Tuchman, Mitch. "Close Encounter with Steven Spielberg." *Film Comment* 14, no. 1 (1978): 49–55.

Tudor, Andrew. *Monsters and Mad Scientists: A Cultural History of the Horror Movie*. Oxford: Blackwell, 1991.

Tullock, John, and Henry Jenkins, eds. *Science Fiction Audiences: Watching Doctor Who and Star Trek*. London: Routledge, 1995.

Turkle, Sherry. *Life on the Screen: Identity in the Age of the Internet*. Guernsey: Phoenix, 1997.

Turner, Bryan S. *The Body and Society*, 2d ed. London: Sage Publications, 1996.

Tyler, Parker. *The Hollywood Hallucination*. New York: Creative Age Press, 1944.

Verne, Jules. *From the Earth to the Moon*. 1864. New York: Barnes and Noble/Aegypan Books, 2006.

Verne, Jules. *Twenty Thousand Leagues Under the Sea*. 1869. London: Puffin Books, 1993.

Vernet, Marc. "The Fetish in the Theory and History of Cinema." In *Endless Night,* edited by J. Bergstrom. Berkeley: University of California Press, 1999, pp. 88–95.

Vest, Jason P. *Future Imperfect: Philip K. Dick at the Movies*. Westport, CT: Praeger, 2007.

Virilio, Paul. *The Vision Machine*. Translated by Julie Rose. Bloomington: Indiana University Press, 1994.

Virilio, Paul. "The Last Vehicle." In *Looking Back on the End of the World,* edited by Dietmar Kamper and Christoph Wulf. New York: Semiotext(e), 1989. 106–19.

Vollmann, Jochen and Rolf Winau. "Informed consent in human experimentation before the Nuremberg code." *British Medical Journal* 313 (December 7, 1996): 1445.

Walker, Alexander. "A Movie Beyond the Bounds of Depravity." *London Evening Standard*, 6 June 1996.

Walker, Janet. *Couching Resistance*. Minneapolis: University of Minnesota Press, 1993.

Wallace, Edwin R., IV, and John Gach. *History of Psychiatry and Medical Psychology*. New York: Springer, 2008.

Walter, G. "Portrayal of ECT in movies from Australia and New Zealand." *Journal of ECT* 14 (1998): 56–60.

Wasko, Janet. *Hollywood in the Information Age*. Austin: University of Texas Press, 1995.

Weinberg, Robert. *Horror of the 20th Century*. Hong Kong: Collectors Press, 2000.

Wells, H.G. *The First Men in the Moon*. 1901. Cutchogue, NY: Modern Library Classics, 2003.

Wells, H.G. *The Invisible Man*. 1897. Harmondsworth, Middlesex: Penguin, 2002.

Wells, H.G. *The Island of Doctor Moreau*. 1896. Boston: Adamant Media, 2006.

Wells, H.G. *The Shape of Things to Come*. 1933. Harmondsworth, Middlesex: Penguin, 2006 (first published 1933).

Wells, H.G. *The War of the Worlds*. Cutchogue, NY: Modern Library Classics, 2002 (first published 1898).

Whitton, Blair. *American Clockwork Toys 1862–1900*. Exton, PA: Schiffer, 1981.

Wiener, Norbert. *Cybernetics: Or Control and Communication in the Animal and Machine*. 1948. Cambridge: MIT Press, 1965.

Wilson, Louise. "Cyberwar, God and Television: Interview with Paul Virilio." CTheory.www.ctheory.com/a-cyberwar_god.html.

Wilson, Richard Guy, Dianne H. Pilgrim, and Dickran Tashjian. *The Machine Age in America: 1918–1941*. New York: Abrams, 1986.

Wolfe, Gary. *The Known and the Unknown: The Iconography of Science Fiction*. Kent: Kent State University Press, 1979.

Wood, Robin. *Hollywood from Vietnam to Reagan*. New York: Columbia University Press, 1986.

Wright, Judith Hess. "Genre Films and the Status Quo." In *Film Genre Reader II*, edited by Barry Keith Grant. Austin: University of Texas, 2012. 41–9.

Wright, Will. *Sixguns and Society: A Structural Study of the Western*. Berkeley: University of California Press, 1975.

Wylie, Philip. *Generation of the Vipers*. 1942. Normal, IL: Dalkey Archive Press, 1996.

Žižek, Slavoj, ed. *Lacan: The Silent Partners*. London: Verso, 2006.

Internet Sources

http://www.Atkinsononfilm.com.
http://imdb.com (Internet Movie Database).
http://imdbpro.com (Internet Movie Database Professional).
http://mentalhealth.gov/statistics.
http://www.nimh.nih.gov/statistics.
http://www.ProPublica.org.
http://www.psychflix.com.
http://www.ptsd.va.gov/professional/pages/epidemiological-facts-ptsd.asp
www.yivoinstitute.org/index.php?tid=45&aid=193.

Index

Page numbers in **_bold italics_** indicate pages with illustrations.

A-bomb 108
Abbott and Costello 32, 49, 57
Abbott and Costello Meet Dr. Jekyll and Mr. Hyde 57
Abbott and Costello Meet Frankenstein 49
Abby Normal 32, 51
abstract art 2
ACA (Affordable Care Act) 83, 253n4
Academy Award 104, 128, 132, 136, 158, 172, 197, 200, 204, 231
Acid Dreams: CIA, LSD, and Sixties' Rebellion 225, 251n17
action-adventure 25, 29, 44, 74–5, 81, 133, 141, 149, 156, 163–4, 167, 169, 171, 212, 215–6
activist 19, 31, 73, 82, 99, 119, 130–1, 144, 151, 158, 210, 211, 241–2, 256ch7n11
Adams, Joe 160
Adderall 180, 182; *see also* amphetamine; meth (crystal)
addiction 14, 37–9, 51, 54, 128, 156, 173, 180, 186, 200, 208–9, 212–3, 216, 218, 222, 224, 229, 231, 242, 251n5
ADHD (Attention Deficit Hyperactivity Disorder) 180, 183, 213, 228
administrator 128, 134, 202
adoption 15, 35, ***181***
aerospace 77, 135
The Affluent Society 103
Afghanistan 43, 111
Africa 83, 85–6, 228; South Africa 32
African American 99, 132, 136, 160, 182, 201, 222, 228
afterlife 199
Agar, John ***109***
Age of Aquarius 168
Age of Exploration 64
agent (CIA, FBI or secret) ***44***, 159, 169, 189, 198, 202, 215, 231
aggression 28, 30, 95, 108, ***109***, 149, 152, ***153***, 184–5, 208, 212, 219, 220, 225–6, 231
aging 43, 59, 82–3, 90–1, 95, 110, 181, 227; *see also* anti-aging
Agrippa, Cornelius 47, 65

AIDS (Acquired Immune Deficiency Syndrome) 2, 80, 83, 110, 198–9, 223; *see also* HIV; retrovirus
Air Loom 144, 256n7
air raid 104
Alabama 31, 130
Alanon 208
Alaska 183–4
Albert Einstein College of Medicine 2, 255n34
Albertus Magnus 47, 65–6
alchemy 47, 65–6, 68, 224
alcohol 25, 51, 68, 103, 132, 146–7, 180, 186, 208, 219, 228, 251n5
alcoholism 68, 77, 103, 136, 168
Aldini, Giovanni 48
Algernon 184
Alice-in-Wonderland 146, 160, 201, 226
alien 12–3, 23–4, 37, ***44***, 96–9, 105–6, 108–9, ***112***, 112–4, 116–9, ***120***, 120–2, 127, 143, 166, 178, ***179***, 189, 222–3, 255n30
Alien (film) 39
alienist 22, 47
Allegory of the Cave 201, 226, 229; *see also* Plato
Allen, Woody 104
Alsace-Lorraine 66
alter ego 55, 217
Altered States 37, 55
ALZ-112/3 84–5, 118
Alzheimer, Alois 188
Alzheimer's Disease 12, 43, 52, 82–4, 136, 139, 156, 177, 181–2, 188, 253n3
amanita (*Amanita muscaria*) 218; *see also* fly agaric
Amazing Stories 63, 72
American Hustle 163, 227, 231
American Indian 154, 165
American Journal of Psychiatry 28, 103, 106, 168
American Psychiatric Association (APA) 2, 15, 18, 19, 25, 28, 31–2, 36, 57, 103, 144, 156, 168, 173, 209, 251n5, 256ch9n5
American Psycho 227
amitriptyline 227
amnesia 41, ***44***

amphetamine 168, 179, 218–9, 222, 224, 228–31, 251n5
amputee 6, 79, 214
Amsterdam 209
amygdala 8, 28, 152
amyloid 181
anabolic steroid 95, 179, 231, 251n5
Analyze That 23
Analyze This 23
"anatomy is destiny" 35, 87, 140
androgen 90, 95; *see also* anabolic steroid; low "T" syndrome; testosterone
android 39, 65
Androids, Humanoids and Other Science Fiction Monsters 141, 256ch8n1
The Andromeda Strain (book) ***26***, 28
Andy Warhol's Frankenstein 50
anima 76
animation 27, 39, 46, 49, 66, 76–7, 123, 127, 193, 201, 226, 229, 255n36
anthropology 2, 16, 28, 59, 62, 103, 138, 205, 249ch1n3, 256ch8n1
anti-aging 43, 90, 95, 110
antibiotic 90, 214
anti-psychiatry 14–5, 29–31, 34, 129–30, 229, 253n22, 255n3, 255n7
anti–Semitism 71–2, 92, 132
anti-war 15, 30, 50, 150–1
Antwone Fisher 158
anus 110, 214
anxiety 18, 42, 83, 94, 105, 174, 228
APA *see* American Psychiatric Association
ape 12–3, 23, 37, 43, 55, 60, 80, ***81***, 82–7, 89, 91–4, 96, 133, 136, ***138***, 138–9, ***181***, 181–2, 184, 188, 196, 252–3n2, 253n9, 256ch7n11, 257ch10n6, 257ch10n7
The Ape 92
The Ape Man 93
apocalypse 9, 26, 41, 63, 192, 198, 200–1
Apollo 11 125
Aquinas, St. Thomas 65, 76
Arbus, Diane 115–6
archaeologist 62

"Are We Automata?" 67
Aricept 182
Aristotle 76, 176, 195
Arkansas 112, 130
Arkham, Dr. Jeremiah 213
Arkham Asylum 213
Arlen, Richard **58, 85**
Armstrong, Neil 133
arrest 77, 98, 151, 154, 161, 227
art 2, 43, 50, 69, 132, 103, 143–4, 147, 157, 166, 192, 205, 192, 250*n*19, 256*n*7, 256*n*8, 256*n*10, 257*ch*11*n*8; see also Art Deco; outsider art
Art Deco 69
artificial intelligence (AI) 64–5, 177, 241
artificial limb 6, 61, 79
The Artist's Dream 192
Aryan 85, 134–5
Asian death syndrome 199
Asimov, Isaac 77, 251*ch*2*n*7
Asperger's *see* Autism-Spectrum Disorder
assassination 80, 130–1, 136, 157, 159, 161, 176, 183, 198, 215, 223–4, 230–1, 241, 243
Assyria 205
astronaut 80, 82, 100, 104–5, **138**, 193, 252–3*n*2, 254*ch*5*n*2
The Astronomer's Dream (aka *Man in Moon*) 192
asylum 9, 22, 47, 50, 73, 86, 102, 117, 144, 213, 250*n*6, 250*n*8; superintendent 22, 47; see also Arkham Asylum
atavism 47, 199, 239
Atlantis (film) 192
Atlas Shrugged 103
Atomic Age 39
Attack of the 50 Foot Woman 108
attorney 20, 133, 180, 199
Atypical Anti-Psychotic (AAP) 57, 157
auditory 15, 118, 145, 159; nerve 145
Australia 171, 198, 251*n*5
autism *see* Autism-Spectrum Disorder
Autism-Spectrum Disorder (ASD) 95, 101, 121, 128, 186, 213; see also Asperger's; autism
automatic talking 72
automatic writing 72
automaton 11, 23, 35, 38, 61, 67–9, 73, 79, 127, 157, 159, 192, 194
avatar 7, 100, 208, 210, 236
The Avengers 8
aversion therapy 219
Axelrod, Julius 31
Aykroyd, Dan 104
Ayres, Lew 106

baby 42, 84, 101, **142, 181,** 186–8, 228, 236, 257*ch*10*n*9; see also crack, crack baby; *Rosemary's Baby*
Baby Boomer 43, 45, 50, 82, 99, 101, 104, 111, 181
Babylonia 201, 205

Bacon, Francis 197, 225, 257*ch*11*n*8
Bacon, Kevin 199
bacterial meningitis 111; *see also* meningitis
The Bad Seed 15, 35
BAFTA 200
Baggot, (William) King 54
Bajoran 236
Balaoo
Baldessarini, Ross 31
Baldwin, William 199
Bale, Christian 227–8
Ballard, J.G. 101, 192, 254*n*5
ballet 38, 61, 68–70, 192, 206, 230, 242
Banner, Dr. Bruce 8–10, 23, 55
Bardo 197, 225
Barnard, Dr. Christian 32
Barnes, Bucky 243
Baron Frankenstein 127
Baron Munchausen's Dream 192
Barrymore, John 54–5
Bates, Norman 56, 241
Bateson, Gregory 230
Batman 2, 70, 145, 213, 227, 255*n*25
Batman 74, 117, 123, 145–7, 157, 161, 211, 213, 243, 252*ch*4*n*4, 252*ch*4*n*10
Batman and Robin 199
Batman: Arkham City 213
Batman Begins 41, 204
Batman Forever 199
batteries 6, 41, 226, 235
Battlestar Galactica 24
Baudrillard, Jean 201
La Bayadère 242
BBAs (Big-Brained Aliens) 13, 96–7, 116
BCI (Brain-Computer Interface) 163
Beach Boys 147
Beatles 50
Beaubien, Jason 112
A Beautiful Mind 96
Beauty & the Beast 204
Beckinsale, Kate 171
Bedlam (Bethlem Royal Hospital) 144
Beer Hall Putsch 71
Beethoven 219–21, **221**
The Beggar's Dream 192
behavior 10, 13–5, 19, 23, 27, 29, 35–7, 50, 52, 58, 60–1, 73–5, 79, 84, 86, 92–6, 103, 106, 108, 113, 116–7, 123, 125, 129–30, 139–40, 144–6, 149, 156, 158, 165, 167, 174, 177, 188, 202, 210, 212, 220, 230, 249*ch*1*n*3, 250*n*11, 257*ch*11*n*5
behavioral conditioning 11, 23, 158, 160, 196, 219–20
behavioral science 1–2
Bekhterev, Vladimir 165
BEM (Bug-Eyed Monster) 97, 105, 116
Ben Casey 123
Benham, Henry 54
Benzedrine 219, 224, 257*ch*10*n*3; *see also* amphetamine

Berger, Hans 6
Bergin, Patrick 51
Bergman, Ingmar 229
Bergman, Ingrid 56, 218
beta-endorphin (β-endorphin) 37, 151, 223; *see also* endorphin
Bethke, Bruce 63
Bethlem Royal Hospital (Bedlam) 144
"better living through chemistry" 151
Beyond Boundaries 194
Beyond Freedom and Dignity 219
Bible 26, 29, 69, 77, 135, 184, 201, 205, 222, 224–5, 229, 257*ch*10*n*6
Big-Brained Aliens (BBAs) 13, 96–7, 116
Big Pharma 61, 82–3, 157, 180, 213; *see also* Pharma; pharmceuticals
Big Tobacco 212
billionaire 6, 19, 78–9, 107, 155, 163, 204, 210
biochemistry 77, 183
bioengineering 1, 6–7, 11, 61, 73–7, 79, 194, 235
bioethics 83; *see also* medical ethics
biological psychiatry 1, 3, 5, 19–21, 103, 142, 199, 212, 253*n*20; *see also* neuropsychiatry
biology 14–5, 18–9, 29, 34–5, 58, 60, 73, 76, 87, 95, 98, 101–3, 105–6, 123, 128, 139–40, 145, 148, 151, 165–6, 173, 182, 188–9, 192–4, 199–200, 207, 236–7, 240; *see also* molecular biology
bionic ear 6
Bionic Woman 7
bio-port (bioport) 214–5
biopsy 16
bio-science fiction 13
bipolar disorder 56
Birmingham, Alabama 130
birth defect 222; *see also* mutation
bisexuality 222–3
The Black Door **17**
Black Like Me 133
Black Muslim 158
black op 183
Black Panthers 222
black shakes 157
The Black Sleep 118
Black Swan 230
Blade Crawler 74
Blade Runner 7, 23, 38, 49, 61, 63, 74–7, 80, 114, 194–5, **195**, 227, 252*n*14
blaxploitation 135–6, **137**
A Blind Bargain 89
Block, Jerrold 208
Blom, August 192
blood 93–4, 125, 128, 173, 183, 194, 198, 211, 223; blood flow 125, 194, 213; blood pressure 64, 193, 196, 235; blood sugar 33, 64, 92; blood tests 93; blood transfusion 223, 258*n*7; blood vessel 125, 196; bloodstream 135, 249*ch*1*n*3; clot 249*ch*1*n*3
Blood of a Poet 204

body horror 188
Boesky, Ivan 163
Bogart, Humphrey 56
Bond, James 25, 146, 185
Bonham Carter, Helena 51
Borderline Personality Disorder (BPD) 121, 186–8
The Borg 236
Borscht Belt 32, 51
Bosch, Hieronymus 2
Boston Children's Hospital *112*
Boulle, Pierre 81
The Bourne Legacy 177, 183–4, 231
bra burnings 82
Bradbury, Ray 148
Braga, Alice 176
brain 16–45, *17*, *33*, *38*; *see also* Decade of the Brain; Traumatic Brain Injury (TBI))
B.R.A.I.N. 96
brain chip 12, 30, 40, 50, 141–4, 149, 151, 157–61, 16-4, 210, 231
Brain-Computer Interface (BCI) 163
brain damage 28, 43, 136, 166, 173, 189; *see also* Traumatic Brain Injury (TBI)
brain death 12, 16, 36, 175, 250n13
brain drain 12, 23, 91, 104, 106, 141–3, 144–7, 149, 161, 164, 210
The Brain Eaters 106, 109–10, *113*, 113–4
brain exchange 12–3, 18, 23–4, 39
The Brain from Planet Arous 13, 106, 108, *109*
brain implant 6, 28, 30, 79, 151–2, 154–5, 157, 159, 162, 171, 232
brain machine 7, 12, 70, 120, 140–2, 146, 161, 164, 210, 252ch4n4, 252ch4n10
The Brain That Wouldn't Die (comic) *100*, 115
The Brain That Wouldn't Die (film) *17*, 100, 106, 114, *115*, 121, 125
brain wave 6, 61, 79, 193, 249n7
Brainstorm (1965) 194
Brainstorm (1983) 7, 39, 42, 194–8, 200, 202, 204, 226
brainwash 34, 98, 105, 129, 158–60, 197, 243, 251n20, 254n13
Brake, Professor Mark 71
Branagh, Kenneth 51
Brando, Marlon 59, 86
Brave New World 218
Bread of Dreams 221
Breton, André 72
Breughel, Peter the Elder 2
Bride of Frankenstein 49, 145
Bridges, Beau 230
A Brilliant Madness 96
Broadway 15, 53, 55, 149
Broca, Paul 59, 138–9
Broderick, Matthew 206
Bronx 49, *115*, 116
The Brood 36, 179, 187
Brooks, Mel 32, *33*, 50
Brown v. Board of Education 99, 130
Brown-Séquard 89–90; Brown-Séquard syndrome 89–90

Brugada syndrome (Asian death syndrome) 199
Buck Rogers in 21st Century 24
Bug-Eyed Monster (BEM) 97, 105, 116
Burgess, Anthony 219
Burke, Katherine **58**
Burning Chrome 154–5
Burroughs, William 37, 214, 218
Burton, Tim 82
Bush, George, Sr. 18, 27, 142, 250n14
Butenandt and Ruzicka 96
Butler, Gerard 210
Butterfield, Asa 67
Byron, Lord George 47
BZ 219

The Cabinet of Dr. Caligari 9, **48**, 50, 54, 107, 116–7, 143, 204, 257ch10n7
Caesar *81*, 84–5, *181*, 182, 188, 257ch10n6–7
Cahn, Edward 119
Cain 224
Caine, Michael 40, 56–7
California Substance Abuse Treatment Facility and State Prison 200
call girl 40
Cambodia 198
Cameron, Ewan 27, 34
Canadians 34, 90, 122
cancer 43, 250n15, 251n6
Cape Canaveral 100
Captain America 183, 243
Captain America: First Avenger 231, 243
Captain America: Winter Soldier 241–2
Capt. Kirk 57, 176
Captive Wild Woman 94
Carey, Benedict 171
Carmel, Eddie *115*
Carradine, John 94, 119
Carrel, Dr. Alex 87
Carrera, Barbara 40
Carrey, Jim *172*, 172–3, **189**
Carrie 224
Carroll, Lewis 201
Cartesian dualism 55, 66–7; *see also* Descartes, René
Casablanca 56
"The Cask of Amontillado" 178
Cat People 94, 192
catatonia 80, 154, 190
catharsis 10, 249n10
Catholicism 131
The Cell 18, 41, 202
Centers for Disease Control (CDC) 110; CDC.gov 112
Central Nervous System (CNS) 6, 23, 78, 110–1
cerebral cortex 61, 67, 116, 119, 129, 138
Cerebral Spinal Fluid (CSF) 31, 37, 89, 93, 110, 135, 214, 253n24
Cerebrovascular Attack (CVA) *see* stroke

Cerletti, Ugo 92, 253n21
Cesare 9, 22, 50, 54, 107, 115–7, 257ch10n7
CGI (Computer-Generated Imagery) 7, 12, 27, 40, 55, 171, 191, 204, 206
Chan, Charlie 145
Chaney, Lon, Sr. 89
Change of Mind 31, 133–4
chaplain 220
character flaw 77
Charly 18354
chemicals 15, 51, 54–5, 57, 74, 84–5, 219, 151, 168, 171, 173, 178, 182–3, 185–8, 223–5, 231; biochemicals 38; chelation 173; neurochemicals 6, 31, 50, 78, 84, 150, 158; restraints 102; warfare 145; *see also* alchemy
Chestnut Lodge 19–20, 33, 36, 250n9, 251n15–6
Chicago 50
Chicago Seven 151
child psychiatry 102
chimpanzee (chimp) 60, 81–4, *138*, 226, 257ch10n6
China 64, 145–6, 155, 159, 179
Chinese Opium Den 216
Christianity 107, 236
The Christmas Dream 192
chromosome 224
Chung, David 223
CIA 33–4, 105–6, 108, 129, 134–5, 183–4, 198, 225, 243, 254n1, 254n13
cigarettes 25, 212
Cimino, Michael 149
cinematography CGI (Computer-Generated Imagery) 11, 77, 108, 132, 183, 191–2, 195, 204, 230
circus 60, 94, 115, *115*
Civil Rights 31, 80, 82–3, 86, 98–9, 121, 125, 130–2, 134, 136, 157, 160–1, 252ch5n1; Civil Rights Bill of 1964 131; civil rights marches 82
Clarity 186
Clarke, Mae 48
class conflicts 161
classic SF 12–3, 39, 81, 98, 104–5, 116, 125, 133, 182, 222
classical conditioning 219; *see also* behavioral conditioning
Claymation 27
Clift, Montgomery 128
clinic 21, 95, 110, 184
clinicaltrials.gov 7
Clive, Colin 48
clock 66–7, 164, 176
The Clockmaker's Dream 192
A Clockwork Orange 219–20, *221*
Close Encounters of Third Kind 24, 105, 195
club kids 222
CNN 112
cocaine 37, 39, 42, 51, 54, 57–8, 167, 170, 182, 186, 222, 224, 251n5; Cocaine Papers 51, 57–8
cochlear implant 6, 145

The Cocoanuts 91
Cocteau, Jean 204
codeine 38
coffee 25
cognition 15, 17, 27, 92, 94, 106, 179
Cognitive Behavioral Therapy (CBT) 202
Cole, Jack *100*, 115
collective unconscious 37, 77, 237, 239–40
College of Charleston 131
The Colossus of New York 120–2, *127*, 242
Columbine 208
coma 14, 33, 36, 92, 96, 106, 118, *175*, 175–6, 202, 205
The Combine 154
comedian 32, *38*, 50–1
comedy 4, 23, 25, 32, 44, 68, 91, 125, 136, 171, 173–5, 180, 184, 189, 216
comic book (comics) 2, 6, 8, 10, 39, 55, 66, 77–8, 99, *100*, 17, 115, 122, 133, 145–7, 157, 206, 243, 252n10, 255n25; Comic-Con 2; Comics Code 99
Communism 98, 99, 101, 104, 158, 160
The Company 224; *see also* CIA
Computer-Generated Imagery *see* CGI
computers 6–7, 12, 18–20, 23–4, 27–8, 38–42, 44, 49, 55, 61, 63–5, 79, 119–20, 142, 149, 152, 154–5, 162–6, 171, 177, 196–7, 201–2, 205–7, 210, 212, 215, 221, 226, 233–7, 241–3, 249n6, 256–7n1; games 41; hackers 154–5, 201, 206, 226, 233; programmers 23, 152, 201, 210, 221, 233; virus 64
Conan Doyle, Arthur 51
concentration camp 31, 104
The Condemned 210
conditioning *see* behavioral conditioning
Conehead 104
conformity 34
Congress 21, 99, 130, 157, 192
Congressional Medal of Honor 158
Connecticut 73, 140, 208
Connery, Sean 25, 222
Conrad, William 194
consciousness 12, 38–9, 65, 70, 72, 76, 82–3, 98, 105, 117, 132, 151, 164, 173, 176–7, 193, 205, 208, 228, 233–4, 236–7, 239, 241–2; *see also* collective unconscious
conspiracy 73–4, 83
Conspiracy Theory 33, 184, 231
Contagion 163, 196
control 6–7, 10, 12, 21, 28–30, 33–4, 39, 41, 52–4, 57, 60–1, 63–5, 70, 74, 77, 79, 81, 83–4, 94–5, 98, 101, 103, 105–7, 111, 117, 120–3, 127, 129, 138, 142, 147–8, *150*, 151–2, 158–9, 161–4, 166–9, 177, 180, 182, 184, 192, 202, 205, 208–12, 215–6, 220–1, 233–5,

235, 236–7, 241, 249n6, 255n7; mind 30, 33, 44, 98, 101, 105, 116–7, 151–2, 161, 168, 184; thought 120, 147–8, 249n6
controlled medicines 95, 151, 180
convict 29, 47, 87, 89, 92, 95, 98, 132, 186, 198, 210
Cooper, Bradley *179*, 179–80, 231, **234**
Cooper, David 14, 129–30, 255n3
Cooper, Gary 25, 222
Coppelia 61, 68–70
Coppola, Francis Ford 221
Corinthians 229
Corman, Roger 24, 109, *113*, 117, 136, 146, 157, 255n31
cornea 32
Cornell University 2, 249ch1n1
corpse 107, 223
Corrigan, "Crash" 93–4
cosmetic psychopharmacology 169
"couch cure" 5, 10, 14, 165, 22, 102
counter-culture 15, 67
counter-transference 10
court 16, 92–3, 132, 135, 160, 176, 180, 199, 250n12
Court, Hazel *133*
Coyle, Jake 23, 25–6, 204–5
Crabtree, Arthur 122, *126*
crack 39, 42, 182, 186, 224, 228; crack baby 42, 182, 257ch10n9; epidemic 39, 42, 186, 228
cranium 49, 104, *113*
Crash 213
Craven, Wes 198–9
Crawford, Joan 99
Creature Features 119
Creature with the Atom Brain 106–7
cretinism 95, 250n7; *see also* myxedema (hypothyroidism)
Creutzfeldt-Jakob disease (CJD) 110–1, 254n20, 254n21
Crews, Frederick 129
Crichton, Michael 25, *26*, 26–30, 43, 50–1, 152
crime 29, 39, 43, 47, 49, 55, 57, 67, 87, 91, 93, 98, 108, 134, 145–6, 155, 164, 178, 182, 185–6, 192, 204, 219–20, 222, 224, 250n15
The Crimson Stain 43, 178
Cronenberg, David 27, 36, 110, 144, 161, 179, 187–8, 195, 209, 212–4, *214*, 215, 222, 224
Cruise, Tom 164, 178, 186
Cruz, James 54
crystal 64, 116, 183, 182, 216, 227
CSF *see* Cerebral Spinal Fluid
cult 28, 38, 41, 56, 62–3, 74, 80, 197, 200, 222, 226
The Curse of Frankenstein 49, 127, *133*
Cushing, Peter 127, *133*
Cybermen 236
cybernetic (surgery) 155, *156*, 236
cyberpunk 7, 13, 19, 23–4, 38–9, 41, 49, 63, 65, 120, 149, 154, 164, 185, 201, 226
cyberspace 11, 19, 36, 63, 154–5, 171, 185, 241

Cyberwar 185
cyborg 122, 147–9, *150*, 236
Cyborg 2087 147–9, *150*
cysticercosis 110
Czech 66

Daedalus 65, 78
Dafoe, Willem 215
Daka, Dr. Tito 117, 145–7, 161, 253
Dalí, Salvador 7, 12, 25, 108, 191, 193
Damon, Matt 161
A Dangerous Method 37
Daniel (person) 25
Daniel, Book of 25–26, 201
The Dark Knight 41, 204
The Dark Knight Rises 41, 227
DARPA (Defense Advanced Research Projects Agency) 7, 162–3, 169, 171, 175, 256n15, 256ch9n2
Darrow, Clarence 87
Darwin 12, 23, 37, 55, 59–60, 80, 86–7, 90
Daughter of Dr. Jekyll 57
David and Lisa 23
Dawley, J. Searle 48
Dawn of Planet of Apes 83
DBS (Deep Brain Stimulation) 145
The Dead Zone 36, 39, 195
death 51, 56–7, 69, 73, 86, 89, 92, 101, 105, 107, 110–1, 113, 115–6, 121–3, 130, 132, 143, 151, 162, 175, 178, 180, 186–7, 189, 196–7, 199–200, 210, 222–3, 225, 229–30, 242–3
death camp 132
deathbed 225
Decade of the Brain 16, 18–9, 27, 40, 76, 96, 123, 142, 164, 199
Dedalus, Stephen 65; *see also* Daedalus
The Deer Hunter 149, 195
Defense Advanced Research Projects Agency (DARPA) *see* DARPA
Defiance 159
The Defiant Ones 132
Delgado, Jose 152
delirium 75
delusion 9–10, 34, 108, 143–4, 154, 161, 170, 176, 207, 235
demagogue 71
dementia 32, 43, 52, 73, 75, 80, 82–4, 110, 119, 136, 139, 166, 171, 181–2, 188, 253n3, 257ch11n5; *see also* Frontotemporal Dementia (FTD)
Demme, Jonathan 157–8
demography 83
demon 13, 15, 22–3, 35, 50, 70, 149, *153*, 177–8, 197, 215, 223, 225, 235–6
Demon Seed 15, 23, 35, 137, 177, 235–6
"Demon with a Glass Hand" 149
De Niro, Robert 51, 179, 182
De Palma, Brian 164
Department of Defense (DOD) 183, 206

Department of Health (DOH) 112
Depp, Johnny 234, 241–3
depression 18, 20, 32–3, 42, 56, 90, 92, 95, 145–6, 152, 157, 167, 174, 186, 189–90, 227–8, 250n7; *see also* major depressive disorder
depth psychology 52, 101, 240
Dern, Bruce 135–6
Descartes, René 55, 66, 76; *see also* Cartesan dualism
desegregation 99, 130, 139
detective 40, 51, 63, 77, 164, 178
determinism 35, 87, 148, 237
Deuteronomy 56
Deutsch, Helene 142
developmental psychology 101
Dexedrine 219, 257*ch*10*n*3; *see also* amphetamine
diabetes mellitus (DM) 56, 90; *see also* sugar sickness
Diagnostic and Statistical Manual (DSM) 19, 36, 52, 57, 151, 156, 209, 249n4
Dial M for Murder 136
DiCaprio, Leonardo **203**, 204
Dick, Philip K. (PKD) 38, 40, 44, 63, 74–6, 167–70, 185–6, 216, 218, 224, 229
Dietrich, Marlene 132
differential diagnosis 1, 213
Dilaudid 38
diphtheria 104
The Discovery of Unconscious: History of Dynamic Psychiatry 104
Disney 73–4, 100, 104, **142**; Disneyland 100
dissociation 188
Dissociative Identity Disorder (DID) 52
divinity 46, 61, 114
Dmytryk, Edward 94
DNA 6, 24, 183, 242
Do Androids Dream of Electric Sheep? 63, 74
D.O.A. 229
Dr. Banner *see* Banner, Dr. Bruce
Dr. Coppelius 61
Dr. Frankenstein 32, **33**, 46–8, 50–1, 68, 121, 131
Dr. Fu Manchu 146
Dr. Jekyll 51–3, **53**, 57, 87, **88**, 89, 54–9, 216–7, **217**, 218, 226
Dr. Jekyll and Mr. Hyde 53, **53**, 87
Dr. Jekyll and Mr. Hyde (1973) 57
Dr. Jekyll and Mr. Hyde Done to a Frazzle 54
Dr. Jekyll and Sister Hyde 57
Dr. Jekyll vs. Werewolf 57
Dr. Jekyll's Dungeon of Death 57
Dr. Mabuse 22, 40, **71**, 108
Dr. Moreau 34–5, 43, 51, **58**, 58–9, **85**, 85–6, 93, 177–8
Dr. No 146
Dr. Renault's Secret 93
Doctor Who 236
The Doctor's Experiment aka *Reversing Darwin's Theory* 87
Doctors' Trial 31, 134
The Doll (Die Puppe) 69

Domergue, Faith 117, **118**
Donnie Darko 223
Donovan's Brain 13, 39, 106–7, 134
The Doors of Perception 170
dopamine 32, 61, 152, 213, 235
doppleganger 70
double bind 229–30; "doublebinding mothers" 101
double feature 13, 63, 104
Downey, Robert, Jr. 5, **8**, 77, 200, 229, 257n12
Dracula 131, 158
dream 3, 13, 25, 27, 39–42, 44, 62, 67, 72, 76–7, 93, 108, 122, 130, 141, 158–9, 161, 166, 168–9, **175**, 184, 191–4, 197–201, **203**, 204–4, 226–7, 233, 235, 254n5, 257ch11n2
The Dream of a Hindu Beggar 192
The Dream of a Poor Fisherman 192
Dream of a Rarebit Fiend 192
The Dream of an Opium Fiend 192
The Dream of Ballet Master 192
Dream Street 192
Dreamcatcher 165
Dreams in Myth, Medicine and Movies 2–3
Dreamscape 197–8, 200, 202, 204
dreamtime 62, 198
Dressed to Kill 40
Drew, Ellen 92
drive-ins 13, 104, 119, 149
A Drowned World 192
drug culture 15, 37, 50, 224, 229
Drug Themes in Science Fiction 216
drugs (illicit, non-medicinal, non-prescribed, recreational) 12, 20, 25, 39, 51–2, 54–7, 59, 77, 87, 118, 151, 155, 169, 174, 185–6, 195, 216, 219–31, 251n5, 252ch3n5, 258n10
The Drunkard's Dream 192
DTC (Direct-To-Consumer) advertising 180
The Duality of Man 53
Duke University 224
Dune 224
Dunst, Kirsten **172**
Duvall, Robert 221
dybbuk 13
dystopia 12, 29, 35, 122, 152, 154, 168, 216, 218, 221, 223, 228

Earth vs. Flying Saucers 117
Earthling 13, 104, 108
East End (London) 130
East Village 159, 168
Ecclesiastes 161
economics 19, 49, 53, 64, 70–1, 83, 99, 103–5, 146, 148, 161, 163, 207–8, 237, 250n2
ECT (Electroconvulsive Therapy) 6, 14–5, 28, 44–5, 92–3, 96, 102, 106, 144, 154, 173–4, 190, 196
Edge of Sanity 57
Edison Studios 32
EDS (Excessive Daytime Sleepiness) 180
Edwards, Vince 123

EEG (Electroencephalogram) 6, 16, 93, 193, 200
Efron, John 85
ego 19, 52, 59, 217, 237; ego psychologist 237
Egyptian 16, 167
Eichmann trial 132
Einstein, Albert 2, 71, 83
Eisenhower, Dwight D. 11, 98, 117
Eisner, Lotte 69
EKG (Electrocardiogram) 16, 193, 200
electric shock 72; *see also* ECT
electricity 6, 28, 30, 32, 41, 46, 49, 51, 63, 69, 72, 74, 76, 98–9, 118, 131, 145–6, 170, 173, 193–4, 201, 220, 249–50n4
Electroconvulsive Therapy *see* ECT
electrode 6
Electroencephalogram *see* EEG
electromagnet 6, 49, 78, 156
elephant 1
Eli Lilly 42, 90, 186
Ellenberger, Henri 104–5, 252ch3n3
Ellis, Warren 6
Ellison, Harlan 149
Elysian Fields 161
Elysium 61, 107, 161–3, 221
Emancipation 201, 131, 252ch5n1
embryonic stem cell transplant 32
EMG (Electromyelogram) 16
Emory University 6
emotion 15, 27, 29, 34, 37, 52, 61, 74–6, 80, 92, 94, 98–9, 16, 114, 123, 127–8, 139, 149, 157, 174, 179, 192–3, 196–7, 213, 227–8, 233–5, 249n10
empathy 41, 59, 75, 114, 121–2
encephalin 223
encephalitis 110, 112, 113, 223; *see also* primary amoebic meningoencephalitis
endocrinology 12–3, 21, 89–90, 94, 103, 125, 140, 167
endorphin 37, 151; *see also* beta-endorphin
England 47, 49, 101, 118
Enterprise 117, 176
Entertainment Weekly 184
entheogen 218, 254n14
environmentalism 19, 161
ephemeral 42, 222
EPI–fMRI (Echoplanar Imaging–functional Magnetic Resonance Imaging) 145
epidemic 2, 39, 42, 110, 186, 223, 228
epidemiology 83
epileptic (ictal) 28; *see also* ictal affect
epileptoid personality 28; *see also* ictal affect; personality
epinephrine 31
Equilibrium 220 1, 227 8
ER (TV show) 27
Eros 108
escapist 12, 25, 96, 213

estrogen 95
E.T. Extra-Terrestrial 101
Eternal Sunshine of Spotless Mind 25, 43, 171, *172*, 173, 184, *189*
ether 19, 63
ethology 35, 58
eugenics 35, 103
euthanize 84, *181*
Evers, Jason *17*
Evers, Medgar 130
Everything You Ever Wanted to Know about Sex* But Were Afraid to Ask 104
The Evil of Frankenstein 127
eXistenZ 37, 41, 110, 161, 212, *214*, 214–5
exopthalmos ("bug-eyes") *33*, 94
exoskeleton 162
experiment 1–2, 6, 12, 28, 30–1, 33, 35, 37, 46–7, 49, 51–2, 57–60, 73, 79, 84, 86–7, 89–92, 94, 98, 105–7, 118–9, 122–3, 132, 134–5, *137*, 139, 144–5, 148–9, 151–2, 158–60, 170, 173–4, 177–8, 181–5, 190, 195, 200, 206, *207*, 209, 218–9, 224–6, 231, 234, 236, 239, 241, 243
Exserohilum rostratum 111
Extra-Sensory Perception (ESP) 224
extraterrestrial 101
Extremis 6, 10, 78, 233
Eyes Without a Face 119

Facebook 11, 36
Fahey, Jeff *207*
Fahrenheit 451 148, 228
Fairbanks, Douglas, Sr. 205
family romance 32, 130, 251*n*14
family therapy 114, 128
The Fantastic Four 163, 187
Faraday, Michael 48
Farmer, Frances 40
Farrell, Colin 40, 63, 79, 171
fashion 223
Fatal Attraction 225
father 37, 47, 52, 56, 59, 63, 65, 67–8, 70, 72, 83–4, 98, 105, 116, 119–21, *127*, 144, 159, 163, 178, 181–2, 188–9, 192, 200, 230–1, 242; father of anatomy 59 father of cyberpunk 63; father of media studies 144; Father of Science Fiction 72
FBI 159, 175, 202, 209, 231
FDA (Food and Drug Administration) 145, 157, 180, 182, 187, 202, 228
Fear Strikes Out 56, 102
FEAST (Focal Electrically-Administered Seizure Therapy) 145
FEAT (Focal Electrical Alternating Current Therapy) 145
Feldman, Marty *33*, 51
feminist 35, 47, 53, 73–4, 86–7, 129, 139–40, 143, 148, 236, 255*n*6
The Feminist Mystique 73, 255*n*6

femme fatale see woman, evil
Fentynl 38
Ferenzi 37
Fetal Alcohol Spectrum Disorder (FASD) 186
Fetal Alcohol Syndrome (FAS) 186
fetus 42, 186, 188, 222
fever therapy 31
Fiala, George *115*
fiancée *17*, 28, 52–3, *53*, 68, *85*, 93, 108, *109*, 116, *133*, 152, *217*
Fiend Without a Face 122, *126*, 179
film critic 1, 5, 9, 22, 163–4, 175
Film Forum 23, 250–1*n*4
film noir 22, 63, 74, 93, 107, 134, 164, 194, 257*ch*11*n*7
fin-de-siècle 18, 55, 89, 183, 250*n*2
Final Solution 92
Firestarter 224
First Person Shooter (FPS) 208
Fishburne, Laurence 201, 226
Fisher, Terence *133*
Fissure of Rolando 109
Fixmer, Andy 249*ch*1*n*1
flapper 53
flash drive 12, 161, 164–5, 169, 175
flash-forward 12, 164
Flash Gordon 146
flashback 12, 22, 39, 44, 92–3, 122, 161, 164–5, 170, 173, 183, 194–5, 225, 250*n*1
Flatliners 16, 40, 199
Fleming, Alexander 31
Fleming, Victor 5, 56, 143–4, 204, 257*n*14
Fletcher, Louise 129, 154, 196–7
floppy baby syndrome 186
flower children 168, 219
fly agaric 218
*f*MRI (functional Magnetic Resonance Imaging) 15, 145
Food and Drug Administration *see* FDA
Forbidden Planet 120, 176, 178, *179*
Ford, Harrison 63, 74–5, *195*, 227
Foster, Jodie 162
Foucault, Michel 14
Fountain of Youth 177
FPS *see* First Person Shooter
framing device 9, 81, 114, 117, 193, 249*n*8, 249*n*9
France 66, 71–2, 93, 104, 108, 230
Frances 40
franchise 39, 49, 61, 146, 160, 198, 221, 239, 243
Franco, James 83, 181
Franju, Georges 119
Franken, Al 157
Frankenheimer, John 34, 59, 86, 220
Frankenstein 32, 39, 46–7, *48*, 50–1, 65–8, 121, 131, *133*, 136, 146
Frankenstein (monster) 46–51, 66–8, 148, 158, 234
Frankenstein, Dr. Victor *33*, 46–7, 50–1, 121, 127, 131, *133*
Frankenstein and the Monster from Hell 127
Frankenstein Created Woman 127

Frankenstein Meets Wolf Man 49, 243
Frankenstein Must Be Destroyed 49, 127
Frankenstein: Or, Modern Prometheus 46–7, 65
Frankenstein: True Story 50
Frankenstein's Army 51
Frankfort, Germany 150
Frankl, Viktor 104
Freddy (Kruger) 158, 198–9, 257*ch*11*n*10
free will 61, 117, *118*, 120, 220, 226, 234
Freedom Rides 130
Freeman, Walter J., II 30, 34, 96, 102–3, 106, 122, 128, 175
Fremen 224
The French Connection 231
"French Freud" *see* Lacan
Freud 2, 32, 15, 18–9, 21–2, 30, 34–5, 37, 42, 47, 51–2, 57–9, 68–9, 72–3, 75–6, 86–7, 94, 97, 105, 114, 128–30, 138–41, 143, 164–5, 191, 199, 218, 224, 237, 239–40, 249–50*ch*1*n*4, 250*n*8, 250*n*19, 251*n*14, 251*ch*3*n*2, 252*ch*3*n*3, 253*n*11, 255*n*6, 256*ch*8*n*2
Freud-bashing 129
Freudianism 11, 14, 97, 101–3, 114
Friedan, Betty 73, 255*n*6
From Caligari to Hitler 22, 72
From Earth to Moon 104
Fromm, Erich 19
Fromm-Reichmann, Frieda 20
frontal lobe 52, 103, 167, 186; *see also* Frontotemporal Dementia (FTD)
frontier 25, 74, 100, 204, 222
Frontier Town 74, 100
Frontotemporal Dementia (FTD) 52, 188
Frye, Dwight 48
FTD *see* Frontotemporal Dementia
fungal meningitis 111, 255*n*24; *see also* meningitis
funny farm 102
The Future of an Illusion 73
futurism 7, 25, 69, 72, 81, 83, 92, 100, 106, 188, 149, *150*, 152, 157, 162, 173, 164, 214, 219, 226, 228–9, 231, 236, 239, 242

Gabriel 200, 225
Gagarin, Yuri 100, 125
Galbraith, John Kenneth 103, 105
galvanism 33, 129, 131
The Gamer 236
gaming 157, 206–10, *211*, 213–5, 242; gaming addiction 209; gaming-anon 208; *see also* online gaming
gamma ray 8
Gandhi 130
gangster 56, 92, 107, 178, 218–9; *see also* convict
Gates, Bill 210
Gaumont 87

"gay plague" 223
Gaye, Gregory 107
gender 29, 53, 58, 86, 140, 201, 214
general paresis of the insane (neurosyphilis) 31, 73, 95
genetic engineer 83, 159
genetics 21, 24, 27, 35, 37, 83, 253n24
genocide 35
germ theory of disease 86
German Expressionism 3, 9, 40, **48**, 50, 54, 74, 107, 134, 143, 164, 252n10
Germany 9, 30–1, 54, 59, 60, 66, 69–70, 72, 74, 106–7, 114, 132, 134–5, 143, 150–1, 164, 166, 175, 187, 222, 243, 252ch4n9, 256ch9n6, 258ch13n4
Gernsback, Hugo 72, 189
Ghost 197, 225
Gibson, Mel 184
Gibson, William 19, 24, 36, 40, 63, 154–5, **156**, 157, 161–2, 196, 231, 256ch8n7; books 24
Girard, Bernard 29
gland 12, 18, 89–91, 93–4, 119, 125, 167, 253n17, 253n18
Glass, Philip 204
glucose 15, 92, 125, 194, 213
Gnosticism 224
Go and Get It 89
Goffman, Erving 14
The Golden Age of Automata 67–8
Golden Gate Bridge **81**
Golden Globe 128
"Golden Years of Cinema Psychiatry" 102, 128
Golem 66, 68
Goodall, Jane 138
gorilla 81, 84, 93–4
government 7, 14, 19, 33–4, 40, 56, 70, 74, 87, 99, 107, 110, 134–5, 147–8, 151, 157, 160, 162–3, 168, 171, 187, 194, 208, 216, 221–2, 224–5, 228, 231, 237
graft 24, 31, 87, 90–1, 105, 119, 136, 141, 215; graft host reaction 91
Grand Guignol 39
grandiosity 10, 224, 241
Graphic Medicine 2
Great Recession 64
Greek 65, 252ch3n9; Greek drama 39, 52, 59; Greek myth 29, 65, 162, 201, 226, 249n10
Green, Joseph **17**, 115
Greenberg, Joanne 19
Greenwich Village 223
Grier, Rosey 135–6, **137**
Griffin, John Howard 133
Griffith, D. W. 192, 257ch11n3
Grim Reaper 229
group therapy 102–3, 114
growth hormone 90, 95, 110, 167
Grunewald, Matthias 3
Guam 110
Guess Who's Coming to Dinner 132
Gulf War 158, 160

hacker 154–5, 201, 206, 226, 233
Haddonfield, Illinois 109

Hades 69
Haight-Ashbury (The Haight) 168
Haiti 223
HAL 149, 177
Haldol (haloperidol) 30, 57, 151; see also neuroleptic
Haley, Jack 5
Hall, Michael 210
Hall, Rebecca 78, 241
Halloween 48
Halloween 72, 109
hallucination 10, 34, 102–3, 111, 113, 144, 155, 185, 197, 200, 213, 225, 230–1
hallucinogen 33, 106, 129, 168, 170–1, 218, 224–5, 231–2, 251n5
Hammer, Mike 40
Hammer horror film 32, 49, 57, 127, 131–2
Hannibal see Lecter, Dr. Hannibal
The Happiness Cage 15, 29, 50, 146, 149, 152, **153**, 256n12
hard drive 155, 165, 233
Harley Quinn 213
Harrison Narcotics Act 54, 57, 151
Harry, Debbie 213
Harvard University 16, 28, 31, 67, 152, 168, 239
Hasselhoff, David 53
The Haunted Screen 69
Hauser's Memory 31, 107, 133–4
Hayden, Charles J. 54
Hays Code 55–6, 87; see also Production Code
Hayward, Louis 57
He, She, It 73
The Head That Wouldn't Die **17**, 114–5; see also *The Brain That Wouldn't Die*
headtrip 168
health care 25, 53, 102, 161–3, 202; health care delivery system 202
hearing aid 118
heart 5–6, 16, 19, 32–3, 35, 51, 61, 78, 170, 186, 193, 196–7, 233, 235
heathen 69
Hebrew 66, 201, 222, 224
Heche, Anne 163
hedge fund 155
Heinlein, Robert A. 109, **113**
Hell 63, 69, 127, 185, 197, 225–6
Hell's Angels 168, 219
Helm, Brigette 70, **147**
helminth (worm) 110
hemodialysis (dialysis) 173
hemophilia 223
Henderson, Lucius 53
Hepburn, Katharine 128
Herbert, Frank 224
the herd 236, 239
heroic age 70
heroin 37–8, 200, 213, 222–3, 228–9, 251n5
Herophilus 59
Heston, Charlton 82, **138**, 138–9
High Noon 25, 222
Hillel 135
Hindu 192, 236

Hippie 129, 218
hippocampus 165, 194
Hiroshima 100
historian 1, 33, 53, 71, 85, 131, 144, 199, 250n5, 255ch7n7
history of medicine 2, 12, 110
history of psychiatry 2, 251n1
Hitchcock, Alfred 4, 25, 56–7, 72, 119, 136, **150**, 183, 194
HIV 223
hive mind 236, 239–40
Hobart, Rose **53**
Hoffman, Herman 119
Hoffmann, ETA 68–9
Hollywood 5, 11, 19, 81, 101, 145, 160–1, 230
Hollywood Ten 160
Holocaust 35, 107, 132, 135, 145
Holy Ghost 236
home health aide 84
L'Homme au Cerveau Greffe 31
Homo sapiens 86, 138
homophobia 128
homosexual 223; see also bisexual
Honest Abe 160
Hong Kong 216
Hopkins, Anthony 158
Hopkins, Miriam **53**, 55, **88**
Hopper, Edward 74
hormone 4, 13, 23–4, 90–1, 94–5, 110, 119, 125, 167, 250n7, 254n21; see also gland
horror 4, 23, 33, 35, 47, 49, 51, 57, 65, 72, 79, 89–93, 106–9, 116, 118–9, 121, 123, 127–8, 131–2, 134–5, 141, 146, 184, 187–8, 198–9, 212, 225, 233
The Horror of Frankenstein 49, 127
horror–SF hybrid 23–4
hospital 2, 15, 20, **26**, 29, 75, 94, 96, 102, **112**, 119, 121, 123, 128–9, 136, 144, 150, 157, 159, 163, 176, 197, 200, 227, 249n4, 250n12
House of Frankenstein 49
House of Pain 59
House Un-American Activities Committee (HUAC) 98
Hudson, Rock 199
Hughes, John 223
Hugo 67, 192
Hugo Award 63, 134, 154, 189
The Hulk 8–10, 55, 163, 187
human 5–7, 11, 13, 15, 23, 26, 28–9, 31, 33–9, 41, 43, 46–7, 49, 52, 55, **58**, 58–64, 74–8, **78**
Human Growth Hormone (HGH) 90, 95, 110, 167, 254n21
The Human Machine (*L'Homme Machine*) 67, 69
human potential movement 184
human rights 182, 210, 222
humanitarianism 55, 63, 121–2, 162, 183
The Hunchback of Notre Dame 89
Hungarians 37, 86, 130
The Hunger Games 163
Hunter, Kim **138**
Huxley, Aldous 76, 170, 218
Hyams, Leila **85**

hybrid 23, 93, 119, 131, 133, 141, 184, 233, 236
Hyde, Mr. Edward 51-3, **53**, 54-8, 87, **88**, 89, 216, **217**, 218, 226
Hydra 243
hydrocephalic idiot 186, 218
hypnosis 9, 14, 22, 50, 54, 72, 165, 191, 146
hysteria 139, 165, 249ch1n1, 258ch13n4

I, Frankenstein 51
"I Have a Dream" 130
I, Jury 40
I Never Promised You a Rose Garden 19
I, Robot 77, **78**
Ibsen, Henrik 176
Icarus 65
Ice-T 155
ictal affect 28
ICU (Intensive Care Unit) 193; ICU psychosis 200
id 8, 52, 55, 178
identity 6, 10-1, 36, 4, 52, 56, 75-8, 86, 93, 105, 135, 146, 166-7, 169, 233, 237, 258ch14n1
Illinois 109, 251n6
The Imaginarium of Dr. Parnassus 25, 42
imagineer 73, **142**
imipramine 227
immigration 110, 161-2
immune response 91, 110, 121
immunology 21
immunosuppression 91
In Dreams 200, 255n32, 257n12
in utero 84, 95, 182, 186
inanimate 6, 49, 76
Inception 25, 41-2, **203**, 204-5
The Incredible Two-Headed Transplant 31, 135
incubi(us) 13
Independence Day 223
India 64
individuality 34, 114, 167, 236
Industrial Age (Industrial Revolution) 48, 64
infantile paralysis 111; *see also* polio
Infectious Disease (ID) 111, 114
The Infinite Worlds of H. G. Wells 178
inflation 70
influencing machine 142-5, 152, 1544, 159, 161, 256n7
infomercial 7-8, **234**
Information Age 20, 36
information mining 64
ingestion 110
inhalation 110
Inherit the Wind 87
inhibition 42, 52, 54, 219, 227
injection 110
inoculation 110
insanity 9, 29, 31, 73, 95, 117, 204, 256n8, 256ch8n10
insider trading 155
Institutional Review Board (IRB) 7, 44, 173

insulin coma 14, 92, 96, 106; Insulin Coma (shock) Therapy (ICT) 14
insurance 41, 57, 83, 209
intelligence 13, 42, 64-5, 80, 84-5, 95-6, 108, 120, 122-3, 127, 135, 138, 140, 149, 166, 177-8, **179**, 180-5, 188, 201, 206, **207**, 221, 241-2, 257ch10n6-7
Intensive Care Unit *see* ICU
International Harvester 91
Internet addiction 156, 209
The Interpretation of Dreams (book) 42, 76, 165, 191, 199
inter-titles 54, 191
intrathecal 110, 214
intrauterine 186, 188, 218, 228; *see also* in utero
Invaders from Mars 116
Invasion of the Body Snatchers 34, 74, 114
Invasion of the Saucer-Men 119, **120**
The Invisible Boy 110, 119-20, 177
iodine 95, 103, 250ch1n7
iPhone 64, 202, 216
IRB *see* Institutional Review Board
Irish American 61
Iron Legion 79, 233
iron lung 78-9, 101, 111, **112**
Iron Man 5-7, **8**, 10-1, 23, 41, 62, 77-9, 97, 233, 240, 249n9
Iron Man (noun) 5-6, 10-1, 77-9
The Island of Dr. Moreau 34, 59, **85**, 86
Island of Lost Souls **58**, 59, **85**, 86, 89
Israelite 69, 77
It Conquered World 117
Italian 67, 92, 192, 221
IV drug use 223

"jacking in" 154
Jacob's Ladder 197, 199, 219, 225, 231
JAMA 208
James, William 67, 239
James Bond 25, 146, 185
Der Januskopf (*Janus Head* or *Janus-Faced*) 54
Japan 145-6, 155, **156**, 158, 176
Japanazi 117, 145-6
Jarvik, Robert 233
Jarvik Heart, Inc. 233
J.A.R.V.I.S. 233
Jason 158
Java 93
The Jazz Singer 72
Jekyll and Hyde 56
Jekyll & Hyde (television) 57
"Jekyll and Hyde" personality 56-7
Jekyll and Hyde ... Together Again 57
The Jewish Giant **115**; *see also* Carmel, Eddie
Jews 14, 71, 236
Jezebel 225
JFK *see* Kennedy, John Fitzgerald
John Q 163
Johnny Mnemonic 24, 40, 154-5, **156**, 157, 161

Johnson, Lyndon B. 131
Johnson & Johnson 157
The Joker 213
Jones, Tommy Lee 189
Jordan, Neil 200
Journal of Psychotherapy Practice and Research 143
Journey to Center of Earth 104
Joyce, James 65
Judgment at Nuremberg 132
Jukes family 15
Jung 6, 22, 37, 52, 55, 65, 218, 224, 236-7, 240
Jupiter 25
Juran, Nathan 108, **109**
Jurassic Park 28
juvenile delinquency 99, 132

Kallmann, Franz J. 102
Kandel, Eric 5, 18, 67, 76, 249n5, 252n12
Kanner, Leo 103
Kansas 101, 205
Kant, Immanuel 166
Kaposi's Sarcoma Opportunistic Infections (KSOI) 223
Karloff, Boris **48**, 49, 57, 91-2, 146, 148
Kaufman, Philip 34
Kaufmann, Fritz 30, 220
Kaufmannization 30, 72, 220, 249ch1n1
Kefauver, Senator Carey Estes 99, 255n29
Kennedy, John Fitzgerald (JFK) 125, 131, 224
Kent State 151
Kenton, Erle C. 59, **85**, 86
Kesey, Ken 28, 40, 92, 106, 129, 152
Khmer 198
kidney 32, 119, 121, 255n35
Kilmer, Val 59, 86
kinetograph 216
King, the Rev. Dr. Martin Luther, Jr. 80, 130
King, Stephen 36, 165-6, 184-5, 195, 206-7, 224, 229
King Kong 91
Kingsley, Sir Ben 68, 77-8
Kinnaman, Joel **62**, 234, **235**
Klein, Donald 20
Klein-Rogge, Rudolf 70, **71**
Klerman, Jerald 20, 249ch1n2, 251n16
Klingon 236
Koch, Robert 86
Korea 98-9, 105, 156, 158, 160, 209, 254n13; Korean War 98-9, 160-1
kosher 135
Kosterlitz, Hans 223
Koyaanisqatsi 204
Kracauer, Siegfried 22, 72
Kraeplin, Emil 188
Kramer, Peter 42
Kramer, Stanley 132
Krypton 101
KSOI *see* Kaposi's Sarcoma Opportunistic Infections

Kubrick, Stanley 219–20, *221*
Kunis, Mila 230

laboratory *17*, *38*, 47, 51, 53, 58–9, 67, 70, 83, 90, 95, 116, 130, 136, 141, 148, 165, 204, *217*, 218
Lacan, Jacques 22
lactation 95, 167
Lacuna, Inc. 171, *172*, 173, *189*
Ladd, Cheryl 57
The Lady and the Monster 107, 134
Laemmle, Carl 54, 89
Laing, R.D. 14, 129, 229–30, 255n3
La Mettrie, Julien Offray de 67
Lancaster, Burt 132
The Lancet 91
Lang, Fritz 22, 35, 39, 69, *71*, 72–4, 81, 136
language 46, 52, 59, 82, 86, 132, 138–9, 149, 208, 251n2
Lanza, Adam 208
Lanza, Anthony 135
larva(ae) 110
Lasker Award 38, 223
laudanum 51, 216
Laughton, Charles *58*, 86
Law, Jude *175*, 176, *214*, 215
The Lawnmower Man 183–5, 206, *207*, 226
Lawnmower Man 2: Beyond Cyberspace 185
lawyer *see* attorney
lead 188, 257n11
Leary, Timothy 50, 168, 257ch11n9
Le Borg, Reginald 118
Lecter, Dr. Hannibal 2, 22, 40, 158
Lee, Christopher *133*
Lee, Martin A. 225, 251n17
Leigh, Jennifer Jason *214*, 242
Leipzig (Germany) 239
Leith, Virginia *17*
Lerman, Logan 210
Leroux, Gaston 93
LeRoy, Mervyn 15, 35
leucotomy 14, 96, 230; *see also* lobotomy
leukemia 107, 162–3
Levin, Ira 73, *142*
Lewis, Jerry 57
Li, Choh Hao 223
Liberia 228
libido 19, 28, 55, 90, 95, 218
Library of Congress 21, 192
Librium 218, 227–8, 258n9
Life 101, 106, 168
Life Is Worth Living 103
"life lies" 176
Life Without Soul 49
Limitless 43, 177–84, 224, 231, *234*
Lincoln, Abraham 160
Linklater, Richard 229
Liquid Sky 27, 37–8, 222–4
LIRR *see* Long Island Railroad
Listening to Prozac 42
Lister, Joseph 86
literature 1, 11, 13, 18, 24–5, 27–8, 37–8, 46, 49, 51, 53, 60, 62, 65–6, 105, 141–3, 145, 164, 178, 188, 216, 218, 221, 239, 250n19

Lithgow, John 83
Little Albert 219
"little green men" *120*
Little Italy (New York City) 67, 192
Little Rock, Arkansas 130
liver 32
lobby card *53*, *58*
lobotomy 14–5, 30, 34, 50, 80, 82, 96, 102–3, 106, 122, 128–9, 138, 154, 157, 159, 176, 196, 230
localization 59, 76, 109, 111, 139, 165, 230, 251n2
Loew ben Bezalel, Rabbi Judah 66
Loki 108
London 52, 55–8, 69, 130, 219
The Lonely Crowd 103
Long Island Railroad (LIRR) 172
Loomis, Dr. Sam 109
Looper 149
Lopez, Jennifer 18, 41, 202
Lord of the Flies 210
Los Angeles 74, 161
loss of consciousness 205
Lost in Space 123
The Lost Weekend 136
Loughery, David 197
Lourié, Eugène 120
love potion 177
Lovecraft, H. P. 39
low "T" syndrome 95
Lower East Side 179
LSD 25, 33, 50, 106, 129, *153*, 168–9, 171, 184, 225, 251n17
Lubitsch, Ernst 68
Lucas, George 221–2
lucid dreaming 204
Luddite 20, 49
Ludlum, Robert 183
Ludovico technique 219–20, *221*
Lugosi, Bela 93
Luhrmann, Tanya 102
Luke Cage 2
Lumet, Sidney 157
Lumière Brothers 67
Lundgren, Dolph 155
Lynch, David 224
Lyne, Adrian 197, 225
Lysergic Acid Diethylamide *see* LSD

MacGuffin 6, 67, 162, 181, 230
machine 5–7, 11–2, 35, 38–9, 41–2, 44, 49, 61, 67, 81, *112*, 117, 120, 122, *127*, 142–8, *150*, 152, 154, 157, 159, 161, 164, 166–7, 173, *175*, 176, 193–4, 201, 205, 210, 218, 234, *235*, 252ch4n4, 252ch4n10, 256ch8n7, 257ch11n6; *see also* brain machine; influencing machine; man-machine
Machine Age 64, 66, 69–70
"mad cow disease" *see* Creutzfeldt-Jakob Disease (CJD)
Mad Hatter 123, 146
Mad Max 162
Mad Monster Party 57
The Mad Room 29, 251n11
mad scientist 49, 69–70, 72, 86, 93, 102, 119, 136, 143, 178

Madoff, Bernie 163
Madonna-*putana* 55
magazine 103, 106, 168, 171, 207, 216
magic 47, 66–9, 143, 168, 185, 191–2, 204–5, 252ch4n8, 254n14; magic lantern 143; "magic mushrooms" 168, 254n14
Maharal of Prague 66
Mai Lai massacre 151
major depressive disorder 90, 227
make-up man *115*
Malcolm in Middle 109
Malcolm X 131, 158
malpractice suit 33, 249ch1n2
The Maltese Falcon 230
Mamoulian, Robert 52, *53*, 55–6, 59, 87, 89, 216–8, *217*
The Man from U.N.C.L.E. 134
The Man in the Gray Flannel Suit 103
The Man in the Moon (aka *Astronomer's Dream*) 192
man-machine 11, 39, 78, 122, *127*
The Man of 1,000 Faces 89; *see also* Chaney, Lon, Sr.
The Man Who Changed His Mind 91
The Man with the Transplanted Brain 31
The Man with the X-Ray Eyes 136
The Man with Two Brains *38*, 39, 107
managed care 41, 257ch11n5
Manchuria 145, 158, 160
The Manchurian Candidate 23, 34, 59, 130, 146, 157–61, 169, 176, 194, 204, 211, 220, 223, 228
The Mandarin 77
mandible 110, *113*
Manhattan 40, 67, 69, 222; *see also* New York City
Manhunter 22
Manila 183
Mankiewicz, Stanley 128
Man's Search for Meaning 104
MAOI (monoamine oxidase inhibitor) 227
March, Fredric 52, *53*, 55, 82, 87, *88*, 216–7, *217*
March, Steve 108, *109*
March of Dimes 111, 255n25
Marcus Welby 35
marionette 68, 236
Mars 116, 168–9, 171
Martian 39, 116
Martin, Steve *38*, 106–7
Marvel Comics 6, 8, 55, 57, 66, 77–9, 143, 163
Marx, Karl 211
Marx Brothers 91
Mary Shelley's Frankenstein 48, 51, 65
masked facies 30
masochism 143, 213
mass media 34, 186
mass murder 105, 132
Massachusetts General Hospital 20
Massive Multiplayer Online Role-

Playing Game (MMORPG) 208, 210
The Matrix 25–6, 41, 49, 63, 154–5, 177, 200–2, 210, 221, 226–7, 233, 235–6
Max Headroom 7
Max Payne 230–1
Mayer, Louis B. 54
McCallum, David 134
McCarthy, Senator Joseph 34, 98, 101, 105, 148, 160; McCarthy Era 34; McCarthyism 101, 104
McCormick, Harold 91
McCoy, Dr. Leonard 202
McCutcheon, Wallace 192
McDowell, Malcolm 219–20, *221*
McLuhan, Marshall 144
McMath case 16
McMurphy 40, 129, 154, 190
Meadows, Joyce *109*
mechanical doll 38, 61, 65, 68–70
Med-Bay 162–3
Medawar, Peter 121
media studies 2
medical ethics 32, 77, 175
medical psychoanalysis 2, 18
medical psychotherapy 2
medical student 25, 28, 43, 72, 125, 152, 199–200, 213, 251*n*6
medication 12, 20, 24–5, 30–1, 34, 42–3, 57, 84, 91, 95–6, 111, 119, 146, 151, 157, 167, 169, 177, 179–83, 186–8, 206, 218, 222, 226–8, 230–1, 249*ch*1*n*4, 253*n*24
"the medium is the message" 144
medsploitation 31, 59, 135–6
Meduna, Ladislaus 92
megalomania 106, 242
Mein Kampf 71
Mekong Delta 225
Méliès, Georges 25, 27, 67–9, 192–3, 216
melodrama 25, 31, 39, 93, 117, 119, 136, 184, 213, 216
Memento 7, 41, 43, 75, 178
memory 4, 7, 10, 12, 22, 39–41, 43–4, *44*, 51–2, 56, 75–6, 82, 93, 96, 104–5, 107, 132–5, 146, 151, 154–5, 157–9, 163–71, *172*, 173–7, 184, 188, *189*, 190, 194–5, 197, 206, 218, 222, 231, 233, 243, 250*n*1; false memories 75, 146, 169; memorable *33*, memory erasure 41, 44, 172–4, 184, *189*; repressed memories 22, 75, 93, 169, 250*n*1; screen memories 75
Men in Black *44*, 45, 149, 189–90, 243; *Men in Black 3 44*, 189
"The Menagerie" 176
Mencken, H.L. 136, 253*n*11
Mengele, Josef 59, 134, 145
meningitis 110–1, 113, 214, 255*n*24; meningoencephalitis 113
Mental Deficiency 10
Menzies, William Cameron 116
meprobamate (Miltown) 218
Merck & Company 216
Meredith, James 130
Merry Pranksters 129

mescaline 103, 106, 168, 254*n*11
message-in-a-bottle story 81
metaphysics 18, 55, 166, 194, 206, 237
meth (crystal) 182
methylphenidate 219, 257*ch*10*n*3
methylprednisolone 111, 255*n*23
Metrazol 92
Metropolis 23, 35, 39, 69–70, *71*, 71–4, 117, 146, *147*, *195*, 221, 252*n*10
Metuluna 104, *117*, 118; Metuluna Mutant 117, *118*
Mexico 106, 110, 133, 180, 254*n*14
Meyer, Dina 155
MGM 54
MI (Myocardial Infarction) 196
microcomputers 6, 79
Microsoft 210
Mideast 160
A Midsummer Night's Dream (film) 192
Midwestern 25, 50, 110
military 7, 14, 19, 29–30, 43, 64, 72, 99, 102, 113–4, 119, *120*, 122–3, *126*, 149, 151, 155, 158, 160, 162, 183, 2185, 196–7, 206, 209, 225–6, 231, 243, 249*ch*1*n*1
military-industrial complex 151, 196
Milk Plus 219–20
Milken, Michael 163
Milland, Ray 136, *137*
millennium 18, 41, 154, 200, 215, 226
Miller, Frank 39, 122
millionaire 106–7
Miltown (meprobamate) 228, 258*n*9; *see also* meprobamate; Soma
mind-body split 6, 55
mind control 30, 33, 44, 98, 101, 105, 116–7, 151–2, 161, 168, 184; *see also* control
The Mind Snatchers 15, 29–31, 36, 39, 50, 149, 151–3, *153*, 195
"mindfuck" film 41, 226
Ming the Merciless 146
Mini-Mental Status Exam (MMSE) 74
Ministry of Fear 136
Minority Report 42, 185–6, 218, 228
Mission: Impossible 164
Mr. Hyde *see* Hyde
Mr. Spock *see* Spock
MIT Technology Review 6
MK-ULTRA 33, 105, 129, 184, 225
MMORPG (Massive Multiplayer Online Role-Playing Game) 208, 210
"mnemonic courier" 155, *156*, 157, 162
modafinil 179, 231
molecular biology 21, 166, 240
Molly Millions 154–5
Moloch 69
Moloko Plus 219; *see also* Milk Plus
momism 101

Moniz 96, 230
monkey 7, 12, 60, 80, 87, 89–91, 94, 119, 125, 134, 149, 162, 171, 242
Monkey-Doodle-Doo 91
"Monkey Gland Man" 12, 80, 87, 89–90, 94, 119, 125
The Monkey's Paw 242
monoamine oxidase inhibitor (MAOI) 227
Monopoly 209
Monroe, Marilyn 148
monster 32, 46–7, *48*, 49–50, 57, 66, 68, 92–3, 97, 105–7, *115*, 116, 119, 127, 131, 134, 136, 141, 148, 178–9, 243, 252*ch*4*n*5
The Monster and the Girl 92–3
Montauk 172–3
Montgomery Bus Boycott 99, 130
morning sickness 222
Morpheus 25, 226
morphine 38, 92, 216, 226–7, 251*n*5; withdrawal 92
Morrissey, Paul 50
mortality 82, 115
Moses 70, 77, 257*ch*10*n*6
Moss, Carrie-Anne 41
mother 42, 55, 70, 84, 89, 95, 98, 101, 105, 128, 157, 159–60, 176, *181*, 182, 186, 188–9, 192, 208; Mother Mary 70; "mother's little helpers" 228
Motion Picture Production Code of 1930 ("Hays Code") 56
movement disorders 30, 57
Movies and Modern Psyche 2, 76
Moynahan, Bridget 41
MPD (Multiple Personality Disorder) 10, 52, 121, 128, 173, 187–8, 254*ch*6*n*11
MRI 15, 52, 145, 194
MS (Multiple Sclerosis) 111
Ms. Magazine 73
MSLT (Multiple Sleep Latency Test) 193
MST (Magnetic Seizure Therapy) 145
MUD (Multi-User Dungeon) 212
Multiple Personality Disorder (MPD) 187
Multiple Sclerosis (MS) 111
mummy 149, 167
The Mummy 131
Munoz case 16, 250*ch*12–3
murder 9, 28–9, 31, 33, 37, 40, 46, 50, 52, 54, 56, 59, 72, 92–3, *100*, 105, 115–6, 130, 132, 136, 152, 158–9, 185–6, 198, 208, 211, 218–20, 223, 230–1
Murnau, F.W. 54
museum 3, 6, 66, 82, 144, 206–7
mushroom 95, 106, 121, 168, 254*n*14
musical 56–7, 65, 134
mutation 123, *126*, 222, 224
MWT (Multiple Wakefulness Test) 193
My Fair Lady 65
Myers, Michael 72, 100, 158
mysticism 224, 236

myth 65, 162, 205, 226, 230–1, 255*ch*7*n*4
myxedema (hypothyroidism) 90, 95; *see also* thyroid

Naegleria fowleri 112
Nagasaki 100
Naik, Gautam 173, 256*ch*9*n*4
Naish, J. Carrol 93, 145
Naked Lunch 37, 214
naltrexone 146
nanite 210, *211*, 212–3, 236, 242
nanny 47
nanoprobe 236, 240; *see also* nanite
nanotechnology 159, 236; *see also* nanite; nanoprobes
narcissism 10
narcolepsy 219, 257*ch*10*n*3, 257*ch*11*n*5
narkidrine 224
NAS ("black shakes") 156–7
NASA 107, 243
Nash, John 96
Natalizumab 111
National Conference of Commissioners on Uniform State Laws 16
National Film Registry 114, 192
National Guard 99, 130, 151
nausea 107, 113, 187, 220, *221*
NCV (nerve conduction velocities) 16
Nebuchadnezzar 26, 201
Nebula Award 63
"Nerve Attenuation Syndrome" (NAS) 156
nerve doctor 22
nervoin 218
nervous breakdown 55
Netherlands 173
neuralyzer 43, *44*, 45, 189–90
neurochemistry 21, 50
neurodegenerative disorder 213
neuroendocrinology 13, 21, 94, 14
neurofibrillary tangles 181
neuro-genetics 21
neuro-imaging studies 15, 40
neuroin 228
neuroleptic 30, 57, 102, 230
neurologist 1–2, 10, 15–6, 21, 28, 35, 47, 52, 59, 73, 75–6, 89, 111, 128, 139, 165, 167, 170, 202, 239, 250*n*6, 250*n*8, 250*n*19, 251*n*2
Neuromancer 24, 63, 154–5, 161, 233
neuromodulation 144, 232
neuropsychiatry 2–3, 5, 10–3, 16, 18–20, 24, 27, 30–1, 35–6, 41, 44, 52, 56, 76, 94, 96, 102–3, 110–1, 122, 140, 144–5, 157, 175, 185, 196, 199, 202, 210, 230; *see also* biological psychiatry
neuropunk 24
neurosurgeon 1, 24, 28, 61, 76, 123, 128, 152, 167, 170; *see also* surgeon
neurosyphilis 31, 103, 151
neurotransmitters 5, 10, 31, 38, 61, 93–4, 135, 152, 194, 230, 235, 253*n*24

Neuss, Alwin 54
neutrophilic meningitis 111; *see also* meningitis
"The New Accelerator" 177–8
New Age 37
New School 2
New Wave Science Fiction 216, 218
New York (magazine) 66, 126
New York Academy of Medicine 2
New York City 2, 23, 92–3, 95, 120, 123, *127*, 130–1, 135, 149, 159, 172, 178–9, 180, 182, 192, 210, 222–3, 242; *see also* Manhattan
New York Times 6–7, 31, 53, 56, 91–2, 93, 169, 171, 180, 206, 223
Newman, Joseph P. 117, *118*
Nicholson, Jack 40, 129, 154, 190
Nicolelis, Miguel 194
Die Nieberlungen 70
Nietzsche 236, 239–40
Nigeria 111
Nighthawks 74
nightmare 116, 159, 182, 198, 254*n*5
A Nightmare (film) 192
Nightmare on Elm Street 198
NIMH (National Institute of Mental Health) 20
Nimoy, Leonard 34, 109
Nintendo 212
9/11 2, 77, 223, 228
1950s 13–4, 39, 96, 98, 111, 114, 117–8, 121–5
1984 (book) 147, 168
19th century 13, 18, 22, 24, 34, 37, 46–7, 51, 57, 60, 86, 90, 104, 114, 131, 138, 143, 154, 165–7, 188–9, 191, 216, 226, 236, 239, 242, 250*n*2
The Ninth Configuration 23
Nobel Prize 5, 12, 31, 73, 87, 90, 95–6, 119, 121, 134, 160, 196, 220, 230
noir 22, 63, 74, 76, 93, 106–7, 162, 164, 194, *195*, 230
Nolan, Christopher 41, *203*, 204
Noonan, Tom 224
nootropic 179, 182
Nordisk 54
Norse mythology 231
North Carolina 130
Not Guilty by Reason of Insanity (NGRI) 136
nuclear power 123
Nuke 224
Nuremberg 132, 134; Nuremberg Code 134; Nuremberg Laws 31, 71, 343; Nuremberg Trials 31, 132, 243
nurse *112*, 129, 154, 193, 196, 200; *see also* Ratched, Nurse
nursing home 83–4
The Nutty Professor 57
Nuvigil (armodafinil) 180; *see also* modafinil
NYPD 230
NZT 179, 180, 182, 224, 231, *234*

Obamacare 83, 163, 202, 253*n*4
Obsessive-Compulsive Disorder (OCD) 202
obstetrics 42, 252*ch*3*n*3
occipital lobe 167
occult 42, 191–2, 195, 197–200, 222, 224, 252 *ch*3*n*6, 258*n*8
An Occurrence at Owl Creek Bridge 225
OCD (obsessive-compulsive disorder) 202
The Octave of Claudius 89
Oedipal complex 19, 101, 128, 159
Of Two Minds: Growing Disorder in American Psychiatry 102
off-Broadway 149
off-world 74–5, 107, 162, 169
Office of Homeland Security 228
Officer Murphy 61, *62*, 122, 194, 231, 234, *235*
OI (Opportunistic Infections) 223
Ol' Miss 130
Old Testament 201
Oldham, John 18
Oldman, Gary *62*, *235*
OLG *see* online gaming
OLG-anon (Online Gaming-Anonymous) 208
Olson, Dr. Frank 33
Omni 154
On Aphasia 59, 138
"On Being Sane in Insane Places" 29
On Origin of Species 86
"The One" 201
One Flew Over Cuckoo's Nest 15, 28, 40, 92, 129, 152, 196
online gaming (OLG) 208, 210
operant conditioning 220; *see also* behavioral conditioning
"Operation Annihilate" 117
Operation Headstart 139
Operation Paperclip 107–8, 125, 135, 243
opioid (opiate) 14, 38, 54, 146–7, 151, 212, 221–3, 228, 251*n*5, 258*ch*13*n*5; *see also* opium
opium 51, 54, 57, 181, 192, 216, 218, 227; Opium Wars 216
optic chiasm 167
Oral Polio Vaccine (OPV) 83, 101, 111
orangutan 81–2
organ transplant 32, 133, 175–6, 223
The Organization Man 103
orgasm 37, 223
Orwell, George 168
Oscar 55, 149
Osheroff, Dr. Raphael 15, 20, 33, 36, 199, 250*n*10
Osheroff v. Chestnut Lodge 20, 250*n*9, 251*n*15, 251*n*16
The Outer Limits 123, 149
outer space 9, 13, 19, 25, 27, 98–9, 101, 104 5, 222
Outland 25, 222
Outline of History 189
outsider art 144, 256*n*10

OxyContin 38, 95
oxytocin 95, 121

pacemaker 152, 235
pacifist 131
Pain, Barry 89
Pakistan 111
Palance, Jack 56
pancreas 32, 91; pancreatic islet cells 91
Panther Woman **58**
Paracelsus 47
paradigm 3–4, 12, 18, 21, 27, 40, 62, 72, 129, 187, 218
paralysis 6, 31, 61, 73, 78–9, 89, 101, 111–2, 145
Paramount 89, 93, 198
paranoid 34, 64–5, 73, 83, 101, 105, 107, 114, 143, 164, 168–70, 177, 187, 197, 219, 225, 230
paranormal 36, 101, 107, 187, 197; *see also* parapsychology
paraplegic *see* paralysis
parapsychology 7, 91, 185
parasite 109, 110, 112–3, **113**, 117, 255*n*27
Paris 67, 90–1, 253*n*15
Parker, Edward **58**, **85**
Parker, Kim **126**
Parkinson's Disease (PD) 30, 32, 145, 151–2, 232, 257*ch*11*n*5; pseudo–Parkinson's 30, 151
Parks, Rosa 99
parody 23, 32, **38**, **39**–40, 50, 73, 104, 107, 109, 145, 258*n*9
parole officer 161, 163
paroxitene *see* Paxil
Parton, Regis 117, **118**
Pasteur, Louis 86
Pathé 87, 192
pathologist 122
pathology 14, 103, 122–3, 128–30, 167, 193, 239
patient 1, 10, 14–5, 22, 25, 28–9, 33–4, 40–1, 44, 47, 64, 72, 75, **78**, 78–9, 103, 109, 111, 119, 143, 152, 154, 168–70, 173–5, 179, 196, 199–200, 202, 211, 214, 227, 235, 239, 251*n*16, 255*n*7
Pavlov 130, 157, 160, 196, 220, 251*n*20; *see also* Pavlovian conditioning
Pavlovian conditioning 157, 251*n*20; *see also* behavioral conditioning; classical conditioning
Paxil (paroxitene) 42, 186; *see also* Selective Serotonin-Reuptake Inhibitors (SSRIs)
PCE (Prenatal Cocaine Exposure) 186; *see also* cocaine
PD *see* Parkinson's Disease
PDE (Polydichloric Euthymol) 222
peace rallies 82; *see also* anti-war
Peale, Norman Vincent 103
Pearce, Guy 41, 78
Pearl Harbor 145–6
peasant 46, 221
Pena, Elizabeth 225
Penfield, Wilder 76, 167, 170

Pentagon 116
pentagram 70
Percodan (oxycodone/aspirin) 38; *see also* opioid
performance enhancer 90, 169, 182
performance psychopharmacology 169
Perkins, Anthony 57
persona 52, 57, 63
Persona 23
personality 13, 52, 55–7, 113–4, 128–9, 132, 224; dual personality 56; epileptoid personality 28; schizotypical personality 64; *see also* personality disorder
personality disorder (Axis II) 10, 254*n*11; antisocial personality disorder 172–3; Borderline Personality Disorder (BPD) 121, 187–8; Multiple Personality Disorder (MPD) 128, 187
personalized medicine 211
Pert, Candace 223
PET scan 15, 40, 52, 194, 213
Peter Bent Brigham Hospital 121
The Phantom of Opera 93
Pharma 31, 61, 82–3, 157, 179–80, 183, 230, **234**; Pharma-Kon 156–7; *see also* Big Pharma
pharmaceuticals 19, 82, 90, 157, 179, 213, 227, 230–1; *see also* medication
pharmacy 83
phenothiazine 14, 30; *see also* neuroleptic
philanthropist **127**, **142**
Philip K. Dick Award 63, 154
Philippines 183
philosophy 1, 10–2, 14, 16, 20, 26, 31, 35–6, 47, 49, 52, 54–5, 59, 61–2, 66–7, 76, 194–5, 201, 209, 229, 236–7, 239–40
phobia 54, 128, 165, 174, 215, 219
photograph 108, **109**, 111, 191, 205; *see also* spirit photography
photographer 73, 115–6
phycomelia ("flipper limbs") 42, 187, 222; *see also* thalidomide
physical restraints 102
physician 1–2, 7, 14–5, 25, **26**, 33, 47, 51–2, 64, 90, 92–3, 104, 116, 121, 134, 143, 148, 157, 160, 170, 176, 187, 193, 199, 202, 209, 233, 235, 239, 242, 249*ch*1*n*4, 250*n*19, 252*ch*3*n*3, 256*n*14, 257*ch*12*n*2
physician-extender 64
Piaget, Jean 130
Pick, Arnold 188
Pickford, Mary 192
Pierce, Ambrose 225
pituitary gland 90, 94, 115, 167, 254*n*11, 254*n*21
placenta 31, 188
Planet of Apes 43, 60, 80, **81**, 81–3, 85–6, 133, 136, **138**, 138–9, 177, **181**, 184, 188, 252*ch*5*n*2, 256*ch*7*n*11, 257*ch*10*n*6, 257*ch*10*n*7
plasmapharesis 173

plastic surgery 59, 93, 119
Plath, Sylvia 145
Plato 12, 166, 170, 201, 219–20, 226, 229
platoon 158–9, 161, 169, 219, 225–6
Platt, Oliver 199
play 15, 29, 48, 53, 65, 128–9, 132, 149, 172, 192, 197, 250*n*10; screenplay 54, 81, 106, 128, 172, 197, 252*ch*5*n*2
Pleasance, Donald 221
Plummer, Christopher 198
PML (Progressive Multifocal Leukoencephalopathy) 111
PMS (Pre-Menstrual Syndrome) 95
pneumoencephalogram 16
pod people 113
Poe, Edgar Allan 178, 255*n*36
poet 47, 57, 72, 155, 166, 168, 204, 242, 253*n*11
Poitier, Sidney 132
police 39, 61, 74–5, 116, 119, 123, 135, 180, 220–1, 229, 230
Polidori, Dr. John 47
polio 78–9, 83, 101, 111–2, **112**, 255*n*25; *see also* infantile paralysis
Polydichloric Euthymol (PDE) 222
Pong 212
Poole, F. Scott 128, 131, 199
Poor Little Rich Girl 192
Popular Science 39
populist 129, 161
Porter, Edwin S. 192
Portman, Natalie 230
Portrait of the Artist as a Young Man 65
Portugal 96
positivism 166
post-modern 41, 63, 172, 225
post-psychoanalytic society 5, 11, 15
Post-Traumatic Stress Disorder (PTSD) 43–4, 158, 174–5, 190, 199
post–war 2, 98, 101, 103, 114, 134, 250*n*5; post–World War II 2
La Poupee 73
poverty 70, 101
Poverty Row 92
POW *see* Prisoner of War
Powaqqatsi 204
The Power of Positive Thinking 103
Power to the People 184
Pre-Code 55
Precogs 185–7, 218, 228
pregnancy 35, 42, 84, 95, 186–8, 221, 250*n*12, 257*ch*10*n*6
prehensile thumb 138
The Premature Burial 136
"premature senility" 110
premonition 186
prequel 83, 182
presenile degeneration 188; *see also* Alzheimer's Disease
president 15–6, 18, 32, 36, 98, 117, 125, 131, 158–9, 162, 198, 250*n*14
priest 184–5
primary amoebic meningoencephalitis 112; *see also* encephalitis

Prinzhorn Museum 144
prison 35, 71, 154, 161, 170, 182, 200, 210, 219–20, *221*
Prisoner of War (POW) 209
Production Code 55–6; *see also* Hays Code; Motion Picture Production Code of 1930; Pre-Code
professor 2, 16, 25, 29, 37, 57, 71–2, 131, 144, 148–9, 168, 177–8, 221–3, 225
progesterone 95
prolactin 167; prolactinoma 167
Prometheus (film) 193
Prometheus (myth) 46–7, 65
Promised Land 201; *see also* Zion
propanolol 174
Proust, Marcel 75, 164
Provigil 180; *see also* modafinil; Nuvigil
Prowse, David 127
Prozac 18, 42, 186, 227–8
Prozium 221, 227–8
Prussian 72
pseudo–Parkinson's disease 30; *see also* Parkinson's Disease
PSG (Polysomnogram) 193
psilocybin 218
psyche 2, 74, 114
psychedelics 51, 74, 168, 197, 257*ch*11*n*9
psychiatric medicine 1–2, 10
psychiatric patients 72, 152; *see also* patient
psychiatric survivors 14
Psychiatric Times 1–2, 252*ch*4*n*3
psychic 64, 72, 185–7, 197–8, *207*, 207, 218, 228
Psycho (1960) 4, 56–7, 72, 119
psychoanalysis 1–5, 8, 10–6, 18–23, 25, 27, 29, 33, 34, 35–7, 40, 42–3, 55, 57–8, 59, 60, 63, 66, 71–3, 76–7, 86, 87, 92–3, 97, 101–4, 106, 114, 123, 128–30, 141–3, 159, 164–5, 182, 187–8, 191, 194, 199, 212, 218, 220, 224, 230, 236, 249*n*5, 249*n*8, 249*n*10, 249*ch*1*n*2, 249–50*ch*1*n*4, 250*ch*1*n*8, 250*ch*1*n*19, 250*ch*2*n*1, 252*ch*3*n*3
The Psychoanalytic Century 18, 21
Psychoanalytic Quarterly 143
psychodynamic 2, 8, 11, 75–6, 114, 212; psychodynamic psychotherapy 2
psychology 5, 7, 10–1, 15, 148, 160, 164–5, 168, 170, 176, 181, 184, 188, 207, 219–20, 229–30, 236–7, 239–40; psychologist 81
psychoneuroimmunology 21
psychopathology 14, 130, 239
psychopharmacology 1, 18–21, 21, 24, 31, 33, 40, 52, 63, 169, 187, 199, 212, 231, 254
psychosis 29–31, 42, 52, 64, 72, 73, 102, 103, 110, 116, 117, 118–9, 122, 127, 135–6, 143, 144, 149, 151, 152, 157, 160, 180, 185, 190, 197, 200, 207, 213–15, 222, 230–1, 242

psychosurgery 14–5, 33, 96, 103, 157, 167, 169, 251*n*20; *see also* leucotomy; lobotomy
psychotherapy 2, 5, 11, 18, 41, 103, 143, 187, 202, 249*n*9; psychodynamic 2; supportive 2
PTSD (Post-Traumatic Stress Disorder) 43–4, 158, 174–5, 190, 199
Puerto Rican American 41
pulmonary hypertension 186
puppet 48, 109, 113
Puppet Masters 109, *113*
Purgatory 63
Pygmalion 65
pyramid 77, 222

Quaaludes 222
quadriplegic 7; *see also* paralysis
Quaid, Dennis 198
Quaid, Douglas (*Total Recall*) 168–9, 171, 218, 256*ch*9*n*3
Quaid, Randy 51
Quaker 47
quarantine 176
Queen for a Day 99
Queens 149
Queensborough Bridge *127*
Quinzel, Dr. Harleen 213

race 31, 80, 82–3, 125, 130–2, 136, 160
race science 85, 253*n*5
racial unconscious 37, 237
racism 80, 132–3, 181, 257*ch*11*n*3
radiation 107, 122–3, *126*, 156, 162–3, 167, 187, 242
radioactivity 101, 103, 163, 242, 242; *see also* radiation
The Rajah's Dream (*Le Rêve du Radjah ou La Forêt Enchantée*) 192
Rand, Ayn 103
Rank, Otto 32, 251*n*14
rape 35, 154, 219, 236
Raspberry (Award) 155
Ratched, Nurse 154, 196
rauvolfia serpentina (snakeroot) 118
reactive psychosis 52; *see also* psychosis
Reagan, Nancy 106
Reagan, Ronald 18–9, 199; Reagan era 18
reality testing 12, 215
reanimate 46, 127
Re-Animator 39, 76
Reardon, Dennis 149, 256*n*12
Reason, Rex 117, *118*
reboot 11, 39, 61–2, 157, 194, 231
reconsolidation 174
recreational psychosurgery 169
Red Dragon 40
Red Light District 171
Red Pill 201
Red Planet 171
Red Queen 160
Red Scare 98, 101, 105
The Red Shoes 69
Redford, Robert 19, 40
Reeves, Keanu 155, *156*, 201, 226, 229

"refrigerator mother" 101
refugee 26, 130, 162, 198, 250*n*5
rehab 77, 111, 209, 219, 222, 229
reimagining 25, 29, 34–5, 40, 59, 62, 80, 83, 133, 157–9, 181–2
Reiner, Carl 39
rejuvenation industry 90; *see also* anti-aging
Rekall, Inc. 40, 168–9, 171, 218
religion 52, 61, 63, 67, 73, 101, 104, 106, 110, 121, 163, 200–1, 212, 215, 224
REM sleep 193, 198, 257*ch*11*n*5
remake 62, 80, 83, 114, 122, 160–1, 168, 171, 175–6, 194, 204, 222, 234, 252*ch*4*n*1
Remembrance of Things Past 75, 164
removable drive 233; *see also* flash drive
Renner, Jeremy 183
Rennie, Michael *150*
replicant 7, 11, 61, 65, 68, 74–5, 114, 140, *195*, 227
Repo Men 43–4, 159, 163, 172, *175*, 175–6
representational art 2; *see also* art
"Resistance Is Futile" 236
respirator *235*
resurrection 107
retina 167
retrovirus 223; *see also* AIDS; HIV
The Revenge of Frankenstein 49, 127
Revolutionary Independence from Technology *see* R.I.F.T.
Rick's Café 56
Rieff, Philip 101
Riesman, David 103
R.I.F.T. (Revolutionary Independence from Technology) 242
Rise of Planet of Apes 43, 78, 80, *81*, 83, 136, 177, 181–2, 188, 196, 257*ch*10*n*7
Ritalin 219, 257*ch*10*n*3; *see also* methylphenidate
Robbins, Tim 225
Robby the Robot 120, 178, *179*
Robert-Houdin, Jean Eugène 67, 252*ch*4*n*8
Roberts, Julia 56, 184, 199–200
RoboCop 11, 23, 39, 40, 49, 61, *62*, 65, 77, 122, 140, 194, 196, 221, 224, 231, 234–5, *235*, 256*ch*9*n*3; *RoboCop 2* 40, 61, 224; *RoboCop 3* 40
robot 6–7, 23, 35, 39, 61, 63, 65, 68–70, *71*, 73–5, 77, *78*, 79, 94, 120–2, *127*, 140, *142*, *147*, 154, 161, 178, *179*, 194, 221, 242; robotics 6, 23, 61, 221, 242
Rockefeller laws 182
Rogers, Buck 24
Rogers, Steve 183, 243
Rollerball 210
Rolling Stones 228
Rollins, Henry 155
romance 5, 23, 25, 32, 68, 70, 75, 77, 105, 141, 148–9, 171, 178, 175,

184, 198; family romance 130, 251n14; romantic comedy 68, 171, 174–5, 184; romantic era 131, 198
Romanticism 47; German Romanticism 69; romantic era 131, 198
Romeo and Juliet 242
Romulan 236
Roosevelt, Franklin Delano (FDR) 111
Rosemary's Baby **142**
Rosenberg, Juliu, and Ethel 98, 105, 254ch6n2-3
Rosenhan, David 29
Rosie the Riveter 99
Ross, Katharine *141*
rotoscope 229
Rotwang 69–71, *71*, 72, 91, 117, **147**
rTMS (repetitive Transcranial Magnetic Stimulation) 145
Ruben, Joseph 197
Rubin, Bruce Joel 197, 225
Ruffalo, Mark 8
The Running Man 210
Russell, Ken 37
Russia 27, 72, 90, 149, 158, 160, 165, 168, 180, 222, 230
Ryder, Wynona 229

Sabin, Dr. Albert 111, 113
Sabshin, Mel 15, 20, 32
sadomasochism 213
Sakel, Manfred (Menachim) 14, 92, 96
Salk, Dr. Jonas 101, 111, 113
saloon 53, 55, **88**, 216
same-sex sex 214
Samsung 6, 249n6
San Francisco *81*, 168, 219, 223
The Sandman 68
Der Sandmann 68
Sandoz Labs 168
Sanity, Madness and Family 229
Sargant, Dr. William 34, 251n20
Satan 178, 185, 191
Saturday Night Live (SNL) 104
Saturn (Award) 170, 200
Savior 77, 163, 201, 243
Scandinavian 130
A Scanner Darkly 229–30
Scanners 36–7, 40, 42, 188, 212, 222
Schelde, Per 16, 46, 141, 185, 205, 256ch8n1
Scheuermann, Jan 7
schizoid embolism 169
schizophrenia 34, 64, 93, 96, 101–2, 108, 110, 143, 148, 154, 159, 166, 187–8, 229–30
schizotypal personality 64; *see also* personality disorder; schizophrenia
Schneiderian first rank symptoms 143
school shooting 208
Schreiber, Liev 158–9, 176
Schumacher, Joel 199
Schwarz, Jonathan 169, 180, 256ch9n1, 258ch13n6

Schwarzenegger, Arnold 40, 149, 167–8, 171, 256ch9n3
Science Fiction Hall of Fame 195
Scientific American 90
scientist 1, 5, 16, 19, 25, 28, 30–1, **33**, 38, 41, 44, 46, 49, 51–2, *62*, 65, 69–70, *71*, 72–3, 76, 78, 82–4, 86, 90, 92–3, 95–6, 99, 102, 106–8, **108**, 113–7, 118–21, 123, 125, 134–6, 138, 141, 143, 145, **147**–8, 159, 165–6, 170, 173–4, 177–8, 181, 183–4, 185, 192, 194, 195–8, 204, 213, 233–6, 231, 233, 235, 241–3, 249ch1n3; neuroscientist 1, 5, 28, 76, 83, 138, 145–6, 173–4, 192
Scopes Trial 87, 90
Scorsese, Martin 67, 192, 204, 257ch11n4
Scott, Ridley 39, 63, 65, 74, 76
Scottish 51, 119, 130
Sears, Fred F. 117
Second Life 41
Second Manifesto 72; *see also* Breton, André; *Surrealist Manifesto*
Second Sino-Japanese War 145
Seconds 59
Seduction of the Innocent 99, 255n29
seele 114, 166
Segal, George 28, 152
seizure 36, 92, 110, 113, 145, 152
Selective Serotonin Reuptake Inhibitors (SSRIs) 42, 227–8; *see also* Paxil (paroxitene); Prozac
self 34, 26, 42, 51, **53**, 72, 75, 110, 117, 161, 166, 171, 177, 180, 187–8, 201, 208, **211**, 222, 237, 241; self-help 34, 208
Selig, William 53
Selig Polyscope Company 54
Semmelweis, Dr. Ignaz 86
sensory deprivation 200
sequel 30, 41, 43, 49, 51, 60–2, 80, 83, 107, 122, 127, 134, 185, 189, 200–1, 206, 243, 256ch7n11
serial killer 202
serials 43, 70, 93, 117, 145–7, 161, 178, 202, 211, 243, 252n10
Serkis, Andrew *81*
Serling, Rod 81, 252–3ch5n2
Sertoli cell 91, 253n18
Serturner, Adam Friedrich Wilhelm 216, 226
The Seven-Per-Cent Solution 51
sex 31, 37, 41–2, 55, 90, 94–5, 101, 108, 121, 143, 184–5, 222–3
Sex Reassignment Surgery (SRS) 201
sex therapy 40
shadow self 52, *53*
sham rage 28, 152
shaman 239
Shammai 135
The Shape of Things to Come 189
Shaun, Ben 32
Shaw, George Bernard 65
Shearer, Moira 69
Shechina 236

Sheen, Bishop Fulton J. 103
shell-shock 14, 30; *see also* war neurosis
Shelley, Mary Wollstonecraft 32, 46–7, **48**, 48–51, 65–6, 76, 131, 252ch3n3
Shelley, Percy Bysshe 47
Sheppard, Alan 100, 125
Sherlock Holmes 51
Shoah (Holocaust) 132
Shock Theater 49
shock therapy *see* ECT (Electroconvulsive Therapy)
Showscan 194
sibling rivalry 29
Siegel, Don 34, 114
The Silence of Lambs 22, 158
Silverberg, Robert 216
"simian cinema" 13, 23–4, 97, 134
Simmel, Ernest 14, 72, 249ch1n4
The Sims 41, 73–4, 154, 210
"simstim" (simulated stimulation) 154
simulacra 74
Simulacra and Simulation 201
Sinatra, Frank 158
Singapore 212
singer **53**, 55–6, 72, **88**, 217
Singh, Tarsem 202
"Singin' in the Rain" 219
Sinner, Alyse (Alice) 213
Siodmak, Curt 39, 106–8, 117, 134, 256ch7n10
Siodmak, Robert 106–8
Sir Lancelot 7
Six Million Dollar Man 7
Skinner, B.F. 219–20, 230
skull 222, 229, 62, 116, 149
Skulldugger 146
Slain, Bruce 225
slasher 198
Sleaze-o-Rama 135–6
Smith, Will **44**, 77
Smith Kline and French (SKF) 31, 219, 257ch10n3
Snow, John 86
SNP (Single Nucleotide Polymorphism) 211
Snyder, Solomon 223
social class 161
social media 11, 36, 64
social networking 36
social phobia 56
social problem film 23, 31, 37, 107, 121, 131–2, 135–6, 139–40
social realism 132
social work 18, 41, 202
society 5, 10–1, 16, 18–20, 24, 34–5, 37, 40, 50–3, 55, 64, 76, 81, 103, 119, **150**, 154, 156, 160, 168, 171, 181, 188, 198, 206, 208, 210–1, 218, 220–2, 227–8, 233, 250
sociopath 172–3, **221**
soldier 14, 30, 36, 43, 54, 72, 82, 90, 97, 99, 101–2, 114, 140, 150–1, 157, 160–1, 176, 183, 219–20, 225–6, 231, 243, 250ch1n4; *see also* military; platoon
soma 218, 187; Soma (brand name)

218; Somafree Institute of Psychoplasmics 187
somatiker 97
somnambulist 9, 22, 54, 107, 116, 257*ch*10*n*7
Son of Dr. Jekyll 57
sorcery 16, 69–70, 72, **147**, 177, 185, 191–2, 198, 205, 239
soul 16, 34, 40, 49, **58**, 59, 68–9, 76, **85**, 86, 89, 91, 121, **137**, 166, 178, 197, 225, 242–3
South (American) 99, 128, 130–1, 133, 151
South Africa 32
South America 134, 180
South Carolina 131
South London 52
South Pacific 145
Soviet 39, 98, 100, 104–5, 120, 125, 129, 160, 222; *see also* FSU; Russia; USSR
space 9, 12–3, 19, 25, 27, 39, **48**, 98–9, 101, 104–5, 108, **120**, 121–3, 125, 133, 149, 162, 252–3*ch*5*n*2; space age 25; space alien 97, 104, 118; space capsule 147–8, 181; space cowboy 25; space travel 39, 81, 104, 118, 125, 138; spaceship 25, 82, 100, 104–5, 121, 176, 178, 181–2, 233, 252–3*ch*5*n*2, 257*ch*10*n*6; *see also* cyberspace; outer space
Spanish 134, 152
special effects 11, 24, 28, 77, 105, 109, 141, 192–5, 255*n*31
SPECT scan 15, 52
speed (amphetamine) 168, 219, 231
Spellbound 25, 108, 193
Spice 224
Spider-Man 163, 187
Spielberg, Steven 42, 101, 185–6
Spielrein, Sabrina 37
spinal cord 6, 23, 37, 44, 79, 89, 92, **112**, 122–3, **126**; spinal cord injury 44
Spinrad, Norman 216
spirit photography 191
splash page **100**
Spock (*Star Trek*) 34, 114, 176
Spock, Dr. Benjamin 101
Sprawl 154
Sputnik 12, 24, 97, 100, 120, 125, 222
spy 98, 105, 168, 171, 202, **203**, 204, **214**
SSRIs *see* Selective Serotonin Reuptake Inhibitors
Stallone, Sylvester 149
standards of practice 4, 209, 211
Stanford University 29, 129
Stanwyck, Barbara 99
Star Trek 24, 34, 81, 100, 114, 117, 123–4, 149, 176, 202, 236–7, 239–40; *see also* Trekkies
Star Trek: First Contact 149, 236
Star Wars 15, 24–5, 27, 35, 105, 127, 141, 146, 198, 221
Stark, Tony 5, 6, **8**, 8–10, 3, 77–9, 233

state hospital 96, 102
status epilepticus 152; *see also* seizures
steampunk 26
Steinach, Eugene 89–91, 253*n*11, 253*n*15
The Stepford Wives 35, 61–2, 73–4, 139–40, **142**
Stevenson, Robert Louis 51–8, 87, 216, **217**, 226
Stewart, Patrick 184
Still of Night 40
Stone, Sharon 168–9, 171
stop-motion animation 57, 123
straitjacket 9
Strange, Dr. Hugo 146
The Strange Case of Dr. Jekyll and Mr. Hyde 51–2, 56, 58, 87, 89, **217**, 226
The Strange Case of Dr. RX 93
Strangers on a Train 183
Strasbourg, France 66
Strasbourg Museum of Decorative Arts 66
Strausbaugh, John 51
Streep, Meryl 159
Strickfaden, Kenneth 51, 146
stroke 6, 111, 138, 171
Substance D 229
substance-induced disorder 52
substantia nigra 235
suburbia 34, 61, 99, 114
succubae(us) 13
Suddenly, Last Summer 128
Suffragette 53
sugar sickness 90; *see also* Diabetes Mellitus (DM)
suicide 30, 33, 43, 101, 115, 143, 145, 159, 194, 200, 204, 220
Sullivan, Henry Stack 20
Sulloway, Frank 129
Summer of Love 50, 74, 128, 151, 168, 219, 254*n*15, 256*n*13, 258*ch*13*n*2
Sunset Boulevard 172
Sunshine Laws 157
superego 2, 52, 172, 218
superego lacuna 172–3
superhero 2, 5–6, 8, 77–9, 99, 107–8, 163, 183, 187, 206, 213, 243
Superheroes and Superegos: Minds Behind Masks 2
Superman 99, 107, 122, 255*n*25
The Superman 122
supernatural 16, 36, 66–9, 185, 198–9, 205, 239
superpower 6, 9, 78, 107, 197
supportive psychotherapy 2
surgeon 1, **17**, 28, 31, 63, 76, 89–91, 94, **100**, 107, 115, 118–9, 121, 123, 128, 152, 167, 170
surreal 25, 27, 37, 41, 72, 108, 143, 173, 193, 204
Surrealist Manifesto 72; *see also* Breton, André
Sutherland, Kiefer 199
Swan Lake 242
swastika 227
Sybil 128

Symbiote 2
Synanon 222
syphilis 31, 73, 95, 103, 119, 151; *see also* general paresis of the insane; neurosyphilis
Szasz, Thomas 14, 129, 130, 255*n*3–4, 255*n*8

tACS (transcranial Alternating Current Stimulation) 145
Taenia solium 110
Tale of Grandmother and Child's Dream 192
talk therapy 8, 19, 15, 23, 42, 103, 191
talkies 56, 69, 72
talking cure 22–3
Talmud 52, 129, 135
Tanhouser 53
tapeworm 110
Tardive Dyskinesia (TD) 30–1; *see also* movement disorders
tattoo 41, 158–9, 230–1
Tausk, Viktor 142–4, 151–2, 154, 159, 161, 256*ch*8*n*5–6
taxidermy 56, 82, 241
Taylor (*Planet of the Apes*) **138**, 139
Taylor, Don 59, 86
Taylor, Elizabeth 128
TBI *see* Traumatic Brain Injury
Tchaikovsky 242
TCMS (Trans-Cutaneous Magnetic Stimulation) 17, 117, 146, 157
tDCS (transcranial Direct Current Stimulation) 145
tearjerker 158, 184, 192, 278*ch*10*n*8
teaser 8
technician 66, 103, 202, 218, 235
technology 6–7, 19–20, 26, 28, 32, 36, 41, 49, 64, 93, 118, 156, 159, 178–9, **179**, 193–4, 196, 202, 205–6, 210, 213, 215, 221, 236–7, 241–3
telekinesis 122, 185, **207**, 222
telepathy 13, 42, 116, 148, 185, **207**, 222
telepsychiatry 41, 63–4, 252*ch*4*n*3
television 7, 24, 29, 34, 49–51, 57, 80, 99, 101, 103–4, 107, 111, 117, 123–4, 132, 134, 136, 143–4, 149, 159, 185, 194, 213, 236
temperament 10
temporal lobe 52, 76, 170, 188
Tennessee 87, 90, 111
TENS (Transcutaneous Electrical Nerve Stimulation) 145
teratogen 42, 187
The Terminal Man 25, **26**, 27–9, 32, 50–2, 152
The Terminator 61–2, 149
Terminator 2 27, 40, 61
terrorism 6, **8**, 13, 77–8, 82, 108, 136, 159, 178, 186, 209, 228
test tube babies 76
The Testament of Dr. Mabuse 108
testicle 89, 91, 95
testosterone 90–1, 95–6, 253*n*25, 253*n*27; *see also* androgen; low "T" syndrome

Teva Pharmaceuticals 179
Texas 131, 133, 250n12
Thalberg, Irving 89
thalidomide 42, 187, 222
theology 54, 77
They Saved Hitler's Brain 108
The Thing 66
The Thing with Two Heads 108, 135–6, *137*
Third Person Shooter (TPS) 112, 208, 210
Third Reich 14, 59, 71–2, 106, 125
This Island Earth 104, 117, **118**
Thompson, Marshall **126**
Thor 108, 254n17
Thorazine (chlorpromazine) 14, 30, 34, 57, 102, 106, 18, 122, 128, 230
Thoreau, Henry David 220
thought broadcasting 64
thought transfer 18, 117, **118**, 202
three blind men 2
Three Faces of Eve 128
thriller 36, 56, 179, 183, 197, 200
Through a Glass Darkly 229
thumb, prehensile 138
THX-1138 220–1
thyroid 90, 94–5, 250n7
Tibetan Book of Dead 168, 257ch11n9
Tibetan Buddhism 197, 225
Till, Emmett 80, 130, 255ch7n9
Tilly, James Matthew 143–4
Time 91
Time Machine 41, 81
time travel 147–9, 182, 257ch10n6
Timecop 149
Times Square 123
Tin Man 5
Tina (crystal meth) 182
Tomorrowland (World of Tomorrow) 100
Tone, Andrea 33, 251n19
Total Recall 40, 43–4, 75, 161, 163, 167–71, 175, 186, 189, 194, 218, 224, 256ch9n3, 258ch14n1
totalitarianism 34, 40, 148–9, **150**, 160, 211, 220–1, 227–8, 237
Tourneur, Jacques 192
Tourneur, Maurice 192
toxin 188
TPS (Third Person Shooter) *see* Third Person Shooter
Tracy, Spencer 56, 87, 132, 218
trailer 8, 93, 107, 136, 234, 241
Tramadol 38
trance 148, 155, 159, 189, 255n32
tranquilizer 14, 102, 187, 222, 228, 258ch13n9
Transcendence 234, 241–3
transplant 12, 31–2, 49, 60, 87, 89–91, 93–4, 119, 121, 133–4, 136, 170, 175–6, 223, 253n18
transvestite 40, 57
Traumatic Brain Injury (TBI) 43, 163, 166
Trekkies 53, 80; *see also Star Trek*
Trenton State Hospital 96
tricyclic antidepressant 42

Trinity 201
A Trip to the Moon 69
The Triumph of Therapeutic: Uses of Faith After Freud 101
Tron 206
Truffaut, François 148
Truman, Harry 98
Trumbull, Douglas 194–5
Tsukerman, Slava 27, 223
Tukes, William 47
Turner, Lana 218
Tuskegee, Alabama 31, 119, 151
TV *see* television
12 Monkeys 149
20th century 3, 11, 18, 21, 23, 35–6, 40, 60, 65, 73, 81, 86–7, 94, 131, 138, 177, 191, 219, 226, 237, 250ch2n2
Twenty Thousand Leagues Under Sea 104
21st century 5, 18, 20, 23, 36, 41–3, 60, 77, 83, 90, 125, 131, 155, 171, 177–8, 180, 182, 191, 201, 204, 206, 224, 233
The Twilight Zone 81, 123, 252–3ch5n2
Twin Towers 223; *see also* World Trade Center
Twitter 36
Two Faces of Dr. Jekyll (1960) 57
2001: A Space Odyssey 149, 177

ultra-violence 219
umbilical cord 214
umbyCord **214**
U.N. (United Nations) 122, **127**, 242
The Uncanny 68
unconscious 14, 37, 41, 47, 72, 77, 104, 158, 178–9, 185, 196, 199, 202, **203**, 204–5, 237, 252ch3n3
underground railroad 226
The Unearthly 119, 125
Uniform Determination of Death Act 16
Unit 731 145
United States 14, 16, 30–1, 54, 61, 92, 96, 98, 102, 106–8, 110–2, **112**, 118, 123, 125, 128, 130–1, 134–5, 157, 159–61, 182–3, 187, 198, 206, 222, 230, 243, 249n5
Universal (Studios) 32, 49, 54, 131
University of Oregon 129
University of Pittsburgh 7
University of Prague 188
unsafe sex 223
uranium 117
Urban's Kinemacolor Company 54
U.S. Public Health Service 31
U.S.S.R 105, 206; *see also* Russia; Soviet
Utopia 218

VA hospital 64, 129, 150
vaccination 83
Vader, Darth 127
Vagus Nerve Stimulation (VNS) 145
Valium 218, 228, 259n9

Valkyr 231
Die Valkyrie 230–1
Valley of the Dolls 228
vampire 47, 197–8
The Vampyre 47
The Varieties of Religious Experience 67
Vaughn, Vince 202
VCR 144
Vedas 29, 218
Veidt, Conrad 54
Velvet Underground 50
Verhoeven, Paul 39–40, 122, 167, 169, 257ch9n3
Verne, Jules 72, 104–5, 189
vertebral artery 111
Vicodan 38
Vidal, Gore 128
video games 37, 154, 156, 171, 185, 206–10, 212–3, 215, 230–1, 258ch12n1, 258ch12n3
Videodrome 144, 213, 215
videotapes 39, 110, 144
Vienna Psychoanalytic Society 164
Viet Cong 82, 225
Vietnam 30, 82, 151, 225
Vindication of Rights of Woman: With Strictures on Political and Moral Subjects 47
violence 56, 130, 185, 208, 212, 218–20, **221**, 224, 252n5, 256n29
virility 90–1
virtual reality 12, 110, 171, 185, 206–8, **207**, **214**, 214–5, 226
virus 64, 78, 84, 110–1, 183; retrovirus 223
vital signs 64
vivisection 35, 59–60
VNS *see* Vagus Nerve Stimulation (VNS)
"Voight-Kampff" test 75, 114
Von Braun, Dr. 107, 243
von Sydow, Max 198
Voronoff, Serge 87, 89–91, 93–5, 125, 253n15–16; *see also* "Monkey Gland Man"
voyages extraodinaires 104
Vulcan 34, 236
Vyvanse 180; *see also* amphetamine

Wachowski Brothers 200
Wagner, Richard 231
Wagner-Jauregg, Julius 14, 20, 30–1, 73, 94–6, 220, 251ch1n4, 251ch1n7; Wagner-Jauregg Trial 30, 251ch1n4
Wahlberg, Mark 230
Walden Two 219
Walken, Christopher 15, 29, 30, 36, 39, 50, 149–51, **153**, 195–7
Wall Street Journal 14, 173–5
war neurosis 13–4, 30; *see also* shell-shock
WarGames 206
Warhol, Andy 50
Washington, Denzel 158, 160, 163
Washington, D.C. 185
Washington Post 223
Wasson, G.W. 168, 255n14

Index

Watson, John B. 130, 219–20
"We Can Remember It for You Wholesale" 168–9, 171, 224
Web of Evil 99, **100**, 115
weepie 39, 117, 184
Weimar 22, 74, 108, 134
Weine, Robert **48**, 50, 54, 143, 204
Weisz, Rachel 183
Wells, H.G. 34–5, 41, 51, **58**, 59–60, 72, 81, **85**, 86, 177–9, 183, 189, 258*ch*10*n*2
Wendt, George 198
Wernicke, Carl 59, 138–9; aphasia 59
Wertham, Fredrik M.D. 99, 256*n*29
Western 23, 25, 50, 56, 76, 105, 110, 119, 141, 189, 191, 204, 222; genre 22, 25–6, 56, 105, 141, 204, 222
Westworld 27–8
Whale, James **48**, 49, 51
What About Bob? 23
wheelchair 111, 176
When Clouds Roll By 56, 143, 204–5
Whitaker, Forest 175
white-collar crime 182
whodunit 29
Whyte, William H. 103
Widmark, Richard 132

Wilder, Gene 51
Willis, Bruce 149
Wilson, Michael 81
Wilson, Sloan 103
Winslet, Kate **172**, **189**
Winters, Shelley 29
Wired 171
Wiseman, Joseph 146
The Wizard of Oz 5, 56, 143, 194, 205, 257*n*14
Wolf Man 106, 131
Wolf of Wall Street 163, 204
Wolff, Ed **127**
Wollstonecraft, Mary 46–7
woman, evil 56, 162, 217
Wonder Woman 73
Wonderland 146, 201, 160, 226
Wood, Natalie 195–7
Woods, James 144, 213
Woodstock Music Festival 74, 255*n*2
worker 34, 41, 69–70, 130, 132, 176, 184, 202, 221
World of Tomorrow (Tomorrowland) 100
World Trade Center (WTC) 78, 228; *see also* Twin Towers
World War I 13–4, 30, 54, 70, 72, 90, 220, 243, 250*ch*1*n*1

World War II 3, 11, 14, 30, 35, 39, 82, 9–3, 98–9, 106–7, 111, 125, 134, 145–6, 148, 164, 183, 189, 209, 219
World War III 227
Wright, Jeffrey 158
wrong man 29
Wundt, Wilhelm 239

X-Men Origins: Wolverine 159
X-ray 16, **75**, 136

Y2K 41, 215
Yakuza 155, **156**, 176
Yale University 152
Yellow Menace (Yellow Peril) 146
Yellow Submarine 50
Yippees 151
York Retreat 47
Young, Sean 75
Young Frankenstein 32, **33**, 51
youth culture 15, 43, 82, 149, 229

Zelig 188
Zion 201
zombie 34, 107–8, 161, 197
zoo 82, **138**
Zucco, George 93
Zuckerman, Mark 210

www.ingramcontent.com/pod-product-compliance
Lightning Source LLC
Chambersburg PA
CBHW081542300426
44116CB00015B/2725